NOVELS
for Students

Advisors

Jayne M. Burton is a teacher of English, a member of the Delta Kappa Gamma International Society for Key Women Educators, and currently a master's degree candidate in the Interdisciplinary Study of Curriculum and Instruction and English at Angelo State University.

Tom Shilts is the youth librarian at the Okemos branch of Capital Area District Library in Okemos, Michigan. He holds an MSLS degree from Clarion University of Pennsylvania and an MA in U.S. History from the University of North Dakota.

Amy Spade Silverman has taught at independent schools in California, Texas, Michigan, and New York. She holds a bachelor of arts degree from the University of Michigan and a master of fine arts degree from the University of Houston. She is a member of the National Council of Teachers of English and Teachers and Writers. She is an exam reader for Advanced Placement Literature and Composition. She is also a poet, published in *North American Review*, *Nimrod*, and *Michigan Quarterly Review*, among others.

NOVELS
for Students

**Presenting Analysis, Context, and Criticism
on Commonly Studied Novels**

VOLUME 49

Sara Constantakis, Project Editor

Foreword by Anne Devereaux Jordan

GALE
CENGAGE Learning·

Farmington Hills, Mich • San Francisco • New York • Waterville, Maine
Meriden, Conn • Mason, Ohio • Chicago

Novels for Students, Volume 49

Project Editor: Sara Constantakis

Rights Acquisition and Management: Moriam Aigoro, Ashley Maynard

Composition: Evi Abou-El-Seoud

Manufacturing: Rhonda Dover

Imaging: John Watkins

Digital Content Production: Edna Shy

© 2015 Gale, Cengage Learning

WCN: 01-100-101

For product information and technology assistance, contact us at
Gale Customer Support, 1-800-877-4253.
For permission to use material from this text or product,
submit all requests online at **www.cengage.com/permissions**.
Further permissions questions can be emailed to
permissionrequest@cengage.com

Gale
27500 Drake Rd.
Farmington Hills, MI, 48331-3535

ISBN-13: 978-1-57302-301-6
ISSN 1094-3552

This title is also available as an e-book.
ISBN-13: 978-1-57302-304-7
Contact your Gale, a part of Cengage Learning sales representative for ordering information.

Printed in Mexico
1 2 3 4 5 6 7 19 18 17 16 15

Table of Contents

The Informed Dialogue: Interacting with Literature

When we pick up a book, we usually do so with the anticipation of pleasure. We hope that by entering the time and place of the novel and sharing the thoughts and actions of the characters, we will find enjoyment. Unfortunately, this is often not the case; we are disappointed. But we should ask, has the author failed us, or have we failed the author?

We establish a dialogue with the author, the book, and with ourselves when we read. Consciously and unconsciously, we ask questions: "Why did the author write this book?" "Why did the author choose that time, place, or character?" "How did the author achieve that effect?" "Why did the character act that way?" "Would I act in the same way?" The answers we receive depend upon how much information about literature in general and about that book specifically we ourselves bring to our reading.

Young children have limited life and literary experiences. Being young, children frequently do not know how to go about exploring a book, nor sometimes, even know the questions to ask of a book. The books they read help them answer questions, the author often coming right out and *telling* young readers the things they are learning or are expected to learn. The perennial classic, *The Little Engine That Could, tells* its readers that, among other things, it is good to help others and brings happiness:

"Hurray, hurray," cried the funny little clown and all the dolls and toys. "The good little boys and girls in the city will be happy because you helped us, kind, Little Blue Engine."

In picture books, messages are often blatant and simple, the dialogue between the author and reader one-sided. Young children are concerned with the end result of a book—the enjoyment gained, the lesson learned—rather than with how that result was obtained. As we grow older and read further, however, we question more. We come to expect that the world within the book will closely mirror the concerns of our world, and that the author will *show* these through the events, descriptions, and conversations within the story, rather than *telling* of them. We are now expected to do the interpreting, carry on our share of the dialogue with the book and author, and glean not only the author's message, but comprehend how that message and the overall affect of the book were achieved. Sometimes, however, we need help to do these things. *Novels for Students* provides that help.

A novel is made up of many parts interacting to create a coherent whole. In reading a novel, the more obvious features can be easily spotted—theme, characters, plot—but we may overlook the more subtle elements that greatly influence how the novel is perceived by the reader: viewpoint, mood and tone, symbolism, or the use of humor. By focusing on both the obvious and more subtle literary elements within a novel, *Novels for Students* aids readers in both analyzing for message and in determining how and why that message is communicated. In the discussion on Harper Lee's *To Kill a Mockingbird* (Vol. 2), for example, the mockingbird as a symbol of innocence is dealt with, among other things, as is the importance of Lee's use of humor which "enlivens a serious plot, adds depth to the characterization, and creates a sense of familiarity and universality." The reader comes to understand the internal elements of each novel discussed—as well as the external influences that help shape it.

"The desire to write greatly," Harold Bloom of Yale University says, "is the desire to be elsewhere, in a time and place of one's own, in an originality that must compound with inheritance, with an anxiety of influence." A writer seeks to create a unique world within a story, but although it is unique, it is not disconnected from our own world. It speaks to us *because* of what the writer brings to the writing from our world: how he or she was raised and educated; his or her likes and dislikes; the events occurring in the real world at the time of the writing, and while the author was growing up. When we know what an author has brought to his or her work, we gain a greater insight into both the "originality" (the world of the book), and the things that "compound" it. This insight enables us to question that created world and find answers more readily. By informing ourselves, we are able to establish a more effective dialogue with both book and author.

Novels for Students, in addition to providing a plot summary and descriptive list of characters—to remind readers of what they have read—also explores the external influences that shaped each book. Each entry includes a discussion of the author's background, and the historical context in which the novel was written. It is vital to know, for instance, that when Ray Bradbury was writing *Fahrenheit 451* (Vol. 1), the threat of Nazi domination had recently ended in Europe, and the McCarthy hearings were taking place in Washington, D.C. This information goes far in answering the question, "Why did he write a story of oppressive government control and book burning?" Similarly, it is important to know that Harper Lee, author of *To Kill a Mockingbird,* was born and raised in Monroeville, Alabama, and

that her father was a lawyer. Readers can now see why she chose the south as a setting for her novel—it is the place with which she was most familiar—and start to comprehend her characters and their actions.

Novels for Students helps readers find the answers they seek when they establish a dialogue with a particular novel. It also aids in the posing of questions by providing the opinions and interpretations of various critics and reviewers, broadening that dialogue. Some reviewers of *To Kill A Mockingbird,* for example, "faulted the novel's climax as melodramatic." This statement leads readers to ask, "Is it, indeed, melodramatic?" "If not, why did some reviewers see it as such?" "If it is, why did Lee choose to make it melodramatic?" "Is melodrama ever justified?" By being spurred to ask these questions, readers not only learn more about the book and its writer, but about the nature of writing itself.

The literature included for discussion in *Novels for Students* has been chosen because it has something vital to say to us. *Of Mice and Men, Catch-22, The Joy Luck Club, My Antonia, A Separate Peace* and the other novels here speak of life and modern sensibility. In addition to their individual, specific messages of prejudice, power, love or hate, living and dying, however, they and all great literature also share a common intent. They force us to *think*—about life, literature, and about others, not just about ourselves. They pry us from the narrow confines of our minds and thrust us outward to confront the world of books and the larger, real world we all share. *Novels for Students* helps us in this confrontation by providing the means of enriching our conversation with literature and the world, by creating an *informed* dialogue, one that brings true pleasure to the personal act of reading.

Sources

Harold Bloom, *The Western Canon, The Books and School of the Ages,* Riverhead Books, 1994.

Watty Piper, *The Little Engine That Could,* Platt & Munk, 1930.

Anne Devereaux Jordan
Senior Editor, TALL (Teaching and Learning Literature)

Introduction

Purpose of the Book

The purpose of *Novels for Students* (*NfS*) is to provide readers with a guide to understanding, enjoying, and studying novels by giving them easy access to information about the work. Part of Gale's "For Students" Literature line, *NfS* is specifically designed to meet the curricular needs of high school and undergraduate college students and their teachers, as well as the interests of general readers and researchers considering specific novels. While each volume contains entries on "classic" novels frequently studied in classrooms, there are also entries containing hard-to-find information on contemporary novels, including works by multicultural, international, and women novelists. Entries profiling film versions of novels not only diversify the study of novels but support alternate learning styles, media literacy, and film studies curricula as well.

The information covered in each entry includes an introduction to the novel and the novel's author; a plot summary, to help readers unravel and understand the events in a novel; descriptions of important characters, including explanation of a given character's role in the novel as well as discussion about that character's relationship to other characters in the novel; analysis of important themes in the novel; and an explanation of important literary techniques and movements as they are demonstrated in the novel.

In addition to this material, which helps the readers analyze the novel itself, students are also provided with important information on the literary and historical background informing each work. This includes a historical context essay, a box comparing the time or place the novel was written to modern Western culture, a critical essay, and excerpts from critical essays on the novel. A unique feature of *NfS* is a specially commissioned critical essay on each novel, targeted toward the student reader.

The "literature to film" entries on novels vary slightly in form, providing background on film technique and comparison to the original, literary version of the work. These entries open with an introduction to the film, which leads directly into the plot summary. The summary highlights plot changes from the novel, key cinematic moments, and/or examples of key film techniques. As in standard entries, there are character profiles (noting omissions or additions, and identifying the actors), analysis of themes and how they are illustrated in the film, and an explanation of the cinematic style and structure of the film. A cultural context section notes any time period or setting differences from that of the original work, as well as cultural differences between the time in which the original work was written and the time in which the film adaptation was made. A film entry concludes with a critical overview and critical essays on the film.

To further help today's student in studying and enjoying each novel or film, information on media adaptations is provided (if available), as well as suggestions for works of fiction, nonfiction, or film on similar themes and topics. Classroom aids include ideas for research papers and lists of critical and reference sources that provide additional material on the novel. Film entries also highlight signature film techniques demonstrated, and suggest media literacy activities and prompts to use during or after viewing a film.

Selection Criteria

The titles for each volume of *NfS* are selected by surveying numerous sources on notable literary works and analyzing course curricula for various schools, school districts, and states. Some of the sources surveyed include: high school and undergraduate literature anthologies and textbooks; lists of award-winners, and recommended titles, including the Young Adult Library Services Association (YALSA) list of best books for young adults. Films are selected both for the literary importance of the original work and the merits of the adaptation (including official awards and widespread public recognition).

Input solicited from our expert advisory board—consisting of educators and librarians—guides us to maintain a mix of "classic" and contemporary literary works, a mix of challenging and engaging works (including genre titles that are commonly studied) appropriate for different age levels, and a mix of international, multicultural and women authors. These advisors also consult on each volume's entry list, advising on which titles are most studied, most appropriate, and meet the broadest interests across secondary (grades 7–12) curricula and undergraduate literature studies.

How Each Entry Is Organized

Each entry, or chapter, in *NfS* focuses on one novel. Each entry heading lists the full name of the novel, the author's name, and the date of the novel's publication. The following elements are contained in each entry:

Introduction: a brief overview of the novel which provides information about its first appearance, its literary standing, any controversies surrounding the work, and major conflicts or themes within the work. Film entries identify the original novel and provide understanding of the film's reception and reputation, along with that of the director.

Author Biography: in novel entries, this section includes basic facts about the author's life, and focuses on events and times in the author's life that inspired the novel in question.

Plot Summary: a factual description of the major events in the novel. Lengthy summaries are broken down with subheads. Plot summaries of films are used to uncover plot differences from the original novel, and to note the use of certain film angles or other techniques.

Characters: an alphabetical listing of major characters in the novel. Each character name is followed by a brief to an extensive description of the character's role in the novel, as well as discussion of the character's actions, relationships, and possible motivation. In film entries, omissions or changes to the cast of characters of the film adaptation are mentioned here, and the actors' names—and any awards they may have received—are also included.

Characters are listed alphabetically by last name. If a character is unnamed—for instance, the narrator in *Invisible Man*—the character is listed as "The Narrator" and alphabetized as "Narrator." If a character's first name is the only one given, the name will appear alphabetically by that name.

Variant names are also included for each character. Thus, the full name "Jean Louise Finch" would head the listing for the narrator of *To Kill a Mockingbird*, but listed in a separate cross-reference would be the nickname "Scout Finch."

Themes: a thorough overview of how the major topics, themes, and issues are addressed within the novel. Each theme discussed appears in a separate subhead. While the key themes often remain the same or similar when a novel is adapted into a film, film entries demonstrate how the themes are conveyed cinematically, along with any changes in the portrayal of the themes.

Style: this section addresses important style elements of the novel, such as setting, point of view, and narration; important literary devices used, such as imagery, foreshadowing, symbolism; and, if applicable, genres to which the work might have belonged, such as Gothicism or Romanticism. Literary terms are explained within the entry but can also be found in the Glossary. Film entries cover how the director conveyed the meaning, message, and mood of the work using film in comparison to the author's use of language, literary device, etc., in the original work.

Historical Context: in novel entries, this section outlines the social, political, and cultural climate in which the author lived and the novel was created. This section may include descriptions of related historical events, pertinent aspects of daily life in the culture, and the artistic and literary sensibilities of the time in which the work was written. If the novel is a historical work, information regarding the time in which the novel is set is also included. Each section is broken down with helpful subheads. Film entries contain a similar Cultural Context section because the film adaptation might explore an entirely different time period or culture than the original work, and may also be influenced by the traditions and views of a time period much different than that of the original author.

Critical Overview: this section provides background on the critical reputation of the novel or film, including bannings or any other public controversies surrounding the work. For older works, this section includes a history of how the novel or film was first received and how perceptions of it may have changed over the years; for more recent novels, direct quotes from early reviews may also be included.

Criticism: an essay commissioned by *NfS* which specifically deals with the novel or film and is written specifically for the student audience, as well as excerpts from previously published criticism on the work (if available).

Sources: an alphabetical list of critical material used in compiling the entry, with full bibliographical information.

Further Reading: an alphabetical list of other critical sources which may prove useful for the student. It includes full bibliographical information and a brief annotation.

Suggested Search Terms: a list of search terms and phrases to jumpstart students' further information seeking. Terms include not just titles and author names but also terms and topics related to the historical and literary context of the works.

In addition, each novel entry contains the following highlighted sections, set apart from the main text as sidebars:

Media Adaptations: if available, a list of audiobooks and important film and television adaptations of the novel, including source information. The list also includes stage adaptations, musical adaptations, etc.

Topics for Further Study: a list of potential study questions or research topics dealing with the novel. This section includes questions related to other disciplines the student may be studying, such as American history, world history, science, math, government, business, geography, economics, psychology, etc.

Compare and Contrast: an "at-a-glance" comparison of the cultural and historical differences between the author's time and culture and late twentieth century or early twenty-first century Western culture. This box includes pertinent parallels between the major scientific, political, and cultural movements of the time or place the novel was written, the time or place the novel was set (if a historical work), and modern Western culture. Works written after the mid-1970s may not have this box.

What Do I Read Next?: a list of works that might give a reader points of entry into a classic work (e.g., YA or multicultural titles) and/or complement the featured novel or serve as a contrast to it. This includes works by the same author and others, works from various genres, YA works, and works from various cultures and eras.

The film entries provide sidebars more targeted to the study of film, including:

Film Technique: a listing and explanation of four to six key techniques used in the film, including shot styles, use of transitions, lighting, sound or music, etc.

Read, Watch, Write: media literacy prompts and/or suggestions for viewing log prompts.

What Do I See Next?: a list of films based on the same or similar works or of films similar in directing style, technique, etc.

Other Features

NfS includes "The Informed Dialogue: Interacting with Literature," a foreword by Anne Devereaux Jordan, Senior Editor for *Teaching and Learning Literature* (*TALL*), and a founder of the Children's Literature Association. This essay provides an enlightening look at how readers interact with literature and how *Novels for Students* can help teachers show students how to enrich their own reading experiences.

A Cumulative Author/Title Index lists the authors and titles covered in each volume of the *NfS* series.

A Cumulative Nationality/Ethnicity Index breaks down the authors and titles covered in each volume of the *NfS* series by nationality and ethnicity.

A Subject/Theme Index, specific to each volume, provides easy reference for users who may be studying a particular subject or theme rather than a single work. Significant subjects, from events to broad themes, are included.

Each entry may include illustrations, including photo of the author, stills from film adaptations, maps, and/or photos of key historical events, if available.

Citing Novels for Students

When writing papers, students who quote directly from any volume of *NfS* may use the following general forms. These examples are based on MLA style; teachers may request that students adhere to a different style, so the following examples may be adapted as needed.

When citing text from *NfS* that is not attributed to a particular author (i.e., the Themes, Style, Historical Context sections, etc.), the following format should be used in the bibliography section:

> *"The Monkey Wrench Gang." Novels for Students.* Ed. Sara Constantakis. Vol. 43. Detroit: Gale, Cengage Learning, 2013. 157–193. Print.

When quoting the specially commissioned essay from *NfS* (usually the first piece under the "Criticism" subhead), the following format should be used:

> Holmes, Michael Allen. Critical Essay on *"The Monkey Wrench Gang." Novels for Students.* Ed. Sara Constantakis. Vol. 43. Detroit: Gale, Cengage Learning, 2013. 173–78. Print.

When quoting a journal or newspaper essay that is reprinted in a volume of *NfS,* the following form may be used:

> Bryant, Paul T. "Edward Abbey and Environmental Quixoticism." *Western American Literature* 24.1 (1989): 37–43. Rpt. in *Novels for Students.* Vol. 43. Ed. Sara Constantakis. Detroit: Gale, Cengage Learning, 2013. 189–92. Print.

When quoting material reprinted from a book that appears in a volume of *NfS,* the following form may be used:

> Norwick, Steve. "Nietzschean Themes in the Works of Edward Abbey." *Coyote in the Maze: Tracking Edward Abbey in a World of Words.* Ed. Peter Quigley. Salt Lake City; University of Utah Press, 1998. 184–205. Rpt. in *Novels for Students.* Vol. 43. Ed. Sara Constantakis. Detroit: Gale, Cengage Learning, 2013. 183–85. Print.

We Welcome Your Suggestions

The editorial staff of *Novels for Students* welcomes your comments and ideas. Readers who wish to suggest novels to appear in future volumes, or who have other suggestions, are cordially invited to contact the editor. You may contact the editor via e-mail at: **ForStudentsEditors@cengage.com.** Or write to the editor at:

Editor, *Novels for Students*

Gale

27500 Drake Road

Farmington Hills, MI 48331-3535

Literary Chronology

1894: Dashiell Hammett is born on May 27 in St. Mary's County, Maryland.

1896: F. Scott Fitzgerald is born on September 24 in St. Paul, Minnesota.

1903: Erskine Caldwell is born on December 17 in Moreland, Georgia.

1906: John Huston is born on August 5 in Nevada, Missouri.

1922: F. Scott Fitzgerald's *The Beautiful and Damned* is published.

1923: Gloria Whelan is born on November 23 in Detroit, Michigan.

1929: Dashiell Hammett's *The Maltese Falcon* is published.

1932: Erskine Caldwell's *Tobacco Road* is published.

1936: Mario Vargas Llosa is born on March 28 in Arequipa, Peru.

1937: Rudolfo Anaya is born on October 30 in Pastura, New Mexico.

1938: Ngũgĩ wa Thiong'o is born on January 5 in Limuru, Kenya.

1940: F. Scott Fitzgerald dies of a heart attack on December 21 in Hollywood, California.

1941: The film *The Maltese Falcon* is released.

1948: Ian McEwan is born on June 21 in Aldershot, England.

1950: Gloria Naylor is born on January 25 in New York City, New York.

1956: Ruth L. Ozeki is born on March 12 in New Haven, Connecticut.

1957: James McBride is born on September 11 in Brooklyn, New York.

1961: Dashiell Hammett dies of lung cancer on January 10 in New York City, New York.

1961: Laurie Halse Anderson is born on October 23 in Potsdam, New York.

1966: Jodi Picoult is born on May 19 in Nesconset, New York.

1967: Ngũgĩ wa Thiong'o's *A Grain of Wheat* is published.

1971: Kiran Desai is born on September 3 in New Delhi, India.

1976: Rudolfo Anaya's *Heart of Aztlan* is published.

1985: Gloria Naylor's *Linden Hills* is published.

1987: Erskine Caldwell dies of lung cancer on April 11 in Paradise Valley, Arizona.

1987: John Huston dies of pneumonia on August 28 in Middletown, Rhode Island.

1987: Mario Vargas Llosa's *The Storyteller* is published.

1998: Ruth L. Ozeki's *My Year of Meats* is published.

2000: Gloria Whelan's *Homeless Bird* is published.

2001: Ian McEwan's *Atonement* is published.

2002: Laurie Halse Anderson's *Catalyst* is published.

2006: Kiran Desai's *The Inheritance of Loss* is published.

2007: The film *Atonement* is released.

2007: Jodi Picoult's *Nineteen Minutes* is published.

2008: Dario Marianelli is awarded the Academy Award for Best Original Score for *Atonement*.

2008: James McBride's *Song Yet Sung* is published.

2010: Mario Vargas Llosa is awarded the Nobel Prize in Literature.

Acknowledgements

The editors wish to thank the copyright holders of the excerpted criticism included in this volume and the permissions managers of many book and magazine publishing companies for assisting us in securing reproduction rights. We are also grateful to the staffs of the Detroit Public Library, the Library of Congress, the University of Detroit Mercy Library, Wayne State University Purdy/ Kresge Library Complex, and the University of Michigan Libraries for making their resources available to us. Following is a list of the copyright holders who have granted us permission to reproduce material in this volume of *NfS*. Every effort has been made to trace copyright, but if omissions have been made, please let us know.

COPYRIGHTED EXCERPTS IN *NfS*, VOLUME 49, WERE REPRODUCED FROM THE FOLLOWING PERIODICALS:

Booklist, Vol. 103, nos. 9-10, January 1, 2007, p. 57.—*Book Riot*, April 8, 2014. © 2014 Kelly Jensen. Reproduced by permission.—*Christian Science Monitor*, December 14, 2000, p. 21.—Copyright 2010 from *Critique* by David Wallace Spielman. Reproduced by permission of Taylor & Francis Group LLC. (http://www.tandfonline.com)— *Encore*, Vol. 26, No. 2, February 2008, pp. 10. © 2008 Bob Ellis. Reproduced by permission.— *Horn Book*, Vol. 78, No. 6, November-December 2002, p. 746.—*Kirkus Reviews*, Vol. 70, No. 17, September 1, 2002, p. 1300.—*Library Journal*, Vol. 132, no. 1, January 1, 2007, p. 97.—*Mother Jones*, Vol. 28, no. 2, March-April 2003, p. 86. © 2003 *Mother Jones*. Reproduced by permission.— *New Republic*, Vol. 202, nos. 2-3, January 8, 1990, p. 41.—*O* Magazine, February 2008.— *Pittsburgh Tribune-Review*, February 17, 2008. © 2008 Tribune Total Media. Reproduced by permission.—*Publishers Weekly*, January 31, 2000, p. 107.—*Publishers Weekly*, Vol. 249, No. 29, July 22, 2002, p. 180.—*Publishers Weekly*, Vol. 254, No. 1, January 1, 2007, p. 31.—*Publishers Weekly*, Vol. 255, No. 1, January 7, 2008, p. 34.— *School Library Journal*, Vol. 47, No. 3, March 2001, pp. 52-55.

COPYRIGHTED EXCERPTS IN *NfS*, VOLUME 49, WERE REPRODUCED FROM THE FOLLOWING BOOKS:

Reprinted by permission of copyright owner, the Modern Language Association of America, from "Texts and Contexts: Teaching 'A Grain of Wheat' and 'Matigari' in Kenya," *Approaches to Teacher the Works of Ngui wa Thiong'o*, pages 206-208.—Beja, Morris. From *Film & Literature: An Introduction*. Boston, MA: Longman, 1979, pp. 129-131. © 1979 Pearson. Reproduced by permission.—Bus, Heiner. From *Rudolfo A. Anaya: Focus on Criticism*, Cesar A. Gonzalez-T., ed. Tempe, AZ: Lalo Press, 1990, pp. 118-125. © 1990 Bilingual Press. Reproduced by permission.—Chavkin, Laura. From *Conversations with Rudolfo Anaya*, Bruce Dick and Silvio Sirias, eds.

Jackson, MS: University Press of Mississippi, 1998, pp. 164-167. © 1998 Laura Chavkin. Reproduced by permission.—Chiu, Monica. From *Filthy Fictions: Asian American Literature by Women*. Lanham, MD: AltaMira Press, 2004, pp. 135-140. © 2004 Rowman & Littlefield. Reproduced by permission.—Ellam, Julie. From *Ian McEwan's "Atonement."* New York, NY: Continuum, 2009, pp. 67-75. © 2009 Continuum. Reproduced by permission.—Hindus, Milton. From *F. Scott Fitzgerald: An Introduction and Interpretation*. New York, NY: Holt, Rinehart and Winston, 1968, pp. 30-34. © 1968 Harcourt. Reproduced by permission.—Jameson, Richard T. From *The A List: The National Society of Film Critics' 100 Essential Films*, Jay Carr, ed. Boston, MA: Da Capo Press, 2002, pp. 176-179. © 2002 De Capo Press. Reproduced by permission.—Knight, Deborah. From *The Philosophy of Film Noir*, Mark T. Conrad, ed. Lexington, KY: University Press of Kentucky, 2006, pp. 207-212. © 2006 The University Press of Kentucky. Reproduced by permission.—O'Bryan-Knight, Jean. Frrom *Vargas Llosa and Latin American Politics*, Juan E. DeCastro and Nicholas Birns, eds. New York, NY: Palgrave Macmillan, 2010, pp. 56-59. © 2010 Palgrave Macmillan. Reproduced by permission.—Lane, Richard J. From *The Postcolonial Novel*. Cambridge, UK: Polity Press, 2006, pp. 47-49, 57-58. © 2006 Polity Press. Reproduced by permission.—Marcus, Laura. From *Ian McEwan: Contemporary Critical Perspectives*, Sebastian Groes, ed. New York, NY: Bloomsbury, 2013, pp. 87-90. © 2013 Laura Marcus. Reproduced by permission.—Mixon, Wayne. *The People's Writer: Erskine Caldwell and the South*. pp. 59-63. © 1996 by the Rector and Visitors of the University of Virginia. Reprinted by permission of the University of Virgina Press.—Marshall, Marguerite Mooers. From *Conversations with F. Scott Fitzgerald*, Matthew J. Bruccoli and Judith S. Baughman, eds. Jackson, MS: University Press of Mississippi, 2004, pp. 26-29. © 2004 University Press of Mississippi. Reproduced by permission.—Montgomery, Maxine Lavon. From *Gloria Naylor's Early Novels*, Margot Anne Kelley, ed. Gainesville, FL: University Press of Florida, 1999, pp. 60-63. © 1999 University Press of Florida. Reproduced by permission.—Munoz, Braulio. From *A Storyteller: Mario Vargas Llosa between Civilization and Barbarism*. Lantham, MD: Rowman & Littlefield, 2000, pp. 90-94. © 2000 Rowman & Littlefield. Reproduced by permission.—Whitt, Margaret Earley. From *Understanding Gloria Naylor*. Columbia, SC: University of South Carolina Press, 1999, pp. 67-73. © 1999 University of South Carolina Press. Reproduced by permission.

Contributors

Susan K. Andersen: Andersen holds a PhD in English and is a former university professor of literature. Entry on *The Storyteller*. Original essay on *The Storyteller*.

Bryan Aubrey: Aubrey holds a PhD in English. Entries on *Catalyst* and *Heart of Aztlan*. Original essays on *Catalyst* and *Heart of Aztlan*.

Cynthia A. Biley: Bily is a professor of English at Macomb Community College in Michigan. Entry on *Linden Hills*. Original essay on *Linden Hills*.

Rita M. Brown: Brown is an English professor. Entry on *The Beautiful and Damned*. Original essay on *The Beautiful and Damned*.

Catherine Dominic: Dominic is a novelist and a freelance writer and editor. Entries on *Homeless Bird* and *Nineteen Minutes*. Original essays on *Homeless Bird* and *Nineteen Minutes*.

Klay Dyer: Dyer is a freelance writer and editor who specializes in topics relating to literature, film, and popular culture. Entry on *Atonement*. Original essay on *Atonement*.

Kristen Sarlin Greenberg: Greenberg is a freelance writer and editor with a background in literature and philosophy. Entry on *Song Yet Sung*. Original essay on *Song Yet Sung*.

Michael Allen Holmes: Holmes is a writer with existential interests. Entries on *A Grain of Wheat* and *My Year of Meats*. Original essays on *A Grain of Wheat* and *My Year of Meats*.

David Kelly: Kelly is an instructor of creative writing and literature. Entry on *The Maltese Falcon*. Original essay on *The Maltese Falcon*.

Amy L. Miller: Miller is a graduate of the University of Cincinnati and currently resides in New Orleans, Louisiana. Entry on *The Inheritance of Loss*. Original essay on *The Inheritance of Loss*.

Bradley A. Skeen: Skeen is a classicist. Entry on *Tobacco Road*. Original essay on *Tobacco Road*.

Atonement

2007

Based on Ian McEwan's best-selling 2001 novel of the same name, Joe Wright's film adaptation of *Atonement* was released in 2007, starring Keira Knightley (Cecilia Tallis), James McAvoy (Robbie Turner), and a series of three different actors to represent the film's catalyst, Briony Tallis, at various points in her life: Saoirse Ronan (Briony age thirteen), Romola Garai (age eighteen), and Vanessa Redgrave (elderly).

Filmed on an estimated budget of $30 million (gross earnings exceeded $125 million), *Atonement* had a very strong run throughout the 2008 awards season, winning an Oscar for Best Original Score (Dario Marianelli) and being nominated in six other categories, including Best Picture and Best Adapted Screenplay (Christopher Hampton). The film went on to add two Golden Globes (Best Picture—Drama and Best Original Score), two BAFTA Film Awards (Best Film and Best Production Design), as well as many other awards and nominations from around the world.

A tragic story of two young lovers whose lives are torn to shreds by the power of words mismanaged and by imagination unchecked, *Atonement* is also a deeply unsettling exploration of the possibility of true atonement, and of making amends for the consequences of decisions as distinct from the decisions themselves. To apologize for actions is one thing, the film suggests, but is it enough? Does an apology for an action

© Focus Features | The Kobal Collection | Bailey, Alex

counterbalance the impact of that decision on an entire life or family? And if atonement is possible, what role does art play in this process? Does Briony's fictional reimagining of Robbie and Cecilia's love transcend the reality that her decision destroyed forever the possibility of that love being realized? The fact that these questions linger in the mind long after the final scenes of the film is a testament to the power of its art and the importance of its message. The film is rated R for disturbing war images, language, and some scenes of graphic sexuality.

PLOT SUMMARY

Part One

The film opens with the sound of a mechanical typewriter being loaded with paper, and the slow staccato rhythms of typing as the word "Atonement" appears (white type on black background). Typing continues, this time against a close-up of an elaborate model of a country estate. The scene is set for the first part of the

movie: England, 1935. Thirteen-year-old Briony Tallis sits at a desk in her bedroom, typing slowly but determinedly on the final pages of a play she is writing titled *The Trials of Arabella*. With finished product in hand, she strides powerfully through the halls and stairways of the large estate house in which her family lives. Looking for her mother, she announces to the kitchen staff that she has finished her play. They direct her to the drawing room. En route she passes an open side door, where she spots the gardener, Robbie Turner, preparing for work. The two chat, obviously comfortable with each other, and she invites him to watch the family performance of her play. Continuing on her way, she enters the drawing room and closes the door. Leaping ahead briefly, the scene concludes with her mother, Emily, announcing that the play is stupendous.

The film shifts to a wide exterior shot of the country house. Briony is lying on the expansive lawn with her older sister Cecilia, who is obviously bored with both the book she is reading and the conversation with her younger, overly dramatic sister. Briony talks more about how she

FILM TECHNIQUE

- A tracking shot (also known as traveling shot or dollying shot) takes place when a director shoots a scene or part of a scene in a continuous shot that engages a camera that is being moved either by wheels or some other mechanical means. Wright uses the technique in *Atonement* for a long (over five-minute) shot that focuses on Robbie's descent into the hellish scene at Dunkirk and his subsequent exploration of this chaotic landscape. Using over one thousand extras for the five takes of this single shot (reportedly the third take made the final cut of the film), Wright deploys a Steadicam operator on foot and via a series of traditional and makeshift dollies (including a rickshaw) across the beach, up a ramp, and across a pier before he enters a crowded bar. This shot has proven to be a point of contention among critics (some see it as monumental, others as self-serving), but the impact of the slow tracking is undeniable, creating an almost trance-like blend of the real and surreal as Robbie is shown walking past bombed-out shells of buildings, a beached barge, a stranded show horse, a singing choir, and a spinning Ferris wheel. The positioning of Robbie within the frame shifts as well during the scene, with some sections opening outward to capture the broad expanse of inhumanity as Dunkirk awaits evacuation and others with Robbie at the extremes of the frame, which tends to evoke a feeling of constriction or even imprisonment.

- An extreme close-up (ECU) is when the details of a shot fill the entire frame, allowing a director to focus on a certain body part or element of a location. Typically, an ECU is used to create a dramatic impact through intimacy or through providing a hyper-focused moment of information. Wright skillfully deploys ECU in *Atonement* with two particular targets. The first is Briony's eyes, which fill the screen on a number of occasions by way of underscoring that it is her perception of the world and how she sees (or does not see) incidents that will prove critical to the story that will unfold. The second focal point is the obscene word that Robbie types in his letter to Cecilia. Impactful in its vulgarity and sexual explicitness, it eventually proves a read-but-never-spoken catalyst to Robbie's downfall when Briony presents it to her mother as evidence of his depravity.

- A voice-over is a narrative technique (adding to both characterization and the creativity of a film) in which an unseen actor's lines are heard over visual elements in a scene. Wright uses voice-over on a number of occasions in *Atonement*, but most effectively when he has the voice of Robbie reading his letter to Cecilia (or parts thereof) over a number of scenes set in wartime France. "Dearest Cecilia, the story can resume. The one I had been planning on that evening walk. . . . I will return. Find you, love you, marry you and live without shame." Robbie's words illustrate two important focal points of his story line: his devotion to Cecilia and commitment to getting back to her so that the two of them might have the life they have dreamed of; and, the connection between life and story. In contrast to Briony, who tinkers with the lives of others while creating her stories, Robbie is living his story directly in an English prison, in the fields of France, and amidst the chaos of Dunkirk. While Briony is the film's most powerful teller of stories, Robbie is a man who lives his story powerfully.

---

understands the power of words to create worlds and realities outside the one she lives in. When Robbie passes by, pushing a wheelbarrow, Briony asks her sister why she does not speak to the gardener anymore; Cecilia replies that she does, but they move in different circles these days.

The scene shifts back to Briony's bedroom, where she is working with her three cousins—twins Jackson and Pierrot, and the precocious Lola Quincey—on preparing the play for presentation. Lola corners Briony into letting her play Arabella, relegating Briony to the role of director and narrator. Their rehearsal is interrupted by the arrival of Danny Hardman, an employee of the family. The interruption gives the twins a chance to declare a break to go swimming, and the room empties.

Left alone, Briony is drawn to her bedroom window, from which she witnesses a heated exchange between Robbie and Cecilia at the garden fountain. The scene intensifies as Cecilia suddenly strips down to her underwear and climbs into a fountain to retrieve something from the water. Briony watches as Cecilia, soaked and clothed only in now transparent lingerie, dresses quickly and pushes past Robbie on her way to the house carrying a large vase that had been sitting by the edge of the fountain.

A flashback shows Cecilia running through the woods, a bunch of wildflowers in hand. She enters the kitchen and goes to the drawing room, where she puts the flowers in the same vase shown in the previous scene. Catching a glimpse of Robbie in the yard, Cecilia picks up the vase, fixes her hair in the mirror, and heads to the garden fountain to get water for the flowers. Robbie joins her for the walk. The conversation between them is awkward and charged with a latent sexual energy that neither is comfortable with. The conversation turns to the fact that Robbie's Cambridge education has been paid for by Cecilia's father, a point of contention that lingers. As Robbie tries to help with the flowers, the vase chips and a piece falls into the fountain. The scene that Briony has witnessed is replayed, with a new context and full dialogue.

The arrival of Leon Tallis and the obviously upper-crust Paul Marshall marks a shift from discussions of art to discussions of business. The backstory of Robbie's rise to Cambridge is recounted. Coming across the Quincey children, Marshall enters into a lecherous flirtation with the adolescent Lola.

Robbie, meanwhile, struggles to capture his feelings for Cecilia as he types a series of apologies in his cottage bedroom. None of the letters satisfy him, and in a burst of raw emotion he writes a sexually explicit letter (caught in extreme close-up) that he immediately pulls from the typewriter.

He clearly never intends for Cecilia to see this letter, and he handwrites a much more formal note of apology for his actions earlier in the day. But in his rush to dress for a dinner party at the Tallis estate, he puts the wrong note into an envelope. In what proves a devastating decision, he entrusts the delivery of the note to Briony, who reads the sexually charged note. Her schoolgirl crush on Robbie twists suddenly toward revenge. Briony later walks in on Robbie and Cecilia consummating their love in the Tallis library (a scene captured in flashback as well), which solidifies her misunderstanding of the adult world and of Robbie as a predatory sex maniac.

Later that evening, Lola is sexually assaulted on the estate grounds, an act that is wholly unconnected with either of the lovers or their previous actions in the library. Briony connects the events in her own imagination, however, and makes a false accusation against Robbie, who is arrested and imprisoned for a crime he did not commit. The accusation splits the family, as Cecilia supports Robbie while her mother is aggressive in advancing the punishment.

Part Two

Released from jail five years later (though the type-over suggests four years), Robbie is shown as a private among the troops trapped in northern France during the 1940 retreat of Allied forces during World War II. A flashback to six months earlier recounts Robbie's brief reunion with Cecilia, estranged from her family and now a nurse in London, prior to shipping out to war. Their stilted conversation cannot hide their feelings for each other, and the scene ends with a declaration of love and promise to be reunited upon Robbie's return (as Robbie's voice-over iterates, the story can resume). Back in France, Robbie leads two of his comrades toward the beach at Dunkirk. Their journey takes them through a field full of dead schoolgirls, each marked with a single bullet wound to the head. Robbie's travails are intercut sporadically with scenes of Cecilia and Briony (in nurse's training) in London, and, more tellingly, with scenes from a past summer that explain Briony's crush on Robbie.

Reaching the crowded beach at Dunkirk, Robbie finds himself in a chaotic world of fire, cruelty, and surreal juxtapositions as a choir sings, a Ferris wheel turns, and half-crazed soldiers twirl on a carousel. Suffering from exhaustion and battle fatigue, he hallucinates about seeing his mother before falling asleep in an abandoned building.

Part Three

The timeline shifts to three weeks earlier in St. Thomas's Hospital (London), where eighteen-year-old Briony is in nurse training and is being chastised for making the care too personal, too much about herself and her own story. Sneaking away from the nurses' residence with her type-writer, Briony hides away writing a novel titled *Two Figures by a Fountain*. Discovered by another probationary nurse, Fiona Maguire, she talks about the novel in progress, which is clearly the story of her own youthful misreading of the incident involving Robbie and Cecilia at the fountain. Briony is also shown writing a letter to Cecilia, trying to explain her own struggles with past decisions and their consequences. As the wounded pour into the hospital, Briony finds her resolve and compassion tested, and her own storytelling tendencies challenged by the hallucinations of Luc Comet, a young French soldier dying from a devastating brain injury.

Later, during a viewing of a newsreel, Briony sees a story on Paul Marshall and his fian-cée, Lola Quincey. Leaping ahead in time, Briony is seen at the wedding of Paul and Lola. Seeing the two of them triggers a memory of the fateful night of the assault, and through a series of brief flashbacks, Briony realizes that it was Paul who had raped her cousin that night, not Robbie. Tracking down Cecilia at her run-down flat, she discovers her sister and Robbie living together. Briony declares that she wants to go in front of a judge to change her evidence about that night, to tell everyone about the terrible thing she did. Robbie and Cecilia respond in anger, and demand that she go to her parents and to a lawyer, and confess fully what she has done. Their thinking is that the perpetrator was Danny Hardman, an employee of the estate, but when told that it was Marshall, all chances of atonement are lost, given that Lola cannot be forced to testify against her new husband. Their hopes shattered yet again, Robbie and Cecilia dismiss Briony from their lives forever.

Part Four

In the final shift, the film leaps ahead to a mod-ern television studio, where an interviewer is speaking with an elderly Briony about her most recent novel, *Atonement*. Her twenty-first novel,

it is also her last. Suffering from vascular demen-tia, Briony is gradually losing her capacity to think, to write, and to create the stories that have defined her life. She admits to the novel being autobiographical, and emphasizes repeat-edly that she has told the absolute truth about her past decisions and their implications for others. But such is not the case. She goes on to admit that she was too much of a coward to visit her sister during the war, making the scene in which she confessed wholly invented. There is no way the scene could ever have happened, she goes on to explain. Robbie Turner had died of septicemia on the last day of the evacuation from Dunkirk. Her sister Cecilia had also been killed during a bombing that destroyed an under-ground train station. The film ends as it had begun, then, with a nearly obsessive focus on the manipulative power of words, and with Bri-ony creating an ending (Robbie and Cecilia alive, together, and deeply in love) that she wished to be true rather than one that is actually true.

The film ends with a scene, wholly imagined, viewers now know, of Robbie and Cecilia on the beach, laughing and playful, as they make their way to a cottage to continue their story as they had always wished it to be.

CHARACTERS

Luc Comet

Luc Comet (Jeremie Renier) is the French sol-dier that Briony is asked to sit with as he lies dying in St. Thomas's Hospital. Initially drawn into the story that he unravels about knowing her from another place and time, Briony is forced to confront her own romanticizing ten-dencies when she realizes that he is, in fact, hal-lucinating due to a devastating brain injury. This realization impacts Briony deeply, and his death seems to trigger a series of events that culminates with Briony realizing that it was Paul Marshall, not Robbie, who attacked Lola so many years earlier.

Danny Hardman

Danny Hardman (Alfie Allen) is the slow-witted, socially awkward handyman on the Tallis family estate. Robbie and Cecilia suspect him of the crime for which Robbie is falsely accused, but in the end Danny is also innocent. A subtle parallel to Robbie, Danny is also judged prematurely and incorrectly because of his lower status within the estate hierarchy.

Interviewer

The interviewer (Anthony Minghella) plays a small but critical role in *Atonement*. Ostensibly generating the forward motion of his interview with an elderly Briony, he is effectively relegated to the role of audience. Her interview is more of a dramatic monologue through which she confesses to past transgressions (the false accusation) as well as to her inability to recount events without rhymes or embellishments. As she admits to the interviewer, the ending of her final, autobiographical novel is wholly invented.

Corporal Frank Mace

Frank Mace (Nonso Anozie) is Robbie's eye-patch-wearing companion during the journey toward Dunkirk. Once on the beach, he is appalled by the shooting of the military horses. He disappears from the scene suddenly and without clear explanation.

Fiona Maguire

Fiona Maguire (Michelle Duncan) is a probationary nurse who shares training and residence with Briony during her time at a London hospital. She discovers Briony writing late one night in a hideaway that the aspiring writer retreats to with her typewriter. In this shared secret space, Briony tells Fiona her own version of the happy ending that Briony hopes will shape the story of her life.

Paul Marshall

Paul Marshall (Benedict Cumberbatch) is a young heir to a food manufacturing empire with strong ties to the British military. As he explains to Leon and Cecilia upon his arrival at the country estate, he stands to become very wealthy as tensions in Europe push inevitably toward war, and conscription is more and more a possibility. To the Tallis family, whose own fortunes are in decline, he is seen as a possible marriage candidate for Cecilia, despite the fact that his morals are highly questionable. He is revealed as a sexual predator, with hints of sadism implied, when Briony realizes years later that he was, in fact, the perpetrator of the rape that Robbie is punished for. He will never be held accountable for his crime, given that under British law at the time his marriage to Lola renders her an unreliable witness (and gives her immunity) even if Briony were to change her evidence in the case.

Corporal Tommy Nettle

Tommy Nettle (Daniel Mays) is the talkative but caring companion who accompanies Robbie on his journey to Dunkirk. Helping Robbie find a place to rest as they await the ship to take them back to England, Tommy is the last person to see Robbie before he dies, and he gives him a brief blessing.

Jackson Quincey

Jackson Quincey (Charlie von Simson, Ben Harcourt) is one of the twin cousins from the North, whose night escapades lead indirectly to Marshall's rape of Lola and Briony's false accusation of Robbie.

Lola Quincey

Lola Quincey (Juno Temple) is the sexually precocious fifteen-year-old cousin from the North who comes to visit the Tallis family as the film opens. Strong-willed, she convinces Briony that she should play the lead in the amateur play that is scheduled to unfold (but never does) as part of the evening's entertainment. She is raped later that evening during a search for her missing brothers, and is convinced by Briony that it was Robbie who committed the assault. Five years later, Lola marries Marshall in a small ceremony that Briony observes.

Pierrot Quincey

Pierrot Quincey (Felix von Simson, Jack Harcourt) is one of the twin cousins from the North, whose night escapades lead indirectly to Marshall's rape of Lola and Briony's false accusation of Robbie.

Briony Tallis

Briony Tallis begins the film (played by Saoirse Roman) as the youngest of the Tallis children, and a girl with two traits that play key roles in the fates of Robbie and Cecilia: an intense schoolgirl crush on Robbie and an overly active imagination. Her misreading of an exchange between Robbie and Cecilia that she witnesses from a window is exacerbated when she opens a misplaced letter that she has been asked to deliver to her sister. Creating in her mind a story that positions Robbie as a sexual predator, she falsely accuses him of a rape, for which he is arrested and imprisoned.

Following the career path established by her sister, eighteen-year-old Briony (Romola Garai) signs on for nurse training in London. Beginning to realize the implications of her earlier decisions as well as her proclivity for creating stories that define her reality (rather than living in the real world), Briony continues to hold true to her role as a writer. Witnessing the marriage of Paul Marshall and Lola Quincey, Briony confronts directly the falsity of her memory of the rape. It is a realization that viewers are led to believe triggers Briony into action, as she visits her sister and Robbie to acknowledge her role in their struggles and to make amends the best she can for what she has done. Tellingly, she comes to this realization *after* the marriage, when Lola is protected by spousal immunity under British law and cannot be made to testify against her husband.

When an elderly Briony (Vanessa Redgrave) sits down for a television interview to promote her twenty-first and final novel, *Atonement*, viewers are suddenly made aware of a number of key elements of the film. The first, of course, is that Briony has never given up her storytelling ways, but has, in fact, made a wonderful career for herself as a writer of novels. Secondly, viewers learn that much of what they have been watching has been a story created by Briony, a direct contradiction of her earlier claim that *Atonement* is a truly autobiographical novel. "Consequently," as Bruno Shah notes in his essay "The Sin of Ian McEwan's Fictive Atonement: Reading His Later Novels," "both Robbie and Cecilia are casualties of war before Briony could own up to her sin against their love and receive actual, that is, personal forgiveness." Moreover, the fact that the novel, and her interview, is her final chance to atone for her false accusation, shows that Briony is still compelled to change the reality of the story (Robbie and Cecilia are both dead) in order to satisfy her own desire for a kind of redemption through fiction. "What sense of hope or satisfaction could a reader derive from an ending like that?" she ponders aloud.

Finally, viewers are left wondering if Briony has ever truly learned from her past or if her foregrounding of her own quest for atonement is a kind of authorial posturing. Her final sentence to the interviewer resonates with viewers

long after the film ends. She would "like to think" that her invention of a happy ending "isn't weakness or evasion, but a final act of kindness," and that, in the end, she "gave them their happiness." Despite all the damage that was done due to her storytelling, Briony is determined, even at the end of her own writing life, to play God for those who have suffered the most. "I wanted to give Robbie and Cecilia what they lost out on in life," she states with conviction but without ever acknowledging her direct and powerful role in denying Robbie and Cecilia their happiness and, after the death, the dignity of a story told accurately and without embellishment.

Cecilia Tallis

Cecilia Tallis (Keira Knightley) is the daughter of the privileged family for whom Robbie's mother works. Her passion for Robbie is thinly veiled and kept at bay only through a veneer of aloofness and disinterestedness that drops dramatically when she reads his sexually explicit note. Admitting their love, Cecilia and Robbie consummate their relationship only to have their world torn apart by Briony's false accusation. Despite pressures from her family and her lover's imprisonment, Cecilia believes in his innocence, dividing herself from the family and its sense of moral and social superiority.

Devoting her life to nursing victims of war, and living in substandard conditions for a young woman of her social standing, Cecilia carries a deep burden for the entirety of her short life. It is she who works desperately to atone for her family's mistreatment of Robbie and to use her life as a corrective to the social snobbery of the day.

Emily Tallis

Emily Tallis (Harriet Walker) is the judgmental matriarch of the Tallis family, whose declining fortunes weigh heavily on her sense of social standing. Never comfortable with her husband's decision to underwrite Robbie's Cambridge education, she is quick to condemn on the basis of a thirteen-year-old's testimony.

Leon Tallis

Leon Tallis (Patrick Kennedy) is the ambitious older son of the family who sees in his friendship with Paul Marshall the opportunity to revive the family fortunes. He fades from view in the film after the fateful night of Lola's rape.

Grace Turner

Grace Turner (Brenda Blethyn) is Robbie's mother and long-term kitchen worker for the Tallis family. Raising Robbie on her own after being abandoned by her husband, she is a gentle woman who is deeply worried about her son's foray into an upper-class world that will never accept him. She returns to care for Robbie during his hallucination, showing her concern for her son even during the final moments of his life.

Robbie Turner

Robbie Turner (James McAvoy) is the son of the Tallis family cook, Grace Turner, and has benefited from a Cambridge education through the financial support of Mr. Tallis. Portrayed with what Peter Travers in *Rolling Stone* describes as "ardent precision," he is a man whose singular decision to ask a thirteen-year-old girl to deliver a misplaced note rips him from his anticipated future. His love for Cecilia is unquestionable, as is his intelligence, which is proven during his tenure at Cambridge.

Given the choice of completing a prison term for a crime he did not commit or joining the army, Robbie opts for the latter, only to find himself trapped on the beach at Dunkirk awaiting evacuation. As with Cecilia, his story is doubled in the film. Initially, viewers are led to believe that he survives Dunkirk and returns to a life with Cecilia. Later, however, an elderly Briony admits that the version of his life is pure fiction, and that he died the day before an evacuation was possible.

THEMES

Atonement

The English word atonement carries a twofold meaning. The first focuses on reconciliation, and specifically refers to a Christian model of reconciling humankind with God through the sacrificial death of Jesus Christ. The second, and more secular meaning, pertains to the possibility of making reparation or amends for an injury or wrong that has been done. In either case, the endpoint of atonement is not that the making of amends can or will return everything to the way it was before, but to provide a kind of spiritual cleansing that, while powerful, will never undo what has been done.

But what happens when the consequences of one's actions are so devastating and so deeply destructive as to be almost unimaginable? Briony's decision at the age of thirteen is such an action. It is a twisting of truth so powerful that it leaves two lives in ruins and triggers a series of events that culminates five years later with Robbie dying on the beach in Dunkirk and Cecilia in a bombing raid in London, alone and disconnected from her family. Briony's response to this damage is not to apologize (she admits to being too cowardly to do that) but to continue to write and create stories (twenty-one novels) well into her seventies. And it is only when vascular dementia threatens her ability to write and to remember that she takes it upon herself to write the novel that might, in some sense, be seen as making amends for the damage done so many decades earlier. The delay is troublesome in itself. Can atonement be realized fifty years after the fact? But even more troubling are the adjustments that Briony makes to this final story in order to provide Robbie and Cecilia with the happiness that her actions denied them. Are her revisions an act of kindness, as she suggests, or a complicated and disrespectful act of erasure that replaces the true story (death) with a fictional one of her own making (happily ever after).

As Brian McFarlane concludes in his essay, "Watching, Writing and Control: *Atonement*," Briony's apparent quest for atonement through her writing raises far more questions than answers:

> If "atonement" means "reparation for wrong or injury," isn't it merely fanciful of Briony to think she has achieved it? Is the title ironic? Or is her real act of atonement in having lived the rest of her long life with the knowledge of the irreparable harm she has done to two people?

Class Conflict

Thanks to the generosity of Cecilia's father, Robbie is elevated from being the son of a servant to the educational equal of Cecilia (and perhaps even superior to her), a move that lays the groundwork for the romance that seems destined to blossom between them. But as literature has long shown (William Shakespeare's *Romeo and Juliet*, for instance), the realities of class disparity, economic inequality, and perceived social standing are far more powerful than even the passion and sexual desire that fires the spirit of young love. As Peter Mathews notes in his essay, "The Impression of a Deeper Darkness:

READ. WATCH. WRITE.

- Dario Marianelli's award-winning score for *Atonement* was often singled out for praise by critics, who describe it variously as "romantic, kinetic" (Derek Elley in *Variety*) and a "percussive, even violent, aural ostinato" (Ann Hornaday in the *Washington Post*). (*Ostinato* is a musical term derived from the Italian word for stubborn, suggesting a strongly repetitive piece played at the same tone and pitch throughout.) Of particular interest is the ways in which Marianelli incorporates the sounds of the typewriter keys throughout the soundtrack, often "conjoin[ing] the clack-clacking of mechanical composition with the steady plink of a repeated piano note," writes Peter Travers in *Rolling Stone*. Select a story or poem that you have studied, and create a soundtrack (music, sound effects, or some combination) to accompany a reading of it. Think about what sounds make the most sense in order to support the themes explored in the work you have chosen or to capture its tone or voice. Be prepared to present your soundtrack to your class.

- Benedict Cumberbatch (Paul Marshall in *Atonement*) also stars in director Alex Holmes's three-hour dramatized docudrama *Dunkirk* (2004), which focuses on what has often been described as one of the more spectacular rescue operations in military history. Research the history of the Dunkirk rescue, and build a multimedia time line of the events leading up to and including the successful extrication of over four hundred thousand troops trapped in and around the port of Dunkirk. Include on this time line both visual and textual references to the scenes of *Atonement* that take place in and against this chaotic time, bringing art and history together in your project. Share this time line with your classmates and discuss the similarities and differences that you discovered in your research.

- Laura Hillenbrand's *Unbroken: A World War II Story of Survival, Resilience, and Redemption* (2010) is an acclaimed work of nonfiction (also adapted to film in 2014) that recounts the story of Louis Zamperini, a juvenile delinquent whose dreams of Olympic track records are interrupted by the outbreak of World War II. Athlete turned Army Air Corps bombardier, Louis is stranded at sea for forty-seven days following a military plane crash. Battling sharks and dehydration, he is eventually captured and held as a prisoner of war in brutal conditions. Write an essay in which you discuss the theme of resilience as it applied to Louis and the character of Robbie Turner in *Atonement*.

- Australian author Markus Zusak's *The Book Thief* (2005) is a young-adult novel (also adapted to film in 2013) narrated by the character of Death but dominated by the life-affirming power of books, even in such a culture as Nazi Germany that regularly banned or burned books as a show of power. *Atonement* is similarly obsessed with books and words. As Anthony Lane suggests in his *New Yorker* review of *Atonement*, this obsession presents director Wright with a fundamental but challenging "conundrum: how do you film a story about language and not leave it reeking of books?" As a personal homage to the power of books in your life, create a poster that either (a) celebrates a book that has been of particular importance or significance to you, or (b) presents a book that has frequently been challenged or banned in schools. In either case, be sure to develop a clear message about why the book is so powerful, what themes are especially evocative, and how your selection might influence readers to think differently about themselves or the world in which they live.

Ian McEwan's *Atonement*," "however benevolent" the support of Robbie "may be, it is impossible for him to overcome fully the fact that [the] liberality places Robbie in a position of obligation." McFarlane concurs, observing that

> Robbie and Cecilia's feeling for each other—they have grown up together, been remote from each other at Cambridge where he has done a better degree, and have been re-drawn together on [a] hot summer day—has at every turn been influenced by their different class associations.

This unwavering awareness of an archaic class structure is underscored tragically when Robbie is falsely accused of rape. Mathews writes, "The benevolence of the Tallis family evaporates" almost immediately, and Emily Tallis, the matriarch of a family in decline, is "forceful and relentless in the prosecution" of the young man whose education her family has underwritten. Certain of Robbie's innocence, Cecilia cuts herself off from her family and its morally stultifying sense of superiority, choosing to live and die alone in London rather than continue along a pathway that has veered dramatically from one of compassion and moral responsibility. Years later, when Briony imagines a conversation with Robbie (she can never actually confront him), it is a confrontation rife with the politics of class conflict. Robbie challenges,

> Five years ago, you didn't care about telling the truth. You and all your family, you just assumed that for all my education, I was still little better than a servant, still not to be trusted. Thanks to you, they were able to close ranks, and throw me to the . . . wolves.

STYLE

Denouement

A French word meaning "unknotting," denouement refers to the point at which the central conflict or plot complexities of a film or novel are resolved or explained. Wright deploys what can be best described as a doubled denouement in *Atonement*, creating a film that has, in effect, two very distinct and even contradictory endings.

The first denouement takes place during a television interview, in which an elderly Briony discusses her final novel, titled *Atonement*. More confessional than interrogative, the scene clarifies much of what the audience has long suspected: that Briony did, in fact, falsely accuse Robbie of rape, thereby triggering the horrific series of events that culminated, in her novel at least, with a tentative but reaffirming reunion of Robbie and Cecilia. But the happy ending of the novel is not actually the case, as Briony explains in the film's first unknotting. In real life (that is, life outside her novel), Robbie and Cecilia died alone and very much separated from each other. The happy ending that Briony imagines in her novel is simply an attempt at atonement, she admits.

It is an admission that delivers a powerful dramatic impact as viewers are forced to realize the depth of the illusion they have been witness to and the unwavering confidence with which Briony continues to rewrite lives to suit her own needs. Bruno Shah condemns Briony's self-proclaimed act of kindness. "The dramatic denouement" that Briony's novelistic ending feigns, he argues, "is merely the narrating expiration of a contrite but effete and solipsistic sinner, who, at any rate, is ambiguously culpable for a 'crime' she committed at age thirteen."

It is important to note, however, that Wright's film itself does not end with the story of the deaths of Robbie and Cecilia or even with the unraveling of Briony's ambiguous act of kindness. Rather, as James Schiff summarizes in his essay, "Reading and Writing on Screen: Cinematic Adaptations of McEwan's *Atonement* and Cunningham's *The Hours*," the film itself concludes with a scene of Robbie and Cecilia on a beach—playful, tender, deeply in love, and heading toward the "lingering image of the seaside cottage, framed beneath white cliffs" into which the two lovers disappear. The film ends, in other words, with an expression of Briony's false ending.

The impact of this doubled unknotting is at once powerful and unsettling. "The film," as Schiff explains, "demonstrates how cinema romanticizes and deceives" through the confessions of Briony as storyteller, but then turns immediately upon this revelation by giving viewers "a romantic ending that we know is not true but nevertheless is persuasive and desirable." Viewers are challenged by this denouement, forced to reflect upon their own willingness to suspend disbelief so readily in support of happy endings and clear resolutions that run counter to much of what is experienced in life beyond the movies.

Flashback

A flashback is a segment of a film that breaks established chronological order by shifting to time past, thereby providing the filmmaker with the opportunity to introduce a new subjective perspective (showing a character with a premonition of something that might happen before it does happen) or for an objective way of supplying details from the past. Wright uses the latter technique often in *Atonement* so that viewers come to understand the power of Briony's imagination and, more specifically, the power of her imagination to misread events and circumstances with potentially devastating effect.

Whether it is the retelling of the fountain scene, or the flashback to Robbie's selection of the wrong letter to slip into the envelope, or, most tellingly, the use of a time shift to explain more fully the passionate lovemaking in the library, Wright uses flashback as a kind of corrective or counterbalance to Briony's restrictive and hyper-moralizing imagination that sees predation in flirtation and lower-class immorality in natural sexual behavior.

Perspective

Atonement creates an intricate web of narrative perspectives, each relating to the four major parts or movements of the film. Parts One (1935 summer house), Two (Dunkirk, 1940), and Three (London, 1940) are all presented as a third-person perspective that recounts the actions as though being watched by a detached observer. The brief fourth section, however, reveals that the film has, in fact, been the narrative construction of an explicit and direct first-person narrator, an elderly Briony who is the creator of the story of Robbie and Cecilia as it has been shared with readers. Peter Mathews's comments on McEwan's original use of this perspective shift are equally applicable to Wright's film: it is "a tactic that requires the [viewer] continually to revise their view of particular events and characters." Are there, in fact, two narrators in *Atonement*, or only one—the elderly Briony— whose perspective shifts across the film but whose consciousness (and purpose in storytelling) remains consistent? Is *Atonement*, in other words, all told from Briony's perspective, and, if so, how does that impact a viewer's understanding of the events recounted? Has this film been the real story of Robbie and Cecilia or simply another of Briony's recreations of their story,

told from her perspective and driven (perhaps) by her unusual (and untrustworthy) blend of imagination and fact?

CULTURAL CONTEXT

Wright's *Atonement* offers a challenge to viewers trying to establish a clear sense of cultural context to the film. On the one hand, the film is dominated by a period from the summer of 1935 through to October 1940, when Cecilia dies in the bombing that flooded the Balham underground station in London. In this context, *Atonement* can be viewed is a powerful commentary on the class structure that shaped British culture of the day. In this sense, Robbie is the perfect foil for a character like Paul Marshall. The son of a kitchen worker, Robbie is, as he suggests, "thrown to the wolves" based on Briony's false accusation, while the wealthy Marshall is seen as beyond reproach (and possible suspicion) given his social standing, which in the world of the Tallis family is mistakenly equated with an equally superior moral standing. (Interestingly, in Briony's version of the story, Cecilia and Robbie never suspect Marshall but focus their attention instead on another member of the rural working class, Danny Hardman.) The contrasts build across the length of the film: while Robbie is offered the opportunity to fight at the front line (in exchange for release from prison), Marshall stays safely ensconced in the North, increasing his wealth by supplying the troops with chocolate bars. And in an ironic twist, Marshall is free to marry the woman he raped, while Robbie dies at Dunkirk before every getting his chance to resume his own love story with Cecilia.

On the other hand, the cultural context for *Atonement* is much more contemporary, given that Briony's confessional interview takes place around 2001, the same year that McEwan published his novel. In this context, the film's emphasis on Briony's disruptive, confessional interview is very much aligned with postmodern questioning of the relationship between art and truth, history and story, and the moral implications of art generally. Manipulating reality freely throughout her life as a writer, Briony remains until the end of her creative life an artist whose commitment to delivering a sense of hope or satisfaction overrides her relationship to

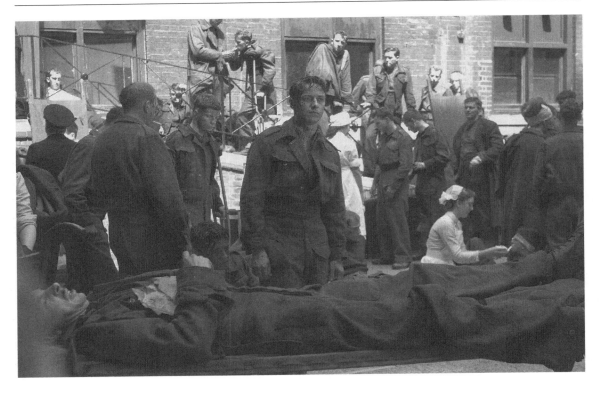

truthfulness or even the lesser goal of veracity. Although this focus on creativity is in itself not problematic, it does pose some challenges for a writer looking to use her writing as atonement for past transgressions, or who sees her storytelling as at least partial reparation for damage done. In this sense, *Atonement* is to be viewed in the context of a postmodern culture searching for a stable sense of right and wrong, order in the face of chaos, and truth.

Despite Briony's obvious skill and her determination to deliver hope, she never realizes atonement in the classic sense of providing a model for others to follow. As Robbie says to her (albeit in Briony's own version of the story):

> How old do you have to be before you know the difference between right and wrong? Do you have to be eighteen? Do you have to be eighteen before you can bring yourself to own up to a lie? There are soldiers of eighteen old enough to be left to die on the side of the road! Did you know that?

This moral weakness is underscored by the fact that even late in her life, Briony cannot seem to shake the moral malaise that seems to define her life and her art. As Shah notes, "There is something sinister (as well as disappointing) about an author whose effects are achieved at the expense of his characters," and even more profoundly, in Briony's case, at the expense of her own self-proclaimed desire for atonement. There is something disappointing, too, about a world in which a falsely accused young man of promise cannot be held up as a model of a life lived nobly and bravely despite his mistreatment.

CRITICAL OVERVIEW

Film adaptations of critically acclaimed novels often pose a particular challenge for reviewers, and Joe Wright's reimagining of *Atonement* is no exception, with critics relatively split in their opinions of its success as a film and, more importantly, as a film based on a novel. *Rolling Stone*'s Peter Travers, for instance, is unflinching in his praise of the film, noting that it is "[w]ritten, directed and acted to perfection." Sweeping an audience "up on waves of humor, heartbreak and ravishing romance," it "is literary in the best possible sense: It's obsessed with the power of words"; and it speaks elegantly to "what's time-less about passion, art, and redemption." Travers's review is rich with praise for all involved in the film: Knightley is "stunning," McAvoy "a dynamo," together they "are heaven-sent acting partners, radiating a heroic spirit that insists on the primacy of love," and director Wright exudes talent that is "combustibly exciting." But Travers saves his most dynamic praise for the young Saoirse Roman (adolescent Briony Tallis), whose performance "simply takes your breath away" and is "the film's glory."

Peter Bradshaw, in the *Guardian*, also praised the film, calling it a "lavish and spectac-ular screen version" of an equally spectacular novel. "Clever, ambitious, compassionate," it is a film that treats an audience "like grownups" both intellectually and emotionally. Derek Elley of *Variety* opens his review with the bold state-ment that "rarely has a book sprung so vividly to life, but also so enthrallingly in pure movie terms." This sentiment is also expressed by Anne Hornaday in the *Washington Post*, who writes that this film "has achieved that to which every literary adaptation should aspire, to respect the original material while freeing it from confining reverence." It is, she declares in closing, "a film that is almost too exquisite for words." Calling the film "relentless," Roger Ebert in the *Chicago Sun-Times* declares it sim-ply "one of the year's best films," while Joe Mor-genstern in the *Wall Street Journal* celebrates the film as "a singular achievement—romantic, sensuous, intelligent and finally shattering in its sweep and complexity." Lou Lumenick of the *New York Post* went so far as to call it "a sweep-ing epic that speaks to the 21st-century soul."

Not all critics were enthralled with the film, however. Lisa Schwarzbaum closes her tepid review in *Entertainment Weekly* with the obser-vation that "it's a nice movie where magnificence is in order," while Anthony Lane in the *New Yorker* frames his concerns slightly differently, acknowledging that while there is much to admire in the film, one is left wondering initially if it might not be "too self-conscious for its own good." More poignant still, he asks, "what hap-pened to its heart"? Following the elderly Bri-ony's revelations that close the film, Lane is left even more troubled by the film in its entirety: "her last, beneficent lie," he acknowledges, "made me look back over the expanse of the

film and realize, to my dismay, that I hardly believed a word of it." In the end, he suggests, *Atonement* is a "beautiful, unsatisfying film" held together not by passion and artistry but "with smoke and mirrors." Geoff Pevere of the *Toronto Star* takes a similar view, labeling it a "handsomely tidy and earnestly dull" film that amounts to little more than "a prettily cast, pro-fessionally performed, impeccably mounted bore."

The most direct criticism, however, came from A. O. Scott, the influential critic of the *New York Times*. Noting that it is "not a bad literary adaptation," he calls *Atonement* "an almost classical example of how pointless, how diminishing, the transmutation of literature into film can be." He sees the war scenes set amidst the chaos of Dunkirk, in particular, as marked by only "an empty, arty virtuosity." Oscillating between murkiness and gimmickry, *Atonement* "fails to be anything more than a decorous, heavily decorated and ultimately superficial reading of the book on which it is based."

CRITICISM

Klay Dyer

Dyer is a freelance writer and editor who special-izes in topics relating to literature, film, and popu-lar culture. In the following essay, he explores the tensions between what is seen and what is imagined in Joe Wright's film adaptation of Atonement.

A critical scene early in *Atonement* has thir-teen-year-old Briony Tallis sitting across the table from a police detective who has been called to the family estate to investigate the rape of fifteen-year-old Lola Quincey. The detective is gentle but forceful and persistent in his question-ing, with particular emphasis on one key point: did Briony see the perpetrator well enough to identify him despite the darkness and the stress associated with the situation? Initially Briony wavers, unwilling to commit herself to the cer-tainty associated with a visual identification. But the wavering soon subsides, and she utters the words that seal the fate of not only Robbie Turner, but her sister Cecilia and, with some irony, herself. "Yes," she says with confidence, "I saw him. I saw him with my own eyes."

These words resonate throughout the film, which pays direct homage to the power of Bri-ony's eyes through a series of extreme close-ups.

WHAT IS CERTAIN, THOUGH, IS THAT
THROUGHOUT *ATONEMENT*, VIEWERS ARE ASKED TO
BEAR WITNESS TO THE POWER OF BRIONY'S
PERCEPTION-MAKING PROWESS AS HER STORIES
SWEEP RAGGEDLY THROUGH THE LIVES OF THOSE
AROUND HER, DESPITE THEIR PLEADINGS FOR NO
MORE RHYMES AND NO MORE EMBELLISHMENTS."

More importantly, these words highlight one of the most compelling tensions shaping the film: the tension between what is seen and what is true.

Viewers of *Atonement* are repeatedly made aware of the perilous crossroads of perception and misperception, especially when the events are viewed through Briony's eyes. The film opens, for instance, with the much-discussed fountain scene, which Briony watches unfold from her bedroom window. She immediately begins to misinterpret the interaction, perceiving Robbie's actions as a volatile combination of threat and sexual power directed toward her sister. The implications of this scene are significant, especially given that what viewers know or will soon know about the younger Tallis sister: left to her own devices to make sense of the world, she is an energetically imaginative writer with a very keen concern for the intricacies and overall impact of her presentations. When she later opens a letter from Robbie to Cecilia and discovers a vulgar, sexually charged word, her earlier misperceptions are reinforced. And later still, when she walks in on them in a passionate sexual embrace in the library, her vision of Robbie is solidified: he is, at least, a sex maniac, and at worst, a member of the morally depraved underclass (despite his Cambridge education) or a predator.

Perception is unleashed more tragically when Lola is attacked during a stressful evening of searching for lost children. Briony's past perceptions guide her to imagine Robbie as the only possible suspect, although her older brother Leon and visiting industrialist Paul Marshall would, to a less tainted eye, be equally valid possibilities. But Leon, as a Tallis family member, is

beyond reproach, and Briony sees in Paul a kindred member of the upper class, and a man, therefore, wholly incapable of such actions.

Briony is successful in her accusation of Robbie because, as a member of an established local family, she is already perceived to be in a position of some clarity and power by the local police, especially in class-conscious England of the 1930s. She is also a child, which would give her no reason to lie, and especially about a friend of the family whom she has known for years.

But what viewers also know, and a fact that slips through the perceptional net of the adults in this moment, is that Briony has been harboring a deep crush on Robbie, which she admits later during a casual conversation with another probationary nurse at St. Thomas. With eyes still wide from her discoveries of that day (in connection with the fountain, the letter, and the library), Briony is seeing the world through the distorting lens of sexual and romantic jealousy. Contrary to the belief of her mother (from whom Briony has learned much about class and morality, it seems), Briony is not of clear vision on this night.

Further still, as an avid reader and writer of such romantic melodrama as *The Trials of Arabella*, Briony has the benefit of truly believing what she has seen to be true, since it is a view of the world that has been planted deeply into her overactive and uncritical imagination. What Briony thinks she sees with her thirteen-year-old eyes is compelling and unquestionable evidence: Robbie uses vulgar language and has sex with Cecilia, therefore is a depraved man or, as she states to Lola, a sex maniac. And what Briony thinks she knows, and what is reinforced by the romance-fueled logic that guides her perception, is that wicked men do wicked things, and will continue to do them until they are caught by someone of noble character or higher class.

So what Briony sees that evening in the hills is the perfect story unfolding before her eyes. A young girl is raped while searching for her lost siblings, which is an act of almost unimaginable depravity. The Robbie that she saw that same day pinning her sister to the bookshelves, in what she perceives as an act of sexual predation, is clearly depraved. The clues line up, and Briony sees the truth of the situation with what she believes to be unwavering clarity, and speaks the words that trigger the undeniable tragedy of Robbie's imprisonment.

WHAT DO I SEE NEXT?

- Wright's adaptation of Jane Austen's *Pride and Prejudice* (2005, rated PG-13) also stars Keira Knightley in an admittedly more genteel exploration of many of the themes that shape *Atonement*: wealth and class, especially as they come to impact the dynamics of love and romance, the fragility and power of reputation, and the journey toward self-knowledge.

- Arguably one of the greatest war films of all time, *Casablanca* (1942, rated PG-13) is also a story of a couple (played by Humphrey Bogart and Ingrid Bergman) caught between two worlds: one defined by love and one by the expectations of duty or virtue during a time of war. Like *Atonement*, it is a story fraught with emotions associated with sacrifice, jealousy, and life-changing decisions. Unlike *Atonement*, it ends with a life-affirming decision.

- Like Wright's *Atonement*, Anthony Minghella's 1996 film adaptation of Michael Ondaatje's award-winning novel *The English Patient* (1992, rated R for sexuality, violence, and language) is a passionate love story set against the backdrop of World War II. It is also an exploration of the power of love, misunderstanding, storytelling, and healing told through a series of flashbacks.

- Based on British writer Louis de Bernières's 1994 novel of the same name, *Captain Corelli's Mandolin* (2001, rated R for some violence, sexuality, and language) is set in 1941 after Italy has allied with Germany to conquer Greece. An Italian garrison is established on a remote Greek island, but when Italy surrenders to the Allies, an Italian officer must defend his newfound community (and the woman he loves) from a German invasion. Like *Atonement*, this is a story of a love that is forced to overcome insurmountable obstacles during a brutal war.

- James Cameron's *Titanic* (1997, rated PG-13 for violence, nudity, and sensuality) explores the theme of love and social class, but with a compelling twist as a beautiful young aristocrat, facing marriage to a rich heir at the arrangement of her mother, falls in love with a poor artist who is traveling as a third-class passenger aboard the ill-fated *Titanic*. As in *Atonement*, the story is recounted by an elderly woman as she recollects and struggles to reconcile powerful memories.

- Written and directed by Cameron Crowe, *Say Anything* (1989, rated PG-13) is a contemporary American take on the theme of social class and love set against high-school graduation in Seattle, Washington. An aspiring kickboxer sets out to begin a romance with the school valedictorian, despite the fact that her father does not approve and she is heading to England on a scholarship.

- Starring Helena Bonham Carter, Colin Firth, and Geoffrey Rush, *The King's Speech* (2010, rated R for some language) is an inspiring film about the power of words and the power of friendship set against political turmoil, personal scandal, and pending war. When King Edward VIII abdicates the throne to marry divorced American socialite Wallis Simpson, his brother George reluctantly assumes the throne. Painfully self-conscious due to his stammer, George turns to an unorthodox speech therapist for assistance, and, as time passes, for friendship and advice.

Tellingly, age and relocation from the family estate to wartime London does little to expand Briony's abilities to see the world, and by extension, her past as clearly as she might. As she notes in a letter to Cecilia, her decision to do nurse training instead of following the family

© *Focus Features | The Kobal Collection | Bailey, Alex*

pathway to Cambridge is, however honorable, underwritten with a sense of the melodramatic:

> I decided I wanted to make myself useful, do something practical. But no matter how hard I work, not matter how long the hours, I can't escape from what I did and what it meant, the full extent of which I'm only now beginning to grasp.

The words here ring hollow, especially when one considers that they are written five years after the false accusation, which also means five years into Robbie's prison/military term as well as five years into Cecilia's estrangement from the Tallis family.

It is clear that Briony's eyes have not yet adjusted to the real world. On her own and left to her own devices to manage in the world, she continues to take solace in her writing and in her perceptions of the world as a romantic melodrama. When asked to tend to Luc Comet, a mortally wounded French soldier, she overcomes her initial hesitation and allows herself to be drawn into his story, despite the fact that she has never been to his hometown of Millau or met his family. Recognizing that his brain damage is

extensive, she willfully imagines herself into the dual role of angelic nurse and lost lover. Later, when asked if she has ever had a serious crush, she recounts the incident during which Robbie was forced to save her from the pond with a tenderness unbecoming the reality of the situation.

Throughout the novel, Briony perceives the world as a series of unstructured events that she can bend and shape into satisfying (for her, at least) stories. Sadly, it is only through these stories that Briony can define herself and bring coherence and meaning to her perceived realities.

Moreover, and as viewers realize in the brief fourth part of the film, it is only through projecting herself into the stories of Robbie and Cecilia (both of whom die in 1940) that Briony is able to reconcile her perceptions in preparation for her own declining health. Spurred to write her final novel by a diagnosis of vascular dementia, Briony uses her closing story not as a correction for past damage or expression of some transcendental truth, but as an opportunity to create a self-proclaimed "act of kindness." By rewriting reality, Briony is freed to perceive it as such, just as by calling her final novel *Atonement*, she is freed to "see with her own eyes" that she has given to "Robbie and Cecilia what they lost out on in life." In the end, misperception gives what misperception has taken away, which, to Briony's way of seeing at least, means that atonement as been achieved.

By overtly emphasizing the tension between perception and imagination, director Joe Wright creates a film that blossoms into a matrix of perceptional uncertainties and perpetually shifting options. At the same time, he shows the audience that with the power to shift perception comes a great responsibility that transcends art, or politics, or business. In the end, the question of Briony's successful reparation is an open one. Does her appropriation of the deaths of Robbie and Cecilia activate atonement through, as she suggests, an act of kindness, or does it constitute yet another example of her unwillingness to allow reality to stand as it is? Is it possible for a story to atone for actions that can never be undone? What is certain, though, is that throughout *Atonement*, viewers are asked to bear witness to the power of Briony's perception-making prowess as her stories sweep raggedly through the lives of those around her, despite their pleadings for no more rhymes and no more embellishments.

Source: Klay Dyer, Critical Essay on *Atonement*, in *Novels for Students*, Gale, Cengage Learning, 2015.

Laura Marcus

In the following excerpt, Marcus examines the relationship between time and knowledge in Atonement.

. . . The ironies of *Atonement*'s retrospective composition are unlikely to be fully comprehended at a first reading. The intense jolt to the first-time reader occurs at a late stage in the novel when it is made clear that we have been reading the final 'draft' of a novel, written by the central character Bryony [sic] Tallis, who makes her initial appearance, as an aspiring 13-year-old writer, on the novel's first page. The two characters—Cecilia and Robbie—whose destinies have become a matter of such moment, have not survived within historical time. Their lives have been extended only in Bryony's narrative, the consolatory nature of which is presented in coded form in the third section of the novel when Bryony, nursing a dying Frenchman, Luc Cornet, tells him of her sister and the man she is

> **ISSUES OF KNOWLEDGE AND VISION FUNCTION AT TWO LEVELS IN THE NARRATIVE: THEY RELATE TO THE QUESTION OF WHAT CHARACTERS KNOW AND SEE, OR IMAGINE THEY KNOW AND HAVE SEEN, AND TO THE QUESTION OF NARRATION ITSELF AND THE WORKINGS OF NARRATIVE OMNISCIENCE."**

to marry. In readings beyond the first, the insistent use of prospect and retrospect, and the invocation of 'posthumous ironies', will point to a knowledge initially concealed by the power of the narrative drive. Time becomes the medium and instrument of irony and pathos, as the lineaments of the 'present' are imagined from the perspectives of a future which neither Cecilia nor Robbie, the characters who are represented most fully in this mode of anticipated retrospect, will in fact live out—'the unavailable future', in a phrase used later in the novel in connection with the dead Luc (McEwan 2002: 311). Cecilia envisages a future vantage point from which she will look back at a present which has become the past: 'Cecilia wondered, as she sometimes did when she met a man for the first time, if this was the one she was going to marry, and whether it was this particular moment she would remember for the rest of her life—with gratitude, or profound and particular regret' (McEwan, 2002: 47). Robbie projects himself forward into the man he will never in fact become, imagining his future as he walks to the Tallis's house for an evening whose outcome will be the destruction of every plan he has made: 'The hard soles of his shoes rapped loudly on the metalled road like a giant clock, and he made himself think about time, about his great hoard, the luxury of an unspent fortune. He had never before felt so self-consciously young, nor experienced such appetite, such impatience for the story to begin' (McEwan 2002: 92). Our stories, though, are not always ours for the making.

In the long first section of the novel, which recounts the events of a single day, the third-person narration enters, in turn, the consciousnesses of four of the characters depicted:

Bryony, her sister Cecilia, their mother Emily, and Robbie, son of their cleaning woman Grace Turner. If Cecilia and Robbie, who first become lovers during the evening of this day, are caught in the imaginings of time and subjected to its failed possibilities and ironies, Bryony and Emily inhabit, and are inhabited by, another set of terms, in particular those of knowledge and vision, knowing and seeing. Bryony is explicitly represented as the fabulist, the maker-up, and the writer, of stories. Writing is her way of ordering the world, and its initial pleasures are those of miniaturization—to be compared with the satisfaction of her neatly arranged model farm—and the satisfactions of completion. Yet as the day progresses, Bryony begins to understand something of complexity of the role of fiction in representing multiple and conflicting points of view.

An author often cited by McEwan as an influence on his work, Henry James, proclaims: 'The house of fiction has in short not one window, but a million—a number of possible windows not to be reckoned, rather' (James 2003: 45). Throughout *Atonement* Bryony, like Henry Perowne in *Saturday*, is represented as a watcher from windows. James, writing at the turn of the nineteenth and twentieth centuries, represented such ways of seeing as central to the 'architecture' of the modern novel. The intense focus, in the work of James and his contemporaries, including Joseph Conrad and Ford Madox Ford, on the relationship between consciousness and vision and its multiple perspectives, challenged the idea that there is a single, objective way of viewing and describing events, objects and people. Bryony's witnessing of 'the scene by the fountain'—the encounter between Cecilia and Robbie which lies at the novel's heart—already witnessed by the reader through the eyes of a seemingly omniscient narrator, and her failure to comprehend what she sees, leads to a new understanding of writing: 'she sensed she could write a scene like the one by the fountain and she could include a hidden observer like herself' (McEwan 2002: 40):

> She [Bryony] could write the scene three times over, from three points of view [. . .] She need only show separate minds, as alive as her own, struggling with the idea that other minds were equally alive [. . .] And only in a story could you enter these different minds and show how they had an equal value. That was the only moral a story need have. (McEwan 2002: 40)

Yet this is not a fully or finally achieved vision: Bryony subsequently finds herself unable to deal with contradiction and imposes an interpretative 'order' on events, which has fatal consequences for those around her.

Emily writes nothing and sees nothing from the bed to which illness confines her, yet possesses a form of 'sixth sense', which she describes as

> a tentacular awareness that reached out from the dimness and moved through the house, unseen and all-knowing [. . .] What to others would have been a muffling was to her alert senses, which were fine-tuned like the cat's whiskers of an old wireless, an almost unbearable amplification. She lay in the dark and knew everything. The less she was able to do, the more she was aware. (McEwan 2002: 66)

Lying in bed, she hears the sound of a man's voice in the room in which her niece Lola is staying. She 'beamed her raw attention into every recess of the house. There was nothing, and then, like a lamp turned on and off in total darkness, there was a little squeal of laughter abruptly smothered. Lola, then, in the nursery with Marshall' (McEwan 2002: 69). She is reassured by her identification of the sounds of the house: wrongly so, for it is Marshall who will be responsible for the damage that follows. The novel thus puts into question the very concept of narrative omniscience, of the 'unseen and all-knowing' narrator. Emily is indeed aware that she 'could send her tendrils into every room of the house, but she could not send them into the future' (McEwan 2002: 71).

The terms of 'knowing' and 'seeing/unseeing' are brought together with those of Bryony's 'crime' at the close of the day, the false identification of Robbie as Lola's rapist: 'the understanding that what she knew was not literally, or not only, based on the visible' (McEwan 2002: 169). Bryony's dangerous 'knowledge' results from her need for a story that makes sense of the events she witnessed earlier in the day but whose meaning she has not understood: Cecilia and Robbie at the fountain, the 'obscene' word in the letter she carried from Robbie to Cecilia, their love-making in the library which Bryony interprets as Robbie's assault upon her sister. Throughout the first section of the novel, she understands sexual passion as coercion and violence.

Issues of knowledge and vision function at two levels in the narrative: they relate to the question of what characters know and see, or imagine they know and have seen, and to the question of narration itself and the workings of narrative omniscience. This is brought into relationship with 'telepathy' and 'clairvoyance', the 'shilling's glimpse of the future' (with all the irony that this phrase imparts, in a novel of 'unavailable futures') provided by Robbie's mother Grace (McEwan 2002: 88). 'A story was a form of telepathy', Bryony thinks, as she contemplates the question of 'intention' and of minds other than her own: 'By means of inking symbols onto a page, she was able to send thoughts and feelings from her mind to her reader's. It was a magical process, so commonplace that no one stopped to wonder at it' (McEwan 2002: 37). The thought chimes with Nicholas Royle's argument that narrative 'omniscience' is a misnomer, bringing with it an inappropriate religious baggage, for the ways in which communication occurs between author and character, author and reader—the reading of minds, the entry into the minds of others, and the communication of the contents of these minds to readers—is not 'omniscient', Royle argues, but telepathic. The category of the 'omniscient narrator', so familiar that its presuppositions go unquestioned, conceals the 'magical process', the magical thinking that lies at the heart of literary writing and reading (Royle 2003: 261) . . . .

Source: Laura Marcus, "Ian McEwan's Modernist Time: *Atonement* and *Saturday*," in *Ian McEwan: Contemporary Critical Perspectives*, edited by Sebastian Groes, Bloomsbury, 2013, pp. 87–90.

Julie Ellam

In the following excerpt, Ellam compares the film with the novel and lays out the "lukewarm reception" that the film received.

In terms of sales, *Atonement* is a national and international bestseller and has been translated into a number of languages including Spanish, Dutch and Portuguese. Its sales were increased due to the tie-in publication with the release of the film version and it has been the recipient of a number of awards. These include the WH Smith Literary Prize, the National Book Critics' Circle Award, the Santiago Prize for the European Novel and the Los Angeles Times Prize for Fiction.

McEwan already has a connection with the film industry, having written screenplays, and some of his works have also been adapted for

> AS BRADSHAW SUGGESTS, WHETHER IT RECEIVES HIGH BOX-OFFICE SALES OR NOT, THE QUALITY OF THE ADAPTATION WILL ENSURE IT A LONGEVITY OF ITS OWN APART FROM ITS CONNECTION WITH THE WELL-SOLD NOVEL."

film prior to *Atonement* (2007). These include *The Comfort of Strangers* (1990), *The Cement Garden* (1993) and *Enduring Love* (2004). As a measure of his kudos, the screenplay for the latter was written by Harold Pinter. It is perhaps in keeping with the popularity of the novel that *Atonement* the film has so far been the most high-profile of his works to be adapted.

The Working Title Films adaptation of *Atonement* premiered at the Venice Film Festival in September 2007 as part of an extensive publicity drive. The reception from the critics may have been mixed, but for a time it was the great British film of the year as it was nominated for seven Academy Awards in 2008 and won a Golden Globe and a BAFTA for Best Film. Reviews varied from claiming it is 'masterly', by Philip French in the *Observer*, to proposing it demonstrates how 'pointless' adaptations can be (A. O. Scott, 2007).

In his review of the novel, Tom Shone sees the opening as having the potential of being a Merchant Ivory production in the future with its setting of the English country house and the centrality of the Tallis family (Shone, 2002). As he goes on to concede, this would never be possible given the material, but the film version *Atonement* (2007), directed by Joe Wright and adapted by Christopher Hampton, capitalizes on its depiction of an upper middle-class English family in the 1930s in these early pre-war scenes. The elderly Briony is played by Vanessa Redgrave and her inclusion, along with Keira Knightley and James McAvoy, invites us to see this as a British star vehicle for the international market.

THE RECEPTION OF THE FILM

In comparison with the favourable book reviews, the adaptation to film in 2007 had a more lukewarm reception. James Christopher for *The Times* points out it was one of the 'great hopes' for British cinema for that year, but thinks it fails to merit the attention it has been given, particularly when the action moves from 1935 to the Second World War: 'The moment Robbie is jailed, the credibility of Wright's him starts coming apart. The story takes a rude melodramatic knapsack off to war, and an older Briony (played by Romola Garai) signs up as a nurse and tries to atone for her ghastly sin' (Christopher, 2007).

A similar criticism is made in the *New York Times* by Scott who also regards it as becoming weaker as it moves away from the first scenes of 1935. Scott argues that it is not that this is a 'bad literary adaptation', but that it is instead 'an almost classic example of how pointless, how diminishing, the transmutation of literature into film can be. The respect that Mr Wright and Mr Hampton show to Mr McEwan is no doubt gratifying to him, but is fatal to their own project' (Scott, 2007). This loyalty to the novel has also meant that the abrupt shift to the war has not translated to the screen as would have been hoped. Visually, the separate sections have the effect of making the film disjointed, and if a smoother movement through time is required, the adaptation needs to steer away from the novel more obviously.

Cosmo Landesman offers another negative perspective and suggests this is a film that has nothing new to offer: 'Irritatingly, *Atonement* gives us the worst of two worlds stylistically: it exploits the taste and nostalgia for 1930s and 1940s Hollywood melodrama, yet it has an annoying postmodern knowingness to it. At its heart is a concern with the unreliability of narrative, be it that of a 13-year-old girl one hot summer's day or that of British history. Thus, when Robbie, who chooses the army instead of prison, winds up at Dunkirk, waiting for evacuation, we see that episode in a different light. Instead of a heroic exodus, we get a nightmarish vision of horses being shot and men going crazy' (Landesman, 2007). Both the book and film elaborate on a version of the retreat that goes against the traditional view that it was as Landesman claims 'a heroic exodus', which has been the prevailing British ideology since the Second World War. Robbie is constructed as a hero, but no comfort in defeat is offered for the viewers or readers, as this episode is captured as bloody and

ultimately wasteful. By representing this significantly precarious moment in British history in such a way—that is, not patriotically—McEwan and Wright will be open for criticism (and especially from those who see such depictions as disloyal). When the film is seen as a critique of destruction, however, it is not so easy to condemn.

For a more positive account of the film, French in the *Observer* considers the later sequences of the 1935 section as being handled with 'immense narrative verve' and praises the process of adaptation overall despite the occasional melodramatic touches: 'What the film brings to the book, apart from excellent performances, are fine images and a powerful period atmosphere' (French, 2007, p. 18). It is also of note that whereas Scott and Landesman question the use of the long tracking shot of the beaches at Dunkirk, French regards this as one of the finest aspects of the film: 'There is a virtuoso long take, lasting five to six minutes, that belongs beside long takes by Hitchcock, Welles, Jancso, Antonioni, and Angelopoulos' (French, 2007, p. 18). By promoting this particular shot, French makes the case for the artistic remit as well as defending this deconstruction of the Dunkirk spirit.

ANALYSIS

Negative criticisms levelled at the adaptation include the accusation by Scott that it follows the novel too closely, yet superficially, and describes it as being 'piously rendered' by Hampton (Scott, 2007). His main dispute with the film comes at the expense of a comparison with the novel: 'Mr McEwan's prose pulls you in immediately and drags you through an intricate, unsettling story, releasing you in a shaken wrung-out state. The film, after a tantalizing start, sputters to a halt in a welter of grandiose imagery and hurtling montage' (Scott, 2007). An interpretation such as this is in opposition to Brian McFarlane's *Novel to Film* (1996), which explains how 'fidelity criticism' has tended to favour novels over films as it 'depends on a notion of the text as having and rendering up to the (intelligent) reader a single, correct "meaning" which the filmmaker has either adhered to or in some sense violated in tampered with' (McFarlane, 1996, p. 8). By questioning the primacy of the novel, McFarlane enables an analysis of the adaptation in its own right: 'The stress on fidelity to the original undervalues other aspects of the film's intertextuality. By this, I mean those non-literary, non-novelistic influences at work on any film, whether or not it is based on a novel' (McFarlane, 1996, p. 21). He follows this up by explaining that the novel is just one element of the film's intertextuality and aspects such as the actors used, the 'cultural climate', the director's influence and the 'prevailing parameters of cinematic practice' should also be brought into the evaluation (McFarlane, 1996, p. 22). Although he refutes a straightforward hierarchy of a novel being preferred over the film, he also adds that the adaptation does not stand alone either and comparisons are inevitable if the book has been read before viewing the film.

As a film that is concerned with the way a writer manipulates narratives, it should be said that it is difficult to separate the connectedness between this particular novel and film, even when one takes McFarlane's point into account about showing fair recognition to adaptations. The opening credits and first scene inform the viewers immediately of the role the writer takes in this work, as a tap of keys from a typewriter spells out the title and the opening scene of summer 1935. When the camera then shifts from the nursery toys to focus on Briony typing her final version of *The Trials of Arabella*, her youthful yet earnest ambition to be a writer is imprinted on the screen. French interprets this opening as a wider metaphor for the film and the novel: '*Atonement* begins with the film's title and its setting (the summer of 1935) loudly printed out by a manual typewriter, thus implanting in our minds that what we are about to experience is a literary work and indeed it is about fiction itself, its purpose and its morality' (French, 2007, p. 18).

The main score, which is composed by Dario Marienelli (and who is the recipient of the only Academy Award for the film), also includes the thread of the sound of typing to add urgency. This occurs, for example, when Briony is searching for her mother to show her this new venture as a playwright. In an otherwise condemnatory review, Scott interprets these early scenes in the country house as relatively praiseworthy and makes reference to the unifying effect of the typist at work: 'This charged, hardly unfamiliar atmosphere provides, in the first section of the film, some decent, suspenseful fun, a rush of incident and implication. Boxy

cars rolling up the drive; whispers of scandal and family secrets; coitus interrupts in the library, all set to the implacable rhythm of typewriter keys' (Scott, 2007). Because Robbie is also shown sat typing his letter to Cecilia . . . the connection and difference between Briony and Robbie is made graphic. Both have been captured as authors, but it is Briony who takes and keeps control of the plot.

As with the novel, her influence on the arrangements of events in the 1935 section is explained with subtlety as it maintains a similar shift between points of view, and this is done through the replaying of key scenes. This is given most attention when Briony looks through the window and sees Robbie and Cecilia at the fountain. Her shock, which is based on misinterpretation, is explained by the replay where the viewers hear the dialogue between Robbie and Cecilia which Briony has been excluded from. The clue remains that this is her story, though, as her appearance at the window frames both versions of this narrative of the two figures by the fountain.

The centrality of Briony and the theme of her dangerous literary imagination are both maintained in the film and, as mentioned in the bonus scenes, this is brought about visually by giving the three different actors who play her at 13, as a young woman, and at the age of 77, the same hairstyle of a bob and a noticeable facial birthmark. Because it is unlikely that Briony's hair has stayed the same for over 60 years, this also has the effect of emphasizing that this is a fiction that she, McEwan and Wright have created. As with the novel, her final revelation acts as a conclusion and is allowed to have the same unsettling impact as it undoes the reality that we have already seen, of Robbie and Cecilia reunited in her flat. The use of the visual medium is made relevant as Briony gives away the secret that this is her refashioning of the story in an interview for television with Anthony Minghella playing the part of interviewer.

As well as holding the narrative together with Briony and the theme of writing, immersion in water is another recurring motif and this is used to create a chain of signifies that signal figurative rebirths and the death of Cecilia. When Cecilia plunges into the fountain to retrieve the broken pieces of the vase, and to demonstrate her recently learned maturity to Robbie, and when Robbie is viewed bathing and Cecilia drowns after the explosion at the underground station, the film uses this element as an equalizer and as a trope to deconstruct the apparently stable hierarchies of class difference. Water washes away the sins, perhaps, but it is also used to form a connection between the lovers. This is used most effectively with the cut from Cecilia diving into the lake to Robbie sitting up in the bath after being immersed.

It is also the means for heightening Robbie's hallucinatory state at Dunkirk, as well as emphasizing his and his mother's virtue. This comes when he imagines his mother has taken off his boots and then washes his feet. The image of the mother showing love for her son is overlaid with the idea that she and Robbie are above reproach as the washing of feet also alludes to Jesus' selfless service.

Peter Childs regards the use of 'water, mirrors, and the transparency of barriers' as a 'series of identity motifs' and also demonstrates this with reference to the cut from Cecilia diving to Robbie surfacing from the bath water (Childs, 2008, p. 151). As stated, he points out that windows act as transparent barriers, and this is made particularly significant when Briony watches Robbie being taken away after being arrested. This barrier is also in place when she watches him and Cecilia at the fountain.

One of the key features of the film is the long tracking shot of the recreated chaos on the beach at Dunkirk as the Allies attempt to make their escape. The uneven reception given to the film on its release may be measured by critics' views of this scene. Whereas French regards this as evidence of 'masterly' cinematography, others have been lukewarm at most in their appraisals. It lasts for just over five minutes as the panorama includes fear and violence and a moving Ferris wheel, and it is as though the film stands still in time to encompass this landscape where horses are shot and Bibles are burned so they will not fall into enemy hands.

Peter Bradshaw wonders in his review if this film will not be populist enough to be as successful as he thinks it deserves to be: 'There are moments—delirious, languorous, romantic moments—when this film appears to have the lineaments of a classic. Yet could it be that its epic, haunting story of tragic love in the Second World War is too oblique and opaque, with too complex an enigma at its heart, to press the right commercial buttons?' (Bradshaw, 2007, p. 9). As

Bradshaw suggests, whether it receives high box-office sales or not, the quality of the adaptation will ensure it a longevity of its own apart from its connection with the well-sold novel.

Source: Julie Ellam, "Novel's Performance and Adaptation," in *Ian McEwan's "Atonement,"* Continuum, 2009, pp. 67–75.

Bob Ellis

In the following excerpt, Ellis praises the performances of the entire cast of the film, as well as the direction.

... Ian McEwan's books concern those moon-dark split-seconds that change a life on earth forever. With algebraic post-Christian remorselessness he shows how bad things can get if you once take your eye off the ball, and what Hell awaits you in a modern, godless universe if you are English, reticent and underinformed.

Because so much of his work is copious, ornate interior monologue (I defy even Ozon to make *On Chesil Beach*) he's really hard to film. *The Comfort of Strangers* and *Enduring Love* both failed despite Harold Pinter and James Bond, and *The Cement Garden*, though good, barely made it across the line.

Christopher Hampton's reduction of *Atonement*, however, is grippingly effective. With time-shifts, differing points of view and what T.S. Eliot called visions and revisions (not only what happened but what should have happened), it flings us down three lifetimes and 60 years with a clarity, suspense and erotic force that impels and enmeshes audiences of all ages and educational standards. Rarely have the questions 'What happens next?' and 'What did I just see?' been more urgent. As with *Army of Shadows* perhaps, or *North by Northwest*, the plotline overwhelms you, and the fate-cursed characters' comeuppances haunt you for days after.

The story's first premise, a country house full of mischievous upperclass children, randy young adults and imperious old-money parents, seems in style a mixture of Noel Coward and J.M. Barry: rapid, natty, double-entendre dialogue between gorgeous spoiled brunette Cecilia Tallis, forever fending off suitors, and Robbie Turner, the housemaid's overeducated uppity son, while 13-year-old Briony, a rabbit-eyed blonde, writes steamy Arcadian romances on her typewriter, and her 14-year-old cousin Lola, a simmering redhead bruised by her parents' famous divorce, is in need, at the very least, of a swoop around the stratosphere with Peter Pan. Her twin redhead brothers Pierrot and Jackson fester with boredom, plot their escape. A young millionaire, Paul Marshall, arrives in a car with Leon Tallis, to woo Cecilia perhaps, like all the other rich drones she despises.

The tone is lightly comic, mischievous, erotic, unthreatening. Then four things happen, all of them ambiguous but of a sexual nature, all of them observed and misunderstood, perhaps wilfully understood, by envious, pubescent Briony, which soon involve the police and alter the atmosphere to Henry James with hints of Agatha Christie, and change forever the lives of everyone present, shockingly, for the worse.

This all happens in 1936. Four years later Robbie, battle-worn in France, stumbles past 50 schoolgirl corpses and through a wrecked and smoking landscape towards the awesome confusion of Dunkirk. Thousands of soldiers, some shooting horses, some singing hymns, some dismantling beached boats, some drinking and groping barmaids, fill the screen.

In London meanwhile Cecilia and Briony are both nurses tending the war-wounded but estranged, not speaking; on the newsreel screen Paul Marshall is showing the King and Queen his new chocolate factory; Cockneys in the Underground sleep through the Blitz; and England, dear old England, is probably, probably losing the war. Now, as they say, read on.

Rarely has a wartime Home Front been as well portrayed as here: the crowded, hushed canteens; the brisk hospitals thronged with silent wounded; Briony's midnight conversation with a dying young Frenchman who in delirium thinks she's his first love, come back at last to say sorry and marry him; the grubby coldwater tenements, with pigs in the front yard, to which girls take randy soldiers on leave for brief joyless sex. Rarely too has the godless hell of pointless battle been better shown: in *Forbidden Games* perhaps, or *Saving Private Ryan*, or *Gone With the Wind*.

The director Joe Wright, last year unknown, is already a swaggering master of world cinema, flaunting a swag of effects from Hitchcock, Lean, Fellini, Clayton, Renoir and Cukor from his crammed quiver of styles and a gift for casting and tuned performance as good as James Ivory's. We see the new Vanessa Redgrave,

Romola Garai, wonderfully at work, and the old Vanessa Redgrave too, and the remarkable Saoirse Ronan, all of them as Briony, unchanged yet always recognisable at different ages down 60 years; and Keira Knightley, quiveringly English, frisky, unforgiving and impelled as Cecilia; and James McAvoy, whose Spitfire-pilot handsomeness belies an infinitude of simmering hinterland, which he showed as the neurotic Lord Balcairn in *Bright Young Things* and the wild-hearted young buccaneering doctor in *The Last King of Scotland*, as Robbie, the sharp-witted boy from below stairs whom triple accident cheats of life and love.

Brenda Blethyn's two minutes as his morose life-withered mum is utterly memorable too, as are the five minutes of Benedict Cumberbatch, all sideward glances, thin moustache and festering perversity, as Paul, and Juno Temple as Lola (a name suggestive of Lolita), knowing, flighty, under-age, proud and brazen as Unity Mitford.

McEwan's fascination with Englishness and what its crisp unspokenness can do for you is wonderfully displayed here as it is in the seasoned adapter Christopher Hampton's other period screenplay Carrington, that Englishness whose reticence ennobles, ensnares, destroys.

Oscars all round, if there is any justice....

Source: Bob Ellis, "The Complexity of Being Human: The Tinseltown Awards Season Is in Full Swing and This Month Bob Ellis Reviews Three Much-Vaunted and Uncompromising Films That Deal Intrinsically with the Human Condition," in *Encore*, Vol. 26, No. 2, February 2008, p. 10.

SOURCES

Bradshaw, Peter, Review of *Atonement*, in *Guardian*, September 7, 2007, http://www.theguardian.com/film/2007/sep/07/romance.keiraknightley (accessed July 13, 2014).

Ebert, Roger, Review of *Atonement*, in *Chicago Sun-Times*, December 6, 2007, http://www.rogerebert.com/reviews/atonement-2007 (accessed July 27, 2014).

Elley, Derek, Review of *Atonement*, in *Variety*, August 29, 2007, http://variety.com/2007/film/reviews/atonement-6-1200556868/ (accessed July 27, 2014).

Hornaday, Ann, "'Atonement': Word-Perfect Pictures," in *Washington Post*, December 7, 2007, http://www.washingtonpost.com/wp-dyn/content/article/2007/12/06/AR2007120602695.html (accessed July 27, 2014).

Lane, Anthony, "Conflicting Stories," in *New Yorker*, December 20, 2007, http://www.newyorker.com/magazine/2007/12/10/conflicting-stories (accessed July 27, 2014).

Lumenick, Lou, "Heartbreaking Work of Staggering Genius," in *New York Post*, December 7, 2007, http://nypost.com/2007/12/07/heartbreaking-work-of-staggering-genius/ (accessed July 27, 2014).

Mathews, Peter, "The Impression of a Deeper Darkness: Ian McEwan's *Atonement*," in *English Studies in Canada*, Vol. 32, No. 1, March 2006, pp. 147–60.

McFarlane, Brian, "Watching, Writing and Control: *Atonement*," in *Screen Education*, Vol. 49, Fall 2008, pp. 8–16.

Morgenstern, Joe, "*Atonement* is Epic Storytelling without Apology," in *Wall Street Journal*, December 7, 2007, http://online.wsj.com/news/articles/SB119697891561216318?mg=reno64-wsj&url=http%3A%2F%2Fonline.wsj.com%2Farticle%2FSB119697891561216318.html (accessed July 27, 2014).

Pevere, Geoff, "*Atonement*: Words without passion," in *Toronto Star*, December 7, 2007, http://www.thestar.com/entertainment/movies/2007/12/07/atonement_words_without_passion.html (accessed July 27, 2014).

Schiff, James, "Reading and Writing on Screen: Cinematic Adaptations of McEwan's *Atonement* and Cunningham's *The Hours*," in *Critique*, Vol. 53, No. 2, 2012, pp. 164–73.

Schwarzbaum, Lisa, Review of *Atonement*, in *Entertainment Weekly*, http://www.ew.com/ew/article/0,,20163015,00.html (accessed July 27, 2014).

Scott, A. O., "Lies, Guilt, Stiff Upper Lips," in *New York Times*, December 7, 2007, http://www.nytimes.com/2007/12/07/movies/07aton.html?_r=0 (accessed July 13, 2014).

Shah, Bruno M., "The Sin of Ian McEwan's Fictive *Atonement*: Reading His Later Novels," in *New Blackfriars*, Vol. 90, No. 1025, January 2009, pp. 38–49.

Travers, Peter, Review of *Atonement*, in *Rolling Stone*, December 14, 2007, http://www.rollingstone.com/movies/reviews/atonement-20071214 (accessed July 13, 2014).

FURTHER READING

Groes, Sebastian, ed., *Ian McEwan: Contemporary Critical Perspectives*, 2nd ed., Bloomsbury Academic, 2013.
This book is included in the Contemporary Critical Perspectives series and provides a valuable collection of new critical essays that set out to provide textual readings, cultural analysis, and explication of key ideas and themes found in McEwan's fiction. This volume includes a previously unpublished interview with McEwan.

Head, Dominic, *Ian McEwan*, Manchester University Press, 2008.
Part of the Contemporary British Novelist series, this eminently readable survey positions McEwan as a rare writer whose body of work has achieved both popular and critical respect. With his trademark economy of prose, McEwan takes such important and deeply complex issues as politics, gender relations, and male violence, and presents them in novels that are profound and accessible. An important figure in the contemporary history of British fiction, McEwan is presented as a serious thinker who tells a great story.

Roberts, Ryan, ed., *Conversations with Ian McEwan*, University Press of Mississippi, 2010.
This engaging and eclectic book captures McEwan's views on a vast range of topics, from the writing process to music, film, science, and the state of literature in general. The bonus in this book lies, too, in the people with whom McEwan converses. The list is a veritable who's who of contemporary culture: Martin Amis, Zadie Smith, and Stephen Pinker, to name only three.

Summers-Bremner, Eluned, *Ian McEwan: Sex, Death, and History*, Cambria Press, 2014.
This is a somewhat dense but fascinating book that explores what Summers-Bremner suggests is a common theme in McEwan's books: the tendency for characters to act and feel in ways that are out of character depending on context and the demands of the moment.

SUGGESTED SEARCH TERMS

Atonement AND film

Ian McEwan

Joe Wright

World War II AND film

Dunkirk AND film

guilt AND film

redemption AND film

storytelling AND film

memory AND film

adaptation AND literature

The Beautiful and Damned

The Beautiful and Damned is F. Scott Fitzgerald's second novel and his most difficult and disputed one. It tells the story of the Jazz Age (a name for the 1920s of Fitzgerald's coinage) with its glittering young society. At a deeper level, though, it is also a subtle criticism of the consumer culture that emerged in the 1920s, with consumption replacing production as a measure of social worth. It reveals the paradoxes of Fitzgerald's life and art. A socialist and a believer in Thorsten Veblen's critique of consumer society, Fitzgerald destroyed himself through a life of conspicuous waste and pleasure-seeking, eventually drinking himself to death. The same unresolved division dominates *The Beautiful and Damned* as his characters play out a reflection of his own life.

F. SCOTT FITZGERALD

1922

AUTHOR BIOGRAPHY

Francis Scott Key Fitzgerald was born on September 24, 1896, in St. Paul, Minnesota. Fitzgerald spent his childhood in Buffalo, New York, but his family returned to St. Paul when he was ten years old. He determined to be a writer at an early age and produced a mass of surviving juvenilia (youthful writings). He attended Princeton and worked intensively on writing, both in course work and publishing in student publications. His grades were poor, however, and he was forced to

F. Scott Fitzgerald (© *Pictorial Parade* / *Archive Photos* / *Getty Images*)

withdraw in 1917. He enlisted in the army at the start of World War I, and he hastily wrote a novel, *The Romantic Egoist*, so that his literary genius would not perish if he should die in the war, a gesture as typical of adolescence as of Fitzgerald's egoism. He was sent to an army base in Alabama for basic training; there, he met Zelda Sayre, his future wife. He never saw action, and after the war he worked as an advertising writer in New York City, also publishing short stories. He finally returned to live with his parents in Minnesota and revised his early novel as *This Side of Paradise*. This time it was accepted by the publishing house Scribner's and rapidly became a best seller.

Fitzgerald and Zelda were married in 1920 and moved to New York. He had a large income from book sales and from selling short stories to popular magazines like the *Saturday Evening Post*, but the young couple spent money much faster than it came in, living in expensive hotels and rented houses and hosting wild parties at ruinous expense. His next novel, *The Beautiful and Damned* (1922), is generally considered an autobiographical exploration of this period. In his fiction, Fitzgerald made it painfully clear how his life was going wrong, but he seemed unable to bring about any change in his life. He wrote a satirical essay, "How to Live on $36,000 a Year," lampooning the waste that could outspend even what was, at the time, a vast income. (In 1921, Fitzgerald made and burned through $21,000, the equivalent of half a million dollars today.) Fitzgerald coined the phrase "the Jazz Age" to describe the hedonism (pleasure-seeking) of the 1920s and is generally thought to be the leading voice of the "lost generation" of American writers and artists, who felt they had lost their center with the breakdown of traditional American culture in the 1920s. Zelda is considered a flapper, the new woman of the 1920s who took enormous strides toward liberation and equality by breaking out of traditional moral strictures.

Almost as soon as they were married, Zelda began showing symptoms of schizophrenia, and her medical care became an exponentially increasing cost as Fitzgerald's income dwindled. Sales of *The Beautiful and Damned* did not match those of *This Side of Paradise*, nor did those of *The Great Gatsby* (1925), Fitzgerald's masterpiece. Zelda was institutionalized (for the first time in 1930 and permanently in 1935) and Fitzgerald descended deeper into alcoholism. In 1934, he published his last complete novel, *Tender Is the Night*, based on Zelda's medical condition and treatment. Living alone, he moved to Hollywood and continued to increase his income through film work, which is not considered especially important artistically. Drinking took its toll on his body, and Fitzgerald had a series of heart attacks, the fatal one coming on December 21, 1940. He left behind an unpublished novel, *The Last Tycoon*, which was edited by his friend the literary critic Edmund Wilson and published in 1941.

PLOT SUMMARY

Book One

I. ANTHONY PATCH

Anthony Comstock Patch is a young man with a degree from Harvard and a comfortable income of $7,000 a year (the equivalent of about $100,000 today) supplied from family money.

MEDIA ADAPTATIONS

- *The Beautiful and Damned* was filmed immediately after the book's publication in 1922 by director William Seiter. Fitzgerald and his wife, Zelda, were seriously considered for the lead roles, but these were finally played by Clarence Burton and Louise Fazenda. Like many films of the 1920s, it has been lost.

- *The Beautiful and Damned* was produced as an independent film in 2010 by Australian filmmaker Richard Wolstencroft.

- An audiobook version was produced in 2010, read by Kirby Heyborne. The running time is fifteen hours and twelve minutes.

His profession is waiting for his hated grandfather, Adam Patch, to die, at which time he will inherit $30 million. Adam thinks his grandson should enter business as he did, but Anthony puts him off with the pretense that he is busy writing a history of the Renaissance popes. While Anthony waits, he socializes with his old friends from college in New York aristocratic society. A dinner party with his friends Maury Noble and Richard Caramel shows the aimless wandering of his existence. They talk pleasantly, but nothing noteworthy happens.

Gloria Gilbert is introduced to the reader through a sort of mythological dialogue that prophetically reveals that she is the prototype of the flapper and destined to marry Anthony.

II. PORTRAIT OF A SIREN

Caramel introduces Anthony to his cousin, Gloria Gilbert. She makes an overwhelming impression on Anthony, and they begin dating, then a new and shocking custom.

III. THE CONNOISSEUR OF KISSES

Through Gloria, Joseph Bloeckman, a film producer who does business with Gloria's father, is introduced into Anthony's social circle. Anthony is obsessively jealous of Bloeckman, who is also romantically interested in Gloria.

Book Two

I. THE RADIANT HOUR

Gloria's parents had disapproved of Bloeckman as suitor because he is Jewish, but they approve of Anthony. Anthony and Gloria become engaged and are soon married. Meanwhile, Richard Caramel's novel, *The Demon Lover*, is published. It is a great success and, within their circle of friends, steals some of the spotlight from the wedding.

II. SYMPOSIUM

Disappointed in his pursuit of Gloria, Bloeckman nevertheless arranges a screen test for her, although she does not go through with it at this time. Anthony and Gloria's married life becomes characterized by a crushing inertia, as they feel they have nothing to do but wait for Adam Patch to die.

Gloria wants to leave a party they are attending at a neighbor's house near their country home. Anthony agrees, and they get as far as the platform of the train to go back to their own house. Since he seems too drunk to buy the tickets, Gloria asks him for the money so she can do it, but he is seized by a sudden desire to enforce his will and refuses. Realizing she has enough money in her purse to buy her own ticket, she says she intends to do just that, but he grabs her arm and will not let her go, causing a terrible scene. They eventually take a cab back to their house. Gloria feels that the incident killed some vital part of her love for Anthony, but nothing in their lives seems changed.

One of the common criticisms of *The Beautiful and Damned* is that it is rather sprawling, meaning that it contains innumerable plots and stories that, while interesting in themselves, do not contribute to the main plot and are essentially self-contained stories. Perhaps the most commented on of these concerns the Patches' Japanese butler, Tanalahaka or Tana, who is introduced in this chapter. His character is established in minute detail but serves no larger function in the novel. Maury Noble thinks it is a good joke to say that Tanalahaka is really a German spy, Maurice Tannenbaum, and starts to send him a letter that is supposed to be from the German general staff filled with a mocking imitation of Japanese characters.

III. THE BROKEN LUTE

Directed by his secretary, Edward Shuttleworth, Adam Patch visits his grandson's country house and finds him and his friends in the midst of a drunken party. Tana is playing on his flute the one song he knows, a Japanese children's song meant to imitate the sound of a train, while Gloria and one of the guests dance. Adam considers this a moral outrage and disinherits his grandson, destroying the prospect of their future life that Anthony and Gloria had spent the years of their marriage carefully cherishing. Adam dies soon after this, and the terms of his will leave his fortune to a charitable trust to be used to promote reform, overseen by Shuttleworth. Anthony immediately starts a lawsuit to claim the inheritance.

Book Three

I. A MATTER OF CIVILIZATION

Anthony and Gloria both have some money of their own from other inheritances, so they intend to live on that and on loans from their friends, until the lawsuit is settled. They must take a smaller apartment in a less fashionable neighborhood. The sad monotony of their lives is broken when Anthony is drafted into the army at the outset of World War I. Leaving Gloria in New York, Anthony reports to Camp Boone in Mississippi. He soon acquires a mistress, Dorothy Raycroft, a lower-class girl from the nearby town who has already been through several officers at the camp.

II. A MATTER OF ÆSTHETICS

Gloria continues to live in their apartment in New York while Anthony is in Mississippi. She becomes increasingly conscious that most of the love that animated their courtship and marriage has vanished. Gloria decides that because she has nothing else to do, the best thing for her to do is to become a film star. Through her connections with Bloeckman, she arranges for a screen test that would lead to a part in a film playing a flapper. The result is disappointing because she is already too old to have the smooth and polished sort of beauty that was then fashionable in film. On her twenty-ninth birthday she is offered a part, but as a rich widow. She does not accept it, but instead rushes to her mirror and finds for the first time the marks of age. She laments, "Oh, my pretty face! Oh, I don't want to live without my pretty face! Oh, what's *happened*?"

The war ends before Anthony can be shipped off to Europe, and he returns to New York. Anthony is reduced to having to find a job; at least, Gloria wants him to do that, but he is not very eager to do so. They are abandoned by their former acquaintances; for the most part, Anthony drives them off because in his straitened circumstances he feels ashamed before them.

III. NO MATTER!

As their situation becomes so desperate that buying food is their chief concern, Gloria mentions the matter of her screen test to Anthony. He feels that Bloeckman, who has changed his name to Black, gave Gloria a deadly insult by not casting her as a younger woman. Already drunk, Anthony takes a cab to a party Bloeckman is throwing at a swank hotel. During their argument, Anthony calls him a "Goddam Jew," provoking Bloeckman to thrash him. He has the hotel staff throw Anthony out into the street.

In a scene played out before Muriel Kane, who is the only one of the Patches' old friends who continues to visit them, it becomes clear that the marriage is descending into constant drinking and constant fighting. Anthony still sees no point in taking any kind of job that would support them on a merely middle-class income, but waits only for the resolution of the lawsuit, which is grinding through the courts. In the end, Anthony is successful and inherits $30 million. The rival claimant, Shuttleworth, shoots himself. The Patches' society friends flock back to them. But Anthony is left mentally and physically broken (probably he suffers a stroke), confined to a wheelchair. The only thing left for him is to want back his youth, even his childhood, which no money can buy. The final words of the novel are his self-congratulation as he and he Gloria set out on an ocean liner for Italy: "I showed them.... It was a hard fight, but I didn't give up and I came through!" But the sense is entirely ironic, since what he has is worthless to him. Gloria is in even worse condition, as is revealed through a snippet of conversation about her Anthony overhears: "I can't stand her, you know. She seems sort of—sort of dyed and *unclean*, if you know what I mean."

CHARACTERS

Joseph Bloeckman

Bloeckman is a film producer who is an acquaintance of Gloria's father, whose company manufactures celluloid products, including film stock. At one time he courted Gloria. He is the opposite of Anthony, a man who started poor and made a fortune by his own efforts. He is Jewish, and eventually changes his name to Black to deflect the anti-Semitism (prejudice against Jews) that was common during the 1920s, represented by Anthony's taunting of him.

Richard Caramel

Caramel is one of Patch's closest friends from Harvard. He is professional writer, and during the course of this story he writes *The Demon Lover* (the title Fitzgerald originally intended for *The Beautiful and Damned*). He does not seem nearly the stand-in for Fitzgerald that Patch is, but he shares one of the author's characteristics: he considers his everyday life to be the material from which he constructs his novels. He carries this further than Fitzgerald does, actually taking notes on conversations with his friends while they are going on, and asking them to repeat what they had just said so he can get it all down. Fitzgerald similarly considered his own life his literary material and even became jealous of his wife, Zelda, when she began to use incidents from their life in her writing.

Gloria Gilbert

Gloria is presented, quite literally, as the ideal type of the new woman of the 1920s. It what should probably be taken as a satirical swipe at spiritualism (which was fashionable in 1920s, perhaps more so than today), Gloria is introduced through a supernatural séance in which the abstract concept of Beauty is told by a mysterious but no doubt divine Voice that she will be incarnated in the flesh on earth, both as the new woman, and as Gloria in particular. The Voice tells Beauty, "You will be known during your fifteen years as a ragtime kid, a flapper, a jazz-baby, and a baby vamp." The fifteen years refers to Gloria's youth. Her vanity has a horror of age. As she approaches her twenty-ninth birthday, she looks upon the fading of her youthful beauty as indistinguishable from death. As Anthony is reduced to looking for work after being disowned by his uncle, Gloria is reduced to longing for children, which she had avoided since it would

have, in her mind, inevitably attacked her beauty, but she still cannot break her habit of preserving her beauty at any cost. Her damnation comes precisely from the fading of her beauty.

Muriel Kane

Muriel is a school friend of Gloria's from Kansas City. When they were girls, she once saved Gloria from drowning. Unlike their society friends in New York, she does not abandon the Patches when they fall into relative poverty.

Maury Noble

Noble is Anthony's best friend from Harvard. He is more cultured and sophisticated than Anthony, but seems no less idle.

Adam Patch

Adam, in his seventies, is Anthony's grandfather. He possesses a vast fortune he made in business as a young man. He likes to tell Anthony stories of how he crushed and bankrupted his rivals. He is now keenly concerned with reform, which he thinks of as purging society of anything he considers sinful, such as smoking and drinking. The attitude of the younger generation to Adam Patch's character is summed up in a conversation about him between Anthony and Gloria:

> "Did they bar cigarettes? I see the hand of my holy grandfather."
>
> "He's a reformer or something, isn't he?"
>
> "I blush for him."
>
> "So do I," she confessed. "I detest reformers, especially the sort who try to reform me."

Anthony despises his grandfather but is flattering and subservient to him.

Anthony Comstock Patch

A great deal about Anthony's character is revealed in a monologue he delivers to his mistress, Dot:

> Once I wanted something and got it. It was the only thing I ever wanted badly.... And when I got it it turned to dust in my hands.... I've often thought that if I hadn't got what I wanted things might have been different with me. I might have found something in my mind and enjoyed putting it in circulation. I might have been content with the work of it, and had some sweet vanity out of the success. I suppose that at one time I could have had anything I wanted, within reason, but that was the only thing I ever wanted with any fervor.

In an attempt to wound her, Anthony tells Dot he is talking about her, but she is too innocent to understand him. What he is talking about is his own possession by desire; the only thing that gives him satisfaction is wanting, not having. If he had produced his history of the popes, he would have had no more satisfaction from that than from anything else. But even with this insight into his own character, Anthony is not able to see his true nature. He thinks of desire as some outside force. He says, "Desire just cheats you," but desire is within him, it is the only thing he truly has, the only thing he truly is. He is finally damned when he receives the ultimate satisfaction, his inheritance, and there is nothing left to desire.

Dorothy Raycroft

Dorothy, or Dot, becomes Anthony's mistress while he is doing his military service in Mississippi. She is a poor girl, and has been previously taken in by many officers whom she was convinced loved her. Anthony brings her back to New York, but he savagely rejects her shortly before the end of the novel.

Edward Shuttleworth

Shuttleworth is Adam Patch's secretary. A sinner reformed by Christian conversion, he is responsible for Adam dropping in on Anthony's debauched party. Adam changes his will to set up a trust to carry on the work of Christian reform under Shuttleworth's direction. When he loses the lawsuit over the inheritance to Anthony, he shoots himself.

Tanalahaka

Tanalahaka is an unfortunate instance in *The Beautiful and Damned* of the racism that Fitzgerald shared with the mass culture of the 1920s. The name *Tanalahaka*, for instance, is not a real Japanese name. It contains the letter *L*, which does not occur in the Japanese language and is no doubt meant to mock the fact that many Japanese speakers who acquire English as a second language have difficulty pronouncing it. Anthony adopts a generally condescending tone over his butler's English. The narrative voice of the novel calls attention to its denigration of Tana (as he is generally called) by mentioning that he regularly reads a comic strip whose humor depends on mocking a Japanese butler, but it is hard to call this self-criticism.

Tana seems to be a caricature of the Fitzgeralds' houseboy, also called Tana, who worked for them in their house in Westport, Connecticut, while Fitzgerald was writing the novel.

THEMES

Romanticism

From a strictly formal viewpoint, romanticism refers to the literature of the late eighteenth and early nineteenth centuries; it often valued heights of feeling inspired by nature. This type of literature made a profound impact on Fitzgerald. In a letter to his daughter of August 2, 1940, Fitzgerald reveals the depth of his appreciation for the works of the romantic poet John Keats in particular,

> Poetry is either something that lives like a fire inside you . . . or else it is nothing. . . . "The Grecian Urn" is unbearably beautiful with every syllable as inevitable as the notes in Beethoven's Ninth Symphony or it's just something you don't understand. . . . "The Eve of St. Agnes" . . . has the richest most sensuous imagery in English, not excepting Shakespeare. . . . Knowing these things, one could scarcely ever afterwards be unable to distinguish between gold and dross in what one read. . . . For awhile after you quit Keats all other poetry seems to be only whistling or humming.

It comes as no surprise, in view of Fitzgerald's estimation of Keats, that many themes in *The Beautiful and Damned* are derived from Keats, particularly from his short epic, *Lamia*. At one point, Fitzgerald had intended to call the novel *The Demon Lover*, a reference to the female demon who takes a mortal man as her lover. This was preserved as the title of Richard Caramel's novel within the story. Briefly, in Keats's mythological poem, Lamia is an immortal serpent who is transformed into a woman by the god Apollo after she falls in love with the young philosopher Lycius. She ensnares him into her illusory palace created through her magical powers, a place of bliss. There she hopes to captivate him by making him completely happy in herself alone, but Lycius is inevitably called back to the world and begins to treat her sadistically. He eventually forces her to go through a marriage ceremony in front of his friends and family. At the banquet, Lycius's teacher, a philosopher and magician, sees what she really is and, in exposing her, destroys her.

TOPICS FOR FURTHER STUDY

- Before and during the Chinese civil war and the Japanese invasion, Shanghai was a center of westernization in China. One of its typical products was the *Ling Long* women's magazine. This presented a model of modernization and westernization to Chinese women, offering, for example, the image of the flapper as an ideal. Scans of nearly the complete run of the magazine have been archived by the Center for History and New Media of George Mason University. They are available online at http://chnm.gmu.edu/world historysources/d/134/whm.html, along with links to explanatory and analytical articles. Make a presentation to your class using images from *Ling Long* to show how it modeled some of the cultural ideals presented in *The Beautiful and Damned*.

- *Ingenue* (2012) is part of the Flappers series of young-adult novels by Jillian Larkin. Write a paper comparing Larkin's presentation of Jazz Age culture with the more authentic view presented by Fitzgerald in *The Beautiful and Damned*.

- Use the Internet to find illustrations, especially photographs, of fashionable young people and swank parties from the 1920s. Possible sources include popular magazines such as *Life* or *Saturday Evening Post* and the picture postcards that enjoyed an immense popularity in the 1920s. Use these images to create a presentation for your class illustrating the world of *The Beautiful and Damned*. The names of popular film stars, such as Louise Brooks and Rudolph Valentino, or important photographers of the period, such as Edward Steichen and Alfred Stieglitz, might be useful search terms.

- Read Fitzgerald's short-story collection *Tales of the Jazz Age*. Write a paper comparing the main themes and their various treatments in *The Beautiful and Damned* and one or more stories from Fitzgerald's *Tales of the Jazz Age*. Topics might include youth, beauty, the Roaring Twenties, wealth, or leisure.

Lycius dies too, though whether from the shock of the truth being revealed or from a broken heart is not clear.

In *The Beautiful and Damned*, Gloria is like a supernatural creature (Beauty) given human form for the purpose of loving Anthony. Anthony is not so much in love with Gloria as with the idea of her. Anthony only wants what is unreasonable, what he cannot have. It is the act of desiring that he is in love with. For one instant, Gloria becomes the perfect image of his desire, appealing "to that part of him that cherished all beauty and all illusion." Anthony mistakes this for love. When he tells his mistress Dot that she is the one thing he wanted, only to have her disintegrate when he got her, he is really talking about Gloria, or rather about the constant episodes of desirous longing that are followed by unfulfilling possession that make up his life, of which Gloria is only the chief example. Gloria's love for Anthony is equally an illusion. When Anthony is to return from his military service, Gloria thinks of "that illusion of young romantic love to which women look forever forward and forever back." When they finally meet again after their separation, "like a figure in a dream he came back into her life across the ballroom on that November evening—and all through long hours that held familiar gladness she took him close to her breast, nursing an illusion of happiness and security she had not thought that she would know again."

Anthony and Gloria fulfill for each other the role of the lovers in the common romantic narrative. They are paralyzed by this illusion, and it prevents them from ever really being in love. Anthony breaks the spell of their illusion by treating her sadistically, failing her as much by being unable to sustain his role as by his physical manhandling of her (which he wrongly thinks will make her love him more, since he is acting more like a brutish masculine stereotype). By the end of the novel, they have faded out of existence as much as Lycius and Lamia.

Leisure

For most people in a traditional society, the goal of life was work to the degree necessary to maintain life. The majority of people before the nineteenth century were farmers, and the primary product of their work was food and other

The story takes place in New York City. *(© Everett Collection / Shutterstock.com)*

necessities of life for themselves. Only the wealthy, who lived from the work of others, had leisure. By the 1920s, though, leisure or freedom from work had become the goal of more people. Ordinary people working in factories did so because they needed the wages to live, but they did not produce their own means of life and had no particular investment in their work. A worker in a Ford plant who tightened the same nut on a thousand identical cars each and every day could not weave the fabric of life from that experience. The commercial interests that had become professionalized by industrialization were largely in the business of selling leisure time activities to workers. But the wealthy were in a different situation. Adam Patch, for example, had an adequate income to support himself without work and so had nothing but leisure. He filled his time, therefore, with the pursuit of pleasure as an end in itself. This was recognized in the 1920s as part of a general social crisis. Workers objected to supporting a class of people who were seen as devoting themselves to drinking and socializing and were in no way productive themselves. There was a growing perception that rich young men and their flapper companions were taking over society and creating a new and destructive pattern of life.

What Anthony Patch becomes is something new, but he has an entirely different model of aristocratic leisure that competes (though not very effectively) in his mind with pure hedonism. Because of his education, he has access to an aristocratic theory of leisure meant to be filled with productive artistic or scholarly work. The aristocratic class in the Roman Empire called their leisure *otium*, and they had a very definite idea of how to fill up their idle hours. The ideal of the Roman gentleman was to devote himself to *belle lettres*: the composition of serious literary work, whether it was poetry, drama, philosophy, or something similar. This ideal, and particularly the Romans' shortcomings in living up to it, is pointed out again and again in the letters of the Roman writer Pliny the Younger. It is exemplified in the life of the Roman philosopher Cicero, who was banned from public life after Julius Caesar seized control of the government. He lived in a forced retirement on his country estate and produced a large number of philosophical essays, such as the *Tusculun Disputations*, which is among the foundational works of literature of Western civilization. The first emperor Augustus provided an income to poets such as Horace and Virgil, providing them with the *otium* that was necessary for them to write.

This is precisely what Patch and his friends think they ought to be doing. This is the reason Patch is constantly announcing his intention of writing a history of the Renaissance popes, although he fails in his intentions because the lure of modern life calls him away from his work. His friend Richard Caramel produces his novel *The Demon Lover*, which even gains a certain popularity.

The 1920s saw the end of this conflict about what leisure time ultimately meant: a productive life of writing and thought, or pure pleasure and fun. The leisure of hedonism finally won out; no one today expects the rich, in particular, to produce literature.

STYLE

Naturalism

Realism and naturalism were the predominant literary styles in American literature in the 1920s. Under these categories, literature was supposed to deal with everyday life, with the conflicts that shaped the lives of recognizable human beings. In the age of social reform, realism took as its special subject matter social and ethical problems. A prototypical realist novel was Sinclair Lewis's *The Jungle* (1906). Not more than a step removed from journalism, it dealt with the abuses of the meat packing industry and the exploitation of immigrant workers. In *The Beautiful and Damned*, Fitzgerald took on the mantle of realism to a remarkable degree. Although its characters are true aristocrats,

removed from the reading audience by their wealth, education, and social prestige, Fitzgerald makes his fiction out of the most mundane events of their everyday lives. Indeed, it is recognized by critics that Fitzgerald went too far in this direction, a mistake he corrected in *The Great Gatsby*. Fitzgerald placed some of the smallest details of his own life into his fiction, calling his life his material. The problem addressed by *The Beautiful and Damned* is no single social abuse, but what might be termed the general crisis of the 1920s, when consumer culture replaced traditional culture. Naturalism required that Fitzgerald not shy away from any aspects of his character's lives, and he explored even their sexual lives in a way that was considered scandalous in the 1920s.

Satire

James L. W. West, in his article in *The Cambridge Companion to F. Scott Fitzgerald*, comments: "Stylistically *This Side of Paradise* seems daring; it mixes genres in a fashion that even today looks unconventional, shifting from fictional narrative to rhymed or free verse, then moving to dramatic dialogue and slipping toward the end into interior monologue." Precisely the same is true of *The Beautiful and Damned*, though not of Fitzgerald's later novels. This style of composition, indiscriminately mixing together genres, is highly unusual, and in English literature it is a mark of great sophistication. Herman Melville's *Moby Dick* is perhaps the outstanding example. The style is so rare that it does not have a generally recognized name in English. It originated in Latin literature; the Romans called it *satire*, meaning a meal of mixed foods. The more usual modern meaning of *satire* as a comic genre derives from the use the Romans made of it in late antiquity. A common literary exercise at that time, practiced by leisured aristocrats, was to compile anthologies of mixed prose and poetry; placing them side by side produced a comic effect.

In *This Side of Paradise*, Fitzgerald more or less stumbled onto this form of composition, since he hurriedly cobbled together any worthwhile writing he had produced in whatever genre, but in his more thoughtful composition of *The Beautiful and Damned*, he continued it for stylistic effect. The section called "A Flash-Back in Paradise" is perhaps the most important of the dramatic episodes in the novel. This scene introduces Gloria into the novel, but in no ordinary way.

COMPARE
&
CONTRAST

- **1920s:** The advent of radio creates a new era of mass market advertising.

  Today: Advertising completely dominates popular culture. Traditional ads are played on the radio and television, before movies in the theater and on DVDs, and on the Internet. Advertising is also seamlessly integrated into entertainment content through product placement and the creation of new genres, such as the music video, that are mainly advertising in the shape of entertainment. On the Internet, most websites contain ads, and even search results are shaped by commercial concerns.

- **1920s:** The "new woman," or flapper, strikes out boldly for increased personal freedom.

  Today: The fruits of second-wave feminism have more nearly than ever before brought women into a state of equality with men in education, civil rights, and employment.

- **1920s:** Prohibition (something Adam Patch worked for earnestly) outlaws the sale of alcohol. The law does little to stop the sale of liquor, but it does give rise to a new criminal class.

  Today: The failed experiment of Prohibition was repealed in 1933. Today, many states have ended the prohibition on cannabis as well, in part to remove the criminal element in its sale.

Presenting the scene as a drama has many advantages for Fitzgerald. It takes place in some sort of supernatural realm and is essentially mythological in character. But this doesn't undercut the realism of the novel, since, because of its presentation in dramatic form, the reader can take it as a fiction within the larger fictional world of the novel. Elevating a section of the novel to drama naturally makes it seem more serious, but here Fitzgerald undercuts that expectation with satire in the modern sense. This allows him to elevate Gloria into a supernatural figure, which the beloved naturally is for the lover, without the text becoming a mere cliché.

HISTORICAL CONTEXT

Anthony Comstock

Anthony Comstock Patch's name was chosen by his grandfather in honor of Anthony Comstock (1844–1915), indicating Adam Patch's own moral and political concerns. Anthony Comstock considered himself a political and social reformer and was the founder of the New York Society for the Suppression of Vice. This organization became one of the chief proponents of censorship in public life in nineteenth- and early twentieth-century America. Comstock and his followers objected to any language that they considered obscene and to any depiction of nudity or sexuality. In part because Comstock was a high-ranking postal inspector, the society was often able to persuade various levels of government to enforce its standard of censorship. The budding film industry, in particular, had to carefully compose a code of what was and was not acceptable in motion pictures in negotiation with the society in order to prevent it lobbying for even stricter laws regulating films.

The society did nothing to promote virtue but wanted to control the speech of others. In particular, the society wanted to control women's lives by preventing the spread of information about abortion, birth control (the knowledge of which would, ironically, have prevented many abortions), and venereal disease. The society prevented the publication in the United States of many great works of literature, such as James Joyce's *Ulysses*, and caused many seemingly innocent authors like Erskine

Caldwell to be tried for obscenity. Fitzgerald's attitude toward the society (whose influence even in the 1920s imposed severe restrictions on him as a writer) is no doubt reflected in Patch's reaction to his own name: "When he went to Harvard, the Comstock dropped out of his name to a nether hell of oblivion and was never heard of thereafter." Fitzgerald suspected that similar reformers would try to ban *The Beautiful and Damned*, though it turned out that this did not happen.

The Flapper

The "new woman" of the 1920s was called, in the language of that era, a flapper. Gloria Gilbert, like her inspiration Zelda Fitzgerald, is a proto-type of the flapper. The image of the flapper, both in the 1920s and as it persists, was most clearly given life by Fitzgerald. In a newspaper article interviewing Fitzgerald in the *Des Moines Capital* in 1923, the reporter begins by stating: "When F. Scott Fitzgerald . . . wrote *The Beautiful and Damned*, he did more than merely write one of the cleverest stories ever done by an American; he immortalized the flapper." Fitzgerald, speaking in the interview, is quite aware that the flapper is one of the images that most clearly links his work to his generation: "'I sometimes wonder,' says Mr. Fitzgerald, 'whether the flapper made me or whether I made her.'" But what is, or was, a flapper? Fitzgerald's mentor, H. L. Mencken, in a supplement to his linguistic study, *The American Language*, traces the word back to Victorian England, where it meant "a very immoral young girl in her early teens." The softened American usage relies on the flapper's flouting of convention, as Fitzgerald observes: "I picked on the flapper because she is independent and bravely unconventional. She has more lee-way, and is a bit of an iconoclast in regard to a thousand and one things of daily life." The flap-per was a step beyond the suffragette (an agita-tor for women's right to vote) in the direction of the liberated woman. The flapper did not yet aim at a professional career as a lawyer or engineer, but she chafed against the control of patriarchal society. This was immediately clear from the flap-per's typical appearance. Nineteenth-century fashion stressed control: the body was locked into a corset, and long hair was intricately braided in a style that might take an hour or more each morning (time spent on hairdressing was time that could not be spent productively).

The Beautiful and Damned portrays the elite of New York City during the Jazz Age. (© Olena Zaskochenko | Shutterstock.com)

Mencken stresses the looseness and shortness of the flapper's hair. In the 1920s, this seemed boy-ish. It was a signal that the flapper wanted the same freedom to run her own life as boys had. They wanted to not be controlled, but to be free.

CRITICAL OVERVIEW

Today, Fitzgerald is ranked among the greatest American novelists, alongside William Faulk-ner and Ernest Hemingway in his own genera-tion, and with the greatest of his predecessors and successors, such as Mark Twain and Tho-mas Pynchon. The height of Fitzgerald's repu-tation somewhat obscures his own history. Fitzgerald's first novel, *This Side of Paradise*, was immensely popular, as were his short sto-ries, but his later novels did not have the same widespread appeal. From the beginning, Fitzgerald was supported by a small group of critics, including his mentor Mencken and his Princeton classmate Edmund Wilson. Their opinions of Fitzgerald's work are influential today, but their enthusiasm for the young writer was variable. By 1940, Fitzgerald's obituaries treated him as a long-forgotten figure. In 1945, Wilson edited *The Crack-Up*, a collection of Fitzgerald's essays and unpublished writings relating to his own decline. This began what is known as the Fitzgerald renaissance, which elevated him to his current status by the 1950s.

With regard to Fitzgerald's critical reception, *The Beautiful and Damned* presents special difficulties. Jackson R. Bryer, writing in *F. Scott Fitzgerald in Context*, notes, "Given the response to *This Side of Paradise*, expectations for Fitzgerald's second novel were enormous—and probably impossible to satisfy." In the initial reviews, opinions were certainly mixed, even among Fitzgerald's closest supporters. His Princeton classmate John Peale Bishop, writing in the *New York Herald* (as quoted in *F. Scott Fitzgerald in His Own Time: A Miscellany*) had to work to find praise for the novel. Comparing it with *This Side of Paradise*, he declares: "If, stylistically speaking, it is not so well-written, neither is it so carelessly written." In the end, he must conclude that Fitzgerald's "ideas are too often treated like paper crackers, things to make a gay and pretty noise with and then be cast aside; he is frequently at the mercy of words with which he has only a nodding acquaintance; his aesthetics are faulty; his literary taste is at times extremely bad." A more neutral reviewer like Henry Seidel Canby, originally writing in the *New York Post* and quoted in the same volume, also wanted to praise the novel, but nevertheless found himself concluding:

> *The Beautiful and Damned* is not so much a novel as an irresponsible social document, veracious, in its way, as photographs are always veracious in their way, but often untruthful, and with about the same relation to the scope and significance of life that is possessed by a society drama in the films.

(Bear in mind that film was not widely accepted as an art form at the time.) A generation older than Fitzgerald, Canby is one of the few reviewers to condemn *The Beautiful and Damned* on moral grounds.

James L. W. West, in his article in *The Cambridge Companion to F. Scott Fitzgerald*, gives an unusually detailed account of the novel's composition and initial reception. Some of the harshest criticism for *The Beautiful and Damned*, however, comes from Kenneth Eble's volume in Twayne's United States Author Series. Eble believes "the book's main weakness—and it is a devastating one—is that the central characters Anthony Patch and Gloria Gilbert only feebly enlist the reader's interest or sympathy." The book is so flawed, in his view, because "Fitzgerald was not prepared to write serious fiction, he had no real idea how to go about it, and he invariably disclosed his weaknesses when he became serious." Recently, the novel has been studied from a variety of postmodern perspectives. Jonathan Enfield, in his article "'As the Fashion in Books Shifted': *The Beautiful and Damned* as Arc Light Fiction," takes a complaint of reviewers in the 1920s that Fitzgerald had debased literature by imitating film and turns it on its head, presenting an analysis of *The Beautiful and Damned* that makes sense of its widely recognized tonal deaf ear in light on a more sensitive understanding of Fitzgerald's use of cinema as a model for literature. Suzanne del Gizzo, in her article "Ethnic Stereotypes," explores Fitzgerald's racism, as openly expressed in his letters as in his novels. These feelings manifest in *The Beautiful and Damned* through the conflict between the blue-eyed Anthony Patch and the Jewish emigrant businessman, Joseph Bloeckman. Despite his sympathies, Fitzgerald shows whites in decline and non-whites (like many of his time, Fitzgerald would have categorized Jewish people as "not white") ascending.

CRITICISM

Rita M. Brown

Brown is an English professor. In the following essay, she examines the thematic use made of Thorsten Veblen's economic theories in The Beautiful and Damned.

Thanks to F. Scott Fitzgerald, the 1920s is known as the Jazz Age. That name is a little deeper than one might think. The decade before might be associated in the same way with the musical genre of ragtime, and each decade since has its corresponding musical form: swing, rock, grunge, rap, and so forth. Still looking at the surface, one can easily see that each style is the type of dance music preferred by young people at

IN *THE BEAUTIFUL AND DAMNED*, IT IS ANTHONY PATCH AND GLORIA GILBERT WHO FLEE THE POLITICAL AND ECONOMIC WORLDS FOR THE PURSUIT OF PLEASURE, NOT FITZGERALD HIMSELF."

the time. But why should that trivial fact be singled out as a particular signifier? Looked at more objectively, one can see that each style is a commodity owned by recording companies. The music left an indelible mark on its era not because of any inherent quality (and indeed only a few people today listen to the popular music of eras before they were born, or, more to the point, from before their own teen years) but because of the bombardment of mass market advertising made possible by radio and later by television each new product entered popular consciousness. While in the past, popular music had been part of a folk tradition, in the twentieth century it became a creature of corporate advertising.

Typically, the popular music of the twentieth century was something produced by large corporations. The corporation carefully selects a composer (who generally remains unknown to he general public), and matches his or her music with a performer, such as the Andrew Sisters, Elvis Presley, or Britney Spears, whose public persona is carefully controlled and even more carefully promoted by the corporation. Since the music is owned by the corporation, the corporation reaps the profit from sales of recordings. It would have been useless to have Elvis sing a Mozart aria, not only because he lacked the basic musical training to do so but because the music was not covered by copyright law: if the piece had become popular, anyone could have performed it and recorded it without having to pay the corporation. Popular music was transformed from an expression of folk culture to a commercial commodity.

Each decade has its own music not because of any natural evolution of style but because the corporations constantly require new commodities to sell. Their barrage of advertising creates the popular consciousness in each generation

that associates it with a particular musical style. It is no secret that the young are most easily influenced by advertising. The 1920s is the Jazz Age, then, not because of the style of music then popular but because it was the first decade in which corporate advertising became an important factor in shaping popular culture. Music is only a microcosm of the transformation of American culture in the twentieth century into a consumer culture dominated by corporate interests.

If the culture of modern America is a consumer culture, or perhaps better expressed as a corporate culture, its prophet was the economist Thorsten Veblen. His book *The Theory of the Leisure Class: An Economic Study of Institutions* (1899) had made a profound impact on Fitzgerald at Princeton University. In Veblen's view, society was dominated not by a Marxist class struggle but by a struggle to display or gain social class. The wealthy demonstrate their class superiority by displays of luxury and idleness. The aim of the lower classes becomes to imitate the lifestyle of the rich. While industrial production is more than sufficient to guarantee the security of each member of society, poverty exists in practice not only because of the redirection of wealth away from labor to capital, as Marx had it, but because a good deal of the wealth produced in a modern economy is wasted on showy display. The wealthy do not need to control the poor through violence or its threat, but simply by making them want the trappings of a class higher than their own.

These factors obviously operated in Veblen's day during the nineteenth century, but the problem became much more acute in the 1920s. The level of industrial production and wealth increased, as shown, for example, by the spread of the automobile. Class consciousness and the wasteful displays of wealth that accompanied it increased even faster. Advertising had always been a tool to spread envy of the upper classes, but the advent of the radio created for the first time a mass medium that could spread its message far more widely. Advertising is, as Upton Sinclair (another follower of Veblen) had already stated in his novel *The Jungle*, "the ultra-modern profession...the science of persuading people to buy what they do not want," and, one must immediately add, what they do not need. Advertising exists to create demand for otherwise useless products. To return to the theme

WHAT DO I READ NEXT?

- *The Real Story of Ah-Q* (available in many translations, including in *The Real Story of Ah-Q and Other Tales of China*, translated by Julia Lovell in 2009) by Xun Lu is a Chinese novel that shares many of the themes of *The Beautiful and Damned* and was also originally published in 1922. Like Fitzgerald's heroes Anthony Patch and (in *The Great Gatsby*) Jay Gatsby, its main character is a young man whose chief drive is to experience life's pleasures to the fullest. Whereas the freedom offered by American society allows Fitzgerald's characters full exercise of their desires to the point of self-destruction, Ah-Q finds himself stifled by the controlling, regimented nature of traditional Chinese culture.

- *Diva* (2013) is part of the Flappers series of novels by Jillian Larkin. It presents a vision of Jazz Age culture for young-adult readers.

- *The Great Gatsby* (1925) is Fitzgerald's masterpiece. Like all of Fitzgerald's works, it explores the cultural upheavals that rocked America in the 1920s, including the period's unprecedented hedonism and the formation of new cultural roles, especially the icon of the flapper.

- Evelyn Waugh's *Vile Bodies* (1930) is a satire of the new culture of "bright young things"—wealthy, cultured young people indulging themselves in the new modern world—in Great Britain, equivalent to the Jazz Age in America.

- *Fitzgerald's New Women: Harbingers of Change* (1988), is a study of Fitzgerald's depiction of the new woman, or flapper, that scandalized and transformed American culture in the 1920s.

- Paula Fass's *The Damned and the Beautiful* (1977) is a historical study of the transformation of American culture in the 1920s.

of music, there is nothing to be gained by listening to the latest singer, as opposed to a Beethoven symphony or a performer expressing the authentic tradition of one's own community, except for the recording company who will make a profit if a large number of people listen to the music they own. Advertising, in Lewis's view, is the means by which corporations deceive the ignorant and vulnerable into buying their products that otherwise no one would want. The same is true of any other aspect of the economy. The prototypical industrial product of the 1920s was the automobile, the purchase of which was the sign that one had arrived in a higher class, but the automobile in time became destructive to the economy and society, creating urban sprawl and causing the decay of once vibrant city centers, and as a chief producer of greenhouse gas emissions which are threatening the very ecology of the earth. The production and sale of the automobile enriches the corporation that produces it but damages many other things. In a traditional culture, personal meaning was constructed by integration into a small, tightly knit society at the village level. Industrialization and the move from the village to the city created a situation where each family was living among strangers. Veblen's class imitation is a response to the lack of meaning that comes from the isolation of the individual in industrial society. Given a definite shape by advertising, it is meant to take the place of social, even spiritual, meaning. In the 1920s, American society changed from a traditional one to a commercial one.

One does not at first think of Fitzgerald as a political writer and still less an economic one. Rather, one's first impression of Fitzgerald is that he is escaping the political and the economic into a world of pleasure for its own sake and a comedy of manners in which taste is dictated by a minute observation of the latest styles and the social hierarchy. But this is superficial. In *The Beautiful and Damned*, it is Anthony Patch and Gloria Gilbert who flee the political and economic worlds for the pursuit of pleasure, not Fitzgerald himself. Anthony does not work, does not produce anything, and does not want to. His and Gloria's life is centered around the consumption of luxury goods that mark them as members of the upper class. Once they are plunged into relative poverty, their chief concern is that their friends will drop them because they can no longer maintain the display of wealth. At their lowest point, as Anthony descends into

World War I brings an end to the carefree days of the Jazz Age. (© NatUlrich | Shutterstock.com)

alcoholism, he insists on becoming drunk only on whiskey that is too expensive for them to afford. The first thing that Gloria does once they inherit Adam Patch's fortune is to buy the most expensive genuine Russian sable coat tailored by a French designer. This is indicated through the comment of a middle-class woman who recognizes the style because she wants one too, even if she cannot afford it. Not yet. Anthony's character is the perfect reciprocal of mass advertising. He wants, does nothing but want, and wants only what he cannot have. He becomes damned when he finds himself in a position where he can buy anything he wants and there is nothing left to desire, no higher display that he can make, no higher class that he can aspire to. Fitzgerald is obviously all too aware of the message, matching Veblen's analysis, of *The Beautiful and Damned*. His paradox is that the novel is for him the product of literary naturalism. The novel truly reflects the material of his life. Even when he made a small fortune as a writer, every penny he made and more went on an ostentatious display of luxury. He was

constantly in debt for the money to throw ever swankier parties. He must have seen the self-destructive character of his own existence, but as with his drinking, he was powerless to stop it.

Source: Rita M. Brown, Critical Essay on *The Beautiful and Damned*, in *Novels for Students*, Gale, Cengage Learning, 2015.

Marguerite Mooers Marshall and F. Scott Fitzgerald

In the following interview, Fitzgerald gives his rather dated views on the role of a woman in marriage.

"New York is going crazy! When I was here a year ago I thought we'd seen the end of night life. But now it's going on as it never was before Prohibition. I'm confident that you can find anything here that you find in Paris. Everybody is drinking harder—that's sure. Possessing liquor is a proof of respectability, of social position. You can't go anywhere without having your host bring out his bottle and offer you a drink. He displays his liquor as he used to display his new car or his wife's jewels. Prohibition, it seems to me, is having simply a ruinous effect on young men."

It is a young man himself who is speaking— no clergyman, no social reformer, but a "regular" young man. Most of you know his name— F. Scott Fitzgerald, who wrote *This Side of Paradise*, a book that managed to be both brilliant and popular, when he was just out of Princeton, two years ago; whose second novel, *The Beautiful and Damned*, is newly published. (A reader of both suggests that, in view of the first tale, the second could have been called, consistently, "Next Stop Is Hell!")

The frank Mr. Fitzgerald undoubtedly set the fashion of holding the mirror up to the flapper. Some of us, in two years, have grown a bit weary of studying her reflection. So we welcome the fact that, in his second novel, Mr. Fitzgerald turns his attention to other representatives of his generation—to the "younger marrieds," in the locution of the society columns. They out-flap the flapper! With youth, health, beauty, love, friends, money, pleasure, his Anthony and Gloria, typifying the prosperous, newly married couple in New York, are hopelessly, irretrievably "damned," broken in body and spirit; one an accomplished, the other an incipient dipsomaniac, before the end of the story.

"But why?" I asked the young novelist, when I met him at the Plaza Hotel, where he and his wife are staying for a few days. Their home is in St. Paul, Minn. "In some ways your pair were a special case. But we all know scores of young men and women here in New York who marry under the happiest auspices, and who, in a few years, manage to throw away all their chances of lifelong happiness and security together. What is the matter with our young married couples?"

"First of all, I think it's the way everybody is drinking," replied the blue-eyed, frank-faced, fastidiously dressed author. His stories are world weary, but he himself is as clean and fresh and boyish as if he'd never had an idea or a disillusion. Then he gave the candid, impartial impression of New York life of the present quoted at the beginning of this interview.

"There's the philosophy of ever so many young people to-day," he went on, thoughtfully. "They don't believe in the old standards and authorities, and they're not intelligent enough, many of them, to put a code of morals and conduct in place of the sanctions that have been destroyed for them. They drift. Their attitude toward life might be summed up: 'This is ALL. Then what does it matter? We don't care! Let's GO!'"

A little nervous movement of Mr. Fitzgerald's cigarette finished the sentence.

The young wife in his book remarks, even before entering the state of matrimony, that she does not want to have responsibility and a lot of children to take care of. "Evidently," observes her creator, with a nuance of sarcasm, "she did not doubt that on her lips all things were good." So I asked him how far he considered the young married woman to blame for the "damnation" of her own life and that of her husband.

"She's very largely to blame," he responded promptly. "Our American women are leeches. They're an utterly useless fourth generation trading on the accomplishment of their pioneer great-grandmothers. They simply dominate the American man. You should see the dowagers trailing around this hotel with their dependent males! No Englishman would endure one-eighth of what an American takes from his wife.

"I've often asked myself the question, 'To what is a woman entitled from life?' The answer, obviously, is 'All she can get!' And when she marries she gets the whole thing. She makes a man love her, then proceeds to hog all his emotions, to get all the money out of him she can, to keep him at her beck and call. She makes a monkey of him, in many cases, and he has to stand it unless he wants a continuous verbal battle."

Mr. Fitzgerald took another whiff of his cigarette.

"What chance have they, these men and women of my generation who come from families with some money!" he exclaimed. "I'm not blaming them. What chance has the young man, unless he has to work for his living? If he were born in England there would at least be a tradition behind him and a background. Here he is born in a Middle Western town. His grandfather, perhaps, was a farm laborer. He—the third generation—is brought up to be absolutely helpless. He is sent to a fine private school, near New York, and before he's through he knows everything every boy ever knew and every chorus girl in town. His idea of happiness is to have one of them on the back seat of a limousine. Then his family resolves that he must go to Yale. He goes there to raise hell. When he's through—if he gets through—he's absolutely ruined.

"He ought to do something. But what can he do? Suppose he thinks that he might try to help govern his country." But what he would think next is so perfectly summed up in *The Beautiful and Damned* that I shall quote it word for word:

> He tried to imagine himself in Congress, rooting around in the litter of that incredible pigsty, with the narrow and porcine brows he saw pictured sometimes, those glorified proletarians babbling blandly to the Nation the ideas of high school seniors! Little men with copybook ambitions who by mediocrity had thought to emerge from mediocrity into the lustreless and unromantic heaven of a government by the people—and the best, the dozen shrewd men at the top, egotistic and cynical, were content to lead this choir of white ties and wire collarbuttons in a discordant and amazing hymn, compounded of a vague confusion between wealth as a reward of virtue and wealth as a proof of vice, and continued cheers for God, the Constitution and the Rocky Mountains!

"Nevertheless," I said, "all our younger married set cannot be 'damned.' Surely you can suggest some way in which they may be 'saved'?"

"Work!" at once exclaimed Mr. Fitzgerald, his blue eyes earnest. "Work is the one salvation for all of us—even if we must work to forget there's nothing worth while to work for, even if the work we turn out—books, for example—doesn't satisfy us. The young man must work. His wife must work"—

"How?" I interrupted. "At bringing up an old-fashioned family?"

Scott Fitzgerald IS a boy, and married happily, and not too long.

"I think," he confided, ingenuously, "that just being in love, really in love—doing it well, you know—is work enough for a woman. If she keeps her house the way it should be kept and makes herself look pretty when her husband comes home in the evening and loves him and helps him with his work and encourages him—oh, I think that's the sort of work that will save her. It's not so easy, you know, being in love and making it go."

Evidently the younger generation, whatever the vagaries of its head, still believes in keeping its heart in the same old place!

Source: Marguerite Mooers Marshall and F. Scott Fitzgerald, "F. Scott Fitzgerald, Novelist, Shocked by

> "
> THE BASIC COMMON DENOMINATOR OF MOST
> OF THE WOMEN IN FITZGERALD'S STORIES IS THEIR
> INTENSE SELF-CENTEREDNESS."

'Younger Marrieds' and Prohibition," in *Conversations with F. Scott Fitzgerald*, edited by Matthew J. Bruccoli and Judith S. Baughman, University Press of Mississippi, 2004, pp. 26–29.

Milton Hindus

In the following excerpt, Hindus discusses Fitzgerald's treatment of women in his fiction.

. . . In at least one passage, he jabs at a favorite target—what he was to call in *Tender Is the Night*: "the American Woman (whose) clean sweeping irrational temper . . . had broken the moral back of a race and made a nursery out of a continent." In *The Beautiful and Damned*, he calls America

> the most opulent, most gorgeous land on earth—a land whose wisest are but little wiser than its dullest; a land where the rulers have minds like little children and the law-givers believe in Santa Claus; where ugly women control strong men. . . . Yes, it is truly a melancholy spectacle. Women with receding chins and shapeless noses go about in broad daylight saying "Do this!" and "Do that!" and all the men, even those of great wealth, obey implicitly their women to whom they refer sonorously either as "Mrs. So-and-so" or as "The wife."

Gloria Patch, in this second of Fitzgerald's novels, is one of his most interesting feminine creations. Like all of the novelist's heroines, she is beautiful and, like so many of his girls, there is a corrosive cynicism in her verbal expression which is merely the outward form that her profound nihilism takes. Her husband Anthony seems to be speaking for both of them (and for many others in their prematurely life-weary generation) when he says to his friend Maury Noble: "It being a meaningless world, why write? The very attempt to give it purpose is purposeless." In such a directionless universe, the logical credo, quite obviously, is that of Gloria when she denies the existence of any moral standards whatever: "I don't know anything about what you should do or what anybody should do." As

Amory Blaine had said in *This Side of Paradise*: "Very few things matter and nothing matters very much." Gloria coins epigrams like some belated follower of George Moore or Oscar Wilde: "There's only one lesson to be learned from life and that is that there's no lesson to be learned from life."

The whole truth about her incurably narcissistic personality is clearly divulged in a speech which she makes while lying ill with double pneumonia and raving feverishly. *In delirium veritas*—the depths of her subconscious are revealed by her wild and whirling words:

> Millions of people, swarming like rats, chattering like apes, smelling like all hell . . . monkeys! Or lice, I suppose. For one really exquisite palace . . . on Long Island, say—or even in Greenwich . . . for one palace full of pictures from the Old World and exquisite things—with avenues of trees and green lawns and a view of the blue sea, and lovely people about in slick dresses . . . I'd sacrifice a hundred thousand of them, a million of them . . . I care nothing for them—understand me?

Gloria manages to be even more antisocial than Anthony, who is critical of her: "What he chiefly missed in her mind was the pedantic teleology—the sense of order and accuracy, the sense of life as a mysteriously correlated piece of mechanism." As for Anthony himself, the sense of order that he possesses appears to be minimal and his "philosophy" is as pessimistic in its orientation as that of the philosopher Schopenhauer, to whom he seems indebted for some of his formulations of his feeling: "Desire just cheats you. It's like a sunbeam skipping here and there about a room. It stops and gilds some inconsequential object, and we poor fools try to grasp it—but when we do, the sunbeam moves on to something else, and you've got the inconsequential part, but the glitter that made you want it is gone."

Connected with this pessimism, this almost complete despair of the possibility of more than ephemeral satisfactions in existence, is Fitzgerald's disgusting picture of old age in his account of Adam J. Patch, Anthony's father. The only comparable example in modern literature is that passage in Proust's last volume *Le temps retrouvé*, in which the narrator describes so poignantly and satirically the changes wrought by age in the physiognomies, manners, and even the spirit of his contemporaries. Fitzgerald says of old Adam J. Patch:

The span of his seventy-five years had acted as a magic bellows—the first quarter century had blown him full with life, and the last had sucked it all back. It had sucked in the cheeks and the chest and the girth of arm and leg. It had tyrannously demanded his teeth, one by one, tweaked out his hairs, changed him from gray to white in some places, from pink to yellow in others, callously transposing his colors like a child trying over a paintbox. Then through his body and his soul it had attacked his brain. It had sent him night-sweats and tears and unfounded dreads. It had split his intense normality into credulity and suspicion.

One of the crudest ironies of the social order stressed by Fitzgerald is that the same man who has seventy-five "winters on his head" also possesses, thanks to the $75,000,000 he has accumulated, privileges and prestige enjoyed by few others among us. He alone, who has lost all taste for living, retains the motives that make life worthwhile: "This feeble, unintelligent old man was possessed of such power that, yellow journals to the contrary, the men in the republic whose souls he could not have bought directly or indirectly would scarcely have populated White Plains, . . ." In *The Beautiful and Damned*, we have the tragic spectacle of youth, which ought to be an end in itself, compelled by social exigencies to spend much of its time plotting and planning to lay hold of the old man's $75,000,000. By the time Anthony and Gloria have succeeded in reaching their ignoble objective, anything in them that even faintly promised to make them worthwhile people is hopelessly lost. Instead of the gay and attractive creatures they had first impressed the world as being, they are as hideous and disfigured as the penurious old capitalist whose will they have spent their lives fighting and have succeeded in breaking at last in death.

In Fitzgerald's writings, the pathos of age and the sense of reverence due to the aged is constantly overweighed by a realization of its unaesthetic qualities. These qualities are illustrated not only in the unflattering portrait of Adam J. Patch but in the one (produced in the same period) of the hero's father in Fitzgerald's only play, *The Vegetable*. Jerry Frost's old father "Dada" in that play is described as having "faded, vacant eyes. . . . Half the time his mind is a vacuum, in which confused clots of information and misinformation drift and stir—the rest of the time he broods upon the minute details of his daily existence."

The fact that the characters a novelist creates bear a resemblance to each other was never more true than of Fitzgerald's women. The mayhem which the author performs upon Gloria Patch is so similar to that done upon Rosalind, the debutante in *This Side of Paradise*, upon Daisy Buchanan in *The Great Gatsby*, upon Nichole Diver in *Tender Is the Night*, and upon numerous girls in his shorter stories that the subject deserves at least brief discussion.

In the short story "The Adjuster," Luella Hemple, who says to a woman companion: "Even my baby bores me." is a variation upon Daisy Buchanan in her habitual mood when she says: "What shall we do with ourselves this afternoon, and the day after that, and the next thirty years?" (The ennui and purposelessness of this are echoed in Eliot's "Waste Land" which Fitzgerald admired very much. "What shall we do tomorrow?/ What shall we ever do?" and also in Auden's line: "What does it mean? What are we going to do?")

In "The Adjuster," Fitzgerald makes a generalization which, no doubt, illuminates his life and work: "It is one of the many flaws in the scheme of human relationships that selfishness in women has an irresistible appeal to many men." The basic common denominator of most of the women in Fitzgerald's stories is their intense self-centeredness. The best example of this other than Gloria Patch is probably Daisy Buchanan, and Daisy's most symbolic action is caught by Fitzgerald in his sentence: "Daisy took her face in her hands as if feeling its lovely shape...."

In the story "May Day," Edith's attitude to Gordon Sterrett is essentially like that of Daisy to Gatsby. Like Daisy, Edith is morally weak and abandons her interest in her lover as soon as she realizes that he is in real trouble. She simply gets scared and runs out on him. In the story "A Short Trip Home" (from *Taps at Reveille*) the character Ellen reminds the reader both of Daisy and of Edith. Like them, she abandons Joe Jelke when the latter is hit by a "hard-looking customer" with brass knuckles. "'It was Joe's own fault,' she said surprisingly, 'I told him not to interfere.' This wasn't true. She had said nothing, only uttered one curious little click of impatience."

In *The Vegetable*, the wife of the hero, Charlotte Frost, is described in the following terms:

> She's thirty, and old for her age, just like I told you, shapeless, slack-cheeked but still defiant. She would fiercely resent the statement that her attractions have declined ninety per cent since her marriage, and in the same breath she would assume that there was a responsibility and shoulder it on her husband. She talks in a pessimistic whine and, with a sort of dowdy egotism, considers herself generally in the right. Frankly I don't like her, though she can't help being what she is.

The American Woman, then, as she emerges from Fitzgerald's pages, is a badly battered ideal. If he had ever managed to finish his projected novel, "The Boy Who Killed His Mother" one may surmise that the hero's action would have appeared wholly understandable. *This Side of Paradise* had opened with the sentence: "Amory Blaine inherited from his mother every trait except the stray inexpressible few that made him worthwhile." These words begin the procession of phenomenally unappealing females (in the moral rather than the physical sense) that were destined to populate his books.

Yet Van Wyck Brooks could ask with seeming justification in *The Opinions of Oliver Allston*: "Who had ever been more romantic than Scott Fitzgerald?" As with other romantics, however, the let-down was directly proportional to the extreme illusion which had preceded it. In this respect, Fitzgerald has something in common with both Schopenhauer and Proust. His disillusion, like theirs, goes so far that he calls the value of life itself into question. Like them, too, he seems to have become something of a misogynist. He is, of course, not quite so outspoken as Schopenhauer in his contempt for "the narrow-shouldered, broad-hipped, short-legged, unaesthetic sex," nor is he a dissembler of his real feelings like Proust, who worshiped the embalmed memory of his mother's goodness while acting as a sexual deviate who could not form satisfactory relations with other members of her sex. Fitzgerald at first glance appears to be much more conventional than either of these writers, but when the surface is critically penetrated and his conformity to heterosexual mores is dissolved by analysis, he appears to exhibit quite as much anger as any writer has at what he regards as the betrayal of his capacity for love by unresponsive, narcissistic, designing women.

Source: Milton Hindus, "*The Beautiful and Damned*," in *F. Scott Fitzgerald: An Introduction and Interpretation*, Holt, Rinehart and Winston, 1968, pp. 30–34.

SOURCES

Barks, Cathy W., "Biography," in *F. Scott Fitzgerald in Context*, edited by Bryant Mangum, Cambridge University Press, 2013, pp. 3–15.

Bishop, John Peale, "*The Beautiful and Damned*: Mr. Fitzgerald Sees the Flapper Through," in *F. Scott Fitzgerald in His Own Time: A Miscellany*, edited by Matthew J. Bruccoli and Jackson R. Bryer, Kent State University Press, 1971, pp. 320–24; originally published in *New York Herald*, March 5, 1922.

Bruccoli, Matthew J., *F. Scott Fitzgerald: A Life in Letters*, Scribner, 1994, pp. 46, 460–61.

Bryer, Jackson R., "Contemporary Critical Reception," in *F. Scott Fitzgerald in Context*, edited by Bryant Mangum, Cambridge University Press, 2013, pp. 66–77.

Burroughs, Catherine R., "Keats' Lamian Legacy: Romance and the Performance of Gender in *The Beautiful and Damned*," in *F. Scott Fitzgerald: New Perspectives*, edited by Jackson R. Bryer, Alan Margolies, and Ruth Prigozy, University of Georgia Press, 2004, pp. 51–77.

Canby, Henry Sidel, "*The Beautiful and Damned*: The Flapper's Tragedy," in *F. Scott Fitzgerald in His Own Time: A Miscellany*, edited by Matthew J. Bruccoli and Jackson R. Bryer, Kent State University Press, 1971, pp. 317–19; originally published in *New York Post*, March 4, 1922.

Canterbery, E. Ray, and Thomas D. Birch, *F. Scott Fitzgerald under the Influence*, Paragon, 2006, pp. 111–32.

del Gizzo, Suzanne, "Ethnic Stereotyping," in *F. Scott Fitzgerald in Context*, edited by Bryant Mangum, Cambridge University Press, 2013, pp. 224–33.

Drowne, Kathleen, "Postwar Flappers," in *F. Scott Fitzgerald in Context*, edited by Bryant Mangum, Cambridge University Press, 2013, pp. 245–53.

Eble, Kenneth, *F. Scott Fitzgerald*, Twayne's United States Author Series No. 36, Twayne Publishers, 1977, pp. 68–75.

Enfield, Jonathan, "'As the Fashion in Books Shifted': *The Beautiful and Damned* as Arc Light Fiction," in *Modernism/Modernity*, Vol. 14, No. 4, 2007, pp. 669–85.

"F. Scott Fitzgerald and His Popular Novel," in *Des Moines Capital*, February 18, 1923, p. 33.

Fitzgerald, F. Scott, *The Beautiful and Damned*, Charles Scribner's Sons, 1922.

Mencken, H. L., *The American Language, Supplement One*, Alfred A. Knopf, 1945, pp. 514–15.

Prigozy, Ruth, "The Fitzgerald Revival," in *F. Scott Fitzgerald in Context*, edited by Bryant Mangum, Cambridge University Press, 2013, pp. 78–88.

Sinclair, Upton, *The Jungle*, Upton Sinclair, 1906, p. 404.

Veblen, Thorsten, *The Theory of the Leisure Class: An Economic Study of Institutions*, B. W. Huebsch, 1899, pp. 35–67.

West, James L. W., "The Question of Vocation in *This Side of Paradise* and *The Beautiful and Damned*," in *The Cambridge Companion to F. Scott Fitzgerald*, edited by Ruth Prigozy, Cambridge University Press, 2002, pp. 48–56.

FURTHER READING

Allen, Fredrick Lewis, *Only Yesterday: An Informal History of the 1920s*, Harper and Row, 1931.

    Allen's history of the 1920s has all of the advantages and limitations of having been written by an eyewitness to the period described. The complete text of the book is available many places online, including http://gutenberg.net.au/ebooks 05/0500831h.html.

Dumenil, Lynn, *The Modern Temper: American Culture and Society in the 1920s*, Hill and Wang, 1995.

    Dumenil provides a historical investigation of the transformation of the American culture and economy that is illustrated in *The Beautiful and Damned*.

Fitzgerald, F. Scott, *Tender Is the Night*, Charles Scribner's Sons, 1934.

    Fitzgerald's last complete novel is based on the medical treatment of his wife, Zelda.

———, *This Side of Paradise*, Charles Scribner's Sons, 1920.

    This Side of Paradise was Fitzgerald's first novel. Like all of his work, it is largely autobiographical, examining the destructive elements of the culture of the 1920s that Fitzgerald viewed with an analytical distance, but to which he could not help being drawn like a moth to a flame.

SUGGESTED SEARCH TERMS

F. Scott Fitzgerald

The Beautiful and Damned

naturalism

realism

Jazz Age

Jazz Age AND Fitzgerald

flapper

Thorsten Veblen

Catalyst

LAURIE HALSE ANDERSON
2002

Catalyst is a young-adult novel by American writer Laurie Halse Anderson, published in 2002. The story begins in the spring, when the seniors at Merryweather High are anxiously awaiting their college acceptance letters. Kate Malone has set her heart on going to Massachusetts Institute of Technology. But MIT turns her down, and she also has to cope with an unwelcome change in her life when Teri, a high-school senior whom she does not like, moves temporarily into Kate's house after her own is damaged by fire. Kate has a choice of either letting her life spin out of control or finding a new purpose that is not so rigidly focused on academic achievement. As the title of the novel suggests, the unexpected events turn out to be the catalyst for a dramatic change that takes place within Kate. The novel has won praise for its sharp portrait of the science and math geek Kate and her high-school world. A word of caution to teachers who might assign this book to middle-school readers: Teri's son turns out to have been fathered by her own father. However, the author does not dwell on this, mentioning it briefly only a couple of times. Teri's father does not appear directly in the story, and the relationship between him and Teri is not examined.

AUTHOR BIOGRAPHY

Anderson was born on October 23, 1961, in Potsdam, New York. Her father was a Methodist minister, and her mother was in management.

Laurie Halse Anderson (© *David Livingston | Getty Images Entertainment | Getty Images*)

She attended Onandaga County Community College, receiving an associate of arts degree in 1981, and then Georgetown University, from which she received a bachelor of science in language and linguistics in 1984.

Anderson knew as a child that she wanted to become a writer, and she decided to write for children and young adults. Anderson writes on her website: "I get new ideas constantly. Generally, it's a person trapped in an interesting situation, or facing a conflict that forces her to change and grow." Her first work was a picture book, *Ndito Runs*, published in 1996. Her first young-adult novel was *Speak* (1999), which is narrated by a high-school student who is being ostracized by other students. The novel won the Michael L. Printz Award Honor Book citation from the American Library Association (ALA). It was also a finalist for the National Book Award and the *Los Angeles Times* Book Prize.

Since then, Anderson has written eight more young-adult novels. *Fever 1793* (2000) is a historical novel set during a yellow-fever epidemic in Philadelphia. *Catalyst* followed in 2002. It received an ALA Best Book for Young Adults

citation in 2003. Andersen then wrote five novels in as many years: *Prom* (2005), *Twisted* (2007), *Chains* (2008), *Wintergirls* (2009), and *Forge* (2010). In 2014, she published *The Impossible Knife of Memory*. She has also published eight picture books and fifteen novels in the Wild at Heart series for older elementary-aged readers as part of the American Girl library.

Anderson married Gregory H. Anderson in 1983. They had one child and were divorced in 2002. Anderson married Scot Larrabee in 2004. They live in northern New York.

PLOT SUMMARY

Part 1: Solid

CHAPTER 1: ELEMENTAL

The story is related by high-school senior Kate Malone. After a late-night run, she returns home to where she lives with her father, who is a minister, and her fourteen-year-old brother, Toby, and finishes the laundry. Kate is a top student and has applied to MIT. She is waiting to hear whether she has been accepted. It is the only college she has applied to. She does some ironing, watches TV, and at two in the morning gives Toby his cough medicine. Then she goes to bed but for some while cannot sleep. She suffers from insomnia.

CHAPTER 2: DELAYED REACTION

The next morning she oversleeps and knows she will be late for school. Her dad says they need to have a talk about college. He does not know that MIT is the only college she has applied to. She drives to school in her battered old car, arriving late for her advanced placement chemistry class with Ms. Cummings, her favorite teacher. Mariah Yates announces she has been accepted by Stanford, while some of the others tell Kate her odds of getting into MIT are four to one against.

At lunchtime Kate sits with her boyfriend, Mitch Pangborn (who has been accepted by Harvard); her friend Sara Emery; and Sara's boyfriend, Travis Baird, in the cafeteria. The football players start taunting the unpopular Teri Litch, and a fight breaks out. Teri throws a book at Art Smith and punches Brandon Figgs in the head. There is a general melee, which ends only with the arrival of security and the principal.

MEDIA ADAPTATIONS

- Random House Audio released an audio version of *Catalyst* in 2002, read by Samantha Mathis.

Kate suffers from boredom in English class. Later, she takes part in a 5K cross-country race but gets lost in the woods because she did not wear her glasses and finishes last. When she gets home she finds Betty, the church secretary, searching for spoons for a church dinner that evening. Kate helps to serve food at the dinner. Teri is also there, and later, after Teri has left, Kate believes that Teri has taken her watch.

Kate follows Teri, planning on confronting her about the watch. As Teri reaches for the doorknob of her house, Kate sees her watch on Teri's wrist. She is startled, however, when Teri invites her in to meet the family, along with Ms. Cummings, who has brought food. Kate meets Teri's mom and her two-year-old brother, Mikey. Kate's father arrives to talk to Mrs. Litch about the fight in the cafeteria. He is surprised to see Kate there. Kate demands Teri return the watch, but Teri says she cannot prove it is hers. Exasperated, Kate leaves and goes for a run.

Part 2: Liquid

CHAPTER 3: GALVANIZE

Kate is notified that she has not been accepted by MIT. Her father and then Mitch try to console her, but she is devastated. Everyone thinks that she can go to another school; no one knows that MIT is the only school she applied to. She thinks her only option is a state school, and only if they have rolling admissions. She tries to see a guidance counselor at school, but they are all busy. She attends calculus class. She wants to go for a run, but the coach says that they are to do conditioning in the weight room. Kate runs so hard on the treadmill that she passes out. Back home that evening, she gets it into her head that MIT has just made a mistake

and that all she has to do is drive three hundred miles to MIT and talk to an admissions officer about her case.

Toby tells her that the Litches' barn is on fire, and the flames are spreading to the house. Teri and Mikey have fled the house and are downstairs. Kate's dad tells her that they will be staying the night and may have to stay for a week. Teri is to stay with Kate in her room. Mrs. Litch will stay at Betty's house. Kate protests, but her father insists. Teri and Mikey take the bed, while Kate sleeps on a cot, but Mikey's snoring keeps her awake.

CHAPTER 4: OXIDIZING AGENT

In the morning, Teri helps Mikey wash and complains about what Kate offers for breakfast. Kate says she has to go to her job at the pharmacy but is informed that her father has called her boss and told him she will not be in. She must stay at home and help to cope with the emergency situation. Kate goes to the Litch property. Her father is there with some workers and has plans for the barn to be rebuilt. The house is still standing but there is much work to be done. It looks like Teri could be staying for weeks. Teri arrives, and while Kate looks after Mikey, Teri gets some toys for him from the house. Kate starts to like Mikey. Then she takes them in her car to a fast-food place for breakfast, followed by a trip to the car wash and other errands. Teri complains all the time. Kate buys contact lenses for the first time, which greatly improve her vision.

After going home for lunch, they go to buy groceries. In the store, Kate runs into Sara and Travis, and also Mitch, who urges her to accept that she has been rejected by MIT and pick another school. Even Mitch does not know that she only applied to MIT. Kate has to leave in a hurry because Teri is outside, honking the horn. (She has hot-wired the car to start it.) They drive off, and Kate thinks Teri may have stolen some food, but Teri claims she was merely trying to help Kate get away from Mitch, because she thought Mitch was hassling her. Kate decides to convince her father to let Teri, who has learned some construction skills, to help in the rebuilding of her house.

CHAPTER 5: ALCHEMY

Kate attends church with Toby, Mrs. Litch, and Mikey. She does not pay much attention to her father's sermon but instead prays to all the gods she can think of that she should be accepted to MIT.

CHAPTER 6: ELECTROSTATIC FORCES

Teri decides to take the day off from school to work on the rebuilding project. Kate drops Mikey off at preschool. After school, she takes Mikey and visits the Litch house. Teri shows her around, talking about how the house is going to be rebuilt. At school, Kate's guidance counselor tells her to apply for a school with rolling admissions or take a year off. To get away from the chaos at home, she runs for miles at night.

CHAPTER 7: NUCLEAR STABILITY

After working at the pharmacy until the afternoon, Kate goes to the Litch house, where workers and volunteers from the church are hard at work. Kate and Toby help out. Kate learns that Teri's father, Charlie Litch, died a year ago in jail. Mitch arrives with pizza. After everyone has eaten, Teri notices that Mikey is missing. Mikey is found lying dead; he has been electrocuted after his fire truck toy and his fingers come into contact with a faulty electrical outlet. All efforts to resuscitate him fail. A stunned Teri tells Kate that Mikey was her son, not her brother.

Part 3: Gas

CHAPTER 8: PHOTOELECTRONS

After the ambulance takes Mikey away, Kate and her friends stay. They light candles and sit together in a huddle, each handling the situation in his or her way. Kate and Toby, and then Sara and Travis, put their fingers in a paint can and paint the walls in a kind of tribute to Mikey. After midnight, Teri returns to the Malone house, sedated. But then she goes back to her own home, where Kate finds her sitting on the floor where Mikey died. Little is said between them, but they sit back to back and their fingers intertwine.

CHAPTER 9: RADIOACTIVE

The next day, Sunday, Kate can do nothing but watch cartoons on television. During the night Teri returns from Betty's, where she has been visiting her mother, and she and Kate then go to Teri's house and sleep on the floor of Mikey's room.

CHAPTER 10: PHASE TRANSITION

Kate and Teri both go to school. Needing Kate's support, Teri decides to accompany her to her classes. In Ms. Cummings's class, Teri falls asleep. Kate is unable to concentrate and wonders what Teri will do in the future. They go

to the cafeteria and sit with Sara and Travis. Mitch is absent. He never misses school, so they wonder what has happened to him. Kate struggles through the rest of the day. Later, Mrs. Litch and Teri are in the kitchen with the funeral director, picking a casket for Mikey.

Kate calls MIT, pretending to be her own mother, and asks an admissions officer why she was turned down. She is told that, while smart, she lacked the "extra something" needed for admission, and her essays were poor. Kate visits Mitch and confesses that MIT was the only college she applied to. Mitch is sympathetic. Then he tells her that he has been affected by the death of Mikey and wants to study something at Harvard that is more practical and useful than history, so he has switched his major to economics.

CHAPTER 11: ALPHA DECAY

The funeral service for Mikey is well attended. After the funeral, people assemble at the Malone house. When everyone has left, Toby asks Kate if their mother's funeral, nine years' prior, was similar. Kate is evasive at first but then confesses that she ran from the church after the funeral and did not attend the burial. She was too upset.

Kate finds Teri pummeling the kitchen in the Litch house to bits with a sledgehammer. Because she is in so much pain over what happened, she aims to destroy as much of the house as she can, including doors, windows, and walls. Kate says she needs counseling, but Teri scoffs. Kate returns home.

CHAPTER 12: ACTIVATED COMPLEX

For the next few days Teri lives in her own house and continues to destroy it. Kate lives in a kind of haze. At the track meet, when the starter's gun goes off, her legs refuse to move. She does not respond to Mitch's e-mails because he told everyone that she had only applied to one college. She still does not know what she will do the following year.

CHAPTER 13: CRITICAL PRESSURE

On Saturday, Sara takes charge and insists that Kate go with her to a diner for breakfast. Mitch and Travis are also there. The waitress turns out to be Teri, who has just started working there. Teri is not gracious, but she sits with them for a few minutes while on her break. Mitch tells her not to be rude to Kate, but Kate does not approve of his intervention. When Teri returns, she drops a necklace she took from Kate on the table. Teri leaves the diner.

Kate visits Teri at her home. She apologizes to Teri for Mitch's bad behavior. After a little more conversation, Kate says she wants to help Teri rebuild the house, for as long as it takes. She has forgotten about college and discovered something else that she really wants to do. Teri accepts the offer, and Kate is ready to start straightaway.

CHARACTERS

Travis Baird
Travis Baird is Sara's boyfriend. They have been dating for four years. He has a shaved head and lots of tattoos. He works the night shift at a supermarket and finds it hard to stay awake during school.

Betty
Betty is the church secretary and organist. Something of a busybody, she helps to organize the chicken and biscuit dinner at the church.

Ms. Cummings
Ms. Cummings is Kate's favorite teacher. When she first arrived during Kate's freshman year, she organized a science geek club. She has supervised all Kate's science fair entries, and Kate thinks of her as her "fairy godmother in a lab coat and goggles." She also attends the Reverend Malone's church and sings in the choir.

Miss Devlin
Miss Devlin is a student teacher of English at Kate's high school. She is only three years older than Kate. Kate is bored in her class.

Sara Emery
Sara is Kate's best friend. She describes herself as a Wiccan Jewish poet. She and Kate always keep in close touch, and when Kate goes into a funk after Mikey's death, Sara helps her to pull out of it by insisting that she go out to breakfast with her friends. Sara is a top student and has won an early decision place at Bryn Mawr.

Brandon Figgs
Brandon Figgs is a high-school football player. Kate dated him for a while a year back but

thought he was dumb. In the fight in the cafeteria, Teri punches Brandon in the head.

Mr. Freeman
Mr. Freeman is the art teacher at Merryweather High. He supervises the building of a statue in the school's lobby.

Charlie Litch
Charlie Litch was Teri's father. He does not appear in the story. He died in jail a year before the story begins, although why he was imprisoned is not stated. Charlie was abusive to his wife and child. He is the father of Teri's son, Mikey.

Mikey Litch
Mikey Litch is Teri's two-year-old son, although Teri lets everyone believe he is her brother. The truth comes out after Mikey is electrocuted by touching a faulty electrical outlet. His father is Teri's father, Charlie.

Mrs. Litch
Mrs. Litch is Teri's mother. She was violently abused by her husband, and it seems like she has never fully recovered. She has a scar above her eyebrow. She is tiny and does not see well. After the fire, she stays at Betty's house.

Teri Litch
Teri Litch is a high school senior. Kate has known her for years. Teri used to beat her up in elementary school, after which Kate learned to avoid her. Teri is from a poor family and lives with her mother and two-year-old brother Mikey (who is actually her son) in a dilapidated old house not far from the Malones. Teri was bullied in ninth grade after she put on weight, but since then she has slimmed down and acquired muscle. She can handle herself in a fight.

Teri is blunt-spoken and not very communicative when Kate talks to her. Kate believes that Teri has stolen her watch, and it appears that Teri also stole a necklace that Mitch had given Kate. (Teri later gives the necklace back.) Tragedy strikes Teri's life when Mikey is accidentally electrocuted. She tears the house apart in anger and grief. Having stayed with Kate for a while immediately after the tragedy, she and Kate, outwardly rather hostile to each other, inch their way to a relationship that is sealed when Kate offers to help rebuild the house and Teri accepts.

Mr. Lockheart

Mr. Lockheart is an old handyman who repairs the broken boiler at Kate's home. Some of the church ladies are wary of him because he drinks whiskey.

Rev. Jack Malone

Rev. Jack Malone is Kate's father. His wife died of pneumonia nine years before the story begins. He throws himself into his church activities and feels most useful when he is helping others or dealing with some humanitarian crisis. He organizes a band of church volunteers, for example, to help the Litches when their house burns. Although he is usually charming with other people, he does not have an easy relationship with his daughter, who does not share his religious faith. They do not seem to be able to communicate well with each other. He also suffers from migraine headaches, which may suggest he is under some stress and not in the best of health.

Kate Malone

Kate Malone is the narrator of the story. She is a very smart high-school senior whose burning ambition is to go to MIT. She does not even bother to apply to any other college. She is set on MIT partly because her late mother attended that college, and she has some reason to hope that she can follow in her mother's footsteps. She ranks third in her senior class, and her science fair entry won a national award. She excels at chemistry and math and also standardized tests. Kate lives a hectic, fast-paced life and does not seem to know when to stop, as a result of which she suffers from insomnia. One thing that does calm her down is running. Like everything else she does, she is good at it.

Kate is devastated when MIT turns her down and has a hard time accepting the setback. She has no idea what she will do as an alternative. Her world is further disrupted when Teri Litch comes and stays at her house following a fire at the Litch home. Kate finds herself having to share a room with a girl she has never gotten along with and who steals from her. Kate does develop a fondness for Teri's young son, Mikey, however. After he dies in a tragic incident, Kate and Teri are thrown together again,

Toby Malone

Toby Malone is Kate's fourteen-year-old brother. He suffers from asthma, and at the beginning of the novel he also has a cough. Kate has to make

sure he takes his medicine. Later, he shows an interest in his late mother and asks Kate a lot of questions about her. He starts to write a biography about her for an English class.

Mitchell A. Pangborn III

Mitchell A. Pangborn III, known as Mitch, is Kate's boyfriend. He has been accepted by Harvard and plans to major in history. He and Kate have a playfully antagonistic relationship and have been fierce academic rivals since sixth grade. Less than a year before the story begins, they went on a date and Kate found she liked him, because he was smart, laughed at her jokes, and was a great kisser. After Mikey is killed, Mitch is angry. He thinks someone must be to blame and should be held accountable. This incident radically affects his outlook on life. He decides not to major in history but to study economics and then go to business school. He feels this is a more practical and useful approach to life.

Mrs. Pangborn

Mrs. Pangborn is Mitch's mother. She works as a real estate agent.

Coach Reid

Coach Reid is the sports coach at Merryweather High.

Art Smith

Art Smith is a football player who is involved in the fight in the school cafeteria. Teri throws a heavy book at him. It hits him in the mouth, and he loses a tooth.

Diana Sung

Diana Sung is Kate's lab partner in chemistry. She has a 3.86 GPA and has been accepted by Rennselaer Polytechnic Institute.

Mariah Yates

Mariah Yates is another top student at the school. She gets accepted to Stanford.

THEMES

Ambition

The atmosphere in the senior class at Merryweather High is extremely competitive. Getting accepted by a prestigious school is considered a

TOPICS FOR FURTHER STUDY

- Take four or five of the chapter headings or subheadings, all of which describe some chemical process, and in a class presentation show why the author chose them as headings. How do the events of the chapter illustrate the chemical process?

- The most well-developed character in the story is Kate, because she is the narrator, but Teri is important too. Teri is seen entirely through Kate's eyes, but what if she were to tell her own story? The reader would have insight directly into her thoughts and feelings and see Kate entirely from Teri's perspective. Take a chapter or section of a chapter, and rewrite it from Teri's point of view.

- Kristen Walker's young-adult novel *A Match Made in High School* (2010), like *Catalyst*, features a female high-school senior. Like Kate in Anderson's novel, Fiona is difficult for some people to get along with. When the school requires that all students take a course on marriage in order to graduate, Fiona finds herself in a challenging situation, to say the least. Write an essay in which you compare and contrast these two heroines. What do they have in common? How do they differ? What do they both learn?

- In a blog, design ten multiple-choice questions to assess how stressed a student is. Invite your classmates to respond to it, anonymously. Present the results in a class presentation, and lead the discussion that follows.

---

badge of honor; failure results in the possibility of being scorned or mocked by one's classmates. Kate is well aware of the GPAs of the other top students and the schools they are getting into. One student, Ed Davis, has been accepted by all fifteen schools he applied to. Others are headed to Dartmouth or Howard University. Kate's boyfriend, Mitch, has already been accepted by Harvard in an early decision the previous September, and her friend Sara is going to Bryn Mawr. There is a lot of stress associated with this competition for college. Mariah Yates, for example, is "wound up tighter than a psychotic terrier on crack. If she doesn't get into her top school she'll snap." Another student faints and cracks her head on a desk when she hears she has been rejected by Georgetown.

Kate is herself one of the most ambitious students. She has set her heart on going to MIT and will not even consider the possibility of going to a less prestigious school. It is not as if she has her entire career mapped out in her mind, but she has been planning on MIT for a long time, probably since her mother, an MIT alumna, died nine years prior. When Kate is turned down by MIT, she is devastated and hardly knows which way to turn. She feels humiliated by what she regards as a personal failure. However, she eventually discovers that living with such narrow ambition, as if nothing mattered but academic success, is not the recipe for happiness. In the end, it is the despised Teri Litch who proves to be the catalyst for the change that Kate did not even know she needed.

Social Class

Many of the students at Merryweather High come from middle-class, perhaps even quite wealthy homes, where success is expected of them. This can be seen from the rush of parents who descend on the guidance counselor's office when their sons and daughters do not get accepted by the schools of their choice. Kate thinks they are "ready to body-slam the nearest administrator because their Precious Babies did not get into The Right School. These folks have been *robbed*. Do you know how much they pay in taxes?"

These high-achieving folks are sharply contrasted by Teri Litch. Teri comes from a poor family and has no advantages in life. Unlike the others, she is not college-bound. There is prejudice against her among the students that seems to be based on class, not who Teri is as a person. The football players tease and harass Teri, although she gives as good and often better than she gets. Kate seems prejudiced against her, though. In one of her less generous moments,

Like many of Anderson's novels, Catalyst *focuses on the stresses and worries of high-school students.*
(© Cynthia Farmer | Shutterstock.com)

she refers to Teri "eating her federally subsidized breakfast" in the cafeteria. In the first chapter, Kate looks out of her window in the middle of the night and sees a light on in the farmhouse at the bottom of the hill, where the Litches live. She thinks Teri must be up, but it is unlikely that "she's angsting about college acceptance letters. She's probably planning a bank robbery."

There is a certain stereotyping of lower-income people going on here, although Kate's narrative also makes it clear that Teri has had a very difficult life and was abused by her father, as was her mother. Of course, Teri does not exactly help herself by stealing Kate's watch—Teri lost hers in the fight in the cafeteria—and adopting a gruff, hostile manner that makes her hard to approach. However, there is clearly a class divide between the Malones and the Litches. Kate's father, a minister, does not seem to notice or care about class differences; he sees the Litches simply as people who are in need of assistance.

Eventually, Kate learns to see beyond her prejudice too. This occurs at the end of the novel, when she decides not to think about college applications for the time being and offers to work with Teri to rebuild her house, which has been badly damaged by fire. In this new emerging situation, Teri, the one who was born on the wrong side of the tracks, has a great deal to teach the academically smart Kate, who is hopeless with a hammer, and both girls seem to recognize it.

STYLE

Chemistry Metaphor

Kate excels at chemistry, a science that deals with the composition, structure, and properties of matter and how they interact, combine, and change. Chemical substances or processes are alluded to in all the section headings and chapter titles, as well as the subdivisions within chapters. These chemical processes act as loose metaphors for the human interactions and situations that take place in the story. Each chapter also has a "safety tip" immediately under the chapter title, which suggests, following the metaphor, that dealing with life can be as dangerous as dealing with chemicals. A person must know the rules in order to avoid disaster. One example of the chemistry metaphors is covalent bonding, which is the title for the subsection of chapter 13, in which Teri and Kate, although completely opposite in circumstance and personality, agree to work together. *Covalent bonding* refers to a chemical bond in which electron pairs are shared between two atoms to form a stable molecule.

First-Person Narrator

The story is told by Kate in the first person. The first-person voice can be recognized by the use of the word "I" by the narrator. A first-person point of view imposes certain restrictions on the narrative. The narrator can only tell of events that take place when she is present, although of course she can be informed by another character of something that happened that she did not personally witness. First-person point of view allows insight only into the thoughts and feelings of the narrator, in this case Kate. All the other characters are seen entirely through her eyes. The reader thus gets to know them through their actions, their words, and Kate's perception of them. They are seen, so to speak, from the outside, while Kate the narrator can reveal herself from the inside.

The author has given Kate an engaging narrative voice that conveys her smart, driven, tense, and restless nature. Kate shows a lot of insight into herself, as when she writes of Good Kate (the well-behaved, dutiful daughter), and Bad Kate (an altogether wilder, less agreeable person). The tone of the narrative is informal and captures the edgy attitude of an eighteen-year-old student who imposes huge pressures on herself to succeed. Passages that contain the rush of her thoughts when she is alone often contain sentence fragments, which help to convey her thoughts realistically as they occur. A fragment is a phrase that begins with a capital letter and ends with a period but does not contain a complete independent clause, often due to the lack of subject and verb. One example is, "Third period English. Hell." "The humiliation. Searing, scarring humiliation" is another.

HISTORICAL CONTEXT

College Admissions

One prominent element in *Catalyst* is the anxiety and stress that high-school students go through during the college admissions process. In the twenty-first century, there has been plenty of comment in the media about the pressure students feel as competition for top-level colleges increases. The economic recession of 2008–2009, from which the US economy was still struggling to recover in the mid-2010s, created a perception that academic success was more important than ever for young people who aimed to get a decent foothold in the job world.

As Martha Irvine noted in a *Huffington Post* article on January 31, 2013, more students were taking college courses in high school and also enrolling in advanced placement (AP) classes to earn college credit. (In *Catalyst*, this is exactly what Kate does; she is enrolled not only in AP chemistry but also AP European history and AP French.) Irvine writes, "The intensity of school has become so great, says one mom in Paoli, Pa., that she and her family have dubbed the senior year of high school 'the crying year.'" Irvine also notes that high schools across the country have tried to address "what some call an epidemic of stressed-out, overwhelmed students" by offering yoga or other relaxation classes, homework-free nights, or free time between classes. The purpose is to help students "slow down and cope with their problems in an overpacked, 24-7 world, where many students stay up late to finish homework and fall asleep with their cellphones in their hands."

Brian Harke, dean of students at University of Southern California School of Cinematic Arts, has dubbed the period when students wait to hear about their applications as "March Madness." Harke writes in the *Huffington Post*,

> Each year high school seniors spend the month of March in a nail-biting, gut-churning, adrenaline-fueled state of anticipation. It's the anxiety that each March brings as thousands wait for their college acceptance letters.

Harke advises students to keep a sense of perspective; it is not a disaster, he says, if they do not get into their preferred schools. "Too often I see students who don't get admitted into their first pick college beat themselves up, think they did something wrong, or succumb to the belief that they weren't good enough," Harke writes.

Kate is a long-distance runner, but her midnight runs hint at serious emotional distress. (© Halfpoint / Shutterstock.com)

Harke's description fits Kate in *Catalyst* closely. In the first rush of disappointment at failing to get into MIT, she makes a list of alternative career possibilities: janitor, soup-kitchen employee, crack cooker, or shirt presser at a dry cleaners. Mitch has a better attitude, and he gives her advice similar to what Harke must give his students at USC: "It's not like the world has ended. They can't take all the geniuses that apply." However, another comment by Harke may have some relevance for the future of Mitch and Kate as a couple: "I've heard of friendships that end because one student got admitted to the college and the other didn't," Harke writes.

Teenage Motherhood

In contrast to the high-achieving, college-bound kids in *Catalyst*, there is Teri, the working-class teenage single mother. Births to unmarried women have been increasing in the United States since 1980, according to the "Out of Wedlock Pregnancy Fact Sheet." In 2007, nearly 40 percent of all births in the United States were to unmarried women, up from 18.4 percent in 1980. Of these births, 48 percent were to teenage women. According to Rebecca A. Maynard, in *Kids Having Kids* (1996), the US teen pregnancy rate was more than twice as high than any other advanced country. In the mid-1990s, half a million teens gave birth each year, and over 175,000 of them were under seventeen. (Teri in the novel must have been sixteen when she gave birth to Mikey, although her situation is different from the vast majority of teenage mothers, because she is a victim of incest, and her baby was fathered by her own father.) Maynard also points out that teenage mothers are more likely than others to raise their children in poverty and be dependent on government welfare.

CRITICAL OVERVIEW

Since Anderson had had great success with her two previous young-adult novels, *Catalyst* attracted some attention from reviewers, who generally praised the book, although some had reservations about it. The reviewer for *Publishers Weekly* comments that the obstacles Kate faces in her life, and the way she deals with them, will probably engage readers, and Kate is a likable heroine. The reviewer also notes, however, that the novel "starts off promisingly, then loses its pacing about midway through" and leaves "unclear" exactly how Teri and Kate change in such a way that allows them to be reconciled. As a result, readers "may be confused about what makes [Kate] tick."

Ilene Cooper, reviewing *Catalyst* for *Booklist*, has similar reservations about the latter part of the novel. Cooper has praise for the "bright and sharp" writing, and the book "is involving and incisive." However, when Mikey is killed and turns out to have been Teri's son, "unfortunately, drama becomes melodrama," and from that point on, "the girls seem to lose some of their identity." Paula Rohrlick, writing for *Kliatt*, offers the opinion that *Catalyst*, "with its rather melodramatic plot, is not quite as mesmerizing as Anderson's masterpiece, *Speak*." However, Anderson "is a gifted writer who makes the complex worlds of teenage girls real to the reader."

Lauren Adams, in a review for *Horn Book*, has no reservations about the novel. She comments, "An unlikely friendship as a catalyst for change is a common element of adolescent literature, but Anderson's take on human relations succeeds through her fresh writing and exceptional characterization." Equally positive was the reviewer for *Kirkus Reviews*, who comments, "The first-person voice is gripping, with the reader feeling as though she's crouching inside Kate's head," while the novel as a whole "confronts moral issues, religious conundrums, and the dynamics of emotions in young adult lives as two girls driven by the past and present realize their impact on the future."

CRITICISM

Bryan Aubrey
Aubrey holds a PhD in English. In the following essay, he discusses the character development of Kate Malone, the protagonist and narrator of Catalyst.

> SHE MUST OPEN HERSELF UP TO WHAT LIFE GIVES HER RATHER THAN SEEK JUST ONE NARROW OUTCOME THAT SHE THINKS IS THE BEST AND ONLY COURSE FOR HER. THIS PROVES TO BE A PAINFUL LESSON FOR THE PREVIOUSLY SELF-CONFIDENT, ALL-CONQUERING KATE."

During the course of *Catalyst*, the protagonist and narrator Kate Malone goes through a profound transformation that could not have been predicted at the beginning of the novel. As she starts to tell her story, Kate presents herself as a highly driven, focused, ambitious individual. Every hour, every minute of her day is accounted for, she notes as she consults her agenda book. Kate thinks she has everything in her life under control, and that is how she likes it. She has no time for the messy ambiguities, contradictions, and unanswerable questions that she is faced with in her humanities classes, such as Greek mythology or advanced placement European history, in which the topic is the Balkan Wars of 1912–13. She does not have a questing mind in that regard. She prefers things that are abstract, precise, and predictable, such as mathematics:

> Math reminds me of pebbles, a whole beach of smooth, wet pebbles that you can pick up turn over, taste, set down. They can be stacked, subtracted, divided, they can be arranged into patterns, into forms, into meaning.

Given her gift for math and science, especially chemistry, she is convinced that she will be accepted by MIT.

In addition to her academic credentials, Kate has a smart, Harvard-bound boyfriend, and she manages to keep her too-religious (in her eyes) father at arm's length. She gets through her household chores efficiently and makes sure her younger brother takes the medicine he needs. She also loves to run. She is very competitive and desires only to win. It seems that life is almost perfect for Kate, except for the fact that she has difficulty sleeping—a warning sign, perhaps, but not one that she is prepared to take any notice of.

WHAT DO I READ NEXT?

- Anderson's *Speak* (1999) was her first young-adult novel. As in *Catalyst*, the protagonist is a student at Merryweather High School. Melinda is shunned by the students for calling the police to an out-of-control party. She becomes isolated and barely able to speak until she decides to fight back and reveal what happened to her at the party.

- *Fever 1793* (2000) is a historical novel for young adults by Anderson that is set in Philadelphia in 1793 during an outbreak of fever.

- *The Impossible Knife of Memory* (2014) is Anderson's young-adult novel about Hayley, a teenage girl, and the difficulties she encounters living with her dad, a war veteran who suffers from posttraumatic stress disorder.

- *Hate List* by Jennifer Brown (2010) is a young-adult novel that tells the story of Valerie, a high-school senior, whose boyfriend shot several students in the school cafeteria a few months prior. Valerie must deal with the guilt she feels over the issue.

- *American Born Chinese* (2008) is a graphic novel by Gene Luen Yang, featuring the attempts of an Asian American middle schooler to fit in with his white classmates.

- *It's Complicated: The Social Lives of Networked Teens* by Danah Boyd (2014) is an engaging analysis of how today's teens use technology and especially social media.

Indeed, she rather seems to like it: "Insomnia rocks, actually," she says. "You can get a lot done if you don't sleep."

Another warning sign that everything about Kate's life may not be quite as it seems occurs when she is out at night running through the streets. "I fly almost naked, breathless, running out of the empty night into a place where I can't hear myself think." The reader may well wonder what those thoughts are that Kate does not want to hear. What is she running from? Yet another signal that all is not well comes when she enters an interschool cross-country race. Kate runs as hard as she can, but she discards her glasses and ends up finishing last. It transpires that she got lost in the woods. The metaphor is plain: Kate, for all her accomplishments and skills, is something of a lost soul.

Given these early hints that there are some chinks in Kate's armor and that her lifestyle is ultimately unsustainable, the rest of the novel is devoted to describing the events that conspire to puncture Kate's illusions of control. In this, the author, Laurie Halse Anderson, has shown some skill in presenting a realistic scenario that can account for the change Kate undergoes while avoiding sentimentality. First, Kate is turned down by MIT. Then she finds that Teri, a girl in her school with whom she has had a troubled history, is to share her bedroom following the fire at Teri's home.

Slowly, by fits and starts, Kate has to rethink her life and accept that she is being led in a direction that is very different from the one she had in mind. She must open herself up to what life gives her rather than seek just one narrow outcome that she thinks is the best and only course for her. This proves to be a painful lesson for the previously self-confident, all-conquering Kate. At first she is simply annoyed by the situation, and with some cause, it would appear. As she drives Teri around town on errands, the belligerent Teri maintains "a running monologue mocking my car, complaining about my driving, and bitching about the fire." Teri seems to be one of those people who are perpetually angry about something

There is one incident on this trip that the author clearly wants to carry some symbolic weight. Kate has revealed several times that she is short-sighted and wears glasses. One of the reasons she came last in the cross-country race was that she chose to run without her glasses. Now she gets some long-awaited contact lenses, and she finds that the world is instantly transformed:

> I can see *everything*: the numbers on the license plates, the small print on the signs in the music store window, the price of gas at the Sunoco. . . . I can see cardinals flying. I can see the cardinal's beak, the twig in the cardinal's beak, the flash in the cardinal's eye.
>
> I have magic eyes.

Kate takes on many of her mother's household chores, such as cooking and doing laundry. *(© Yuriy Rudyy / Shutterstock.com)*

The metaphorical suggestion is that Kate is already in a process of transformation in the way she sees life, although the metaphor acts more as a foreshadowing, because as yet she has little awareness of what is going on.

Having given her readers this hint, Anderson carefully prepares the way for Kate's change of direction in life. It does not come with absolute suddenness, without preparation. To begin with, Kate develops a fondness for Mikey and takes some responsibility in caring for him. She is ready to accept that he will be staying for a while. She also expresses the wish, continuing the vision metaphor, that her new contact lenses "could see into his head, see the world through his eyes." This is a new notion for Kate—seeing the world through the eyes of someone else. She has not, up to this point, shown much empathy

for anyone else, being too obsessed with the game plan for her own life. It seems that her emotional range is beginning to widen.

One of the major catalysts for change is, of course, Mikey's tragic death. Kate feels this deeply (as do her friends who are present in the house when it happens). However, Kate and Teri have an antagonistic relationship, and it would be unrealistic and sentimental if they were to be presented as immediately embracing and saying comforting words to each other. Instead, the author presents an image of the two of them together that is quite believable and indeed touching. In the middle of the night following the tragedy, the two girls are alone in the Litch house, in the room where Mikey died. They sit on the floor, leaning against each other, back to back. No words are exchanged, but Teri reaches out behind her, her hand searching for Kate's hand. Their fingers intertwine. Teri's hand is very hot, but Kate does not pull back. The image perfectly conveys the situation. Sitting back to back, they are facing different ways, as they have done all their lives, and yet the interlinked hands now acknowledge how tragedy has brought them into a new kind of relationship, albeit a tentative one in which much of the old antagonism, at least on Teri's side, will remain. But it is a start.

A week or so later, Kate realizes with the force of a revelation what she wants to do now. College is no longer on her mind, at least not for the next year. Even though she has few practical skills, she has decided she wants to help Teri rebuild the house and will devote herself to the project for as long as it takes. Before, Kate has simply done what she is good at, but now she is prepared to learn something new, in an area for which she seems to have little natural aptitude, from a girl who has up to this point been an antagonist rather than a friend. With this, Kate overcomes the dichotomy in her nature between what she calls Good Kate and Bad Kate. These are categories that she means somewhat ironically and probably derive from the fact that her father is a minister. With her offer of help to Teri, however, she is not merely being "good" out of a sense of duty but is responding to an authentic inner prompting that comes from her true self. This is not just Good Kate; it is another person altogether.

Source: Bryan Aubrey, Critical Essay on *Catalyst*, in *Novels for Students*, Gale, Cengage Learning, 2015.

Kelly Jensen and Laurie Halse Anderson
In the following interview, Anderson talks about some of the difficulties faced by female authors.

It's fifteen years since Laurie Halse Anderson's young adult novel *Speak* was first published. *Speak* is an enduring novel that has a significant place in YA fiction's history, and Anderson herself has been a champion of YA lit, as well as a champion of those who advocate on behalf of YA readers.

In honor of this anniversary, and in conjunction with April being Sexual Assault Awareness Month, Anderson has teamed up with the Rape, Abuse and Incest National Network (RAINN) in the #Speak4RAINN15 campaign to raise $30,000 that supports victims of sexual violence.

> SEEK OUT BOOKS THAT TOUCH YOUR HEART AND MAKE SURE THAT YOU ARE CASTING YOUR READING NET WIDELY."

In light of this campaign, as well as the book's anniversary, I was eager to ask Anderson a few questions about the book's legacy, including its regular appearances on "most challenged" book lists; about how she's seen YA fiction mold and grow over the last decade and a half; and I was eager to pick her brain about gender and gender disparity within the book world and beyond.

Speak turns 15 years old this year. Can you talk a bit about the life of this book?

The book was turned down by the first publisher I sent it to. When it was published, my then-editor warned me against getting my hopes up because she felt the book had little chance at being a Big Success. The book took off because booksellers, librarians and teachers got behind it strongly. Teens handed it to each other and said, "You have to read this."

The movie version that came out in 2004 (starring Kristen Stewart) brought a lot of new readers to the book and then English teachers started to put it in curriculum. They saw firsthand that if you give students a book that they can connect with, they are more open to learning about things like symbolism and metaphor.

I think we're approaching 2 million copies sold and the last time I checked it had been translated into 27 languages. Right now artist Emily Carroll (http://www.emcarroll.com/) is working on the graphic novel version of the book, which I hope will be published in 2016. Nearly every day I hear from readers for whom the book is a touchstone that helped them find the courage to speak up about their sexual assault and begin their journey from victim to survivor.

When I was growing up, "rape" was a word that was whispered, if it was spoken at all. Around the time that *Speak* was published, America started to talk about rape and began to move away (slowly) from the destructive notion of victim-blaming. The Internet can be a real cesspool of sexual abuse and hatred, but it has also allowed victims of sexual assault to find help and healing. Their ability to speak up is leading to a revolutionary shift in attitudes about sexual assault. We still have a long way to go, but I am very optimistic.

It's hard to wrap my head around all of this. I'm intensely grateful that the story poured through me and that—thanks to the hard work of lots of people and the stars lining up at the right time—it continues to be a source of strength and hope.

What changes have you seen in the YA Lit world since Speak *published?*

Everything has changed! The field has dramatically expanded, both in scope and in depth. When authors like Joyce Carol Oates started writing YA, I knew we had entered new territory. When adults started reading YA for fun, I knew we were looking at a brave new world.

Speak *is a title that's regularly challenged in schools across the country. What goes on in your mind when you hear about these attempts at censorship?*

It makes my blood boil.

I worry about the teachers and librarians who are at danger of losing their jobs and I worry about the students being denied access to a good book that has saved lives. I'm baffled by people my age (and younger!) who are so terrified at their inability to talk about rape, a crime that affects 1 in six women and 1 in 33 men, that they would rather ban the book than tell their kids the truth and prepare them for the harsh realities of the world.

Book banners make me fight harder.

Is there a connection with Speak, *the imprint of Penguin, and your own book* Speak? *If so, how did that come to be?*

The background includes a bit of publishing history. Farrar, Straus & Giroux published *Speak* in hardcover in 1999. At the time, FS&G was not in the business of publishing paperbacks; they contracted out to other publishers for that. Penguin won the auction to become the paperback publisher of *Speak* and negotiated a 10-year license. It's important to remember that at this point, *Speak* had been nominated for the National Book Award, but no one had a clue about the book's future popularity.

Penguin threw a lot of energy and love at *Speak* and when the time came a few years later to name a new teen imprint, they called it Speak, which was a huge honor. Then the book sort of went supernova. When the 10-year paperback license ended, Penguin negotiated hard, but Macmillan (which had acquired FS&G in the meantime) turned down all of their offers. (When I sold *Speak* to FS&G I did not yet have an agent, so when it came to this contract, I was not a part of the decision-making process.)

So now *Speak* is a Macmillan book, the rest of my "resilience lit" is at Penguin, and Simon & Schuster publishes my historical fiction (which is a whole other story.)

Speak *reaches a tremendous number of readers each year. What do you think gives the book staying power?*

I think it's because everyone has had a bad thing happen to them and has struggled to figure out how to speak up. Everyone has felt alone and not-heard.

Over the last year, you've begun to call what you write "Resilience Lit." Can you talk a bit about what that label means and what it might mean to readers?

The term comes from a high school teacher, whose name I, unfortunately, forgot to make note of. She took a photo of her whiteboard after a classroom discussion of *Speak*. It was covered with plot details, symbolism, and character notes, and in the top left corner, the teacher had written "resilience literature." That was such a better description of what I write than "contemporary realistic YA" that I started using it immediately. Resilience is the quality that I hope all teenagers can develop so that they are ready when the world comes at them. Literature is a fantastic way to learn about the kinds of hardships you may have to deal with; watching characters grow and change is a great way to strengthen yourself for your own challenges.

You recently did a Reddit AMA and one of the questions that came up was about the "John Greenification" of YA fiction. It's impossible not to think about, especially since you're a female author who has been writing and selling young adult books, including realistic titles, for 15 years. There are other female authors writing contemporary books who have been publishing as long as you have, and selling the huge numbers of backlist you have—Sarah Dessen and Meg Cabot, to name a couple. Why do you think that traditional media pursues the "John Green has influenced the YA world" when there are and have been equally powerful other writers, both male and female?

Because traditional media is largely edited and vetted by a much older, male-dominated generation that can't or won't recognize that women writers are just as powerful and important as men. Or that writers of all ethnic backgrounds, of every type of gender identity and sexual orientation, are as powerful and important.

However traditional media is crumbling, in part because there is such a large disconnect between it and most people under age 40. We all have the capability to promote the books and authors we care about. That is amazing and so exciting!! I enjoy shaking my fists at traditional media as much as the next person, but I know that I can achieve more change by taking advantage of the opportunities that New Media offer.

Do you think the contributions of female authors and female-centric novels in YA are downplayed or undermined?

Within the worlds of book selling, librarianship and education I see less evidence of this kind of undermining. I think the leadership of traditional media is where the problem lies.

Given the power and influence Green has had not only on the New York Times *list, but also in mainstream outlets like* Vanity Fair *(which noted he is beginning a revolution in bringing realistic teens to the big screen with his book-to-film adaptations), it's clear he's a household name not just to teenagers, but to their parents and other adults as well. What do you think it would take for a hypothetical "Jean Green" to do the same thing? Could it happen?*

It will take a while, but it will happen.

I stand in this interesting place on the timeline of equality for women. My grandmother often told the story of the first time her mother voted, in 1920, and what a huge influence that had on her. I remember reading the newspaper want ads in third grade and asking my mom why there were Jobs for Women separate from Jobs For Men. My mom said "It's not right, but that's the way it is." I was in that generation of girls who benefited tremendously from Title IX and other changes wrought by earlier generations of feminists. I was one of the only girls who worked on a dairy farm in my county and was the only

woman in the stock brokerage I worked at after college.

Americans who are younger than 35 have taken the torch from my generation and continue to run towards equality for everyone. I'm thrilled to see how many guys are working towards this, as well as women, and how we are finally beginning to talk about true equality that encompasses gender identity, sexual orientation, ethnic background and faith community.

It's still not right, but we are changing it.

There is a lot of focus on the newest titles. We tend to want what's hot right now and we want to talk about those books. But, as Speak *shows, there are always going to be titles that resonate with readers for a long time, and I think that shows itself, too, on the* Times *list, as the majority of those books aren't titles that came out in the last year or two. With that in mind, I'd like to hear what some of your favorite older YA titles?*

Dinky Hocker Shoots Smack by M.E. Kerr, *The Chocolate War* by Robert Cormier, *Hush* by Jacqueline Woodson, *Weetzie Bat* by Francesca Lia Block, *Annie on My Mind* by Nancy Garden.

Who are some of your current favorite young adult authors?

These authors are amazing and their work deserves a lot more attention: Kekla Magoon, Coe Booth, Alex Sánchez, Jason Reynolds, Mitali Perkins, Nikki Grimes, Malinda Lo, Cynthia Leitich Smith, Jaime Adoff, Octavia Butler, Eric Gansworth, Jacqueline Woodson, Sumbul Ali-Karamali. Rita Williams Garcia and Meg Medina.

For my final question, I want to know how we—as adults, as readers, as advocates for young adult fiction—can help amplify the voices of females, especially teen girls like Melinda in Speak *who don't find themselves being heard?*

Seek out books that touch your heart and make sure that you are casting your reading net widely. Look for books being brought out by smaller publishers. Follow blogs that make a point of review books about all kinds of characters and by all kinds of authors. Participate in discussions like the Vida Count and [Maureen Johnson's] Cover Flip.

Call out the owners and decision-makers of traditional media when you see them choosing to review titles by one kind of author or featuring only one kind of narrator. Share their contact information with your friends and increase the visibility of your protest. Use New Media outlets to discuss and promote the books you are passionate about.

To remain silent is be complicit. We must all speak up and be the change we want to see.

Source: Kelly Jensen and Laurie Halse Anderson, "15 Years of *Speak*: An Interview with Laurie Halse Anderson," in *Book Riot*, April 8, 2014.

Kirkus Reviews

In the following review, the anonymous reviewer praises Anderson's use of first-person narrative.

Newton's law proclaims to every action there's always an equal reaction. For Kate Malone, life is a matter of scientific exactness, except that she is driven by her obsession to get into MIT. The conflict between running her life with the preciseness of scientific equations (calculations) and the religious beliefs and blessings of her minister father separates her into Good Kate and Bad Kate. When the rejection letter arrives (and she's forced to admit she didn't apply to any back-up schools), both Kates begin a meltdown; the catalyst is a destructive fire of a classmate's house and barn. Teri, the senior-class toughie and bruiser with whom nobody messes, and her two-year-old brother, come to stay at Kate's house while a corps of volunteers rebuilds theirs. An already combative relationship between the girls builds even as Teri throws herself into the renovation project. A terrible tragedy will shock readers as much as it threatens to unravel the progress folks have made. The first-person voice is gripping, with the reader feeling as though she's crouching inside Kate's head. Numbered like an outline, 2.3, 7.0, the chapters are labeled with scientific terms and safety tips that anticipate the introspective reactions. Intelligently written with multi-dimensional characters that replay in one's mind, this complex, contemporary story carries much of the intensity and harshness of *Speak* (2000). It confronts moral issues, religious conundrums, and the dynamics of emotions in young adult lives as two girls driven by the past and present realize their impact on the future.

Source: Review of *Catalyst*, in *Kirkus Reviews*, Vol. 70, No. 17, September 1, 2002, p. 1300.

Publishers Weekly

In the following review, Kate's aloofness is pointed out as distancing and potentially confusing to readers.

Like its cross-country-running heroine, Anderson's (*Speak*) latest novel starts off promisingly, then loses its pacing about midway through. The narrator, 18-year-old Kate Malone, has placed all of her eggs in one basket: she has applied only to her late mother's alma mater, MIT. Calculus is a cinch, chemistry is her favorite subject, even physics comes easily to her, but when her MIT rejection arrives, it acts as catalyst for the slow unraveling of her delicately balanced life. A preacher's daughter, she struggles between "Good Kate" and "Bad Kate" as she singlehandedly keeps the household running (her mother died nine years ago). Anderson excels in conveying Kate's anxieties and her concomitant insomnia, and frequently intersperses evidence of Kate's sharp humor (she calls Mitchell A. Pangbom III "my friend, my enemy, my lust"). But Kate's relationships with others remain hazy. While this seems to reflect Kate's state of mind, since she slowly shuts everyone out as her MIT-less fate becomes clear, her detachment may create a similar effect for readers. This aloofness becomes most problematic in the dynamics of her relationship with Ten Litch, who once beat her up habitually. After Ten's house burns down, she and toddler Mikey Litch come to live with the Malones, and the action escalates to the point of melodrama. Yet another tragic event spurs a reconciliation between Kate and Ten, but the underlying changes in the individuals that lead up to this event remain unclear. Teens will take to Kate instantly, but as the novel continues, they may be confused about what makes her tick. Still, the universal obstacles she faces and the realistic outcome will likely hold readers' attention.

Source: Review of *Catalyst*, in *Publishers Weekly*, Vol. 249, No. 29, July 22, 2002, p. 180.

Lauren Adams

In the following review, Adams praises Anderson's work as "believable" and "readable."

An unlikely friendship as a catalyst for change is a common element of adolescent literature, but Anderson's take on human relations succeeds through her fresh writing and exceptional characterization. High-school senior Kate is a self-described science geek, an outstanding student who also runs the house for her minister father and cares for her asthmatic younger brother. She has friends, rivals, a boyfriend, and one supreme ambition—to get into MIT. Kate is near the edge at admissions time, running miles or ironing laundry at night instead of sleeping—a "super Kate, the fiber-Kate," poised to collapse. Teri Litch is at the opposite end of the spectrum—a beefy girl in "vo-tech" who fights back with her fists when teased, regularly, by the jocks. Kate is appalled when her do-good dad brings Teri and two-year-old Mikey Litch home to stay with them after a fire, but changes are only beginning. The novel is gently shaped by the chemistry terms that are Kate's second language; section titles "Solid," "Liquid," and "Gas" are an apt metaphor for Kate's loss of grounding. Well-chosen quotes from a chemistry textbook foreshadow events and set the tone for things to come: "The rate of a chemical reaction depends on the frequency and force of collisions between molecules." The collision with the Litches proves enormous, as the many tragedies of Teri's life culminate in the most unthinkable one—the death of a child. Anderson treats the tragedy—as well as serious issues of abuse—with respect and a steady hand, always remaining true to her characters. The changes wrought are human-scale and fully believable. Anderson returns here to the same high-school setting of *Speak* (now-verbal Melinda makes a cameo appearance); readers will return for Anderson's keen understanding and eminently readable style.

Source: Lauren Adams, Review of *Catalyst*, in *Horn Book*, Vol. 78, No. 6, November–December 2002, p. 746.

SOURCES

Adams, Lauren, Review of *Catalyst*, in *Horn Book*, Vol. 78, No. 6, November–December 2002, p. 746.

Anderson, Laurie Halse, *Catalyst*, Penguin Group, 2003.

———, "Writing and Life F.A.Q.," Official author website, http://madwomanintheforest.com/laurie/ (accessed July 9, 2014).

Cooper, Ilene, Review of *Catalyst*, in *Booklist*, Vol. 99, No. 2, September 15, 2002, p. 222.

Harke, Brian, "March Madness: College Admissions," in *Huffington Post*, March 11, 2013, http://www.huffingtonpost.com/brian-harke/college-admissions-time_b_2850652.html (accessed July 15, 2014).

Irvine, Martha, "From Pets to 'Recess': High School Stress Relief," in *Huffington Post*, January 31, 2013, http://www.huffingtonpost.com/2013/01/31/from-pets-to-recess-high-_n_2593553.html (accessed July 16, 2014).

Maynard, Rebecca A., ed., *Kids Having Kids: Economic Costs and Social Consequences of Teen Pregnancy*, Urban Institute Press, 1996, http://www.urban.org/pubs/khk/summary.html (accessed July 16, 2014).

"Out of Wedlock Pregnancy Fact Sheet," First Things First website, http://firstthings.org/out-of-wedlock-pregnancy-fact-sheet (accessed July 15, 2014).

Review of *Catalyst*, in *Kirkus Reviews*, Vol. 70, No. 17, September 1, 2002, p. 1300.

Review of *Catalyst*, in *Publishers Weekly*, Vol. 249, No. 29, July 22, 2002, p. 180.

Rohrlick, Paula, Review of *Catalyst*, in *Kliatt*, Vol. 36, No. 5, September 2002, p. 6.

FURTHER READING

Chbosky, Stephen, *The Perks of Being a Wallflower*, MTV Books, 1999.

This coming-of-age story about a high school student, told in the form of letters, has received high praise from reviewers.

Hile, Lori, *Bullying*, Heinemann-Raintree Middle School Nonfiction, 2012.

Bullying is only a minor issue in *Catalyst*, but it is a problem in many schools. Hile shows how students should deal with it.

Lieberman, Susan Abel, *The Real High School Handbook: How to Survive, Thrive, and Prepare for What's Next*, Mariner, 1997.

This handbook supplies students with plenty of useful information about how to get the best out of their high school years.

Pope, Denise Clark, *Doing School: How We Are Creating a Generation of Stressed-Out, Materialistic, and Miseducated Kids*, Yale University Press, 2013.

Pope conducted research at a California high school and assessed how five motivated students regarded their educational experience. She found that many students employ unethical methods to get the results they need and also suffer from anxiety and breakdowns.

SUGGESTED SEARCH TERMS

Laurie Halse Anderson

Catalyst AND Laurie Halse Anderson

high school AND stress

college admissions AND stress

chemistry AND glossary

Catalyst AND chemical terms

sexual abuse

teen pregnancy

A Grain of Wheat

NGŨGĨ WA THIONG'O
1967

A Grain of Wheat is one of the greatest works of Kenyan writer and postcolonialist theorist Ngũgĩ wa Thiong'o, as well as in all of African fiction. When the novel was first published in 1967, the author was known by his Christian name of James Ngugi, but his political and cultural inclinations led him to officially re-Africanize his name a decade later. By then his literary renown was established, on the foundation of some four novels, five plays, a short-story collection, and a book of essays, with much more to follow. His name is often mentioned alongside two contemporaries in particular, the great Nigerian authors Wole Soyinka and Chinua Achebe.

Ngũgĩ's earliest literary concerns were with the volatile historical situation in which he was raised, the period leading up to Kenya's achievement of independence from Great Britain in 1963. *A Grain of Wheat* focuses on the dozen or so years prior to independence, which were shaped above all by the armed insurgency known as Mau Mau, led by the Kenya Land and Freedom Army (KLFA), and by the state of emergency that the British colonial government declared in dealing with it. The emergency period was rife with atrocities on the part of the British. The novel portrays how Gikuyus—also known in English as Kikuyus—took heart in Mau Mau, as led by heroic individuals, and then coped with extensive British reprisals against suspected rebels and innocent peasants

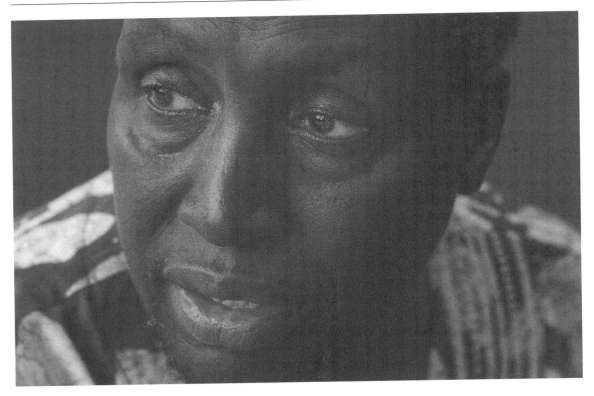

Ngũgĩ wa Thiong'o (© *Nikki Kahn* | *The Washington Post* | *Getty Images*)

alike. Thrown off balance by the profoundly unstable social climate, several of Ngũgĩ's characters make regrettable choices that alter their lives. When Uhuru—independence—arrives, justice must be served. By and large a discreet novel, *A Grain of Wheat* does contain oblique references to sexual activity and occasionally explicit mention of the appalling torture carried out by the British in their vain attempts to preclude Kenyan independence.

AUTHOR BIOGRAPHY

Ngũgĩ was born as James Ngugi on January 5, 1938, in the community of Kamiriithu, in Limuru, Kenya. His mother was the third of four wives, and the family had twenty-seven siblings in all. When he was ten, his mother separated from his father, taking Ngũgĩ and three brothers and sisters with her. He attended both Christian and Gikuyu schools and was a student when the state of emergency was initiated in 1952. His deaf stepbrother was killed in precisely the way that Gitogo is killed in *A Grain of Wheat*. After two years, Ngũgĩ's older brother Wallace joined the Mau Mau forest fighters, and their mother was tortured for some three months as a result. Ngũgĩ attended Alliance High School, one of Kenya's premier mission schools, and was for a time devoutly Christian. In literature, he was fond of Robert Louis Stevenson—whose *Treasure Island* planted the seed of literary ambition when he was around age fifteen—Charles Dickens, and Leo Tolstoy, among others. In 1955, Ngũgĩ returned home from boarding school to find that his village had been destroyed—part of Britain's "villagization" containment strategy to cut forest fighters off from domestic support—with the entire community forced to relocate to a smaller area.

After graduating, Ngũgĩ briefly taught primary school and then enrolled at Makerere University College, in Kampala, Uganda. In 1961, he was married to Nyambura, and they would have six children. By this time, Ngũgĩ was writing, having published his first story, "The Fig Tree," in the Makerere literary magazine *Penpoint* in 1960. Most intently studying African and Caribbean literature, he chose the worldly European author Joseph Conrad as his special focus for his bachelor's degree. His play *The Black Hermit* was produced by the Uganda National Theatre for independence celebrations in 1962, and his first major publication, the novel *Weep Not, Child*, was issued a year later. Also that year, he engaged in postgraduate studies at Leeds University in England, where he wrote *A Grain of Wheat*, his third novel, which was published in 1967. That year he became the first African faculty member of University College, Nairobi, in the English Department; in 1973 he became the first African department head, and he oversaw a shift in focus toward African literatures. He legally changed his name to Ngũgĩ wa Thiong'o in 1977.

Outspoken with regard to not only British colonialism but also the shortcomings of the newly instituted Kenyan government, Ngũgĩ got into trouble in 1977 both with the politically charged novel *Petals of Blood* and with the culturally oriented Gikuyu-language play *Ngaahika ndeenda* (*I Will Marry When I Want*), cowritten with Ngũgĩ wa Mĩriĩ. The government deemed the works subversive, and Vice President Daniel arap Moi signed Ngũgĩ's detention order; he was imprisoned without due process for one year. Upon his release, he found himself out of favor in the educational system—he was denied his former teaching position, and his books were removed from curricula—and after five otherwise active years, marked by international lectures, publications, and play productions, he moved permanently to London. In later life, he has concentrated on his African audiences, writing more often in Gikuyu and also producing films to better reach the illiterate masses. Moving to the United States in 1989, he taught at Yale University and then New York University. Briefly returning to Kenya in 2004, after Moi's reign had ended, Ngũgĩ and his wife were attacked by hired gunmen and nearly killed. Ngũgĩ's most recent professorship has been with the University of California, Irvine.

PLOT SUMMARY

One

Mugo awakes from a nightmare in his hut in Thabai; he walks toward his *shamba*, or farm plot, at dawn, bringing a *jembe*, or long-bladed

MEDIA ADAPTATIONS

- A CD audiobook of *A Grain of Wheat* was produced in 2005 by Recording for the Blind & Dyslexic.

hoe, and *panga*, or machete. In the village, Warui asks if he is ready for Uhuru—the independence celebrations—and Githua greets him overeffusively. Mugo mulls over the deaths of Gitogo and Waitherero, the aunt who raised Mugo. Unusually, he is uninspired with farming. That evening, Warui, Wambui, and Gikonyo visit him on behalf of the Party and the Movement.

Two

The narrator reviews the history of the Movement. Mugo once attended a meeting where, with Jomo Kenyatta absent, Kihika spoke and stirred much nationalist fervor. Mugo was repulsed. Kihika later led the storming of the Mahee police garrison. Kihika was somehow captured alone by the Kinenie Forest. He was hanged.

Three

In his hut, Mugo warily listens to the three visitors. General R. and Lieutenant Koina also arrive. The general produces Kihika's Bible, with salvation passages underlined in red. General R. reveals his belief that Mugo sheltered Kihika the night Kihika killed District Officer Robson; the general asks if Mugo learned who Kihika was meeting a week later—was it Karanja? Mugo only shakes his head. Gikonyo asks Mugo to speak on Independence Day, December 12, 1963. After they leave, General R. tells Koina that Kihika's betrayer must be found. Loath to see Mumbi at home, Gikonyo heads back to Mugo's hut—but shies away after all. At their home, Gikonyo and Mumbi clash, in part over a child.

Four

At the Githima forest research station, John Thompson summons Karanja to deliver a (deceitful) message to his wife. Margery warmly welcomes the nervous Karanja. At the Githima eating house, Karanja reconciles with Mwaura, who startled and irritated him earlier. At the station, Thompson watches as, outside, Dr. Lynd's dog corners a man, who picks up a stone in defense. Dr. Lynd appears and chastises the man; it is Karanja. Descending from his office, Thompson escorts Dr. Lynd away and exculpates Karanja. Dr. Lynd recalls how her old houseboy (Koina) had viciously slaughtered her previous dog. Thompson later regretfully pacifies Karanja.

Five

John Thompson broods over leaving Kenya; Margery recalls her affair with Dr. Van Dyke. She considers having a heart-to-heart talk with John but just goes to bed. John, after reviewing his colonialist notes on Kenya, considers likewise, but Margery is asleep.

Six

The day after visiting Mugo, Gikonyo visits the area's Member of Parliament (M.P.) in Nairobi to see about a loan for cooperatively purchasing the farm of a departing Briton. The M.P. expresses the difficulty and says he will contact Gikonyo about any results. Mugo is distressed. He recalls the one (disingenuous) speech he had been obliged to make after the Emergency ended. He imagines he has been chosen to speak so that he might reveal he betrayed Kihika, which he did. Gikonyo visits Mugo and mourns having sold his soul for a changed Mumbi and a changed life.

Seven

At Rung'ei Trading Centre, near Thabai, trains between Mombasa and Kampala would meet every Sunday. Youths would convene there and dance in the forest afterward. Gikonyo tells Mugo of the time he missed the train. A carpenter, he silently loved Mumbi. One day she visits and admires Gikonyo's guitar playing, and sings along. She asks Gikonyo to repair a panga for her mother. Arriving with Kihika and Gitogo, Karanja proceeds to chivalrously escort Mumbi home.

Gikonyo repairs the panga (gratis) and delivers it, and Mumbi flirts with him. Karanja and Kihika arrive and talk politics. The narrator recalls Kihika's education; Kihika speaks with revolutionary zeal. Njeri and Wambuku arrive. Njeri spies the train from afar, and they begin rushing off; Karanja and Gikonyo both wait for Mumbi, then trail her as she dashes away. Karanja soon races ahead, but when Gikonyo too passes Mumbi, she calls to him to stop. They enter a wood and make love.

Effectively alone at the station, Karanja has a vision of mass panic. He finds Kihika giving an oration and challenges him; Kihika takes it in stride. In the forest after, Karanja plays guitar with a passion reflecting his angst over Mumbi and Gikonyo's absence together. Wambuku, walking off with Kihika, is disappointed that he only talks politics; but she commits to him, and he to her.

Speaking with Mugo, Gikonyo recalls his early marital happiness; then the State of Emergency was declared. A few months after the declaration, Kihika takes to the forest with other Movement leaders, to Wambuku's dismay. Scornful of Wambuku, Njeri devotes herself to Kihika. Soon, in a roundup (the night Gitogo is killed), Gikonyo is led away. Six year later, he returns, recalling life in detention. At Yala, Gatu kept spirits up, but administrators hanged him. Gikonyo relied on thoughts of Mumbi—which led him to confess the oath. Refusing to confess names, he was detained for four more years.

At last returning home, Gikonyo finds Mumbi with a baby, surprised to see him "so soon." The child is Karanja's. Numb, Gikonyo cannot sleep. In the morning, he walks out to visit the chief to report his arrival; the chief is Karanja. When Gikonyo advances threateningly, Karanja draws a pistol. Leaving, Gikonyo decides to kill Mumbi; he charges through their door, slams his head on the hearthstone, and foams at the mouth.

Eight

Gikonyo concludes in telling Mugo he resolved to live with Mumbi but chastely. After Gikonyo leaves, Mugo uncertainly regrets having not told his own story. He recalls a day when he envisioned himself as Moses; a week later, Kihika shot Robson. Going to a bar, Mugo is obliged to buy the pathetic Githua a drink and then leaves. Mugo dreams of being back in detention in Rira.

Nine

The narrator recounts how Mugo, after his arrest, ended up at Rira. Meeting John Thompson (again) there, Mugo is singled out because he at least responds verbally to interrogations; also,

Thompson eventually recognizes him. Mugo bears whippings stoically (feeling he deserves them), inspiring a detainee hunger strike. After throwing stones, they all suffer prolonged beatings; eleven die.

Mugo visits Gikonyo's home but finds only Mumbi. They talk of dreaming and Wambuku's and Njeri's deaths. Mumbi starts speaking of her married life. She recalls how after the fall of Mahee, in Gikonyo's absence, her and Wangari's huts were burned down, when during forced relocation she built a new one too slowly. Karanja began helping them by bringing food. After Kihika's death, during the trench digging, twenty-one people died. After an assassination, Karanja became a chief. Mumbi imagined Gikonyo would never return. Yet she learned from Karanja that Gikonyo would indeed return and, not in her right mind, let Karanja take advantage of her. General R. and Koina arrive at the home. General R. asks Mugo to help expose Karanja during Uhuru, but Mugo refuses to speak that day and leaves.

Ten

Karanja fears Thompson is truly leaving Kenya. Mwaura visits and talks up the Uhuru celebration at Rung'ei; Karanja will join him. Thompson arrives very late and, confronted by Karanja, confirms he is leaving. Mwaura teases Karanja.

Eleven

At the Thompsons' going-away party, the white people review their concerns. After leaving, John tells Margery his conviction that Africa still needs Europe.

Twelve

At their home, Gikonyo pushes Mumbi's son and abuses her; Wangari steps in. Gikonyo just learned that Richard Burton's farm now belongs to their M.P. Gikonyo visits Warui and reports Mugo's refusal to give a speech. They walk to Mugo's hut.

From earlier that day, Mugo has left Mumbi's home, and in the village, Warui relates that Gitogo's ghost has been visiting his mother. Mugo envisions blood on the walls of his hut. That evening, Mugo tells Gikonyo and Warui he feels unwell. Departing, Gikonyo determines to truly thrash Mumbi now but finds she has left for her parents' home.

Thirteen

That Wednesday, Mugo is seen bearing a sack through heavy rain, provoking wonder among the villagers. Wambui sends Mumbi to persuade Mugo to speak the next day. Mumbi has sent a note telling Karanja not to attend the celebrations. Mugo invites Mumbi inside. Pressed, he claims that he killed Kihika; when she tries to leave, he starts strangling her until she asks what is wrong.

In May 1955, Robson is killed by a disguised assassin. In his hut, Mugo hears the forest fighters' whistling, gunshots, and screams. Later awoken by knocks, he lets in not homeguards, as expected, but Kihika, the assassin. Mugo thinks of calling for help. Kihika insists that Mugo visit him in one week at Kinenie Forest. The next day, Mugo despairs that Kihika's visit has condemned him to death; imagining himself as vital as Moses, Mugo tells District Officer Thompson when and where to find Kihika—then reels over his betrayal.

Fourteen

With overcast skies, the Uhuru day races are subdued—until a surprise three-mile race elicits bold competitors, including Karanja (who has been lured to the festivities by Mumbi's note) and Gikonyo. Mumbi is watching. While racing, General R. recalls his family; Koina, his wartime service and Dr. Lynd. During the final lap, Gikonyo, leading with Karanja on his heels, trips, downing both men; General R. wins. Gikonyo's arm is broken.

The evening crowd anticipates a speech by Mugo. When it is said he will not be arriving, an uproar leads to two elders being sent to fetch him. Meanwhile General R. speaks, insisting on true change. When he calls for Kihika's betrayer's exposure, Mugo steps forward; the crowd, believing he has simply appeared to speak, is shocked when he affirms his traitorous guilt.

Karanja

Leaving his mother's hut for a bus to Githima, Karanja encounters Mumbi, who rejects him one last time. At the Githima eating house, Karanja recalls realizing, during the general's speech, that he was the suspected betrayer. He remembers exposing and murdering other Mau Mau revolutionaries. He is nearly hit by a train.

Mugo

The next afternoon, Mumbi recalls visiting Gikonyo in the hospital. Wangari encourages her to stay loyal to him. That morning, Mugo sets off to begin life again in Nairobi—but rain starts, and he stops to visit Gitogo's mother, who recognizes him as Gitogo and promptly dies. Shaken, Mugo returns to his hut, where, later, General R. and Koina fetch him for a trial, with Wambui as judge.

Warui, Wambui

In Wambui's hut, Warui wonders about Gitogo's mother's death. Mumbi arrives and wonders about Mugo's disappearance; Warui and Wambui both express not knowing his whereabouts. Mumbi and Warui leave; Wambui laments the trial.

Harambee

In the hospital, Gikonyo recalls his last year of detention and confessing the oath. He imagines having children with Mumbi. After she misses a visit on the fifth day because her son is ill, Gikonyo appeals for reconciliation. He thinks of the stool he means to carve for her.

CHARACTERS

Richard Burton

Richard Burton is the departing colonial whose farm Gikonyo wishes to jointly purchase.

Gatu

In the Yala detention camp, Gatu keeps up morale with his defiant parodies of the British. Gikonyo discovers that Gatu's brashness stems in part from his having failed to unite with his beloved back home. Recognizing his value to the other prisoners, the camp administrators hang Gatu.

Gikonyo

Gikonyo's story is among the novel's most central. A quiet, industrious carpenter, he manages to impress Mumbi with his labor as well as his music, and the two marry. After falling in with the Movement, however, Gikonyo is detained for a total of six years. Returning burdened by guilt over his confession of the oath, his troubles are compounded when he discovers that Mumbi has borne Karanja's child. Crucially, he never

allows her to explain, allowing himself to dwell on an inaccurate image of intentional adultery. He channels all his energy into market trading, becoming a locally esteemed businessman. Whether he subconsciously recognizes that Mugo, too, is burdened by guilt, or simply reveres him as a compatriot of Kihika's, Gikonyo is moved to discuss his past and present with Mugo. In the end, Gikonyo is able to see past Mumbi's momentary marital lapse and envision creating their own family.

Githua

Githua is emotionally unrestrained and unpredictable, When beseeching Mugo to buy him a drink, he describes losing his leg in battle. But General R. affirms that Githua, a driver, lost his leg in a car accident.

Gitogo

A powerful and highly esteemed deaf and dumb man who works as a village laborer, Gitogo is shot in the back when he unwittingly ignores a soldier's order to halt.

Gitogo's Mother

After her son's death, Gitogo's mother, often called the old woman, evokes the sympathy of Mugo (a son without a mother). He helps her out, though she also repulses him. She seems to hallucinate visions of Gitogo near the time of Uhuru, such that when Mugo shows up at her door, she believes Gitogo has finally come to fetch her away—and she dies.

Karanja

Though he is not Kihika's betrayer, Karanja betrays his people in so many other respects that he becomes the novel's most vilified figure. His role is foretold when he has a vision of chaos at the train station, in which he imagines having no compunction about trampling others to save himself. While his peers devote themselves to the Movement, Karanja is motivated by his infatuation with Mumbi to survive at any moral cost. During the punitive trench digging, Karanja decides to join the homeguards, the African security personnel, and anonymously identifies Mau Mau adherents to the authorities. He eventually becomes a chief and commits beatings and even murder as his British-supported station demands. He also takes advantage of Mumbi. Once the Emergency is lifted and independence looms, Karanja oversees the beating of a former detainee who owed two years' poll tax, a standard treatment; in response, the District Officer advises him to resign his chiefdom. He ends up inscribing labels on books at Githima, pathetically dependent on the authority of John Thompson. After Uhuru, Karanja makes one last appeal to Mumbi, who has borne his son, but she finally quashes his hopes.

Kariuki

The younger brother of Kihika and Mumbi, Kariuki spends much of the novel obtaining an education, eventually in Uganda, much as Ngũgĩ himself spent the Mau Mau period and the years beyond.

Reverend Jackson Kigondu

A revivalist who supports the British, Kigondu is murdered by his own people.

Kihika

Though he appears only a few times in the novel, Kihika is a fount of revolutionary fervor, speaking of saving the people and of self-sacrifice almost constantly. He commits to Wambuku, but his heart is with the Movement. He achieves the Agikuyu's most celebrated victories, but he brings about his own death when he insists on Mugo meeting him at the forest, though he must have recognized Mugo's uncertainty. Indeed, Kihika may have willed the betrayal, to make himself a martyr. With a bounty on his head, Kihika is caught and hanged.

Lieutenant Koina

A cook by profession, Koina served in World War II but feels slightly inferior for not having seen battle. He later works for Dr. Lynd until electing to join the Movement, slaughtering her dog before her eyes as a last vengeant act. Koina becomes General R.'s right-hand man.

Dr. Lynd

A British botanist with a sense of entitlement, Dr. Lynd is content to believe that she has every right to claim and control her Kenyan land, property, and servants.

Mbugua

Kihika's father, a proud man, cries at the news of his son's death.

Mugo

The novel revolves around Mugo's tale, beginning with the day he is approached to speak for Uhuru, peaking first with the night he sheltered Kihika and then with his public confession, and finally suggesting his fate. Mugo's life was largely shaped by his orphan's upbringing. He became devoted to simply attaining a decent existence through hard farmwork.

When the Emergency comes about, Mugo, disdainful of Kihika's bold words and preoccupied with his own life, tries to forge ahead, being among the first to finish his new hut during the village relocation. Thus, when Kihika shows up after killing Robson, Mugo is incensed that he has been dragged into the Movement; he now must either act as Kihika's accomplice, a capital offense, or expose him, a betrayal of his people. In a panic, relying on logic that holds water just long enough to allow it, he chooses betrayal. His later actions belie his betrayal, as he tries to save Wambuku from a fatal beating in the trench, and he becomes the figurehead of a pivotal hunger strike at Rira. But his self-negating stoicism is repeatedly mistaken for more than it is, fueling his public image as a hero. After he confesses, his fate is only implied; the reader may presume he has been executed, one way or another.

Mumbi

Kihika's sister Mumbi is the novel's most essential feminine presence. Her name, as suggested by the repeated song "Gikuyu na Mumbi," is that of the Gikuyu equivalent of Eve. A natural beauty, she attracts both Karanja and Gikonyo in her youth; she chooses Gikonyo, but Karanja never gets over her. She persists proudly in Gikonyo's absence and supports his mother, but the burden of building them a new hut leaves her overwhelmed. She resents Karanja's offers of food and support but must allow herself to survive. He later manages to take advantage of her, which she immediately regrets but which nonetheless produces a child. When Gikonyo is so distraught by this state of affairs that he begins abusing her, she leaves him and scorns her own mother's traditionalist advice that she simply bear the abuse. Her womanly appeal comes into play one more time when the inchoate sexual tension between her and Mugo spurs him to open up to her—violently at first. Yet her instinct for compassion saves her, as her asking Mugo what is wrong causes him to cease his attack. The novel ends with the fairly feminist suggestion that Mumbi will accept Gikonyo back, but on her own terms.

Teacher Muniu

Like the Reverend Kigondu, Muniu is killed for aiding the British.

Mwaura

An associate of General R. and Koina's who works in Githima, Mwaura helps get Karanja to the Uhuru celebration.

Njeri

Wambuku's best friend, Njeri also has eyes for Kihika. She joins him in the forest and eventually dies in battle.

Old Woman

See Gitogo's Mother

General R.

Named Muhoya, General R. (for Russia) is the novel's most upstanding military figure, one who fought with the British in World War II and has contributed his knowledge and abilities to the independence movement. In the wake of the State of Emergency, he is committed to unmasking Kihika's traitor. Despite his suspicions, it is not Karanja but Mugo, yet the general nonetheless sees justice served.

District Officer Thomas Robson

Said to abduct and kill native Kenyans essentially at random, District Officer Thomas Robson is seen as a terror. He is assassinated by Kihika.

District Officer John Thompson

A longtime district officer, John Thompson is demoted from public administration to Githima after the hunger strike in the Rira concentration camp, under his supervision, leads to eleven deaths from beatings. Preparing to leave Kenya, he mournfully imagines what will become of the precious research station.

Margery Thompson

A sensually charged figure, Margery has an affair with Dr. Van Dyke and, perhaps out of boredom, fosters intrigue when Karanja delivers a message from her distracted husband. John seems unaware that she had that affair.

Dr. Henry Van Dyke

A fat, drunken meteorologist, Dr. Van Dyke has an affair with Margery Thompson, but he fulfills his oath to kill himself after Jomo Kenyatta's release from prison when, whether intentionally or not, his car collides with a train.

Waitherero

Mugo's aunt, bitter over the absence and seeming indifference of all her married daughters, vents her drunken frustration on her adoptive charge, the young Mugo, regularly ridiculing him. Just when he is ready to kill her, she dies of her own accord.

Wambui

Like Warui, Wambui is an elder who has been involved in the Movement since her youth. Representing a council of women, Wambui asks another woman, Mumbi, to persuade Mugo to speak for Uhuru, ultimately leading to the truth coming out. For Mugo's trial, Wambui is the judge. Afterward, she leads Mumbi to believe she knows not Mugo's fate, but her numbness and regret suggest that Mugo is dead.

Wambuku

Adoring Kihika, Wambuku unites with him despite her misgivings about his focus on the Movement. Despairing after Kihika dies, Wambuku gets reckless and pregnant. She is the woman whom Mugo tries to defend in the Thabai trench; she dies from her wounds.

Wangari

Wangari fled to Thabai after her husband, preferring his later wives, sent her and her son, Gikonyo, away. She adores Mumbi and does what she can to preserve their union.

Wanjiku

Wanjiku is the mother of Kihika, Mumbi, and Kariuki.

Warui

An elder, Warui has been involved in the Movement since the 1923 Procession, a tragic protest march. He has wise words for the likes of Mugo and Gikonyo, and important news is channeled through him. He is involved in imploring Mugo to speak for Uhuru, but notably he is left out of Mugo's trial, suggesting the supremacy of his female counterpart, Wambui, in matters of justice at least.

THEMES

Colonialism

Maintaining a keen historical focus—through primarily fictional characters—on the roles and lives of Gikuyu people in Kenya's quest for independence, Ngũgĩ's novel cycles through a series of interconnected themes. Foremost is the issue of colonialism. Ngũgĩ is hardly sympathetic in his portrayals of the British, with the text bearing out numerous atrocities, along with everyday slights, inflicted by a people who self-servingly inserted themselves into the native culture with utter disregard for their impact. Apparently (and justifiably) seeing little reason to treat the British presence with critical evenhandedness, Ngũgĩ offers no serious debate about whether colonialism was positive or not—though in Western societies such debate took place—and no British character who suggests a truly positive influence. Instead, much as the Nazis are the obvious villains in any tale of World War II, the characters of Thomas Robson and John Thompson are patently evil—killing and torturing without restraint, treating Africans as less than human—while the likes of Margery Thompson and Dr. Lynd are possessive and condescending at best. John Thompson is at least given a humane background, marked by literary affection for Rudyard Kipling—author of the notorious colonialist poem "The White Man's Burden"—and by a belief (based on interactions with just two Gold Coast men) that the most intelligent Kenyans appreciate being colonized, are *proud* of being Westernized. Notwithstanding his fairly utopian visions, in practice Thompson rules with typically racist cruelty. The reader can be left with little wonder that the Mau Mau adherents resorted to violent means in their quest to at last overthrow their colonizer.

Religion

Stirred into the theme of colonialism is the role of religion, though Ngũgĩ only touches on the society-wide impact of Christian missionaries and their particular designs. Of more import in his narrative is the way Christian stories have fixed themselves in the minds of Gikuyu men like Kihika and Mugo. Although the British certainly never intended biblical stories to inspire Kenyans to revolt, Kihika's underlining of key passages makes clear that, if one pays selective attention to, say, Moses's leading of the Israelites out of slavery in Egypt, the spiritual

ground for revolution is there; furthermore, in descriptions of Jesus's role as savior, the ground for martyrdom is evident. If one considers the theological argument that Jesus, being the son/embodiment of an all-knowing God, must have known that Judas would betray him and bring about his crucifixion, one easily imagines that Kihika is deliberately playing out such a betrayal–crucifixion script here.

The narration makes clear the animosity Mugo felt when he first heard Kihika speak and also made pointed eye contact with him—animosity that Kihika likely felt. When Kihika, after killing Robson, finds Mugo in his hut, he expresses having "always wanted to speak to" him; but given Mugo's staid and practical life, marked not at all by revolutionary fervor, what other motive could Kihika have honestly had other than to accomplish his own martyrdom? Mugo's hesitance and uncertainty throughout this conversation add to the sense that Kihika would have understood where Mugo's concerns truly lay. Mugo, too, has been influenced by Christian stories, having, like Kihika, identified himself with Moses, leading a people to freedom. But in Mugo's case, it seems his visions deceive him; or perhaps he allows himself to believe in his own importance to the world simply as an excuse for turning Kihika in and, he hopes, preserving his own life. He does temporarily become a hero to the people, but only because through his later deeds they remain unaware of his treachery; and while he shows the potential for great leadership and is favored to become a chief, the fact of his betrayal would have always blocked his psychic ability to assume any leadership role. Thus, while religious stories may provide a blueprint for spiritually inspired action, this is no guarantee that the action taken will prove morally sound.

Rebellion

If a people are being systematically oppressed, especially in the case of a native majority under a foreign elite minority, they basically have three options for resolving the situation: they can endure the drawn-out, uncertain process of diplomatic talks, they can resist nonviolently, and they can resist violently. In *A Grain of Wheat*, it is the third option, violent resistance, that is undertaken. While an assessment of the historical situation makes clear why this path was chosen by Mau Mau, Ngũgĩ offers little such background to enlighten the non-Kenyan reader.

TOPICS FOR FURTHER STUDY

- Write an essay in which you consider who, in the absence of Mugo, might make the best new chief of Thabai, drawing on the descriptions, thoughts, and deeds of characters with potential. Warui, Wambui, Gikonyo, General R., and Mumbi all merit consideration. Feel free to include cultural research on whether the Gikuyu or other East African ethnic groups would allow a woman chief in such circumstances, or simply argue as if they would.

- Read the young-adult novel *The Mzungu Boy* (1990; originally published as *Little White Man*), by prolific Kenyan author Meja Mwangi, which provides a look at the Mau Mau period through the eyes of Kariuki, a twelve-year-old whose father works as cook for a white planter with a grandson, Nigel, who visits for the summer. Write an essay considering the themes and style of this story and comparing the treatment of white characters with that in *A Grain of Wheat*.

- The chronological arrangement of *A Grain of Wheat* is exceedingly complicated. Compile a chart specifying the time frames of the action throughout the novel, including mention of flashbacks as short as a paragraph (or shorter), and, if appropriate, also produce by hand or computer a more graphic representation of the chronological trajectory. Add a written analysis of the nature of Ngũgĩ's framing strategies and how they affect the reader's absorption of the narrative.

- Create a website featuring a sort of map or time line of all the historical figures mentioned in the course of *A Grain of Wheat*—there are at least thirteen—and provide subsections or links giving relevant biographical capsules and a photo or two for each figure. Be sure to include a bibliography listing sources.

- Write a research paper on postindependence Kenya, focusing on either the way Mau Mau and its adherents were viewed and treated, or the extent to which the common people were disappointed by the actions of the new government.

The resistance movement, as he does indicate through occasional narrative excursions from the second chapter onward, had existed ever since the incoming British moved beyond honeyed words to unveil their swords and their true intents—plunder and pleasure. By Kihika's time, the grievances had mounted to the point where enduring British rule was, for many, no longer acceptable. This of course sounds much like another famous episode of violent resistance, the American Revolution. In Ngũgĩ's novel, Kihika and many others are willing to sacrifice their very lives in order to secure a future of freedom for their fellow countrymen. In Kihika's words, "a few shall die that the many shall live. . . . Choose between freedom and slavery and it is fitting that a man should grab at freedom and die for it." Notably, Ngũgĩ has not sensationalized the action-oriented aspects of Mau Mau but has rather focused on ordinary people's endurance of the British response to the conflict—in circumstances rife with possibilities for betrayal.

Betrayal

The fact that so many betrayals take place in the novel—Gikonyo's revealing the oath, Karanja's joining the British as a loyalist, Mumbi's marital lapse with Karanja, and, above all, Mugo's betrayal of Kihika—points to how the colonial situation fostered these betrayals. With uncertain numbers of Kenyans taking the Mau Mau oath of resistance, the British reacted with maximum aggression, communicating through the

The novel is set in a village in Kenya during the country's struggle for independence.
(© nutsiam / Shutterstock.com)

murder of Kenyans practically at random that the slightest indirect affiliation with Mau Mau—even the mere *suspicion* of such affiliation—would be grounds for execution. Thus, the life of every Kenyan citizen was in imminent danger, leading many to the choice that Karanja and Mugo consciously consider: whether to support Mau Mau and risk execution, or support the British and betray their people. Interestingly, while Karanja, Gikonyo, and Mugo all commit betrayals, each comes at a different junction in the context of rebellion. Karanja permanently sides with the British as soon as it becomes convenient, in the most morally reprehensible betrayal; Mugo, upon essentially being forced to aid Mau Mau, betrays only the one individual responsible, Kihika; and Gikonyo, committed to the resistance but driven to the psychic brink by indefinite detention, betrays only the oath he swore. It is worth recognizing here that one of the primary intents of the British in suppressing resistance in Kenya, as with elsewhere in colonial Africa, was to keep the people divided; this historical fact, like others, is not much expanded upon in the novel, with little more than Kihika's

rhetorical allusion in speaking to Mugo: "Our fathers fought bravely. But do you know the biggest weapon unleashed by the enemy against them? . . . It was division among them." Even though the novel's narrator does not specifically address how the British went about this, the Kenyans' often succumbing to the temptation of betrayal illustrates how their opposition to one another, even within ethnic groups, made united resistance all the more difficult.

Leadership

One of the most unsettling aspects of *A Grain of Wheat* is the manner in which the novel closes. Ngũgĩ has made clear, starting with the biblical allusion in the title, that his focus is not just on Kenyan resistance but also on what the results of resistance will mean for the common people. That they will not be altogether positive is suggested by, for example, the M.P.'s taking possession, probably illegitimately, of the farm that Gikonyo had sought to legitimately buy. While running in the race, Koina, haunted by colonial ghosts, laments that already "the cool Uhuru drink had turned insipid in his mouth." In his speech, General R. reveals his concern that the needs of the common people be addressed by the new Kenyan government, suggesting the justified fear that they will not be. Indeed, "the sensation of imminent betrayal was so strong that General R. trembled in his moment of triumph."

Thus arises the question of leadership; historical figures like Jomo Kenyatta and Oginga Odinga remain at the top of the chain, but in the immediate community of the book, the resistance has left behind a void of leadership. Kihika was crucified; Karanja damned himself by siding with the British; the less-guilty Gikonyo has withdrawn into business, not politics; General R., in turn, is not a politician but a militarist who disappears from the scene after closure is achieved through the exposure of Kihika's betrayer; and as for Mugo, the man with the most potential, justice supposedly had to be served. Wambui seems to recognize the vacuum that has been left behind when she thinks that perhaps they should not have tried him. Even as the book closes, the question of Kenyan leadership remains open.

STYLE

Surrealism

While *A Grain of Wheat* is generally regarded as written in a realist mode, especially in contrast with Ngũgĩ's later allegorical novels, there is a vein of surrealism that colors the reader's appreciation of what the characters endure. The sense of a reality that has been shifted, to somewhere beyond where it ought to be, begins with the opening chapter, where Mugo walks through town unable to comprehend why people are looking at him the way they do, and what their words and gestures mean. Without knowing that Mugo is profoundly affected by guilt, the reader can only, like Mugo, feel confused and displaced in the reality presented. With Mugo this sense is sustained throughout the novel, such as when he visits a bar and "he was in a reverie, the ground on which he walked, the people in the bar, were all unreal." Among other characters, Karanja is able to take advantage of Mumbi because, as she reports, "I was in a strange world, and it was like if I was mad." Gikonyo's detention, too, is marked as a surreal experience: "Was he dead? . . . He was both in and outside himself." His decision to confess the oath leaves him feeling that

"he had woken from an unreal dream in which he had walked and walked ever since Gatu was hanged." But when Gikonyo returns after six years of detention to an entirely new Thabai village, and to his wife and a baby he has nothing to do with, his world once again turns surreal, as "Thabai was just another detention camp; would he ever get out of it?"

Sometimes the sense of surreality is achieved through striking images, such as where the stricken Gikonyo sees life as "one endless blank sheet, so flat"; where Mugo hallucinates blood dripping down the walls of his hut; and where Karanja vividly sees his own hooded self before him in the dark. Generally speaking, the significance of such images is discounted by Gikonyo when, upon hearing of the old woman being visited by her dead son Gitogo, he remarks, "It's only pictures in the head." But the proof that such images can have an impact on reality comes when the old woman imagines that the visiting Mugo is Gitogo, come to fetch her away, and indeed, she at last allows herself to be ushered to death. In all cases, the surreal circumstances experienced by the Kenyans have been fostered by colonialism, and Ngũgĩ's literary style aptly conveys the unsettled, unsettling nature of those experiences.

Postcolonial Literature

It may be said that any literary work that takes as its subject the transition of a colonized nation toward independence and its ensuing statehood, typically written after independence has been achieved, is a postcolonial work. As many academics have observed, however, the term *postcolonial* is open to criticism, as it necessarily situates any work of literature from a colonized nation, such as Kenya, in the context of its past subjugation, foregrounding the significance of the colonizer, in this case Britain, in the nation's history. And yet it is true that the colonial experience so comprehensively shaped the cultures of African nations in particular—with regard to everything from infrastructure to economics to politics—that most aspects of modern African society can be related back to colonialism in some sense or another. In fact, Ngũgĩ lends colonialism full global significance in the preface to his nonfiction volume *Something Torn and New: An African Renaissance*: "There is no region, no culture, no nation today that has not been affected by colonialism and its aftermath." Ngũgĩ is perhaps as well known as a critical commentator on postcolonial literature, politics, and culture as he is as a novelist.

In *A Grain of Wheat*, Ngũgĩ demonstrates how postcolonial commentary can be encapsulated in a fictional work without any more than cursory attention being devoted to the actual colonizer. John Thompson is characterized just fully enough for the reader to recognize him as a human being with genuine and even idealistic interests; but in the colonial situation his idealism evaporates, signifying the unbridgeable divide between colonizers' expressed interests—bringing religion and civilization to Africa (as if those were not already present in African cultures, which they were)—and colonizers' actual deeds, as characterized by appropriation (theft), differentiated treatment (racism, discrimination), the institution of law and order (oppression), and capital punishment (murder). Even writing as early as the 1960s, as part of the first cresting wave of English-language African literature, Ngũgĩ saw fit to reduce colonial discourse to ironic asides that lay bare the duplicity of the British. When the deaf Gitogo is murdered for failing to heed a soldier's order, "Another Mau Mau terrorist had been shot dead"—surely Britain's official take on what transpired, even if entirely untrue. Another British line of thought is subtly derided when Queen Victoria is referred to as "the great woman whose Christian hand had ended the tribal wars," reflecting the self-glorifying British conceit that colonization ushered African out of endless internecine warfare into an era of peace. When the tyrannical Robson is assassinated by Kihika, the newspapers duly report, with the usual colonial slant, that "a District Officer had been senselessly murdered by Mau Mau thugs." But the reader understands that Kihika was no mere thug, and the murder of that appallingly murderous man was one of the most sensible acts he committed. Overall, while dismissing British propaganda with such cutting one-liners, Ngũgĩ fully engages in the more important aspects of the postcolonial state through his thematic exploration of such ideas as religion, rebellion, and leadership and their roles in Kenya on the verge of independence. He also occasionally uses Gikuyu or Swahili terms without explanation—including *sufuria*, *uhuru*, and *harambee*—leaving the English-language reader to try and keep up with the African words, instead of vice versa.

HISTORICAL CONTEXT

Colonialism, Mau Mau, and Kenyan Independence

While Arabic traders had been frequenting as well as settling on the Kenyan coast, especially around the city of Mombasa, since the Middle Ages, and the Portuguese made temporary inroads in the sixteenth and seventeenth centuries, it was in the late nineteenth century that Britain asserted its presence there. It first permitted a commercial enterprise, the Imperial British East Africa Company, to wield authority in the region and then, in 1895, established the East African Protectorate. A primary goal was overcoming civil hostility and Masai military resistance in order to secure fertile farmland in the central highlands. Firearms and a newly built railroad greatly aided the endeavors of the British, who deliberately lured civilian settlers and granted additional land to ex-soldiers after World War II. With too little land left for native Kenyans, many were obligated to work on British farms for extremely low wages, under deplorable conditions. Ngũgĩ writes in *A Grain of Wheat* of several individuals who made their names in the early period of resistance, going back to Waiyaki wa Hinga, who successfully attacked a British garrison after the British broke a peace treaty, but was captured and killed in 1892; Harry Thuku, who in 1921 led the expansion of Gikuyu resistance into cross-ethnic resistance under the new East African Association; and Jomo Kenyatta, who would be Kenya's first president.

In the words of R. Mugo Gatheru in *Kenya: From Colonization to Independence, 1888–1970*, Kenyatta was "a man of extrovert personality, a vigorous speaker, physically strong, with eyes burning like fire, generous but ruthless when aggravated, independent in his thought." A colleague of Thuku's who remained after Thuku was arrested and banished to the north, Kenyatta became a political leader with the Kikuyu Central Association and later the Kenyan African Union, making a key diplomatic trip to London in 1929 and studying there from 1933 to 1936. When the Emergency broke in 1952, he was convicted (in a spurious trial) of leading what had become known as Mau Mau and held as a prize captive until 1962.

While the British made far-reaching efforts, both in Kenya and internationally, to discredit

COMPARE
&
CONTRAST

- **1950s:** Led by Governor Philip Mitchell—who favors equal representation for Africans in a new East African assembly—until 1952, Kenya is subsequently led by Evelyn Baring, who almost immediately declares a state of emergency to deal with the Mau Mau uprising and otherwise minimizes African political representation.

  1960s: After a transitional period, Jomo Kenyatta becomes the first president of independent Kenya in 1964. With the banning of the primary opposition party, which was led by Oginga Odinga, the nation's first vice president, in 1969, Kenyatta will manage to remain in office until his death in 1978.

  Today: The sons of Kenya's founding fathers are at the forefront of the political scene, with Deputy Prime Minister Uhuru Kenyatta narrowly defeating Prime Minister Raila Odinga in the 2013 presidential election.

- **1950s:** Through the early part of the decade, Mau Mau rebels actively fight against the British colonial government and settlers, as well as Kenyan loyalists (homeguards). Military operations end for the most part when Field Marshal Dedan Kimathi is executed in 1956.

  1960s: Civilian Kenyan leaders politically and peacefully negotiate for independence, which is achieved in 1963. The situation is stable until 1969, when Minister Tom Mboya is assassinated, in the wake of which Kenya effectively becomes a one-party nation; political violence will not be uncommon in the ensuing decades.

  Today: Kenyan soldiers have been dispatched to Somalia in attempts to root out Islamist al-Shabab militants, who, among other attacks, kill over thirty people in a shopping center bombing in Nairobi in 2012, and sixty in a mall bombing in 2013.

- **1950s:** Mau Mau adherents and many innocent Kenyans are rounded up and either murdered or shuttled through a series of detention camps and years of torture, often with no criminal charges ever brought.

  1960s: With Britain having suppressed the Mau Mau revolt and banned the organization, the new Kenyan government sustains the ban for political reasons and discounts the role of Mau Mau in the quest for independence.

  Today: Numerous histories have both demonstrated the legitimacy and practical contributions of Mau Mau and illustrated the extent to which the British committed wartime atrocities in suppressing it. In 2013, Britain apologizes for the atrocities and promises twenty million pounds in compensation.

Mau Mau as mere savage brutality, Ngũgĩ's novel demonstrates what historical study has borne out, that the armed resistance of Mau Mau was entirely honorable, and what savage brutality could be found in the era was primarily that of the British. The term *Mau Mau* remains one of history's great curiosities, having been coined not by the group responsible for armed resistance, the Kenya Land and Freedom Army, but in the context of a trial conducted after oathing ceremonies in Naivasha were crashed by the police. *Mau Mau* is speculated to have been derived perhaps from onomatopoetic reference to whispering; or repetition of the Gikuyu word *uma*, meaning "out" (a direction for the British); or a police officer's inability to pronounce the Gikuyu word *muma*, meaning "oath." Regardless, by 1950 the rebel generals and forest fighters identified themselves as Mau Mau.

Gikonyo spends six years in a detention camp. *(© Gwoeii | Shutterstock.com)*

Guerilla War

The Mau Mau war was largely a prolonged guerrilla resistance, interspersed with various battles, with the Kenyan fighters far overmatched in manpower and armaments. Mau Mau rebels did, at times, elicit condemnation from the British for such practices as dismembering corpses. At the forefront of Mau Mau was Dedan Kimathi, whom Harish Narang, in "Prospero and the Land of Calibans: *A Grain of Wheat*," recognizes as one of the movement's "number of truly great soldiers by any standards of military warfare." Thinking beyond the battlefields, Oliver Lovesey, in *Ngũgĩ wa Thiong'o*, observes that Ngũgĩ has sought "to elevate revolutionary national intellectuals such as Dedan Kimathi into a position of spiritual leadership." Kimathi himself wrote from the forest in 1953, in a letter published in the widely circulating *East African Standard*, that ultimately Kenyan independence would have to be achieved politically. Meanwhile, Mau Mau fighters would continue armed resistance, leading to piecemeal improvements in African political participation throughout the 1950s.

As historians' reports attest, Ngũgĩ's treatment of the brutality and inhumanity of the British response to Mau Mau in *A Grain of Wheat* is accurate; if anything, he has softened his accounts, perhaps for aesthetic reasons. As Lovesey reports, colonial troops were given cash payments for every murder of a Mau Mau suspect. As a diary from a tortured detainee in Carol Sicherman's sourcebook *Ngũgĩ wa Thiong'o: The Making of a Rebel* reveals, individuals would be restricted to cells with standing water up to their ankles for days on end, entirely preventing sleep and causing serious medical complications, with only kale and maize meal for food. This particular detainee was led into experiences under hypnosis which may have been either real or hallucinations—he was never sure. The massacre of eleven detainees at the Hola camp in 1959—Ngũgĩ's Rira camp in *A Grain of Wheat*—which helped turn international opinion in favor of the Kenyans, was one of several such massacres. Some eighty thousand Kenyans were forced through the system of concentration camps, while over ten thousand, perhaps as many as thirty thousand, were killed;

unknown are the numbers who were injured or permanently disabled through torture. Perhaps fewer than one hundred Europeans were killed in the conflict.

Mau Mau military operations were hampered through Britain's Operation Anvil in 1954, which saw the arrest of tens of thousands of suspected adherents in Nairobi. This led to the British discovery and detention of the members of the Mau Mau Supreme Council, which had been running military actions from the capital; thenceforth the forest fighters took more direction into their own hands and lost unity as a result. Active Mau Mau resistance was dealt a crippling blow in 1956, when Kimathi was captured, tried, and executed. The state of emergency would continue for four more years, and not until 1963 would Kenya achieve independence. Nonetheless—and despite the fact that leaders such as Kenyatta went on to disown the movement and its violence when doing so was politically expedient—Mau Mau has been recognized as an indispensable stage of the resistance and Kenya's road to independence. In the words of Bildad Kaggia (cited in Narang), who was writing in 1978, at a time when perceptions of the movement were yet to be fully corrected from those first propagated by the British:

The Mau Mau struggle, whether one likes it or not, will stand in history as one of the greatest liberation struggles in Africa. It was the first of its kind on the continent. Its heroes will be remembered by generations to come.... It is time to recognise their achievements. Long live "Mau Mau": Long live the freedom of Kenya, which it fought for and brought about.

CRITICAL OVERVIEW

Ngũgĩ is one of the most admired writers in African history. His novels have been critically well received, his plays have been highly popular in East Africa where they are usually staged, and his essays are considered a foundational part of the growing international body of postcolonial literary theory and criticism. In *Ngũgĩ wa Thiong'o*, Oliver Lovesey recognizes Ngũgĩ's place seemingly just below, but perhaps rather alongside, the Nigerian literary stars:

Although he has not written an acknowledged masterpiece, a staple of college and university syllabi like Achebe's *Things Fall Apart*, or, like Soyinka, won the Nobel Prize in Literature,

Ngũgĩ has inspired a generation of writers and is celebrated for his stand on political and linguistic issues.

Lovesey reveals the thematic relevance of *A Grain of Wheat* to Ngũgĩ's broader artistic vision: "Much of Ngũgĩ's work conveys a sense of both the transcendent hope of independence and freedom, *uhuru*, and also the absolute despair that followed when this hope was compromised."

Reviewing *A Grain of Wheat* along with Ngũgĩ's preceding and ensuing novels for the *Times Literary Supplement*, Helen Hayward declares, "These three novels are important documents in the history of postcolonial writing, distinguished by the urgency of their political engagement and the subtlety of their historical grasp." Focusing on the style of *A Grain of Wheat*, Arthur Ravenscroft, in *Contemporary Novelists*, observes,

A great strength of this finely orchestrated novel is Ngũgĩ's skillful use of disrupted time sequence to indicate the interrelatedness of the characters' behavior in the Rebellion and the state of their lives (and of the nation) at Independence.

Govind Narain Sharma, in his essay "Ngugi's Christian Vision: Theme and Pattern in *A Grain of Wheat*," affirms that the novel is marked by "extraordinary richness and complexity," and notes that "it is precisely the possession of this depth and subtlety which constitutes the singular distinction of Ngugi's novel." Considering the novel in the context of its predecessors, Lovesey finds that Ngũgĩ's first two novels only hint "at the sustained and multifaceted brilliance of *A Grain of Wheat*, a novel that completes and concludes his first stage as a novelist." Lovesey characterizes the third novel as "a great, mournful song of freedom" with "a wide epic sweep, bringing together individual and communal aspirations and despair." David Maughan-Brown, in the *Dictionary of Literary Biography*, calls *A Grain of Wheat* "one of the major accomplishments of African literature," and Angus Calder, in the *New Statesman*, calls it "arguably the best, and certainly the most underrated, novel to come from Black Africa."

Maughan-Brown more generally observes that throwing off

the mental shackles of his colonial education... has brought Ngũgĩ persecution and an enforced exile, but it has also led to the production of a body of fiction, drama, and essays so original, technically assured, politically committed, informative, and influential that many of Ngũgĩ's admirers regard him as the most important African writer.

Maughan-Brown concludes that "courage and commitment, combined with a technical mastery of fictional forms and a total command of both English and Gikuyu, make Ngũgĩ wa Thiong'o preeminent among African writers." Peter Nazareth, in his introduction to *Critical Essays on Ngũgĩ wa Thiong'o* from the turn of the twenty-first century, goes so far as to declare, "It is not inaccurate to say that Ngũgĩ wa Thiong'o is the most famous African writer today."

CRITICISM

Michael Allen Holmes

Holmes is a writer with existential interests. In the following essay, he considers how Mugo remains precariously poised between good and evil throughout A Grain of Wheat *and how his moral trajectory is ultimately determined.*

While many classic novels follow a single main protagonist, *A Grain of Wheat* follows an ensemble cast through and beyond the Mau Mau rebellion leading up to Kenya's independence. Many wartime novels distribute the character focus in such fashion, since war is one circumstance that produces vastly different experiences for those who are more or less involved, and only with attention to multiple characters can the full experience of the era be captured. Mugo, Gikonyo, Mumbi, and Karanja all get roughly equivalent narrative attention devoted to them—but it is Mugo whose deeds and destiny are of the utmost import. The revolutionary Kihika, a lesser character in the narrative context, is unmistakably rendered the Gikuyus' Mao Mao hero, such that resolution regarding his death is of profound historic and even folkloric relevance: when ensuing generations of Gikuyus sing his praises, how will the story end? For General R., this is above all a matter of justice. Heroes, he affirms, must be both praised and protected; the traitor who cost the Gikuyu their veritably mythic leader cannot be allowed to go unpunished. Mugo's story line, in accord with his crucial role, is the most complex, with his betrayal of Kihika first hinted at, then subtly disclosed by the narrator, then claimed by Mugo himself, and only in the last quarter of the book portrayed directly. His scenes

> AT THIS POINT, BOTH NARRATIVELY AND EXISTENTIALLY, MUGO IS CAPABLE OF ANYTHING."

are wrought with the most tension, largely because of the hanging question of his guilt and his uncertain way of interacting with everyone. Ngũgĩ might have crafted Mugo with little more than this matter of his guilt and eventual exposure, and on the whole such a simple characterization could have sufficed. But part of Ngũgĩ's genius is that, much more ambitiously, he also made Mugo arguably the most psychologically complex and unique character, one whose mindsets and actions make clear, by the end, just why he has played the monumental role that he has.

That Mugo occupies a mental state poised somewhere between good and evil is suggested very early in the book, such as in the third chapter, as he converses with the several visitors who have just arrived. Trying to decide whether to speak for Uhuru, Mugo realizes that making decisions—rationally electing to take a course of action based on an expected outcome—has never come easy to him. Rather, in general, "he allowed himself to drift into things or be pushed into them by an uncanny demon; he rode on the wave of circumstance and lay against the crest, fearing but fascinated by fate." There are certainly negative connotations to this frame of mind, as further suggested when "that devilish fascination now seemed to light his eyes." One might characterize this approach as living by impulse, that is, in Freudian terms, in accordance with the carnal whims of the id, to the extent that they are practicable. This is the part of the psyche that is capable of enacting violence for personal gain—as in primitive man hunting and slaying an animal for food—or, in wartime, killing other humans for the sake of survival. Tragically, some people's experiences lead them to inhabit this part of the psyche in the course of normal civilized life. In morally anchored modern humans, the id is almost entirely submerged; for example, excluding farmers and hunters, very few modern Americans have had the experience of personally killing the animal that they eat for dinner. Mugo is no hunter or herder, of course; he is a

WHAT DO I READ NEXT?

- While Ngũgĩ's earlier novels *Weep Not, Child* (1964) and *A River Between* (1965) both treat aspects of Kenya's colonial situation, the ambitious reader might turn next to Ngũgĩ's translated epic *Wizard of the Crow* (2006), published in six volumes in the original Gikuyu as *Murogi wa kagogo* (2004–2007). As opposed to his earlier realist works, this novel features myth, satire, and magical realism, following a populist wizard in a fictional modern-day African republic.

- Ngũgĩ's affiliations with Joseph Conrad have been well discussed by critics, especially regarding *A Grain of Wheat*, which can be considered a postmodern reflection of Conrad's *Under Western Eyes* (1911), a treatment of betrayal in revolutionary Russia.

- Another non-African writer who made a significant impact on Ngũgĩ was George Lamming, a Barbadian novelist with a similar postcolonial agenda. His masterpiece is *In the Castle of My Skin* (1953), a semiautobiographical treatment of colonial race relations and the awakening of a village's social consciousness.

- Historically, Kenya's next best-known author is Grace Ogot, a Luo woman whose tales often reach back into the precolonial past in Luoland, in western Kenya. She is most admired for her short stories, such as in

the collections *Land without Thunder* (1968) and *The Other Woman* (1976).

- One of the earliest historical treatments of Kenya's 1950s rebellion is *Mau Mau from Within: Autobiography and Analysis of Kenya's Peasant Revolt* (1966), written by Karari Njama with Donald Bartlett, offering perspective on daily life for Mau Mau fighters and on the singular person of Dedan Kimathi.

- Perhaps the most famous Mau Mau history in Western circles is Caroline Elkins's Pulitzer Prize–winning volume *Imperial Reckoning: The Untold Story of Britain's Gulag in Kenya* (2005), which characterizes the British approach to containing Mau Mau as genocide.

- The first president of independent Kenya was also an anthropologist: Jomo Kenyatta's *Facing Mount Kenya* (1938) is a study of his own people, the Gikuyu, that addresses customs and social history as well as considering the culture in relation to foreign ones.

- An admired Kenyan author of young-adult fiction is Emmanuel Kariuki, whose titles include *The Salem Mystery* (2001), which won the Jomo Kenyatta Prize, and its sequel, *The Red Coat* (2008), which follow two adolescents whose skill at criminal investigations outshines that of the police.

---

farmer of the soil, and a devoted one, and such a person might have spent his life safeguarded from the psychic zone dominated by the id. But Mugo's childhood, unfortunately, did propel him into a morally ambiguous state of mind.

Orphaned at a young age, Mugo ended up with an aunt who clearly had no vested interest in raising him to be a happy, healthy individual. Disappointed with the distance, and apparent indifference, of her married daughters, Waitherero

is the sort who makes herself feel better by making someone else—Mugo—feel worse. It is in the very first chapter, in fact, that the reader learns about how Mugo responded to his aunt's constantly badgering and belittling him:

> His one desire was to kill his aunt.
> One evening the mad thought possessed him. He raged within.... Blood rushed to his finger-tips, he was breathless, acutely fascinated by the audacity and daring of his own action.

Beyond demonstrating Mugo's interest in and capacity for fatal action, whether justified or not, this passage also subtly suggests Mugo's visionary capacity: he imagines killing his aunt so vividly that the narration, reflecting his mind, vacillates between the conditional—"he would get her"—and the simple past—"he watched her struggle"—until by the end his blood and thoughts alike run as if he is actually committing the deed in question. This scene also suggests Mugo's transparency when in such a state, with his aunt, upon noticing his stare, voicing the accurate suspicion that he is imagining murder.

To characterize Mugo as evil based on these passages, however, would be entirely inaccurate, because he also shows a great capacity for good. That he is, in a fundamental sense, a good person is certain: he is a hard-working, honest laborer, one who, in the absence of any meaningful family members, projects his innate sympathy onto a lonely old woman—whose son, Gitogo, was killed—helping her out at least once by bringing food and firewood. More significantly, Mugo occasionally envisions, as did Kihika, being a savior of the people, one who "shall save the children of the needy, and shall break down in pieces the oppressor," as Psalm 72 has it. Thinking that this description might apply to him, "the words thrilled him; a flicker once more danced within him. He stood, transfixed." Later again, after Githua has (prematurely) hailed him as "Chief," Mugo

> felt he could embrace the whole night, could contain the world within his palms. For he walked on the edge of a revelation.... He would speak at the Uhuru celebrations. He would lead the people and bury his past in their gratitude.

That Mugo might even have the opportunity to "lead the people" is largely due to how, when Wambuku was being assaulted with lethal force in the trench, he committed the truly heroic deed of sacrificing his own freedom and well-being, subjecting himself to years of detention and torture, in a futile attempt to save the defenseless pregnant woman.

By now it is apparent that Mugo occupies a liminal state, an in-between place where he is liable to tilt either toward evil or toward good, depending on the circumstances and his precise state of mind. The question that thus suggests itself is, what is it that determines which way he will tilt, toward good or evil? The question is highly relevant because the novel yet has two key moral decisions on Mugo's part to show the reader: whether he will betray Kihika—a foregone conclusion by the time the scene is reached—and what he will do when Uhuru comes.

Mugo's reasoning with regard to whether and why to betray Kihika is explored at length in the narrative disclosure of Mugo's thoughts after the rebel leader's visit. These thoughts by and large revolve around Mugo's desire for self-preservation. It makes sense that this would be his priority, given the precariousness of his very identity early in life, under a derisive aunt who left him "haunted by the image of his own inadequacy." Left to his own devices, Mugo naturally ends up with the libertarian belief that the one thing a man has a right to is his own life: "His argument went like this: if you don't traffic with evil, then evil ought not to touch you; if you leave people alone, then they ought to leave you alone." Kihika, however, has threatened Mugo's life by involving him with insurgent activity, a capital crime, and thus Mugo feels justified in preemptively taking Kihika's life, by turning him over to the British authorities. The text makes clear that this decision of Mugo's is founded in evil, since the poster of Kihika's face "awakened the same excitement and terror he once experienced, as a boy, the night he wanted to strangle his aunt." That is, subconsciously he recognizes that turning Kihika in is as good as committing murder; and yet his self-centered rationale holds long enough for the evil impulse to be carried out.

Once the novel has disclosed this pivotal scene, about which suspense has been building all along, a more immediate suspense overtakes the narrative, since in the days leading up to Uhuru the reader has no clues as to what Mugo will do next. The scenes of his betrayal operated within preestablished boundaries—the reader knew, for example, that he would not kill Kihika with his own hands—but at this point, both narratively and existentially, Mugo is capable of anything. What will happen on Uhuru day may be foremost in the reader's mind, but a more private drama is enacted just before, one with the utmost significance with regard to the drama to follow. Indeed, one might argue that the interaction between Mugo and Mumbi the night before Uhuru is what determines Mugo's course of action the following day.

From their first meeting on, interaction between Mugo and Mumbi is marked by a certain sensual tension, as they both at times become acutely conscious of each other's physical presence and the potentiality between them. Love, in fact, has proven a serious sticking point for Mugo thus far. In the scene when he feels great irritation, even hatred toward Kihika, upon hearing a speech that so moves everyone else in the audience, Mugo's repulsion seems triggered by Kihika's reference to familial love: "A day comes when a brother shall give up his brother, a mother her son, when you and I have heard the call of a nation in turmoil." At this point "Mugo felt a constriction in his throat. He could not clap for words that did not touch him." Whether deliberately or subconsciously, his thoughts glaze over *why* the words did not touch him, but the reader may imagine that it is because he cannot relate to the idea of a loving brother or a loving mother at all anymore. Kihika has unintentionally excluded him from the larger Mau Mau family of which he wants all Gikuyus to be a part. Mugo is later similarly irritated by his own speech, made spontaneously at a postdetention rally that he only attended because it would have seemed impolitic not to. He finds himself speaking words he hardly means:

> We only thought of home.
> We longed for the day when we would see our women laugh, or even see our children fight and cry. When we thought that one day we would return home to see the faces and hear the voices of our mothers and our wives and our children we became strong.

Mugo soon abandons his speech midsentence, thinking to himself, "I did not long to join my mother, or wife or child because I did not have any. Tell me, then, whom could I have loved?"

Indeed, another aspect of Mugo's character that is only gradually revealed, and thus affects his actions beneath the surface for much of the novel, is his lack of any romantic life. Romantic interest is a key aspect of the characters of Gikonyo and Karanja, as both make moral or immoral decisions based on their love for Mumbi. Gikonyo even has a fairly transcendent experience in the first throes of their shared love, while hammering, as it happens: "Suddenly the wave of power broke into an ecstasy, an exultation. Peace settled in his heart. He felt a holy calm; he was in love with all the earth." This is the power not just of love but of religion, the power to inspire in the individual a perfectly compassionate relationship with not just a single other person but all the rest of the world.

As for Mugo, the reader can only gradually discern that such an experience of love/transcendence has eluded him for the first quarter century of his life. Unlike with the other main characters, the novel provides no scenes of youthful sentimental thoughts or exchanges in Mugo's life. He seems to have some level of romantic interest in Mumbi—though, again attesting to his goodness, it seems that he entirely excludes the idea of acting on his interest, as if because she is already married—and yet that interest is characterized in curiously loaded terms. When he visits her, looking rather for Gikonyo, "He became conscious of her well-formed body; her dark eyes, infinitely deep, swallowed him, unsettled him, and he feared her." Mumbi has "dark power" over Mugo, and the story of her marital transgression leaves him "weak with pain and longing." Only after Mugo and Mumbi's later dramatic confrontation is the reader furthermore made aware that Mugo "rarely went out" at nighttime; that, facing the idea of death, he can think of himself, "I have not even lived"; and that, finally, "he had never before considered women in relation to his man's body." This presumably excludes the possibility of any actual romantic experience. Thus, one can imagine how wholly sensitive Mugo would be to Mumbi's feminine presence.

What romance would most essentially offer Mugo, what Mugo really needs, it seems, is not mere physical satisfaction—evidently a strong and handsome man, if he wanted as much he might have sought someone out by now—but rather a compassionate connection. Even Mumbi finds herself on the brink of being unable to offer this to Mugo, as a friend: he distrusts her precisely because of the powerful femininity she is deliberately wielding, and it is only in the absence of a strictly compassionate connection that he can nearly kill her. But once her life is threatened and she forgets about trying to seduce him into speaking for Uhuru, she does speak with pure compassion: "What is it, Mugo? What is wrong?" One imagines that no loving family member or friend has yet seen fit to ask Mugo this question; and in the event, as the reader later learns, Mumbi's compassion opens

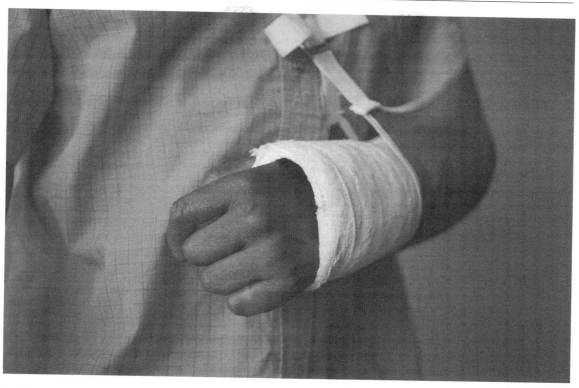

While recovering in the hospital, Gikonyo thinks about how to talk to Mumbi and begin to rebuild their marriage. (© *bikeriderlondon* / *Shutterstock.com*)

a floodgate of benevolent emotion—his murderous intent falls away like a too-heavy cloak, and he releases her. Beyond this immediate result, Mugo, rather than acting to preserve his own life now that his traitorous secret is out, is led to simply remain in the village in his hut, awaiting his fate.

Brought forth by elders, Mugo does end up speaking for Uhuru, and, remaining in an emotionally open state after unburdening himself to Mumbi, he publicly reveals the shameful truth, rather than attempting any self-serving deception. He does at last make an attempt, afterward, to flee to Nairobi. But that old woman—he had realized days earlier, in the first chapter, that "perhaps there was something fateful in his contact with this old woman"—incidentally disrupts his final self-serving mind-set when he is compelled by rain to stop at her hut. Inside, Mugo, unintentionally standing in for the ghost of Gitogo, escorts the old woman, her mind as pacified as it could ever be, into death. Actually, for a moment he thinks of throttling her, as he

had with his aunt; there is a window when he might well have begun acting out evil impulses. But when the old woman dies of her own accord, it is as if Mugo realizes that fate could not have found a more fitting end for the old woman's life—as if people's intertwined destinies must achieve collective closure. Deep down, Mugo surely knows that the end of Kihika's life, which he so regretfully brought about, is yet intertwined with his own. If fate has anything to say—and early on Mugo reveals himself to be allied with fate—the fitting end is not for Mugo to successfully flee to Nairobi, for the guilty party to get away.

Throughout the novel Mugo has shown himself to be as capable of visionary good as he is of cold-blooded evil, and in the novel's closing days he might have tilted either way. But thanks to the modicum of compassion extended him by a compassionate woman, not just fate, or any old devilish inclination, proves to direct his actions, but rather his heart and his conscience ultimately take control; and if the only way he can atone for his sin of betrayal and placate the hearts of his people is not to lead them but to sacrifice himself, to let himself be sacrificed in the name of Kihika, then he is capable of choosing that fate.

Source: Michael Allen Holmes, Critical Essay on *A Grain of Wheat*, in *Novels for Students*, Gale, Cengage Learning, 2015.

Peter Simatei

In the following excerpt, Simatei describes the reactions of his Kenyan students to A Grain of Wheat.

Ngũgĩ wa Thiong'o's texts constitute a staple in literature courses at universities in Kenya. One obvious reason is his pioneering status and intense engagement with Kenya's colonial and postcolonial histories. In two undergraduate courses that I teach—one on the African novel, the other on Kenyan fiction and history—his work is central to any understanding of how the African novel evolves into a complex literary genre through appropriation of the oral narrative traditions of Africa and the domestication of European novelistic traditions and culture. His work also offers a rich site for the study of the ever-changing political project of African literature. In our local contexts, it offers critical interventions in the persistent discourses of history, nationhood, citizenship, and cultural identity. Ngũgĩ is an overtly political writer, and for a background lecture I give my students an overview of his thematic concerns, explore the nationalist and socialist ideologies that frame the politics of his engagement with the histories of colonization and decolonization in Kenya, and discuss his radical ideas about the political functions of art. I then settle on *A Grain of Wheat* and *Matigari* for in-depth analysis.

My choice of these two novels is guided by their very differences and by the fact that each represents a turning point in Ngũgĩ's writing career. It is generally agreed that *A Grain of Wheat*, with its sophisticated narrative techniques associated with European literary models, confirmed his stature as a major writer, but it is also a transitional novel in the sense that Ngũgĩ would abandon its kind of complexity for the simple, folkloric form crystallized in *Matigari*. *Matigari*, although coming after *Devil on the Cross*, is Ngũgĩ's Gĩkũyũ-language novel that best blends African oral narrative techniques with elements of Western written traditions. My students, who in most cases have already

> THE NOVEL RESISTS ANY SIMPLISTIC CORRELATION OF VIOLENCE AND LIBERATION BY IRONIZING THE PROCESS OF DECOLONIZATION SO THAT THE POSTCOLONIAL MOMENT BECOMES AN INVERSION AND DENIAL OF THE VIOLENCE THAT USHERED IT IN."

encountered *The River Between* and *Weep Not, Child* in introductory courses, are able to see the complexity in theme and style of *Grain* and then the subtle simplicity of *Matigari*. I introduce *Grain* as the novel that best captures the ironies of decolonization in Kenya in the sense that while it indicts colonialism, it both celebrates and questions the triumph of the nationalist project. With a knowledge of Ngũgĩ's earlier novels, students can see the link *Grain* makes between the writer's past themes and his future concerns. Set four days before *uhuru*, its time structure is fluid, traveling to the colonial past and beyond to understand the anxieties haunting the present and their implications for the future. It is this intermediary status that makes *Grain* unique in Ngũgĩ's oeuvre.

Whenever I ask students to list striking stylistic or thematic features of this novel, they always point to Ngũgĩ's appropriation of Judeo-Christian texts, the theme of betrayal, and the multiple narrative voices. Therefore I begin analysis of the novel by first addressing the significance of the use of biblical texts in the novel. I consider, in general, African writers' appropriation of European texts and culture, where intertextual references become acts of transgression rather than an affirmation of whatever truths are expressed by such texts and cultures. Students begin to realize that *Grain* mimics the Judeo-Christian concept of salvation, but they initially have different explanations for this mimicry. One student thought that the use of the Bible showed Ngũgĩ's Christian faith, but she was perplexed when I called her attention to his disavowal of Christianity. Even assuming that he was deeply Christian when he wrote the novel, his use of Judeo-Christian texts has more to do with the possibilities for dissent offered by notions of biblical justice than with the author's faith. The class comes to understand that *Grain* mimics Christian acts of salvation in order to inaugurate its own narrative of national liberation as well as subvert the way colonial discourse reinscribes biblical texts in order to legitimate the colonial system.

The epigraph derived from the Gospel of Saint John, which yields the title of the novel, exploits the Christian concept of death and resurrection to show the inevitable sacrifices involved in any war of liberation and that selective deployment of the Old Testament enables Kihika to imagine the liberation of his people as a divine mission akin to Moses's liberation of the Jewish people from Egyptian bondage. The juxtaposition of these verses with other narratives of anticolonial struggle also translates episodes from the Judeo-Christian history of salvation into a discourse of liberation. The recasting of these verses in secular and political terms makes them assume the role of a metalanguage that envisions a new Kenya with nonviolent, Indian characteristics. In Kihika's oppositional theology, Mahatma Gandhi answered the call of Christ to "deny himself, and take up his cross." Gandhi's personal sacrifice leads not to the abstract kingdom of God where Christ wants to take his adherents but to the liberation of India. For Kihika, the kingdom of heaven can be attained only through messianic sacrifice:

> "Take up my cross, is what Christ told his people," Kihika resumed in a more light-hearted tone. "If any man will come after me, let him deny himself, and take up his cross, and follow me. For whosoever will save his life shall lose it: and whosoever will lose his life for my sake shall find it. Do you know why Gandhi succeeded? Because he made his people give up their fathers and mothers and serve their one Mother-India. With us, Kenya is our mother."

Kihika's radical rereading of Christ's death connects with Kihika's belief in violence as a legitimate means to end colonialism and establish a new society: "Had Christ's death a meaning for the Children of Israel? In Kenya we want deaths which will change things, that is to say we want true sacrifice." Colonial violence and its effects on the colonized is one of the subjects in *A Grain of Wheat* that we discuss. Students explore instances of colonial violence in the text as narrated by the victims and give their views on the legitimacy of violent response to oppression. I introduce Frantz Fanon's thesis that violence is a legitimate tool of liberation and suggest that

Ngũgĩ's representation of decolonization as a violent process may be influenced by it. In *The Wretched of the Earth*, decolonization was violent because it involved "quite simply the replacing of a certain 'species' of men by another 'species' of men.... [T]here is a total, complete, and absolute substitution." To what extent, I ask students, is Kihika guided by Fanon's assertion that colonialism "is violence in its natural state, and it will only yield when confronted with greater violence?" *Grain* interconnects with Fanon's thesis in many respects. Fanon's contention that anticolonial violence is a consequence of settler violence is affirmed by Kihika:

> We only hit back. You are struck on the left cheek. You turn the right cheek. One, two, three—sixty years. Then suddenly, it is always sudden, you say: I am not turning the other cheek any more.... [Y]ou strike back.... We must kill.

The question of redemptive violence turns out to be quite controversial in class. Most students feel that while Ngũgĩ has an obvious affinity to Fanon and seems convinced of the necessity of revolutionary violence, *Grain* does not celebrate or exalt it. The novel resists any simplistic correlation of violence and liberation by ironizing the process of decolonization so that the postcolonial moment becomes an inversion and denial of the violence that ushered it in. I discuss irony in the novel in general and how it enables Ngũgĩ to gesture toward his future concerns such as the betrayal of the ideals of independence. The class agrees that one of the greatest ironies in the novel is Mugo's false heroism, the role Mugo plays in the unfolding drama of reversed expectations that characterizes independence celebrations....

Source: Peter Simatei, "Texts and Contexts: Teaching *A Grain of Wheat* and *Matigari* in Kenya," in *Approaches to Teaching the Works of Ngugi wa Thiong'o*, edited by Oliver Lovesey, Modern Language Association of America, 2012, pp. 206–208.

Richard J. Lane

In the following excerpt, Lane characterizes A Grain of Wheat *as the definitive novel about the Kenyan struggle for independence.*

As a study in arrested decolonization, Ngũgĩ wa Thiong'o's novel *A Grain of Wheat* (1967) arguably remains unsurpassed; through complex and sensitive character development, and a narratology that functions to build a form of community writing, the novel explores the eruption of independence ('Uhuru') in Kenya, gained on 12 December 1963. The struggle for independence is revealed in the novel to be complex and contradictory, liberating and imprisoning; the central protagonist, Mugo, appears to be a hero, but in reality is a traitor, and Mugo's narrative is also symbolic of the ways in which decolonization can be arrested or even transformed into neo-colonialism. Mugo's narrative has intertextual links with Joseph Conrad's *Under Western Eyes*, but critics have long since shown how Ngũgĩ develops a unique, powerfully tragic and original protagonist in the *character* of Mugo, partly because of the ways in which he is inextricably linked with the emergence of a new nation and a new community. Kofi Owusu notes that Ngũgĩ 'employs a narrative strategy that allows his characters to pick up and pass on the narrative thread in a way that is obviously intended to suggest that the narrative is as much theirs as it is the author's.' The image of the 'thread' is derived from early on in the novel: after one of the community leaders, Warui has spoken, there is a silence: 'Each person seemed engrossed in himself as if turning over the words in his mind. The woman cleared her throat, an indication that she was about to take up the thread from Warui.' The implication here is that none of the characters within the novel should be considered entirely in isolation; they are implicated in, and contribute to, the independence of their nation, and, as such, are deeply interrelated.

A Grain of Wheat opens with Mugo lying on his back, dreaming and feeling nervous. He dreams of a drop of water that is suspended above him, slowly gathering in size, and picking up soot from the roof as it draws towards him. Mugo wants to close his eyes or move out of the way, but he can do neither: 'He tried to move his head: it was firmly chained to the bed-frame.' His own body refuses to obey his will to escape the drop of water, but then the power of his despair enables him to wake up. This powerful existential opening to the novel (*existential* because it is the power of despair that *moves* Mugo) creates a finely balanced tension: between immobility and mobility; imprisonment and freedom; the world of dreams and fantasies and the waking world of reality; and finally between a nihilist and a an affirmative will-power. Later on in the novel, the reader learns the long-suspected truth: that Mugo actually betrayed a leading revolutionary called Kihika,

> EAST AFRICAN LITERATURE APPEARED TO HAVE FINALLY COME INTO ITS OWN WITH THIS NOVEL WHICH CAPPED NGŨGĨ'S BURGEONING CAREER."

who had visited Mugo after assassinating the District Officer, a man called Thomas Robson, or Tom the Terror. The arrival of Kihika to Mugo's hut, and the latter's response, contrasts with Mugo's earlier fantasies that he would somehow become a Messiah-like figure:

> [Mugo was] . . . revelling in the dreams he loved, dreams which often transported him from the present to the future. He had come to see in them a private message, a prophecy. Had he not already escaped, unscathed, the early operations of the Emergency? Kenya had been in a state of Emergency since 1952. Some people had been taken to detention camps; others had run away to the forest: but this was a drama in a world not his own. He kept alone, feeling a day would come when horns, drums and trumpets would beat together to announce his entrance into the new world.

The problems with Mugo's fantasies reflect neatly the external misunderstandings concerning Kenyan community. To explain further, on closer reflection, Mugo's Messiah fantasies reveal a detachment from society, with his belief that the bad things happening in society are taking place in a world separate from his. The central phrase here is that he 'kept alone' in an adjacent sphere of activity: tending to his crops, going through the motions of a model citizen, but fundamentally isolated. In temporal terms, Mugo has rejected the time of the crisis that society is experiencing (i.e., the crisis of colonialism and its violent rejection, and the concomitant increase in repressive counter-measures) in favour of the time of prophecy, where he merely waits for 'destiny.' Egocentrically, the destiny for which he awaits is his entry back into society, but this time as some kind of indeterminate saviour announced by 'horns, drums and trumpets.' How does this make Mugo's vision akin to external misunderstandings? Kofi Owusu argues that close analysis of point of view and narrative strategy can explain such a mechanism where the novel, 'in its entirety, gives a forceful impression of an implied "they" against whom "we" react.' Owusu gives some powerful examples: '"They" say, for example, that "another Mau Mau terrorist had been shot dead," when "you" and "I"—in effect, "we"—know that the person "murdered," Gitogo, is innocent. What "they" call "detention camps" are what "we" see as "concentration camps."' In other words, the external perspective is that of the colonists, attempting to denigrate the quest for independence and freedom. The community or social perspective of the novel— the 'we'—reveals not some idealized, perfected indigenous society, but one that is fundamentally human, with all of the concomitant contradictions and problems, yet still moving unstoppably towards transforming the ideals of independence and freedom into everyday realities. From Mugo's isolated perspective, the process whereby those ideals are transformed is messy, troubling and problematic. He wants to rely on some undefined transcendent force, some external agency that will eventually put everything right. But such a reliance is also a denial of the injustices which the community suffers daily. As such, Ngũgĩ posits the revolutionary over the Messianic; given that British colonialism and missionary activity were bedfellows, this distinction is crucial for the novel, even though biblical text permeates the entire narrative. Owusu regards the narrative strategies that reveal the differences and shared values of isolation and colonialism as also being important for questions concerning authorial identification:

> These observations, almost inevitably, raise some of those questions which have bedevilled the criticism of African literature for decades: for whom does the African writer write? On whose authority is a story told? Is it on the authority of the author as an individual artist or the author who, as spokesperson, gives expression to a communal, collective consciousness?
>
> The author of *A Grain of Wheat* gives the impression that he is writing on behalf of, and communicating with, his people. (His decision, after publication of his fourth novel in English, to write in his native Gikuyu is in consonance with this stance.)

The question remains: how does Ngũgĩ write through and for community?

How does he allow the narrative 'thread' to be taken up?

. . . Kenneth Harrow asserts that with the publication of Ngũgĩ's *A Grain of Wheat*, 'the African viewpoint on the struggle for independence in Kenya was given its fullest, most complex, and most moving expression. East African literature appeared to have finally come into its own with this novel which capped Ngũgĩ's burgeoning career.' Critics have long debated the role of intertextuality and 'influence' upon postcolonial writing through Ngũgĩ's novel: for example, countering the arguments for or against the influence of Conrad's *Under Western Eyes* on *A Grain of Wheat*, Byron Caminero-Santangelo suggests that 'part of the "originality" of Ngũgĩ's novel lies in his critical appropriation of Conrad's text into an evolving Kenyan culture.' In other words, Ngũgĩ's novel is counter-discursive, radically reworking a canonical author from a Kenyan perspective. Other novels and key thinkers are intertextually examined by *A Grain of Wheat*; perhaps the most noted of these thinkers is Franz Fanon. But the situation concerning Ngũgĩ's relationship with Fanon's work is complex, as Simon Gikandi suggests:

> It is hard to say whether Ngũgĩ started writing *A Grain of Wheat* after encountering Fanon's book, or whether he had already started working on it when he read *The Wretched of the Earth*. Nevertheless, the genealogy of the novel raises questions that are germane to its interpretation: does the (Marxist) aesthetic ideology of the novel mark a radical break with Ngũgĩ's previous narrative and cultural practices? Does this novel initiate the socialist ideology and aesthetic that culminated in later works such as *Petals of Blood* and *Devil on the Cross?* Or is it a continuation of the cultural nationalist project . . . that reaches its apotheosis in the troubled temporality of decolonization?

The complexities of Ngũgĩ's writing demand that there 'are no categorical answers to these questions.' For Gikandi, this is also the case because of Ngũgĩ's 'conflicting intentions': 'The novel itself is caught between its author's desire to trace the history and consequences of cultural nationalism—and thus provide a paradigm for representing decolonization—and the imperative to proffer a cultural grammar for understanding the new postcolonial state.' Such a new 'cultural grammar' is at times more postmodern than modern (for example, the multiple perspectives of the novel, and the play of competing signifiers concerning Independence/arrested decolonization) and this aspect of Ngũgĩ's writing has more recently intrigued scholars. Drawing upon the work of Henry A. Giroux, Kathy Kessler, for example, argues that '[i]n redefining concepts of difference and otherness, a task which . . . Ngugi wa Thiong'o participates in, we "step beyond the modernist celebration of the unified self, totalizing notions of history and universalistic models of reason".' Kessler adds that even with his more Marxist stance, ' . . . Ngugi's later fiction contributes to a shift away from the "Eurocentric notion of society that subordinates the discourse of ethics and politics to . . . an unproblematic acceptance of European culture as the basis of civilization, and a notion of the individual subject as a unified, rational self which is the source of all cultural and social meaning".' The intersection here of the postcolonial and the postmodern may be a key reason as to why Ngũgĩ's writing continues to have relevance and interest for current-day readers.

Source: Richard J. Lane, "National Consciousness: Ngugi wa Thiong'o's *A Grain of Wheat*," in *The Postcolonial Novel*, Polity, 2006, pp. 47–49, 57–58.

SOURCES

Calder, Angus, "Fresh and Whole Vision," in *New Statesman*, Vol. 84, No. 2170, October 20, 1972, p. 562.

Gatheru, R. Mugo, *Kenya: From Colonization to Independence, 1888–1970*, McFarland, 2005, pp. 16–23, 48–56, 138–47.

Hayward, Helen, "A New Dispossession," in *Times Literary Supplement*, No. 5163, March 15, 2002, p. 25.

Jabbi, Bu-Buakei, "The Structure of Symbolism in *A Grain of Wheat*," in *Critical Essays on Ngũgĩ wa Thiong'o*, edited by Peter Nazareth, Twayne Publishers, 2000, pp. 142–68.

"Kenya Profile," BBC News website, http://www.bbc.com/news/world-africa-18503598 (accessed July 27, 2014).

Lovesey, Oliver, *Ngũgĩ wa Thiong'o*, Twayne's World Authors Series No. 890, Twayne Publishers, 2000, pp. 1–22, 39–45.

Maughan-Brown, David, "Ngugi wa Thiong'o," in *Dictionary of Literary Biography*, Vol. 125, *Twentieth-Century Caribbean and Black African Writers, Second Series*, edited by Bernth Lindfors and Reinhard Sander, Gale Research, 1993, pp. 145–69.

Narang, Harish, "Prospero and the Land of Calibans: *A Grain of Wheat*," in *Critical Essays on Ngũgĩ wa Thiong'o*,

edited by Peter Nazareth, Twayne Publishers, 2000, pp. 123–43.

Nazareth, Peter, ed., "Introduction: Saint Ngũgĩ," in *Critical Essays on Ngũgĩ wa Thiong'o*, edited by Peter Nazareth, Twayne Publishers, 2000, pp. 1–16.

Ngũgĩ wa Thiong'o, *A Grain of Wheat*, African Writers Series No. 36, Heinemann, 1986.

—————, *Something Torn and New: An African Renaissance*, Basic Civitas Books, 2009, p. ix.

"Ngugi wa Thiong'o: A Profile of a Literary and Social Activist," Ngũgĩ wa Thiong'o website, http://www.ngugiwathiongo.com/bio/bio-home.htm (accessed July 27, 2014).

Ogude, James, "Ngugi's Portrayal of the Community, Heroes, and the Oppressed," in *Ngugi's Novels and African History: Narrating the Nation*, Pluto Press, 1999, pp. 126–52.

Ravenscroft, Arthur, "Ngugi wa Thiong'o: Overview," in *Contemporary Novelists*, 6th ed., edited by Susan Windisch Brown, St. James Press, 1996.

Sharma, Govind Narain, "Ngugi's Christian Vision: Theme and Patter in *A Grain of Wheat*," in *African Literature Today*, Vol. 10, *Retrospect & Prospect*, edited by Eldred Durosimi Jones, Heinemann, 1979, pp. 167–76.

"Torture Diary (1986)," in *Ngugi wa Thiong'o: The Making of a Rebel; A Source Book in Kenyan Literature and Resistance*, edited by Carol Sicherman, Hans Zell Publishers, pp. 424–28.

FURTHER READING

Bennett, Huw, *Fighting the Mau Mau: The British Army and Counter-Insurgency in the Kenya Emergency*, Cambridge University Press, 2013.

> This very recent history, which takes advantage of manifold sources made available through document discoveries and the Freedom of Information Act, seeks to clarify once and for all the extent to which the British shamed themselves through their unjust and inhumane treatment of Kenyans during Mau Mau.

Hedva, Beth, *Betrayal, Trust and Forgiveness: A Guide to Emotional Healing and Self-Renewal*, 3rd ed., Wynword Press, 2013.

> This book is highly respected for its insight into the psychological impact of betrayal, whatever form it may take, and how to cope with it.

Ngũgĩ wa Thiong'o, *Dreams in a Time of War: A Childhood Memoir*, Knopf Doubleday, 2010.

> Ngũgĩ's first autobiographical volume treats his earliest life, leading up to Mau Mau and the state of emergency declared just when he reached his teens.

———, *In the House of the Interpreter: A Memoir*, Pantheon Books, 2012.

> This second autobiography focuses on Ngũgĩ's formative late adolescent years, between 1955 and 1959, during the latter half of Mau Mau and the emergency period.

Odinga, Oginga, *Not Yet Uhuru: The Autobiography of Oginga Odinga*, Heinemann, 1967.

> Written and published several years into Kenya's independence, Odinga's memoir explores his role in the Kenyan republic's earliest political endeavors and his contention that the government was failing to meet the needs of the masses.

SUGGESTED SEARCH TERMS

Ngugi wa Thiong'o AND A Grain of Wheat

Ngugi AND Mau Mau

Ngugi AND socialism OR communism

Ngugi AND Conrad OR Lamming OR Achebe

Kenyan literature

African literature AND independence

Ngugi AND interviews

Ngugi AND postcolonial theory

Ngugi AND exile

Heart of Aztlan

RUDOLFO A. ANAYA

1976

Heart of Aztlan is a novel by Rudolfo A. Anaya, published in 1976. Set in a Mexican American neighborhood in Albuquerque, New Mexico, in the mid- or late 1950s, it tells the story of Clemente Chávez and his family, who move to the city from the small town of Guadalupe, New Mexico. The entire novel takes place within a period of no more than six months or so. The Chávez family must adapt to life in a big city, which is very different from what they were used to. Jobs are scarce, and soon a serious labor dispute erupts at the railroad where many of the men work. Chávez's two teen-age sons, Jason and Benjie, respond to their environment in very different ways. Their father, after going through a period of turmoil, finally emerges as the leader of his people in the ongoing labor dispute. Characteristically for Anaya, the novel also draws on myths and legends about the Aztlan land and people. Aztlan is considered to the ancient home of the Aztec people before they migrated south to present-day central Mexico. In the novel, Aztlan is presented as representing the soul of the Mexican Americans who otherwise find themselves losing their traditions in an alien Anglo culture that exploits them.

AUTHOR BIOGRAPHY

Novelist, short-story writer, poet, and essayist Rudolfo Anaya was born to Martin and Rafaelita Mares Anaya on October 30, 1937, in Pastura, a

Rudolfo Anaya (© *Steve Snowden | Getty Images Entertainment |*
Getty Images)

1970s: *Heart of Aztlan* (1976) and *Tortuga* (1979). The latter won the Before Columbus American Book Award from the Before Columbus Foundation in 1980. The novella *The Legend of La Llorona* was published in 1984. *Lord of the Dawn: The Legend of Quetzalcóatl*, about the god worshiped in Mexico before the conquest, followed in 1987. Anaya also published a collection of short stories, *The Silence of the Llano*, in 1982, and an epic poem, *The Adventures of Juan Chicaspatas*, in 1985. Anaya's second-short story collection, *The Man Who Could Fly and Other Stories*, was published in 2006.

Anaya's fourth novel, *Albuquerque* (1992), received the PEN Center USA West Award the following year, which was also the year Anaya retired from teaching. The novels *Zia Summer* and *Rio Grande Fall* followed in 1995 and 1996, respectively, and *Jalamanta: A Message from the Desert*, in 1996. As of 2014, Anaya's most recent work was the novella *The Old Man's Love Story* (2013). Anaya has also written ten children's books; a travel journal; six plays, including *Matachines* (1992); and several nonfiction essays, thirteen of which appeared in *The Anaya Reader* in 1995.

Anaya has received many awards and fellowships. These include the New Mexico Governor's Public Service Award (1978 and 1980), the New Mexico Governor's Award for Excellence and Achievement in Literature (1980), and the President's National Salute to American Poets and Writers (1980). In 2011, Anaya received the Robert Kirsch Award, which is presented to a living author with a connection to the American West who has made a substantial contribution to American literature. Anaya married Patricia Lawless in 1966, and as of 2014, the couple resides in Albuquerque.

village in eastern New Mexico. The family moved to Santa Rosa soon after Anaya's birth. Anaya was the youngest of four brothers, and he had six sisters. (Three of these siblings were from his parents' previous marriages.) The family moved again in 1952 to Albuquerque, New Mexico, where Anaya attended a public school, graduating in 1956. He attended Browning Business School for two years and then enrolled in the University of New Mexico, from which he received a bachelor of arts degree in 1963. He then taught English for five years in Albuquerque's public schools while continuing to study. He received a master's degree in English from the University of New Mexico in 1968 and a master's degree in guidance and counseling from the same university in 1972, after which he was appointed director of counseling at the university.

Anaya's first novel, *Bless Me, Ultima*, a coming-of-age story that reflected his Mexican American heritage, was published in 1972. It received the Premio Quinto Sol National Chicano Literature Award and established Anaya's literary reputation. In 1974, he began teaching in the Department of English at the University of New Mexico. Two more novels followed in the

PLOT SUMMARY

Chapter 1

Because of hard economic times, Clemente Chávez, a Mexican American, or Chicano, is forced to sell his ranch in the small town of Guadalupe, New Mexico, and move his family west to Albuquerque, where his eldest son Roberto lives. He is unhappy at having to the land he has known for so long, but his wife, Adelita, convinces him it will be good for the children, who will have more opportunities in the big city.

Clemente and Adelita have two younger sons, Jason and Benjie, and two daughters, Juanita and Ana, all of whom are between the ages of fourteen and eighteen. Arriving in Albuquerque, in the Chicano part of town known as Barelas, they meet Roberto and his wife Rita. They move into the house they are to rent, and in the evening go to the house of Crispín, an old blind man who plays spellbinding melodies on his blue guitar. The men talk about an old woman who lives in the *barrio* (neighborhood) and who possesses a magic rock that sings and knows the secrets of a man's heart. Some think the rock is evil. Clemente is wary of life in the new city, but his sons and daughters are ready to enjoy themselves.

Chapter 2

Roberto, who works for the railroad, takes Clemente to the railroad depot so that he can find a job. A worker named Sánchez is killed there in an accident involving a crane. Jason, who has brought lunch for his father, witnesses the accident. Some of the workers blame the accident on the railroad management, which has laid off a number of workers, and also on their trade union, which fails to protect them. Upset, Jason runs to visit Crispín, who plays a lament on his guitar. Back home that evening, the family is pleased that Clemente has a job at the railroad but sad that it was available only because of Sánchez's death. Jobs are scarce.

Chapter 3

At the railroad, a wildcat strike not supported by the union has resulted in some workers being fired. Clemente tries to stay out of political issues such as this. He is distressed, however, at how his children are becoming independent and no longer look to him for guidance. At supper, he quarrels with his older daughter, Juanita. That night, there is a wedding dance in the community, and the Chávez family attends. Outside, however, there is trouble. Benjie has been selling marijuana on behalf of a gang led by Frankie, but when they come to collect the money, Benjie cannot pay them. Frankie starts to beat Benjie up, but Jason intervenes, getting the better of both Frankie and his fellow gang member Flaco. Jason's friends celebrate his victory, but Clemente is displeased with Benjie for getting involved with marijuana. He takes him to a shed at the back of the house and beats him with a belt.

Chapter 4

Jason talks with his friends Chelo, Pato, Pete, Dickie, and Willie outside on a Saturday afternoon in late summer. Except for Chelo, who prefers to go to confession at church, they agree to go to the town brothel that evening. Pato buys some wine, even though he is underage, and Willie is sent to the drugstore to buy condoms. They go to the brothel, prove their manhood with the women there, and return home with a feeling of emptiness.

Chapter 5

Pato gets himself and his friends invited to a party at the home of Cindy, an attractive blonde girl from a wealthy family. Cindy has seen Jason and likes him. At the party, Cindy and Jason dance together, although Jason is more interested in another girl, Cristina, the daughter of Sánchez, the worker who was killed. Also at the party is Sapo, a violent friend of Frankie and Flaco who knows what happened between his friends and Jason. He and Jason have a tense encounter.

Chapter 6

Still in late summer, Sapo, Frankie, and Flaco confront Jason and Willie in the park. Sapo is armed with a zip gun (an improvised weapon made by adapting existing materials). After a brief fight in which Jason kicks the gun out of Sapo's hand, Jason and Willie run. They reach Willie's house, and Jason meets Henry, Willie's severely developmentally disabled brother, and Rufus, Willie's father.

Chapter 7

Ana has dropped out of high school and taken a job as a waitress. Her sister, Juanita, works as a clerk at a cosmetics store. They like work and the freedom the money brings. They are looking forward to going to a dance that evening, but after they have finished supper Clemente arrives home drunk and in a bad mood. He is angry that he has to eat alone and he refuses to allow the girls to go to the dance. He accuses his wife of encouraging the children not to obey their father. He is frustrated because he feels he has lost control of his own family. The girls stand up to him, and later Adelita tells them that Clemente has been fired from his job because he challenged Kirk, the corrupt union leader.

Chapter 8

There has been another unofficial strike at the railroad and more men have been fired. There is a struggle between the union and the breakaway group led by Lalo. At a meeting in a bar, Lalo and the workers discuss what they can do to improve their position. Manuel says they must choose a leader, but the men do not wholly trust Lalo, whose rhetoric is too violent for them. Crispín plays his guitar and sings of the legends of the land of Aztlan and of the desire of those ancient people for freedom. Clemente is fascinated. He wonders where Aztlan was, and even whether he is the destined leader of his people. He goes to see La India, the old woman who possesses the magical rock that can foretell the future. When he touches the rock he gets a painful jolt, as if fire is exploding in his body. The next day, he abandons all thoughts of becoming a leader.

Chapter 9

At the state fair, a fight breaks out between rival gangs, pitting the Chicano boys from the barrios against a gang of Anglo kids from the large ranches on the river valley. During the fight, Jason gets slashed across his cheek, but Chelo comes to his rescue.

Chapter 10

In the fall, the newborn son of Roberto and his wife is returned home after being baptized, and the neighbors gather to celebrate. Roberto says his dream is that his son should have a good education and become a leader among his people and help them achieve things. Some of the men fear, however, that those who are educated will leave the community and seek their fortunes elsewhere. They say the only way to help the people is to return to the traditional ways. That night the baby becomes ill, but it is too late for the doctor to come. Manuel's wife Dorotea applies some traditional remedies to the baby, who soon recovers.

Chapter 11

Under a full moon in November, Willie's brother Henry escapes from the house. Jason and Chelo are unable to catch him. Henry dances under the moon and then leaps into the river, trying to reach the moon's reflection on the water. The current sweeps him away, and he drowns.

Chapter 12

Henry's body is recovered from the river, and his father, Rufus, carries the casket home from the mortuary on his back. Neighbors arrive, bringing food. A wake is held all night. An old man named Lázaro comes and sings the old prayers for the dead.

Chapter 13

It is a harsh winter. Half the men of Barelas are out of work. Clemente is in despair, but Crispín helps him, and Clemente is inspired to search for the heart of the ancient land of Aztlan. Crispín tells him all the legends that relate to Aztlan and its people. Clemente wants to find the source of their strength. Accompanied by Crispín, he goes once more to La India, the old witch. Crispín gives Clemente some pins and needles to put on the magic rock before he touches it. When he does, he is transported on a visionary journey in which he feels he becomes one with the ancient land of Aztlan and its people.

Chapter 14

After his overwhelming experience, in which he thinks he climbed a mountain and saw visions, Clemente is sick for some weeks. He keeps saying he has found a way to unite his people. He goes to see Father Cayo at the church, convinced that the priest will be aware of the people's suffering and agree to help the striking workers. However, the priest says he respects the existing order of things; he is concerned with the salvation of souls and will not take part in political revolution. At a meeting that night, it becomes known that men are being blacklisted and cannot find jobs anywhere. Lalo calls for action. Clemente calls for a new movement that would be based on principles of universal brotherhood. He makes a reference to rekindling the fire in the soul, but the men misinterpret the word *fire* and think it is a call to violent action. A riot ensues in which the angry men burn down railroad property. The police arrive and open fire. Several of the workers are killed or wounded.

Chapter 15

The police seek Clemente, but he evades them. He visits Mannie, a rich and powerful Chicano who owns a supermarket and has political connections. Clemente appeals to him for support but Mannie has no interest in helping the people. He is interested only in advancing his own business interests.

Chapter 16

Jason and his friends enter a café, where they listen to the men talking about the strike and the lack of employment. Clemente has been arrested but is free on bail. One man says they need an educated man as a leader, while another says they should organize a general strike. Jessie speaks about his disturbing experiences in the Korean War, in which he was awarded a Silver Star for his service. The war did no one any good, he says, because now there are no jobs.

Chapter 17

It is the Christmas season. Willie tells Pato and his friends that the city businessmen tried to bribe Clemente to leave town, but Clemente refused. He touched the bag of money and it went up in flames. In the church, Jason helps Cristina put up decorations, but he is denounced by Mannie's wife, a gossip who says Jason is responsible for getting Cindy pregnant. Cristina's mother believes the malicious story and tells Jason he must never see Cristina again. Father Cayo shouts at Jason that he is damned and tells him to leave the church. Jason, who has been protesting his innocence, leaves the church with Chelo.

Chapter 18

Jason and Cristina miss each other. Sapo returns from reformatory school and is seeking revenge on Jason. He tells Cristina that he will leave him alone if she will go to the New Year's eve dance with him. He also tells her that is was Benjie, not Jason, who got Cindy pregnant.

Chapter 19

One the last day of December, Willie signs up to join the army. Jason's mother sends him to Mannie's store to buy some meat. Mannie insults him and his father, deriding Clemente's attempt to give his people hope. Jason wants to answer him but cannot find any words. On the way home, in frustration he tosses the meat to the dogs. He tells his mother the store was closed.

Chapter 20

The workers' movement in the barrio is growing as more men join the strike. Jason, Chelo, Pato, Pete, and Dickie go to the dance. Jason sees Sapo there with Cristina; Jason confronts him and sends him sprawling. A general fight breaks out. Sapo leaves the dance with Cristina and drives off. Jason and Chelo follow, searching

for him. At a café, they find Frankie, who has just been shot by Sapo, his former friend. Sapo is after Benjie, Frankie says. Jason and Chelo eventually find Sapo near the city water tank. Cristina rushes to Jason, telling him that Sapo has forced Benjie to climb the steel ladder of the water tank. Challenged by Jason, Sapo shoots at Benjie, who is hit in the hand and falls from the tower. He is alive but paralyzed.

Chapter 21

The men of the barrio gather in Manuel's yard. He tells them what happened the previous night. He says that Frankie will live. Also, after Benjie's accident, Clemente took a sledgehammer and caused as much damage at the railroad as he could. Then he hammered at the water tank until the sledgehammer splintered. The story spreads around town. Lalo calls for a violent uprising, but the men regard Clemente as their leader, not Lalo. Clemente goes outside, mingles with the people, and says that injustice and oppression must end that night. He rejects violence, saying that love is stronger. He and his wife lead a torchlight procession down the street, while Crispín plays a tune of liberation on his guitar.

CHARACTERS

Father Cayo

Father Cayo is the old Roman Catholic priest in the barrio. He refuses to help the striking workers and calls them troublemakers. He prefers things to remain as they are, arguing that radical protest will just make everything worse for all the people in the barrio. Later, when Clemente approaches him directly for help in unifying the workers, he refuses. He also supports the attempt to buy Clemente off and get him to leave town.

Adelita Chávez

Adelita Chávez is Clemente's wife. She is devoted to her husband and is used to making the best of every situation. She loves to have her family around her. She nurses Clemente when he is sick and has the courage to accompany him at the head of the torchlight procession at the end.

Ana Chávez

Ana Chávez is the younger of the two daughters of Clemente and Adelita. She drops out of high school and gets a job as a waitress. She asserts her independence, starting to identify more with the subculture of the barrio.

Benjie Chávez

Benjie Chávez, a son of Clemente and Adelita, is one year younger than his brother Jason. Despite his father's advice to stay out of bad company, he soon gets involved with a gang and sells marijuana for them. His father strongly disapproves when he finds out, and he beats Benjie. Later, after Sapo forces Benjie to climb the water tank, he is paralyzed after he falls.

Clemente Chávez

Clemente Chávez is very reluctant to leave the small town where he and his family have lived for many years. He feels connected to the land there and fears what a move to the city may bring, but he is forced by economic necessity to make the move. Initially he does not adjust well. With the help of his son Roberto, he gets a job at the railroad but he loses it after a dispute with Kirk, the union leader. After that, Clemente's life seems to disintegrate for a while. He hates the fact that his children are becoming more independent and no longer do what he tells them. At one point he even strikes Juanita during an argument. He also drinks too much. However, when he hears Crispín tell of the legends of the Aztlan people, he is fascinated. He has never heard this before. Although he has never been interested in politics, he wonders whether he may be the one who is to lead his people toward a better future. Twice he visits an old woman, La India, who possesses a magic rock that can give visions and predict the future. On his second visit, he touches the rock and is taken on a visionary journey that inspires him to take on a leadership role in the Chicano community, especially among the striking workers. The men respect him and decide to follow his lead as he calls for a spirit of love and brotherhood rather than the violent course advocated by Lalo.

Jason Chávez

Jason Chávez is quiet, strong, and thoughtful, unlike his more impulsive younger brother, Benjie. He thinks seriously about life and what he expects to get from it. Benjie thinks Jason is moody and that his moods are like those of a poet. When Jason arrives in Albuquerque, he quickly makes friends with a group of boisterous but good-natured boys. He stands up to the bully Sapo and starts to date Cristina, even though the attractive Cindy hopes he will take up with her. Going with Cristina gives him a feeling of peace and calm. He adjusts well to the change of environment from small town to big city.

Juanita Chávez

Juanita Chávez is the older of the two Chávez sisters. She gets a job in a cosmetic store and likes having the independence to live her own life. She stands up to her angry father when he tries to exert control over her. She points out that she has a job and brings in money, and she wants to be allowed to come and go as she pleases.

Rita Chávez

Rita Chávez is Roberto's wife. She gives birth to a baby boy during the course of the novel.

Roberto Chávez

Roberto Chávez is Clemente's oldest son. He has lived for some time in Albuquerque before the rest of his family arrives. He works for the railroad. After he loses his job, he helps Clemente to organize the workers into a tight group. He believes in the power of education to create a new generation of leaders.

Chelo

Chelo is one of Jason's friends, possibly his best friend. He goes to Jason's aid after he is injured in the gang fight with the stompers and on several other occasions too.

Cindy

Cindy is an attractive blonde girl from a wealthy family. She is a cheerleader. She takes a fancy to Jason, but Jason prefers Cristina. Later, Cindy gets pregnant, and apparently the father is Benjie.

Conio

Conio is the owner of a café that bears his name and is a local meeting place for the Chicano community.

Crispín

Crispín is an old blind man in the barrio who is known for playing his blue guitar and for telling of the old legends of the Aztlan people. He encourages Clemente in his spiritual quest.

Dickie

Dickie is a member of Jason's group of friends. He plays his part in their boisterous pursuit of fun in the barrio.

Dorotea

Dorotea is Manuel's wife. When Roberto and Rita's baby gets sick at the celebration that follows the baptism, Dorotea says that someone has put the evil eye on him, but she cures the baby by using some traditional folk medicine.

Flaco

Flaco is a thin boy who hangs out with Freddie and Sapo, part of the gang that Benjie gets loosely attached to when he sells marijuana for them.

Frankie

Frankie is a boy in Sapo's gang. He is strong and aggressive, but after he starts to beat Benjie up for not handing over money from drug sales, Jason gets the better of him. Frankie eventually falls out with Sapo and is shot by his former friend, but he survives.

Henry

Henry is the son of Rufus and brother of Willie. He is severely developmentally disabled, but he is kept chained up at home rather than being institutionalized. The family tried putting him in an institution in Las Vegas, Nevada, but Henry became very sad there and refused to eat. He is playful and harmless, but he is fascinated by the moon, and one night he escapes and is drowned in the river while trying to reach the moon's reflection.

La India

La India, sometimes referred to as a witch, is an old, shriveled, hunchbacked woman who lives in a mud hut near the canal and keeps some mangy dogs. She possesses a magic rock, sometimes called a black rock or a singing rock, that can foretell the future. Clemente goes to visit her so he can touch the rock.

Jessie

Jessie is a former US Marine who fought in the Korean War. He suffers from posttraumatic stress disorder. At Conio's café, he tells the men about his distressing war experiences.

Kirk

Kirk is a corrupt union leader who does not represent the best interests of the workers.

Lalo

Lalo is one of the spokesman for the striking workers. He is fired from his job and thinks the workers should be more aggressive in fighting for their rights. He is willing to advocate violence in pursuit of their goals. However, the men do not entirely trust him, and eventually they reject his violent rhetoric and follow Clemente instead.

Lázaro

Lázaro is an old man who attends the wake for Henry after the boy drowns. He sings the traditional prayers for the dead.

Mannie

Mannie, also known as *el Super*, owns the only supermarket in the barrio. He is rich and drives a Cadillac, and he is also well connected politically. He helps others only if he can profit from it himself, so if he helps a man find a job, he demands some payment. When Clemente appeals to him to help his people, Mannie refuses, making it clear that he has a low opinion of the people in the barrio and will risk nothing to help them.

Mannie's wife

Mannie's wife is a gossip who spreads the rumor that Jason is the one who got Cindy pregnant.

Manuel

Manuel is a woodcutter in the barrio and a neighbor of the Chávez family. He is already a friend of Roberto and Rita, and he helps the newcomers to move in.

Pato

Pato is a member of Jason's group of friends. He buys a flashy 1948 Ford and claims that, as a result, he has the pick of the girls at the dance.

Pete

Pete is a member of Jason's small group of friends.

Primo

Primo is a man from the barrio who makes friends with Clemente. Like Clemente, he drinks too much, and he may have cancer.

Rufus

Rufus is the father of Willie and Henry. He is not liked in the barrio as he has a reputation for being a dog killer and for feeding his family dog meat. This belief, though, may be untrue. He has been forced into isolation partly because he insists on keeping Henry at home rather than institutionalizing him. Willie says his father is an honest man and a hard worker.

Sánchez

Sánchez is a railroad worker who is killed in an accident while on the job.

Cristina Sánchez

Cristina Sánchez is Sánchez's daughter. Jason likes her and they begin to date. She rejects him when she falsely believes that he got Cindy pregnant. When the truth comes out, she and Jason are reconciled.

Sapo

Sapo is the leader of a small gang that sells drugs in the barrio. When he is high on drugs, he is dangerous to be around. After Jason gets the better of him in defense of Benjie, Sapo wants his revenge. He is sent to a reformatory but comes back and starts taking heroin again. He has a falling out with his old friends Flaco and Frankie, and even shoots Frankie. He also pursues Benjie and forces him to climb the water tank.

Willie

Willie is the son of Rufus and brother of Henry. He is also a friend of Jason. In school, Willie is in a special education program, but he is no less intelligent than his friends. At the end of the year, he joins the army.

THEMES

Political Protest

The novel paints a picture of Barelas, a Chicano neighborhood in Albuquerque, as a poor community where unemployment is high and opportunities are few. This becomes apparent in the very first evening that the Chávez family arrives in Barelas. At a gathering at Crispín's house, an unnamed young man comments on the kind of lives people lead in the barrio: "We're in the same pinch all the time, just holding our noses above debts so we won't drown, hoping things at the shops don't get worse." The main employer appears to be the railroad company, but it is a bad employer that does not even take care of the safety of its workers. This is also apparent early in the novel. In chapter 2, after Sánchez is killed in an accident involving a crane, there are expressions of discontent among the men. Sánchez's work crew had twice been cut, making working conditions unsafe. One unnamed worker says, "The blame lies with those bastards that treat us like animals and our rotten union that won't protect us!" Conditions are ripe for social unrest and political action to improve the situation. Indeed, this is what happens as things get rapidly worse. The workers call a strike, unsanctioned by their labor union, to protest poor working conditions and the corruption in their union leadership. The company responds by firing many of the men, who are left jobless and receive no support from their official union representatives, who enjoy a cozy relationship with the employer. The men cannot find other jobs in the city because they have been blacklisted—that is, their names have been circulated to other employers as undesirable workers. Some even have to leave the city and return to the rural areas they came from. Another wildcat strike takes place in the fall, but the railroad ruthlessly exploits the divisions in the ranks of the workers. It fires the strikers and hires replacements. A vote on a new contract offered to the workers by the company is fixed by the union bosses and so is officially approved, even though it does not improve the workers' conditions.

In this situation, the workers must find a way to fight for their rights. They are very much on their own. They can get no support from the local Catholic church, where the priest sides with the employers, or from successful local businessmen like Mannie, who only care about themselves. (This amounts to a criticism of capitalism on the part of the author.) The workers rule out legalistic maneuvering as being ineffective, after which two different approaches to achieving their goals are developed in the novel. First, there is the violent, radical approach advocated by Lalo. However, when

TOPICS FOR FURTHER STUDY

- In a world in which science and technology are considered the most important factors in advancing human progress, does mythology have any role to play? Why do people need ancient stories? Are they of any practical use? If so, in what way? Choose a legend or mythological story from your tradition that appeals to you. Create a blog entry explaining why you like it, and why others, and even a society as a whole, might benefit from knowing it. Invite comments on this post from your classmates and respond to them.

- Read *Muchacho: A Novel*, a 2011 novel for young adults by Louanne Johnson. Eddie, the main character, is a high-school junior who lives with his Mexican American family in a town in New Mexico. Write an essay in which you compare and contrast Eddie and his story with the story of the young people in *Heart of Aztlan*. Who does Eddie most resemble, Jason or Benjie? Or is he actually closer to Sapo, the gang leader?

- Create a time line of Mexican American history from the 1600s to the present. Include at least twelve important events. Give a class presentation in which you explain the time line and talk about several of the most important dates.

- *Heart of Aztlan* emphasizes the importance for Mexican Americans to connect with their cultural heritage. In 2012, the school district of Tucson, Arizona, which has a high percentage of Mexican American students, suspended its course in Mexican American studies. The Arizona state legislature had declared such courses illegal, saying they were too political. Conduct Internet research on this controversy, and then give a class presentation in which you describe the issues and the latest developments. Start your research with this March 14, 2013, report from the *Huffington Post*: http://www.huffingtonpost.com/2013/03/11/arizona-mexican-american-studies-curriculum-constitutional_n_2851034.html. Also read this NPR report from July 24, 2013, which explains how the program was reinstated for the 2013–2014 school year: http://www.npr.org/blogs/codeswitch/2013/07/24/205058168/Tucson-Revives-Mexican-American-Studies-Program.

the workers follow that course, the result is disastrous. There is a riot, and railroad property is set afire and destroyed. Police fire on the rioters, killing two men and wounding others. The state governor threatens to call out the national guard. Clemente, who has been wrongly associated with the violence, is jailed, later to be freed on bail after the people of the barrio raise the necessary money. Clemente thinks he has a better way of ending injustice and oppression. After the visionary experiences granted to him by the magic rock, the people accept him as their leader, and he inspires them with a nonviolent strategy of mass protest, made possible by a faith in the soul of his people and a belief in love and universal brotherhood. The novel ends on this note

of hope and solidarity, as the people march down the street, shouting, "*Adelante!*" (Forward!). The author chooses not to show any details of how this strategy is going to be any more successful than previous ones, but he clearly intends readers to embrace it as the superior and right path to social change.

Coming of Age

Part of the story is the coming of age of Jason and Benjie, and to a lesser extent (because their characters are not developed in depth in the novel) Juanita and Ana. Coming of age is about the transition from childhood to adulthood. All four of the Chávez children start to grow out of dependence on their parents as the novel progresses. Juanita graduates from high school and takes a job, valuing her newfound independence and alarming her father with it. Ana, on the other hand, drops out of high school, seeing no point in continuing. She, too, gets a job and starts to contribute to the family income. Both girls insist on having the freedom to come and go as they please to and from the family home. They are becoming young adults, even though they both realize they are stuck in low-paying jobs with few prospects.

The boys present more complicated cases, and the author is clearly more interested in their development than in that of the girls. As teenage boys coming to live in the city for the first time, Jason and Benjie have to create new lives for themselves as they mature. They are younger than their sisters and are both still in school. They both quickly find new friends and acquire girlfriends too. But that is about all they have in common. Jason shows how growing up should be done, while Benjie fails the crucial test. Benjie is fearless, but he makes the mistake of falling in with a gang of toughs who are also involved with drugs. He starts to sell and, presumably, use marijuana. He also disobeys the rules of the gang regarding distribution of the profits, and he gets beaten up for it. At the end of the novel, Benjie is paralyzed by his fall from the water tank, an incident that stemmed directly from his involvement in the wrong crowd. It is a clear symbol of the fact that he has been going in the wrong direction in life; there is no future in it.

Jason, on the other hand, goes in the right direction. He is naturally a more serious, reflective individual than his more impetuous younger brother, and he matures quickly. One important incident happens on his first full day in Albuquerque, when he witnesses the death of Sánchez. He is grief-stricken, even though he did not know the man. He runs to Crispín, who comforts him with the melodies of the blue guitar and some timely words of wisdom about life and death. Jason shows that he is able to absorb this mature perspective. A little later, he takes a leadership role in his new group of friends. When trouble hits, he comes to Benjie's aid against Flaco and Frankie, and he knows how to fight. He is attractive to girls, too. For a little while, Jason feels that life is moving too fast for him, but his relationship with Cristina calms him down, and he meets every challenge he is faced

At the beginning of the novel, the family moves from a small rural community to a barrio in Albuquerque. (© photoBeard / Shutterstock.com)

with. While Benjie's growth is literally stunted, Jason shows every sign that he will grow into a wise, responsible adult.

STYLE

Myth and Legend

Into the sometimes harsh realism of life in the barrio, Anaya injects elements of myth and legend. These stories show that there is more to life than the daily grind of trying to survive or to escape reality through alcohol or drugs or superficial entertainment. The myths are conveyed through the character of the old, blind guitar player, Crispín. The fact that Crispín is blind has a symbolic significance. Like the blind prophets in classical mythology, he is blind to the material world, but he sees the depths of the inner world. Crispín lays out the myths of the Aztlan people in such a way that deepens people's awareness of who they are and where they come from, although few people who hear them understand them or see their relevance to life in Albuquerque in the 1950s. Bringing these legends into the narrative allows Anaya to suggest that Chicanos should dig deeper into their cultural roots to find their true nature and destiny, rather than passively becoming either marginalized by the dominant Anglo culture or assimilated into what essentially is an alien culture. Anaya communicates this theme not only via Crispín but also through Clemente. Clemente is drawn to the magic rock, which according to legend has power because it was a gift to the people from the gods. The rock knows secrets and can reveal the future. When Clemente experiences the full power of the rock, he is transported, at least symbolically, to another realm of existence. The soul of the ancient Aztlan people enters him, he is at one with all of nature, and he seems to be anointed in some sacred fashion as the leader of his people. These passages in which the myths of Aztlan are described and Clemente gets insight into his destiny are all presented in high-flown language that is quite different from the ordinary talk in the barrio, and is also marked typographically by the use of italics.

English and Spanish Languages

The novel is written in English, but in almost every chapter there are also Spanish words and phrases, usually but not always printed in italics, which are not translated into English. These Spanish words serve a purpose similar to that of the italicized sections that deal with the Aztlan myths and legends, in that they establish for the reader the feeling that the Chicano culture is quite distinct from the Anglo culture, having its roots in a different place and a different language. (Anaya himself grew up in a Spanish-speaking family and spoke Spanish exclusively until he was six years old.) Sometimes the meaning of the Spanish words can be guessed from the context even for those readers who know no Spanish. Other terms may need explanation. Some of the Spanish words used include *vatos* (the young men from the barrio, rather like "guys"), *toda madre* (a slang expression that means roughly "totally awesome"), *mota* (marijuana), and *pachuco* (Chicano guys from the barrio). Occasionally a sentence may be written that mingles the two languages, such as "The children who had earlier shared in the merriment now fell asleep in the arms of a mother, a sister,

una tía or an abuelita, anyone." (The Spanish words mean aunt and grandma, respectively.)

HISTORICAL CONTEXT

Aztlan and the Chicano Movement

The Chicano movement, also sometimes called the Mexican American civil rights movement, began in the late 1960s and continued into the 1970s. It was in part inspired by the African American civil rights movement of the 1950s and 1960s. Activists in the Chicano movement campaigned on issues such as farm workers' rights, the need to improve education for Mexican Americans, and political and voting rights. The Chicano movement was very active in many cities in the Southwest, including Albuquerque, the setting for *Heart of Aztlan*, although the events described in the novel take place earlier, in the 1950s.

When Anaya used Aztlan myths and legends when he wrote *Heart of Aztlan* in the 1970s, he was not merely wanting to add depth and richness to his novel. He was following the practice of the Chicano movement, which in the late 1960s declared Aztlan to be the Chicano homeland. This was a reference to a pre-Columbian people who had lived in what is now the southwestern United States, including parts of California, Arizona, New Mexico, and Texas. Those ancient people at some point migrated south to present-day Mexico and created the Aztec civilization. The Chicano movement identified with Aztlan as a way of creating knowledge about what they regarded as their true cultural heritage. Although they lived in an Anglo-dominated society, they were not Anglo, but neither were they entirely Hispanic in ethnic and cultural origin either. They preferred to refer to themselves as Indo-Hispano, indicating their dual heritage from the native people of North and Central America as well as the Spanish conquerors of Mexico in the sixteenth century. (Those of dual Indian and Spanish heritage are also referred to as *mestizo*, which means "mixed race.")

Anaya discusses Aztlan and the Chicano movement in his 1989 essay "Aztlán: A Homeland without Borders." He writes that when the Chicano community named Aztlan as its homeland, it was a significant event because such a naming "creates a real sense of nation, for it fuses the spiritual and political aspirations

COMPARE
&
CONTRAST

- **1950s:** Barelas is an old neighborhood in southwest Albuquerque that is going through difficult economic times. The Atchison, Topeka and Santa Fe Railway, one of the main employers, maintains many shops (maintenance facilities) in Barelas, but as steam locomotives are replaced by diesel, jobs start to disappear.

  1970s: In 1970, the railway shops close and fifteen hundred workers lose their jobs. An urban renewal program begins, leading to industrial development in the area.

  Today: The old railway yards are empty. They were bought by the City of Albuquerque in 2007, and there are plans to redevelop the area.

- **1950s:** Mainstream publishers in the United States have no interest in publishing Chicano writers. *Mexican Village* by Josephina Niggli (1910–1983), published in 1945, is the only work by a Mexican American author that reaches a general audience.

  1970s: Several publishing houses are formed during the Chicano movement that are designed to give Mexican American writers an outlet for their work. These include Quinto Sol, in Berkeley, California, which creates a national award for Chicano literature, Premio Quinto Sol (Fifth Sun Award). The first winner is the novel *Y No Se Lo Trago la Tierra/And the Earth Did Not Devour Him* (1970), by Tomás Rivera (1935–1984).

  Today: Leading Mexican American writers include poets Lorna Dee Cervantes (born in 1954) and Gary Soto (born in 1952); novel and short-story writers Sandra Cisneros (born in 1954), Daniel Olivas (born in 1959), Benjamin Alire Sáenz (born in 1954), and Sergio Troncoso (born in 1961); novelist and playwright Denise Chavez (born in 1948); and poets and novelists Luis Alberto Urrea (born in 1955) and Rigoberto González (born in 1970).

- **1950s:** Mexican Americans continue to migrate to the cities in the Southwest in a trend that began during World War II because of labor shortages. In 1954, in the case *Hernandez v. the State of Texas*, the Supreme Court recognizes the discrimination faced by Mexican Americans and other nonwhite racial groups. The court rules that such minorities have the right to equal protection under the Fourteenth Amendment to the US Constitution. This is the first Supreme Court case argued by Mexican American lawyers.

  1970s: The Chicano movement continues to advocate for greater opportunities for Mexican Americans. In 1974, Congress passes the Equal Educational Opportunity Act, which prohibits discrimination and segregation by race in public schools. The act also requires schools to promote equality by offering bilingual education to Hispanic students. In 1970, fewer than one million Mexican Americans reside in the United States.

  Today: According to Pew Research Center, in 2012, 33.7 million Hispanics of Mexican origin reside in the United States. This figure includes 11.4 million immigrants born in Mexico. Of that figure, 51 percent are in the United States illegally. Efforts to legalize the status of such immigrants stall in Congress during the 2010s.

---

of a group and provides a vision of the group's role in history." According to Anaya, the need for a new national identity was important in situations such as those experienced by the Chicanos in the 1960s. They felt their existence threatened both by assimilation into Anglo culture and by political and economic exploitation. Anaya writes,

Crispín, a blind poet and musician, leads Clemente on a mystical journey. (© Umkehrer | Shutterstock.com)

Leaders within the Chicano community—educators, poets, writers, artists, activists—rose up against the majority presence of Anglo America to defend the right of the Hispanic community to exist as a national entity within the United States.

He emphasizes that the artist played a central role in this process, embodying the new vision in symbol and metaphor. Through adopting Aztlan as its homeland, the Chicanos found a way of acknowledging their Native American heritage, as a result of which they "could more clearly define the mestizo who is the synthesis of European and Indian ancestry." As a result of embracing Native American legends, the Chicanos could "find the psychological and spiritual birthplace of their ancestors." (In the novel, this is what happens to Clemente after he touches the magic rock.) According to Anaya, "The naming of the homeland created a Chicano spiritual awareness which reverberated throughout the

Southwest." He believed that this embrace of their Indian origins was a better solution for the Chicanos than merely emphasizing their Spanish heritage, which "suited the powers that dealt with this community as a tourist commodity and as a community that could do service work for the society in power."

CRITICAL OVERVIEW

In general, *Heart of Aztlan* did not receive positive reviews, certainly not as good as those of *Bless Me, Ultima*, Anaya's first novel and the one that established his reputation. Margarite Fernández Olmos, in *Rudolfo Anaya: A Critical Companion*, notes that "the attempt to blend a sociopolitical theme with mystical elements was perceived as contrived and simplistic." For Cordelia Candelaria, in *Dictionary of Literary*

Biography, "the wide array of characters lack verisimilitude and are sketched as literary types—from traditional *machos* and *mamacitas*, to melodramatic healers and artists." Candelaria regards the attempt to employ mythological themes similar to those used in *Bless Me, Ultima*, as being "at the heart of the second novel's failure." Marvin A. Lewis, in *Revista Chicano-Riqueña*, writes, as quoted by Candelaria,

> The novel attempts to accumulate and to assess the myths, legends, and social realities reflecting the totality of Chicanismo. Unfortunately, the author falls short of the mark due to a conceptual disparity between form, content, and overall meaning.

However, Roberto Cantú, in a later volume of *Dictionary of Literary Biography*, had a more positive assessment. Cantú writes that by the end of the novel, "one senses that Anaya has transformed the Chicano barrio of Barelas (to which this novel is dedicated)—and by extension Albuquerque—into the collective protagonist of this novel." Nonetheless, Cantú adds a caution: "If *Heart of Aztlán* achieved its own degree of success, it also pointed to the limitations of an overtly ideological novel or criticism."

Juan Bruce-Novoa shares the common view that the novel was less than successful. He comments in an introduction to an interview he conducted with Anaya in 1979, and which was published in 1980, that Anaya's first novel "produced expectations that *Heart of Aztlan* did not satisfy." The later novel is "less polished, less accomplished." However, Bruce-Novoa adds that "Anaya should be admired for having the courage to explore a new space—*Heart* is set in the city—instead of remaining within the circumference of the secure area established in *Ultima*."

WHAT DO I READ NEXT?

- In *Randy Lopez Goes Home: A Novel* (2011) by Anaya, a Mexican immigrant to the United States feels that something is missing in his life. He returns to his ancestral home in Mexico to reconnect with his past.

- *Bone* (1993) is a novel by Chinese American author Fae Myenne Ng. It is set in San Francisco's Chinatown and tells the story of one Chinese American family over two generations.

- *Growing Up Chicana/o* (1995), edited and with an introduction by Tiffany A. Lopez, and a foreword by Anaya, contains twenty stories about growing up Mexican American in the United States.

- *Crazy Loco* (2001) by David Talbot Rice contains nine stories about Mexican American teenagers growing up in a small town in South Texas.

- *Mexicanos: A History of Mexicans in the United States* (revised and updated edition, 2009), by Manuel G. Gonzales, surveys more than two centuries of Mexican American history. Gonzales shows how the culture of the Mexican immigrants was shaped by their Indian and Spanish ancestry, and he assesses the impact Mexican Americans have had on American society.

- *Lord of the Dawn: The Legend of Quetzalcóatl* (1987), by Anaya, explores the Aztec legends and mythology that form such a large part of *Heart of Aztlan*.

CRITICISM

Bryan Aubrey

Aubrey holds a PhD in English. In the following essay, he discusses the mythological background of Heart of Aztlan *and whether it contributes to the effectiveness of the novel.*

Many commentators have regarded *Heart of Aztlan* as a flawed novel, and it is not difficult to see the reasons for this majority view. The novel is somewhat disjointed as it switches back and forth from the stories of the young people,

with their gangs, love affairs, and boisterous and sometimes violent behavior, to the increasingly bitter labor dispute and the sudden transformation of Clemente Chávez from a state of aimlessness and despair into the new leader of the Chicano workers. The latter plot twist in particular strains credulity because before his mystical encounter with the magic rock, Clemente has shown no leadership qualities at all. He is a relative newcomer to the barrio and works at the rail yard only for a short while before being fired, and he admits that he has no interest in politics. Not only this, he knows little about urban life, since he comes from a rural area—and yet this man suddenly becomes the leader of a the emerging nonviolent political protest movement in the streets of Barelas.

Anaya himself has acknowledged that this aspect of his plot was a challenge. In a 1979 interview with David Johnson and David Apodaca, Anaya said that Clemente's transformation was "the most difficult" part of the novel, "because he's caught up in a very realistic setting and then how in hell do you take him into this visionary trip that I attempted to do." Anaya acknowledged that he might have created that trip through a dream, or "in some kind of revelation," but chose instead to do it "through Crispín and the old woman, the keeper of the rock." It is this and other mythological elements in the novel that some readers have found hard to integrate with the otherwise realistic framework. Little reason is given for why the workers, struggling to feed their families as a harsh winter sets in, would have any time for these strange-sounding stories, or why they would think that Clemente's visionary journey qualifies him as their leader. Furthermore, how would knowledge of these mythological stories be of any practical use to the workers in their struggle for their rights? Other than in the notion that it is somehow better for a people to have knowledge of their own roots, of where they came from, this question is not addressed in the novel. Indeed, when at a workers' meeting Crispín sings of the legends, the general feeling among the men is that the old tales "didn't put beans and meat on the table for the family. Sure the stories helped to pass the time and ease the despair of going jobless this winter, but that was all."

These criticisms notwithstanding, it may be that Anaya has not received sufficient credit for the diligent and careful way he has tried to inject greater psychological and spiritual depth into his novel by drawing on the legends of Aztlan as well as Native American and Hispanic mythology. If the overall results are not entirely satisfactory, he has at least tried to go beyond the surface of things and give expression to what he sees as the deeper springs from which the Chicano culture he depicts arises. He brings these elements in very early in the novel and tries to keep them in

> THROUGH THIS PASSIONATELY ENACTED VISION—AND THERE ARE NEARLY THREE PAGES OF IT—ANAYA ENDEAVORS TO CONVEY IN A TONE OF RISING ECSTASY THE HUGE TRANSFORMATIONAL MOMENT THAT CLEMENTE EXPERIENCES."

the reader's mind quite frequently. For example, in chapter 1, there is an allusion to the legend of *La Llorona* (a Spanish term that means "weeping woman"), which is found in Hispanic cultures in the Americas. In the myth, La Llorona mourns for her lost sons and cries for her "demon-lover." All the young men in the barrio have heard of La Llorona, and she is identified with the sirens of the police cars as they try to track down those who possess the illegal drug marijuana. La Llorona cries out, "*You cannot flee from me. . . . I seek you out in all new lands. I am the essence of your smoke, I am the spirit of your past.*" This is undoubtedly a clever and effective way of incorporating an old myth into a modern setting. Native American mythology is also alluded to early, in the reference to the "white deer" and later the "golden deer" that run across the sky, which as pointed out by Margarite Fernández Olmos in *Rudolfo Anaya: A Critical Companion*, "combines the solar symbolism of Aztec myths with the totemic animal of Native-American Pueblo culture."

Also in chapter 1, Anaya introduces both the blue guitar and the magic or singing rock, known to some as *la piedra mala* (meaning "evil stone"). The blue guitar symbolizes the songs of the poet that tell the mythological history of the people. It was "carved from the heart of a juniper tree" and has been passed from poet to poet over the ages. Anaya is careful to point out how deeply people connect to the songs and melodies they hear played on the blue guitar. "Some men said its music could stop death in his tracks." Others say it can stop time. Certainly, "the magic music stirred the soul." As for the singing rocks, the legend is that "they had much power because they were part of the gods' gifts to the people." In his interview with Johnson and Apodaca, Anaya explained the concept behind the magic rocks.

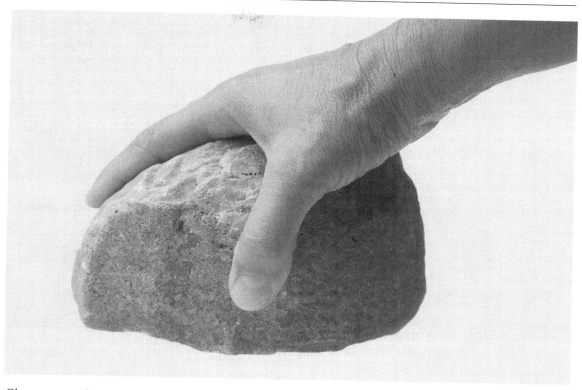

Clemente touches a magical stone and is transported to Aztlan. (© hans.slegers / Shutterstock.com)

The rocks embody the power of the Aztec god Quetzalcóatl, which "is the power of the blending or the merging of the dichotomies" of life. By this Anaya means "the polarities of God and earth, of spirit and flesh," which "cooled off... and congealed into rocks." The task of the writer is to "reinfuse [the rocks] with life and mythology." This is what Anaya tries to do in the novel, especially in long passages in chapters 8 and 13, where through his characters Crispín and then Clemente, he gives some details of the myth. The people from the land of Aztlan, Crispín tells the assembled men at the workers' meeting in chapter 8, traveled southward in a great exodus after receiving an instruction from a "burning god" who "fell from the sky." When they saw "a giant bird in whose claws would be ensnared the poisonous snakes which threatened the people," they were to build a new civilization. This "plumed bird" (which is the god Quetzalcóatl, although Crispín does not identify him by name), would protect them. Crispín then likens the trains of the modern-day railroad to the serpents that enslaved the people. In ancient times, "a giant bird sent by the guardian sun, a bird to mate the snake and steal its fear" protected them, and now a man is needed "who will rise like the eagle and melt the power of the steel snakes!" Thus does Anaya, through his blind seer Crispín, attempt to give the myth some contemporary relevance.

Then in chapter 13, Anaya tries to provide a mythological background that will explain how Clemente becomes the anointed leader of his people. In his visionary journey, Clemente penetrates to the very core of life, its creative heart, as presented in the Aztec mythology. In the passage that leads up to this defining experience, it is as if Clemente has been able to embrace the dichotomies of life that Anaya mentioned in the interview with Johnson and Apodaca, and thus in a way become godlike himself.

The passage has to be quoted at some length in order to convey the flavor of it. After Clemente asks the keeper of the rock for a sign:

> *Two forms rose from the lump of the earth. One was a man clad in shining scales and the other was a woman dressed in feathers. They mated, twisting together like snakes, forming the tree which Clemente climbed, and from which he soared like*

a giant bird. He saw the burning desert of the legend! He saw the sacred mountain to the east! And he caught a glimpse of the sacred lake!

A little later he reaches a sacred river and immerses himself in it until he sees the seven springs that arise from it. At that point, *"He had come to the source of life and time and history."*

Through this passionately enacted vision—and there are nearly three pages of it—Anaya endeavors to convey in a tone of rising ecstasy the huge transformational moment that Clemente experiences. Readers must decide for themselves whether or not it is successful in explaining Clemente's emergence as a leader and providing the Chicanos with a mythology they can identify with, but it is certainly written with spirit and conviction.

Anaya is aware of the criticism made of his novel, but he has insisted that the mythological elements and the concept of Aztlan are important in laying the groundwork for a sense of shared community and national origin for Chicanos. In a 1986 interview with John F. Crawford, Anaya responded to the criticism that the novel was a failure because it lacked a political ideology that would be able to propel the workers forward. Anaya acknowledged the importance of such political structures but also said, "If they're not shored up by some common respect and a common goal we have as human beings, they don't last long." He identified love as an essential part of what he calls "that old sense of value that has sustained all communities on earth throughout history." It is that sense of value and of love that is imbued in Clemente through his vision and with which he inspires the workers to join him in the march through the streets in the final chapter of the novel. In his 1989 essay "Aztlán: A Homeland without Borders," Anaya, who has studied comparative mythology, noted that throughout history, "the collective soul of the group renewed itself through myth." As an attempt to show this process in action in a contemporary setting, *Heart of Aztlan*, flawed though it may be, has earned its place in Chicano literature.

Source: Bryan Aubrey, Critical Essay on *Heart of Aztlan*, in *Novels for Students*, Gale, Cengage Learning, 2015.

Laura Chavkin and Rudolfo Anaya

In the following interview excerpt, Anaya discusses his writing process and his background.

LC: Can you tell me a little about your background and your career?

> THE PROCESS OF REVISION SHOWS HOW IDEAS AND SYMBOLS COME FROM THE SUBCONSCIOUS AND THEN ARE REFINED IN REVISIONS. TO ME THAT'S A VERY IMPORTANT PROCESS, SO ANYONE LOOKING AT THOSE DIFFERENT DRAFTS CAN GET AN INSIGHT INTO THE WORKING OF MY MIND."

RA: I was born in New Mexico. Actually, I was born in a very small town, Pastura, which, by the way, worked its way into my first novel *Bless Me, Ultima.* I was raised in Santa Rosa, which is on the eastern side of the state. I went to school there through the eighth grade. It's a small town on Highway 66. I spent most of my childhood either going to school or playing along the river, or in the hills playing with friends, or listening to community and family telling stories. I guess that's when I got my yearning to be a writer, although I didn't know it at the time.

My family moved to Albuquerque in 1952, after World War II. That was happening to a lot of the communities in the state. People were going to bigger cities where there was more opportunity for work, and so we left the small town and wound up in Albuquerque. We lived in a barrio which is called Barelas.

LC: Can you tell me what motivates you to write?

RA: I've always said that all people have a creative spirit. We're all creative in one way or another. I guess in my case reading a lot and finding ideas in literature and being a student at the university as a young man and trying to emulate some of the poetry and stories that I was reading sparked that spirit of creativity. At that point in my life I was introverted, quite alone, and so writing was a way of expressing my feelings, my ideas. Reading the ideas of others slowly worked its way into looking back on my childhood and seeing it as something that I could use as the subject matter for a novel.

LC: When did you decide you wanted to become a writer?

RA: I don't think that's a decision that was very clear cut in my life. I really trained to become a teacher because that meant that I could get a job. I knew very little about the life of a writer, where you went to work, or what would happen if you just sat around and just wrote stories. In a sense I was pragmatic about my education and getting a degree that I could use. I was writing all the time at night, and so it was an evolution instead of an overnight decision. My writing evolved.

LC: When you first started writing, were there any writers who influenced your work or served as models?

RA: Almost everyone that I read, especially during my university years, I would say was important because that's when I really realized the power of literature. I was reading everything, everyone.

LC: Do you write for yourself, or your family, or friends, or an ideal reader?

RA: Writers write to communicate their ideas, so their audience is always the widest audience possible. I think there are times when we might focus in on a family, group, or community, but at the same time the story or whatever we're working on has to make a leap to the world.

LC: Are you conscious of a political message when you write? Do you deliberately try to include a social message or political message in your fiction?

RA: Probably so, since we live in a social and political context, we can't help but respond to it, and perhaps all that is wrapped up in our literature. I think the difference is how one does it. If it's a goal of a writer to be very direct about conveying a social and political message, that's one way to approach literature. On the other hand, one's atmosphere, one's social life, feelings, or ideas about the society can also appear in more subtle ways in what one writes.

LC: Are any of your stories somewhat autobiographical?

RA: I think my first three novels are the most autobiographical because there I am in settings that I know intimately, and I'm using people I knew as models for characters. After the first three novels, it seems that I begin to get away from a very strict autobiographical setting. On the other hand, characters always reflect the author so writing never quite escapes autobiography.

LC: Is there a religious foundation for your works?

RA: I think there is a spiritual foundation in my work.

LC: What do you see as your particular strength as writer? Do you see any weaknesses you'd like to correct?

RA: Oh, sure. Writing is, for me at least, never completely learned, and so every manuscript I do, I revise over and over, and I'm always learning. It's a process of learning and every element that there is in fiction I can always improve on.

LC: How elaborate are your outlines before you begin writing? Do you depart much from your original plans?

RA: I don't do outlines.

LC: Where is your greatest effort made? In your first draft or in the subsequent revisions?

RA: The first draft. If I can put a lot of time and concentrated energy and focus into that first draft, once I have that draft I am relieved because revision is a lot of work, but it's a good feeling to have that first draft done.

LC: At what part do you begin revising? Do you write a whole draft and then rewrite or do you revise as you write?

RA: I finish a complete manuscript, and then I start revising. I have to add that now that we use computers it's easier to revise while working on a first draft. I find myself doing that. I'll be on chapter ten and I'll go back and straighten out chapter two. With the computer I can just flip over to it and revise it.

LC: When you compose a novel, do you find yourself moving scenes to different parts of the novel as you write the various drafts?

RA: I don't do that much in the first draft. The first draft usually seems to flow, and the scenes seem to come where they should be. But when I revise, there's always the possibility that I'll take out scenes or move them.

LC: Would someone comparing your early drafts with your published story gain insight into your process of revision or thinking?

RA: Oh, yes, anyone might learn a lot by comparing the first draft to the published version. Since I really try to get through the first draft to have it in hand, to finish it, the first draft is usually very rough. The process of revision shows how ideas and symbols come from the subconscious and then are refined in revisions. To me that's a very important process, so anyone looking at those different drafts can get an insight into the working of my mind.

LC: Do you get advice and suggestions for changes before you submit a story for publication?

RA: Yes. It's important who is giving the advice. The person that I trust to give me that advice happens to be my wife. I'll finish a manuscript, and I'll give it to her to read and she'll give me her feedback on it.

LC: Can you describe a typical working day?

RA: On a typical working day, I get up, take a walk, have breakfast, and ask my wife if there's any work I need to do like washing dishes before I start writing. I write for about three hours and then have lunch and then spend the afternoon either answering letters or doing community work or projects or going visiting schools.

LC: Do you try to write seven days a week?

RA: I used to write seven days a week and through the holidays. Recently, I give myself more breaks on weekends, and I'll take a weekend off and maybe go to the mountains and just get away from work.

LC: How many pages can you write on an average day?

RA: When I am working on the first draft of an original manuscript, it would be maybe three or four pages.

LC: Do you ever write in long hand or always use a word processor?

RA: Word processor.

LC: Do you complete a project before moving on to the next one or do you work on several things at the same time?

RA: I can work on a couple of projects at the same time but not novels. If I'm working on a novel, I can't be working on two novels. I could be working on a novel and a children's story or a novel and an essay. That works. I can do that.

LC: Some writers have stated that writing is a painful exhausting, and frustrating process for them; what's your experience?

RA: It is painful; there is a lot of intense mental work involved, but it's also a meditative type of work. One learns to focus one's mental energy. It's also a process of discovery. We learn about ourselves, we learn about human nature,

> THE EMERGENCE OF A LEADER CLEARLY PRESENTS ITSELF AS A SURRENDER, AS A PROCESS OF IDENTIFICATION AND INTERACTION, DEFINITELY NOT AS A SOLITARY QUEST OF A SELF-APPOINTED CANDIDATE."

and I think in a sense that's why I write, that process is a journey of revelation . . . .

Source: Laura Chavkin and Rudolfo Anaya, "A Conversation with Rudolfo Anaya," in *Conversations with Rudolfo Anaya*, edited by Bruce Dick and Silvio Sirias, University Press of Mississippi, 1998, pp. 164–67.

Heiner Bus

In the following excerpt, Bus traces the theme of leadership in Heart of Aztlan.

. . . In *Heart of Aztlán*, a leader emerges only gradually and reluctantly after the old values have been modified and complemented by new insights. When the Chávez family arrives in Albuquerque, Clemente still makes the major decisions, but his position, not totally undisputed in Guadalupe, is very soon threatened by his children and even by his wife whose responses prove to be more appropriate to the new challenges. Clemente's dependence on *la tierra* and rituals fails to assess and counterbalance the attractions of city life; "the old earth of his valley" does not seem to mix easily with "the hard city soil."

The quick accommodation of his eldest son, Jason, who bade an equally painful farewell to Guadalupe and to his mentor, the old Indian, suggests to the reader that by the change of place, leadership has been handed on to the next Chicano generation. Jason demonstrates a remarkable acuteness, inquisitiveness, and alertness to interpret the phenomena of his new environment to maintain islands of human dignity and self-determination. During their first meeting, he recognizes continuities between Crispín and the old Indian of Guadalupe before actually learning that "the poet of the barrio" knew the man. His pre-eminence becomes evident when his own father is about to attack his sisters and Jason is ready to interfere. As for himself, Jason rejects the opportunity of passing into the mainstream through Cindy, the rich Anglo girl. So much prudence and firmness must be rewarded: In a number of scenes he feels "composed," "complete," and "calm."

However, despite these virtues, in the end Jason considers himself a failure because he cannot prevent his younger brother's tragedy. This outcome has been prepared for: When his family discusses Sánchez's fatal accident in the railroad yards, he does not reveal himself as an eyewitness and interpreter of the scene. Later in the novel, after he faced el Super, who blamed him and his father for violating barrio conventions, he tries to redeem his irritation by a symbolic gesture which he hides from his people. These reactions set him in direct contrast with his father as depicted in the last chapters of the novel: Jason also comprehends the water tank as a symbol of human perversion, exploitation, and lost faith, but he cannot deduce a larger vision. At this moment Jason, who initially proved to be the superior character, is tormented by self-reproaches, a stage his father had left behind. Yet some passages in the novel promise Jason future leadership on the basis of his barrio experience and the model of his father's slow and painful re-emergence: "Clemente looked at his son. There was something about his son that reminded him of himself when he was young. Sometimes he felt awkward when he talked with Jason, because he felt as if he was talking to himself."

In stark contrast to the domineering protagonist of *Marching Men*, Anaya's troika of Jason, Crispín, and Clemente has to be interpreted in their mutual interdependence. From the outset, Crispín, the blind singer of the barrio, accompanies the efforts of the Chávez family to settle down and survive decently in Barelas. He serves them and the community by connecting their actuality to the past and the group experience; he and his guitar are "constantly reshaping things as they are," striving for continuity and enlargement through memory and recognition. Though he can read the signs and make reality transparent, he is a searcher himself and merely acts at the inspiration of an authority beyond human grasp. Crispín is on a quest for the missing link between past, present, and future in

order to complete one cycle and begin a new one. To fill in the gap, requires a leader united with his people in suffering and the desire to reform life along an ethnic myth. The message is persuasive in its simplicity as it permeates the emotions of brotherhood based on the individual *movidas* characterized by an undeserved *tristeza de la vida*. The myth of Aztlán as proclaimed by Crispín relates this common experience to history, as the people have been unjustly punished and the benevolent gods promised to restore life "in peace and harmony with the earth and her gods." Though in many ways Crispín plays an active part in the barrio and closely ties his personal fate to that of the community, the blind seer remains detached from the daily activities of his people—just an attendant at the birth of a leader, indispensable as a transmitter of energy and knowledge, but never claiming leadership for himself.

Clemente Chávez development to such stature is not foreshadowed in the first chapters of the novel. His unproblematical integration into barrio life seems to promise an easy realization of his modest demands. So he does not feel compelled to question his role as paterfamilias or to explore the mechanics of the new place beyond the limits of random actuality and his individual horizon. Such general content even compensates his slight irritation when Crispín hints at a deeper alliance between Barelas and Guadalupe, the past and the present. On Clemente's momentary level of awareness, the last bond between the two places is threatened when his position in the family declines step by step. As he lacks the resources to prevent this process, he resorts to violence, self-accusations, and alcohol. His identity is totally ruined when he becomes financially dependent after losing his job in an effort to preserve his honor in a labor dispute. Significantly, an individual and separate act within a collective action—by coincidence in unison—pushes him to the low point of his career and self-esteem: "Somehow he had lost command over his life and destiny."

At this point, Crispín, Jason—even Father Cayo, Lalo, and el Super—outrank him through their firmer grip on barrio affairs. Clemente's wife, Adelita, characterizes him as "a man lost in a foreign land." By referring back to Guadalupe, she probes the degree of his divergence and indirectly suggests the cure—an eventual acceptance of the foreign land as part of the homeland:

> "...I remember watching the Chávez brothers walk on that llano-land of theirs. My God, you would have sworn that they were gods themselves the way they held themselves and walked upon that earth.... And there were also the people, los compadres, los vecinos, the people of the small pueblos, they understood and lent their support, so a man was never lost, never separated from his soul."

In this situation, Anaya exposes Clemente to scenes in which the workers of Barelas discuss the need for leadership in their fight for self-determination. Basically, these encounters depict the various stages of Clemente's gradual growth of insight into the demands of his people, of joining his individual with the common cause.

Manuel's equating the family with the people both includes and excludes Clemente as a candidate because of his recent failures in the smaller unit. Options depend on varying definitions of leadership. At the same meeting during a wildcat strike, Crispín's storytelling and singing of the *corridos* offer relief by relating the oppressions of the present not only to the miseries but also to the heroic acts of liberation in the collective past. This call for identification is taken up by Clemente only reluctantly, though he asks the barrio poet to explain further the legends and the myth. His deeply-rooted llano heritage makes him particularly sensitive for Crispín's concepts and their applicability in the present situation. So his position as an uncommitted outsider is gradually undermined by his unexpectedly strong responses to the myth:

> There was something very true and very essential in the story and it kept calling to him to find its meaning. He was bound up with the people of the story, and with the legend of the eagle and the serpent, and all that related somehow to him and to the strikers who sought justice, but he didn't know how. And the place they called Aztlán was like a mysterious word, latent with power, stretching from the dark past to the present to ring in his soul and make him tremble.

Clemente's physical and spiritual reverberations send him on a search for further revelations, yet without being equipped with a proper method. His unassisted individual approach to the energizing sources ends in utter disappointment. Nevertheless, he learns something about the interrelationship and continuity between larger and smaller units. These new insights are

not yet powerful enough to sever the lifelines of his old identity. In spite of the declaration of his insolvency, there is still room for escapist acts. During *la fiesta del bautismo*, the blind Crispín, under strange circumstances, picks out Clemente as the future leader. One of the old men in attendance defines criteria which are met for the first time by Clemente, while they disqualify other contenders: "To be a leader a man must know the traditions of his father;" he must have "that spiritual attachment to the earth." The following successful healing, Henry's sacrificial death, and his *velorio* demonstrate the validity of the old ways in an urban environment, and they indirectly confirm Crispín's choice without persuading Clemente to take over responsibilities. He has yet to reach the deepest point in the valley of his despair in order to connect unconditionally his own identity to the communal myth: "He reviewed his life and found that it no longer had meaning.... There was no reason to go on living.... He had lost his land and his family, and nothing else really mattered. He smiled and welcomed death."

Significantly, it is Crispín who becomes his savior and interprets Clemente's experience of life in death as a rebirth. Crispín now has at his disposal a person in urgent need of an effective set of values and with the potential of becoming a powerful symbol of suffering and survival to persuade the barrio people to identification. By reconstructing Clemente's personality, Crispín hopes to accomplish his mission of filling the gap between the past and the present. The emergence of a leader clearly presents itself as a surrender, as a process of identification and interaction, definitely not as a solitary quest of a self-appointed candidate.

So it is appropriate that the reborn once again has to listen to the myth which reflects his own fall and Crispín's promise of wholeness restored. In the myth, the people's suffering is explained as a consequence of their refusal to fulfill the demands of the cruel gods for human sacrifice. As a reward for this philanthropic act, the good gods made a convenant with them predicting an eventual return to Aztlán and the rise of a more sane civilization. The new quality of interdependence among the myth, Crispín, and Clemente is shown in the second visit to the old woman of the barrio and *las piedras malas* which open the gates for a visionary trip to the river of human suffering and the heart of

Aztlán. Clemente acknowledges *injusticia, miseria*, and *pobreza* in Barelas as a description of his own and of his people's situation. Through re-enactment and the fusion of his ego with the fate of his people, he achieves a state of heightened awareness preparing him for his leadership position. Like Moses, he returns from the mountain evoking feelings of awe and respect. Still, Clemente is not yet convinced of the paradoxical idea of becoming a powerful leader through defeat and surrender. His reluctance is quite understandable as, according to mainstream teachings, traditional leadership in the barrio is considered to be founded largely on individual achievement. So, the next stage is one of self-persuasion and of extending the small group of the faithful.

Clemente temporarily feels encouraged when he is able to set his new concept of *el alma de la raza* [the spirit of the common people] and universal brotherhood against Lalo's militancy. But his persecution, for a violent strike he tried to prevent, exposes the ambiguity of his situation as an undisputed leader in terms of false criteria. At this point Clemente both suffers and benefits from outside influences because they strengthen the symbolic character of his experience. This is particularly true for his turning down the bribe money from the alliance of established leaders and for his final translating of his private pains into an articulate public gesture of defiance. Both actions, denying the separation of individual and collective fate, persuade the people and Clemente himself into common action. He finally accepts the extension of his parish from his family to the people of Barelas by including himself and the barrio in the myth: "I held a fiery sword...and with that sword I cut down the snakes that suck the blood of our people and poison their will!" In the end, pity and respect for Clemente's suffering, his persistence in identifying with the group, which in turn evokes their compassion, make them respond to his call for action. They are united in a dream of brotherly sharing, of acknowledging one's weaknesses and strengths, in "the fire of love . . . the pure fire that gushes from the soul of our people, from the foundations of our history . . ."

> They could never be beaten! Never! Not as long as a single man dared to look for his humanity in the corners of his heart. That infusion of spirit into flesh which generations of wise men had described throughout the ages was the

simple bond of love that gave the river its strength to surge and roar and cut its new channel into the future!

In the final scene, Clemente leads the workers and their families, but the will for liberation and self-realization along the lines set by the myth has become self-propellant and no longer needs the traditional leader. In his review of *Heart of Aztlán*, Marvin A. Lewis criticizes this conclusion and incidently reminds us of *Marching Men* joining David Ormsby's and el Super's evaluations: "The final act is not convincing since the only things that can change the social order are money and power. The people of Barelas have neither and are not likely to achieve these means in the future. But there is a certain amount of strength involved in togetherness . . . ."

Source: Heiner Bus, "Individual Versus Collective Identity and the Idea of Leadership in Sherwood Anderson's *Marching Men* (1917) and Rudolfo A. Anaya's *Heart of Aztlan* (1976)," in *Rudolfo A. Anaya: Focus on Criticism*, edited by César A. González-T., Lalo Press, 1990, pp. 118–25.

SOURCES

"Albuquerque Rail Yards, Albuquerque, New Mexico: Redeveloping the City's Rail Yards," Urban Land Institute, February 24–29, 2008, http://www.cabq.gov/council/documents/1uli_final_report.abq_rail_yards_advisory_services_panel.pdf (accessed July 3, 2014).

Anaya, Rudolfo, *Heart of Aztlan*, University of New Mexico Press, 1976.

———, "Aztlán: A Homeland without Borders," in *The Essays*, University of Oklahoma Press, 2009, pp. 119–22, 125; originally published in *Aztlán: Essays on the Chicano Homeland*, edited by Rudolfo A. Anaya and Francisco Lomelí, El Norte Publications/Academia, 1989.

Bruce-Novoa, Juan, "Rudolfo A. Anaya," in *Conversations with Rudolfo Anaya*, edited by Bruce Dick and Silvio Sirias, University Press of Mississippi, 1998, pp. 11–12; originally published in *Chicano Authors: Inquiry by Interview*, University of Texas Press, 1989, pp. 184–202.

Candelaria, Cordelia, "Rudolfo A. Anaya," in *Dictionary of Literary Biography*, Vol. 82: *Chicano Writers, First Series*, edited by Francisco A. Lomelí and Carl R. Shirley, Gale Research, 1989, pp. 24–35.

Cantú, Roberto, "Rudolfo A. Anaya," in *Dictionary of Literary Biography*, Vol. 278 *American Novelists Since World War II, Seventh Series*, edited by James R. Giles and Wanda H. Giles, Thomson Gale, 2003, pp. 11–20.

Crawford, John F., "Rudolfo Anaya," in *Conversations with Rudolfo Anaya*, edited by Bruce Dick and Silvio

Sirias, University Press of Mississippi, 1998, p. 112; originally published in *This Is about Vision: Interviews with Southwestern Writers*, edited by William Balassi, John F. Crawford, and Annie O. Eysturoy, University of New Mexico Press, 1990.

Fernández Olmos, Margarite, *Rudolfo Anaya: A Critical Companion*, Greenwood Press, 1999, pp. 1–11, 45, 59.

Gonzalez-Barrera, Ana, and Mark Hugo Lopez, "A Demographic Portrait of Mexican-Origin Hispanics in the United States," Pew Research Hispanic Trends Project, May 1, 2013, http://www.pewhispanic.org/2013/05/01/a-demographic-portrait-of-mexican-origin-hispanics-in-the-united-states/ (accessed July 4, 2014).

Johnson, David, and David Apodaca, "Myth and the Writer: A Conversation with Rudolfo Anaya," in *Conversations with Rudolfo Anaya*, edited by Bruce Dick and Silvio Sirias, University Press of Mississippi, 1998, pp. 41, 43; originally published in *New America*, Vol. 3, No. 3, Spring 1979, pp. 76–85.

"Latino-Americans: Timeline of Important Dates," PBS website, 2013, http://www.pbs.org/latino-americans/en/timeline/ (accessed July 4, 2014).

Mendoza, Valerie, Review of *Chicano! History of the Mexican American Civil Rights Movement*, in *Journal for Multimedia History*, Vol. 3, 2000, http://www.albany.edu/jmmh/vol3/chicano/chicano.html (accessed July 3, 2014).

Peredes, Raymund, "Teaching Chicano Literature: An Historical Approach," in *The Heath Anthology of American Literature Newsletter*, No. 10, Fall 1993, http://www9.georgetown.edu/faculty/bassr/tamlit/newsletter/paredes.html (accessed July 4, 2014).

FURTHER READING

Anaya, Rudolfo, *The Anaya Reader*, Warner Books, 1995.
    This volume contains a wide variety of Anaya's writings, including novel excerpts, short stories, essays, and poems.

Tatum, Charles M., *Chicana and Chicano Literature: Otra voz del pueblo*, University of Arizona Press, 2006.
    Tatum surveys the history of Mexican American literature, from the earliest Spanish documents in the sixteenth century to the growth of fiction and poetry in the nineteenth and twentieth centuries, the Chicano movement of the 1960s and early 1970s, and the post-Chicano movement.

———, *Chicano Popular Culture: Que hable el pueblo*, University of Arizona Press, 2001.
    In this overview of Chicano popular culture, Tatum discusses a wide array of sources: music, film, newspapers, radio, and television. He looks at literary genres, such as fiction, poetry, and theater, and cultural products such as fiestas, celebrations, and art. He also presents different theories of popular culture.

Vargas, Zaragosas, *Crucible of Struggle: A History of Mexican Americans from the Colonial Period to the Present Era*, Oxford University Press, 2010.
    Vargas surveys Mexican American history from Spanish colonial times to the present.

SUGGESTED SEARCH TERMS

Rudolfo Anaya

Heart of Aztlan

Aztlan

Mexican American history

Chicano

Chicano movement

Indo-Hispanic

Mexican immigration to the United States

New Mexico

Quetzalcóatl

Homeless Bird

GLORIA WHELAN

2000

Gloria Whelan's young-adult novel *Homeless Bird* explores the plight of a teenage widow in India. When Koly is thirteen, her parents arrange a marriage for her, as is customary among the Hindi population in India. Anxious but hopeful, Koly is resolved to not bring shame to her family and so accepts her fate.

She soon learns that her new husband is both very young and gravely ill, and his family arranged the marriage only to receive her dowry, which would pay for a trip to the Ganges River. The river is revered by faithful Hindus for its healing powers. Her husband dies not long after he bathes in the river, and Koly is forced to return to her husband's parents' home, where she lives essentially as a servant. When her father-in-law dies, her mother-in-law deceives her, telling Koly they will be going to live with relatives. Koly is instead deposited in the city of Vrindavan, alone and nearly penniless. She is taken in by a benefactor who cares for some of the large population of poor and abandoned widows in the city. There, she attempts to make a new life for herself. She finds work and eventually plans to marry a young man with whom she falls in love.

In this work, Whelan explores the interplay between cultural traditions, familial duty, and personal identity, as the young Koly must navigate her family's expectations, the societal dictates of her culture, and her own burgeoning

Gloria Whelan (© *AP Images | Mark Lennihan*)

sense of selfhood. *Homeless Bird* was published in 2000 by HarperCollins and won the National Book Award.

AUTHOR BIOGRAPHY

Whelan was born on November 23, 1923, in Detroit, Michigan, to William and Hildegarde Rewoldt. As a child she was confined to her bed for a year as she recovered from rheumatic fever. Whelan attended the University of Michigan and received a bachelor of science degree in 1945 and a master of social work degree in 1948. She married Joseph L. Whelan in 1948 and would go on to have two children with him. For the next three decades, Whelan worked as a social worker, both in Minneapolis, Minnesota, and in Detroit, Michigan. Whelan and her husband moved from the metropolitan Detroit

area in 1972 to a cottage on Oxbow Lake in a remote wooded region of northern Michigan.

In 1978, Whelan published her first children's novel, *A Clearing in the Forest*, which was concerned with the oil industry. The story was inspired by her experience of an oil company drilling on her property. Over the years, Whelan continued to write and publish for children and young adults, penning both short fiction and novel-length works. In 2000, Whelan published *Homeless Bird*. It won the National Book Award for Young People's Literature. She continues to write from her home near Lake St. Clair in Michigan.

PLOT SUMMARY

Chapters 1–3

Homeless Bird begins when Koly, the protagonist, is thirteen years old. The opening scene establishes Koly's family's poverty and the pressing matter of finding a dowry for Koly so that she can marry once an appropriate suitor is found. Koly's brothers, Gopal and Ram, tease Koly about having to marry. Koly is not allowed to go to school like her brothers but is educated in matters pertaining to maintaining a home. She also learns the craft of embroidery. As Koly begins to embroider the garment she will one day wear when she marries—a wedding sari—her parents search for a husband for her. They sell what few valuable possessions the family has in order to provide a dowry for Koly.

Before long, Koly becomes betrothed to Hari Mehta. The family receives little information about Hari from his parents. After traveling to the Mehta's home for the wedding, Koly and her parents are introduced to the Mehta family—Hari's parents and sister, Chandra, but not to Hari himself. The first time Koly sees Hari is at the wedding. Koly soon learns that Hari is much younger than she anticipated and quite ill.

As Koly's new life begins, she finds that her role is more that of servant than wife. She attends to cooking and cleaning in the Mehta household and is only rarely permitted by her mother-in-law to spend time with Hari. Still, they manage to share a few conversations. Hari explains that his parents intend to take him to the Ganges River, which they hope will heal him. Chandra later elaborates and tells Koly that her

MEDIA ADAPTATIONS

- Whelan's *Homeless Bird* is available as an unabridged audio CD recording read by Sarita Choudhury. It was published by Listening Library in 2003.

parents needed money to pay for the doctor and for Hari's journey, which is why they arranged the marriage.

Hari argues with his parents until they allow Koly to accompany them on their journey. After a long train ride, the group rests for the night and prepares to complete their journey to the Ganges the next morning. Hari is assisted into the water and initially enjoys himself, splashing about. However, he soon grows cold and tired, and the party returns to the home of Mr. Lal, and old friend of Mr. Mehta's. Hari dies that night. He is cremated in the morning, and the mournful party returns home.

Chapters 4–6

Not long after Hari's death, Mrs. Mehta instructs Koly to put on her white widow's sari and takes her into the village. They visit with a government official, and Koly is instructed to sign papers, which she cannot read. As the weeks pass, Koly continues to be treated like a servant, and she is verbally accosted by Hari's mother. Koly's only happiness comes from her sisterly relationship with Chandra. Occasionally, they slip away to swing on a rope tied in the mango tree. Koly examines Hari's old books, but she has not been taught to read. Mr. Mehta agrees to teach her to read.

Koly begins to dream of running away. Her desire to escape the drudgery of the household increases when a husband is found for Chandra. Chandra is given Koly's wedding sari, and Koly is asked to give the Mehtas the silver earrings she wore for her own wedding as part of Chandra's dowry. Koly refuses; she has hidden the earrings and insists she has lost them.

Privately, Mr. and Mrs. Mehta discuss Koly. As Koly listens, Mr. Mehta defends Koly against Mrs. Mehta's accusations of laziness and lack of gratitude. Mr. Mehta speaks of money that Koly has been provided by the government, a widow's pension, or a monthly allotment of money. Mrs. Mehta has been collecting it without telling Koly. The money has been used for Chandra's dowry. Chandra asks Koly if she will make her a quilt for her dowry, and Koly agrees, pleased to be working at her embroidery again.

Things change for Koly in the household after Chandra leaves to begin her new life with her husband. Mr. Mehta mourns the loss of his son and now the departure of his daughter. Time passes slowly for Koly. Mr. Mehta's job is threatened. He is a teacher, but once the school gets electricity and computers are installed, his work responsibilities decrease. Koly begins to form a plan to leave and figures out how she can get her widow's pension paid directly to her once she moves. The day Mr. Mehta loses his job, he dies.

Chapters 7–9

Chandra returns home for the funeral; it has been more than a year since her wedding. After the funeral and Chandra's departure, Koly's life becomes even more miserable. Without Mr. Mehta's income, the family falls further into poverty. Koly offers Mrs. Mehta her silver earrings so that Mrs. Mehta will not sell Mr. Mehta's book, which is a cherished object to Koly because she learned to read from Mr. Mehta. After a letter arrives, Mrs. Mehta's demeanor changes. She informs Koly that they will be moving to stay with her brother in Delhi. Koly is excited for the journey, but a little sad to leave the house and its fond memories of time spent with Chandra.

They arrive in the city of Vrindavan, where they are supposed to spend the night. They stow their belongings at the train station and hire a rickshaw to take them to a temple at Mrs. Mehta's insistence. Koly notices all the women wearing the white sari designating a widow, women just like her, congregating at the temples. Mrs. Mehta gives Koly money and tells her to go find them some food; she tells her she will wait in the temple. Koly is surprised to have been trusted with a relatively large amount of money. She buys two samosas and returns to the temple but cannot find Mrs. Mehta. She waits for hours.

At dusk, Koly leaves the temple. She tries not to panic as she searches for her mother-in-law. Koly returns to the train station and claims her basket and bedroll but still cannot find Mrs. Mehta. Seeking a familiar face, Koly spots the young rickshaw driver from earlier in the day and asks him if he has seen her mother-in-law. He informs her that she returned to the train station and got on a train to Delhi less than an hour after he had dropped them both at the temple. The boy explains that this type of thing happens frequently. Widows young and old, not wanted by the families into which they married, are abandoned in the city. Most spend their days chanting at the temples and in return are fed by the monks.

Koly observes that many other people have settled down to sleep for the night on sidewalks throughout the city. She finds a scrap of space for herself and spends the night there, alone and afraid. Koly spends a week sleeping on the same doorstep, eating bits of food tossed out of the door by the woman who lives in the adjacent home. Koly spends her days attempting to find work. She is told she cannot begin receiving her pension until she has an address.

Eventually, Koly sees the rickshaw boy again. He offers to help her and tells her of a place where she might be taken in. After he finishes work for the day, he returns. He explains that he owns a little land left to him by his father and that when he saves enough money for seeds, he plans to return to his village. At the home to which the boy brings Koly, a woman address him as Raji. She introduces herself as Maa Kamala and says she will take Koly in.

A young woman named Tanu assists Koly by providing her with clothing from a chest and telling her about Maa Kamala and how she helps widows find jobs and begin new lives for themselves. Koly is instructed to go with Tanu in the morning to her job at a bazaar. There, Tanu strings marigolds for garlands. Koly works diligently and is helpful in finding creative solutions when there is a marigold shortage. The girls are later given a job stringing beads.

As time goes on, Koly and Tanu become close friends. They earn money to pay for their room and board, and the remainder is saved for them. Raji comes to visit. When Koly learns that he cannot read, she vows to teach him. They become close friends, and Koly's feelings begin to deepen. They spend time together alone by the river, and Raji mentions that when he has saved enough to return home, he will want a wife. Koly is uncertain how to respond, and she does not see much of Raji after this conversation.

Mrs. Devi, the wealthy woman who owns the home where Koly and the others are staying under Maa Kamala's care, comes to visit and to see the girls. When Mrs. Devi sees the quilt Koly has made, she admires Koly's embroidery skill and offers her the opportunity to meet with someone who might employ her in this capacity.

Chapters 10–11

After Mrs. Devi introduces Koly to Mr. Das, the sari maker, and shows him her work, Mr. Das hires Koly. She earns three times what she did stringing marigolds. She works with a young woman named Mala, whose work Mr. Das greatly admires. Mala takes advantage of his high opinion of her and often comes into work late.

Mala invites Koly to her apartment for a party. While at Mala's apartment, Koly sees an embroidered wedding veil that has been stolen from Mr. Das's shop. She is approached by a young artist who wants to paint her; he offers her bhang, made from marijuana. She declines. When the artist, Kajal, returns to her with a glass of lassi (a traditional drink made with yogurt), Kali soon feels dizzy and nauseous. The sitar player from the party sees Koly and helps her to the cinema where she is to meet Tanu. He tells her that Kajal put bhang in her lassi.

Just after Koly returns from work after missing time for being ill, Raji returns. Koly finds him waiting for her when she leaves work. He tells her that he will need to return to the village soon to plant the lentils. He has left his rickshaw job and asks to speak with her. They make their way to the river where Raji asks Koly if she will marry him. Koly cares for him deeply but suggests they wait. She enjoys her independence and her embroidery work and is wary of returning to a life where cooking and cleaning are her only occupations. Raji is disappointed but agrees to wait.

Koly and Tanu move into their own apartment. Koly and Raji write to one another, and he tells her of the room he has built for her, where she can continue to do her embroidery. At work, Mr. Das discovers that Mala has stolen from him, and he fires her. Koly begins to sew a quilt for her dowry. Koly tells Mr. Das of her marriage plans and proposes the idea of doing her work from home. He enthusiastically agrees with the plan. The novel ends with Koly eagerly anticipating her new life with Raji.

CHARACTERS

Baap

Baap is Koly's father; the word *baap* is the Hindi term for father. Koly has great respect for her father's ability to read and write. Although the family does not have much wealth—they are so poor that finding a husband for Koly is in part spurred by the fact that there will be more food for her parents and brothers when she is gone—they are of the highest caste in Hindi society.

Binu

Binu is the sitar player at Mala's party. He escorts Koly from Mala's room after she is drugged by Kajal.

Mr. Das

Mr. Das is the owner of the sari shop where Koly is employed.

Mrs. Devi

Mrs. Devi is the wealthy woman who owns and funds the home where Koly and the other widows live. She takes a particular interest in Koly and her embroidery and finds her a job embroidering saris for Mr. Das.

Gopal

Gopal is one of Koly's brothers.

Mr. Govind

Mr. Govind runs a stall in the market. Tanu and Koly string marigold wreaths for him, and he is depicted as a fair boss.

Kajal

Kajal is the artist who puts a drug in Koly's drink at Mala's party.

Maa Kamala

Maa Kamala runs the home for widows to which Raji brings Koly. She is kind but strict, and Koly is grateful to be taken in and given the opportunity to work. Maa Kamala shows Koly more affection and care than Mrs. Mehta did and in

this way becomes a sort of surrogate mother figure for Koly and the other widows.

Koly

Koly is the protagonist of *Homeless Bird*. When the novel opens, she is thirteen years old. Her parents are in the process of arranging a marriage for her. Koly is anxious but dutiful, and she is hopeful that her husband will be someone with whom she can enjoy her life. Upon meeting him on her wedding day, Koly learns that Hari is gravely ill with tuberculosis. Following his death, Koly attempts to cope with her position as a widow within her in-laws' home. She works like a servant and dreams of escape.

After the death of her father-in-law, Koly is abandoned by her mother-in-law in the city of Vrindavan. Here, after a few days and nights of homelessness, she is taken into a home for widows. A job is found for her, and Koly begins to rebuild her life. Throughout this difficult time, Koly demonstrates her sense of duty and respect to her family and her husband's family, as well as a desire for happiness for herself. This resolve is reflected in her work ethic and in her efforts to improve her situation. By the novel's end, she has, after a period of time that allowed her to pursue her work, accepted Raji's marriage proposal.

Mr. Lal

Mr. Lal is an old friend of Mr. Mehta's. It is in Mr. Lal's home that the Mehta family stays when they travel to the Ganges River in hopes of healing Hari.

Maa

Maa is Koly's mother. Maa is the Hindi word for mother. Koly's mother has traditional Hindi values. She does not think her daughter should attend school or learn to read and write. She believes that Koly should be married at the age of thirteen. Although the book does not center on Koly's relationship with her own parents, the fact that she expresses how much she misses them attests to her love for them. Her unwillingness to return to them after her husband's death demonstrates her respect for her parents; she refuses to bring shame upon them by returning.

Mala

Mala works for Mr. Das. She comes in late often, but Mr. Das is lenient with her because her work is excellent. She seems mature to Koly because she has her own apartment. Mala invites Koly to a party. There Koly is given a drugged drink by an artist friend of Mala's. While at the party, Koly sees a wedding veil Mala has stolen from Mr. Das. Mala is later fired for the theft.

Chandra Mehta

Chandra is Hari's sister and the daughter of Mr. and Mrs. Mehta. She and Koly become friends. Koly finds her to be a bit spoiled and must do much more of the household work than Chandra does. Koly, though, is glad to have a sister, and Chandra is the only bright spot in the drudgery of Koly's life, particularly after Hari's death. Chandra soon marries and leaves the household, returning only when her father dies. Koly misses her deeply.

Hari Mehta

Hari is the only son of Mr. and Mrs. Mehta. He is sick with tuberculosis and is near death when he meets and marries Koly. She finds him to be spoiled, yet she seems to feel some affection for him and wonders what their life could have been like if he had not been ill. Hari insists on Koly coming with him and his parents to the Ganges River. After a few moments of frivolity in the river, Hari becomes chilled and weak. He soon dies.

Mr. Mehta

Mr. Mehta is Chandra's and Hari's father and Koly's father-in-law. He is referred to in the novel as Sassur, the Hindi term for father-in-law. He is more affectionate with Koly, particularly after his son's death, than his wife is. Mr. Mehta assures Koly after Hari's death that she will be treated like a daughter in their home, but Koly already knows from Mrs. Mehta's treatment of her that this will not be the case. Mr. Mehta responds to Koly's thirst for knowledge and teaches her how to read and write. Mr. Mehta is grief-stricken by the loss of his son, and his sadness only increases after his daughter, Chandra, marries and leaves the home. He is a teacher, and the school where he is employed relies increasingly on computers. His responsibilities are diminished. On the day he loses his job, he dies.

Mrs. Mehta

Mrs. Mehta is Chandra's and Hari's mother and Koly's mother-in-law. She is referred to by Koly as Saas, the Hindi term for mother-in-law. Mrs. Mehta's affection is focused almost exclusively on her dying son. She is barely polite to Koly from the moment she arrives. Mrs. Mehta is resentful of Koly's presence in her home; she only wanted her son to marry so that the dowry money could be used for the trip to the Ganges River. The Mehtas hope Hari will be cured there.

After Hari's death, Mrs. Mehta's resentment of Koly increases; she is just another mouth to feed. Mrs. Mehta tricks Koly by having her sign papers so that her widow's pension will be mailed to their home, but she does not tell Koly that the money is rightfully hers. Koly spends her days cooking and cleaning and being criticized by Mrs. Mehta, who is also resentful of her husband for teaching Koly to read and write. After Mr. Mehta's death, Mrs. Mehta lies to Koly, telling her they are going to live with her relatives. She then abandons her in a city where many widows are deposited by relatives in this same manner.

Raji

Raji operates the rickshaw that takes Mrs. Mehta and Koly to the temple where Mrs. Mehta abandons Koly. Later, Koly finds Raji, and he tells her that Mrs. Mehta returned to the train station and boarded a train for Delhi. Raji later brings Koly to Maa Kamala in the hopes that she will take Koly in. Raji owns land in a village but cannot afford to plant seeds. He saves as much money as he can so that he can return to the village. After learning to read from Koly, Raji suggests that one day, he will be looking for a wife to share his home and farm. Koly does not know how to reply, but when Raji returns to the city, he seeks out Koly and asks her more directly to marry him. He is disappointed when Koly asks for more time but promises that he will wait for her. Honoring Koly's desire to remain employed with Mr. Das, Raji adds a room on to his house where Koly can continue to embroider. He shows himself to be dedicated to Koly and considerate of her wishes.

Ram

Ram is one of Koly's brothers.

Saas

See Mrs. Mehta

Sassur

See Mr. Mehta

Tanu

Tanu becomes Koly's friend at Maa Kamala's home for widows. Maa Kamala instructs Koly to go with Tanu to her flower-stringing job at Mr. Govind's stall. As coworkers and roommates, the girls spend most of their time together and become close. Tanu helps Koly sneak away to go to Mala's party and waits for her to escort her back. She is sad to hear that Koly plans to leave and marry Raji.

THEMES

Duty

In *Homeless Bird*, Koly's choices are shaped by a familial and cultural sense of duty. In many ways, this sense of duty imposes itself upon Koly so firmly that she feels she has no choices. The book opens with Koly's mother, her maa, discussing with Koly her duty to the family to marry. Koly is thirteen, her mother reminds her: "It's time for you to have a husband." As Koly goes on to consider her mother's words, she places this mandate within the context of her family's poverty. She feels a sense of duty to alleviate their suffering by leaving home so there will be more food left for her brothers and her parents.

In the second paragraph of the story, the cultural duty to marry is again emphasized. Koly understands that her father, her baap, "like all fathers with a daughter to marry off, had to find a dowry for me." Koly accepts that a marriage will be arranged for her; it is simply what is done in her culture. Her brothers tease her about having to obey her new husband and how she will have to lose to him when they play cards. As Koly contemplates her future she thinks, "A part of me hoped they would be successful and that someone wanted me," as her relatives and friends aid her parents in the search for a husband. At the same time, Koly thinks, "A part of me hoped no one in the world would want me enough to take me away from my home and my maa and baap and brothers." She realizes that after she is married, her new home will be that of her husband's family. Koly is afraid, but resolved, as she contemplates her fate.

Once Koly is wed to Hari, these conflicting feelings remain. Hari is gravely ill. The marriage

was arranged by his family solely for the purpose of gaining Koly's dowry money, so that efforts could be taken to save Hari. Once Koly learns this, she is rightly concerned with what her place in her new family is and will be. Mrs. Mehta, her mother-in-law, makes it clear that Koly is there to help maintain the household. Mrs. Mehta treats Koly as an inconvenience. Koly was a means to an end, a way of getting money to help Hari, and now Mrs. Mehta acts as if Koly's presence is a necessary unpleasantness that needs to be endured for the sake of her son.

After Hari's death, and in particular after Hari's sister, Chandra, is wed and leaves the home, Koly's position worsens. She has no one to talk to and is even more like a servant than before. Her own widow's pension is stolen from her by Mrs. Mehta, who, after the death of her husband, abandons Koly to the fate of other unwanted widows. While Koly honored her sense of duty by remaining with Mrs. Mehta and not fleeing, Mrs. Mehta never treated Koly as a true daughter-in-law. Despite her fate, Koly refuses to return to her own family. Not only does she not wish to dishonor them, but she is aware that her departure has enabled them to redistribute their meager resources among fewer family members. Koly, throughout the novel, is defined by this strong sense of duty.

Coming of Age

Koly matures from a child to a young woman in *Homeless Bird*. Though the work is framed by her two marriages, she enters the first marriage as a frightened girl, whereas she contemplates her upcoming second marriage, at the novel's end, as competent young woman. For much of the novel, she faces the major life-changing events as a child who does what she is told to do, first by family and then by the strangers who take her in and help her. These experiences make her stronger, so that when she is provided with the opportunity to make a choice about her future, she feels equipped to handle the decision as an adult.

Koly is told she must marry Hari, which she does, with trepidation but without complaint. She follows her mother-in-law's orders to care for the household, as she is expected to do. She accompanies Hari to the Ganges because he wishes it, even though his mother is not happy about her son's decision. After Hari's

TOPICS FOR FURTHER STUDY

- In *Homeless Bird*, Whelan references the Indian caste system. Research the way this system classifies people in Indian society. Make a diagram that illuminates the class distinctions, and write an accompanying report that explains the religious basis for the divisions. Consider and research the impact of these social structures on Indian society.

- Koly is taught the craft of embroidery, and it is this skill that enables her to pursue her own livelihood. Styles of embroidery vary by region and village in India. Research the different traditional styles of Indian embroidery, and create a web page, PowerPoint presentation, or Prezi report in which you discuss the differences among the various styles and include images or links to images of examples of these styles.

- Lensey Namioka's *Ties That Bind, Ties that Break* was published in 1999. In this novel, a young girl who was born in China is rejected for an arranged marriage because she has not participated in the practice of foot binding. With a small group, read Namioka's novel. In particular, focus on the protagonist, Ailin, and compare her with Koly in *Homeless Bird*. How are the girls alike in terms of their attitude toward their cultures' traditions of arranged marriages? What are the similarities and differences in the ways they relate to their families? What other parallels can you observe? Create a blog you can use as a forum to discuss these and other questions with your group.

- Whelan wrote about India and Indian culture without ever having visited India. Form a small writing group. Pick a place you have not been to, and write a short story that takes place there. Using print and online sources, research the location, its traditions, and its customs. Find images that will assist you in describing the landscape and the people. When you have finished writing your stories, share them with other members of the group, and discuss the challenges you may have had as you attempted to write a detailed description of a place you have never been to.

---

death, Koly attempts to cope with her new circumstances as a widow in her husband's home, even though she has never been entirely welcome. Mrs. Mehta endures Koly's presence in her home only as long as Mr. Mehta is alive.

During the span between Hari's death and Mr. Mehta's death, Koly contemplates running away. Her existence is joyless after Chandra, her one companion, departs to begin her new life as a married woman. Koly does convince Mr. Mehta to teach her to read, and these lessons prove invaluable to Koly. The request is a significant step in her journey toward adulthood; it prepares Koly to eventually redirect her widow's pension, after Mrs. Mehta has stolen it. It also gives Koly a sense of power to be able to read, a skill that typically only male members of her society possess.

Still, after Mrs. Mehta has abandoned her, Koly remains, in many ways, a frightened child. She allows strangers to advise her on where to sleep. It is Raji who takes Koly to the home where Maa Kamala cares for the homeless widows. Maa Kamala finds Koly a job and gives her food and shelter. Later, Mrs. Devi sees Koly's embroidered quilt and guides her toward a new job. In this way, Koly is still a child, directed toward the next phase in her life by the adults in it. She makes the mistakes a child would make when she goes to Mala's party. Not yet a good judge of character, Koly puts herself in a situation that makes her uncomfortable, and she is

Koly's marriage is arranged when she is only thirteen years old. (© *Aman Ahmed Khan* / *Shutterstock.com*)

rescued by the sitar player and guided back to her friend, Tanu, and finally back home.

In contrast, when Raji proposes marriage, Koly has finally settled into her life. She has friends and a job, and she is saving money. She finds that she is not ready to be done with this part of her life, and she makes her first adult decision when she tells Raji she will not marry him yet. By the novel's end, she has finished making a new quilt, for the dowry she is providing for herself to offer Raji. Now she decides she is ready to marry. The decision to wait until she feels ready signals Koly's transformation from someone swept along by the decisions made for her by well-meaning and not-so-well-meaning adults to a young woman able to make decisions for herself.

STYLE

First-Person Narration and Tone

Homeless Bird is written in first person from the point of view of Koly, who is thirteen when the story begins. In first-person narratives, the narrating character refers to himself or herself as "I." In third-person narratives, on the other hand, the point-of-view character is referred to by his or her name, or "he" or "she." There are various types of third-person narratives. The author may chose to provide the perspectives of multiple characters, giving the reader access to the intimate thoughts and feelings of these characters. This is known as omniscient third-person narration. In close, or limited, omniscient third-person narration, the author allows the reader this intimate access only to one or two characters. Close third-person narration is similar to first-person narration in the way it allows for intimate access into a character's interior world. In *Homeless Bird*, Whelan limits access to the perspective of Koly alone. This allows the reader to understand the protagonist in a meaningful way, even while the reader's understanding of the novel's other characters is limited to Koly's view of those characters.

First-person narration typically invites a sense of familiarity between the narrator and the reader. However, even though Whelan incorporates this type of storytelling, the tone of the work is overlaid with a sense of formality. The reader does not have the casual intimacy of friendship with Koly; rather, the reader is kept at a respectful distance through the narrator's language and diction. For example, when Koly recalls peeking into her brothers' school books because she is envious of their ability to go to school and learn to read, she states, "When I stole looks into my brothers' books, I saw secrets in the characters I could not puzzle out." Later, she describes loitering at the windows of the school to hear the lessons. "But the lessons were not like measles. I did not catch them." She does not *glance* at the books or try to *understand* the words—rather she steals looks and attempts to puzzle things out. She does not flip through the books, she turns over the pages, and she wishes she could catch the meaning of lessons like one catches the measles. Her way of describing herself and her own place in her world is marked by lyricism and formality—the tone is not casual or glib.

The distance Whelan establishes through her narrator reflects the formality of Koly's culture, rooted in the deference and respect women are expected to show in public and to men in their society. Throughout the novel, attention is drawn to these notions of respect, duty, and decorum. Although Koly develops close relationships, there is always this sense of deference, a hesitancy to reveal too much of herself to the other characters in the novel. For example, even with Raji, with whom Koly develops a deep friendship and eventually a romantic relationship, Koly is reserved. When he tells her he will one day be seeking a wife, she gives no indication that this might be a role she would desire to fill; she remains quiet and consequently does not hear from Raji again for some time. It is unsurprising, therefore, that the same relationship between Koly and the reader is

similarly established through Koly's reserved first-person narration.

Realism

In interviews, Whelan has recounted the way she developed the idea for *Homeless Bird* after seeing a news story about the widows, dressed in their white saris in the city of Varansi, abandoned by their in-laws. The news story told how the women chanted at the temples in exchange for food from the monks. Later, Whelan states, she saw an exhibit of embroidery crafted by Indian women. She wove these two stories together as the starting point for *Homeless Bird*. The fact that Whelan used elements from a news story and an art exhibit as the basis for the book underscores Whelan's realism.

In both its premise and in the way the story unfolds with details about Koly's daily life, her cultural traditions, and her family dynamic, the work strives to present an accurate picture of life in India for a young woman. The fact of Koly's arranged marriage takes center stage in the story, and it is a hallmark of Indian society. By exploring such elements of culture and tradition and daily life, Whelan writes in the tradition of social realism. The novel is not just about Koly, but her place within her society and her society as a whole. In particular, Whelan focuses on the treatment of widows within Indian society. Whelan depicts the abandoned widows almost as a by-product of the arranged marriage system.

Also present in Whelan's novel to some degree is what is known as psychological realism. Psychological realism is heavily focused on depicting a character's interior world. In *Homeless Bird*, Whelan is concerned with conveying Koly's thoughts and feelings about her marriage and with depicting the trauma Koly endures after she is abandoned by her mother-in-law. This thorough treatment of Koly's psychological state by Whelan allows the reader to understand Koly more precisely, particularly when the narrative highlights the gap between what Koly thinks and what she says or does not say, as when Raji first speaks of marriage.

HISTORICAL CONTEXT

Caste System in India
In India, the caste system divides individuals into different social rankings. The system is

COMPARE
&
CONTRAST

- **2000:** Widows abandoned by their families and living in Vrindavan rely on charity in order to avoid starvation and find shelter. Many must devote themselves to the spiritual practice of singing in temples in order to receive the free food upon which they survive. They are often shunned by society and regarded as unlucky and inauspicious.

  Today: Some progress is being made in changing social attitudes about the widows of Vrindavan. Some are now allowed to participate in a religious celebration from which they had been excluded in the past. About eight hundred widows celebrate Raksha Bandhan for the first time in August 2014, after the group Sulabh International advocates for their participation. Sulabh International works toward assimilating the widows into mainstream society.

- **2000:** Many rural parts of India have traditional needlecrafts associated with them, such as quilting and embroidery. Regions often have styles particular to their location, such as Sujini quilt making in Bihar or Kantha embroidery in West Bengal.

  Today: Sujini embroidery allows women living in poverty, because of social customs that deem many forms of work as not respectable, to help earn money in a way that is socially acceptable.

- **2000:** Arranged marriages are common in India and are often regarded favorably, despite Western attitudes that view the practice as dated and restrictive.

  Today: Recent statistics show that in India, 90 percent of marriages are arranged. A recent survey indicates that about 75 percent of Indians prefer arranged marriages.

---

most commonly associated with Hinduism, but other religions in India similarly adhere to such social classifications. As Tom O'Neill explains in an article for *National Geographic*, "To be born a Hindu in India is to enter the caste system, one of the world's longest surviving forms of social stratification." This system has been a part of Indian culture for over fifteen hundred years.

The most revered rank in Hindu society are the priests and teachers, or Brahmans. Next come the Kshatriyas, or rulers and soldiers. The merchants and traders, or Vaisyas, are next. Then come the laborers, or Sudras. The fifth and final group are known as *achuta*: untouchables. They are the outcasts of society. Whelan references the untouchables in her novel. They live in homes on the edge of town made from "bits of metal and old crates." Mrs. Mehta tells Koly, "You must not let their shadow fall upon you... or it will pollute you."

The untouchables—also referred to by the more politically correct term *Dalit*—are discriminated against. O'Neill states that although this discrimination is considered illegal, many have faced violent consequences for attempting to have the same rights as other members of society. O'Neill cites a case in which a Dalit man—a leatherworker, considered unclean because he works with animal skins—earned enough money to buy a plot of land. When he demanded the use of the village well, members of a higher caste burned his house and beat his family.

Writing for *Diplomat* magazine, Neeta Lal also comments on how ingrained the prejudices of the caste system are in Indian society. Lal cites a study in which it was reported that in some schools, "teachers and students refuse to partake of government-sponsored free midday meals because they are cooked by Dalits." Lal goes to explain that even though

The groom's parents arranged the marriage only to obtain the dowry to pay for the sickly boy's trip to bathe in the healing waters of the river Ganges. (© sudalim | Shutterstock.com)

the caste system has been officially abolished under the Indian Constitution, there's still blatant discrimination and prejudice against the Dalits. They are frequently refused entry to temples, schools, eateries and barred from participating in community gatherings. They are sometimes still even ostracized to the point that they are made to live on the outskirts of villages.

Widows of Vrindavan

The widows Whelan depicts in *Homeless Bird*, unwanted women abandoned by relatives in the city of Vrindavan, are not a fictional creation. In Whelan's novel, the explanations for this phenomenon are lightly sketched; she implies that these widows are left destitute and alone because they are a financial burden on the husband's family. For Koly, this is true—her mother-in-law can barely afford to feed her. At the same time, it is also true that Mrs. Mehta never wanted her son to marry in the first place; Koly was used. For other widows, the reasons they find themselves in Vrindavan are varied. As is explained by the Indian charity Maitri,

In many Indian societies, if a husband passes away, the wife bears the blame for her husband's death which is considered a manifestation of the wife's past sins. Considered a bad omen, widows are often abandoned by their families, left destitute, and forced to beg for their daily survival.

In an article for BBC News, Anthony Denselow describes the situation in vivid detail, noting that in Vrindavan alone, there are approximately six thousand widows. Just as in Whelan's novel, widows gather at temples to receive food. They are paid a small amount for singing in the temples. Some are housed in spiritual communes known as *ashrams*, while others are forced to beg in order to pay for a roof over their heads. Pilgrims who come to the city to pay tribute to the deities Radha and Krishna often take pity on the widows and give them money. As Denselow points out,

> The government and pilgrims can help keep these refugees from family life away from starvation, but they are less able to quell injustices and age-old superstitions in Bengal. For some here, to even cast an eye on a widow is considered deeply unlucky.

CRITICAL OVERVIEW

Homeless Bird was well received upon its 2000 publication; it won a National Book Award that same year. Critics have discussed Whelan's portrayal of aspects of Indian, specifically Hindu, culture. A review by the Smithsonian Asian Pacific American Center states, "Whelan writes deftly of unchallenged traditions that begin with the devaluation of girls which allows for child marriage, abusive in-laws, and ends with disposable widowhood." The reviewer goes on to note, "Clearly aware of her younger audience, Whelan invests Koly with the determination to survive and thrive."

Alethea Helbig and Agnes Perkins summarize and review *Homeless Bird* for the *Dictionary of American Young Adult Fiction, 1997–2001: Books of Recognized Merit*. The critics assert that although "the plot moves on coincidence, characters are transparent, and symbolism is obvious," the book nevertheless is commendable for its "vividly portrayed details of everyday life and customs from the women's point of view in a warm and fluid style."

Susan Gelber Cannon, when assessing the work from a teacher's perspective in *Think, Care, Act: Teaching for a Peaceful Future*, questions the portrayal that Helbig and Perkins praise. Cannon states,

> Reading *Homeless Bird* allows us to explore issues of Indian culture and history, to view commonalities and conflicts in attitudes among rural, urban, traditional, and modern Indians, and to explore a variety of beliefs about marriage and gender roles.

However, Cannon goes on to maintain, "without a teacher's thorough introduction to modern Indian culture in all its diversity, this book could mistakenly convince students that all Indian girls are forced into arranged marriages at age 13."

Martha Davis Beck, writing for the *New York Times*, offers a favorable assessment of the work's style, describing it as "graceful and evocative." Beck further observes that the novel provides a "hopeful and moving answer" to the question of how a young woman begins to define herself in a part of the world in which "a woman's identity is still narrowly tied to the men who claim her as daughter and wife."

> YET FOR KOLY, FROM THE BEGINNING OF *HOMELESS BIRD*, BIRDS ARE ASSOCIATED WITH WORDS, BOTH AS A SYMBOL OF FREEDOM AND AS A POWER TO BE HARNESSED."

CRITICISM

Catherine Dominic

Dominic is a novelist and a freelance writer and editor. In the following essay, she examines Whelan's use of bird imagery in Homeless Bird, *particularly focusing on Whelan's association of bird imagery with the written word.*

Among the most prevalent of the images Whelan employs in *Homeless Bird* is that of bird imagery. She uses various bird images to denote different ideas throughout the novel. The title itself makes use of this imagery and is a reference to a poem Koly reads in her father-in-law's book. Although critics have commented on the book's imagery in general and the bird imagery in particular, the specific relationship between bird imagery and the power of the written word in the novel bears further exploration. In a review of Whelan's *The Impossible Journey* for the University of Manitoba's *CM Magazine*, critic Lorraine Douglas compares the bird imagery in Whelan's *The Impossible Journey* to that found in *Homeless Bird*. Douglas states that in both novels, Whelan "uses images of birds to express ideas of personal freedom and the ability of the human spirit to soar above the realities of living in an authoritarian family or political system." Yet for Koly, from the beginning of *Homeless Bird*, birds are associated with words, both as a symbol of freedom and as a power to be harnessed.

In the first chapter of the novel, Koly describes the way her father would attempt to earn money by writing letters for people who did not know how to write. She notes that her father's customers were typically poor, and he would write for them for a very small amount, one or two rupees. Sometimes, her father let her watch him form the letters. "I watched," Koly states, "as the spoken words were written down

WHAT DO I READ NEXT?

- The young-adult novel *Goodbye, Vietnam*, published by Yearling in 1993, is another of Whelan's novels set in Asia. It is set in contemporary Vietnam and is concerned with one family's struggle to flee the political and economic oppression of Vietnam and escape to Hong Kong.

- Bali Rai's young-adult novel, *(Un)arranged Marriage*, was published by Corgi Childrens in 2001. A Sikh who grew up in England, Rai writes on the theme of the arranged marriage from the intended husband's point of view.

- Vasudha Narayanan's *Hinduism*, published in 2009 by Rosen Classroom, is part of the *Understanding Religions* series. In it, Narayanan introduces the basic aspects of the religion, focusing on the divinities worshiped, the spiritual teachings, and the sacred texts and places connected with Hinduism.

- Adeline Yen Mah is a Chinese author whose memoir, *Chinese Cinderella*, was published for young-adult readers by Ember in 2010. After her mother dies while Mah is a child, Mah is considered bad luck. When her father remarries, she is treated unfairly by her stepmother and feels unwanted and unloved.

- Ksum Ansal's novel *The Widow of Vrindavan,* published by HarperCollins India in 2004, centers on the plight of one of the abandoned widows of the famous city.

- Anand Giridharadas's *India Calling: An Intimate Portrait of a Nation's Remaking*, published in 2011 by Henry Holt, chronicles the author's return to the country of his relatives and ancestors. Giridharadas strives to capture the struggles of the country as it attempts to modernize and retain its cultural traditions at the same time.

to become like caged birds, caught forever by my clever baap." Here, words are captured, and in this act of drawing words from air—so like

catching and caging a bird to Koly—her father has the power to earn money, however little it may be, for the family. Koly admires her father's skill and sees the act of writing as an act of power, of agency over one's own fate.

Just as writing words is an enigma to Koly, so is reading them. Both reading and writing are considered to be men's activities, and women are typically excluded from such learning. Koly envies her brothers' ability to attend school. Her mother tells her such learning is pointless for a girl. She tells Koly that school "was a waste for girls," that such learning "will be of no use to you after you are married. The money for books and school fees is better put toward your dowry, so that we may find you a suitable husband." Her brothers tease her for her desire to learn and say she is lucky to not have to go to school. One of her brothers, Ram, tells Koly, "when a girl learns to read, her hair falls out, her eyes cross, and no man will look at her." With such messages being delivered to Koly about the written word, about literacy, it is no wonder Koly associates them with freedom and power—they are freedom and power for the men who can harness them, but not for her.

After Koly marries Hari and then becomes his widow, Koly's father-in-law agrees to teach her to read and write. Koly becomes increasingly accomplished, and Mr. Mehta shares with her his book of poems by the Indian poet Rabindranath Tagore. He tells Koly of the book's value and how it has been passed down from father to son in his family. To cheer her father-in-law up one day, Koly reads her favorite poem to him. "It was about a flock of birds flying day and night through the skies. Among them was one homeless bird, always flying on to somewhere else." Here, Whelan associates words and bird imagery again. The bird in the poem is a figure with both positive and negative connotations. The bird is free to fly wherever it chooses, yet, unlike the others in the flock, it is described as homeless. It can go wherever it will but has no place to which it seems called to return, no home to go to. The poem as a written text read by Koly provides comfort to Koly and to her father-in-law. At the same time, his depression is in part due to the fact that the school at which he teaches, now that it has electricity, is turning increasingly toward computers and away from books. Mr. Mehta experiences this transition from the written word to an electronic version of it as a loss, and Koly likewise takes on this sorrow for herself because it causes her father-in-law pain.

Just as words are directly compared with captured birds early in the novel, here the correlation is implied by virtue of the fact that the written word captures the image of the homeless bird. Further, the homeless bird is very much like the captured bird in the earlier analogy that Koly imagines. The homeless bird soars and represents freedom in this way, but at the same time, its homelessness suggests a *desire* to be captured. It is not characterized as *free*. Instead, it is marked by what it *lacks*—a place to return to. The reader must ask why this poem in particular appeals to Koly and must keep in mind at the same time the association the author has established between birds and words. Koly clearly feels an affinity toward the homeless bird—she obviously has left her own home and has never felt truly at home in the Mehta household. She, like the bird, feels homeless.

Just as words are associated with usefulness—they have the most power when they are captured on a page in Koly's mind—so is freedom, like that of the homeless bird—less valuable without purpose. What Koly seeks is not just freedom from her circumstance of being trapped within an unhappy position in the Mehta household, but an understanding of what her purpose should be once she is free. When she contemplates escape, it is not for the sake of wanderlust or to simply be free of the work of the Mehta household. Rather, she wonders where she will *go* and what she is to *do*. She is a homeless bird that longs for a home.

Once she has been abandoned by her mother-in-law, Koly finds a way to put written words to use. She shares them with Raji. When he hears her reading the poem about the homeless bird, Koly sees the rapture on his face and asks him if he would like to read more of the poems. He confesses that he cannot read. Koly offers to teach him, and in this way, the friendship between them blossoms.

When the two escape the city so Raji can show Koly his favorite spot by the river, they experience two encounters with birds. Raji spots a kingfisher. When he points and names it, "his voice was proud," Koly notes, "as if he had caused the bird to appear." Although Raji's identification of the bird is not linked to the written word or to a word he has read, Whelan nevertheless demonstrates the way Koly notices the association between the *naming* of the bird and its presence, as if Raji's spoken word caused the bird to come into being. It is a moment when Koly seems attuned to a generative power in words.

Soon after, as Raji flings pebbles into the water, a heron appears and flies away. Koly compares the beating of the bird's wings to the beating of her heart. Here, the bird symbolizes something else entirely different from words, language, meaning, power, or even freedom—the bird is simply emblematic of pure emotion, and Koly will later use *image* rather than *word* to capture this emotion, when she embroiders a heron onto a scrap of cloth as she thinks about Raji. In this way, Koly realizes something new—she begins to comprehend the *limitations* of the written word.

After Raji's marriage proposal and Koly's deferral, the two write letters back and forth; words again are here used to capture meaning and to convey the power of emotion. He finally tells her of the room he built for her where she can work on her embroidery. After hearing about the room, Koly thinks, "My last doubts about the marriage flew from me like a flock of birds starting up from a field to be lost in the distance." Here birds are associated with loss—specifically loss of fear—and with Koly's gaining of confidence in her decision.

As she embroiders the quilt for her dowry, Koly once again draws on the heron image—on the wordless power of her emotion, her love for Raji. At the conclusion of the novel, Koly is asked by Mrs. Devi to embroider something from Tagore's poems on one of her saris. "Immediately," Koly thinks, "I knew that it would be the homeless bird, flying at last to its home." In this way, Whelan ties together, admittedly in a heavy-handed way, the imagery that has threaded its way through the novel. Koly is the homeless bird, who has found her home with Raji. The power of words exemplified in the text of the poem about the homeless bird is underscored. Koly relates to them, is moved and guided by them, and in the end she understands both the power and limitations of the written word as she embroiders the image of the homeless bird onto the fabric.

Source: Catherine Dominic, Critical Essay on *Homeless Bird*, in *Novels for Students*, Gale, Cengage Learning, 2015.

Koly meets Raji when she and Sass hire him to take them to the temple in his rickshaw. *(© Amith Nag /
Shutterstock.com)*

Kathleen T. Isaacs and Gloria Whelan

*In the following interview, Isaacs asks Whelan
about the inspiration and the research needed for
Homeless Bird.*

When Gloria Whelan ventured in her imagination halfway around the world to write
Homeless Bird (HarperCollins, 2000), she captured the feeling of small-town India so clearly
that her novel received the National Book
Award for Young People's Literature, in
November. The book describes the life of Koly,
a young Indian girl, widowed at 13 and abandoned in a holy city by her devious mother-in-
law. The tale's far-flung setting was a departure
for Whelan, who has often written about northern Michigan's woods, where she and her husband, Joseph, have lived for more than 20 years,
beside a quiet lake. Long admired as a local
writer, Whelan has also been honored as Michigan Author of the Year by the Michigan
Library Association for her many novels, which
include *Goodbye, Vietnam* (Knopf, 1992), *The
Indian School* (HarperCollins, 1996), *Forgive*

the River, Forgive the Sky (W. B. Eerdmans,
1998), and *Miranda's Last Stand* (HarperCollins, 1999). We spoke to the 77-year-old writer
in December.

*You've been writing for many years. How did
you get started?*

I've been writing as long as I can remember.
I used to dictate stories to my baby-sitter and she
would type them up. When I was in college, I was
going to write the great American novel. I wrote
short stories for adults; I had a collection published by the University of Illinois Press. I also
wrote poetry for quarterlies. That was all before
I began writing for young people.

When did that happen?

We moved up here to northern Michigan
about 23 years ago from Detroit, because we
loved the quiet, the wild, and the woods. We
were here just a couple of weeks and someone
knocked at our door, with a Texas accent and
cowboy boots, and said, "We want to drill for oil
on your property." We didn't have the mineral
rights, so we had nothing to say about it. They

> IT'S A TREASURE HUNT. YOU BEGIN READING
> ONE THING, AND THAT LEADS YOU TO ANOTHER, AND
> THAT LEADS YOU TO ANOTHER. IT'S LIKE A CHAIN."

cleared three acres and bulldozed a road in, and we watched this big derrick go up. Of course, we hoped that the oil well would not produce because we didn't want any kind of permanent installation on the land. We were lucky: the well didn't produce.

We were so fascinated with the whole process that I wrote a novel about a young boy who worked on an oil rig. Because he was a young boy and I was telling his story, somehow it turned into a young adult novel [*A Clearing in the Forest*; Putnam, 1978]. So that was my first novel. Of course, being up here in northern Michigan, away from the city, gave me so much more time [to write]. I could do novels instead of short stories. That made a difference, too.

The world of Oxbow Lake, where you now live, comes through in many of your stories. What attracted you to such a remote part of the country?

Our family had been coming up here for years in the summertime. I came up here as a child with my father, who was an enthusiastic fisherman. So I knew northern Michigan. It has always been a part of my life. I particularly love a river up here. That river [the Au Sable] comes into almost every book I write, and *Forgive the River, Forgive the Sky* is about that river. My husband, who comes from northern Minnesota, loves the North Country, too. So finally, on a Sunday, we decided we didn't want to go back to the city. We wanted to stay. So, we stayed.

Tell us a little about the land you live on.

We have a couple hundred acres. The nearest house is about a mile away; our mailbox is a half a mile from the house. We're on a small lake, and we're the only cabin on the lake. I look out my window when I'm writing, and I see herons and beaver and deer and fox, trotting around the lake. In the wintertime, we see coyotes out on the frozen lake, sleeping in the sun.

I do a lot of walking in the woods. I'm not out so much this time of year, but fall, spring,

and summer I walk at least three miles a day. I like to fish, when I have time—fly-fish. I don't like to fly-fish so much to catch fish. It's just a good excuse for walking down the middle of the stream. You know, that was Thoreau's passion. He loved to walk down the middle of rivers, and I do, too. I've been involved with the [Grand Traverse Regional Land] Conservancy, and we've actually put an easement on our property, which means that all the property that we have will never be developed. It will always stay just the same. So when I look out there at the lake and woods, I know that it will always remain just as it is.

One of the things that comes through in your books is your empathy for Native Americans. Do you have a personal connection to them?

No. I didn't really have much knowledge of Native Americans when we first moved up to northern Michigan. But I happened to write *Next Spring an Oriole* [Random House, 1987], and Native Americans were a part of that book. Native Americans are so much a part of northern Michigan. In 1812, the time of my books about Mackinac Island, there would easily be a thousand Native Americans camped on the shores of that island. So Native Americans gradually began to be a part of what I was writing. As I began to write about Native Americans, I began to read more. *For Miranda's Last Stand*, I had just read a biography of Chief Sitting Bull. I was tremendously impressed with Chief Sitting Bull, so he found his way into my book, and really was an important part of that book.

There are a lot of people, I know, who say you can't write about these things if you're not a Native American or an African American. But I feel very strongly that that's not true. It seems to me that if we can't understand one another, then our society has very little hope. Compassion comes from our understanding of one another. Imagining yourself into the lives of others is really what makes life tolerable. It's what makes us all human. Do we really want to segregate our literature, like we were once a segregated society? I don't think so.

What was the genesis of Homeless Bird?

I saw an article in the *New York Times* a couple of years ago. It was a description of the city of Vrindivan, the city where widows are abandoned by their in-laws. In the article, it mentioned a girl who had been widowed at age 13. I've always been fascinated by India. I've read lots of novels by Indian writers, as well as novels by English writers writing about India. But I didn't want Koly to have to spend the rest of her life chanting in temples. I had happened to see an exhibition at Asia House, in New York City, of quilts that were embroidered by Indian women. And those two things just came together.

Tell us more about researching the novel?

It's a treasure hunt. You begin reading one thing, and that leads you to another, and that leads you to another. It's like a chain. When I was researching *Homeless Bird*, I had never been to India. I had a lot to learn, a lot of research to do. I would find little odds and ends that were so useful. I wanted Koly's first job to be threading marigolds for special occasions, weddings, and funerals. I came upon a sentence that explained how the fibers of the banana plant were used in the process. So that was useful. I discovered that there are bats that hang out in the temples and lots of snakes appear after the monsoons. Those were little things I had not been looking for. But when I found them, they fitted into the book perfectly.

Other than attending that exhibition in New York, were you able to do the rest of the research in Michigan?

Yes. I did it all in northern Michigan, just reading. We have two very good libraries up here, one in Traverse City and one in Petoskey. The one in Petoskey has a superb Michigan collection compiled by William Ohle, who lived up here in northern Michigan and left it to the library. The library has a small room, where you can read the books. They have been a tremendous help.

Was it difficult for you to write about a place you had never visited?

No, not at all. For some reason, I enter into any book that I'm writing. I was very involved in *Homeless Bird*. But then I had written a book about Vietnam—a book that is used in a lot of schools—and had never been to Vietnam. I was able to find a wonderful book written by some Michigan State professors about life in a small village in Vietnam. They had lived there for several years, and included all sorts of detail. It was a treasure for me. You do find these things. Somebody does your work for you.

Have you heard from young readers of Homeless Bird?

Yes, I have. A wonderful young Indian girl e-mailed me and interviewed me, doing a wonderful job. Her questions were so perceptive; it was fun talking with her. There is evidently a Web site for children who are interested in India or are of Indian background [see www.thinkindia.com/channels/news/features/books.htm]. I have talked with other girls with an Indian background, and they seemed to enjoy the book.

What impact has winning the National Book Award had on your life?

It's been nonstop. I've had many, many calls and interviews. I have a quote taped to my computer: *nulla dies sine linea*—it's Latin for "no day without a line." The Greek Pythagoras could draw a perfect line, but he said if he didn't draw it every day, he would lose the skill. So on my computer I have "no day without a line," and I really make myself write every day. It's what I like best to do, and it's what I do. But lately, it's been a tremendous struggle.

Source: Kathleen T. Isaacs and Gloria Whelan, "Flying High," in *School Library Journal*, Vol. 47, No. 3, March 2001, pp. 52–55.

Christian Science Monitor

In the following review, the happy ending is pointed out as being unrealistic.

A book that wins the National Book Award garners high expectations, which is problematic for the recent young-adult winner, *Homeless Bird*. Gloria Whelan's novel of a doomed but resourceful young Indian woman lacks richness and originality, but the story is emotionally compelling.

At 13, Koly faces a big change: She will marry a boy she has never met and go to live with his family. Koly stitches a dowry quilt, capturing images of her mother in a green sari, father on his bicycle, brothers playing soccer, the tamarind tree, the cow, and the courtyard well. This quilt, a photograph, and her mother's silver earrings will be her only possessions and the only reminders of the home and family she may never see again.

The only blessings she finds in her new marriage are a new sister to confide in, a large rat she tames, and a father-in-law who teaches her to read.

It's hard to imagine that someone could be as cruel as Saas, her new mother-in-law, or that her lot in life could get much worse. But when her sickly young husband dies, Saas abandons Koly in a city teeming with widows, and Koly becomes the homeless bird of her favorite poem.

In a happily-ever-after ending, Koly manages to piece together a life that defies the hopeless aspects of her culture's traditions. But if Whelan had included more authentic details about modern-day India, readers would have gained more than a stereotypical look at a young Indian girl's life. The view here seems more influenced by *National Geographic* than real contact with the country.

Source: "For Young Readers," in *Christian Science Monitor*, December 14, 2000, p. 21.

Publishers Weekly

In the following review, the anonymous reviewer characterizes the novel's feminist themes as "more American than Indian."

Whelan (*Miranda's Last Stand*) blends modern Hindu culture with age-old indian traditions as the profiles a poor girl's struggle to survive in a male-dominated society. Only 13 when her parents find her a husband, Koly can't help feeling apprehensive about leaving home to live in a distant village with her in-laws and husband, none of whom she has met. The truth is worse than she could have feared; the groom, Hari, is a sickly child, and his parents have wanted only a dowry, not a wife for him, in order to pay for a trip to Benares so Hari might bathe in the holy waters of the Ganges. Koly is widowed almost immediately; later, she is abandoned in the holy city of Vrindavan by her cruel mother-in-law. Koly, likened to a "homeless bird" in a famous poem by Rabindranath Tagore, embodies the tragic plight of Hindu women without status, family or financial security. She is saved from a dismal fate by her love of beauty, her talent for embroidery and the philanthropy of others—and by Whelan's tidy plotting, which introduces a virtuous young man, a savvy benefactress and a just employer in the nick of time. The feminist theme that dominates the happily-ever-after ending seems more American than Indian, but kids will likely enjoy this dramatic view of an endangered adolescence and cheer Koly's hard-won victories.

Source: Review of *Homeless Bird*, in *Publishers Weekly*, January 31, 2000, p. 107.

SOURCES

"Arranged/Forced Marriage Statistics," Statistic Brain website, http://www.statisticbrain.com/arranged-marriage-statistics/ (accessed August 11, 2014).

Beck, Martha Davis, Review of *Homeless Bird*, in *New York Times*, January 21, 2001, http://www.nytimes.com/books/01/01/21/reviews/010121.rv085319.html (accessed August 11, 2014).

"Breaking Society's Social Dogmas, Vrindavan Widows Celebrate 'Raksha Bandhan,'" in *Sulabh International Social Service Organization*, August 9, 2014, http://sulabhinternational.org/news/breaking-societys-social-dogmas-vrindavan-widows-celebrate-raksha-bandhan (accessed August 11, 2014).

Cannon, Susan Gelber, "Reading Multicultural, Historical, and Controversial Literature to Enhance Empathy," in *Think, Care, Act: Teaching for a Peaceful Future*, Information Age Publishing, 2011, pp. 65–82.

"The Culture of Arranged Marriages in India," Indiamarks website, http://www.indiamarks.com/the-culture-arranged-marriages-india/ (accessed August 11, 2014).

Denselow, Anthony, "The Indian Town with 6,000 Widows," BBC News website, May 2, 2013, http://www.bbc.com/news/magazine-21859622 (accessed August 11, 2014).

Douglas, Lorraine, Review of *The Impossible Journey*, in *CM: A Reviewing Journal of Canadian Materials for Young People*, Vol. 9, No. 19, May 23, 2003, http://umanitoba.ca/outreach/cm/vol9/no19/impossiblejourney.html (accessed August 11, 2014).

Ghose, Tia, "India's Caste System Goes Back 2,000 Years, Genetic Study Finds," NBC News website, August 8, 2013, http://www.nbcnews.com/science/science-news/indias-caste-system-goes-back-2-000-years-genetic-study-f6C10874609 (accessed August 11, 2014).

Helbig, Alethea, and Agnes Perkins, "*Homeless Bird*," in *Dictionary of American Young Adult Fiction, 1997–2001: Books of Recognized Merit*, Greenwood Press, 2004, pp. 149–50.

"Indians Swear by Arranged Marriages," in *India Today*, March 4, 2013, http://indiatoday.intoday.in/story/indians-swear-by-arranged-marriages/1/252496.html (accessed August 11, 2014).

"Kantha Embroidery," Art of Threads website, http://www.art-of-threads.com/indian-embroidery/kantha-embroidery (accessed August 11, 2014).

Lal, Neeta, "India's Ageless Caste Shadow," in *Diplomat*, June 7, 2011, http://thediplomat.com/2011/06/indias-ageless-caste-shadow/?utm_source=feedburner&utm_medium=feed&utm_campaign=Feed%3A%20the-diplomat%20%28The%20Diplomat%20RSS%29sample (accessed August 11, 2014).

O'Neill, Tom, "Untouchable," in *National Geographic*, http://ngm.nationalgeographic.com/ngm/0306/feature1/ (accessed August 11, 2014).

Review of *Homeless Bird*, Smithsonian Asian Pacific American Center website, http://smithsonianapa.org/bookdragon/homeless-bird-by-gloria-whelan/ (accessed August 9, 2014).

"Sujini Embroidery," Upendra Maharathi Shilip Anusandhan Sansthan website, http://www.umsas.org/en/bihar-arts-crafts/sujini-embroidery/ (accessed August 11, 2014).

Whelan, Gloria, *Homeless Bird*, HarperCollins, 2000.

"Widows of Vrindavan," Maitri India website, http://www.maitriindia.org/?p=505 (accessed August 11, 2014).

FURTHER READING

Chen, Martha Alter, *Perpetual Mourning: Widowhood in Rural India*, Oxford University Press, 2001.

Chen studies the treatment of widows in the villages of rural India, discussing the social and financial challenges the women face and highlighting the impact of Hindu traditions on the treatment of Indian widows.

Forbes, Geraldine, *Women in Modern India*, Cambridge University Press, 2007.

Forbes explores the cultural and political history of Indian women from the nineteenth through the twentieth centuries, after India gained independence from Great Britain. She focuses in particular on how a movement to provide women with access to education transformed the role of women in Indian society.

Jadhav, Narendra, *Untouchables: My Family's Triumphant Escape from India's Caste System*, University of California Press, 2007.

Jadhav describes his family's fight for equal rights and justice in India. Jadhav bases his work on his father's diaries and on family stories. He captures his family's fight for a better life for their children, free from the discrimination of the caste system.

Krishnan, Nandini, *Hitched: The Modern Woman and Arranged Marriage*, Random House India, 2013.

Krishnan's work is based on interviews with women about their arranged marriages. She explores the way the concept of arranged marriages has evolved in modern-day India and comments on the use of the Internet and matrimonial websites as means of simply meeting potential partners, not unlike other online dating sites.

SUGGESTED SEARCH TERMS

Whelan AND Homeless Bird

Whelan and realistic fiction

Hinduism AND caste system

Hinduism AND arranged marriages

widows of Vrindavan

traditional Indian embroidery

India AND women AND education

Hinduism AND age for arranged marriages

Indian society AND untouchables AND discrimination

Rabindranath Tagore AND Indian poetry

The Inheritance of Loss

KIRAN DESAI

2006

Kiran Desai's *The Inheritance of Loss* (2006) follows a group of Indians living in a dilapidated house in the foothills of the Himalayas. A cruel retired judge, an aging cook, an orphaned sixteen-year-old girl, and a gorgeous purebred dog share a cramped and cluttered life inside the house called Cho Oyo. The judge finds himself plagued by memories of his past as a student in England while his granddaughter is consumed in the fire of her first love. The cook's hopes of status and material wealth are pinned on his son, Biju, who has immigrated to the United States. Onto this scene arrives a local insurgency of young Indian-Nepali men demanding their own state in India to be called Gorkhaland. Violence and chaos pull each of the characters further from each other all while Biju, facing no luck as an illegal worker, makes the long journey home to Kalimpong. *The Inheritance of Loss* features sweeping scenery from the peak of the nearby Mt. Everest to a basement apartment in Harlem crowded with illegal aliens. Race, religion, poverty, wealth, love, envy, nationalism, colonialism, terrorism, and globalization are addressed not as abstract concepts but as forces directly affecting the characters' lives.

AUTHOR BIOGRAPHY

Desai was born on September 3, 1971, in New Delhi, India, to Ashvin and Anita Desai. She is one of four children. She spent

Kiran Desai (© *Ralph Orlowski* / *Getty Images News* / *Getty Images*)

her childhood in India, moving to England at the age of fourteen, then to the United States one year later. Desai went to high school in Massachusetts before attending Bennington College as an undergraduate, where she studied creative writing. After graduation she attended both Columbia University and Hollins University. Her first novel, *Hullabaloo in the Guava Orchard*, was published in 1998 to positive reviews. *The Inheritance of Loss*, her second novel, was published in 2006 and won both the Man Booker Prize and the National Book Critics Circle fiction award for books published that year.

Desai's mother is also a successful novelist and has been a major influence on her work. Anita Desai's novels include *Fire on the Mountain* (1977), *Clear Light of Day* (1980), and *In Custody* (1984). On her mother's influence on her work, Desai says in an online interview with *Boldtype*: "All my life I've grown up hearing her talk about writing and literature and books." Desai is an avid reader herself, always willing to read authors from different cultures around the world. Her favorite authors include Truman Capote, Juan Rulfo, Gabriel García Márquez, Tennessee Williams, Flannery O'Connor, R. K. Narayan, and Kenzaburō Ōe.

PLOT SUMMARY

One

The Inheritance of Loss begins in the foothills of the Himalayas, where a retired judge lives with his cook; his orphaned granddaughter, Sai; and his beloved dog, Mutt. The judge is cold and cruel, the cook is subservient, and Sai—a young Indian woman with a Western education—is out of place in the judge's decaying house, Cho Oyu. One night, young rebels from the Gorkhaland movement break into the house. They steal the judge's hunting rifles and humiliate him by making him serve them tea.

Two–Three

The police search the house, more out of their own curiosity than any desire to solve the case. Cho Oyo is an example of ruined wealth, whereas the cook's hut is an artifact of the deepest poverty. The cook's son, Biju, lives in the United States, much to the cook's pride. Biju works in the kitchens of New York City, where he is an illegal immigrant.

Four

As the police turn the cook's hut upside down, suspecting him in the robbery, Sai watches, embarrassed. She remembers first meeting him nine years ago when she was dropped off at Cho Oyo from the convent where she was educated.

Five

Biju bounces from job to job in New York City. With no green card, he is fired at the first hint of an inspection.

Six

Sai's father is working in Russia's space program when a bus hits and kills him and his wife while they are out walking. Sai, who has been left behind at a convent while her parents travel, is delivered to her closest kin—the judge.

Seven–Eight

The judge is pleased when Sai compliments Mutt's beauty, but he otherwise sees the girl as a nuisance. He remembers his own travels as a young man, when he took a ship to England to study law, leaving behind his new wife. In England, ashamed of his Indian heritage and the victim of frequent discrimination, he becomes withdrawn, anxious, and untrusting.

When Sai first arrives at Cho Oyo, the judge hires a tutor for her: a woman named Noni. Sai and the cook walk to the tutor's house, passing their neighbors. The closest neighbor is Uncle Potty, who drinks each night away with Father Booty, the owner of a Swiss dairy.

The next neighbors are two Afghan princesses left without an inheritance because their father returned from vacation one day to find he no longer held a title. Also living nearby is Mrs. Sen, who lives in poverty but has a daughter, Mun Mun, who lives in the United States.

Finally, at the house called Mon Ami, two sisters, Lolita and Nonita, live on a pension. Noni tutors Sai from when she first arrives in Kalimpong, but when Sai turns sixteen, a second tutor must be found for math and science, because Sai becomes too advanced for Noni.

Nine

In the present day, Lola panics when she hears from Sai about the robbery of Cho Oyo. Sai is more upset that her math and science tutor, Gyan, does not show up for their scheduled lesson the night of the robbery. She fears he no longer likes her.

Lola has a daughter, Pixie, who is an announcer for the BBC news out of England. Both Lola and Noni hold on to the British ways, as if Indian independence has not happened. They read British novels and eat British jam. Because her security guard, Budhoo, is Indian-Nepali like the rebels who robbed Cho Oyo, Lola wonders if she should fire him, though he has done nothing wrong.

Ten

In New York, Biju drifts from kitchen to kitchen with no success. He lives in a crowded Harlem basement with other illegal immigrants. Biju meets a coworker from Zanzibar named Saeed Saeed and comes to admire him for his easy confidence in navigating America.

Eleven

The cook drops off Sai at Mon Ami three days a week for tutoring. He spends the day selling his homemade liquor at the market, sharing gossip

along the way. The liquor business is necessary for the cook, because the judge does not pay him enough to support himself and Biju.

At night, the cook tells Sai exaggerated stories about the judge's past. The judge overhears and remembers the truth. He was born into a peasant family and spent his childhood studying. He received a scholarship to study law in England, mostly because the Indian Civil Service did not employ enough Indians in high positions to fulfill its quota. He graduated from Cambridge and returned to India a member of the Civil Service as a district judge, traveling the countryside to hold court. The cook was fourteen when he was hired into the judge's service and remembers how strictly the judge ruled over his travels.

Twelve–Thirteen

Gyan, Sai's tutor in math and science, is a poor Indian-Nepali accounting student. At twenty years old (four years older than Sai), he is the only contemporary Sai has known in years of isolation. When they meet for their first lesson in the dining room of Cho Oyo, they are instantly attracted to each other.

Fourteen

Biju witnesses Saeed's easy way with American women. He becomes paranoid that his father might be hurt or worse back home without his knowledge. In India, the cook is inundated with requests for his son to help others travel to and prosper in the United States.

Fifteen

The cook reads a letter from Biju that makes his job sound much better than the reality. He tells everyone he sees on his way home the good news.

Sixteen

Sai asks the judge about his wife—Sai's grandmother. Though the judge refuses to speak to her of it, he remembers privately. He was married to the daughter of a family much wealthier than his own because he was going to an English university. The dowry from the wedding paid his passage to England. It was an arranged marriage that the judge did not consummate before leaving the country because his new wife was fourteen and terrified. However, before he left the two shared a happy bike ride together.

Seventeen

In New York, men from Zanzibar appear at Biju and Saeed's work, hoping that Saeed will help them start their lives in America. Saeed must hide until they leave. He has nothing to give them and no success to share. The restaurant closes after a health inspection, and Saeed and Biju part ways.

Eighteen

The monsoon season descends on Kalimpong, and the residents of Cho Oyo witness the deteriorating state of the house as leaks spring up and mold grows rampantly. During a break in the storms, Gyan walks to Cho Oyo. He and Sai nervously steal glances at each other over the textbooks until a storm begins. Gyan says he should leave, but Sai asks him to stay. At dinner, the judge is rude to Gyan, who reminds him of himself as a young student in England. Sai apologizes for her grandfather's behavior, but Gyan only stares at her with open desire.

Nineteen

Biju runs into Saeed on the street. Saeed proudly tells him about his green card marriage. Biju cannot believe Saeed's luck. Meanwhile in India, Biju's letters home are getting so wet in the post that the cook cannot read them. When he complains at the post office, the workers are indifferent.

Twenty

Sai and Gyan share their first kiss, then many, many more. As they grow closer, the political unrest that leads to the break-in at Cho Oyo first appears in Kalimpong. The Indian-Nepalis demand their own Indian state. Gorhkaland for Gorkhas is their motto.

Twenty-one

Lola and Noni explain the Gorkhaland movement to Sai—how the Indian-Nepali were left out when Jawaharlal Nehru (the first Indian prime minister) divided India into states. However, the Gorkhas' demand of Kalimpong seems excessive to Lola: "When did Darjeeling and Kalimpong belong to Nepal? Darjeeling, in fact, was annexed from Sikkim and Kalimpong from Bhutan."

Mrs. Sen joins the conversation to the chagrin of Lola. Her daughter, Mun Mun, has a job with CNN in America, making her a rival to Lola's daughter Pixie at the BBC. The women bicker over which is a better place to live, England or America.

Twenty-two

After working in the kitchen of a steak house, a rattled Biju quits in search of a restaurant that does not serve beef (cows are considered sacred to Hindus). He discovers the Hindu-owned and staffed Gandhi Café.

Twenty-three

Sai and Gyan are inseparable, ignoring the differences of their class (for example, Sai uses utensils, but Gyan eats with his hands).

Twenty-four

Biju moves in to the Gandhi Café, where the owner, Hashish-Harry, pays his workers less than a livable wage in exchange for room and board—they sleep in the kitchen among the rats.

Twenty-five–Twenty-six

Sai spends Christmas with Lola, Noni, Father Booty, and Uncle Potty. While at the market, Gyan runs into a group of his college friends marching in a Gorkhaland demonstration. He joins the Gorkha National Liberation Front (GNLF) at a canteen after the march. Surrounded by men like him, he is embarrassed at his indulgences with Sai. He urges the group to take the most extreme action toward accomplishing their goal of reclaiming Kalimpong and Darjeeling as Gorkhaland.

Twenty-seven

The next day Gyan arrives at Cho Oyo enraged by the wealth he sees there. He picks a fight with Sai, irrationally blaming her for their difference in class.

Twenty-eight

The judge remembers his reunion with his wife, Nimi, after returning home from England. He treats her brutally. She fails to learn English, and he leaves her behind when he travels for work. He wants her to be westernized as he is, but traditional Indian culture is all she knows.

Twenty-nine

After their fight, Gyan returns to Sai apologetic, but leaves angry once again. At the canteen with the other Gorkha rebels, he tells them about the judge's guns, leading directly to the robbery of Cho Oyo.

Thirty

When he left for the United States, Biju miraculously obtained his tourist visa to on his first visit to the embassy, whereas others try again and again without luck. Three years later, he slips and falls in the Gandhi Café, injuring his knee. Hashish-Harry will not take him to the hospital because of the cost and because Biju is an illegal immigrant. Luckily Biju mends on his own and is able to walk after two weeks.

Thirty-one

Sai, Lola, Noni, Father Booty, and Uncle Potty go to the market in Darjeeling to exchange their library books before the Gorkhaland movement worsens. While they are in the library, a Gorkhaland march passes by outside. The unrest is driving away tourism—one of the area's largest sources of income.

Thirty-two

The judge reluctantly has dinner with his oldest and only friend, Bose, whom he has not seen in over thirty years. Bose is eager to catch up, but the judge resents being reminded of England. He remembers seeing an Indian being beaten mercilessly outside an English pub and hurrying to pass by rather than taking action. Back home, he considers the fact that Sai resembles him as a Westernized Indian. He decides it is good to have her in the house: "This granddaughter whom he didn't hate was perhaps the only miracle fate had thrown his way."

Thirty-three

Sai sees Gyan marching past in the protest, and Gyan locks eyes with her. Neither speaks. On the way home from the market, Father Booty gets into trouble with the police at a checkpoint for taking a picture of a butterfly with a bridge in the background. The police consider this a security risk and confiscate his camera.

Thirty-four

Suspecting Father Booty of suspicious activity because of the photo, the authorities check his papers and discover that he is an illegal alien. He is forced to leave India despite having lived in Kalimpong for forty-five years.

Thirty-five

The police pick up a drunk for the robbery of Cho Oyo and torture him. They do not necessarily believe he is guilty but are practicing for the violence to come as the Gorkhaland movement gains momentum.

Thirty-six

After hearing of the unrest in Kalimpong, Biju arranges a phone call with his father—a very complex ordeal because the only phone near Cho Oyo is at the house of the MetalBox watchman, and the telephone wire is precariously stretched across the valley. The father and son assure each other that each is all right.

Thirty-seven–Thirty-eight

The situation in Kalimpong grows worse as strikes and roadblocks prevent travel. Lola and Noni are beset with rebels sleeping in their house and building huts on their property.

Thirty-nine

Gyan visits Sai at Cho Oyo. Once more they argue, and Gyan leaves, except this time he does not come back. Sai is relieved when she catches a cold that hides her tears and heartbreak. Finally, tired of waiting for Gyan, she decides to track him down.

Forty

Sai finds Gyan's home, where he lives with his parents, grandmother, and siblings: "It was a small, slime-slicked cube." Gyan reluctantly comes outside to talk. Sai blames him for Father Booty and then suddenly realizes that Gyan is behind the robbery at Cho Oyo. She orders his little sister, who has been watching their fight, to tell his parents what Gyan has done. Back at Cho Oyo, the drunk arrested for the robbery comes with his wife to beg for food. The judge refuses them.

Forty-one

Biju decides to go home to India. He buys a treasure trove of New York City souvenirs and electronic gadgets to bring with him as gifts.

Forty-two

Gyan's little sister tells their parents what she heard during the argument outside, and Gyan is immediately grounded. On the day they plan to burn the Indo-Nepal treaty of 1950, the Gorkhas force each home to send a male representative. Gyan's parents keep him from going. At Cho Oyo, the judge tells the cook to go to the march.

Forty-three

Several thousand men gather for the protest, including the cook. Violence erupts as the marchers and then the police throw stones. A riot breaks out, and the police open fire into the crowd. Three policemen fleeing the melee ask to hide at Mon Ami, and Lola refuses them. The cook escapes the violence but sees the bloody aftermath in the market.

Forty-four

Amid escalating chaos, the drunk and his wife return to Cho Oyo to beg. Again the judge refuses them, feeling he owes them nothing because it was the police that arrested the drunk. The couple steals Mutt, hoping to sell her.

Forty-five–Forty-six

Biju begins his journey home as the Cho Oyo household realizes Mutt is missing. The judge, mad with worry, travels Kalimpong asking after her. Those he asks cannot believe he is worried about a dog during a time as dangerous as this.

Forty-seven–Forty-eight

As the police hunt the GNLF members, there are brutal home invasions, and human limbs are hung from the trees on the road to the market. Biju lands safely in Calcutta: "He looked about and for the first time in God knows how long, his vision unblurred and he found that he could see clearly."

Forty-nine

Desperate for Mutt, the judge even tries to pray. He remembers sending his wife back home to her family because of her unwitting participation in a party welcoming Nehru (and thus Indian independence), bringing shame on the judge. He beats her and sends her to live with her sister and brother-in-law, not realizing she is pregnant. After giving birth, Nimi dies in what appeared to be a cooking accident, though it is possible the brother-in-law murders her to rid himself of an extra mouth to feed. The judge ignores his daughter, sending her to boarding schools. He feels his granddaughter's arrival at Cho Oyo

cancels out a small amount of the shame of his past actions toward his wife and daughter.

Fifty

With all the roads closed and buses to Kalimpong cancelled, Biju takes a GNLF jeep, paying a steep price for his passage.

Fifty-one

After dreaming of Mutt's death, the judge turns on the cook, telling him to find Mutt immediately or be killed. The cook tries to reason with the judge, who will not listen. The cook, feeling miserable and guilty despite his innocence, goes to the canteen to ask about the dog. Gyan overhears his pleas and tells the cook to pass the message to Sai that he will personally find Mutt for her.

Fifty-two

Landslides slow the GNLF jeep that carries Biju toward home. Finally, the men rob Biju of everything—his luggage, money, clothes and shoes—sending him away on foot wearing an oversized women's nightgown.

Fifty-three

The cook returns from the canteen drunk and tells the judge to beat him for his failure to find Mutt. The judge beats him brutally. Sai tries to stop him but cannot. She runs outside the house in a panic. She decides that leaving Cho Oyo is the only way she will have a good life. While returning to the house, Sai spots a figure approaching in the distance. She goes inside to tell the cook, who has survived the beating with red marks from the judge's slipper on his face. The cook goes downstairs to meet the visitor, and finds Biju. Father and son shout for joy to see each other again and embrace.

CHARACTERS

Afghan Princesses

The Afghan Princesses are neighbors of Cho Oyo and Mon Ami. Their father goes on vacation and returns to find the British have replaced him, robbing the two girls of their royal prestige and inheritance.

Biju

Biju is the cook's son. He lives and works in New York City. He is aware of how desperately many young Indians wish to come to America and of how eager both he and his father were for his journey. Yet the reality of life in the United States is grim for an illegal immigrant with no connections. He works a bleak series of restaurant jobs while staying in a basement apartment in Harlem with countless other illegal immigrants. However, his letters home always assure his father of his success and happiness. He has moments of terrible fear when he imagines some great harm has come to his father without his knowledge. After settling into a job at the Gandhi Café, where he sleeps in the kitchen at night and works during the day, he begins to hear of the turmoil in Kalimpong. After arranging a telephone call to his father, Biju decides to return home to India. He makes it home successfully, though he has all of his possessions stolen by the Gorkhas in the process. He and his father embrace in the final scene of the novel.

Father Booty

Father Booty is a Swiss immigrant to Kalimpong, where he runs a popular dairy. He is best friends with Uncle Potty and frequently drinks and dances at Uncle Potty's house at night. Father Booty takes a picture of a beautiful butterfly, unintentionally capturing a bridge in his photo. The police consider this suspicious during the turbulent times of the Gorkhaland movement and reveal that Father Booty is an illegal immigrant. Despite living in India for forty-five years, he has never filled out the proper paperwork to become a citizen. He is forced to leave Kalimpong and to sell his dairy for much less than its value

Bose

Bose is the judge's only friend, from his years as a student in England. They meet for dinner after thirty years apart, but the judge will not participate in Bose's nostalgia. The more Bose talks about the old days, the more enraged the judge becomes.

Budhoo

Budhoo is Lola and Noni's watchman at Mon Ami. After the robbery at Cho Oyo by Gorkhaland supporters, the sisters fear Budhoo will turn on them because he is Indian-Nepali like the rebels.

Cook

The cook is an old servant of the judge who has worked for him since the age of fourteen. He has watched the judge's slow and steady downfall from being a prominent member of the Indian Civil Service to being a grumpy man living friendless in a rundown house. The cook has no education or wealth but survives by supplementing his meager wages from the judge with his own successful bootleg liquor business. His hopes rest on the shoulders of his son, Biju, though he misses him terribly. He pours his fatherly energy into Sai in his son's absence. The cook tells Sai exaggerated stories of his past with her grandfather and pouts when she disrespects him, saying, "Here I bring you up as my own child with so much love and just see how you are talking to me."

The cook is a gossip, trading rumors along with liquor during his trips to the market. He tells everyone he meets the latest news about Biju, leading many to beg him for help with their own children's journeys to the United States. He narrowly avoids death when he is forced to march in the demonstration the day the Gorkhas burn the Indian-Nepal treaty of 1950. After Mutt disappears and the judge threatens to kill the cook if she is not found, the cook gets drunk at the canteen and returns to Cho Oyo begging the judge to beat him for his transgression. Despite all the years they have spent together, the cook and the judge are neither friends nor family. There is no love between them. After the beating, the cook goes to the gate to meet a visitor and finds that it is Biju returned from America. He is overjoyed.

Drunk and His Wife

The drunk is picked up on the side of the road and nominally charged with the robbery of Cho Oyo, mostly as an excuse for the police to beat and torture him in preparation for the growing insurgency in Kalimpong. Afterward, the drunk and his wife visit Cho Oyo to beg for the judge's charity, because the drunk has not committed the crime. Very poor, the couple are desperate and refuse to leave the property right away, lingering in the hills. When they return and are again refused, they steal Mutt in order to sell her.

Gyan

Gyan is Sai's tutor in mathematics and science. A former accounting major in college who cannot find a job after graduation, Gyan is hired by the judge to tutor his granddaughter after she can no longer learn from Noni. Gyan is quiet, well mannered, and intelligent. An Indian-Nepali, he is not as wealthy as Sai and the judge nor as westernized, despite his education. Gyan joins the Gorkhaland movement after seeing his friends from college march in a protest. He has been discriminated against as an Indian-Nepali and enjoys the male camaraderie of the cause. He tells the other members of the movement about the valuable guns at Cho Oyo, betraying Sai. After joining the movement, Gyan sees in Sai all that is wrong with society and is embarrassed about the time he has spent with her sharing the easy luxury of her life. Yet he also cannot deny his feelings for her, frequently visiting Cho Oyo only to end up leaving after a heated argument. After Sai visits Gyan at his home, his parents discover his involvement with the Gorkhaland movement and ground him. Because of this, he misses the large rally for the burning of the Indo-Nepal treaty of 1950. When he hears Sai is looking for Mutt, he vows to bring the dog back for her.

Gyan's Little Sister

Gyan's little sister observes the argument between Gyan and Sai at Gyan's house. When Sai catches her watching, she tells Gyan's little sister what kind of activities Gyan has been up to as a member of the GNLF and commands her to tell Gyan's parents. After Sai storms off, Gyan asks his little sister to keep his secret, but as soon as she gets a chance she tells their parents everything she saw, resulting in Gyan's grounding.

Hashish-Harry

Hashish-Harry owns the Gandhi Café in New York City. He employs Biju. His restaurant is Hindu owned and operated. He has his workers sleep in the kitchen of the restaurant. When Biju is hurt, Hashish-Harry refuses to take him to the hospital and responds scornfully when Biju asks him to sponsor him for a green card. He can be very genial but always has his eye on the bottom line as a business owner.

Judge

The judge, whose full name is Jemubhai Popatal Patel, was a high-ranking member of the Indian Civil Service under British rule, traveling from village to village, holding trials. Educated in England, he was incredibly successful despite being born into a peasant family. However, after sending his wife away and disowning his daughter, the judge began to lose his status and power. He lives in Cho Oyo with his granddaughter, his cook, and his dog, Mutt, the only creature he loves in the world. As much as he has wanted to escape being Indian, he can never become an Englishman. He resents the Indian culture that is part of him, preferring westernized manners. He has treated his traditional wife brutally as a result of her failure to become westernized like him, eventually disowning her and his daughter. His granddaughter, Sai, however, is more like him: Western-educated and out of place in the world. The judge is haunted by memories of his past. He has spent his life so absorbed in the impossible dream of becoming a European that he has missed many opportunities for connections, happiness, or even a brief feeling of peace. Instead, he cannot stand the company of even his only friend from his youth, Bose, or his constant companion for years, the cook. When Mutt is stolen, the judge roams the town asking after her. He has a dream in which Mutt dies. He wakes up blaming the cook and beats him savagely.

Lola

Lola lives with her sister, Noni, at Mon Ami. She was once married, but her husband had a heart attack. Now she lives on a pension and enjoys the finer things in life, cultivating a deep appreciation for English and European art, literature, society, and goods. She has a daughter, Pixie, who works for the BBC in England, which delights Lola to no end. Lola is easily panicked, making the Gorkhaland movement especially hard on her fragile emotions. She is enraged by the rebels who build huts on her property. Lola and Noni love Sai dearly and spend their time socializing with Father Booty and Uncle Potty.

Lolita

See Lola

MetalBox watchman

The MetalBox watchman is the keeper of only telephone near Cho Oyo. He is friends with the cook and helps him set up a phone call with Biju.

Mr. and Mrs. Mistry

Mr. and Mrs. Mistry are Sai's parents. They leave Sai at a convent in India while they travel to Russia for Mr. Mistry's work. He is a candidate to work in the Russian space program, but he and his wife are hit by a bus while out for a walk one day and are killed. Mrs. Mistry is the judge's daughter, though they did not have a relationship. The judge kept her in boarding schools so as not to have her around to remind him of her mother.

Mun Mun

Mun Mun is Mrs. Sen's daughter and lives in the United States. She works for CNN.

Mutt

Mutt is a purebred red setter that the judge loves dearly. She is beautiful and cowardly, eating special meals prepared by the cook and sleeping on the judge's pillow. She is stolen from outside Cho Oyo by the drunk and his wife and sold to a family who ties her to a tree and kicks her when she upsets them.

Nimi

Nimi is the judge's young bride, whom he abandons. Married to the judge at fourteen years old in an arranged marriage, Nimi is a traditional Indian bride. Her husband demands that she learn English and act westernized, but she does not catch on, and he punishes her severely. She is left behind when he goes on trips for work, unlike the other wives of men in the Indian Civil Service. He does not allow her to wear hair oils or style herself in Indian fashions. All of this abuse begins to break her mentally. When she is taken to a rally for Nehru, unintentionally shaming her husband by supporting Indian independence, the judge sends her away to her sister and brother-in-law's home. He does not let her return, even after she gives birth to his daughter. This brings great shame to her family and burdens her brother-in-law with another mouth to feed. She dies in a cooking accident, though her frustrated brother-in-law may actually have murdered her.

Noni

Noni lives at Mon Ami with her sister, Lola. She tutors Sai from her first days in Kalimpong, growing very close to her in the process. Noni is calmer and quieter than her sister, though both women habitually romanticize English life. They read books by European authors and use British products. Noni has never been married. She moved in with her sister after Lola's husband died suddenly.

Nonita

See Noni

Jemubhai Popatlal Patel

See Judge

Pixie

Pixie is Lola's daughter and lives in England. She works for the BBC.

Uncle Potty

Uncle Potty is a drunk who lives near Cho Oyo and Mon Ami. He and Father Booty are great friends, getting drunk together nearly every night.

Saeed Saeed

Saeed Saeed is Biju's friend and fellow immigrant to the United States. Originally from Zanzibar, he seems naturally talented at navigating life in America, much to Biju's admiration. He quickly rises from kitchen worker to retail-store employee before finding a girl willing to marry him so that he can receive a green card. When Biju last sees him, Saeed is collecting shoes. His path in America is remarkably different from Biju's.

Sai

Sai is the judge's orphaned granddaughter and lives with him in Cho Oyo. Her parents die in an accident in Russia, though she had not seen them in years. Sai is educated in a convent in India, where she is given a Western education. While there she learns of her parents' deaths and is sent to Cho Oyo. She is very close to the cook, who treats her like a daughter. Sai is a favorite visitor at Mon Ami and with Uncle Potty and Father Booty. The judge does not hate Sai, a fact he finds remarkable, mostly because he sees himself in her. Noni tutors Sai from the time of her arrival at Cho Oyo until she is sixteen, when Gyan is hired for her math and science lessons. Sai is both intelligent and beautiful, catching Gyan's eye from their first meeting. They fall in love until the Gorkhaland movement tears Gyan from her side. Sai spends her time during the Gorkha uprising alternating between being heartbroken and being enraged, getting into vicious arguments with Gyan only to miss him when they are apart. She pours her sorrow into the search for Mutt. After failing to stop the judge from beating the cook, Sai steps outside and realizes she must leave Cho Oyo in order to find happiness and purpose.

Mrs. Sen

Mrs. Sen is a neighbor of Mon Ami and Cho Oyo. She is less wealthy than her neighbors, yet has a daughter who lives successfully in America, drawing the ire of Lola, who sees Mrs. Sen as low class and inappropriate.

THEMES

Loss

Each of the characters in *The Inheritance of Loss* experiences loss as the novel progresses. The only significant gain is the reunion between Biju and his father, the cook. Other than that, the final moment of the novel, the losses pile high. Sai, after losing both of her parents in the bus accident, loses her first love to the Gorkhaland movement. Gyan loses Sai but hopes to win her back by finding Mutt. The narration reveals, however, that Mutt will be impossible to find. The cook has lost his wife and lives off the hope of Biju's success. The judge loses Mutt, the only thing he loves in the world, and also loses his guns and dignity. Noni and Lola lose their sense of security as the rebels build huts on their property. Father Booty is taken away as an illegal resident of India, and all of the characters lose their lives of comfort as the rebellion grows more powerful. Eventually the telephone lines are cut and the roads are blocked—resulting in the loss of all communication out of Kalimpong.

Other, larger losses in the novel include the judge's loss of self and soul as he tries unsuccessfully to banish his own Indian identity in favor of

an English one. Desai also portrays the loss of community experienced by Saeed Saeed and Biju as they hide from their own countrymen in America, unable to help them get on their feet. The Gorkhas, it is revealed in a flash-forward, fail their mission of statehood, making the great loss of life and damage to their community a futile exercise. The general trend of the relationships in the novel is one of falling away rather than coming together. Each generation inherits the loss from the previous one. Sai's losses have their roots in the judge's loss, which even the judge recognizes in the resemblance he sees in their personalities. Likewise, Biju's losses have been passed down from the cook—both exaggerate to save their dignity. The cook pretends life with the judge was once glamorous, and Biju lies to his father about the quality of his jobs in the United States. If loss is thus inherited, Desai suggests, it cannot be escaped but must be endured as a fact of life.

Memory

Memory is central to *The Inheritance of Loss* as the time shifts forward and backward from chapter to chapter, mimicking a person's own shifting thoughts throughout a day. Though the robbery at Cho Oyo occurs in the first chapter, the narration does not return to the time of the robbery until the twenty-ninth chapter, when Gyan joins the Gorkhaland movement. Sometimes the reader is told what will happen in the future, such as the takeover of the library by the Gorkhaland movement and Mutt's mistreatment by the family that buys her. In general, however, the narration flows unpredictably between present and past. The judge, in particular, battles his memories daily. He does not want to remember his life, yet cannot seem to stop himself. For the judge, memory is a tortuous catalog of his failure to become a truly Western man, escaping India once and for all. Looking back on the promise of his career from the confines of the rotting house, the judge is an embittered creature of memory. He prefers to see his past in England in such negative terms that when his friend Bose reminds him of the good times they shared, he becomes irate. Meanwhile, Biju remembers home fondly as life in America grows more difficult, but his memory is selective: "He didn't think of any of the things that had made him leave in the first place." These forgotten facts confront him upon his return to India when the Gorkha rebels steal

TOPICS FOR FURTHER STUDY

- Read Chetan Bhagat's young-adult novel *Revolution 2020*. What comparisons can you draw between the love story of *The Inheritance of Loss* and the love story of *Revolution 2020*? What comparisons can you draw between the two rebellions featured in the novels? Write an essay in which you compare and contrast the representations of love and revolution in each novel.

- Answer each of the following questions in a writing exercise: What challenges does Biju face as an illegal immigrant in New York City? What is a green card and what makes someone qualified to receive one? How does Saeed Saeed obtain his green card? Why is Biju unable to even apply for a green card? Visit the US Citizen and Immigration Services web page at http://www.uscis.gov/greencard and research the green card application process.

- Using the scenes of the monsoon season at Cho Oyo as an example, compose a scene in which the setting plays a major role in the plot. In the same way that the pounding rain makes Gyan move closer to Sai in order to hear her speak, find a way in your scene to make the setting cause, interrupt, or stop the action of your characters.

- Write an essay relating the title of *The Inheritance of Loss* to the novel itself. What does the title mean? To which of the characters do you believe the title refers? What do the characters lose in the course of the action?

- Choose one of the minor characters—such as Father Booty, Uncle Potty, Lola, Noni, Saeed Saeed, or Hashish-Harry—to examine more closely. Write a summary of the character's history and personality as revealed in the novel. Why does the character live where he or she does? What losses does the character experience, if any? What do you think the character's presence in the novel adds to the story?

- Create a blog on the subject of Kalimpong, India. What kind of city is Kalimpong, and where is it located? What is its history and what is nearby? Post about different aspects of Kalimpong and the nearby area that you find interesting. Choose relevant quotations from the novel to tie in to each of your posts. Be sure to use photos and to cite your online sources. After you have finished your posts, visit a classmate's blog and leave a thoughtful comment on one of his or her posts. Be sure to respond to any comments you receive. Visit blogspot.com to access free blog space.

- Sai and Gyan discuss Tenzing Norgay in great detail after viewing his climbing gear at a museum exhibit. Who is Tenzing Norgay? In a small group, create a PowerPoint presentation explaining who this man is, why he is famous worldwide, and why he is admired by the two young characters in *The Inheritance of Loss*. End your presentation with a summary of the conversation that Sai and Gyan have with the other museum-goers about his contribution to the first known climb of Mount Everest. What do you understand about the debate in the museum now that you did not before doing your research? At the end of your presentation, include a slide that shows sources cited.

every possession he has, including the souvenirs he has brought home—memories of his time across the world. Memory works in the novel as a nagging force, one that pushes and pulls at characters without their consent. As the narrative shifts in time, the characters drift on memory through the past, present, and even the future of their lives in Kalimpong.

Sai lives in the mountains of Kalimpong with her grandfather. (© Attila JANDI | Shutterstock.com)

STYLE

Mood

The mood of a novel is the general feeling or emotion that the novel conveys—in other words, how the novel makes the reader feel while reading it. In *The Inheritance of Loss*, the mood could easily be one of despair and, as the title suggests, loss: The dog is lost, the lovers become foes, the judge beats the cook, and Biju is robbed of every possession. Kalimpong descends into chaos as the characters, with the exception of Biju and the cook, grow farther apart rather than banding together against the hardships each faces. Gigy Alex writes in "They Who Regained the Lost Inheritance:" "Though relieved by much humor, *The Inheritance of Loss* may strike many readers as offering an unrelentingly bitter view." Yet because of this humor, which is as unrelenting as the monsoon season storms, the mood of the novel seems more humane and loving than depressing and hopeless. This is exemplified by the reunion of Biju and his father. Despite the heartbreak of losing everything he owns, including the money he has saved and the gifts from New York City sure to delight his father endlessly, Biju is ecstatic to see his father, and the

cook to see Biju. Yet Biju arrives at Cho Oyo wearing only an oversized women's nightgown. This image is, like the novel itself, as funny as it is sad: both a triumph of the human spirit (he makes his way home despite everything) and a tragedy (he has lost everything up to and including the shirt off his back and is returning home in defeat).

Setting

The setting of a novel is the location where the action takes place. In *The Inheritance of Loss*, the major settings are New York City and Kalimpong. In New York City, the story takes place inside various restaurant kitchens where Biju works alongside other illegal immigrants from many countries. When Biju is not at work, he is walking to or from work, looking for a new job, or sleeping in a crowded room. Thus the setting reveals the trials of his life as an immigrant. His New York City is far different from the New York City of a tourist, of a diner in one of the restaurants where he works, of a businessperson taking a cab everywhere, or of someone enjoying the weekend. The very limited setting of work, street, and bed is all Biju knows. In Kalimpong, the most remarkable setting is the dilapidated, Scottish-built house

Biju, an illegal immigrant to the United States, struggles to find his way. *(© Shyamalamuralinath | Shutterstock.com)*

called Cho Oyo. The house is a reflection of the judge's mental state: crowded with old memories, falling to shambles, but certainly a unique monument to European ways. Uma Jayaraman writes in "John Peter Peterson or Jemubhai Popatlal Patel?: 'The Uncanny' Doubleness and 'Cracking' of Identity in Kiran Desai's *Inheritance of Loss*:" "The idea that the house 'needs repairs' hints at Jemubhai's failed aspirations and his dream to be the model mimic man of the British Raj in India." Both the cook and Sai are stuck in this small world of Cho Oyo, where they are victims of the judge's whims. However, they navigate the judge's sour moods as easily as they navigate the cluttered and rotting rooms of Cho Oyo. In this way, the characters' interactions with the setting of a story can reveal more than is on the surface.

HISTORICAL CONTEXT

Gorkhaland

The movement to establish an Indian-Nepali state called Gorkhaland in *The Inheritance of Loss* is based on an actual movement that took place in the 1980s in West Bengal. The Indian-Nepalis felt they were left out of the state making that occurred after Indian independence in the 1950s. Jawaharlal Nehru, the first Indian prime minister, divided India into new states based on several factors, including language. The Indian-Nepalis were not included in this process. Without a state, they felt they were second-class Indian citizens unable to find jobs or learn their own language in school. They demanded retribution in the form of turning Darjeeling and the surrounding area into Gorkhaland, where Indian-Nepalis would be economically and socially predominant. The Gorkha National Liberation Front (GNLF) relied heavily on violence but ultimately failed to win statehood. As seen in *The Inheritance of Loss*, the GNLF was extremely attractive to young men who had found it difficult to find work or rise in society owing to their ethnicity. Indian-Nepalis make up the majority of the population of Kalimpong yet generally live in poverty. This is why Gyan rages at the thought of the wealth of Cho Oyo, where the judge pays him too little for his services. Yet Gyan struggles to find a job elsewhere, even as a college graduate, because of ethnic discrimination.

Diaspora

Diaspora refers to the scattering across the world of a group of people with a common ancestral home. In *The Inheritance of Loss*, three Indian families are separated: Mrs. Sen and Mun Mun, Lola and Pixie, and the cook and Biju. In each case, the parent has encouraged the child to leave India to search for a better life. Biju especially encounters the diasporas of many countries while working in New York City. He becomes so overwhelmed working side by side with African, South American, Mexican, and Caribbean immigrants, many from places he has not heard of, that he is relieved when a Pakistani joins the kitchen. Falling back on his prejudice and hatred as an Indian against Pakistanis feels warm and familiar to the overwhelmed Biju. Nazneen Khan and Ravi Jauhari write: "Diaspora refers not only to geographical dispersal but also brings in the issues of identity, memory and home which such dispersal causes." Biju quits the steak house to honor his beliefs as a Hindu and finds a restaurant without beef on the menu. There, among the company of other Hindus, he finds the most stable community of his time in America—India in miniature in the kitchen of the restaurant. When he decides to return home, it is against the advice of even his travel agent, because one does not undo such a journey.

Indian diaspora began in earnest after British colonization. When the judge travels to England for school he is one of few Indians to receive a Western education. Later, as Noni and Lola point out, Indian food is more popular in London than is traditional British fare. This speaks not only of the increasing population of Indians in England but also of the success that many have found there.

population in the United States. In "Nationalism in Transnational Space: A Saga of Conflict in *The Inheritance of Loss*," Nibedita Mukherjee writes: "Through the character of Biju and his escapades, Kiran Desai introduces the readers to the actual America seen by the immigrants." It is not the Statue of Liberty or Broadway that Biju tours in his time in the United States but a series of rat-infested kitchens beneath high-end restaurants where illegal immigrants are welcome until the first sign of an inspection.

Of all the characters featured in *The Inheritance of Loss*, the cruel judge has most fascinated critics. Alex writes of the judge that through this grumpy man who "still cherishes everything foreign and cannot come to terms with the Indian atmosphere, Kiran presents the other side of Indians—Those Indians who know everything except India."

Jayaraman, however, sees the judge more as a victim of English colonialism than its cheerleader: "Jemubhai Patel is the sad symbol of the debris of India's colonial history." Because the judge is disliked by both Indians and the English, it is no wonder his cold exterior hides a deep-rooted self-hatred at his inability to fit into either culture.

In a book review for the *New York Times* titled "Wounded by the West," Pankaj Mishra considers the weight of a novel that addresses every walk of life from terrorism at the foot of the Himalayas to New York City's basement kitchens and reaches a strong conclusion: "Despite being set in the mid-1980's, it seems the best kind of post-9/11 novel." In an epic story that spans two continents, *The Inheritance of Loss* simultaneously breaks the reader's heart and delicately mends it.

CRITICAL OVERVIEW

The Inheritance of Loss won both the Man Booker Prize and the National Critics Circle fiction award. Critics hailed the book as a triumph, praising the broad scope of the work and its humanism. Khan and Jauhari write: "Full of pathos and tenderness, the novel presents its characters as ultimately frail human beings struggling in a search for love and happiness."

Much attention has been paid to Desai's masterly treatment in the novel of the immigrant

CRITICISM

Amy L. Miller

Miller is a graduate of the University of Cincinnati and currently resides in New Orleans, Louisiana. In the following essay, she examines how the main characters of Desai's The Inheritance of Loss *struggle with their identity as a result of Western influence in their lives.*

In Desai's *The Inheritance of Loss*, each of the main characters struggles with identity. Biju, the cook, Sai, Gyan, and the judge each struggle

WHAT DO I READ NEXT?

- In *Aging and the Indian Diaspora: Cosmopolitan Families in India and Abroad* (2009), Sarah Lamb studies the large population of elderly Indians living alone owing to the migration of their children to other countries, such as England and the United States. Like Mrs. Sen, the cook, and Lola in *The Inheritance of Loss*, these parents are often the motivators behind their children's move, yet they are left behind in India in the process.

- In Desai's first novel, *Hullabaloo in the Guava Orchard* (1998), an overwhelmed man climbs up a guava tree to think and is mistaken for a holy man. Suddenly famous, the man's little town becomes a circus of those wishing to see the guru in his tree and those wishing to profit from the attraction.

- Chetan Bhagat's young-adult novel *2 States: The Story of My Marriage* (2009) describes the difficulty of marriage for love in India when the boy and girl are from traditional families and two different Indian states. Not only must the two love each other, but also their families must meet and approve the match.

- Zadie Smith's *White Teeth* (2000) is a humorous and poignant novel about two families living in England. Samad Iqbal lives a rocky existence with his young traditional Indian wife by an arranged marriage and their twin sons while his English war buddy Archie Jones marries a Jamaican woman and has a troubled but intelligent daughter, Irie. In this celebration of the growing diversity of English life, the tangles and trials of the two men and their families speak to the confusion and triumphs born from the muddling of cultures.

- Desai's mother, Anita Desai, is also an accomplished novelist. Her novel *Clear Light of Day* (1980) is about a family in Old Delhi that has grown apart with the passing years. When the siblings reunite, they act out old memories and conflicts, coming to a deeper understanding of themselves and each other.

- Salman Rushdie's *Midnight's Children* (1981) tells the story of India's history as a nation through a man born at the stroke of midnight on the day of Indian independence. As the man grows, the ups and downs of his life are matched by rises and falls in the progress, peace, and well-being of India.

- In Rabindranath Tagore's *The Home and the World* (1916), a social movement sweeps over a town in Bengal, causing chaos in the markets and dangers in the street and tearing apart the life of the local maharaja. The goal of the movement is to rid India of all its British goods and to rely instead on Indian-made goods. However, the goal of the movement's charismatic leader is to seduce the wife of the maharaja.

- Angie Cruz's *Let It Rain Coffee* (2005) is the story of a family from the Dominican Republic struggling to form a new life in New York City while remembering their past in the Caribbean. Each member of the Colón family—from the children, Bobby and Dallas, to Don Chan, the family's ancient patriarch—must forge his or her own identity as an American.

with a feeling of disorientation with their reality. This disorientation is caused by various factors. For Gyan it is the social gulf between himself and Sai despite their attraction for each other.

For the cook it is his desire to work for a thriving family rather than a fallen one, which causes him to make up tall tales of the judge's glorious past. Biju's vision clears for the first time in years when he steps foot on Indian soil, despite all advice against leaving the land of opportunity, the United States. Sai, a lonely maiden in a tall tower, must take control of her own life if she ever wishes to escape the stale air of Cho Oyo. Otherwise, she will become her grandfather in miniature. The judge, by far the most disoriented of all, sits day in and day out terrified of his own memories: his failure, his shame, his fear, his cruelty.

What is to blame for the state of this sad group? Desai suggests that the insidious power of globalization, snaking its way into even the most remote mountain peaks in the world, has fractured each of these small lives. Biju shoulders the heavy burden of American capitalism in the basement kitchens of New York City. The judge's schooling in England has destroyed his personality as he obsesses over a Western way of life unobtainable in India. The cook dreams of material wealth in his little hut. Sai, having lost her parents to a brief flirtation between the Indian and Russian governments, feels jealous of what Biju and the cook share. Gyan, Sai's intellectual equal, wishes for a state of his own—a Gorkhaland job, Gorkhaland money, a proud history of Gorkha independence— perhaps subliminally so he can feel he deserves her. Desai does not give the characters conclusions to their crises in identity as much as trajectories. They have inherited the loss of those who came before and must bear it into the future.

Although the cook, Gyan, and Sai have connections to the Western world, they have not been immersed as the judge and Biju have. The stories of the judge's struggles in England and Biju's the United States dig at the heart of the novel. As Alex writes, with the inclusion of the diasporic experience, the novel "becomes a cosmopolitan discourse which discusses the pains of rootlessness and the anxiety of displacement." The judge, from the moment he steps onto the ship to England, becomes acutely aware and hypercritical of the culture he leaves behind. Rather than throw a lucky coconut overboard as his father instructs him, he throws the meal his mother has packed him, embarrassed by the smell. This is the beginning of the end of the judge's humanity. Unable to fit in with the English, yet an obsessive student of their culture, he grows distant from his own until Indian life seems unfamiliar and incorrect. The judge's wife, Nimi, becomes his personal symbol of all

> WHAT IS TO BLAME FOR THE STATE OF THIS SAD GROUP? DESAI SUGGESTS THAT THE INSIDIOUS POWER OF GLOBALIZATION, SNAKING ITS WAY INTO EVEN THE MOST REMOTE MOUNTAIN PEAKS IN THE WORLD, HAS FRACTURED EACH OF THESE SMALL LIVES."

things backward in India, from her squatting over the toilet to the oils she wears in her hair, but no matter how hard he beats her, he cannot beat the Indian out of himself.

All of the judge's energy is expended in this futile mission to become a Western man, making him seem a stranger to both cultures. Jayaraman writes: "By the time Sai meets him, he has been paralyzed by the liminality of his space." This means that caught between two cultures, the judge can no longer move. His memories are aggressive, seeking to avenge those he hurt in the past by torturing him in his old age. Only his pretty dog, Mutt, makes the judge happy. A purebred, effortlessly Western dog, Mutt is useless as protection and more cowardly than the cook, but the judge believes she is perfect and treats her as a queen. It is no wonder that this symbol of all things Western is kidnapped by common Indian beggars, the judge's worst nightmare. Without Mutt, the judge forgets his well-trodden identity of cruel, prideful man and goes door to door in a search for the dog that strikes the other residents of Kalimpong as pathetic. The judge snaps back into his old form when he beats the cook, suggesting that the judge's future aligns with that of Cho Oyo—a slow, lonely decay.

Jayaraman writes: "Cho Oyo becomes an externalization of the judge's guilt-ridden life and career." This includes the mold, the leaks, and the maze of clutter, but two of the most important parts of Cho Oyo are Sai and the cook, who are certainly significant aspects of the judge's terrible past. They struggle with their own identities in part because of the judge's brand of dining-room tyranny. Just the suggestion by the judge that the cook is guilty for

The disgust some feel for traditional Indian ways is symbolized by Judge Patel eating his chapati with a knife and fork. (© szefei / Shutterstock.com)

Mutt's disappearance leads the cook to confess and accept a beating—all while being absolutely innocent. Sai is beside herself with rage when the judge insults Gyan over dinner, only to find Gyan is more concerned with her hair, her wrists, her eyebrows, and her lips. However, the cruel jabs by the judge will return to haunt Gyan as he decides to join the GNLF.

From Sai's Western education to Biju searching the streets of New York, each of the characters is touched by the West—a remarkable feat of globalization, considering they live in the remote mountains beneath the shadow of Mount Everest. Yet there are tourists in the market and European authors at the library. By portraying the characters most sympathetic to the West as the least sympathetic personalities (for example, the fussy and uptight Lola and the judge, whose antisocial behavior drives everyone near him away), Desai suggests that the inward journey is more valuable than the outward. After all, it is Biju who emerges happy and victorious in his women's nightgown at the end of the novel. Sai, however, must skulk away into the shadows, too complicated by her Western upbringing to be rescued from Cho Oyo by Gyan—whom she hopes it is when the figure first emerges from the woods. Mishra writes: "Almost all of Desai's characters have been stunted by their encounters with the West." This applies most thoroughly to the judge, who is stunted beyond repair, but even Sai, Biju, and Gyan suffer indignities and setbacks due to the creeping influence of globalization into what by all logic should be their local world.

The "un-homeliness" of home resulting from an envious encounter with a culture apart from one's own is the subject of Mukherjee's essay: "All these men—the judge, Biju, and Gyan—attempt to be established through the process of migration and suffer the varied aspects of 'un-homeliness.'" Biju simply cannot set down roots in the United States, despite three years of earnest trying. He is a good man: focused, honest, and hard working. Yet the land of opportunity has nothing to give him but kitchen after rat-infested kitchen and a string of bosses with eyes only for the bottom line. He does not feel at home, and rightfully so. When he returns to India, it is a triumphant defeat. Biju chooses family over opportunity when many in India are making the opposite choice at their families' urging. The judge's feeling of un-homeliness comes from his liminal state: Caught between two cultures, he is a member of neither. Gyan, at first an eager member of the Gorkhaland movement, quickly becomes lost between his feelings for Sai and his anger at his condition as a second-class citizen in India. He conflates the two issues, becoming angry with Sai for large, abstract issues, and puts the life of his love in danger by sending the GNLF to her home. A robbery causes a literal feeling of un-homeliness: a personal sanctuary violated. The robbery at Cho Oyo begins the great unraveling of the knots that tie the characters together: loose knots, to be sure, but knots all the same. As the connections between them grow thin, the characters must build new identities for themselves or be doomed, like the judge, to die with Cho Oyo.

Desai's great accomplishment in *The Inheritance of Loss* is presenting the incredible scope of the novel while keeping each jab at modernism, each swing at globalization personal and specific to her struggling characters. Never didactic, Desai uses humor in the bleakest of situations to underscore the humanity at stake. Khan and Jauhari write: "Desai's realistic portrayal of life on two continents, diasporic on multiple levels, demonstrates a deep concern for the human condition." Though each character finds himself or herself disoriented by the complications of globalization during the course of the novel, some hold tighter to their true identity than do others. The hope of the novel is that men like Biju and his father will forever outnumber cruel, old judges and that young love can flourish without a backdrop of violence. The novel's pages may be filled with loss, but life does not always give as much as it takes, especially not in a village overrun with rebels, or in an America without a green card. The human spirit will find humor and light in the darkest valley, as long as, like Biju, one can be true to oneself.

Source: Amy L. Miller, Critical Essay on *The Inheritance of Loss*, in *Novels for Students*, Gale, Cengage Learning, 2015.

David Wallace Spielman

In the following excerpt, Spielman examines how the judge suppresses any contradictions in his thoughts to more easily establish and defend what he knows.

> HE IS SELFISH, ABUSIVE, AND WINDS UP BITTER AND ALONE WITH ONLY HIS COOK TO KEEP HIM COMPANY, BUT HE IS AT HIS MOST SYMPATHETIC WHEN HE OPENS HIMSELF UP TO CONTRADICTIONS."

. . . *The Inheritance of Loss* focuses not on an individual's story but on how several people make sense of themselves, view the world around them, and deal with the difficulties that they have with contradictions. "Contradiction" is a term not much used in postcolonial theory, which tends to be dominated by post-structuralism and hybridity theory. I offer this term because Desai uses it frequently in the novel, and it helps us understand how she presents the conflicts of identity the characters face. By "contradiction" I mean simply an opposition between two ways of thinking. Many of the characters do not deal with contradictions particularly well and prefer (usually unwisely) to avoid challenges to the things they *believe* to be true. This could be said of almost anyone, but the problem is magnified and exacerbated for postcolonial peoples, whose lives are affected by a history of colonialism and the neo-colonialism resulting from globalization, economic disparity between nations, and consumer-driven multiculturalism. The characters tend to define people in broad terms, as "English," "Indian," or "black." Poststructuralists might object to these terms on the grounds that identities are fluid and hybrid, a point with which I do not disagree. I use the terms throughout this essay, however, the way the characters do in order to indicate their understanding of themselves and others. Some of them do not think of identities as very fluid at all. Instead, they struggle to establish "solid knowledge"—a term which Desai uses throughout the novel, not to indicate truth but what the characters believe to be true. Those who pursue solid knowledge do so because it provides a sense of mastery and understanding, a refuge from contradictions. Despite their encounters with people whose attitude or behavior contradicts their solid knowledge, some characters cling to it anyway.

No two characters' responses to contradiction are identical, but they do generally fall into one of two types—suppression and ambivalence. In the first section of this essay, I discuss characteristics and examples of suppression, followed by ones of ambivalence. After showing how the characters handle contradictions, I attempt to identify Desai's opinion of the approaches she offers. She does not state explicitly which one she advocates, so we are left to judge which is preferable based on whether the characters' methods lead them to good or bad outcomes. I present the characters as exemplars of certain types of response to contradictions for the purpose of illustrating those responses. To avoid oversimplifying or distorting how the characters behave, however, I include instances in which they act differently from what we might expect. The point is not to label these characters as ambivalent or suppressive but to understand the various ways in which they handle contradictions and whether their approaches result in positive or negative outcomes.

SUPPRESSING CONTRADICTIONS

The characters who most desire solid knowledge establish and defend its solidity by means of suppression, deliberately pushing a thought out of their consciousness (Rycroft 161). The characteristics of suppression can be seen through examples from its two most frequent users, the judge (Sai's grandfather) and Biju (the cook's son). The section begins with the judge's experience as an immigrant in England and his life and marriage in India upon his return, followed by Biju, his experience in America and a comparison between him and his friend Saeed Saeed.

The judge's story comes to us in flashbacks, usually brought on by his interactions with his granddaughter, Sai, and her math tutor and love interest Gyan. When Gyan stays for dinner one evening, the judge tries to humiliate him by asking him to recite a poem. Gyan recites one that "[e]very schoolchild in India knew," and the judge laughs at him "in a cheerless and horrible manner." Embarrassing Gyan, however, gives him no satisfaction. The narrator comments: "His strength, that mental steel, was weakening. His memory seemed triggered by the tiniest thing—Gyan's unease, his reciting that absurd poem. . . . Soon all the judge had worked so hard to separate would soften and envelop him in its nightmare, and the barrier between this life and eternity would in the end, no doubt, be just

another such failing construct." In truth, Gyan reminds the judge of himself as a young man and of the shame he felt when asked to deliver a poem from memory during his examination at the Institute for Constitutional Studies (ICS) at Cambridge. He feels compelled to belittle Gyan in order to create distance between the two of them and thus between himself and his past. He succeeds only in doing the opposite, recalling the very awkwardness he is keen to forget. He takes medication to help suppress these memories, but he finds that "even the pill could not chase the unpleasant thoughts unleashed at dinner back into their holes."

In the course of his flashbacks, we learn that in 1939, at the age of fifteen, he was sent to England to study law at Cambridge University. After passing his ICS exam, he returned to India as a judge. His experience of being an immigrant was similar to Biju's. He was shy and barely ventured out into the new, unfamiliar territory. He almost never spoke during his years in England and eventually stopped speaking as "I," beginning sentences instead with "one," as if his subject position were that of anyone. As the narrator says, "[h]e had learned to take refuge in the third person and to keep everyone at bay, to keep even himself away from himself."

Upon returning from England, the judge began using his new social position to hide from his past poverty and lack of confidence. The narrator tells us that he "found he began to be mistaken for something he wasn't—a man of dignity," that "[t]his accidental poise became more important than any other thing. He envied the English. He loathed Indians." The judge's anglophilia marks him as a particular kind of postcolonial subject: a self-hating Indian, a would-be Englishman, a foreigner to everyone including himself. He supports assimilation fully and believes in the superiority of the English. To suppress his "Indian" past and elevate himself above others in his community, the judge holds fast to what he has learned of performing English identity.

We see this process of distancing most clearly in the judge's treatment of his wife, Nimi. He projects onto her that which he rejects in himself. He is not English, but distinguishing himself from his Indian wife makes him feel less Indian. Unfortunately, his marriage to her is a constant reminder that he is not in fact English. Everything about her seems Indian to him. He despises "her typically Indian bum—lazy, wide as a buffalo," the "pungency of her red hair oil." Her presence is "disruptive" because she reminds him of the contradictions that he tries to suppress. He hates having sex with her, for example, but finds himself doing it "again and again. Even in tedium, on and on, a habit he could not stand in himself. This distaste and his persistence made him angrier than ever and any cruelty to her became irresistible. He would teach her the same lessons of loneliness and shame he had learned himself." Nimi arouses in the judge ambivalent feelings, in the strictly psychoanalytic sense of the word. He simultaneously desires and rejects his wife, and these feelings are interdependent. His response to this contradiction, as with others, is to suppress it by removing Nimi from his life entirely and forgetting her.

The judge's attempts at distancing himself from Nimi generally involve emotional neglect and physical abuse. The narrator describes a particularly graphic instance of the judge's behavior towards his wife: "One day he found footprints on the toilet seat—*she was squatting on it, she was squatting on it!*—he could barely contain his outrage, took her head and pushed it into the toilet bowl, and after a point, Nimi, made invalid by her misery, grew very dull [. . . .] She peered out at the world but could not focus on it, never went to the mirror, because she couldn't see herself in it." In response to his cruelty, Nimi becomes (like the judge) a crushed shadow, unable to see herself. He does to her what his experience in England did to him. She becomes his suppressed Indian self, though her presence constantly reminds the judge of his failure to suppress her fully. He sends her away, telling her that otherwise he will kill her, and refuses to accept her back. Ultimately, he has her murdered and gets away with it by bribing the police. To avoid feeling guilty for her death, he convinces himself that it was an accident.

At the end of the novel, the judge seems headed toward some kind of redemption. A series of events begins when his dog, a red setter named Mutt, is stolen. Apart from being a status symbol, Mutt was the judge's closest companion, and she ate far better than anyone else in the house. Upon finding her missing, the judge searches frantically all over Kalimpong, asking people to help him look for her. He had long avoided most of these people at all costs. His elitism is less important to him than finding Mutt, however, so he exposes

himself to harsh ridicule. In an ultimate act of desperation, he prays for her return, "undoing his education, retreating to the superstitious man making bargains, offering sacrifices." His loss causes him to reconsider whether he made the right choices in life. He remembers how he rejected his father and wife. Memories resurface and confront him in rapid succession. Finally he wonders "if he had killed his wife for the sake of false ideals. Stolen her dignity, shamed his family, shamed hers, turned her into the embodiment of their humiliation." He then recalls a time he had suppressed, when they were young, and he had liked her.

Throughout most of the novel, the judge is a despicable, unsympathetic character. He is selfish, abusive, and winds up bitter and alone with only his cook to keep him company, but he is at his most sympathetic when he opens himself up to contradictions. At the end of the novel, he recognizes how unjustly he treated his father, his wife, their families, and his daughter (born after Nimi was sent away). Sai, he hopes, might be "something in the past that had survived, returned, that might, without his paying too much attention, redeem him [. . . . H]e felt, in the backwaters of his unconscious, an imbalance in his deeds balancing itself out." He feels a unique kinship with Sai, she having been "westernized" by the nuns who raised her. Unlike the judge, though, Sai does not reject Indian culture or want to elevate herself above others by advertising her background. If anything, she is embarrassed by it, as we see when she eats with Gyan, he using his hands and she silverware. Part of the redemption that Sai symbolizes for the judge, then, involves embracing his Indian heritage and giving up his insistence on the superiority of Englishness . . . .

Source: David Wallace Spielman, "'Solid Knowledge' and Contradictions in Kiran Desai's *The Inheritance of Loss*," in *Critique*, Vol. 51, No. 1, September 1, 2010, pp. 75–78.

SOURCES

Alex, Gigy, "They Who Regained the Lost Inheritance," in *ROMAN Critical Contexts: Kiran Desai's The Inheritance of Loss*, edited by Nilanshu Kumar Agarwal, ROMAN Books, 2013, pp. 74–86.

Desai, Kiran, *The Inheritance of Loss*, Grove Press, 2006.

"An Interview with Kiran Desai," in *Boldtype*, Random House website, https://www.randomhouse.com/bold type/0599/desai/interview.html (accessed June 30, 2014).

Italie, Hillel, "Desai's *Inheritance* Wins Book Critics Circle Award," in *Washington Post*, March 9, 2007, http://www. washingtonpost.com/wp-dyn/content/article/2007/03/08/ AR2007030802042.html (accessed June 30, 2014).

Jayaraman, Uma, "John Peter Peterson or Jemubhai Popatlal Patel?: 'The Uncanny' Doubleness and 'Cracking' of Identity in Kiran Desai's *The Inheritance of Loss*," in *ROMAN Critical Contexts: Kiran Desai's The Inheritance of Loss*, edited by Nilanshu Kumar Agarwal, ROMAN Books, 2013, pp. 32–52.

Khan, Nazneen, and Ravi Jauhari, "Aspects of Immigration and Diasporic Sensibility in Kiran Desai's *The Inheritance of Loss*," in *ROMAN Critical Contexts: Kiran Desai's The Inheritance of Loss*, edited by Nilanshu Kumar Agarwal, ROMAN Books, 2013, pp. 66–73.

Mishra, Pankaj, "Wounded by the West," in *New York Times*, February 12, 2006, http://www.nytimes.com/ 2006/02/12/books/review/12mishra.html?pagewanted = all &_r = 0 (accessed June 30, 2014).

Mukherjee, Nibedita, "Nationalism in Transnational Space: A Saga of Conflict in *The Inheritance of Loss*," in *ROMAN Critical Contexts: Kiran Desai's The Inheritance of Loss*, edited by Nilanshu Kumar Agarwal, ROMAN Books, 2013, pp. 53–65.

FURTHER READING

Gopal, Priyamvada, *The Indian English Novel: Nation, History, and Narration*, Oxford University Press, 2009.
> Gopal considers the history and heritage of the Indian novel written in English, comparing these novels to their counterparts in native Indian languages and in British novels written in the time of colonization.

Sharma, Vijay K., and Neeru Tandon, *Kiran Desai and Her Fictional World*, Atlantic Publishers and Distributors, 2011.
> Sharma and Tandon examine both Desai's *The Inheritance of Loss* and her first novel, *Hullabaloo in the Guava Orchard*, in this in-depth analysis of the author and her work.

Subba, Tanka Bahadur, *Ethnicity, State, and Development: A Case Study of the Gorkhaland Movement in Darjeeling*, Har-Anand Publications and Vikas Publishing House, 1992.
> Subba recounts the history of the Gorkhaland movement for Indian statehood, expanding on the specific politics fueling the protests and unrest in *The Inheritance of Loss* and relating these protests to similar pushes by marginalized groups for their own identity within a larger nation.

Toffin, Gerard, and Joanna Pfaff-Czarnecka, *Facing Globalization in the Himalayas: Belonging and the Politics of the Self*, SAGE Publications, 2014.
> This text explores the globalization of the mountainous and remote Himalayan region. As Desai illustrates in *The Inheritance of Loss*, the modernization of the area did not come naturally or easily. Toffin and Pfaff-Czarnecka use case studies of the region to further identify the challenges, successes, and pitfalls of globalization in the Himalayas.

SUGGESTED SEARCH TERMS

Kiran Desai

The Inheritance of Loss

Kiran Desai AND The Inheritance of Loss

diaspora AND The Inheritance of Loss

India AND The Inheritance of Loss

Sai AND The Inheritance of Loss

Man Booker Prize AND Kiran Desai

The Inheritance of Loss AND 2006

New York City AND The Inheritance of Loss

Linden Hills

GLORIA NAYLOR

1985

Linden Hills is the second novel by National Book Award winner Gloria Naylor, published in 1985. Naylor was part of a wave of African American women writers, including Alice Walker, Toni Morrison, Paule Marshall, and others, who achieved tremendous popular and critical success in the 1980s. Through three novels set in the same fictional city, Naylor explored themes of feminism, homophobia, racism, and the special challenges African Americans face as they strive for the American dream.

The novel is set in an upscale neighborhood called Linden Hills, a development built for African Americans on a hillside with crescent-shaped roads arranged so that the lower a person goes down the hill, the greater the wealth of the residents. *Linden Hills* echoes the structure of Dante Alighieri's thirteenth-century poem *Inferno*, in which a poet visits the nine circles of hell. Here, two young out-of-work poets named Lester and Willie visit the streets of Linden Hills looking for odd jobs. As they witness the torments of those who have chosen to pursue wealth and status and lost their souls, they wonder how they will fit into a world that values money more than art and happiness.

AUTHOR BIOGRAPHY

Gloria Naylor was born into a working-class African American family in Harlem, New York City, on January 25, 1950. Her parents had been

Gloria Naylor (© *AP Images* / *Tom Keller*)

sharecroppers in Mississippi before moving to New York to find better lives; in New York, her father worked in a framing shop and as a transit worker, and her mother was a telephone operator. Her mother did not have much formal education and was denied access to the public libraries in Mississippi, but she always loved books. She encouraged her three daughters to read and keep journals. After high school, Naylor spent six years as a missionary for the Jehovah's Witnesses. She came to reject her religion and returned to New York and to her education at age twenty-five. She enrolled in Brooklyn College, majoring in English, and supported herself by working as a hotel telephone operator while she went to school.

Naylor was in the first generation of college students who had access to courses in women's studies and African American studies. In a literature class, she was exposed for the first time to African America women writers, including Toni Morrison and Zora Neale Hurston. These writers excited her and inspired her to shape her own writing to reflect her African American culture. She also studied other major works of literature in college, including Dante's *Inferno*. She graduated in 1981 and then completed a master's

degree in African American studies at Yale University in 1983, writing a thesis that she later turned into the novel *Linden Hills*.

Naylor's first publications, in 1980, were short stories appearing in *Essence*, a monthly magazine targeted toward African American women. Her first book was *The Women of Brewster Place* (1982), a novel comprising interconnected short stories about the residents of one housing project. The book won the 1983 American Book Award for the best first novel. In 1985, Naylor expanded her fictional geography, setting *Linden Hills* in an upscale housing development next to Brewster Place. She revisited this world with her fifth novel, *The Men of Brewster Place* (1998). Through the 1980s and 1990s, she was popular with critics and with readers and much in demand as a lecturer and writer-in-residence at universities including Princeton, George Washington University, Cornell, Brandeis, New York University, and Boston University. Her work was also supported by a 1985 National Endowment for the Arts fellowship, a 1988 Guggenheim fellowship, and other awards. She was married for less than two weeks while she was in college; she did not have children of her own but took in a teenaged nephew for several years and has shared her homes with her mother and sisters.

Naylor's novels have been recognized as her most important works, but she has also written nonfiction, essays, magazine articles, and screenplays exploring tensions between men and women, struggles for success, materialism, heritage, race, and culture. In 1990, she founded an independent film company, One Way Productions, in New York. Naylor had long been attracted to the Sea Islands along the coasts of South Carolina, Georgia, and Florida and set two of her novels there. In 1996, she moved to St. Helena Island, South Carolina, looking for a quiet place to write and garden. Her fictionalized memoir, *1996* (2006), describes her conflict with a neighbor there and her suspicions that she was a target of National Security Agency surveillance. Naylor returned to New York, taking up residence in Brooklyn.

PLOT SUMMARY

Chapter 1

Linden Hills opens by describing the housing development that gives the novel its title. Linden Hills, as reported by the third-person limited narrator, occupies the V-shaped face of a hillside in Wayne County. Because it is later revealed that two of the characters are executives at General Motors, it seems safe to assume that Linden Hills is in Wayne County, Michigan, in a fictional suburb of Detroit. The land was surveyed and purchased in 1820 by Luther Nedeed, an African American man who, according to rumor, had sold his own wife and children into slavery in Mississippi to come north and buy the land. Nedeed built a home for himself at the base of the hill and built shacks higher up. Poor African Americans became his tenants, and as he prospered, becoming the wealthiest man in the county, he replaced his cabin with a large home with a mortuary in the basement.

Eventually he brought home a wife—no one knew whether she is his first or second wife—an octoroon, or a woman with only one-eighth African American blood and very light skin. She gave him a son, who was dark like his father. The son, also named Luther Nedeed, took up his father's undertaking business and expanded the number of houses in Linden Hills. The second Luther Nedeed also had a light-skinned wife and a dark-skinned son named Luther Nedeed. To keep whites out, Nedeed gave every tenant a lease for one thousand years and a day. He had no love for his tenants, but he saw that African American maids and laborers living on the best land in the county was a way to irritate the white businessmen, who refused to treat him with respect.

During the Great Depression, the third Luther Nedeed founded the Tupelo Realty Corporation to finance fancier houses for fancier folks. He encouraged his neighbors to borrow money, improve their properties, send their children to college, and pursue a black version of the American dream. By the time Luther Nedeed III died, Linden Hills had eight circular drives. The roads near the top of the hill were First Crescent Drive, Second Crescent Drive, and so on; the lower roads near Tupelo Drive were lined with the largest homes and the wealthiest African Americans in Wayne County. The development was featured in national magazines. African Americans from all over applied to live in Linden Hills, and those already there consistently tried to move lower and lower down the hill, closer to Nedeed.

The fourth Luther Nedeed lives during the novel's present. Still an undertaker and land

manager, he is different from his ancestors. He no longer cares whether whites approve of him, and he no longer strives for material wealth. For years, he has watched folks work for money, grasp it, and find no peace. He knows that he will not find satisfaction that way, but he has nothing else to value. He is constantly suspicious and anxious. Also unlike his predecessors, he has married a dark-skinned woman, Willa. His son has clear Nedeed features but light skin, and Luther is sure that his wife has been unfaithful. In the opening chapter, he builds a prison in the basement morgue and locks his wife and son down there. In the last sentence of the chapter, the narrator introduces the novel's protagonists, Willie Mason and Lester Tilson, as they are about to begin "their journey down Linden Hills."

December 19th

The next chapter begins, as the first did, with geography. The narrator describes Wayne Avenue, a busy street that separates Linden Hills from the less prestigious sections of town. Down the street from a few small businesses and churches, Willie and Lester, twenty-year-old best friends nicknamed "White" Willie and "S—," get together in the school yard of Wayne Junior High School, where they first met. They became friends when Willie jumped in to keep Lester from being beaten, and months later their friendship deepened when they revealed their mutual love of poetry. Willie, from the lower-class Putney Wayne neighborhood, dropped out of school after ninth grade. Lester, who lives on First Crescent Circle in Linden Hills, graduated from high school but decided against going to college. Now, they both value writing poetry more than making money; neither has a steady job or solid prospects for the future.

As the two men discuss their lack of money to buy Christmas presents, they run into their friends Ruth and Norman Anderson. Ruth used to be married to another man and lived on Fifth Crescent Drive, where she had cultivated a taste for nice furniture and clothes. However, Norman, the man she now loves, is mentally ill, and when he has attacks of "the pinks" every year and nine months, he breaks everything he can get his hands on and tries to hurt himself. Ruth and Norman live simply, with only three pieces of furniture, three Styrofoam cups that cannot be broken into sharp pieces, and just enough money to get by. Every extra penny goes into the bank, so Ruth will have it for doctors when Norman has his next attack.

Willie and Lester spend the afternoon drinking with Ruth and Norman in their apartment backing up to Linden Hills. Although the feminist Ruth has no wealth or stability, she is beautiful and content, and Willie is a little in love with her. While Norman dreams of getting ahead and moving Ruth back to Linden Hills, she rejects the idea; the people she knew there were hollow and sad and always trying to "make it." Still, she sets the rest of the novel in motion with her suggestion that Willie and Lester might be able to make some extra money before Christmas by knocking on doors in Linden Hills and looking for odd jobs.

Willie and Lester spend the night at Lester's house, even though Lester's mother does not approve of Willie. Mrs. Tilson, who grudgingly invites Willie to dinner, is typical of the people in Linden Hills: self-conscious about her home, worried about how she measures up against her neighbors, and always hoping that her children will climb higher on the social ladder. Lester's sister, Roxanne, comes home from work and criticizes Lester and Willie for their lack of initiative. The two men escape to Lester's room, where they smoke marijuana, recite poetry, and talk. Before falling asleep, they hear a moaning cry drifting up the hill—a cry they have been hearing all day.

December 20th

This chapter opens with a visual clue—a new typeface—showing that an important change has occurred. In the first three paragraphs of the chapter, as well as further sections in this typeface, the narrator focuses tightly on Willa, the wife of the current Luther Nedeed, who is locked in the basement with her son. In this brief introduction, Willa stares at a clock, clutching her son's dead body, fearing the moment when Luther lets her out because she believes she will try to kill him.

The typeface changes back, and now the narrator focuses on Luther, sipping a drink and feeling annoyed with his wife for not giving him a proper son. He thinks the death of the child is "certainly regrettable" but hopes that after Willa stays a while longer in the basement with his body she will get over her anger and accept what it means to be a proper wife.

As morning comes, Lester and Willie prepare for their day of labor, and Winston Alcott prepares for his wedding. He is about to marry a woman named Cassandra, but he does not love her. He and his best man, David, have been lovers for eight years, and it hurts both men terribly that Winston is going through with the wedding. Winston assures David that his new wife means nothing, that he is marrying her only to stop rumors that he is gay. Both men know that Winston would lose his job and his status if the truth got out—in the 1980s, same-sex marriage was not legal anywhere in the United States, and people could easily lose their jobs for being lesbian or gay. David wants Winston to give up his career and his home on Second Crescent Drive to be with him; Winston wants David to ignore his marriage and remain his lover. David's decision is clear: "since I can't be your wife, I won't be your whore."

Lester and Willie talk their way into jobs scraping plates and hauling garbage at the wedding reception. As will happen throughout the novel, this temporary work gives them an opportunity to peer into the lives of the people in Linden Hills. Through the kitchen doors they see the lavish wedding cake, the fancy food, the furs, and the jewelry. Xavier Donnell, Roxanne's boyfriend, is there with a blonde woman, although he told Roxanne he had not been invited. Luther Nedeed is there as an usher, and during the reception he presents the married couple with a diamond necklace and a mortgage on a house on the prestigious Tupelo Drive, near the bottom of Linden Hills. As best man, David rises to give his toast. He recites a Walt Whitman poem, "Whoever Your Are, Holding Me Now in Hand," which Willie recognizes as being a love poem and a good-bye from Whitman to another man. Aside from Winston, no one else in the room seems to understand the significance of David's toast.

Back in the basement, Willa dreams that the wives of the previous Luther Nedeeds are mourning with her. Digging through an old trunk, she finds a bridal veil and uses it to wrap her son for burial. She also finds a Bible, embossed with the words "Luwana Packerville 1837." Inside, someone has written, "There can be no God."

December 21st

The next day's narrative takes place on Third Crescent Drive and begins with the line, "Xavier

Donnell was falling in love with a black woman." The woman is Roxanne, Lester's sister, and his love for her terrifies him because he believes that his status as a highly ranked black executive at General Motors would be in jeopardy if he married a dark-skinned woman or a woman beneath his social class. Looking for advice, he invites his friend and mentor, Maxwell Smyth, to come over. Lester and Willie also come to the house, hired by Xavier's mother to clean out the garage.

Xavier confesses that he has been thinking about marrying Roxanne, and Maxwell launches into a list of the failings of African American women. Maxwell believes that women with college educations are too ambitious and expect too much equality from their husbands. He advises Xavier to find someone else to marry—a woman of any color but black. When Lester and Willie come for their pay, Maxwell and Willie argue about whether being poor and being black are in any way related. Maxwell claims that there is no connection and, as proof, shows the others the latest issue of *Penthouse* magazine, which has a picture of a nude African American woman as its centerfold. To Maxwell, this is clear progress for black women.

Meanwhile, Willa is paging through Luwana's Bible, reading diary entries that Luwana wrote on blank pages. Luwana reports that her Luther intends to keep her and her son as property. She had thought that her marriage would make her a free woman, but she has "only exchanged one master for another." Later, when her son Luther is two, her husband grants the boy his freedom, but he never frees Luwana. Soon after, Luther hires a housekeeper and gardener, worried that Luwana is poisoning him. Luther stops sleeping with Luwana, and he and the boy barely speak to her. Luwana is lonely and miserable, trying to find joy in her Bible.

Willa weeps over the diary. She, too, thought marriage would free her from loneliness, but it has only made it worse. She realized early that her marriage was a mistake, but there was no one she could share her sorrows with. After all, she was Mrs. Luther Nedeed, wealthy, important, and a new mother. As the diary continues, Luwana writes letters to herself and replies to them, in voices that are increasingly insane. She begins to scratch herself with a hatpin, counting in her flesh the number of times she is asked to speak. The diary ends after she speaks

for the six hundred and sixty-sixth time, except for the words "There can be no God."

Lester and Willie find another job, working for Chester Parker on Fourth Crescent Drive. Parker is hosting a wake for his dead wife, Lycentia, and he hires to Willie and Lester to strip the wallpaper from her bedroom while the wake is going on so new paper can be hung the next day during the funeral. Downstairs, people from Linden Hills file through the dining room eating and paying their respects. Someone mentions a rumor that a low-income housing project that Lycentia had fought against is going to be built, and the guests comment that poor people are taking advantage, tax money goes to support lazy folks, public schools are dragged down by remedial students, and so on. Overhearing them, Lester and Willie are disgusted that these wealthy African Americans have turned their backs on the poor. Luther Nedeed arrives, apologizing for his wife's absence. He says she is away visiting relatives.

Looking for more writing from Luwana, Willa finds boxes of handwritten cookbooks that belonged to Evelyn Creton Nedeed, wife of the second Luther. At the bottom of one box, she finds two small books that surprise her.

December 22nd

Willa is reading recipes from Evelyn Creton's secret cookbooks. She learns that Evelyn served her husband tea breads with different ingredients from traditional medicines—powdered dove's heart, snakeroot, shame-weed—trying to lure him back to her bed. Willa remembers her first days as the wife of her own Luther, learning that she and her husband would have separate bedrooms and finally accepting hurried and passionless sex on his schedule. He had not come to her bedroom since their son was born. Suddenly her husband's attitude toward sex seems "unnatural," and she wonders if Evelyn ever used that word. The final section of Evelyn's recipe book reveals that she gained weight early in her marriage and then turned to years of what today would be called bingeing and purging, until finally she ate and starved herself nearly to death. She finished the job by poisoning herself.

Willie and Lester have been summoned to the home of the Right Reverend Michael T. Hollis. Willie remembers fondly the Christmas parties that Hollis threw for poor children when Willie was young, with Hollis dressed as Santa

Claus and handing out food and toys. The men have been hired to drive donations for this year's party from Hollis's home on Fifth Crescent Drive to the church. Hollis has worked his way up from being a young boy at his grandmother's small country church to being pastor at Mount Sinai Baptist, but he has lost his wife because of his many affairs, he has lost his faith, and he is an alcoholic. Riding to the church with Hollis, Willie realizes Hollis is drunk, as his father often was.

When they all arrive at the church, Lycentia Parker's funeral is about to begin, and Luther is finalizing preparations. Luther tells Hollis that he will not be needed to officiate at the high-class funeral he has arranged. Hollis preaches anyway, in the old country style, shouting and weeping. Nedeed delivers the eulogy, praising Lycentia for her success and status, and Hollis knows that this emotionless religion is what his congregation prefers.

After Fifth Crescent Drive, Willie and Lester head for the best section of Linden Hills, the homes along Tupelo Drive. Willie is worried that walking in this section could get them in trouble, and sure enough, two police officers stop them and accuse them of trespassing. Lester argues with the officers until Norman Anderson rescues them by pretending they have a job at the home of Laurel Dumont, the district attorney's wife, and arranges for them to shovel her walk for free the next day in exchange for his help.

December 23rd

Angrily, Willa tears through the books and the boxes in the basement, shredding pages and ripping fabrics. She finds a photo album that belonged to Priscilla Nedeed, wife of the third Luther Nedeed. A series of family portraits shows Willa's husband from when he was a baby. With each subsequent picture, Luther grows taller, and Priscilla's face is increasingly obscured by shadows.

Lester and Willie are shoveling snow at the Dumont home. Willie is in a foul mood because dreams that he was faceless kept him awake the night before. The men hear a voice calling "Laurel" over and over and look up to see an old woman calling out an upstairs window. Now the story flashes back to when Laurel was a girl, visiting her grandmother, Roberta Johnson, in Georgia for the summer. Her father has a new girlfriend, whom Laurel does not like, and her

grandmother loves her as a mother should. At her father's home, Laurel has all the modern conveniences, but she feels most at home with her grandmother. She loves music and the water and learns to swim in her grandmother's pond. Back home, she joins a synchronized swimming team and eagerly shows her grandmother her new skills each summer.

Roberta cashes in her savings to send Laurel to the University of California, Berkeley, and is dismayed when college and Laurel's subsequent career at IBM turn her into a stranger. Laurel marries Howard Dumont of Linden Hills, lives a life of wealth and status, and adds a swimming pool and a music room to their home. Her life is lonely and empty, however, and ten years after her wedding she comes back to her grandmother's cottage looking for comfort. Her grandmother sends her back home, so Laurel goes, but she cannot bring herself to go back to work.

As she withdraws further, Howard leaves her. Roberta comes up to Linden Hills and tries to get Laurel interested in Christmas, but when snow begins falling she becomes immobilized again. As the men are shoveling the snow, Luther Nedeed comes to the house. He tells Laurel that since Howard is no longer living in the home she cannot stay either, because of the terms of the thousand-years-and-one-day lease his family holds. Laurel puts on a swimsuit, climbs the diving platform in the backyard, and dives into the empty pool. Lester runs to Roberta, while Willie climbs into the pool.

A quick scene with Willa shows her looking at the last photo in Priscilla's album. Her face is completely hidden. Then the narrative returns to Willie, who has turned Laurel over and found that her face has been obliterated in her fall. Willie becomes ill, and he and Lester are invited in by Daniel Braithwaite, a neighbor. Willie tells Lester and Braithwaite that footprints in the snow indicate that Luther Nedeed watched Laurel kill herself and did not try to help her. Braithwaite shows the two younger men that from his house he can see everything that happens up the hill and confesses that he has been watching them work their way down all week. He tells them that Luther Nedeed has commissioned him to write a history of Linden Hills.

December 24th

Back in Putney Wayne, Willie is still awake after midnight, in the earliest moments of Christmas

Eve, with the nagging feeling that Luther's wife is waiting for him. He wonders what he was supposed to have learned from his days in Linden Hills. He can feel a poem coming, so he gets into bed and waits for the first line to come as he falls asleep.

Willa calmly but not quite sanely thinks over her thirty-seven years, remembering how and why she chose to marry Luther. She decides to regain her identity as wife and mother and begins to climb the stairs out of the basement.

That evening, Lester and Willie walk all the way down the slope of Linden Hills to Luther Nedeed's home, discussing whether there is a way for a black artist to be successful without accepting the hollow materialism of Linden Hills. Waiting for them, Luther remembers beautiful images of past Christmases and gazes at portraits of the four adult Luther Nedeeds, wondering how he can find contentment. He forgives Willa, accepting that much of the fault is his for choosing an apparently unsuitable wife. Lester and Willie have been hired to help Nedeed decorate his Christmas tree, and as they unwrap each precious antique ornament, he tells them exactly where it should go on the tree. The last step in the process is placing candles, which Luther does himself.

While fetching boxes, Willie accidentally unlatches the lock that keeps Willa a prisoner, so when she gets to the top of the stairs she is able to open the door. Carrying her dead child, she enters the living room and announces, "Luther . . . your son is dead." Luther quickly gets Lester and Willie out of the house and struggles with Willa. The veil shrouding the child catches fire from the candles on the tree, and soon the whole house is in flames. Seeing the fire, Nedeed's neighbors all the way up the hill turn off their lights and lock their doors. They watch the house burn, but no one comes to help.

CHARACTERS

Winston Alcott

Winston Alcott is a gay man who is afraid to let anyone know that he is completely in love with his friend David. To stop rumors about his orientation, Winston marries Cassandra, choosing his law career over his love.

Norman Anderson

Norman is a kind, well-meaning man who is severely mentally ill. Every year and nine months, he suffers from what he calls "the pinks," hallucinations that pink slimy creatures are crawling on him, and he must use any available sharp object to scrape them off. In between these episodes, he works hard and is a loving partner to his wife, Ruth. Willie and Lester are amazed to see that Norman and Ruth share household chores equally and that Norman is not embarrassed to admit it. Years before, Ruth was tempted to leave Norman and the chaos he brought to her life, but she fell ill and Norman was so caring, even as the pinks were forming, that she could not go. Although they are poor, the two are happy, satisfied, and in love.

Ruth Anderson

Ruth was once married to another man and living on Fifth Crescent Drive, but, as she explains it, she lasted only six months with the people in Linden Hills, who were always trying to get ahead. Now she lives in poverty and in harmony with her second husband, Norman, in an apartment on Wayne Avenue just outside Linden Hills. Ruth and Norman work hard and live simply, but Norman's mental illness eats up their savings every time he has an episode of "the pinks." Ruth knows that she will never have children or a stable life. Even so, she loves Norman, and she knows that she is happier not chasing wealth and status. Ruth is beautiful and wise, and it is she who sends Willie and Lester out on their journey through Linden Hills.

Daniel Braithwaite

Daniel Braithwaite is a historian who has been commissioned by Luther Nedeed to write the history of Linden Hills. Retired from teaching, he lives in the lowest part of the hill above Nedeed's home. He invites Lester and Willie into his home to recover after they find Laurel's body.

Cassandra

Cassandra is the woman who marries Winston Alcott, apparently not realizing that he really loves his friend David.

David

David has been Winston Alcott's lover for eight years and serves as best man at his wedding. Unable to persuade Winston to choose their love over his career, he recites a Walt Whitman poem as his wedding toast, telling Winston through the poem that he will not remain in his life.

Xavier Donnell

Xavier Donnell, thirty-one, is vice president of minority marketing for General Motors. He lives on Third Crescent Drive. He is in love with Roxanne Tilson, but he is worried that he should marry someone of higher status and fewer demands in order to move ahead with his career and to have the kind of marriage he wants.

Howard Dumont

Howard Dumont is Wayne County's first black district attorney. He lives on Tupelo Drive, in the best part of Linden Hills, until he leaves his depressed wife, Laurel.

Laurel Dumont

Laurel Dumont is married to District Attorney Howard Dumont. From the time she was a toddler, she has loved music and the water, and she was a competitive synchronized swimmer in high school. Because her mother is gone and her father is remarried, her grandmother, Roberta Johnson, is her surrogate mother. Laurel pulls away from her grandmother after high school, pursuing a more conventional and materialistic life, but finds herself coming back for comfort when her career at IBM and her home in Linden Hills leave her empty. Increasingly depressed, Laurel kills herself by diving into an empty swimming pool on December 23.

Michael T. Hollis

A graduate of the Harvard Divinity School, the Right Reverend Michael T. Hollis is pastor of the Mount Sinai Baptist Church. A resident of Fifth Crescent Drive, he is an alcoholic and a fraud who has lost his faith. Because he was continually unfaithful, his wife has left him.

Roberta Johnson

Roberta Johnson is Laurel's grandmother, who looked after Laurel every summer in her small cottage in Georgia. Roberta is plain-spoken and clear-eyed and loves her granddaughter fiercely.

Willie K. Mason

"White" Willie Mason earned his nickname by being the darkest-skinned student in junior high school. Like his friend Lester Tilson, Willie is twenty years old and a poet, but he memorizes poems instead of writing them down. He dropped out of school after ninth grade, believing that formal education and writing are ways for white people to maintain their power over others, but he has read widely and has memorized 665 poems by great black and white poets. Willie sometimes works bagging groceries; he sets out with Lester to look for temporary work in Linden Hills because Christmas is coming.

As the two work their way down the slope of Linden Hills, Willie constantly challenges what he hears well-off African Americans saying about poorer people. Willie lives in Putney Wayne, a low-income neighborhood near Linden Hills, and he resents stereotypes about poor people being lazy and stupid. He knows that he is smart and talented, and he wonders whether the world has a place for a gifted black poet unwilling to sell out his principles.

Willie is more observant than Lester: He is the one who recognizes the meaning of David's wedding toast and notices Nedeed's footprints in Laurel Dumont's yard. Willie wonders why people talk about Luther Nedeed but never mention his wife, and he notices that Nedeed's explanation for his wife's absence does not quite add up. He comes to feel that Nedeed's mysterious wife is in trouble and waiting for him to help. When Willa and her family die in the fire, Willie cries until he is spent.

Evelyn Creton Nedeed

Evelyn Creton was married to the second Luther Nedeed. In the cookbooks Willa finds in the basement, Evelyn has recorded recipes for tea breads with ingredients she hopes will make her husband love her again. Since the birth of their son, he has shown no interest in her, personally or sexually. Eventually, in her loneliness, Evelyn starves and poisons herself to death.

Luther Nedeed I

The first man named Luther Nedeed bought the hillside land that became Linden Hills in 1820; according to legend, he sold his wife and his children into slavery to get the money to leave Tupelo, Mississippi, and come north. The white man who sold that land believed that he had tricked Nedeed into buying worthless property, but Nedeed built shacks, rented them out to black tenants, opened a funeral parlor, and prospered. He built his own house and funeral parlor at the bottom of the hill, facing up. Eventually, he returned to the South to purchase a wife, an octoroon (one eighth African American) woman named Luwana Packerville, and brought her home with him. He studied the stars and the equinox to determine when to have sex with her, believing they could produce one perfect son if the timing was right. After she gave birth to the second dark-skinned Luther Nedeed, he stopped sleeping with her.

Luther Nedeed II

The second Luther Nedeed, after attending a fancy boarding school, expanded the community and the funeral parlor. He carried on his father's businesses and his father's resentment of white people. He made a fortune selling guns to the Confederacy during the Civil War and used the money to improve his property. When his white neighbors saw the value of his land and tried to acquire it, he gave leases of one thousand years and a day to all of the African American tenants to keep whites out. Nedeed married Evelyn Creton, another light-skinned octoroon, who gave birth to another dark-skinned son, also named Luther Nedeed.

Luther Nedeed III

The third Luther Nedeed came into his own during the Great Depression. He somehow did not lose money during that time and took away the lesson that what Americans value above all else is material success. To increase the irritation that his family created in white people, he founded the Tupelo Realty Corporation, built large and fancy homes to replace the shacks, and attracted the wealthiest and most successful African Americans to live in Linden Hills. This Luther Nedeed laid out the permanent pattern of the development, with eight circular roads descending down the hill and the wealthiest families closest to the bottom. Nedeed followed his father and grandfather's example in marrying a light-skinned woman and having one dark-skinned son.

Luther Nedeed IV

The fourth Luther Nedeed is the owner of the funeral business and the Tupelo Realty Corporation during the action of the novel. Unlike his ancestors, he takes no pleasure in his wealth or status and no pleasure in showing off his success to white people. He has realized that the American dream is a "continually dying dream" and

that the wealthy people in Linden Hills have attained status at the cost of their souls.

He is also troubled at home: he has gone against convention and married a dark-skinned woman, Willa Prescott Nedeed, and the son she has borne him is light-skinned. Nedeed is sure that she has cheated on him, and he cannot bear to look at his son. As the opening chapter ends, Nedeed imprisons Willa and his son in the basement. He regrets the boy dying but hopes his wife will come to her senses and give him another son.

As the most important man in the neighborhood, Luther appears everywhere Lester and Willie go: at the wedding, the wake, the funeral, and even at Laurel's house. He explains away Willa's absence by saying she has gone to visit relatives. On December 24, Luther hires the two younger men to help him decorate his Christmas tree. When Willa escapes from the basement, she and Luther struggle and accidentally start a fire from the Christmas tree candles. Luther and Willa both die as the house burns down.

Luther Nedeed V

The fifth and last Luther Nedeed is the young son of the fourth Luther Nedeed and his wife, Willa. Because the child is light-skinned, his father refuses to acknowledge him. The father locks his wife and son in the basement, where the child dies. After his death, Willa tries not to remember her son asking why he did not resemble his father and why his father never liked him.

Luwana Packerville Nedeed

Luwana Packerville was an octoroon, a term used for someone who had seven great-grandparents who were white and one who was black, and her skin was very light. She was purchased by the first Luther Nedeed and brought to the land that would become Linden Hills; technically, she was his property as well as his wife. After the fifth Luther Nedeed—the child—dies, his mother Willa finds Luwana's bridal veil and uses it to wrap his body for burial. Willa also finds Luwana's Bible, in which she has recorded her sorrow and loneliness and in which she has written, "There can be no God."

Priscilla McGuire Nedeed

Priscilla McGuire married the third Luther Nedeed, the father of Willa's husband. Her photo album contains annual pictures of her, her husband, and her son. As the child Luther appears older and taller in the pictures, Priscilla's face is increasingly in shadow, until her face cannot be seen.

Willa Prescott Nedeed

Willa Prescott married the fourth Luther Nedeed when she was thirty-one years old. Unlike the previous Mrs. Nedeeds, she has dark skin. She married Luther because he could give her wealth and status; he chose her because she was old enough to be undemanding of any man who married her. Willa is the mother of Luther's son, the last Luther Nedeed, whose skin is so light that his father cannot believe he is actually the father. When the child is five, Luther locks his wife and son in the basement so that she will learn obedience and so that he will not have to look at the boy. When the child dies, Willa goes mad with grief. Still in the basement, she digs through boxes of books and papers belonging to the wives of the previous Luthers and discovers that they all suffered the same fate: self-doubt, isolation, and husbands uninterested in sex or companionship. On Christmas Eve, Willa accepts her own culpability for the faults in her marriage and decides to go upstairs and try again with Luther. She manages to get out of the basement, carrying her dead child. As she struggles with her husband a fire catches, consuming Luther, Willa, their son, and the entire house.

Chester Parker

Chester Parker lives on Fourth Crescent Drive. He hires Lester and Willie to strip wallpaper from his wife Lycentia's room upstairs while he is hosting her wake downstairs. Parker says over and over that Lycentia would have wanted him to begin redecorating as soon as possible, but the implication is that he is in a hurry to move a new woman into the house.

Lycentia Parker

Lycentia is the recently dead wife of Chester. Lycentia was a community activist, working to prevent a new housing project from being built in Putney Wayne because she worried that the project would drive down the value of homes in Linden Hills.

Maxwell Smyth

Maxwell Smyth is Xavier Donnell's friend and mentor and an assistant to the executive director of General Motors. He is extraordinarily controlled in every aspect of his life, working toward the goal of becoming the head of General Motors. While those around him accuse Maxwell of trying to be white, he insists that he is only trying to be the best. He believes that race is irrelevant, but he advises Xavier not to marry a black woman, because they do not know how to meet a man's needs.

Lester Tilson

Lester Tilson, twenty years old, lives with his mother and his sister, Roxanne, in a house on First Crescent Drive. Like his best friend, Willie Mason, Lester is a poet. He has graduated from high school but refuses to go to college, to his mother's great disappointment. Lester wants to live among the common people he writes about and fears that more formal education will distance him from them. Unlike Willie, Lester writes his poems down on paper and sometimes earns a few dollars publishing them. He has no steady work, however, which is why he agrees to go with Willie through the streets of Linden Hills looking for odd jobs to earn money for Christmas presents.

Lester is caught between two worlds: as the owner of the home he inherited in Linden Hills, he lives among those who have achieved success, but he rejects the materialism and self-absorption of the people he knows there. Like Willie, he wonders whether the world has a place for him. Lester tends to laugh off the conflicts around him, which Willie sometimes finds irritating. As the two work their way through Linden Hills, Lester shows himself to be less observant and less intuitive than Willie, but he is a loyal friend.

Mrs. Tilson

Lester's mother, whose first name is not given, is a widow, living with her son and daughter in the smallest house on First Crescent Drive. She wants her children to become professionals and is disappointed that Lester refuses to go to college. She pushed her late husband so hard to provide more and better for the family that he held two full-time jobs and finally worked himself to death.

Roxanne Tilson

Lester's sister, Roxanne, is on track to be a success. She has a degree from prestigious Wellesley College, a good job in an ad agency, and a boyfriend, Xavier Donnell, who is an executive at General Motors. In college, Roxanne flirted with the Black Pride movement, wearing an Afro hairstyle and taking black history courses. However, her vision of success now includes straightened hair, bleached skin, and a phony way of speaking. Roxanne still lives at home because she hopes her Linden Hills address will help her land Xavier or another worthy husband; she does not know that Xavier worries that the Tilsons, who live in the most modest home on the most modest street in Linden Hills, might not be a good enough family to marry into.

THEMES

American Dream

The American dream can be thought of as one of the founding myths of the United States, the idea that in a free country, anyone can work hard and succeed and that each generation will do a little better than the one before. Depending on one's view of this idea, the American dream is seen as either a personal quest for the traditional spouse, house, and white picket fence or as a nagging desire to keep up with—or do better than—the Joneses. For the author of *Linden Hills*, it is clearly the latter. The characters in this novel are not seeking just enough to be happy and content but are constantly trying to get more material goods, more prestige, more status. This quest leaves them hollow and lonely.

This idea is not something that the novel develops gradually. Before Lester and Willie even begin their journey, Ruth and Lester discuss what they already know about Linden Hills. Ruth, who lived there with her previous husband, says that she will never go back. Lester, who has a house on the least prestigious street, explains, "those are a bunch of the saddest niggers you'll ever wanna meet. They eat, sleep, and breathe for one thing—making it." Lester is eager to show Willie that he should not be jealous of what the rich people have: "all that glitters ain't gold, baby."

As Lester and Willie work their way down the slope, they meet one person after another who has given up something important to pursue wealth and status. Winston gives up David, the love of his life, so that his firm will not suspect that he is gay and fire him. Winston's father urges him to marry Cassandra, pointing out, "I broke my ass so you and your brother could have it a lot easier than I did." Xavier questions

and then gives up his love for Roxanne because it might interfere with his ability to maintain his image at General Motors. The Reverend Hollis lost both his wife and his faith when he accepted "his new post at Sinai Baptist, the coup of his career, the one that came complete with a home in Linden Hills." When Laurel Dumont moved into her husband's home in Linden Hills, "The couple had everything; she had to believe that because everyone told her so." However, Laurel's life is empty; she has pushed away her grandmother, her husband, and her friends. As her grandmother says, "It's lonely at the top." Luther has realized the hollowness of the dream for years. Near the beginning of the novel, as he thinks about his forefathers' vision and his neighbors' quest, he realizes that "the shining surface of their careers, brass railings, and cars hurt his eyes because it only reflected the bright nothing that was inside of them." In this novel, the American dream is not an image of equality and opportunity, but a false god that leaves people "devoured by their own drives."

Black Culture

To the extent that *Linden Hills* challenges the American dream or materialism, it is a universal story. However, Naylor also focuses specifically on black culture and the sacrifices African Americans make to conform to what can be seen as a white idea of success. The first Luther Nedeeds, as they built Linden Hills, clearly saw their success as both an imitation and an affront to the dominant white culture. The people who move to Linden Hills are trying to "forget the world that said you spelled black with a capital nothing," but their idea of making something of themselves forced them to also "forget what it meant to be black, because it meant working yourself to death just to stand still."

This tension between being successful and being black is one that several of the characters face. When Lester's mother prepares fried chicken for dinner, she apologizes for it: "We're eating like peasants tonight." Lester laughs that the full name his mother gave him is Lesterfield Walcott Montgomery Tilson, which she defends by saying, "I gave you a name that I thought would fit the heights I hoped you'd climb." Roxanne, Lester's sister, has been using "bleaching creams and hair relaxers" in her quest to "marry black, marry well," which seems to mean lightening her skin and making her hair more like a white woman's. Indeed, the

TOPICS FOR FURTHER STUDY

- Watch a few episodes of *Black-ish*, a television program that uses humor to explore some of the same ideas about material success and cultural identity that Naylor addresses in *Linden Hills*. Can humor be an effective way to bring up serious issues? With a group of classmates, create and perform a comedy sketch featuring characters from *Linden Hills*; you may wish to make a video and share it with a wider audience. Write a brief essay reflecting on how well your sketch was able to make serious points.

- Read Naylor's novel *The Women of Brewster Place*, or watch the film version of the novel. Paying special attention to the character of Kiswana Browne, a former resident of Linden Hills, analyze how residents of Brewster Place view those who live in Linden Hills. Write a paper analyzing whether their impressions are fair and accurate.

- Identify other novels that address the tensions that arise when a person belonging to a minority group has to navigate between her or his heritage and the dominant American culture. You might consider *Bless Me, Ultima* (1972) by Rudolfo Anaya, *The House on Mango Street* (1984) by Sandra Cisneros, or *The Absolutely True Diary of a Part-Time Indian* (2007) by Sherman Alexie. Write a dialogue between the main character from your chosen book and either Willie or Lester from *Linden Hills*, in which the characters explain to each other what they are up against.

- The poet Willie Mason in *Linden Hills* writes only the first two lines of an important poem: "There is a man in a house at the bottom of a hill. And his wife has no name." Finish the poem.

- Using clues from the text, draw a map of Linden Hills. Mark the locations of the homes mentioned in the novel.

- Near the end of *Linden Hills*, Daniel Braithwaite explains to Lester and Willie that "the Nedeeds kept going because they felt our people needed a role model. . . . And that was real black pride." Research the Black Pride movement in the United States, focusing on the 1960s and 1970s, when Lester and Willie were growing up. Prepare a PowerPoint or other presentation for your class highlighting the movement, including images and music.

- Read the short story "Everyday Use" by Alice Walker. Write a brief essay in which you compare the short story's character Dee with Laurel from *Linden Hills*. How has college and experience in the wider world changed how each woman views her family back home in the rural South?

first three Mrs. Nedeeds were all chosen for their light skin. At Winston's fancy wedding, the women are dressed in clothes by white designers including Halston and Yves Saint Laurent, and the band is playing slow waltzes. Willie guesses "that they'd dance to nothing more exciting than that the entire afternoon." When the Reverend Hollis gives a rousing sermon from his heart, accompanied by "Amazing Grace" the way "we did it down home," he is met with stony silence and contempt.

Xavier's mentor, Maxwell—the same man who urges him not to marry a black woman—is a little more successful than Xavier at General Motors. Maxwell credits this to "the psychological sleight-of-hand that he used to make his blackness disappear." He does not want to be white, necessarily, but he does not want anyone to think of him as black. Maxwell "had discovered long ago that he doubled the odds of finishing first if he didn't carry the weight of that

Linden Hills seems to be the epitome of the American dream. *(© Dan Thornberg | Shutterstock.com)*

milligram of pigment in his skin." As Luther Nedeed says early in the novel, "Linden Hills wasn't black; it was successful."

Lester and Willie stand out among the other characters because of the great value they place in black culture. Lester's role models are black nationalist leader Malcolm X and baseball great Hank Aaron. In his bedroom, he has a poster of Malcolm X and tapes of his speeches. He listens to music by Aretha Franklin and other black performers and collects books from the Arno Press black history series. Willie memorizes poems because "his aim was to be like the great slave poet, Jupiter Hammon, who memorized thousands of verses because he couldn't read." In fact, Willie can read well but considers it a drawback, since "the written word dulls the mind, and since most of what is written is by white men, it's positively poisonous." Both men are dazzled by Daniel Braithwaite's book collection, showing their knowledge of important figures in black history as they find exciting volumes on the shelves.

When wealthier African Americans make disparaging remarks about the poor and the backwardness that keeps them poor, Willie argues that it is the system, not lack of initiative, that keeps so many African Americans in the lower classes. He believes that inequality is maintained by white oppression and by African Americans trying to imitate the worst of white materialist culture. Braithwaite disagrees, arguing that the early Nedeeds built up Linden Hills "because they felt our people needed a role model.... And that was real black pride." This touches on the existential question of Willie's life. What will black pride mean for him? He asks Lester, "Where's the answer for someone like me?" Braithwaite predicts that someone as bright and talented as Willie will end up in Linden Hills. Recognizing that Linden Hills has not produced any poets or any happiness, Willie is determined to find something else.

STYLE

Allusion to Dante's Inferno

Linden Hills makes several allusions to a great thirteenth-century poem, Dante Alighieri's *Inferno*.

An allusion is a reference to an earlier work of literature or a historical event. Allusions give writers a quick way to bring in a wealth of ideas or imagery without having to explain each detail—at least for those readers who understand the allusion. Naylor takes the basic structure for her novel from Dante's poem; another way to say this is that *Linden Hills* is a modern version of *Inferno*.

There are many parallels. In Dante's poem, Dante the poet is sent out on a tour of Hell by the heavenly figure Beatrice, who summons the ancient Roman poet Virgil to guide him. Virgil and Dante travel through hell, which is arranged as a funnel with nine concentric circles or levels. Each circle is reserved for one particular kind of sinner, and the sins are graver the lower down one goes. At the bottom of Hell, surrounded by a frozen lake, is Lucifer. In the novel, it is Ruth, a woman whose capacity for love seems otherworldly, who sets the poets Willie and Lester on their journey. She suggests that Lester would be a good guide for Willie, since he lives in Linden Hills and knows many of the neighbors. Linden Hills, wedge-shaped instead of circular, has eight circular streets, making nine groups of houses. The houses become more expensive the closer they get to the bottom of the slope, where Luther lives with his frozen moat. As Ruth and Lester explain, "Everybody wants to make it up there," and "up means down in the Hills." As Dante travels through the circles of Hell, he ponders the moral failings of those he witnesses, just as Willie does.

Other characters in *Linden Hills* line up with Dante's. Lester's mother and sister, in their house decorated in shades of green, are like Dante's characters in purgatory, on the knife edge between good and evil. Winston and David are like Dante's star-crossed lovers, Paolo and Francesca. In *Inferno*, Beatrice sends an angel to the fifth circle to rescue Dante; in *Linden Hills*, Ruth sends Norman to rescue Willie and Lester from the police on Fifth Crescent Drive.

Once she has established the allusion, Naylor is free to follow *Inferno* closely or abandon it to serve her own novel. In fact, she explained in a 1991 interview with Donna Perry, "I was with Dante until Second Crescent Drive.... I left Dante there because I had my own schema. Then I picked him up again at Sixth Crescent Drive." Naylor's focus is not on reinterpreting Dante, but on making her own statements about

what it costs people who pursue material wealth at the cost of happiness and fulfillment. She uses Dante, in other words, to support her own artistic purposes. Building her novel on top of Dante's structure, she never has to say directly that chasing the American dream leads people to sell their souls and end up in a kind of hell. The allusion makes that point implicitly.

Point of View

In a novel with as many characters as *Linden Hills*, it is common for point of view to shift often. Naylor uses a third-person omniscient narrator in *Linden Hills* to tell the story from various perspectives. The narrator is third person because she or he is not a character in the story, but someone reporting what happens from outside or up above. The narrator is called omniscient because she or he can see into the thoughts and feelings of more than one character. For example, when Lester, Willie, Ruth, and Norman are sitting around a table together, the narrator tells about Willie's dreams of Ruth, reports conversation with no special insight, gives background information about Norman's condition, enters Ruth's head to explain why she stays with Norman, enters Norman's head to recall the time when Ruth is sick, and then backs off to a neutral perspective once again to pick up the conversation.

The narrator is like a video camera, backing up and zooming in and backing up again. This allows readers to learn more about the characters that Lester and Willie observe than the two men can themselves. On December 20, for example, the narrator renders a conversation in which David tries to persuade Winston not to go through with marrying Cassandra. Willie does not hear this conversation, but because readers have witnessed it, they can see that Lester is correct about the true meaning of David's wedding toast, even though Lester himself is unsure.

The point of view is slightly different in Willa's sections. Here, Naylor occasionally employs what is sometimes called free indirect discourse or free indirect speech. This means that although the narrator remains in the third person, the voice gives Willa's speech and thoughts almost as though in first person. One small passage from December 20 will show how the narrator captures Willa's tenuous hold on reality by shifting the pronouns: "She kneeled slowly by the cot.... Yes, you looked like your grandmother. And the mother before that. And the mother before that. Oh, my baby, what have I done to you?"

It is less common for novels to employ visual tricks to highlight point of view, as this novel does. Turning the page to begin the December 20 chapter, readers are suddenly presented words in a new typeface. In the first edition of the novel, the main story was set in a serif typeface, while Willa's sections were set in a bold sans serif type. This use of two typefaces highlights Willa's separation from the others. Further, with the addition of extra line spaces between sections, the change allows Naylor to move quickly between what Willa is doing and what the others are doing without having to say, "Meanwhile, back in the basement . . ." each time. This is especially important in the December 24 chapter, where there are four sections of Willa's story, quickly intercut with the actions of Lester, Willie, and Luther. In the first edition of the novel, after Willie accidentally leaves the door to the basement unlocked, the sentence "A slow chill breeze trailed behind him from the basement door as it crept open" comes at the bottom of a right-hand page, followed only by three centered asterisks. This arrangement heightens the surprise for readers when, turning the page, they find Willa opening the door—in the regular serif typeface. Now that Willa has come upstairs to be with the others, the narrator backs away from her and no longer enters her mind, and her story is presented in the same type as the main narrative as she and her husband head toward their horrible fate.

HISTORICAL CONTEXT

The 1980s and Black Feminism

The 1980s witnessed a remarkable flourishing of writing by African American women—writing that drew large readership across racial lines and attracted great critical acclaim. Alice Walker's novel *The Color Purple* (1982) won the Pulitzer Prize in 1983 and was made into a movie directed by Steven Spielberg and featuring Oprah Winfrey and Whoopi Goldberg in 1985. In 1987, Toni Morrison published *Beloved*, which won the Pulitzer Prize as well as the American Book Award; Morrison won the Nobel

Prize in Literature in 1993. Young-adult author Mildred D. Taylor was nominated for the American Book Award for *Let the Circle Be Unbroken* (1982), and Virginia Hamilton was nominated the following year for *Sweet Whispers, Brother Rush*. Other African American women fiction writers, including Paule Marshall and Toni Cade Bambara, were celebrated alongside poets June Jordan, Audre Lorde, Gwendolyn Brooks, and others. Naylor wrote three novels during this decade, including *The Women of Brewster Place* (1982), which won the National Book Award for First Novel the same year that *The Color Purple* won the general fiction award, and *Linden Hills* (1985).

These writers depicted the experiences of black women and worked toward a new understanding of feminism that would better reflect that particular experience. Many women had come to believe that the civil rights movement of the 1950s and 1960s had focused too narrowly on the needs of men, while American second-wave feminism (the wave starting in the 1960s) focused too narrowly on the concerns of white women. American feminism especially, they believed, considered the oppression of women to arise only from their gender, ignoring what happens to women from different races or from lower socioeconomic classes. An important anthology published in 1980, *This Bridge Called My Back: Writings by Radical Women of Color*, edited by Cherríe Moraga and Gloria Anzaldúa, collected essays, poems, and fiction from a wide range of women. The original note soliciting contributions for the anthology expresses the frustrations many felt: "We want to express to all women—especially to white middle-class women—the experiences which divide us as feminists. . . . We want to create a definition that expands what 'feminist' means to us."

Interestingly, it was because of the civil rights movement, the feminist movement, and the various calls for inclusion that they led to that so many African American women were able to attend colleges and universities that had been previously closed to them by racist and sexist policies. Male characters in *Linden Hills* speak disparagingly of black women who have attended Brandeis, Wellesley, Yale, Stanford, Princeton, Berkeley—some of the most highly respected institutions in the country. These women have graduated with professional degrees

COMPARE
&
CONTRAST

- **1980s:** In 1980, 72 percent of white adults age twenty-five or older have graduated high school. For African Americans, the number is 51 percent.

  Today: In 2012, 92 percent of white Americans age twenty-five or older have graduated high school, while 86 percent of African American adults have graduated.

- **1980s:** In the equivalent of 2012 dollars, the median white household has a net worth of $82,374 in 1984. In 2012 dollars, the median African American household has a net worth of $7,150, approximately 9 percent of the figure for whites.

  Today: In 2012, the median white household has a net worth of $91,405, while the median African American household has a net worth of $6,446, only 7 percent of white households' worth.

- **1980s:** Marriage between two people of the same sex is illegal in every state in the United States and in every other country.

  Today: At least nineteen states in the United States and at least fifteen countries around the world recognize same-sex marriages, with several more states and countries apparently moving toward marriage equality.

---

and a new awareness of black history and literature. (Naylor herself did not discover African American writers, including her idols Zora Neale Hurston and Toni Morrison, until she went to college.) In the minds of these male characters, especially Maxwell Smyth, these graduates are not prepared to be traditional wives to hard-working men; instead, "they're ready to ask a hell of a lot from the world then and a hell of a lot from" their husbands. There are no happy marriages among the couples living in Linden Hills, because each of the husbands blames his wife for being in some way unsupportive of his needs, and feminists like Roxanne are doomed to remain single.

In her essay "Womanism: The Dynamics of the Contemporary Black Female Novel in English," Chikwenye Okonjo Ogunyemi explains why African American women of the time felt that they fit poorly into the standard feminist framework:

> Black women are disadvantaged in several ways: as blacks they, with their men, are victims of a white patriarchal culture; as women they are victimized by black men; and as black women they are also victimized on racial, sexual and class grounds by white men.

While the idea of "victimhood" fits Naylor's working-class characters in *The Women of Brewster Place* more closely than it fits the privileged women in *Linden Hills*, the two novels together show Naylor thinking her way through the debates about feminism and black feminism.

Naylor provided her own definition of feminism in an interview with Virginia Fowler in 1993: "Feminism is for me the simple belief that all human beings, regardless of gender, are equal.... Feminism to me is political, social, economic equality for all human beings." In spite of the terrible things that happen to many of the female characters in *Linden Hills*, Naylor explains that she does not see them as victims, because they ultimately control what happens to them. She stated, "I've always seen my characters—even if they're driven, like the woman in the basement in *Linden Hills*, to insanity—as somehow resisting in some way, if the resistance is only then to resort to insanity." In the 1980s, African Americans were writing about new opportunities and new challenges, creating texts that explored women's experiences in a rapidly changing world.

No one thinks to question why the homes on Tupelo Drive go back on the market so quickly.
(© *Andy Dean Photography / Shutterstock.com*)

CRITICAL OVERVIEW

After the success of Naylor's first novel, *The Women of Brewster Place* (1982), her second, *Linden Hills*, was eagerly anticipated. The contemporary reviews are mixed. Some reviewers, like Sam Cornish in the *Christian Science Monitor*, are enthusiastic. Cornish describes the novel as "a poignant and moving look at men and women, together and in conflict" and calls Willie and Lester "perhaps the best black male protagonists of recent fiction." In the *New York Times*, Mel Watkins believes this novel is "a much more ambitious work" than Naylor's first and finds that "although flawed, it tackles a controversial subject with boldness and originality." Watkins admires Naylor's willingness to criticize successful African Americans but believes that she is at times too heavy-handed in delivering her message. Joseph A. Brown, however, writing for *Callaloo*, disagrees, placing the novel "in the best didactic tradition."

Perhaps the harshest criticism comes from other African American female writers. In *Ms.* magazine, Sherley Anne Williams questions

Naylor's implicit message that "the only *real* black is a poor black." She also feels the novel is flawed but looks forward to more work from Naylor, "a mature literary talent of formidable skill." Jewelle Gomez, writing in *The Women's Review of Books*, expresses disappointment in the novel's uncritical treatment of the old idea that lighter skin represents a better person; Gomez writes that Naylor's "reiteration of the symbolism here feels like simple acceptance of it." Overall, Gomez concludes that the novel was trying to take on too many issues and too many characters, leaving her "unsatisfied, somewhat like I've felt after my grandmother's *Reader's Digest* condensations." However, Gomez agrees with the other reviewers that Naylor was—or would be—a major talent.

In the twenty-first century, *Linden Hills* has become a staple of women's studies and African American studies courses, and published criticism digs deeper into the three threads that informed discussion of the novel through the 1980s and 1990s: the novel's structure, the role of women, and the issue of racial identity. Critics thoroughly examine Naylor's use of Dante and classical texts in structuring the novel, and more recent attention has expanded to explore her dialogue with other texts. John Noell Moore, for example, finds echoes of German fairy tales, the Bible, and Ovid's *Metamorphoses* in an article published in 2000 in *Callaloo*. At the heart of his analysis is the question, "Why does [Naylor] choose patriarchal narratives as the architectural bases for her novel?" Moore concludes that she chooses these texts precisely because they offer a model of failure, as Lester and Willie learn.

Christopher N. Okonkwo, writing in *African American Review* in 2001, analyzes Willa's imprisonment and death in light of black liberation theology, a religious movement that uses Christianity as a lens for African Americans to understand and overcome oppression. Okonkwo argues that Willa's death is not a suicide and not a failure, but rather "an emphatic positive metaphor of Black women's liberatory activism." He writes, "Willa's rebellion and death exalt the legacy of public and private sacrifice made by 'grassroots' Black women."

Finally, Tim Engles examines *Linden Hills* in the context of the new field of "critical whiteness studies," looking at how *Linden Hills* and other works address whiteness without focusing on any white characters. Engles's article "African American Whiteness in Gloria Naylor's *Linden Hills*," published in *African American Review* in 2009, sees in the novel "a critique of African American 'whiteness' as a generally repressive mode of thought and behavior that paradoxically bleaches away both communal ties and individual distinctiveness."

CRITICISM

Cynthia A. Bily

Bily is a professor of English at Macomb Community College in Michigan. In the following essay, she examines the importance of food in Linden Hills.

In the last hours of his life, Luther Nedeed stands at his window at the bottom of Linden Hills, dreaming of Christmases past. First the decorations: swags of greenery, crystal gleaming in candlelight, wreaths, and bunches of herbs. Then he remembers the food. There has always been punch, and he remembers his father giving

> IN *LINDEN HILLS*, WOMEN WHO PREPARE FOOD ARE STRONG. WOMEN WHO HAVE LOST THEIR CONNECTION WITH THIS TRADITIONAL, SACRED TASK ARE WOMEN WHO HAVE LOST EVERYTHING."

him "small sips and later a whole cup" of the same punch he will soon serve to Lester and Willie. He remembers how "the smell of roast goose and baked ham drifted from the back kitchen," and he remembers "mountainous platters of molasses cookies and sweet potato buns" and "a molasses-cake house, whose roof lifted off to reveal cut rock- and ribbon-candy." He remembers a "feast of time" to talk with his father. What he does not remember is the people who made all that food. What he does not remember is the women.

Charles P. Toombs considers food imagery in the novel in an essay titled, "The Confluence of Food and Identity in Gloria Naylor's Linden Hills: 'What We Eat Is Who We Is.'" Published in 1993 in *CLA Journal*, the essay focuses on the food that Naylor's characters choose and how that food demonstrates their separation from their southern roots and their African American heritage. A central theme of the novel, Toombs points out, is that the residents of Linden Hills are trying to make new identities as upper-class professionals. Although many of them sense a hollowness in their lives, they do not seem to recognize that they are empty because while they are creating new identities they are losing their culture.

Some critics, including Tim Engles and others, have described what these characters are striving for as "African American 'whiteness.'" Toombs addresses that idea with an analysis that is grounded in the everyday lives of the characters. He points to the catered parties, the caviar, the stuffed artichokes, and the Norwegian crystal and sees people who have forgotten who they are. Also, he points out that the only happy or potentially happy people living in the area are the four—Willie, Lester, Norman, and Ruth—who have decided not to pursue what their neighbors

WHAT DO I READ NEXT?

- The structure of the neighborhood of Linden Hills, with its circular roads arranged along a descending slope, echoes the concentric circles of hell in *Inferno*, an allegorical epic poem composed in Italian by Dante Alighieri (1317). The poem has been translated into English many times; highly regarded translations include those of Robert Hollander and Jean Hollander (2000), Allen Mandelbaum (1980), and John Ciardi (1954).

- Gloria Naylor's most well-known novel is *The Women of Brewster Place: A Novel in Seven Stories* (1982), which won a National Book Award. Each of the stories focuses on one woman of color living in Brewster Place, a poor and sometimes violent neighborhood next to the wealthier Linden Hills. As the women interact with each other and with their friends, lovers, and children, they attempt to come together to struggle against abusive men, homophobia, and an economy that offers little hope for them.

- *The Bluest Eye* (1970), by Toni Morrison, was one of the first books by an African American woman that Naylor ever read. Set in Lorain, Ohio, during the Great Depression, it tells the story of Pecola, a young African American girl with an unhappy life. She feels inferior to others because of her skin and eye color and thinks her life would be better if she were white with blue eyes. This highly regarded novel has occasionally been called unsuitable for students because of its themes of racism and child abuse.

- F. Scott Fitzgerald's classic novel *The Great Gatsby* (1925) is one of the most famous fictional examinations of the American dream. It is the story of Jay Gatsby, a poor, uneducated boy from the Midwest who has transformed himself into an enormously wealthy man, throwing elaborate parties at his mansion on Long Island to attract the attention of the woman he loves. Through the eyes of Gatsby's neighbor, Nick Carraway, the book questions whether money can really buy happiness.

- Marisa, the main character in Ashley Hope Pérez's novel *What Can't Wait* (2011), is a seventeen-year-old math whiz with dreams of becoming an engineer. Marisa, whose parents emigrated from Mexico, thinks she could do well in college, but her family needs the money she earns at the grocery store, and her sister needs child-care help. With her family pulling her back, Marisa wonders whether she can ever move up and out.

- *Race: A History beyond Black and White* (2007), by historian Marc Aronson, traces the ways that humans have sorted themselves and each other into "us" and "them" for thousands of years. Racial prejudice is nothing new, but methods of classifying people have changed over time. This well-illustrated book raises interesting questions about how ideas that seem logical and natural are often artificial—and can be dangerous.

---

consider success. These four, Toombs writes, "know that eating barbecue ribs, fried chicken, and collard greens, and drinking beer and cheap wine are intrinsically more important than a manicured lawn, an Olympic-sized pool, and an empty heart." It seems a missed opportunity that

Naylor and Toombs never use the term "soul food" to name what these folks have rejected.

Toombs insightfully observes how food acts as a marker of identity in the novel. However, perhaps there is both less and more to it than Toombs claims. One of the great pleasures of reading literature is that one need not look for one-to-one correspondences and assume that each element in a novel "means" exactly one secret thing. So Toombs is right in what he says, but he does not say everything that can be said about food in *Linden Hills*. For one thing, many of these characters are far from their southern roots anyway. Naylor's parents came north in the late 1940s as part of what is called the Great Migration, a movement of millions of African Americans in the middle of the twentieth century from the rural South to big cities in the North. However, the first Luther Nedeed bought his land in 1820.

By the time of the novel's present, the Nedeed family is four generations removed from the South. Other families have been in Linden Hills since the beginning of those thousand-year-and-one-day leases. Laurel Dumont's husband's family, for example, leased their land in 1903, so Howard and his father both grew up in Linden Hills. By the terms of the leases, this must be true of many of the twenty- and thirty-something characters who live in Linden Hills. Perhaps their parents' or grandparents' generation made conscious choices to scale back on their southern cooking, but more likely they just found it difficult to find collard greens and catfish in the suburbs. It seems more apt to say, then, that what these characters eat stands as an interesting marker of what they have lost, but not necessarily as a marker of what they have rejected.

Another way to look at food in this novel draws attention to the women characters. Most of the food in the novel is made by women or provided by caterers—unlike twentieth-century men, none of the men of Linden Hills seem to know how to prepare a meal (with the peculiar exception of Maxwell Smyth). Luther, it is true, makes the Christmas punch, as the Nedeed men have always done, but all he can scrounge up for Christmas Eve dinner is cheese and crackers. Of course, he blames Willa for the paltry feast: "Cheese and crackers for Christmas Eve. Did she know what she had done?" Luther is so unused to thinking about where food comes from—about who is doing what in that back kitchen—that he brings a store-bought cake to Lycentia Parker's wake and thinks no one will be able to tell it is not homemade.

Lester is a twenty-year-old high school graduate whose mother still cooks for him. Xavier Donnell lives with his aunt, and when Maxwell comes over he offers drinks without so much as a

bowl of nuts to go with it. These men do not prepare food, but they expect to dominate women who will prepare food. The women, for their part, do not fight back; they are happy with having the responsibility and the power to nurture and provide sustenance. In *Linden Hills*, women who prepare food are strong. Women who have lost their connection with this traditional, sacred task are women who have lost everything.

And then there are those caught in the middle. The first meal served in the novel is the dinner prepared by Mrs. Tilson, Lester's mother. The Tilsons live in the smallest house on the least important street in Linden Hills, and Mrs. Tilson is well aware that she is on the edge between belonging and not fitting in. She sighs, "There are homes across Wayne Avenue that are better than this one, and we live in Linden Hills." She and her late husband did not come from wealth, and she tries too hard to be accepted by the rest of Linden Hills. This is shown in various ways. She insists on pointing out to Lester and Willie, who could not be less interested, that she has redone the upholstery. She calls Willie "William," even though that is not his name. She corrects Lester's grammar. Because she does not really know how to act like the person she wants to be, the neighbors laugh at her.

One clear demonstration of Mrs. Tilson's position in between who she is and who she wishes she were is the dinner she has prepared: fried chicken and potatoes. Fried chicken comes right out of the South, right out of tradition, and is everyone's favorite. But Mrs. Tilson has to be sure that no one—not even Willie—thinks that she considers this a suitable meal for guests. "We're eating like peasants tonight," she says, calling the chicken "common food, but filling." She cannot bring herself to serve plain mashed potatoes, though. She says, "I'm trying something a bit daring with the potatoes. A cheese and wine sauce I saw in the papers." This would be heartbreaking if she were a nicer person. A bit daring? In light of the horrors that are yet to come in the novel, Mrs. Tilson's walk on the wild side is just sad. Mrs. Tilson lives at the far edge of Linden Hills, almost outside it, and one wonders if there is still time for her to settle down and accept a simpler life. Her choice of food, and her comments about it, illustrate her struggle.

One generation younger, Roxanne is also struggling. She wants to live in a world of success; she wants to "marry black, marry well—or not at all." Just as her mother does not quite know how to decorate or cook, Roxanne does not quite know how to dress, wearing clothes that are just a bit off, and she wishes she had lighter skin and straighter hair. Like many of the women characters in the novel, Roxanne's main challenges come from men. She is well-educated, she has a good job, and she is (her bickering with her brother aside) a pleasant person. However, the men around her judge her mainly in terms of her body, and this creates an awareness of and a struggle with food that the male characters do not share.

Roxanne is curvy, and "her body gave the impression that it was just one good meal away from being labeled fat." Her own brother tells her she looks like a pig. Maxwell and Xavier disagree about whether "there's a bit too much avoirdupois," or weight, or if she is just "full," before Maxwell launches into an appalling rant about black women, jungle days, and starvation. Roxanne does not hear their discussion, but she gets the message: Thin is in. "So her life consisted of nibbles: bits of lettuce and cucumber, dabs of fish and cottage cheese," interspersed with depression-induced binges on potato chips and Twinkies. While Lester feels free to wolf down the food his mother has cooked and still complain about it, Roxanne eats only "two bites of chicken and [a] teaspoon of potatoes." Roxanne's relationship with food is a marker of her struggles to meet the expectations of men. It is not her heritage she rejects when she takes small bites of fried chicken and then eats French chocolates. Giving up control over what she eats is a sign that she is giving up her own self-image and self-determination.

Of course, many of the women in this novel do not voluntarily give up their traditional relationship with food. Willa had been a willing partner in her marriage of convenience. Accepting her role as wife, "She cleaned his home, cooked his meals," and Luther has to admit to himself that the housekeeper "never made his eggs like his wife had." Once she is locked in the basement, however, Luther controls her food and water, and she has nothing but powdered milk and dry cereal. Luther has taken away the task of preparing food for her family, as well as her ability to choose what she eats.

Willa's husband's interference with her connection to food is one important marker of the connection between her and the previous Mrs. Nedeeds. Luwana Packerville, for example, was owned as a slave by her husband, as was her infant son. But as soon as "the child was weaned," as soon as he "could now take solid food without harm," as soon as his mother was no longer needed to provide his nourishment, Luther signed papers to make the son free. Soon, Luwana was stripped completely of her responsibility for preparing meals, as Luther brought in a housekeeper and a gardener to handle all the food and declared that he and his son would not eat anything Luwana prepared. Even when she prepared molasses cake, her son's favorite (and the cakes the fourth Luther dreams of on Christmas Eve), the boy refused it.

Evelyn Creton Nedeed, collector of cookbooks, tries to use cooking to save herself and her marriage. Willa observes that Evelyn "didn't know that a woman had gone insane because she was barred from the very kitchen that Evelyn Creton later filled with her damned cookbooks." Soon it becomes clear that Evelyn herself was not quite sane. At first Willa sees only that "the woman cooked as if she were possessed," but then she realizes that Evelyn was adding herbs and powders into her recipes to bring her husband back to her bed. When that did not work, Evelyn used the only power she had—control over her food—to binge and purge until she was near death. Her last meal was vanilla ice cream and prussic acid, a roach poison. Like the others, Evelyn's Luther created the conditions that disrupted his wife's connection to food, a marker of the disruption of her happiness and sanity. When Willa decides to go upstairs and rebuild her life, she does it with the most basic form of sustenance, the "cold, rusty water" collected in her pot. She decides consciously to "take small sips, very small sips—and think." Nourished in this simple way, she begins climbing the stairs.

Tracing women's control over food and control over their lives in *Linden Hills* does not yield a neat map or a clear thesis (for one thing, it does not have anything to say about Priscilla), but it highlights connections and raises interesting questions. Other readers have reflected on Naylor's use of mirror and reflection imagery, or references to faces, or shown connections between Willie and Willa. It might also be possible to useful to trace imagery of light and dark or heat and cold or different colors. Digging

Despite their very different backgrounds, Lester and Willie are loyal friends. *(© bikeriderlondon / Shutterstock.com)*

deeply into small details and word choices in a large work can bring out ideas and assumptions that hover, like Willa Prescott Nedeed, just below the surface.

Source: Cynthia A. Bily, Critical Essay on *Linden Hills*, in *Novels for Students*, Gale, Cengage Learning, 2015.

Maxine Lavon Montgomery

In the following excerpt, Montgomery addresses how female characters in Linden Hills *achieve a sense of identity from their domestic chores.*

. . . Whereas the home place in *The Women of Brewster Place* is a potentially revolutionary site revealing urban black women's survivalist tendencies, in *Linden Hills* the home place is an arena under patriarchal domination divorced from the political struggle of contemporary black America. The Nedeed wives are guardians of notions of women's place and duty that bourgeois ideology perpetuates; and as a result, they

become unwitting co-conspirators with their male counterparts in female subjugation. In this context, the Nedeed home, a large, white clapboard structure built during the antebellum era, is a locale where the hierarchical sociopolitical structure responsible for the marginalization of black women is replicated. The Nedeed wives are little more than their husbands' servants, and the Sisyphean housekeeping tasks the women carry out place them in a hell-like state that is even more debilitating than that which the residents of Brewster Place experience.

Naylor levels a stinging indictment of marriage as a social institution in this second novel. Because of societal conditioning, the women who marry into the Nedeed family do so primarily in hopes of finding an identity within a staunchly middle-class setting. What they discover is that marriage to an upwardly mobile, propertied businessman such as Luther Nedeed not only fails to occasion any personal fulfillment, it furthers the women's sense of "otherness." As Angela Davis puts it, "the housewife, according to bourgeois ideology, is, quite simply, her husband's lifelong servant" (1981, 225). The central dilemma that the Nedeed wives face is that they have no self apart from the social role each assumes in her pursuit of marriage and middle-class respectability. Luwana Packerville-Nedeed sums up the irony surrounding the women's plight: "Was she so busy being needed that it never dawned on her she wasn't being married?" Unlike the women of Brewster Place, the Nedeed wives do not have to participate in a paid labor force, so their work all takes place in the confines of their own home. Here, isolated from the larger community, the women fashion tenuous selves that depend on establishing domestic order and harmony.

The Nedeed wives, like the other residents of Linden Hills, fail to look inward at the mirror, which, according to Grandma Tilson, can allow an individual to form an identity apart from the institutions, conventions, and ideals of bourgeois society. "So you keep that mirror," Lester relays his grandmother's timely advice, "and when it's crazy *outside*, you look inside and you'll always know exactly where you are and what you are." While confined to the basement of the Nedeed home, Willa reads herself through a perusal of the documents revealing the "shared domestic tragedies of the Nedeed wives" (Levy 1992, 213). Those documents—cookbooks, diaries, and photographs—reflect who Willa is, or more accurately, who she is not. Only as Willa acknowledges her true self—an act figured by the discovery of her name—does she acquire the self-confidence necessary to ascend the stairs leading to the Nedeed kitchen. In the fictional world Naylor constructs, then, knowledge is liberating, for like slaves whose introduction to literacy brought about a desire for freedom, Willa's newfound knowledge motivates her to rise from her subjugated state, and she does so in the midst of housecleaning.

Narrative emphasis on the daily tasks the women perform, along with a focus on different sites within the home, reveals the imposed limits of female domesticity. The bedroom, for instance, is the place where the Nedeed wives are subjected to male desire and privilege. Once the women help to fulfill their husbands' patriarchal goal of fathering a son, the husbands lose interest in them. Willa tries to put the spark back into her marriage by visiting New York and trying various beauty products designed to enhance her sex appeal, in addition to consulting *Cosmopolitan* and *Ladies Home Journal*. She rejects the shame-weed her great-aunt Mama Day recommends as a way to regain Luther's affection. For all of Willa's efforts at restoring her marriage, though, Luther remains cold and distant. Luther's punishment of Willa and young Luther—confining mother and son to the basement for her alleged infidelity—is his way of ensuring his control in a situation where female sexuality is a potential threat to Luther's hegemonic rule.

Just as the Nedeed men view female sexuality as a threat, so, too, do they consider women's culinary art a possibly subversive medium. The kitchen thus becomes a battleground in the war between the sexes. After learning of a woman in Tennessee who was hanged for poisoning her master's soup, Luwana Packerville-Nedeed's husband feels compelled to hire a housekeeper to cook and wash. Evelyn Creton-Nedeed devotes so much time and energy to cooking that the kitchen is her entire reality: "The woman cooked as if she were possessed. What drove her to make that kitchen her whole world?" Willa recognizes in Evelyn's meticulous handwriting evidence of the woman's fanatical dedication to good housekeeping: "This woman never had a curl out of place, a ribbon knotted loosely, a stick of furniture not glowing with

lemon oil. She gave the right parties at the right time for the right people. There were two sets of china and silverplate, a suit for each occasion, a set of boots for each season—and a porcelain exterior that accented whatever room it was placed in. There were probably a dozen words that the friends and enemies of the Nedeeds used to describe her, but one of them just had to be 'perfect'." When Evelyn's marriage begins to deteriorate further despite her efforts, her attention to cooking becomes compulsive. She spends countless hours at grocery stores purchasing food and then recording the buying of the ingredients she hopes will allow her to restore her marriage. Gradually, as if to indicate the discord that is the ironic end result of Evelyn's fanatical devotion to cooking, her attention to food gives way to overeating and purging, with her recipe books chronicling her retreat into insanity.

The documents that the Nedeed wives author attest to the home as a place of bondage and subjugation. In fact, Willa's awakening to self, which occurs in terms of a rebirth, is occasioned by a knowledge of what Barbara Christian refers to as "herstory," a history both by and about women (1993, 116). In discovering "herstory," Willa discovers herself. This discovery renders Willa's decision to reenter the Nedeed home at the novel's end highly ambiguous. On the one hand, she appears to challenge the place to which bourgeois society would consign housewives; on the other hand, Naylor's rendering of the woman's psychology during the cleaning of the Nedeed home suggests that Willa is still operating within a socially prescribed context. As Naylor points out in an interview with Toni Morrison, Willa enjoys being a housewife, much to the author's dismay (Naylor and Morrison 1985, 587). Willa is either unable or unwilling to abandon externally imposed definitions of domesticity; indeed, the narrator describes Willa's ascent to the home, saying "each step was bringing her closer to the kitchen and the disorder whose oblivion was now inextricably tied to her continuing existence." Consequently, her ascent to the home constitutes only a partial triumph over Luther's hegemonic rule.

Linden Hills thus offers a powerful commentary on the dangers of a domesticity divorced from community empowerment. Rather than being liberating, either for themselves or the larger community, the tasks that the Nedeed wives perform lead to madness, solitude, and despair. The women in the novel affirm the vital sisterhood that Larry Andrews (1993) sees as central to the text, but they fail to enact positive sociopolitical change. In this sense, Willa's housekeeping at the novel's end is both destructive and self-destructive. The entire Nedeed family falls victim to the disorder Willa, alone, tries futilely to contain . . . .

Source: Maxine Lavon Montgomery, "Good Housekeeping: Domestic Ritual in Gloria Naylor's Fiction," in *Gloria Naylor's Early Novels*, edited by Margot Anne Kelley, University Press of Florida, 1999, pp. 60–63.

Margaret Earley Whitt

In the following excerpt, Whitt looks at Naylor's allusions to Dante's Inferno.

. . . WILLIE AND LESTER

Naylor's choice of names—Willie K. Mason and Lesterfield Walcott Montgomery Tilson—for the two who serve as the reader's guides through Linden Hills suggest a comic allusion to the black ventriloquist Willie Tyler and his dummy with an exaggerated Afro, Lester. Tyler, a soft-spoken person, has called Lester his alter-ego, using the dummy to say things that Willie cannot say for himself. Naylor's Willie uses Lester in much the same way. When his mouth gets him in trouble during the visit to Norman and Ruth's, Willie looks to Lester for help.

Willie and Lester also serve as the Dante and Virgil figures, respectively, of the novel. When Dante (1265–1321) was a young man, Italy was almost always under siege. His family was connected in Florence to the Guelphs, a papal party antagonistic to the Ghibellines. The Guelphs split into two factions, the Blacks and the Whites. As a White, Dante was forced into exile by his political enemies in the other faction. For the last twenty years of his life, he lived outside of Florence, wrote *The Divine Comedy*, traveled, and lectured. Willie's nickname, White, given to him because he was "so black that the kids said if he turned just a shade darker, there was nothing he could do but start going the other way," is an ironic physical reminder of what Willie is not, and a link to Dante's political faction.

Just as Virgil serves as the guide to Dante in the excursion through Hell, Lester serves as the one who makes it possible for Willie to have easier access to Linden Hills because Lester and his family live on First Crescent Drive. The first

> **LINDEN HILLS IS LESTER'S NEIGHBORHOOD, AND LIKE VIRGIL WHO KNOWS HELL AND MAKES THE OFFER TO DANTE, HE IS WILLING TO BE WILLIE'S HOST AND HIS GUIDE."**

circle of Hell, Limbo, where the unbaptized dwell because they preceded Jesus Christ, is Virgil's home in the afterworld. As Dante knows Virgil's poetry, Willie first reads Lester's poems before he admits to his friend that he also is a poet. Naylor's use of poetry becomes a vehicle larger than only a connection to the *Inferno*, for Willie and Lester are contemporaries and their knowledge that the other finds solace in writing poetry deepens their friendship: "Giving sound to the bruised places in their hearts made them brothers." Willie keeps his poetry in his head because "his aim was to be like the great slave poet, Jupiter Hammon, who memorized thousands of verses because he couldn't read." Hammon (1711–1806?) published nine pieces of prose and verse, and on each of them he indicated that he was "a Negro Man belonging to Mr. Joseph Lloyd." Though Willie's claim for Hammon is that he could not read, critics have indicated that Hammon was "allowed to acquire skills of reading and writing in the early eighteenth century so that he could assist his masters in commercial endeavors." Willie's formal education stops in the ninth grade.

Willie and Lester have been friends since they were in the seventh grade at Wayne Junior High School. When they meet in front of that school the week before Christmas, they are 20 years old. The words on the bronze plaques over the school's triple doors are a parody of the opening three lines of Canto III of the *Inferno*. When Naylor's lines are placed beside a translation of Dante's, the ironic inversion is clear:

> I am the way out of the city of woe—
> I am the way to a prosperous people—
> I am the way from eternal sorrow—
> Sacred justice moved my architect—
> I was raised here by divine omnipotence—
> Primordial love and ultimate intellect—
> Only the elements time cannot wear—
> Were made before me, and beyond time I stand—

Abandon ignorance, ye who enter here—
Through me you enter the woeful city,
Through me you enter eternal grief,
Through me you enter among the lost.
Justice moved my high maker:
The divine power made me,
The supreme wisdom, and the primal love.
Before me nothing was created
If not eternal, and eternal I endure
Abandon every hope, you who enter.

Willie's comment as he looks at the last plaque indicates that he takes the last line seriously. He knows that he should have stayed in school. He has memorized 665 poems, a number that is only one away from the number of the beast, 666, in Revelations 13:18. Hebrew and Greek letters have numerical equivalents, and the sum of the separate letters of the Antichrist's name equals the number 666.

The poets Willie has memorized—Amiri Baraka (1934–), formerly Leroi Jones, a man who represents the revolutionary mood of the 1960s and changed his name after Malcolm X was assassinated; Wole Soyinka (1934–), a Nigerian poet and playwright, well versed in the Yoruba culture, who received the Nobel Prize for Literature in 1986; and Langston Hughes (1902–67), who was in the vanguard of the Harlem Renaissance—were prolific poets. Their complete canons along with most of Samuel Taylor Coleridge and Walt Whitman (45) total more than 665, a number Naylor mentions at least three times (44, 45, 275), a reminder of its proximity to the beast's number. When Willie composes his poem about the "man in a house at the bottom of a hill," he has 666 poems in his head. The last one is about the Antichrist figure in this novel.

In many ways, Willie is the central character. Through him, the reader discovers the unfolding world of Linden Hills' secrets. Naylor's placement of every detail—the addresses of the houses where Lester and Willie do chores double as allusions to the *Inferno*, the simple act of their spending the night together, and the placement of Willie's dreams—predicts what is to come. As they move through the neighborhood, like Dante and Virgil moving downward in hell, Naylor is careful to identify by address each person for whom the boys work. When Lester invites Willie to his home for the night so that they can get an early start in the morning, the two spend the night in the same bed. Naylor suggests the physical contact they have with each other is the result of innocent sleep patterns; Henry Louis Gates, Jr., on the other hand, explores their connection as homoerotic. Citing examples from the trepidation of divulging their poetry to each other to spending this night in bed together, a night that deliberately precedes the wedding of the declared gay Winston, Gates makes a case for Willie as the sexual cynosure in the novel.

Linden Hills is Lester's neighborhood, and like Virgil who knows Hell and makes the offer to Dante, he is willing to be Willie's host and his guide. Naylor draws Lester as more worldly-wise than Willie. Lester has inherited his grandmother's cynical attitude about Linden Hills. He believes he can see through the hypocrisy of his mother, his sister Roxanne, and her boyfriend. Lester shares Kiswana Browne's view of the world. This young woman, who abandoned the best house on First Crescent Drive for a studio apartment on Brewster Place, was declared by Lester's mother to be "mentally disturbed . . . putting holes in her nose, taking some heathen name." But when Kiswana comes collecting clothes for the Liberation Front in Zimbabwe, Roxanne's comment to her "that the people of Zimbabwe weren't ready for independence" sends Kiswana away quickly and embarrasses Lester. To the chagrin of both sets of parents, Kiswana has chosen to drop out of college, and Lester has chosen not to start. The offspring of First Crescent Drive dwellers understand what the fifth Luther Nedeed banks on nobody knowing—that "they've lost all touch with what it is to be *them*. Because there's not a damned thing inside anymore to let them know."

Lester's cynicism is deepened by his preoccupation with Malcolm X. Though Willie suggests that Malcolm X could be offended by Lester's using his mother's hospitality and insulting her to her face, Lester chooses to express his frustrations of life in Linden Hills by listening to tapes of Malcolm X, an alternate voice to Martin Luther King's during the civil rights movement. With Malcolm's poster on his bedroom wall and a three-foot stack of his taped speeches at the foot of the television stand, Lester chooses "Message to the Grass Roots" to play for Willie. Malcolm X delivered this speech to the Detroit Council for Human Rights several weeks before the November 1963 assassination of President John Kennedy. The fact that Lester listens to—instead of reads—these speeches encourages an antagonistic attitude within him. According to one critic, listening to Malcolm X is "vastly superior to the written text in conveying style and personality of Malcolm at his best—when he was speaking to a militant black audience."

The first dream that Willie reports having, the one that drives "him toward the security of his friend's body," occurs the night before the boys' descent into Linden Hills. Naylor's choice of language predicts the next day's story: Winston, who loves David, chooses to abandon that partnership for the respectability of marriage to a woman he does not love. Willie's "night images . . . the flashes of a huge clock with snakes and spiders for hands and numbers" are similar to Dante and Virgil's meeting with Minos. As a clock would strike time to Willie and Lester, telling them that work awaits this day on Second Crescent Drive, Minos stands inside the second circle, where Hell proper begins, horrible and snarling, listening to sinners confess and determining, by girding himself with his tail, where exactly in Hell the sinner will be sent.

Willie's second dream occurs after overeating Parker's leftover roast beef and Nedeed's cake. Pale hands with bright red fingernails "growing and curling like snakes around the cake" reach out to him from a long row of erect coffins as he runs through a glass door and down a dark corridor. It is the morning he will go to Fifth Crescent Drive. Similarities exist in Canto IX of the *Inferno*, in the corresponding fifth circle. Dante is confronted by three hellish Furies, who beat their breasts and tear at themselves with their nails. They have snakes for hair, and Virgil covers Dante's eyes for him to pass by safely. Willie alone in his dream has no option but to run straight ahead, "trying to avert his eyes from the ghostly fingers [and] bloody snakes," move through the glass door, and wake up in his bed. As in I Corinthians 13:12, Willie sees through the glass darkly, but all too soon, he will see face to face; he will come to know more about the world reflected in Linden Hills. His seeing clearly, however, will have to wait, for in his third dream Willie is told by the saleswoman from whom he tries to buy a Disc camera that he has no face. It is a dream that prevents him from trying to return to sleep in the early hours of the day he and Lester begin their descent onto Tupelo Drive, a day in which he will encounter Laurel Dumont, whose face disappears in her fatal dive into an empty swimming pool . . . .

Source: Margaret Earley Whitt, "*Linden Hills,*" in *Understanding Gloria Naylor*, University of South Carolina Press, 1999, pp. 67–73.

SOURCES

Brown, Joseph A., "With Eyes Like Flames of Fire," in *Callaloo*, Vol. 8, No. 24, Spring–Summer 1985, p. 484.

Cornish, Sam, "Middle-Class Souls on Ice," in *Christian Science Monitor*, March 1, 1985, p. B1.

Dante, *Inferno*, translated by John Ciardi, 1954, Signet Classics, 2009.

Engles, Tim, "African American Whiteness in Gloria Naylor's Linden Hills," in *African American Review*, Vol. 43, No. 4, Winter 2009, pp. 661–62.

Fowler, Virginia C., "Writing as Witnessing: An Introduction to the Life of Gloria Naylor," in *Gloria Naylor: In Search of Sanctuary*, Twayne's United States Authors Series No. 660, Twayne Publishers, 1996, pp. 1–20.

———, "Appendix: A Conversation with Gloria Naylor," in *Gloria Naylor: In Search of Sanctuary*, Twayne's United States Authors Series No. 660, Twayne Publishers, 1996, pp. 144–45.

"Gay Marriage Pros and Cons," ProCon.org, http:// gaymarriage.procon.org (accessed July 25, 2014).

Gomez, Jewelle, "Naylor's Inferno," in *Women's Review of Books*, Vol. 2, No. 11, August 1985, pp. 7–8.

Moore, John Noelle, "Myth, Fairy Tale, Epic, and Romance: Narrative and Re-Vision in Linden Hills," in *Callaloo*, Vol. 23, No. 4, Fall 2000, p. 1410.

Moraga, Cherrié, and Gloria Anzaldúa, Introduction to *This Bridge Called My Back: Writing by Radical Women of Color*, 2nd ed., Kitchen Table Press, 1983, p. xxiii.

Naylor, Gloria, *Linden Hills*, Ticknor & Fields, 1985.

Naylor, Gloria, and Donna Perry, "Gloria Naylor," in *Conversations with Gloria Naylor*, edited by Maxine Lavon Montgomery, University Press of Mississippi, 2004, p. 88; originally published in *Backtalk: Women Writers Speak Out*, Rutgers University Press, 1993, pp. 217–44.

Ogunyemi, Chikwenye Okonjo, "Womanism: The Dynamics of the Contemporary Black Female Novel in English," in *Signs*, Vol. 11, No. 1, Fall 1985, p. 67.

Okonkwo, Christopher N., "Suicide or Messianic Self-Sacrifice?: Exhuming Willa's Body in Gloria Naylor's Linden Hills," in *African American Review*, Vol. 35, No. 1, Spring 2001, p. 128.

"Race in America: Tracking 50 Years of Demographic Trends," in *Pew Research Social and Demographic Trends*, August 22, 2013, http://www.pewsocialtrends.org/2013/ 08/22/race-demographics/ (accessed July 25, 2014).

Toombs, Charles P., "The Confluence of Food and Identity in Gloria Naylor's *Linden Hills*: 'What We Eat Is

Who We Is,'" in *CLA Journal*, Vol. 37, No. 1, September 1993, pp. 1–18.

Watkins, Mel, "The Circular Driveways of Hell," in *New York Times Book Review*, March 3, 1985, p. 11.

William, Sherley Anne, "Roots of Privilege: New Black Fiction," in *Ms.*, Vol. 13, June 1985, pp. 69–71.

Wilson, Charles E., Jr., "The Life of Gloria Naylor," in *Gloria Naylor: A Critical Companion*, Greenwood Press, 2001, pp. 1–13.

FURTHER READING

Butts, Tracy, "Gloria Naylor: A Selected Bibliography," in *Calaloo*, Vol. 23, No. 4, Fall 2000, pp. 1497–1512.
    Although this bibliography is no longer up to date, it is thorough. The lists of primary works include Naylor's early short stories and magazine articles, while the annotated list of secondary sources includes more than one hundred critical articles and reviews.

Cullen, Jim, *The American Dream: A Short History of an Idea That Shaped a Nation*, Oxford University Press, 2004.
    This accessible volume traces how Americans' ideas of how to achieve happiness and success have changed over time. Cullen explains how the Founders' original notion that, under democracy, hard work would lead to upward mobility leads directly to the struggle for racial equality of the civil rights movement. In the twenty-first century, he is concerned that materialism and self-absorption have corrupted the Founders' vision.

Montgomery, Maxine Lavon, ed., *Conversations with Gloria Naylor*, University of Mississippi Press, 2004.
    This is a collection of fourteen interviews and recorded conversations with Naylor, helpfully indexed. The conversations were held from 1983, just after the publication of *The Women of Brewster Place*, to 2000. Among the highlights are a 1985 discussion between Naylor and Toni Morrison, whose work inspired Naylor to write, and another, from 1997, between Naylor and poet Nikki Giovanni.

Russell, Sandi, *Render Me My Song: African-American Women Writers from Slavery to the Present*, St. Martin's Press, 1990.
    This book considers African American women writers from the eighteenth-century poet Phillis Wheatley, through Harlem Renaissance writers such as Zora Neale Hurston, to the generation of black feminist writers that includes Audre Lorde, Paule Marshall, and Naylor.

Ward, Catherine C., "Gloria Naylor's *Linden Hills*: A Modern *Inferno*," in *Contemporary Literature*, Vol. 28, No. 1, Spring 1987, pp. 67–81.
    Several critics have illuminated the connections between Naylor's novel and the epic poem that influenced it. Ward's analysis is perhaps the most thorough and accessible even for readers who may have little knowledge of Dante. Ward concludes that Naylor's choice to echo a medieval moral tale is risky, but that the risk pays off.

Whitt, Margaret Earley, *Understanding Gloria Naylor*, University of South Carolina Press, 1999.
    Part of the Understanding Contemporary American Literature series, this volume gives a basic introduction specifically intended for students and general readers. For each of Naylor's first five novels, Whitt discusses the major characters and themes. Her analysis of *Linden Hills* includes a graphic representation of the streets in the neighborhood and where characters live.

SUGGESTED SEARCH TERMS

Gloria Naylor

Linden Hills

black feminism

Linden Hills AND novel

Linden Hills AND Gloria Naylor

Linden Hills AND Inferno

Gloria Naylor AND Dante

Kiswana Browne

Luther Nedeed

The Maltese Falcon

1941

The Maltese Falcon is an iconic 1941 movie adapted from a 1929 novel by Dashiell Hammett, who is widely considered one of the greatest mystery writers of all time. The plot involves a detective, Sam Spade, who takes on a seemingly simple case at the request of a beautiful female client. When Spade's partner is murdered on the job, the trail leads to a cabal of exotic characters who have traveled the globe searching for a legendary statue of a falcon, cast from gold and encrusted with precious jewels, that is worth more than the human imagination can conceive. As Spade feels his way through lies and threats he falls in love, leaving audiences waiting to see if he will survive, if he will profit, and if a hard-boiled detective like him can ever know satisfaction.

John Huston, who wrote and directed this film, had been writing screenplays for ten years before he made *The Maltese Falcon*, the first film of his long, celebrated directing career. With his choices of camera angles, lighting, and dark themes, many critics credit Huston with beginning the film noir approach that identifies so many crime stories of the 1940s and 1950s. Humphrey Bogart, who plays Spade, is one of the most recognized, admired, and imitated stars in the history of American cinema. *The Maltese Falcon* was his first starring role as a film hero; up to then he had played gangsters and tormented criminals, giving him a dark aura of potential danger that makes Hammett's detective always interesting to watch.

Director John Huston with his father, actor Walter Huston, who made an uncredited appearance in The Maltese Falcon. *(© Warner Bros / First National / The Kobal Collection / Crail, Schuyler)*

The Maltese Falcon was nominated for an Academy Award for Best Picture of 1941. In addition, John Huston's script was nominated for Best Screenplay, and Sydney Greenstreet, making his film debut at age sixty-one, was nominated for Best Supporting Actor.

PLOT SUMMARY

The Maltese Falcon begins, after the opening credits, with text scrolling across the screen explaining the history of the title statue, going back to 1539. Allegedly, the Knights Templar of Malta paid tribute to Charles V of Spain for protection under his realm. They sent him a golden statue of a falcon, encrusted with jewels, but it was stolen by pirates, and its whereabouts were unknown up to modern times.

A title card establishes the setting of the film as San Francisco and several shots of the city are shown. The camera finally settles on the glass window identifying "Spade and Archer," a detective agency. Inside, Sam Spade, the film's protagonist, sits rolling a cigarette. His receptionist, Effie Perine, comes in to announce the arrival of a new client, Miss Wonderly. As she is explaining that her sister has run away from New York with a man named Floyd Thursby, and that Thursby is supposed to come to Miss Wonderly's hotel that night, Spade's partner, Miles Archer, comes in. Showing sexual interest in Miss Wonderly, Archer says that he will personally handle the job of following Thursby for her. She pays them two hundred dollars and leaves, with Archer still grinning after her.

An establishing shot shows the street sign at the intersection of Bush Street and Stockton. Archer stands looking worried for a moment as a hand from off camera, holding a gun, aims at him and shoots. His body rolls downhill into a construction site.

The phone in Spade's apartment rings at two o'clock in the morning, and he answers it groggily. He talks to Tom Polhaus, a police detective. After hanging up he calls Effie and tells her about Archer's death. He tells her to break the news to Archer's wife, Iva, because he does not want to see Iva himself.

At the crime scene Polhaus explains that Archer was shot from close range with an English pistol. Thursby was an Englishman. Polhaus asks why Archer was tailing Thursby, but Spade refuses to tell him about the job. When Polhaus sympathetically suggests that Archer had his good points, Spade comments, without much enthusiasm, "I guess so."

Spade tries phoning Miss Wonderly from a drug store phone booth but is told she has checked out of her hotel. He goes home and pours himself a drink. Polhaus and his superior, Lieutenant Dundy, ring his doorbell. They point out that Spade left the crime scene in a hurry. They know he is lying about going to Archer's house to break the news of the death to Iva. They reveal that Thursby is dead, having been shot in the back outside his hotel at Geary and Leavenworth. Dundy says that he would sympathize if Spade did kill the man who killed his partner (a sentiment that will be repeated in the film's final scene), but that he will prosecute the crime anyway. Spade laughs at the idea, pours drinks for the two policemen, and sneeringly raises a toast to crime.

FILM TECHNIQUE

- Traditionally, a camera shot was focused on objects in the foreground, with things in the background appearing hazy, or on something in the background, with things in the foreground appearing indistinct. In the late 1930s, though, directors experimented increasingly with deep focus, which keeps all of the objects in the frame equally in focus. This was a way to let viewers make their own decisions about what is important in a scene instead of telling them where to look. In *The Maltese Falcon*, John Huston and Arthur Edeson, the director of photography, use deep focus often. When Spade receives the news of Archer's death, for instance, the camera shows the curtain in the window in the background and his alarm clock in the middle ground, then pulls back to show Spade hanging up the phone, without giving up the focus on any image. Spade's walk up the long hall outside Gutman's hotel room keeps him in focus all the way, so that viewers can see his smile as he approaches.

- The interplay between light and dark in film composition is considered the heart of film noir, and *The Maltese Falcon* is considered to be one of the films that defined this style. In many of the scenes, Huston complicates the images by using a distinct light source, so that the eye is drawn to follow not only the characters' movements but also the shadows that they throw, so that even the brightest scenes, such as when Spade is walking down a sunny sidewalk, are half-darkened. In truly dark night scenes, such as the shooting of Archer or the dock where the La Paloma is burning, the film provides enough light for viewers to follow what is going on, but the entire scene is presented in a range from dark grey to black. Windows in the background keep viewers aware of whether interior scenes take place in the day or the night:

usually at night, in keeping with the air of menace that is associated with film noir. They also add to the texture of the indoor scenes by casting lines across the screen caused by light through venetian blinds, an effect that has come to be associated with film noir.

- Huston makes frequent use of low-angle camera shots, with the camera looking up at characters from below, giving them dominance. One strong example of this is when Wilmer, having been knocked unconscious, awakens in Spade's apartment and looks up from the couch into the faces of Cairo, Spade, Gutman, and O'Shaughnessy; he knows that they have all decided to turn him over to the police, and the camera angle helps viewers feel his helplessness. Frequently, Humphrey Bogart is filmed from a low angle. Bogart was not a tall man (five foot eight, according to the Internet Movie Database), but photographing him with the ceiling beyond him makes Sam Spade seem bigger. It helps make him a domineering presence in the film.

- Frequently, this film uses a dissolve: instead of fading to black and then picking up with a different scene, the new scene fades in at the same time that the current scene is fading away. Overlapping scenes like this, instead of stopping and then starting again, creates a sense of continuity and keeps the viewers engaged, following a story that does not give them time to sit back. One particular type of dissolve used in *The Maltese Falcon* is the vertical wipe: instead of the current scene fading, the scene is chased left to right as the new scene takes over the screen, replacing it. Like the dissolve, this movement keeps viewers involved in the story: by the time the new scene begins they are already drawn into the setting.

A newspaper headline announces the related murders of Archer and Thursby. Spade arrives at his office to find Iva Archer there. As soon as the door to the reception room closes she falls into his arms and kisses him hard, implying a long-standing affair between them. When Iva suggests that Spade might have killed Archer to marry her, Spade laughs at her. After she leaves, Effie asks if he does intend to marry Iva, and Spade bitterly tells her that he wishes he had never laid eyes on her. Effie tells him that there is evidence that Iva had not been home at the time of Archer's murder, but Spade is certain that Iva did not kill her husband.

While Effie and Spade are talking, Miss Wonderly phones with her new address and the new name she is living under, Miss Leblanc. Before leaving the office, Spade instructs Effie to have Archer's desk taken out and have his name taken off the door and window. He burns the sheet of paper that has Miss Wonderly/Leblanc's address on it.

Spade goes to Miss Wonderly/Leblanc's apartment, she answers the door in a robe. She confesses that the story she gave at Spade's office was not true. Spade bemusedly says that he and Archer knew that, but that they did not mind because she was paying so well. Her actual name, she tells him, is Brigid O'Shaughnessy. She asks him to shield her from the police, begging for his help, but Spade dismisses her emotions as an act. Cornered, she explains that she met Floyd Thursby in the Orient and sailed from Hong Kong to America with him. She says she is certain that Thursby, who always carried a few guns with him, must be the one who shot Archer. She says that she does not know who might have killed Thursby. Spade becomes frustrated with her convoluted story and rises to leave. While she is out of the room to get all of the cash she has on hand, five hundred dollars, Spade looks inside of her hat and sees that it is from Hong Kong, confirming the truth of at least part of her story.

Back at his office, Spade phones his lawyer to check whether he can legally refuse to answers questions from the police. Effie brings in a card from Joel Cairo. Cairo enters. He is a small, accented man. He says that he hopes Spade can help him recover a black statue of a bird, for which he will pay five thousand dollars. Effie buzzes the office to say that she is going home for the night; when Spade turns back from the intercom, Cairo is holding a gun on him. He

plans to search the office for the bird statue, but Spade overpowers him and knocks him out with a punch. Searching Cairo's pockets, he finds several passports and a theater ticket for that night. Cairo awakens and says he will pay Spade a hundred dollars as a retainer to find the bird; Spade takes two hundred from his wallet. Before leaving, Cairo asks for his gun back. When Spade hands it over, he turns it on Spade and again announces his intention to search the room. Spade raises his hands and laughs.

Later, as he is walking down a crowded sidewalk, Spade notices a young man in an overcoat and hat following him. He has a cab take him to a random apartment building, where he rings all of the doorbells until somebody buzzes him in. His pursuer is trying to find which apartment he went to, while Spade leaves through the back door. He goes to Brigid O'Shaughnessy's apartment. After getting her to admit that she is not as innocent as she pretends to be, Spade tells her that he talked with Joel Cairo and that Cairo offered him five thousand dollars for the black bird. O'Shaughnessy bitterly says that she could not offer that much if she had to bid for Spade's loyalty, making Spade angry; she has never, he says, offered him anything but money for his loyalty. They kiss. She says that she cannot really confide in him until she talks to Joel Cairo, so he phones Cairo's hotel and arranges a meeting at Spade's apartment.

As they enter Spade's building the camera shows Iva Archer, dressed in mourning clothes, watching them. They go up to the apartment and turn on the lights, and Spade looks out to see the young man who was following him across the street, but he does not mention it. When he enters, Cairo mentions the young man, and O'Shaughnessy is frightened. She and Cairo are terse but polite with each other.

O'Shaughnessy explains that she can sell the falcon statue to Cairo in about a week. She says that she is willing to sell it because she is afraid of someone called "the fat man," with whom Cairo is familiar. A fight breaks out when O'Shaughnessy and Cairo discuss a "boy" they both knew in Istanbul. She slaps Cairo, but before he can pull his pistol Spade grabs him and slaps him a few times.

The policemen, Polhaus and Dundy, arrive. Spade refuses to let them in without a warrant, but while they are questioning him about his relationship with Iva Archer they hear Cairo and O'Shaughnessy fighting inside. Cairo screams for help, so they push past Spade. Spade says that they were only pretending to fight, to play a trick on the police, and that O'Shaughnessy works for him while Cairo was an acquaintance of the murdered Thursby. Spade angers Dundy, who punches him, and Spade insists that they leave. Alone in the apartment, O'Shaughnessy describes the falcon but says she does not know why people are willing to pay so much for it. They begin to kiss, and as they do Spade looks out the window and sees the young man standing in a doorway across the street. The camera fades away, implying that they spend the night together, which the novel plainly states.

At Cairo's hotel the next morning, Spade sees the young man sitting in the lobby and confronts him. He calls over the hotel's house detective, Luke, and points out that the young man is a gangster carrying a pistol. He blows smoke in the young man's face as he leaves. Spade sees Cairo entering and talks to him. Cairo says he has been questioned at the police station all night.

At his office, Space receives a message that a man named Mr. Gutman called and said he had gotten Spade's message from the young man in the lobby, leading Spade to conclude that Gutman is the fat man people have been talking about. O'Shaughnessy is at the office; when she went home that morning she found out that her apartment had been searched, which is something that Spade does himself in Hammett's novel. He convinces Effie to let O'Shaughnessy stay at her home. After they leave he phones the district attorney to arrange a meeting. Iva comes in and says she was the one who told the police go to his apartment the night before. He tells her she might be in trouble with the police, and she leaves. Gutman phones and invites Spade to his hotel.

Gutman greets him cordially and gives him a drink and a cigar, as the young man, named Wilmer, lingers in the background. Gutman wants to know who Spade is working for; Spade tells him that he is looking out for his own interests. He asks why the black bird is so important to everybody but Gutman refuses to tell him. Spade stands up shouting and smashes his glass against the table, insisting that he will not do business without being told what all of this is about. When he walks off down the hall,

though, he is smiling, revealing that his anger was just an act. As he gets onto one elevator, Joel Cairo is exiting from the one next to it, unnoticed.

Spade meets with District Attorney Bryan. Spade accuses the police and the district attorney of trying to implicate him in the murders of both Archer and Thursby, and that the only way he can clear his name is by catching the real criminals himself. He says that he will not cooperate without being arrested or subpoenaed.

On his way back to his office Spade is stopped by Wilmer, who takes him to see Gutman. Before entering the hotel room, though, Spade jumps Wilmer and takes away his guns. Gutman gives Spade a drink and tells him a long history of the falcon statue, similar to the one that appeared in print at the start of the film. He describes various sightings of it over the centuries and notes that jewel-rich gold statue acquired its coat of black enamel to hide its value. Most recently, he says, it was found in 1923 by a Greek dealer who was killed and robbed; since that time, seventeen years earlier, Gutman has been following it around the globe.

As they talk, Gutman keeps refilling Spade's drink. Spade agrees to get the falcon for a hundred thousand dollars or more, but when he rises to leave he falls down, drugged. Wilmer kicks him in the head. Gutman, Wilmer, and Joel Cairo, who has been hiding in the next room, leave.

Spade awakens in the darkened hotel room and phones Effie, only to find out that O'Shaughnessy is missing. He searches Gutman's room and finds a newspaper that has a circle drawn around the announcement of a ship, the *La Paloma*, arriving that day from Hong Kong. When he reaches the dock, the *La Paloma* is in flames.

Spade is at his office with Effie when a man stumbles in, carrying a package, and drops dead on the floor. A search of his pockets reveals that he is Captain Jacoby, the master of the *La Paloma*. The package contains the falcon statue.

The phone rings: it is Brigid O'Shaughnessy, frantic, saying that she is in great danger and needs Spade to come help her. The call ends with her scream. Spade stops at the bus terminal and leaves the package containing the falcon at the baggage counter. He receives a claim check, which he mails to himself. When he arrives at the address he was given by O'Shaughnessy, in the far-off suburb of Burlingame, Spade finds an empty lot. This is one of the most significant changes from the novel, though a minor alteration that does not affect the plot. In the book, Spade is sent to Burlingame by Rhea Gutman, the fat man's daughter, whom he finds drugged at Gutman's hotel room after dropping the package at the bus station.

O'Shaughnessy is waiting outside of his apartment building when Spade goes home. She is weak and stumbling. Inside the apartment are Gutman, Cairo, and Wilmer. Gutman gives Spade an envelope with ten thousand dollars in it, much less than expected, but Spade is more interested in satisfying the curiosity of the police. He says that they need a fall guy. He recommends Wilmer. When Gutman objects, Spade says that Cairo could be made to fit the part. Cairo suggests that they can just force Spade to tell them where to find the falcon, but he explains that he cannot talk if he is dead, and that any attempt to torture the information out of him will end in death. Spade taunts Wilmer until the young man draws his gun, then Spade knocks him out. This settles the issue of who will be the fall guy.

While waiting until he can get the falcon, Spade has Gutman fill in the story. Wilmer shot Thursby because he would not give up the falcon, being loyal to O'Shaughnessy, and he shot Captain Jacoby because Cairo had seen Jacoby and O'Shaughnessy together in Hong Kong and reasoned that the falcon must be with him. When they met with Jacoby at the boat, O'Shaughnessy was with him. The boat started on fire by mistake, and Jacoby and O'Shaughnessy escaped with the bird.

Spade calls Effie, tells her to pick up the claim check at the firm's post office box, pick up the package at the bus station, and bring it to his apartment. She arrives with it in a short while. Gutman, perspiring, rips the package open and scratches at the falcon's enamel coating, only to find lead, not gold, underneath. He and Cairo recall a man in Hong Kong they refer to as "the Russian," not previously mentioned in the film. They are certain that he must be the one who made this copy. Gutman determines to carry on with his pursuit of the falcon. He invites Cairo to join him on an expedition to Istanbul in pursuit of the Russian general, and Cairo accepts. He cannot find Wilmer, who has

escaped through the apartment's back door. He pulls a gun on Spade and demands the return of his ten-thousand-dollar down payment, leaving Spade with a one-thousand-dollar bill. He invites Spade to join the expedition to Istanbul, but Spade declines.

As soon as they are gone, Spade calls Sergeant Polhaus and tells him the entire story about Wilmer, Cairo, and Gutman. Before the police can come to his apartment he pressures O'Shaughnessy to confess that she killed Archer. Crying, she throws herself against him, but Spade has no sympathy. He may be in love with her, he says, but a man has to do something when his partner has been killed, regardless of what he thought of the partner.

Polhaus and Dundy arrive, saying that they have arrested the others. Spade turns O'Shaughnessy over to them as Archer's killer. Polhaus asks what the bird statue is, and Spade responds that it is "the stuff dreams are made of." He watches the elevator gate close like a jail cell on O'Shaughnessy, and the elevator takes her away. Hammett's novel includes a brief descrption of Effie Perine showing disgust at Spade for having turned O'Shaughnessy over to the police; in the last line of the book, Iva Archer comes to Spade again.

CHARACTERS

Iva Archer

Iva (Gladys George) is the wife of Miles Archer. She is also the lover of Sam Spade, Archer's business partner. When Archer dies, she puts on a display of proper grief, wearing black mourning clothes and a dark veil, but she comes to Spade's office the morning after her husband's death and kisses him. She believes that Spade might have murdered his partner, her husband, so that he could marry her. Spade treats her with disgust, assigning his secretary, Effie, the task of keeping Iva away from him.

The film does not offer any solution to the question of where Iva was the night Archer was shot, though it does establish that she did not kill him. She was out somewhere and is unwilling to tell Spade where, indicating that she might have had another lover beside him.

Miles Archer

Spade's partner, Miles Archer (Jerome Cowan), only appears in two scenes in this film. In his first scene he walks in as Brigid O'Shaughnessy, then known as "Miss Wonderly," is explaining why she is hiring the Spade and Archer agency, giving Spade an opportunity to summarize what she has been saying to Archer in the direct, no-nonsense way that detectives see their cases. His second scene is even shorter: he is seen from the perspective of his killer as he looks surprised, is shot, and falls backward through a railing.

Archer could be a tragic figure in this story; he is murdered early on, and audiences soon find out that his business partner has been having an affair with his wife, who may be having affairs with other men as well (since her whereabouts on the night Miles is killed by O'Shaughnessy are never established). He is not presented as an innocent victim, however. He leers at O'Shaughnessy when she is in his office, eager to take advantage of her. He offers to handle her case himself, to get closer to her. In the end, Spade deduces that Archer left himself open to being shot because he was sexually interested in O'Shaughnessy and let his guard down.

District Attorney Bryan

At one point, Spade is summoned to the office of District Attorney Bryan (John Hamilton) to give a formal statement about what he knows about the deaths of Miles Archer and Floyd Thursby. He refuses to tell everything that he knows about the case, explaining that he does not trust the police or the district attorney to clear his name, so he is willing to clear it alone. District Attorney Bryan is helpless to force Spade to cooperate.

Joel Cairo

Film great Peter Lorre turns in one of the best performances of his long career as Cairo, a relatively minor role in the film. He is portrayed as a dandy; he is a meticulous dresser, and he almost immediately obtains theater tickets. He has a temper tantrum when he finds out that the falcon statue he and his partners have been chasing is a fake, screaming at Gutman in a rage.

The film uses subtle touches to imply that Cairo is a homosexual. His business card is scented with a floral scent. His handkerchief is scented, too, with something that Spade seems to find amusing when he holds it up to his nose. Although nothing in particular is said of his personal life, much is implied in the way O'Shaughnessy is able to bait him into anger by mentioning the way he "handled" the "boy" who was involved in their last escapade.

Wilmer Cook

Wilmer Cook is a tough hood employed by Kasper Gutman. He is referred to as a young man throughout the film, although Elisha Cook Jr., the actor who plays him, was nearly forty when the film was made. It is clear that Wilmer is trying hard to behave like the image of a movie gangster; he walks with his shoulders hunched and his hands deep in his overcoat pockets where he keeps two pistols, and mumbles insults (identified in Hammett's novel as obscenities).

Spade takes delight in goading Wilmer, first by taking his guns from him and later by casually telling Gutman that a crippled newsboy could take Wilmer's guns from him again without much effort. In the novel, Spade famously calls Wilmer a "gunsel," which was slang for a gunman but also for a homosexual, when he points him out to the house detective at the Hotel Belvedere; in that scene, Wilmer threatens Spade, and the detective blows cigarette smoke in his face.

Although Wilmer is not strong enough to outfight Spade, he actually is a dangerous person. He is the man who shot Floyd Thursby and Captain Jacoby to death.

Lt. of Detectives Dundy

Dundy, played by Barton MacLane, is the detective who is suspicious of Spade throughout the story. Unlike Polhaus, who is Spade's friend, Dundy sees the holes in the logic of the way Spade strings the events together. In one scene, Spade goads Dundy into punching him in the jaw, giving him an excuse to insist that the police leave his apartment. At the end of the story, Spade gloats knowingly that Dundy must be disappointed to find out that he has actually been honest all along.

The Fat Man

See Kasper Gutman

Kasper Gutman

Gutman is played by Sydney Greenstreet in his first movie role, though he had already been a stage actor for almost forty years. Gutman is a major character in the story, but he does not show up until the film is half over. Earlier,

Spade picks up indications of his existence when he hears Brigid O'Shaughnessy and Joel Cairo refer to a "fat man" whom they both encountered in Hong Kong looking for the falcon statue. On a hunch, Spade mentions the fat man to Wilmer Cook, assuming that Wilmer is working for him. Later, when he receives a message that a Mr. Gutman called and left a message, Spade deduces that this is the fat man he has been hearing about.

Gutman is an adventurer who has been seeking the Maltese falcon ever since learning about it seventeen years earlier. He is ruthless in his pursuit of it. There are clear indications that he has killed men or ordered men killed in his quest. He offers to work with Spade to get it, then drugs Spade when he thinks that he can get it without him. He claims to think of Wilmer as his own son, but agrees to turn Wilmer over to the police if that is what is necessary to get the falcon from Spade.

When he talks, Gutman exudes an air of detached bemusement; his desire for the falcon seems to be a sporting person's interest, as if he has to pursue an exotic, expensive item to keep himself amused. In his final scene, that mask drops a little. He thinks he has finally attained the falcon, and when he finds out that he only has a lead imitation he is driven almost to tears with frustration. He quickly recovers his composure, however, and within minutes is ready to begin his pursuit all over again.

In Hammett's novel, this character's first name is spelled Casper, but the film script spells it Kasper.

Captain Jacoby

Captain Jacoby is the master of the *La Paloma*. He does not speak in the film but stumbles into Spade's office bearing the Maltese falcon moments before he dies. He is played by Walter Huston, the director's father (and later Bogart's costar in *The Treasure of the Sierra Madre*) in an uncredited role.

Miss Leblanc

See Brigid O'Shaughnessy

Luke

Luke (James Burke) is the Hotel Belvedere's house detective. In the lobby of the Hotel Belvedere, where Joel Cairo is staying, Spade has a brief conversation with Wilmer Cook. The young man acts tough, so Spade goes to get Luke. They address each other by first name. Spade points out that there is a gangster sitting around the hotel lobby, and Luke makes Wilmer leave.

Brigid O'Shaughnessy

Of all of the characters in this film, Mary Astor's Brigid O'Shaughnessy is the most difficult for audiences to clearly comprehend. She lies to Sam Spade throughout the film, from the false names she goes under (first Miss Wonderly then Miss Leblanc, before she finally tells him her real name) to the nature of her relationship with Floyd Thursby, to her alliance with Gutman and Cairo, to the moment at the end of the film when she admits to Spade that she was the one who killed Miles Archer. From the start, Spade does not believe what she tells him. When Gutman tries to drive a wedge between them by hiding a thousand dollars and making it look like she stole it, however, Spade accepts O'Shaughnessy's word that she did not take it. He does not trust her completely, though, later pressuring her to confess her crimes.

The true mystery at the heart of the story is whether O'Shaughnessy is using Spade out of fear or greed. She says that she felt the need for his protection because the people she had become associated with are such vicious killers, but there is ample evidence to suggest that she is the most dangerous character of them all. The men who do choose to protect her, as she would like Spade to do, all end up dead, including Thursby, Archer, and Captain Jacoby. Spade realizes this, and he balances all of the evidence of her lethal dishonesty against the fact that he might love her, knowing full well that the love he thinks he feels might be something that she has tricked him into feeling. He ends up having her sent to prison for murder without even settling the question of love, simply because making her pay for her crimes is more important than love. To the very end, she acts horrified that he would turn against her like this, as if she cannot believe that such a thing as justice can come between two people who love each other the way she loves him and the way she tells him he loves her.

Effie Perine

Effie (Lee Patrick) is the secretary at Spade and Archer detective agency at the beginning of the film and the Samuel Spade Agency after Miles Archer is killed. She is an idealization of the sort of assistant a detective like Sam Spade should have: part office worker, part girlfriend, part pal. While Spade is out following leads, she watches the office and takes his calls. When he is mulling over the facts of the case she is there, sitting on the corner of his desk, rolling his cigarettes and holding them out for him to lick sealed. He has her hide his witness for him at the house where she lives with her mother after assuring her (wrongly, it turns out) that O'Shaughnessy is a good person. He calls her by affectionate names as if she were his lover, but also tells her "you're a good man" when she contributes a helpful idea.

Detective Sergeant Tom Polhaus
Played by veteran character actor Ward Bond, Polhaus has a relationship with Spade before the film begins. In the middle of the night, when Miles Archer's dead body is found, Polhaus phones Spade at his home to tell him about it. The two discuss the crime scene and the murder weapon as professionals in police work. In his later scenes in the film, Polhaus has to intercede between Spade and his superior, Lt. of Detectives Dundy. Spade and Dundy clearly hate each other, and Polhaus frequently has to ask them each to calm down and be reasonable when they insult one another.

Samuel Spade
The protagonist of this film, Sam Spade, is a private detective in San Francisco. At the beginning of the film he and his partner, Miles Archer, are hired to follow a man. Archer is murdered, and the woman who hired them, Brigid O'Shaughnessy, admits that she lied to Spade about the case, but that she still needs his help against some former murderous associates who are in San Francisco searching for an object of incredible value—the Maltese falcon.

Another man may have turned this whole situation over to the police, but Spade is not that man. The film establishes early on that he is a ladies' man, when his secretary tells Spade that he will want to see this new client because she is beautiful. Soon after that, viewers see that Spade has been conducting an affair with his partner's wife, even though he does not like her very much. While Spade's womanizing makes him a dashing, romantic character to the audience, it also makes him vulnerable to a cunning, beautiful, manipulative woman like O'Shaughnessy.

Spade is also not afraid to go outside of the law for his clients' interest. In his initial interview with O'Shaughnessy, when she warns the detectives that Thursby is dangerous, he smiles and breezily dismisses her fear, telling her that they will know "how to handle him." Later, when the police want to know about his client, Spade calls his lawyer to find out how much legal trouble he might be in if he refuses to cooperate with them. His willingness to skirt the law is an asset to Spade as a private investigator, allowing him to get more involved with the criminals he is investigating than a law-abiding detective might be able to get.

In the end, though, Spade turns out to have a strong moral sense. He pretends that Kasper Gutman, the leader of the group looking for the falcon, can buy him off with a thousand dollars, and that O'Shaughnessy can keep him from telling the police what he knows by making him fall in love with her, but when he knows everything that happened in the few days since she first walked into his office he calls the police and explains it all to them. He gives them the thousand-dollar bribe, since it is evidence in a criminal case, and he turns O'Shaughnessy over to them as a murderer, even though he admits that he might love her.

Before playing Spade, Humphrey Bogart had a career playing criminals. After this film, he was a leading man and a romantic lead, eventually becoming one of the greatest stars in the history of American film.

Floyd Thursby
Thursby is the man that Brigid O'Shaughnessy, going under the name of Miss Wonderly, hires the Spade and Archer detective firm to follow. She tells them that Thursby has come to San Francisco with her underage sister. Actually, she and Thursby were partners. They came together, having made arrangements for the falcon statue to be delivered to them, but O'Shaughnessy suspected that Thursby was planning to double-cross her. She admits to killing Archer so that Spade and the police will suspect Thursby. Later, when talking with Spade, Gutman admits that his hired gun Wilmer Cook killed Thursby.

Miss Wonderly
See Brigid O'Shaughnessy

THEMES

Truth

Sam Spade sets the film's standard for honesty early on, after Miles Archer has been killed and Brigid O'Shaughnessy says that she feels guilty about it. He tells her that neither he nor Archer believed her story, but that the money she paid was enough for them to take the job anyway. After that, viewers can never be sure of the film's stance toward the truth. Audiences are forced to figure out which lies are considered acceptable in the film's moral world and which are considered to be unacceptable. When, for instance, Spade lies to the police and tells them that O'Shaughnessy is his employee, he is valuing his client's freedom over the law. He also plays within the law by telling the truth when he gets Cairo in trouble by telling the police of Cairo's visit to his office.

Of the film's main characters, the one who ends up being most honest is Kasper Gutman. He is assumed to be ruthless beneath his jovial exterior, as implied by the way O'Shaughnessy cringes when she hears that he might be in town. And he is not above drugging Spade if he thinks it will clear his path to the object he is seeking. But in spite of his ruthlessness, he generally adheres to the principles that he states clearly when he first meets Spade and toasts "plain speaking." The one time he does lie, pretending that O'Shaughnessy has stolen one of the thousand-dollar bills he paid Spade, he is caught immediately, indicating that he is more comfortable telling the truth. O'Shaughnessy, on the other hand, seems incapable of telling the truth; every time she expresses her regret at not being more honest with Spade he laughs at her and accuses her of false regret, of just starting one more ruse.

Love

At the end of *The Maltese Falcon*, Brigid O'Shaughnessy tells Spade that he would help her go free if he really loved her. In response, he admits that he might actually love her. This point has not been clearly made in the film up to this point. At first, Spade's interest in O'Shaughnessy was attributed to his interest in a wealthy client who was willing to pay well. As his involvement with her grew throughout the story, so did his understanding of the falcon's presumed value, to such a point that it became impossible for viewers (or readers of Hammett's

novel, for that matter) to tell whether he was developing true feelings for her, using her sexually in the same way that he used Iva Archer sexually before the story began, or just playing along with O'Shaughnessy to get his hands on the falcon. His admission of possibly loving her seems to clarify his motivation throughout the story.

Unlike many stories, however, love does not conquer all here. Spade does not take the time to determine whether he really loves her or not because, as he explains to her, love does not matter; whether what he feels is true love or not, he is still obligated to turn her over to the police.

Antiheroes

Traditional movie heroes are admired by audiences because they show the self-control necessary to act against their own self interests, doing what is necessary for the common good. In *The Maltese Falcon*, though, the main character earns the respect of the audience by ignoring conventional views of morality and acting out of his own self-interest. A character that audiences treat as a hero, even when he or she indulges in unheroic behavior, is identified by literary critics as an antihero.

At the end of the story, there appears to be some possibility that Sam Spade is an actual hero. He turns the bribe that Gutman gave him over to the police, and he gives Brigid O'Shaughnessy over to the authorities to be punished for the murder of Archer, his partner. Both of these actions suggest that Spade might hold an idealist's view of the social order, that he might place the rule of law above his finances or even his own emotions. But if viewers are to believe him, the things he does are not done with anyone but himself in mind. He knows that the police will connect him to Cairo and Gutman and their crimes if he is not completely honest with them. He also knows that his private detective business will suffer if he does not bring O'Shaughnessy, his partner's killer, to justice. He is not upholding the law because he wants to do the right thing; he is doing it only because it serves his purposes.

Legends

Much of the story that Gutman tells Spade about the origin of the falcon statue is true. Emperor Charles V of Spain did in fact grant

READ.
WATCH.
WRITE.

- Writer Megan Abbott is considered one of the best contemporary writers carrying on the film noir tradition in her fiction for teens. Read Abbott's book *Dare Me*, published by Reagan Arthur Books in 2012, about a high-school cheerleading squad. Although the subject matter is completely different, the mood and techniques are similar to ones Hammett used to develop his characters in *The Maltese Falcon* and John Huston carried into the film. Identify which character from *Dare Me* you think would fit into Sam Spade's San Francisco, and explain why before writing a scene with that character interacting with one or more of Hammett's characters.

- Possibly the only film Humphrey Bogart is more widely known for than *The Maltese Falcon* is *Casablanca*, a 1942 film in which he plays a man reunited with his one true love, only to find out that her husband is one of the most important people in the fight against Hitler in World War II. The film also stars Peter Lorre and Sydney Greenstreet. Watch *Casablanca* and use your observations as the basis of an essay about the actor's craft. Compare Bogart's performances in each film. What do you think are the differences between Sam Spade and *Casablanca*'s Rick Blaine? How does Bogart convey those differences?

- In 2010, Joe Gores, with the permission of Dashiell Hammett's estate, published *Spade & Archer*, a prequel to Hammett's novel that takes place seven years before this story. Gores gives background information about characters here, such as Miles Archer, Effie Perine, police lieutenant Dundy, lawyer Sid

Wise, and more. Read Gores's novel and then write a short story for some character, such as Joel Cairo or Kasper Gutman, showing what they were up to seven years before *The Maltese Falcon*. Add to your story an explanation about why you think the person you presented would eventually turn into the person from the film.

- Hammett's style of detective writing has translated to other countries. One prime example is the work of Lisa See, a Chinese writer of young-adult fiction who tells mystery stories as thick with the atmosphere of Beijing as Hammett's was of San Francisco. Read one of See's novels, such as *Flower Net* (2007), about the murder of an American ambassador (among other things) and list the elements of her writing that you find different from Hammett's. In a blog post, explain why each item on your list is different because of the passage of time, the different culture, or both. Allow your classmates to comment.

- *The Maltese Falcon* is often called the first American film noir. Similarly, Orson Welles's *Touch of Evil* (1958), is often identified as the last of the classic film noir cycle. Watch Welles's film and take notes about the characters. Which character would you say is most like Sam Spade? Brigid O'Shanghnessy? Kasper Gutman? Joel Cairo? Make a chart that shows why you think these characters are similar and explains their apparent dissimilarities. At the end, prepare an explanation to your class about how the personality of film noir changed over the course of those seventeen years.

the islands of Malta, Gozo, and Tripoli to the Knights Templar of the Order of the Hospital of St. John of Jerusalem (though in 1530, not in 1539 as stated in the film). The payment he asked

from them actually was a single falcon, to be paid to him each year on All Saints Day. There is, however, no historical record of any golden statue of a falcon encrusted with jewels. Hammett added that part of the story himself while writing the novel, covering the inaccuracy by having Gutman state, as he does in the film, "These are facts—not schoolbook history, not Mr. Wells's history [a reference to the multivolume book *An Outline of History* by popular novelist H. G. Wells] but history nevertheless."

The movie thrives on the fact that the object being sought is not historically a real thing. As the film progresses, the stakes grow higher and higher as the value of the object increases. When Spade knows nothing of it, two hundred dollars seems like a lot of money; Cairo offers to hire him for five thousand dollars to find it; Gutman offers him first fifty thousand dollars, and then a share of its value that could expand Spade's share as high as a quarter of a million dollars. Since the object is not real, audiences cannot put any real value on it, and are free to imagine. It takes on properties that are beyond what a real-world object could have, making it, for audiences as well as for characters in the film, "the stuff dreams are made of."

Underworld

One of the reasons *The Maltese Falcon* has been such a favorite of movie audiences across generations is the amusing but improbable image it presents of the criminal underworld. The criminals in this film are greedy, duplicitous, and ruthless, but they are contained within a small world in which each keeps the company of the others, along with a few, like Spade and Captain Jacoby, who choose to associate with them. They pose no threat to the general public.

The four criminals presented here—Kasper Gutman, Wilmer Cook, Joel Cairo, and Brigid O'Shaughnessy—each represent some exaggerated aspect of criminal thought. Gutman is literally the big boss, the one with the intelligence and financial backing to control a criminal organization. Wilmer is a killer, but only because he wants so badly to be viewed as a dangerous man; he is not competent enough to follow people without being spotted or to keep his hands out of his pockets while walking down a hall with an enemy. Cairo is intelligent and dangerous but also effeminate and vain. O'Shaughnessy uses her charm to make men risk their lives for her, but men who can resist her charms, as Spade can, are not in danger. Each of these members of the film's underworld has character flaws that make them exotic and unique. In making them well-rounded characters for his detective film, Huston, as screenwriter, diverted from reality.

STYLE

Third-Person Limited

Dashiell Hammett wrote his first two novels in the first-person narrative voice, with the main character talking to readers using "I" or "me." To expand the range of the narrative for *The Maltese Falcon*, he used the third-person perspective. Readers can observe Sam Spade's actions and hear what he says, but they do not have access to his thoughts. By doing this, Hammett invited his readers to solve the story's mystery along with his detective, experiencing what Spade experienced. Readers are, in a sense, competing with Spade to find out what the falcon is, where it is, and who is responsible for what actions, using the same evidence he had available.

John Huston retained this style in adapting *The Maltese Falcon* to the screen. Audiences are introduced to Spade when the camera creeps up behind him and looks over his shoulder, and for the rest of the film, no matter where the camera is placed, audiences receive information as he receives it. They learn the legend of the falcon when Spade learns it; they first see the bird when it is brought to his office; they do not know that Wilmer has escaped until Spade sees the couch empty. The one glaring exception to this is when Spade walks onto the elevator at Gutman's hotel without noticing that Cairo is coming off a different elevator. Audiences know then that Cairo is working with Gutman, but Spade does not know it until later. This is a minor change of style, however, because the change in Cairo's status, shifting to Gutman's side, makes no appreciable difference to Spade.

Audiences do not know what is going on in Spade's mind throughout the film, only what he says and does. This makes his refusal to help O'Shaughnessy at the end a surprise ending.

Hard-Boiled Detective

The Maltese Falcon is credited with establishing one of the most uniquely American archetypes in film history, that of the hard-boiled detective. This persona is familiar around the world, with his trench coat, cigarette, and bottle of whiskey in his desk drawer; his attraction to a dangerous woman who can use him to his own detriment if he permits himself any affection; and his skirmishes with the legal establishment. Unlike his predecessors, the hard-boiled detective works outside of the law, guided by his own moral sense.

Raymond Chandler's character Philip Marlowe followed closely after Spade, and he was followed by Mickey Spillane's Mike Hammer; Ross MacDonald's Lew Archer; John P. MacDonald's Travis McGee; and Walter Mosley's Easy Rawlins. The type is often parodied in films and cartoons. Although the image of the hardboiled detective has changed over the course of decades, most of the personal attributes and situations associated with it can be traced back to the mixture of bitterness and bemusement that Humphrey Bogart brought to his interpretation of Sam Spade.

CULTURAL CONTEXT

Darkening the Detective Film
There have been detective films for as long as there has been an American film industry, as seen from such early silent entries as the 1900 short film *Sherlock Holmes Baffled* or vaudeville escape artist Harry Houdini's rare movie appearance in the title role of *Haldane of the Secret Service* in 1923. Soon after the technology for talking movies became widespread in 1927, Warner Bros., the studio that would later produce *The Maltese Falcon*, became known for specializing in gangster movies. These movies, capitalizing on the public's fascination with celebrity criminals such as Al Capone and John Dillinger during the Depression years of the early 1930s, included *Little Caesar* (1931), *Public Enemy* (1931), and *Scarface* (1932). As the decade wore on, though, the public became increasingly tired of glorifying criminals. In 1934, the Motion Picture Producers and Distributors of America adopted strict rules about the sexual and violent content of their films, in order to avoid mandatory censorship from the government. Gangster films fell out of favor, and detective films were on the rise.

The 1930s detective films tended toward light entertainment, emphasizing humor and veiled sexual innuendo. One of the clearest examples of this is Warners Bros.' first version of *The Maltese Falcon*, released in 1931. In it, handsome leading man Ricardo Cortez plays Sam Spade as a grinning, flirting, joking ladies' man. One of the most successful movie franchises of the 1930s, also based on a Dashiell Hammett novel, is the Thin Man series, featuring William Powell and Myrna Loy as a beautiful,

wealthy couple that exchanged witty banter with each other while sipping martinis and solving murder cases. In these films, the mystery was often treated as an afterthought, as an excuse to watch drinking, sexual innuendo, and comedy. In other popular detective series of the 1930s, including those featuring Charlie Chan, the Saint, and Bulldog Drummond, the filmmakers made no effort toward pretending that they were dealing with serious subjects. They focused on giving their audiences a good time, either presenting viewers with a mystery that anybody could follow and solve or presenting a convoluted, improbable tale in which the true culprit was as likely as not decided by the writers after filming had already begun.

The Maltese Falcon of 1941 is notable for its hard edge. Instead of flirtation, Sam Spade is caught between one woman he detests, the married Iva Archer, and one whom he knows is probably setting him up for jail or death, Brigid O'Shaughnessy. Instead of light humor, there is Spade's masochistic grin as he slaps the much weaker Joel Cairo or feigns a violent fit of rage. Instead of being called in to solve the murder of some abstract nonentity, Spade has to solve the killing of his partner.

The Maltese Falcon is sometimes called the first Hollywood film noir, and sometimes it is referred to as the precursor that opened the door for later detective films that featured detectives who were either surrounded by corruption or were trying to save themselves from the corruption they wallowed in. Sam Spade established a new standard for the film detective: instead of trying to show how calm and witty they could be while solving a case, the post-*Falcon* detectives struggled with their own souls. In a few years, Hollywood was putting out such dark fare as *Murder, My Sweet* (1944), *Out of the Past* (1947), *The Big Heat* (1953), and the ruthlessly amoral Micky Spillane film *Kiss Me Deadly*, in 1955.

World War II and Film
The Maltese Falcon was released into theaters in October 1941. The United States entered World War II almost immediately after the bombing of Pearl Harbor on December 7, 1941. As could be expected, being at war changed the practices of film studios as much as it changed audience expectations.

The immediate effect that being at war had on American movies was a notable shift from

© *Warner Bros / First National / The Kobal Collection*

cynicism to optimism. This mood can be seen by contrasting Humphrey Bogart's two best-known films. In *The Maltese Falcon*, released before the war, the Bogart character is cynical and jaded, and in the end he shocks audiences by being even more cynical than expected, turning his back on the woman he loves to follow his own personal code of ethics. In *Casablanca*, released in 1942, the Bogart character is again cynical, having been thrown over by his one true love, but in the end he makes the heartrending decision to forgo his chance to win her back, choosing instead to help the war effort. Throughout the rest of the war and after, Bogart, considered an action star, appeared in numerous movies with military themes.

During the war, Hollywood put out hundreds of films aimed at promoting the war effort. These films varied from ones that were about the war, such as *Sabotage at Sea* and *Thirty Seconds Over Tokyo*, to those with the war in the background of action that could have happened at any time, such as *Mr. Lucky* or *Lady on a Train*.

It is possible to see the film industry's enthusiasm for the war as being a function of government propaganda. The US government did have more powerful control over the content of commercial films then, through the Hayes Office, which had been established to enforce the Motion Pictures Production Code in the 1930s and had the power to hold a film back from release if it were deemed unacceptable. During the war, there was a government film agency, the Office of War Information, working with the studios, encouraging them toward a pro-war stance. Furthermore, the studios that wanted access to the bombers, warships, military equipment, and stock battle footage that the government held would naturally be open to showing a pro-government perspective.

But the studios wanted access to such equipment and material because the public had an interest in seeing portrayals of the war. Support for the war was high, and there was money to be made in films about it, especially in films that presented a positive view of the war in which so many millions of Americans were fighting. Studios cannily shifted their focus during the war years toward bringing Americans a version of the war effort that they knew from their daily lives and showing it to them in a flattering light. There were many films that were not about the war, but all the major studios managed to make the war a part of the product they were putting out, not only to placate the government but also to present the subject that was most interesting to their audiences.

CRITICAL OVERVIEW

Not much was expected of *The Maltese Falcon* when it was released in 1941. It was a film made on a small budget, shot in six weeks, with a lead actor, Humphrey Bogart, who was not an established star, and a director, John Huston, who had never directed a film before. Film critics still remembered the bland adaptation of the novel made ten years earlier. As soon as Huston's version came out, though, critics praised it, and it has been recognized as an important American film since then.

The low expectations helped critics find delight with what they saw. As Bosley Crowther noted in his review for the *New York Times* in 1941, the film "turns out to be the best mystery thriller of the year, and young Mr. Huston gives promise of becoming one of the smartest directors in the field." Huston went on to fulfill that promise in a long, illustrious career that included such classics as *The Treasure of the Sierra Madre*, *Key Largo*, and *The African Queen* (all with *Falcon* star Humphrey Bogart); *The Misfits* (with Clark Gable and Marilyn Monroe); *Reflections in a Golden Eye* (with Elizabeth Taylor and Marlon Brando); and *Prizzi's Honor* (with Jack Nicholson), as well as numerous others.

While Crowther focused on the artistic promise of the director, other reviewers of the time looked at it as entertainment, finding it superb for movie audiences. "This is one of the best examples of actionful and suspenseful melodramatic story telling in cinematic form," began

an unsigned review in *Variety*, a newspaper for show business insiders and theatrical booking agents. That review went on to emphasize

> the standout performance of Humphrey Bogart, an attention-arresting portrayal that will add immeasurable voltage to his marquee values. Bogart not only dominates the proceedings throughout, but is the major motivation in all but a few minor scenes.

Otis Ferguson, writing in *New Republic*, also lauded Bogart:

> He is not a villain here [as he had been in his earlier films], though a pretty hard type; but it doesn't make any difference: he has some of that magnetism you can feel through the screen; he is a villain with appeal.

Decades later, the film still has impact. It is number six in the American Film Institute's list of top ten mystery films of all time, and twenty-third on its list of best American movies ever. In a 2006 review in *Entertainment Weekly*, Jeff Labrecque began by comparing it favorably with *Citizen Kane*, also released in 1941 and frequently cited by critics across the world as the best film ever made:

> While Orson Welles receives credit for redefining visual storytelling in *Citizen Kane*, John Huston's *Maltese Falcon* was equally monumental. Boldly manipulating light and shadow, utilizing drastic camera angles, and introducing Bogart's Sam Spade, the first-time director's detective classic defines *film noir*.

The film was a success upon its release, but it is clear to see that, if possible, critical esteem has grown with time.

CRITICISM

David Kelly

Kelly is an instructor of creative writing and literature. In the following essay, he examines the clues of Sam Spade's life before the story of The Maltese Falcon *begins and finds the film to be one of moral redemption.*

Starting with the portrayal of him that John Huston elicited from Humphrey Bogart in 1941's *The Maltese Falcon*, private detective Sam Spade has given generations of viewers a definitive example of the consummate professional who chooses to work in a dirty business. It was a career-making role for Bogart, a chance to show off the cool intelligence that had always been present under the surface of character after

WHAT DO I SEE NEXT?

- The first film version of *The Maltese Falcon* was released in 1931 by Warner Bros. Ricardo Cortez's Sam Spade portrayed the detective as a flirtatious ladies' man; Bebe Daniels played "Ruth Wonderly" and Dudley Diggs played Gutman. The 1936 adaptation of the book was released under the title *Satan Met a Lady*: liberties were taken with Hammett's plot to make the story into a romantic comedy, with Bette Davis playing "Valerie Purvis," the duplicitous female lead, and Warren William playing detective "Ted Shayne." The Kasper Gutman equivalent in this version is "Madame Barabbas," played by Alison Skipworth. Both are available with the 1941 *Maltese Falcon* in *Humphrey Bogart: the Signature Collection, Volume 2*, from Warner Bros. Neither film is rated.

- Humphrey Bogart also played Philip Marlowe, the one fictional detective that critics generally feel rivals Sam Spade's stature, in *The Big Sleep*, released in 1946. The unrated film, directed by Howard Hawkes, is an American classic and the most acclaimed adaptation of Raymond Chandler's iconic character for the screen. Bogart costars with his wife, Lauren Bacall, as well as John Ridgley, Martha Vickers, and Elisha Cook Jr., who played Wilmer in *The Maltese Falcon*. It is available from Warner Bros.

- The one film adaptation of a Dashiell Hammett novel that can rival *The Maltese Falcon* in popularity is the 1934 unrated movie *The Thin Man*. This comedy/drama about a debonair husband-and-wife crime-solving team, Nick and Nora Charles, was so popular that it spawned five sequels and set the standard for romantic comedies for generations. Directed by W. S. Van Dyke, it stars William Powell and Myrna Loy as the Charleses, as well as Maureen O'Hara and Nat Pendleton.

- Before *The Maltese Falcon*, Humphrey Bogart was known for his portrayals of emotionally complex gangsters. He gave one of his finest performances as Roy Earle, an ex-convict who falls in love with a goodhearted crippled girl but falls back to his thieving ways in Raul Walsh's *High Sierra* (1941), also starring Ida Lupino. It is unrated and available from Warner Bros.

- In 1975, David Giler directed *The Black Bird*, a comic parody of *The Maltese Falcon*, with George Segal playing the son of Sam Spade and Lee Patrick and Elisha Cook Jr. reprising their roles as Effie and Wilmer from the original film. It has not been released on DVD, but some library systems still carry the Columbia TriStar Home Video version, released in 1987. The film is rated PG.

- In 1982, director Wim Wenders and producer Francis Ford Coppola brought to the screen an imagined chapter in the life of Dashiell Hammett, playing off the fact that he had worked for a detective agency before earning fame as a writer. *Hammett* stars Frederic Forrest, Marilu Henner, and Peter Boyle in a story that has the writer called back to continue an old case, including several people he meets in his fictionalized life who prove to be inspirations for *The Maltese Falcon*. It is available on DVD and BluRay from Lionsgate. The film is rated PG.

- The acclaimed television series *The No. 1 Ladies' Detective Agency* (2008–09), adapted for television from a series of popular novels by Alexander McCall Smith, follows the adventures of a Motswana woman, Precious Ramotswe, as she starts her own agency and encounters the kinds of stereotypes that, thanks to Huston's film, are now commonly associated with detective work. The unrated series stars Jill Scott and Idris Elba, and is available from Warner Home Video.

character in a career that had been spotty up to then. Bogart plays Spade as a master of detection who understands what is going on around him at every turn or, when he is unsure, has the instincts to patiently drift toward the right direction. The plot of the film is convoluted and the cast changes over the course of the story—for instance, a main character, Sydney Greenstreet's Kasper Gutman, shows up at almost the exact halfway point, and Captain Jacoby, who has the falcon statue everyone is looking for, comes in late in the film, drops the falcon on the floor, and falls dead. Through it all, audiences feel that they are on track, assured by Bogart's star charisma.

There is so much plot development in the film that audiences tend to forget that they do not really know much about Sam Spade at all. The story progresses chronologically, never looking back. Once the film begins, it barrels ahead over the course of four days and three nights, not taking time to dwell on who its characters were before they came on-screen. That missing information is not very difficult to imagine, and it is important for determining what, aside from the chase for an object that is or is not valuable, this story is all about. From the evidence in the story, and in Dashiell Hammett's novel, which the story follows quite faithfully, it is pretty clear that before this episode in his life—as recently as, say, ten minutes before the film begins—Sam Spade was a rather pathetic, self-destructive, self-loathing creature.

As the film begins, Spade hates his business partner. Throughout the film, people who know both Spade and Miles Archer offer him half-hearted condolences for Archer's murder, which Spade shrugs off. He is quick to have Archer's name removed from the business the day after the man's death. In Hammett's novel, he tells Effie, who was secretary to them both, quite pointedly, "I always had an idea that if Miles would go off and die somewhere we'd stand a better chance of thriving." His dislike for the man seems to have gone much deeper than just the business, too. At the end of the book, explaining to Brigid O'Shaughnessy that he is not motivated to avenge Archer's death out of any personal affection, he spells it out quite clearly: Miles "was a son of a bitch. I found that out the first week we were in business together and I meant to kick him out as soon as the year was up. You didn't do me a damned bit of harm by killing him."

> MAYBE HE CAN SEE THAT UNDER HER PRETENSE TO NEED HIM BRIGID REALLY *DOES* NEED HIM, AND, BEING NEEDED, AS IN EVERY GOOD LOVE STORY, SHAKES SPADE OUT OF HIS SELF-INVOLVEMENT, HIS SELF-LOATHING, AND HIS SELF-DESTRUCTIVE BEHAVIOR. HE BECOMES A BETTER MAN TO SERVE THE WOMAN HE LOVES."

Archer, it seems, deserved Spade's contempt. In his only scene in the book and film, he breezes into the office in the middle of the day, sees a pretty client, and immediately starts flirting with her. He offers to handle her case personally, to put her in his debt—in the novel she at least has to ask for the personal attention of one of the agency's partners, giving him the opportunity to set himself up as her protector, but in the film Archer suggests it immediately, leering. When she leaves he claims her for his own, stating, "You saw her first, but I spoke first." One wonders what Archer's wife might have to say about that, until they meet her a few scenes later in the film. It sounds as if Spade should never have had anything to do with this terrible man. As indicated in the film, though, in a brief shot of Bogart looking across the office at an empty desk, they not only shared a business but sat in the same room together, day after day.

Being in business with Archer is too close. Sharing an office with a man he dislikes is still closer. While Spade would have been smart to distance himself from Archer, he instead, foolishly, made their connection to each other tighter by sleeping with Archer's wife, Iva.

Not much is said about how Spade and Iva began their affair, but it would be difficult to think of a scenario that does not include Spade's contempt for his partner. If he did not begin sleeping with Iva specifically to spite Archer and passive-aggressively act out his dislike for the man, then certainly he must have at least considered that he was justified in the affair because Archer deserved to be cheated on. In the book and the film, audiences are given very little to understand their affair: Effie mentions her jealousy of Iva's shapely body in the novel, but in both versions, when asked if he would think of marrying Iva now that she is a widow, Spade responds, "I wish I had never laid eyes on her."

Iva seems to have earned his contempt, too. The fact that she refuses to say where she was on the night of Archer's death is never connected to the falcon case, leaving the most likely explanation for lying about her absence to be that she was probably having an affair with yet *another* man, hours before throwing herself into the arms of her lover for sympathy about the death of her husband.

The Archers, then, are both lecherous cretins that Sam Spade hates, but he has been spending his days with one of them and his nights with the other. The fact that he would do so marks him as a deeply troubled man with self-esteem issues, not the confident professional who outwits a cartel of international thieves by the end of the film.

Comparing the man Spade was before the film began to the man he is at the end, *The Maltese Falcon* can be viewed as a redemption story. In it, Spade learns to focus on his good points and to leave behind the aspects of his personality that had driven him previously. His entanglement with the people who have come to town in search of the mythic statue has made him realize his potential and stop wallowing in seething hatred of his life.

Assuming that is true, the question arises of what in the story, exactly, leads to his redemption. There are several possible answers that bear consideration.

Throughout history, stories have covered the redemptive power of love, and there is love in this film—maybe. Spade admits at the end of the story that he may be in love with Brigid O'Shaughnessy. She has lied to him throughout the film, changing names at every turn, pretending to be more frightened than she is in order to get him to put himself in between herself and danger. He suspects her of being involved in Archer's death up to the point where she admits that she herself killed him. It is not the traditional kind of self-sacrifice that the word *love* usually brings to mind, but it might be just what Sam Spade needs.

His involvement with Miles and Iva Archer shows him to be someone who is wary of happiness. He seems to gravitate toward suspicious

behavior and the challenges it presents to him. One thing that becomes clear from Humphrey Bogart's portrayal of Spade is the delight he takes from catching Brigid in a lie. Maybe it is a sign of his analytical mind, with an interest in puzzles that draws him to mysteries and liars, rather than to a woman like Iva, who throws herself at him. Maybe he can see that under her pretense to need him Brigid really *does* need him, and, being needed, as in every good love story, shakes Spade out of his self-involvement, his self-loathing, and his self-destructive behavior. He becomes a better man to serve the woman he loves.

Of course, it could never work out between them. She *is* a murderer, after all. And in the end, when he tells Brigid that she will have to suffer for her crimes, Spade is admitting that there are moral imperatives that are more important than love, without fully admitting whether he loves her or not.

It is uncomfortable, at the end of the film, to see Sam Spade admit to a moral hierarchy. Where was this sense of ethics at the start of the film? His original position appears to have been that all is good—he saw no problem with sleeping with a married woman, cheating on his business partner, working with someone who disgusted him, or pretending to love a woman he could not stand. Maybe the moral code that he explains so clearly in his "When a man's partner is killed he's supposed to do something about it" speech at the end is something that he is just coming to realize—the way Bogart plays it, with a furrowed brow and eyes set off, gazing into an unseeable distance, Spade is just putting the pieces of correct behavior together as he is talking. He does coat his talk in cynicism about it being good for business, but that may just be a reflex reaction, borne of years of cynical living.

Something in the movie's hundred-minute running time has either awoken a sense of decency that Sam Spade forgot he had, or has led him to the logical conclusion that decency is important. The obvious explanation is that his love for Brigid O'Shaughnessy, bad woman that she is, was the catalyst that made this change possible. It seems unlikely that Spade himself would accept that explanation, but then, judging from the position he was in at the start of the film, Spade's understanding of his own feelings has never been all that reliable.

Source: David Kelly, Critical Essay on *The Maltese Falcon*, in *Novels for Students*, Gale, Cengage Learning, 2015.

Deborah Knight

In the following excerpt, Knight compares film noir detectives with more traditional detective characters, such as Sherlock Holmes.

An elegant, dark-haired woman in a fur wrap enters the office of the private detective firm of Spade and Archer. Sam Spade's secretary has already told him that he'll want to see her because "she's a knockout." Miss Wonderly, as she initially identifies herself, wants to hire Spade to find her younger sister, Corinne, who has apparently run away to San Francisco with a man named Floyd Thursby. Miss Wonderly insists that Thursby is dangerous and will stop at nothing. Spade's partner, Miles Archer, arrives during the interview, obviously finds Miss Wonderly quite attractive, and agrees to tail Thursby that evening. When Miss Wonderly leaves, Spade and Archer agree that her story is suspicious but that she has certainly paid well, perhaps too generously, for their efforts. Later that night, Spade is awakened by a telephone call from the police telling him that Miles Archer has been shot and killed. At the scene, Spade learns that Miles was shot at point-blank range in a dark alley with his gun still buttoned down in his pocket. Still later that night, Floyd Thursby is shot to death. The police suspect that Spade

> WE TEND SIMPLY TO ASSUME THAT PRIVATE DETECTIVES EXHIBIT A PARADIGMATIC SORT OF RATIONALITY, AND THIS ASSUMPTION TENDS TO OBSCURE THE ROLE THAT EMOTIONS PLAY IN THEIR REASONING."

killed Thursby in retaliation for Miles Archer's murder. Spade must now resolve Miss Wonderly's case while finding out who killed his partner and, in particular, must solve the murder of Thursby to get the police off his back. Even though he wasn't particularly fond of Miles Archer, Spade is fully and ironically aware that, being a private detective, it is bad for business if your partner is murdered and nothing gets done about it.

In this essay, I examine what I take to be the philosophical core of *The Maltese Falcon* (John Huston, 1941), namely, its examination of the relation between reason and passion as exemplified by the two central protagonists, Sam Spade (Humphrey Bogart) and Brigid O'Shaughnessy (Mary Astor), who initially calls herself Miss Wonderly. My approach is to start from certain distinctive conventions and structures of the hard-boiled detective genre. These include the defining characteristics of the hard-boiled detective, the central female character and her relationship to the detective, how the detective enters a story partway into its development, and the strategies used by the detective to uncover the criminals and solve the crimes. With respect to the philosophical status of the emotions, I am a cognitivist and will briefly explain what that position entails. Part of my concern is to debunk the view that hard-boiled detectives are dispassionate reasoners, solving crimes through a detached rationality. Several key scenes from *The Maltese Falcon* will help me make this point. But my ultimate goal is to indicate that there is something special about the hard-boiled detective, as opposed to the classic detective, something that has to do with his personal and emotional investment in the events and people he is investigating, an investment that requires that he act to ensure justice is done even after the crime has been solved. This final step could not be taken, I argue, if the hard-boiled detective were simply a dispassionate reasoner.

THE PRIVATE DETECTIVE AND THE WORLD OF FILM NOIR

Private detectives have a privileged place in the world of film noir, a genre itself identified with stories that take place down dark streets, skirt the edges of the law, and involve deception and double-crossing. Film noir private detectives typically operate among a host of morally dubious characters pursuing their own gain at whatever cost. They are hard-boiled—that is, they are tough, cynical individualists who have a history of ill-will toward more obviously legitimate, although invariably plodding, representatives of the law, such as police detectives and district attorneys. They must inevitably—considering the petty criminals and other lowlifes with whom they associate—look out for themselves. Their self-interest is understandable. Given their clientele and their clientele's particular problems, staying alive and out of jail is not for them as straightforward a process as it might initially appear.

Film noir private detectives typically enter a situation in media res, which is to say that they become involved partway into an ongoing course of action that predates their involvement. Therefore, the most immediate job for them is to figure out just what course of action they have gotten themselves into. This is different from the situation in which classic detectives find themselves, one in which the central crime has typically already been committed and the only questions left to answer are who did it and how. The film noir detective, by contrast, must first discover what the real situation is. A central task for him is to avoid being the dupe of his client, who usually has good reasons not to communicate everything she knows about the situation. Not all clients are duplicitous—one need only think of General Sternwood (Charles Waldron) in *The Big Sleep* (Howard Hawks, 1946). But there is always some risk since even a non-duplicitous client typically does not fully understand the situation she wants sorted out. Thus, the film noir private detective must critically analyze everyone involved: not only his client, but also the people he is investigating. This is where toughness and cynicism pay off. For private detectives, cynicism is more than an attitude; it is something of a life skill, keeping them

properly suspicious of those who might try to take advantage of them. The consequences of miscalculation here are dire, something Miles Archer (Jerome Cowan) plainly should have learned before going down that dark alley. Not understanding the situation can lead to arrest and imprisonment and even, sometimes, death.

Because the private detective enters the situation in media res, he must figure out, from the minimal information that he is originally given, precisely what is unfolding. This means that he is, in effect, operating hermeneutically. Frank Kermode correctly observes that detection narratives feature "a specialized 'hermeneutic' organization." The detective's goal is to piece together the real story from the range of story fragments that he learns about or discovers. One thing he discovers is that the initial object of investigation invariably turns out not to be the central crime or puzzle, although solving this initial situation is necessary if what will later emerge as the main crime is to be properly resolved. So, in *The Maltese Falcon*, the initial object of investigation is Miss Wonderly's sister Corinne and her association with Thursby. But it turns out that Corinne is merely a fictional pretext invented by Miss Wonderly to cause Archer to trail Thursby in order to throw suspicion on Thursby for Archer's murder. Nevertheless, solving Miss Wonderly's involvement with Thursby is an important step in Sam's progress toward finding out who killed Miles.

It is generally agreed that the private detective must have exemplary reasoning skills. This assumption is understandable since his job is to figure out "whodunit," that is, to solve a complex situation, usually a crime, by means of sorting out who has done what to whom. There is obviously good reason to think that the private detective has particularly well-honed skills and that skill at reasoning is high in his repertoire. But we must acknowledge that the sort of reasoning exemplified by a classic detective such as Sherlock Holmes is very different in kind from the sort of reasoning exemplified by a hard-boiled detective such as Sam Spade. As John Cawelti persuasively argues in his analysis of the main differences between classic detective fiction and its hard-boiled variant, classic sleuths such as Holmes are typically upper-class amateurs whose chief satisfaction derives from the demonstration of "superior intellect and psychological insight" in solving the crime.

The hard-boiled detective, by contrast, is much more directly involved, and his participation in the investigation of a crime quickly becomes something more like a personal mission. First, he becomes "emotionally and morally committed" to certain figures at the center of his investigation. Second, his involvement in solving the crime typically requires that he extract himself from a threat to his own life or career. For these reasons, it is not just the solution of the crime that is important to him. Rather, he "remains unfulfilled until he has taken a personal moral stance toward the criminal." Unlike the classic detective's work, the hard-boiled detective's work does not stop with the solution of the crime; instead, there is an important further step, which Cawelti describes as "some kind of personal choice or action," that brings closure to his mission.

While both hard-boiled detectives such as Sam Spade and classic detectives such as Sherlock Holmes rely on guesses and hunches and use the progress of their investigation to test their best guesses, the nature of their involvement with the crime and its investigation is decidedly different. One way to see this difference is to note that Spade is involved emotionally and morally in the progress of his investigation, whereas no comparable emotional or moral commitment is required of Holmes as he sorts out the facts of the case and draws his conclusions. Yet it might initially seem a peculiar thing to emphasize the role of emotion in the hard-boiled detective's investigations, given that we typically think of him as a dispassionate reasoner rather than as a passionate one. In fact, noticing his passionate side allows us to ask what the proper relation between reason and the emotions might be and how that question is resolved in the case of the film noir private detective. Philosophers have often argued that reason is locked in a perpetual struggle against the negative influence of the emotions. This idea has roots that date back at least to Socrates and Plato. Roughly, Plato argues that reason must take precedence over the emotions since, obviously, the emotions corrupt good reasoning. This view has recently been contested by a number of philosophers who argue that emotions are integral to sound reasoning.

The view that the emotions are themselves rational is known as *cognitivism about the emotions*. The basic claim of cognitivism is that our emotions contribute positively to, rather than

inevitably distracting from, our understanding of the world. Furthermore, our emotions are centrally involved in our decision making, since they help us determine what we desire and value. This means that the emotions are prerequisites, not only for right judgments, but also for right actions. Proper moral agency does not result from reasoning conducted in isolation from the rich resources that our emotions provide for us.

Anyone doubtful about this claim should consider the description by Antonio Damasio, the noted neurologist, of the remarkable aftermath of a devastating accident that befell a man named Phineas Gage in 1848. An iron rod with a lot of force behind it pierced Gage's head and in fact traveled straight through, exiting the other side, permanently damaging a quite specific part of his brain, that which is responsible for feelings and emotions. Astonishingly, Gage survived the accident, but crucial aspects of his personality changed as a result of it. Most important from Damasio's point of view, Gage's ability to make decisions and, in particular, to make good choices was completely annihilated. Although "attention, perception, memory, language, intelligence" were all undamaged, Gage's decisions no longer took into account his own best interests or advantage. Worse yet, his respect for social conventions and for ethical matters more generally construed disappeared. Damasio uses this case to illustrate the deep interconnection among our emotions, our judgments, and our ability to operate as moral and social beings.

Still, it is not commonly recognized that emotions play a formative role in at least some key decisions made by film noir detectives. We tend simply to assume that private detectives exhibit a paradigmatic sort of rationality, and this assumption tends to obscure the role that emotions play in their reasoning. Yet philosophers such as Robert Solomon argue that emotions just are judgments about situations that we face, and private detectives are first and foremost figures who must make good judgments, since the consequence of bad judgment could, as mentioned above, very well be death. Private detectives are practical reasoners in the sense that they are professional problem solvers. This means that, in any situation, they must be able to juggle competing answers to the main "whodunit" question. And they must be able to track the implications of various equally plausible answers to that question, at least until they have focused in on the real target of their investigation, the person who really did it. But emotions need not be absent from any of these undertakings....

Source: Deborah Knight, "On Reason and Passion in *The Maltese Falcon*," in *The Philosophy of Film Noir*, edited by Mark T. Conrad, University Press of Kentucky, 2006, pp. 207–12.

Richard T. Jameson

In the following essay, Jameson explains how Huston's direction adds tension to the film's dialogue.

> In 1539, the Knight Templars of Malta, paid tribute to Charles V of Spain, by sending him a Golden Falcon encrusted from beak to claw with rarest jewels—but pirates seized the galley carrying the priceless token and the fate of the Maltese Falcon remains a mystery to this day.

That crawl appears following the opening credits of *The Maltese Falcon*, set to dreamy-sinister music and laid over a dark image of the peregrine statuary seemingly poised in some undiscovered tomb. The grammar is regrettable (surely it should be Knights-Templar?) and suggestive of some haste. Was the foreword perhaps added at the last minute, in an act of desperation, after preview audiences had grown fidgety with reel upon reel of baroque conversations and ornately peculiar comings and goings in a collection of offices and hotel rooms purporting to be modern-day (1941) San Francisco? More than half the film elapses before anyone even mentions the titular bird, let alone accounts for its immense value and lurid history. Yet strike the keynote with that one-sentence prelude and the mantle of legend settles over the entire proceedings.

Of course, *The Maltese Falcon* has become positively encrusted with legend in the six decades since its release. It's *the* classic hardboiled private-eye movie; the nervy maiden offering of its celebrated director, John Huston; the first glamorous star vehicle for Humphrey Bogart, an icon of American cinema and the twentieth century's definition of existential cool; and still the most triumphantly well-cast movie from Hollywood's golden age (rivaled only by *Casablanca*). Watching *The Maltese Falcon* now, everybody and his brother know they're in the presence of something extraordinary. But it's tantalizing to contemplate how easily the brass ring might have been missed—how close the picture might have come to being just another detective thriller, like the two previous screen versions of Dashiell Hammett's groundbreaking novel (respectively so-so, in 1931, and ludicrous, in 1936).

> THE MALTESE FALCON, LIKE ITS ELUSIVE NAMESAKE, IS ETERNALLY IN MOTION, DESPITE THE FACT THAT IT TRANSPIRES IN A FIERCELY INTERIOR ENVIRONMENT."

Private eye Samuel Spade (Bogart) is lolling in his swivel chair and rolling a Bull Durham cigarette when his secretary announces "a Miss Wonderly to see you." The lady in question (Mary Astor)—initially a soft fog behind opaque glass—is an aggressively demure creature all aflutter because her sister Corinne has run off with a shady man named Thursby. Could Mr. Spade do something about it? Mr. Spade's partner Miles Archer (Jerome Cowan), a leering sleaze, shows up just in time to usurp the assignment—and within hours/minutes gets abruptly dead. With the police sniffing after Sam as prime suspect (he had, after all, been sleeping with his partner's wife), the detective starts improvising. He's not the only one: The dainty Miss Wonderly (there is no sister Corinne, by the way) becomes the evasive Miss LeBlanc and soon owns up to the scullery-maid moniker Brigid O'Shaughnessy; she and Spade will become allies, after a fashion, and lovers. A lisping Levantine named Joel Cairo (Peter Lorre) also retains Spade's services, then keeps pulling a gun on him. There are two guns in the trenchcoat pockets of a sullen hoodlum (Elisha Cook Jr.) who always seems to be haunting nearby doorways, and just as the pot is really starting to boil, everything and everyone becomes very still at the mention of "the fat man."

John Huston had been laboring as a Warner Bros. screenwriter for several years, after a genially miscellaneous and gadabout early manhood. A couple of particularly successful assignments (Howard Hawks's *Sergeant York* and Raoul Walsh's *High Sierra*) won him a shot at directing as well as writing something that Warners briefly planned to call *The Gent from Frisco*. The writing came easy: Huston asked a secretary to type out a scene-by-scene breakdown of Hammett's novel; studio boss Jack L. Warner happened to see the "script," congratulated Huston on licking the adaptation, and told him to start shooting next week. Virtually all the film's flavorsome dialogue is Hammett's, and so, of course, is the plot about a slippery private detective and a fractious cabal of outré characters willing to sacrifice anyone, including one another, to possess an ancient artifact beyond price. As it happened, Huston not only had the good sense to be faithful to Hammett's original and capitalize on its myriad strengths; he also found in it a theme and worldview that would define his own body of work.

For Huston, the Maltese Falcon is only the first instance of an unholy grail in pursuit of which a collection of strangers make temporary common cause. Whether prospecting for *The Treasure of the Sierra Madre*, plotting to steal a fortune in diamonds in *The Asphalt Jungle*, aiming to sink a German battleship with *The African Queen*, chasing God and vengeance and *Moby Dick*, hunting wild mustangs in *The Misfits*, getting battered to win a purse in *Fat City*, or dreaming of a kingdom in Kafiristan as *The Man Who Would Be King*, Huston's motley crew of questers never really find anything but themselves. Aspiration makes a beeline for absurdity; defeat and victory alike are mostly a matter of dumb or bitterly ironic luck. It's the journey, not the destination, that counts, and almost always the only achievable triumph is the weary serenity of self-knowledge.

Still, *The Maltese Falcon* is an exemplary first film, and its dominant tone is a sassy smartness, not despair. Indeed, the narrative personality of the film and the personality of its protagonist are one and the same from the moment Spade is introduced. He will dominate every action and interaction and serve as our point-of-view reference for everything that happens. With only a couple of exceptions—the abrupt, abstract depiction of the film's first murder and the fadeouts of two later scenes—we see nothing that Spade does not see himself (a cardinal principle of the private-eye genre). Even more important, we see him seeing it. Sam's ongoing, moment-to-moment assessment of the shifting vectors of allegiance and advantage, the trade-off of truth and hastily adapted fiction on the part of his fellow denizens of the *Falcon's* night-world, is the most privileged spectacle the film has to offer.

The Maltese Falcon, like its elusive namesake, is eternally in motion, despite the fact that it transpires in a fiercely interior environment (even the few street scenes feel like interiors) and an inordinate amount of it consists of people talking about things (or the possibility of things) that occur offscreen. Now, "talky" is usually a bad word when it comes to movies. But Hammett's talk is tensile and exotic, and the way Huston films it, talk is dynamic action. The camera is ever ready to adapt, adjust, to satisfy a lively curiosity about an ever-surprising world. Producer Henry Blanke advised his tyro director to "shoot each scene as if it was the most important one in the picture; make every shot count." Huston did, with the result that nothing, not even the incidental behavior of anonymous passersby or the riffling of fake I.D. plucked from a suspect's wallet, fails to crackle with energy and insinuation. The dialogue scenes play like relief maps of mined terrain. Looming close-ups are juxtaposed against tiny figures tucked away in the distant corners of the same frame. When two police detectives come to brace Spade in his apartment, just their postures, their positions in the frame and the difference in how they're lit, testify to the bulldog antagonism of Lieutenant Dundy (Barton MacLane) and the reluctance and discomfort of Sergeant Polhaus (Ward Bond), who regards Sam as a friend. Among the Falconers, visible tensions are still more fraught, even when the illusion of affability and rapport is being assiduously courted.

Affability and rapport run nowhere higher than in Spade's (and by all means Humphrey Bogart's) scenes with Kasper Gutman, the most obsessive votary of the Black Bird. Gutman, "the fat man," does not make his appearance until midfilm—and Sydney Greenstreet, the sixty-one-year-old stage veteran tapped for the role, was making his own first appearance on a motion picture screen. It's a moment beyond price. Glimpsed in the distant background as his gunsel Wilmer (Cook) opens the door of their hotel suite, he emerges from behind a vase of roses, his bulbous trunk floating on twinkle-toes, his arm capturing Spade's own to draw him into his parlor and his enchantment, snorting companionably.

Gutman is quite mad, but his madness is instinct with grandeur. It is he who, finally, speaks of the Falcon and elevates its pursuit to a cosmic principle. Long after the film has ended, and the sundry on-screen and off-screen corpses have all been accounted for and morality has been satisfied, the viewer realizes that, by the time he does so, Gutman has no practical reason to tell Spade about the Falcon and its fabulous history. It's just that, as he remarks elsewhere, "I must have my little joke now and then." In his heart, Spade deplores him, but John Huston loves him. So do we, and we'll never shake the secret wish that in an alternative universe Sam Spade might yet take him up on his invitation to "join us on the Quest." The Maltese Falcon remains a mystery to this day.

Source: Richard T. Jameson, "*The Maltese Falcon* (1941)," in *The A List: The National Society of Film Critics' 100 Essential Films*, edited by Jay Carr, Da Capo Press, 2002, pp. 176–79.

Morris Beja

In the following essay, Beja discusses some behind-the-scenes details, such as casting.

ON THE NOVEL

The Maltese Falcon (1930) was the third novel by Dashiell Hammett (1894–1961), who is often credited with "inventing" the genre of the tough private detective and who in any case certainly had a major influence on others who wrote in that form, notably for example Raymond Chandler. Earlier novels had been *Red Harvest* and *The Dain Curse* (both 1929); he later wrote *The Glass Key* (1931) and *The Thin Man* (1932)—the latter having as its hero the antitheses of Samuel Spade in the debonair and charming Nick and Nora Charles, characters who appeared in a successful series of films starring William Powell and Myrna Loy.

Hammett had himself been, like Spade, a private detective in San Francisco (for the Pinkerton Agency) before he began writing his stories and novels, many of which were published in the magazine *Black Mask*.

ON THE FILM

John Huston's *The Maltese Falcon* (1941) was actually the third film version of the novel. A film by the same name appeared in 1931, directed by Roy del Ruth and starring Ricardo Cortez as Spade and Bebe Daniels as Brigid O'Shaughnessy. This version was largely played for laughs, but it was otherwise fairly faithful to the original plot line. That was not true of the 1936 version, called *Satan Met a Lady* and directed by William Dieterle, in which for example the Fat Man became the Fat Lady (played by Alison Skipworth); Warren William and Bette Davis starred.

John Huston (b. 1906) had been having a successful career as a screenwriter, working on such films as *Juarez* (1939) and *Sergeant York* (1941), when—to keep him happy, Huston says—the Warner Brothers studio agreed to let him try directing. They stipulated that he choose a relatively inexpensive project, and Warners still owned the rights to *The Maltese Falcon*. At first there was pressure to cast George Raft as Spade. Raft had turned down *High Sierra*, which Huston had helped to write, because he did not want to play a character who dies at the end, thus enabling Humphrey Bogart to break out of the type-cast bad-guy secondary roles he had been restricted to for years. Raft did not want to take chances with a new and inexperienced director, so he turned down *The Maltese Falcon* too. Bogart thus played the role that made him a major star—and he remained one for the rest of his life, just as Huston has remained a major director, if an often controversial and not always successful one.

Huston made important documentaries during World War II, and his first postwar film starred, again, Bogart: *The Treasure of the Sierra Madre* (1948). His other films include *Key Largo* (1948) and *The African Queen* (1951), both also with Bogart, and *The Asphalt Jungle* (1950), *The Red Badge of Courage* (1951), *Moby Dick* (1956), *The Misfits* (1961), and *The Man Who Would Be King* (1975), as well as some films that caused his reputation to decline somewhat, such as *The Bible* (1966) and *The Mackintosh Man* (1973). In any case, *The Maltese Falcon* is almost universally admired and is indeed regarded by many people as the greatest of all detective films; for that matter, it was immediately greeted as such upon its release.

Huston wrote the screenplay in addition to directing the film. The producer was Hal Wallis, then head of production for Warner Brothers; he also produced *Little Caesar* (1930), *Casablanca* (1943), and many other films. Henry Blanke (who went on to produce *The Treasure of the Sierra Madre*) served as the associate producer. The director of photography was Arthur Edeson, whose previous work included *All Quiet on the Western Front* (1930), *Mutiny on the Bounty* (1935), and *Satan Met a Lady*, the earlier version of *The Maltese Falcon*. He would later photograph Bogart, Sydney Greenstreet, and Peter Lorre again in *Casablanca*.

Other credits: music, Adolphe Deutsch; editor, Thomas Richards; dialogue director, Robert Foulk; assistant director, Claude Archer; art director, Robert Haas; sound recorder, Oliver S. Garretson; make-up, Perc Westmore.

Looking back at *The Maltese Falcon* over thirty years and thirty films later, Huston once said, "I've never had a better cast"—and that remark came from someone who is widely regarded as especially good at directing actors. Humphrey Bogart (1899–1957) of course was Sam Spade.... Other films besides those mentioned above for which he is especially remembered include *To Have and Have Not* (1945), *The Big Sleep* (1946), and *The Caine Mutiny* (1954). He won an Academy Award for his performance in *The African Queen* (1951).

Mary Astor (Brigid O'Shaughnessy) received an Academy Award for best supporting actress in 1941, but for her role in *The Great Lie* (1941) rather than for *The Maltese Falcon*. She went on to play understanding mothers in *Meet Me in St. Louis* (1944) and *Little Women* (1949). Sydney Greenstreet was Kasper Gutman, the Fat Man: he was a British actor who had worked in the American theater for many years, and this was his first film role (at the age of sixty-one). He made many other films for Warner Brothers, including *Casablanca* and *The Mask of Dimitrios* (1944), both of which also featured Peter Lorre. Lorre (Joel Cairo) had become famous in the role of a psychopathic murderer in Fritz Lang's *M* (1931). He had also appeared in *Mad Love* (1935) and as Raskolnikov in an adaptation of Dostoevsky's *Crime and Punishment* (1935). Elisha Cook, Jr. (Wilmer) later appeared in such films as *The Big Sleep* and *Shane* (1953).

Other members of the cast: Ward Bond as Detective Tom Polhaus; Barton MacLane as Lieutenant Dundy; Lee Patrick as Effie Perine; Gladys George as Iva Archer; Jerome Cowan as Miles Archer; James Burke as Luke; Murray Alper as Frank Richman; John Hamilton as District Attorney Bryan; and, without a screen credit, Walter Huston (John Huston's father) in the cameo role of Captain Jacobi.

Source: Morris Beja, "*The Maltese Falcon*: Background," in *Film & Literature: An Introduction*, Longman, 1979, pp. 129–31.

SOURCES

"AFI's 100 Years—100 Movies: 10th Anniversary Edition," American Film Institute, 2014, http://afi.com/100Years/movies10.aspx (accessed July 22, 2014).

Crowther, Bosley, Review of *The Maltese Falcon*, in *The Maltese Falcon: John Huston, Director*, edited by William Luhr, Rutgers University Press, 1995, p. 127; originally published in *New York Times*, October 4, 1941.

"The Detective and Film Noir," in *The Maltese Falcon: John Huston, Director*, edited by William Luhr, Rutgers University Press, 1995, pp. 7–9.

Ferguson, Otis, Review of *The Maltese Falcon*, in *New Republic*, October 20, 1941, http://www.newrepublic.com/article/film/100374/tnr-film-classics-the-maltese-falcon-october-20-1941 (accessed July 14, 2014).

Hammett, Dashiel, "The Maltese Falcon," in *Hammett: Complete Novels*, The Library of America, 2001, pp. 387–586.

"Humphrey Bogart: Biography," Internet Movie Database, http://www.imdb.com/name/nm0000007/bio?ref_=nm_ov_bio_sm (accessed July 11, 2014).

"The Knights in Malta," in *Discovering the Maltese Falcon and Sam Spade*, edited by Richard Layman, Vince Emery Productions, 2005, pp. 147–54.

Labrecque, Jeff, "Crime Esprit," in *Entertainment Weekly*, No. 900, October 3, 2006, http://www.ew.com/ew/article/0,,1540539,00.html (accessed July 14, 2014).

MacLaughlin, Robert, and Sally E. Parry, *We'll Always Have the Movies: American Cinema During World War II*, University Press of Kentucky, 2006, pp. 7–22.

The Maltese Falcon, Turner Classic Movies Greatest Classic Films Collection: Murder Mysteries, Warner Home Video, 2009, DVD.

Review of *The Maltese Falcon*, in *Variety*, September 30, 1941, http://variety.com/1941/film/reviews/the-maltese-falcon-2-1200413694/ (accessed July 14, 2014).

"Top Ten Mystery: AFI 10 Top 10," American Film Institute, 2014, http://afi.com/10top10/category.aspx?cat=5 (accessed July 22, 2014).

FURTHER READING

Biesen, Sheri Chinen, *Blackout: World War II and the Origins of Film Noir*, Johns Hopkins University Press, 2005.

While *The Maltese Falcon* is often considered the first major studio example of film noir, much about the way the movement was to develop had to do with America's entry into the war at the same time. Biesen examines the other films of the time in relation to *The Maltese Falcon*, then she examines how the war years and the postwar period practically ensured that the film noir worldview would come to follow.

Borde, Raymond, and Etienne Chaumeton, "The Sources of Film Noir," in *A Panorama of American Film Noir, 1941-1953*, City Lights Books, 2002, pp. 15–28.

This book was originally written in French and published in France, where American film noir has always been appreciated as an art genre more than it has been in the United States. In this chapter, the authors trace the origins of American noir to *The Maltese Falcon* and show how the idea quickly grew out of Huston's concepts.

Brill, Lesley, "Theater, Identity, and Reality in *The Maltese Falcon*," in *John Huston's Filmmaking*, Cambridge University Press, 1997, pp. 143–54.

In this chapter, part of a larger overview of the director's career, Brill focuses on the ways that the characters use external personae to hide their true personalities.

Hogan, David J., *Film Noir FAQ: All That's Left to Know About Hollywood's Golden Age of Dames, Detectives, and Danger*, Applause Theater and Cinema Books, 2013.

As this book's subtitle implies, much has already been written about film noir. This recent publication summarizes decades of film theory in an interesting, focused way.

Huston, John, *An Open Book*, DeCapo Press, 1994.

Anyone interested in the inside workings that went into putting together this film should refer to Huston's autobiography, where he conveys, in the middle of the story of a life spent in Hollywood, some of the sense of wonder and excitement he felt when being given (within limited movie industry standards) the means to control the camera and make a film the way he envisioned it.

Maxfield, James F., "La Belle Dame Sans Merci and the Neurotic Knight: Characterization in *The Maltese Falcon*," in *Literature/Film Quarterly*, Vol. 17, No. 4, 1989, pp. 253–60.

Maxfield examines the film in terms of the type of woman described in the famous poem by John Keats, one of the most noted figures of English romanticism, bringing together high literary art and popular art.

Mooney, William, "Sex, Booze, and the Code: Four Versions of *The Maltese Falcon*," in *Literature/Film Quarterly*, Vol. 39, No. 1, 2011, pp. 54–70.

In this long essay, Mooney traces the evolution of the story from its first appearance in *Black Mask* magazine, through its publication as a book and the three film versions of it, explaining how the censorship code of Hollywood studios in the 1930s affected each film's presentation of the material.

SUGGESTED SEARCH TERMS

The Maltese Falcon AND John Huston

John Huston AND Humphrey Bogart

Humphrey Bogart AND Peter Lorre AND Sydney Greenstreet

The Maltese Falcon AND film noir

Sam Spade AND detective fiction

Dashiell Hammett AND John Huston

The Maltese Falcon AND World War II

The Maltese Falcon AND the Knights Templar

Mary Astor AND The Maltese Falcon

The Maltese Falcon AND adaptation

My Year of Meats

RUTH L. OZEKI

1998

With a title that only hints at the cornucopia of contents to be found within, Ruth L. Ozeki's *My Year of Meats* (1998) is an ambitiously woven tale linking an idealistic Japanese American documentary director, a cowed Japanese house-wife, and a handful of American families through mass media, mixed messages, and, above all, meat. The novel is partly narrated by the director, Jane. Ozeki herself has been a documentary film-maker, a fact reflected in her nuanced portrayal of the workings of the fictional television show *My American Wife!* Every move of the show is governed by the orders of the major sponsor, the Beef Export and Trade Syndicate, or BEEF-EX. In a phrase, "Beef is Best!"

Following developments in Jane's life and the TV show over the course of twelve months, *My Year of Meats* becomes most prominently an exposé of the meat industry's underworld, where hormone treatments and other shady practices put the health of both consumers and producers at risk. The novel also exposes the dubious results of blending corporate interests and "documentary" television: fictional realities all too readily believed. But the novel's feminist heart has an even broader agenda, making major themes of the experience of pregnancy, the trials of miscarriage, spousal abuse, and the places of women both inside and outside the home. In exploring these themes, Ozeki portrays various relevant scenes of sexual activity, with occasional graphic reference; there are two

Ruth Ozeki (© Leon Neal / AFP / Getty Images)

scenes of sexual assault. Also, at times the novel's behind-the-scenes looks at the meat industry are grotesque and appalling, and readers may—indeed, should—find that material disturbing. *My Year of Meats* is appropriate for the most mature readers.

AUTHOR BIOGRAPHY

Ruth Ozeki Lounsbury was born on March 12, 1956, in New Haven, Connecticut. Her white father and Japanese mother met while attending Yale University. She wanted to be a novelist from a very early age. In her youth, people thought of her as Japanese based on her appearance, and so she thought of herself that way, leading her to try to fulfill stereotypes about being attractive, intelligent, and musically proficient, but she could not speak Japanese and had little connection with her mother's homeland.

Attending Smith College, a women's institution in Massachusetts, she started studying psychology but changed direction after spending a year abroad in Japan. She graduated with degrees in English literature and Asian studies. When she received a fellowship from the Japanese Ministry of Education, she went on to study classical Japanese literature at Nara Women's University in Nara, Japan. There, she told interviewer Tom Tivnan, "for the first time people looked at me as a Westerner. I was able to get in touch with my inner American: it was OK to have a sense of humour, to be sort of loud and obnoxious." Spending some eight years in Japan, she worked as a bar hostess, studied Noh theater, started a language school, and taught at Kyoto Sangyu University.

Returning to the United States in 1985, Ozeki worked in New York City as an art director for low-budget science-fiction and horror films, such as *Mutant Hunt* and *Necropolis*. She went on to direct documentaries for Japanese television. Issues regarding commercialism in the media came to the forefront of her mind when she directed a show sponsored by cigarette manufacturer Philip Morris. While she herself was trying to quit smoking, she had to walk the streets offering people cigarettes in order to get the requisite shots of the sponsor's tobacco products being enjoyed. She went on to produce two films independently, the documentary-minded drama *Body of Correspondence* (1994) and the slightly fictional documentary *Halving the Bones* (1995).

Having written short stories through high school and college, Ozeki turned to novel writing, and her debut, *My Year of Meats* (1998), won the Kiriyama Pacific Rim Book Prize. At this time she largely abandoned filmmaking—she had been especially fond of the editing process, that is, the assembling of the story—in order to focus on writing. She proceeded to publish the novels *All over Creation* (2003) and *A Tale for the Time Being* (2013). Ozeki was ordained as a Soto Zen priest in 2010, and she became editor of the website Everyday Zen. Her husband, Oliver Kellhammer, is a German Canadian environmental artist. Ozeki lives part of the year on Cortes Island, outside Vancouver, British Columbia, and part of the year in New York City. She was hired to be a professor of creative writing at Smith College beginning in 2015.

PLOT SUMMARY

Prologue

My Year of Meats opens with Takagi—Jane Takagi-Little—helping a fussy Japanese director arrange a shot of Fred and Suzie Flowers kissing.

1. The Sprouting Month

Despairing over her lack of job prospects, Jane is awakened at 2 a.m. by a phone call from Kato, who offers her work on a Japanese television show to be filmed in the United States. This show, *My American Wife!*, is sponsored by the American export syndicate BEEF-EX. As a coordinator, she will find typical American housewives to present their meat-laden recipes on the show.

2. The Clothes-Lining Month

In Japan, Akiko Ueno, to comply with the wishes of her advertising-executive husband, Joichi, or John—who is in charge of the BEEF-EX account—watches the episode of *My American Wife!* that features the Flowers family and cooks the recipe shown in it. For Jane, that episode's filming is marked by miscommunications, delays, and at last the revelation that Fred Flowers has been having an affair. He leaves his wife. In New York, Jane tells Kenji not to grant Suzie's request for a copy of the show.

3. The Ever-Growing Month

While the crew for the series is steady, the directors rotate. Akiko is reading *The Pillow Book*, a protofeminist millennium-old journal. Under her new meat-heavy diet, she becomes bulimic. John is making her rate the episodes of *My American Wife!* and submit to interrogation afterward. In America, Jane films commercials under the visiting John's intrusive supervision, and then at night she helps get him drunk (and thus pliable for ensuing work). Akiko is having trouble getting pregnant; she has stopped menstruating.

4. The Deutzia Month

Jane regularly meets Sloan, who flies in to places like Nebraska to maintain their relationship. When Oda suffers an allergic reaction to veal in Oklahoma, Jane steps in to direct the episode. She reroutes the crew to Texas and films the Martinez family, including a picture-perfect farmland shot. At home in Japan, Akiko has

MEDIA ADAPTATIONS

- An unabridged audiobook version of *My Year of Meats* was produced by Blackstone Audiobooks on eight cassettes, or nine CDs, in 2003, as read by Anna Fields. The running time is eleven hours. This production is also available for download.

started her own list/poetry-filled pillow book. The Martinez episode moves her to tears.

Jane faxes Kato a proposal, laden with family history, to film the Beaudroux family in Louisiana, a couple with two biological children and ten adopted multiracial (mostly Asian) children. The show is to feature Vern's Cajun baby back ribs (pork). In between filming, the cameraman Suzuki teaches Vern how to cook with the invasive kudzu weed. In Japan, Akiko buys a CD with music from the Beaudroux episode. John shouts at Akiko over that show's cooking husband, inferior pig meat, and excessive number of Koreans. Akiko sees a fertility specialist and is scolded for sabotaging her body; the doctor will report to John. In Louisiana, Grace Beaudroux thinks about her daughter Alison's new baby, her daughter Joy's behavior, and the recent TV shoot.

5. The Rice-Sprouting Month

The historical killing of exchange student Yoshihiro Hattori is recalled. Jane considers her submissive interactions with Sloan. In Fly, Oregon, she asks about his double-condom use; she says she cannot get pregnant and that she is free of sexually transmitted diseases. He cajoles her into having unprotected sex. For work, Akiko writes about pregnancy for a magazine. Her marriage to John was set up by their bosses. John arrives home drunk, shouts at Akiko over the doctor's report, and shakes her until she falls over a chair, which injures her stomach, and she gets a cut above her eye.

Jane and John sit in church in Harmony, Mississippi, where they have been invited by Helen Dawes, who is a candidate to appear on *My American Wife!* John, hungover, fumbles an impromptu speech introducing himself; Jane, who is prepared, speaks eloquently. The day before, Becky Thayer, the show's other potential subject, had proven unsatisfactory in Jane's opinion. That night, John, while very drunk, sexually assaulted Jane, but she fought him off. In Harmony, the sermon, gospel music, and spiritually inspired churchgoers lead both Jane and John to a revelatory experience. However, after they visit the Dawes family, John decrees that the show will feature the Thayers.

6. The Water Month

Jane recounts the history of misguided DES use in medicine and agriculture (DES is a synthetic chemical used to stimulate growth). Helen regrets that Jane has forsaken the Dawes family. Back in Japan, John criticizes Akiko's responses to the Thayer and Beaudroux episodes. He prevents her from closing herself in the bathroom after dinner.

Jane tells of the Bukowskys of Indiana, their lives upended by their daughter Christina's accident. During filming, Suzuki and Oh, the soundman, flirt by chasing Christina in a wheelchair. The crew shoots during her sweet sixteen party. Meanwhile, Jane's period is overdue. The show features lamb chops. Because Australia supplies that meat to Japan, John greets Akiko's faithful cooking by knocking the platter to the floor and hitting her. Akiko eats the chops and keeps them down; her period returns.

7. The Poem-Composing Month

Reviewing her life, Jane recalls learning of stereotypical views of race in an old geography text, finding and marrying Emil, and failing to conceive. She is now pregnant. In Quam, Minnesota, her mother confronts her about it. Jane believes that her mother took DES while pregnant, which actually compromised Jane's uterus. Jane recalls Sloan asking, later that night in Fly, whether she really could not get pregnant; she affirmed as much. Back in New York, she learns that the Bukowsky episode was a sensation in Japan. John and Kenji warn her, though, about BEEF-EX's mandates. Jane thinks she loves Sloan.

8. The Leaf Month

Akiko hides her soiled sanitary pads from John. On camera (in Massachusetts), Lara and Dyann introduce their family. While editing the video, Jane wonders whether the episode will air; the lesbian couple are vegetarians, which is at odds with the show's focus on meat dishes. She had neglected to inform the couple about the show's sponsor. In faxes, John's secretary indicates that the episode will not air and that Jane must resign, and Kato admonishes her. Akiko, watching Lara and Dyann's show (after all) in Japan, is moved to tears. She decides she wants a baby.

Kenji, John, and Jane resolve concerns about the lesbian show over faxes; Jane promises an all-American follow-up in Montana. Akiko buys pornography and imitates poses from it. Jane calls Sloan from jail in Montana and reports the pregnancy; they settle on having an abortion. Filming a train, the crew was arrested as suspected Mexican terrorists. Released and drinking ("only two shots"), Jane tells her crew she is pregnant. Reading some gravestones, she realizes she wants her baby. At home in Japan, trying to seduce John, Akiko bites his finger, and he knocks her to the floor; John then sees and desires her but cannot perform.

9. The Long Month

In a fax, John congratulates Jane on her Montana show. Jane is now aiming for a bombshell exposé. Dyann faxes Jane information on the beef industry's darker side. Jane passes this information and her concerns along to John, who dismisses the matter. Jane faxes an apology to Dyann and Lara for not revealing the show's sponsor. Akiko writes a plaintive and revelatory appeal to Jane for help. Proofing her letter, Akiko recalls getting Jane's number from her informational fax to John, which was found by a meddling laundry woman.

Sloan picks Jane up at the Chicago airport and drives her to Blatzsik Meat Fabricators; they tour the creepy facilities, and Anna is found not to be telegenic. At Sloan's apartment, he and Jane bicker. She flies to Colorado. In Japan, Akiko accidentally reveals to John that she read Jane's fax; she appeases him by implying that she is jealous. After scouting Bunny Dunn's home, Jane returns to New York, and Kenji gives her Akiko's fax number. Jane calls Akiko to secretly learn when she can safely fax her back. John then gets a work-related fax from

Jane. At noon Japanese time the next day, Jane faxes Akiko. Sloan visits Jane in New York; the baby moves in her belly. John, having earlier found Jane's fax to Akiko—hidden in the English dictionary—arrives home very drunk and rapes his defenseless wife. Akiko calls Jane, vaguely revealing what happened and asking about John's upcoming business trip destination, Colorado.

10. *The Gods-Absent Month*

In Colorado, Jane's crew's hired driver, Dave, points out the ill effects of industrial farming. Two days after the assault, Akiko is still nursing her injury; she passes out. Jane ponders the intricacies of filming the curvaceous Bunny and her somehow strange daughter, Rose. Gale Dunn takes them on a tour of the feedlot, cutting off Jane's interrogation about hormones. Cued by Dave, Jane asks about the feeding regimen of the cattle, and Gale proudly reports their efficiency—that is, their use of non-food sources and recycling of animal parts and even waste. John Dunn and Rose arrive. Jane realizes that the hormone-laced dust is perilously infecting her. John Dunn speaks disapprovingly of Gale's chemical-centric management. Gale gives a popsicle from the industrial refrigerator to Rose, who licks her dusty fingers. The crew films the cattle-processing chute, with branding and mysterious injections for new arrivals, as well as a chemically aborted calf fetus on the ground.

At the motel, Suzuki and Oh show Jane footage of Gale fondling the physically hyper-developed Rose. After filming in the Dunns' house, Jane confronts Bunny, who tells Jane to return with her crew after eleven. Then, they film the evidence of Rose's tragically early puberty, which will likely lead to ovarian cysts and cancer. Back at the motel, Jane dreams of having a stillbirth. Riding alone with Gale to the slaughterhouse, Jane confronts him, and he threatens her. Inside, the crew films a cow's torturous death; in an accident, Jane is knocked out cold.

11. *The Frost Month*

Akiko finds herself in the hospital, where Nurse Tomoko suspects abuse. John, however, has left a compassionate note. In Colorado, Jane awakes in the crew's van, and then in the emergency room. A couple of hours later in the hospital, Bunny reports to Jane that the doctors discovered her baby was already dead, before the

accident. Late at night, Jane realizes that John Ueno, who arrived in Colorado earlier, must have discovered and destroyed their tapes. After Jane's morning checkup, Kenji calls her to report that the tapes were actually destroyed in the accident, and that Ueno has fired her. Sloan calls, and he and Jane connect poorly. Dave visits the hospital to relate Ueno's wayward management of the show—and give Jane the tapes that Oh and Suzuki actually saved and copied. Jane flies to New York. In Tokyo, John's mother visits Akiko, who has a fractured rib. Akiko realizes she is pregnant. Tomoko urges her to find someplace else to go; for now, John is in America. In Minnesota, Jane and her mother talk about their miscarriages. After Akiko arrives home in Tokyo, John calls. Akiko then calls a travel agent, in order to fly out just before John returns. A couple of weeks later, she visits Tomoko—sharing a kiss—then rides to the airport.

12. *The End of the Year*

Jane edits the Dunn tapes. Akiko calls from the plane. Jane welcomes Akiko in New York and then helps her off to Louisiana; in preparation, Grace and Joy tidy up Akiko's cabin. Jane sends her finished documentary to Bunny, Dyann and Lara, and Sloan. After Louisiana, Akiko is overjoyed by the southern hospitality on the northbound train. Jane calls Lara and Dyann to apologize further, and they agree to host Akiko. In New York, Jane shows Suzuki and Oh her film, and then they go out drinking. Suzuki mentions that Sloan played at the Mercury Lounge recently; she calls there and learns he will be in Memphis, Tennessee. In Massachusetts, Akiko enjoys having her very own apartment. In Memphis, Jane finds Sloan at a gig and watches him kiss a girl. He sees her, ushers her out, and confronts her; they kiss and make up. Early in the morning, they go to church in Harmony.

Epilogue: *January*

Jane returns to her New York apartment to find a pile of notes under her door and abundant phone messages; Bunny has spread the news about Jane's documentary. Bunny took Rose to her grandmother in Texas, and John Dunn made Gale confess his illegal operations to the Department of Agriculture. Jane's documentary enjoys a frenzy of media attention. John Ueno is demoted. Suzie calls to report that the tape of the Flowers show brought her and Fred back together. Jane closes the book on her Year of Meats.

CHARACTERS

Alison Beaudroux
Alison, Grace's eldest (biological) daughter, is unmarried and pregnant. When she has the baby, they live in a refurbished cottage on the family's estate.

Grace Beaudroux
A demure, number-crunching, forward-thinking southern belle in Louisiana, Grace Beaudroux met her husband, Vern, in a ritual where teenagers drove around and swapped passengers. Once married, they together decided, after having two biological children, to adopt ten multi-racial children. Grace enjoys napping while Vern and their many children cook dinner.

Joy Beaudroux
Joy is the first and most curious of the Beaudroux family's ten adopted children; she has an eyebrow ring and will audition at Juilliard, a prestigious music school in New York City.

Vern Beaudroux
A thin, balding man with a talent for cooking, Vern Senior starts a Cajun restaurant that becomes famous in Louisiana. His eldest (biological) son is called Vernon Junior.

Anna Blatszik
Anna Blatszik, the wife from a Polish meatpacking family in Chicago, is judged by Jane to be too uninteresting to appear on *My American Wife!*

Christina Bukowsky
After being run over by a Wal-Mart delivery truck while biking, Christina seemed condemned to a vegetative state. However, her parents managed a community effort to keep her company, and eventually she started responding to people and recovering. She is described as transcendently beautiful.

Dale Bukowsky
Dale has lost his mining job in Indiana. He and his wife translate their daughter's recovery into financial success, and he becomes mayor of their small town.

Eleanor Bukowsky
Mrs. Bukowsky is denied time off by Wal-Mart to care for her injured daughter, so she quits. She spearheads the successful community effort to

nurse Christina to mental and physical health. She and her husband then start a recovery center and write a book.

Helen Dawes
The athletic but quiet Miss Helen at first says little but "Yes, Ma'am" while Jane and John Ueno are visiting Harmony, Mississippi. Helen leads her eight daughters as pitcher on the family softball team. Her family is rejected by John for being black, having too many children, and serving chitterlings—pig intestines.

Purcell Dawes
When Jane and John are visiting the Dawes family, Helen's husband, Purcell, recalls having suffered ill effects from eating hormone-laced miscellaneous chicken parts.

Bunny Dunn
A buxom former rodeo queen and exotic dancer who was swept up by an older man, Bunny loves her daughter but has been in denial about the girl's accelerated physical development. Jane opens Bunny's eyes and inspires her to take action to protect her daughter.

Gale Dunn
Gale Dunn, John Dunn's son from an earlier marriage, now runs the family's Colorado feedlot Dunn & Son, favoring modern chemical and hormonal management of the cattle, including the illegal use of DES. Jane, realizing that Gale and Rose are suffering ill effects from estrogen absorbed in the course of his work, confronts him, but he lashes out in denial. Gale bows to his father's will in the end, confessing his misdeeds to the government.

John Dunn
The seventy-two-year-old father of Gale and Rose and husband of Bunny is now in a wheelchair and lets his son run their business. But he hates chemically intrusive modern methods and ultimately forces Gale to confess his illegal operations to the Department of Agriculture.

Rose Dunn
Rose is the daughter of John and Bunny Dunn. Although she is just five years old, she has already experienced the onset of puberty owing to exposure to hormones in the medicine-laced dust out on the feedlot.

Dyann

The black woman in the Massachusetts lesbian couple shown on *My American Wife!*, Dyann is more forthright and convivial than her partner. She is a writer and shares some of her research with Jane.

Emil

Jane met Emil, her former husband—a Zairean graduate student—at Kyoto University, when he chased her down on a running path. Jane's failure to conceive a child ended their marriage after five years.

Fred Flowers

Fred Flowers is one member of a couple featured on *My American Wife!* Irritated by the television shoot, Fred casually reveals during an episode that he has been having an affair; he then leaves his wife. In the end they get back together.

Suzie Flowers

Suzie Flowers, the novel's dithering first "American wife," becomes the butt of humor when her reaction to the revelation of Fred's affair is overlaid with a *boing* sound effect. She hounds Kenji's office until he sends a copy of the episode, complete with false happy ending. She shows it to Fred, and, fulfilling that ending, they get back together.

S. Kato

Kato, Jane's former boss at a Japanese TV production company, is the one who hires Jane to work on *My American Wife!* Jane sends proposals to him by fax.

Kenji

Kenji, the producer of *My American Wife!*, lives in New York City, but he would rather be in Tokyo.

Mrs. Klinck

In Oklahoma, Mrs. Klinck's veal sends Oda to the hospital.

Lara

The white woman in the lesbian couple in Massachusetts, Lara is apparently a computer programmer.

Mr. Little

Mr. Little, Jane's father, died of cancer. He met Michi Takagi while working as a botanist with the US Army, examining aftereffects of the atomic bomb dropped on Hiroshima.

Alberto "Bert" Martinez

Bert, as he now prefers to be called (for the name's Americanness), is Bobby's father; he lost his hand in a hay baler accident.

Bobby Martinez

The Mexican American son of Bert and Cathy Martinez is fond of his piglet, as shown in the brief scene depicting him.

Catalina "Cathy" Martinez

Cathy's dream had been to have an American son, so she and her husband moved from Mexico to Texas just before Bobby was born.

Mr. Oda

The most significant of the rotating directors of *My American Wife!*, Oda rubs Jane the wrong way with his superficiality. Jane takes over directing the show when he has an allergic reaction to the antibiotics in some veal.

Oh

Jane's soundman follows Suzuki's lead in the crew's various exploits.

Payne

Mrs. Payne is the Montana wife who makes beef fudge.

Sloan Rankin

Sloan is an internationally known saxophonist who is casually involved with Jane. Their relationship gradually becomes serious, though it happens in fits and starts because of their miscommunications.

Dave Schultz

Dave Schultz is the van driver on the episode featuring the Dunn family. He is an agricultural student at Colorado State University, and originally he says he dislikes talking but later discourses freely about the perils of industrial farming. He helps Jane understand what is going wrong at the Dunns' operation.

Suzuki

Suzuki, Jane's cameraman, matures rapidly when the gravity of Jane's more controversial shows sinks in. He has an instinct for shooting what Jane wants. He seems to love her, or at least he would like to have children with and support her.

Michi Takagi

It is not clear whether Jane's mother took her husband's last name, Little. She was a teacher of ikebana, the Japanese art of flower arranging, when she met Jane's father in Japan. Jane's mother is generally traditionalist in her mindset, though in a modern twist she makes up her own good-luck ritual before conceiving Jane. Michi has miscarried four times, and Jane's own miscarriage brings them to much greater understanding of each other's lives.

Jane Takagi-Little

Jane, who narrates the parts of the book that describe her own life, is the main protagonist and the author's alter ego (they share professions and racial identities). Jane enthusiastically jumps aboard the *My American Wife!* television project, but her documentarian's ideals clash with the commercial imperatives laid out by the show's sponsor. She walks a fine line in deferring to the beef industry's interests while also promoting more liberal views of America. Although she eventually loses her job, her self-produced documentary about the Dunn family and its business becomes a media phenomenon, and though she miscarries her and Sloan's baby, they are committed to trying again.

Becky Thayer

Becky and her picture-perfect bed-and-breakfast in Magnolia Springs are chosen by John Ueno over the Dawes family for *My American Wife!*

Nurse Tomoko

Highly sympathetic toward the injured—and evidently seriously abused—Akiko, Tomoko urges her to leave John. Akiko stops at Tomoko's house on her way to America and, suspecting the nurse might be a lesbian (just as Akiko might be), kisses her.

Akiko Ueno

The novel's secondary protagonist, Akiko is a thin (but formerly heavy) writer for maternity magazines (formerly for gory comics) who currently plays the role of the dutiful wife as well as possible. Her problem is that, perhaps subconsciously sabotaging her fertility, she has grown so thin, partly as a result of bulimia, that she has stopped menstruating. She warms to Jane's episodes of *My American Wife!* and, starting with the lamb chops, starts putting on weight again. However, her husband John is abusive toward

her. When she writes to Jane with a cry for help and John happens to find Jane's response, he goes so far as to rape Akiko, which is the last straw; after recovering at the hospital, she makes her way to America and a new life.

Joichi "John" Ueno

An advertising executive with no moral compass beyond the dictates of his employment, Joichi—who takes a liking to Jane's nicknaming him John (i.e., John "Wayne-o")—insists that "Beef is Best" and chastises Jane every time her shows stray from this motto. He channels his professional frustrations by abusing his wife, whom he also ridicules for failing to conceive a child. John drunkenly rapes Akiko. Akiko leaves him; and after Jane's Dunn exposé surfaces, John is demoted.

Mrs. Ueno

Mrs. Ueno, John's mother, visits Akiko in the hospital.

Wilson

Wilson runs the slaughterhouse near the Dunn & Son feedlot.

THEMES

Japanese Culture

The cultural domain of *My Year of Meats* is quite intricate in that the novel describes a Japanese television show filmed in America according to the dictates of a Japanese advertising agency working for an American syndicate. This setup provides ample space for nuanced interaction between the two cultures. Prominent throughout is commentary on American culture, as documented on film and in writing by Jane, while Japanese culture makes for a more embedded theme, implicitly suggested by, for example, Kato's and Ueno's responses to Jane's direction of the TV show, which are understood to reflect popular and corporate opinion in Japan. In terms of the prominent characters of the novel, the theme is largely contained within Akiko and John Ueno's relationship, as well as in the behavior of Suzuki and Oh.

Based on these three Japanese men, the picture is one of masculinity run amok. In a culture where, as the novel suggests, women are expected to be utterly deferential to husbands

TOPICS FOR FURTHER STUDY

- Write a scene in which Akiko and Jane reunite a year or longer after the end of *My Year of Meats*. Along with the women's conversation about what has happened, incorporate at least two flashback scenes directly showing recent developments, whether with regard to Akiko's pregnancy, Jane's family life, or other aspects of the women's lives.

- With several classmates, pick one of the families shown on or considered for *My American Wife!* during Jane's time as director—the Martinez, Beaudroux, Bukowsky, Dawes, or Thayer family or Lara and Dyann's family—and record your own version of their episode of the show. (The Dunns are excluded because of the graphic nature of the footage recorded there.) Mimic any footage shown or suggested in Ozeki's novel, and fill out the episode with scenes you devise. Reflecting Jane's direction, your treatment of the family should be respectful.

- Read *Candle in the Wind* (1995), a young-adult novel by Maureen Wartski, which depicts how the family of Harry Mizuno copes when, seeking help with his stalled car, Harry is shot by a fearful elderly white man. Also consult at least two news articles on the real-life 1992 killing of Yoshihiro Hattori. Then write an essay exploring the themes of the novel, comparing the real-life and fictional circumstances, and remarking on anything else to be learned from the incident.

- Write a research paper on the current state of industrial agriculture. Cover the latest scientific and political developments with regard to such concerns as bovine growth hormone, genetically modified foods, cloned animals, laboratory-produced meat, and overall consumer awareness.

- Write a research paper on the science and history of bovine spongiform encephalopathy (BSE), also called mad cow disease.

and other male superiors—to the point that a boss's comments on a woman's appearance are taken for granted, as in the 1950s in America— "John" Ueno all too easily slips into what becomes an unquestioned habit of beating his wife. He can, so he does. The male fertility specialist whom Akiko sees helps set up this unbalanced and twisted relationship by directly informing John about Akiko's self-destructive habits, knowing full well that John will punish his wife as he sees fit. The later doctor who realizes the abuse is happening, based on Akiko's injuries, at least implicitly supports Tomoko's efforts to prolong Akiko's hospital stay and help her, but there is clearly no expectation that the abuse should be reported to authorities, as there would be in modern America. Suzuki and Oh, meanwhile, are relatively harmless in their offhand misogynism (prejudice against women), as suggested by their firing air rifles at pornographic pictures; at no point do they treat real women that badly. But their eyes are opened to the idea of sensitivity—something that Japanese housewives broadly attribute to American men, according to Jane—when Jane's assistant makes a lewd comment about Christina Bukowsky, of all people, deeply offending Suzuki in particular. He and Oh, at least, appear ready to modify their ingrained Japanese masculinity.

Consumerism

Though American culture is praised in a sense for softening one or two Japanese men (through the example provided by Vern Beaudroux, for instance, who is a caring person and who is active in cooking, two stereotypically feminine roles), other aspects are slated for ethical demolition at Jane's hands. Foremost on the list of American problems is *consumerism*, an idea that connotes not just consuming things—buying them, eating them—but more fundamentally approaching the world with a consumerist attitude: viewing things, animals, and even people as little more than objects to be consumed. Indeed, this is the attitude at the heart of the dark side of the meat industry exposed by Jane through her documentary work. In the eyes of the manager (Gale) and employees of Dunn & Son, the cows brought to the feedlot and slaughterhouse are not living, breathing creatures: they are already just beef, food items to be consumed by paying customers. Thus, as far as Gale and his employees are concerned, it hardly matters what sorts of hormones, chemicals, and antibiotics are pumped into their bodies, nor does the animals' horrific experience of being slaughtered. In his view, beef is beef, and when it is sold, money is money.

Of course, while this perspective passed muster well through the mid-twentieth century, scientists eventually realized that everything pumped into the cow does not just disintegrate in the animal's body but persists to affect anyone who eats the animal. And this is not simply a matter of natural and harmless contamination, as the meat industry might suggest; some additives, such as DES (a synthetic estrogen that was used in cattle feed to stimulate growth), have been shown to have grave effects on human beings. A gripping irony is that DES was not just given to cows but was given directly to pregnant women, not because it was proven effective but because prescribing doctors dipped their hands into the rich pockets of DES-synthesizing companies; that is, doctors effectively enforced self-destructive consumerism among pregnant women simply because the companies paid them to promote the drugs. Consumerism is intimately linked with capitalism, and Jane singles out both ideologies for criticism.

Art and Society

Beyond the surface attention to both Japanese and American culture and, of course, the meat industry, *My Year of Meats* engages more quietly with a few tangential themes. Perhaps the most prominent such theme is the presence of mass media, specifically television, in modern society. In many respects, products of mass media are worthy of consideration as art. Newspaper reporting is a form of writing, of creating stories with words; fictional movies and television shows are often seen as more explicitly artistic, being created from scratch, or from broad ideas, rather than simply presenting reality as it is found.

A prime question, then, has to do with the degree of art to be found in Jane's documentaries. On the one hand, she strives toward the documentarian's ideal of representing reality as truthfully—if also as eye-openingly—as possible; her art is directly founded in reality. And yet, as the Flowers show most dramatically indicates, the producers of such a television show are not above turning reality into fiction for the sake of entertainment, not to mention, in this case, for the sake of selling the product of the show's sponsor. Indeed, most all forms of mass media

suffer from the influence of consumerism; no matter how much freedom the directors and producers may be given to make the entertaining or informative work they wish to create, the work must always be able to sell whatever the sponsors, the advertisers, are trying to sell. Such is the case with newspapers, magazines, television shows, and now websites as well, all of which depend on advertising. Even big-studio films, despite not usually featuring direct advertisements, use product placement to earn additional profits. Jane wants to see her documentaries as art, but only when she is able to escape the oversight of the Japanese production company—by pushing the envelope until she gets fired—is she able to create a documentary work that is unsullied by the rules of a looming sponsor.

Authenticity

Authenticity is one of Ozeki's favorite words in her debut novel, used pointedly by Jane, John, and Akiko with regard especially to the episodes of *My American Wife!* When and why, John wants to know, does a viewer consider an episode authentic? He tries to answer this question by having Akiko rate each show on authenticity, but her responses frustrate him. He imagines that the Beaudrouxs, for example, should be considered inauthentic, based on the haphazard way their adoptive children have been assembled into a family; and yet Akiko perceives the exact opposite, that based on the way the family members interact with and support each other, the family is entirely authentic. Meanwhile, he imagines that the Thayer episode, with its antique-filled bed-and-breakfast and high-class southern cuisine, ought to merit the highest marks in authenticity, but Akiko, again in contrast, finds the Thayer episode inauthentic. The novel does not really support Jane and Akiko's disparagement of the Thayers as such (without offering evidence, Jane dismisses their existence as "entirely predictable," while Akiko simply "didn't believe it"), but the reader gets the point: John's authenticity is based on the factual trappings of marriage and family—biological children, a well-appointed household, quality foodstuffs—while Jane and Akiko's is based on the emotional bonds one expects to find in a truly happy family. Most readers will agree that Akiko's conception of authenticity in a family is the ethically superior one, based not on materialism and conventionality but on care and loving relations.

Ozeki weaves the observations of Sei Shonagon, an eleventh century author, throughout the novel.

(© Valery Sidelnykov.Shutterstock.com)

Truth

What Jane ultimately wants to get at, in her filming as in her life, is the truth. Early on she thinks, "I believed, honestly, that I could use wives to sell meat in the service of a Larger Truth." She later affirms, "As a documentarian, you must strive for the truth." She recognizes that there are truths people *need* to be exposed to, since otherwise they may unwittingly jeopardize their own lives and their loved ones'—as Gale does in exposing Rose to hormones. And yet Jane also recognizes that sometimes, the clean truth is not good enough: she tries to tell Gale about what is happening, but he impulsively refuses to believe her—the truth is too shattering to him. Thus, with Gale as with many others, not just the truth but the truth wrapped in a rationally and emotionally gripping package seems to be what is needed. Many conscientious people can be satisfied with the truths conveyed by essay writers such as Dyann

and use what they learn to alter their own lives. With others, the truth must be presented dramatically to have the effect it ought to. Thus, even where Jane's documentary work involves the manipulation of sounds and images (and thus emotions), the splicing together of words and pictures for maximum effect, it may be a dramatized version of the truth, but in essence, it is still that same salvational truth.

STYLE

Documentary Fiction

Ozeki is herself an accomplished documentary filmmaker, a fact reflected not only in the career of the character of Jane Takagi-Little but also in the construction of the novel. The book itself is, of course, attributed to Jane, and so a documentary style is logical from within as well as without. One aspect of this style is the abundance of "primary sources" presented to the reader, such as faxes, Jane's journal entries, Akiko's poems, and newspaper and magazine articles. These fabricated documents lend realistic depth to the novel. Jane, in narrating, also takes several opportunities to report actual historical facts, such as regarding the history of DES and the real-life killing of Japanese exchange student Yoshihiro Hattori. Dave Schultz, as well, is inclined to launch into reporter-style digressions about the facts of industrial farming. All of the true facts and history documented in the course of the book serve to support the themes that Ozeki establishes through the plot of her story. The trials and tribulations of Jane, her mother, Akiko, Rose, and others are not mere fiction—they are fiction representing what is often heartbreaking reality.

Notably, Ozeki does not shy away from a bit of commentary on the documentary nature of her book. She gives the standard warning that any resemblance between the fictional characters and reality is "entirely coincidental"—a warning placed prominently in an author's note on its own page, just before the table of contents, rather than buried in the copyright page—with the note that real people and events are indeed referenced. Thus, when the fictional Jane writes, with regard to the 1902 book *Grammar School Geography*, "I'm a documentarian. I'm not making this up," one cannot help but smile and wonder just where the line between fiction and reality should be drawn.

Multicultural Literature

Through the turn of the twenty-first century, as cultural intermixing has become ever more prevalent owing in part to advances in global economic equality, education, transportation, communication, cross-cultural awareness, and acceptance of differences, multicultural novels have become ever more prominent. Often, these modern-day novels do not simply place a person from one culture within another one, like Henry James's *The American* (1877), or directly oppose two cultures through representative characters, like Chinua Achebe's *Things Fall Apart* (1958), but include characters who are themselves biracial or multiracial, scenes taking place in the two or more countries, and characters' passages to and from the different cultural contexts.

The bodies of work of internationally esteemed authors such as Jhumpa Lahiri, Junot Díaz, and Chimamanda Ngozi Adichie reflect the literary benefits of such a multicultural approach. Many, if not most, readers do not have the sorts of cross-cultural experiences that authors straddling more than one background do, so those authors can provide the most comprehensive and awareness-raising experience for readers by approaching the multicultural terrain from as many angles as possible. With *My Year of Meats*, Ozeki highlights a character who makes a point of pondering her identity as a biracial woman in America, as set in opposition to mainstream white Americans as well as a multiracial adoptive family, a Mexican American family, an African American family, and a biracial lesbian couple's family. Furthermore, the parallels and distinctions between the lives of Jane and Akiko offer commentary on how a Japanese American and a Japanese woman may come to both resemble each other and differ in part as a consequence of the cultural environments in which they have grown and matured.

HISTORICAL CONTEXT

The Rise of Organic Agriculture

As documentary fiction, Ozeki's novel makes a point of informing the reader of historical background relevant to the plot, especially with regard to the use of diethylstilbestrol (DES) in pregnant women and in industrial farming—and merely placing those two spheres of life so closely together suggests that something was profoundly wrong—into the late twentieth century. What she reveals about the beef industry is, by and large, unpalatable to say the least, enough to turn many a reader's stomach and perhaps inspire people to vegetarianism, with Lara and Dyann as role models.

On a more positive historical note, the reader might turn away from the grotesque aspects of industrial agriculture and toward the modern development of organic farming. Throughout history, of course, farmers have used natural means to encourage the growth of crops and control weeds and other pests. In the early twentieth century, even before chemical pesticides had come into wide use, agriculture was being industrialized: larger and more efficient machines allowed for the planting and harvesting of crops at amazing rates. Yet by the 1920s, many people recognized that industrial farming, focusing on efficiency and profit, was compromising the health of the organic part of the soil, the *humus*. These farmers took care to use manure and compost rather than synthetic fertilizers, include soil-enriching plants (not just cash crops) in field rotations, and add natural rock dust to enhance the soil's mineral content. By 1940, this style of farming was called *organic* to acknowledge the way farmers' care of the soil mimicked the self-maintenance of a biological organism.

It was around this time that chemicals developed for military use during World War II were recognized as capable of killing insects and redeveloped as pesticides. Given the undeniable effectiveness of such pesticides as DDT and the collective ignorance regarding long-term effects, farmers overwhelmingly adopted such chemical methods of crop maintenance. Organic farmers became a fringe community ridiculed for their backward, unproductive ways. Nonetheless, the movement gathered pace in Britain, spread to Australia, and gained traction in America—especially with the publication of Rachel Carson's environmental study *Silent Spring* (1962), which described the potential for a world without birds owing to the chemical contamination of the environment accomplished by the unchecked use of pesticides. The naturalist orientation of the 1960s counterculture helped sustain the development of a commercial organic niche in the agricultural world.

COMPARE
&
CONTRAST

- **1990s:** While research indicated by 1953 that the hormone DES was ineffective in treating miscarriages and in fact actually caused them, doctors continued to prescribe it until 1971. Thanks to grassroots activism carried out by the nonprofit DES Action USA, Congress passes the DES Education and Research Amendments of 1992, establishing the first national program for research, outreach, and education to improve scientific knowledge and public awareness of DES and its effects.

  Today: In 2012, after extended litigation, more than fifty "DES Daughters"—women exposed to DES in the womb—who developed breast cancer were found in federal court to be entitled to settlements from the drug companies who produced the DES taken by their mothers during pregnancy.

- **1990s:** Bovine spongiform encephalopathy (BSE), known as mad cow disease—caused by cows being fed other dead animals—is found in more than a hundred thousand cattle in Britain through the early 1990s. The British government denies that humans can be infected, until some ten cases of its variant Creutzfeldt-Jakob disease are concluded in 1996 to have been caused in humans by BSE-contaminated meat. Some 4.5 million cows are slaughtered, and Britain's beef industry collapses.

  Today: In the United States, despite bans on using deceased ruminants (animals such as sheep and deer), chicken manure, and restaurant scraps as feed for cows, cases of BSE still arise from time to time. In 2012, Japan bans imports from Brazil based on the case of a single disease-carrying cow's death.

- **1990s:** In 1990, with sales of organic goods reaching an estimated $1 billion, Congress passes the Organic Foods Production Act to create a federal body to define and enforce nationwide rules for organic agriculture, the National Organic Standards.

  Today: In 2013, the Food and Drug Administration proposes a new rule that would require larger farms to wait nine months—increased from four months—before harvesting from a field on which manure has been spread as fertilizer. Scientists say that the disease-causing bacterium *Escherichia coli* (*E. coli*) in manure can survive for up to three hundred days, but Jim Crawford of Pennsylvania's New Morning Farm, one of many organic farmers objecting to the rule, affirms that in forty years his produce has never made anyone sick. An organic spinach contamination in 2006 was determined not to have come from manure.

Through the 1960s and 1970s, organic products were sold farther and farther afield, and organizations evolved to certify that farms were indeed using organic methods. The first was California Certified Organic Farmers, established in 1973 (the year that DDT was finally banned in the United States). By the decade's end, landmark studies were recognizing the benefits of organic agriculture for both the environment and consumers, such as the US Department of Agriculture's *Report and Recommendations on Organic Farming* (1980). Through the 1990s and beyond, organic foods were being sold not just in natural foods stores but in chain supermarkets as well. These include not only fruits, vegetables, and grains but also meats, with the federal National Organic Standards stipulating that there must be no pesticide content in animal feed, no use of hormones and antibiotics, and no genetic modification of either plants or animals, among other requirements. Some products, while not meeting the stringent organic requirements, still make a point of raising food more naturally, such as with grass-fed cows or free-range chickens.

Although Jane is a documentary filmmaker, she takes a job producing a Japanese cooking show.
(© iodrakon | Shutterstock.com)

Ozeki makes only passing reference to the organic movement in *My Year of Meats*—at one point, craving meat while pregnant, Jane decides to buy organic, perhaps because her focus is on documenting the ills of the industrial meat industry. Of course, where those industrial ills are society's collective problem, the solution is organic.

CRITICAL OVERVIEW

Reviewers largely greeted *My Year of Meats* with warm praise, occasionally qualified, with appreciation not only for its bold treatment of important societal issues but also for the quality of the narrative. A *Publishers Weekly* reviewer praises the "fluent, entertaining prose" in this "sharp-witted cross-cultural satire." In a judgment as much of readers as of the book itself, the reviewer observes, "Those captivated by the

novel's initial light, witty tone and romantic sub-plot may balk at the heavy message toward the end." The honorable intent, the reviewer recognizes, is that "readers are forced to face the grim realities of modern-day cattle farming."

Booklist reviewer Joanne Wilkinson was among those least favorable to Ozeki's novel. Wilkinson acknowledges (with what seems a dash of sarcasm at the end) that *My Year of Meats* "has some fine touches, including a pleasing prose style, the feisty, independent protagonist, and her modern relationship with her attractive musician boyfriend." Seeming to resent that a novel should be anything but an entertaining story, Wilkinson continues: "However, in striving for complexity, Ozeki overloads her narrative with too many issues . . . , and her intermittent diatribes on cattle ranching bring her story to a screeching halt." On the other hand, *Library Journal* reviewer Shirley N. Quan finds that Ozeki has "cleverly" constructed the novel, which "skillfully tackles hard-pressing issues" and "is unique in presentation yet moving and entertaining."

Through the late 2000s and into the 2010s *My Year of Meats* has been subject to a steady stream of in-depth criticism, as the novel's array of themes lend it significance from multiple critical perspectives. In "Rational and Irrational Choices: Form, Affect, and Ethics," David Palumbo-Liu observes that generally speaking, "Ozeki's novel has been met with enthusiasm, especially for its wit, intelligence, and progressive politics." Palumbo-Liu's focus is on the ethics promoted by the novel, leading him to affirm that the author "has constructed an ambitious, progressive novel that seeks to educate, persuade, anger, and motivate its readers toward all sorts of what I consider positive action—anticorruption, anticorporate, antimisogynistic, antichauvinist, antiracist, antisexist, the list goes on."

Other critics have considered the novel from economic, sociological, cross-cultural, ecological, and feminist perspectives, among others. Yoo Kim, in a *Foreign Literature Studies* essay, concludes, "This novel stands as a triumphal feat of resistance."

CRITICISM

Michael Allen Holmes

Holmes is a writer with existential interests. In the following essay, he considers how the vocation of

WHAT DO I READ NEXT?

- Readers may find Ozeki's third novel, *A Tale for the Time Being* (2013), to be more palatable than *My Year of Meats*. In this more recent work, Ozeki again employs dual protagonists, one a stand-in for the author—a writer also named Ruth, living in British Columbia—the other a young woman who was living in Tokyo when the 2011 tsunami struck. The novel was short-listed for Britain's prestigious Man Booker Prize.

- *The Pillow Book*, the tenth-century book by Sei Shōnagon so appreciated by both Akiko and Jane, has been translated into several modern English editions, including Meredith McKinney's 2006 edition. The diary of Shōnagon's daily thoughts is considered a major Japanese classic.

- Another Japanese classic is *The Tale of Genji*, written by the noblewoman Murasaki Shikibu in the eleventh century. This novel—considered among world literature's first—relies less on plot than on in-depth characterization over an extended period of time. It was translated in 1998 by Jakucho Setouchi, a novelist with a colorful past who became a Buddhist nun; her translation enhances the focus on the novel's female characters.

- The young-adult novel *The Language Inside* (2013), by Holly Thompson, depicts an American-born teenager who has come to identify with the culture she has been raised in, that of Japan, but must move to Massachusetts when her mother undergoes treatment for breast cancer.

- Julie Otsuka's novel *The Buddha in the Attic* (2011) illuminates the ways Japanese women have historically been regarded and treated by men, especially in the United States, by following the lives of a group of young Japanese women who travel to America as "picture brides"—married off by photograph to Japanese men who have already emigrated—early in the twentieth century.

- A good first-person account of the impact of the DES era is provided in the documentary *A Healthy Baby Girl* (1997), by filmmaker Judith Helfand, whose mother took DES and who underwent a hysterectomy at age twenty-five. The film further delves into familial relationships and attitudes toward motherhood in Jewish American culture.

- Another documentary filmmaker who has approached the meat industry and its extensions is Morgan Spurlock, who, as shown in his film *Super Size Me* (2004), attempted the audacious feat of surviving on nothing but McDonald's food for an entire month. He gained over twenty pounds and lost ground in other markers of general health. The work highlights the willing harmfulness of the fast-food industry and its role in the American obesity epidemic. Spurlock went on to publish the related volume *Don't Eat This Book: Fast Food and the Supersizing of America* (2006).

---

the narrator of My Year of Meats *seems to compromise her personal integrity.*

The moral character of the first-person protagonist of a major novel is one of the most intriguing points of interest in literature. No person, one might argue, is flawless, but when a character is being presented to the reader in his or her own words, it is quite possible that any personal flaws will be either unaddressed, glossed over, or outright lied about. Sometimes the words of such a protagonist are intentionally crafted by the author to make the reader suspicious about the protagonist's credibility; this is the *unreliable narrator*, a device played to the hilt by postmodern authors seeking (sometimes vainly) to redouble the depth of their narratives.

In Ruth L. Ozeki's *My Year of Meats*, Jane does not appear to be an unreliable narrator. If a documentary filmmaker shows the slightest hint of personal deception, the truthfulness of his or her films will be cast into doubt, and then the film is not a documentary any more; it is simply fiction. Director Michael Moore ran into this sort of trouble in manipulating for film the chronology of a pivotal conversation with National Rifle Association president Charlton Heston, seriously marring what could have been a nation-changing documentary on gun control in America, *Bowling for Columbine* (2002). With Ozeki's novel, the reader is certainly not meant to second-guess the conclusions Jane draws and captures on film with regard to hormones and the horrors of the modern meat industry. Nor, it seems, should the reader doubt that Jane has accurately depicted any of the novel's action. Nonetheless, there is a degree of duplicity (deceptiveness) about Jane, which she herself acknowledges, but which may still lead the reader to conclude that she is not as morally upstanding as she would like to consider herself.

The reader familiar with Ozeki's background may be aware that she was ordained as a Zen priest in 2010, and *My Year of Meats* does contain a passing reference to Zen, when Suzuki and Oh are filming Christina Bukowsky by following her in a second wheelchair: "When a cameraman gets under the skin of his subject like that, the resulting images are zen in their oneness." The lowercasing of the typically capitalized word may hint at the looseness with which Ozeki is applying Zen philosophy to the situation at hand. In fact, Zen might be most concisely characterized as something like "full existence in the immediate present," and with just a moment's reflection one sees that Zen and television cannot really coexist: when one watches television, regardless of what is being shown on the screen—a cartoon, a film, a live musical performance, a sporting event, a morally upstanding documentary—one is anywhere but the *here* and now. One is *there*, wherever the image on the TV is; except one is not really there, participating in what one sees, but is merely watching *there* from somewhere else entirely. Some people can get so absorbed in a TV show that they will entirely fail to hear conversation being carried out in the same room, even when their name is repeated several times in

a row; if anything, this is anti-Zen, full existence outside of the immediate present.

Of course, one can *create* a television show without necessarily sinking into the anti-Zen state represented in watching it—or can one? It is hard to know if one has never worked in the television/film industry, and part of the value of *My Year of Meats* is that Ozeki has indeed worked in that industry, and so she can accurately convey not only what the experience is like, but also, intentionally or not, the effects it may have on one's personality.

Morality-wise, fictional filmmaker Jane Takagi-Little is not shy about proclaiming her documentarian's ideals, which are a far cry from the typical commercial TV producer's ideals. In her most pointed comment, she writes, "As a documentarian, you must strive for the truth and believe in it wholeheartedly." (Notably, this formulation depends upon an ideal of truthfulness and yet, in suggesting that it must be *believed* in, implies that the truth cannot be either *known* or *proven*.) When it comes to her interactions with John Ueno, who is in charge of the BEEF-EX account and is thus effectively her boss, Jane is sure to distance herself from his will: "He was base. His wanton capitalist mandate had nothing to do with my vocation." It may be true that his mandate has nothing to do with her self-conception as a documentarian, but the statement is misleading at best, a lie at worst, because to the extent that her vocation is (currently) director of *My American Wife!*, his mandate has everything to do with it; BEEF-EX's money is calling the shots, and she must heed Ueno's words whether she wants to or not. It is all, of course, part of the television business.

The fundamental duplicity in Jane's ambivalent employment under a beef sponsor is quite apparent, and few readers will hold against her the fact that she takes this job and manages it as best she can. Many people know the difficulties that come along with accepting much-needed work despite one's distaste for it, whether intellectual, physical, or moral. But Jane's duplicity goes well beyond this, becoming more evident the more she reveals of the filming and editing of the show's episodes. In filming Lara and Dyann in their home, for example, there is a point where the couple are discussing themselves and their family on camera while Jane acts as custodian of their two daughters, who are sitting on her lap. At just the right moment, when Lara playfully punches Dyann on the arm, Jane "set them on their feet and pushed them forward," and into the blossoming family fray they went. Jane goes on to profess, "I felt the warm smugness that comes over me when I know that there is another heart-wrenching documentary moment at hand, being exquisitely recorded." There are two problems here. First of all, Jane's delight at this scene of inclusive family love appears to be entirely based on self-interest. Her words do not suggest true compassion—the emotional foundation of Buddhism—but rather prideful contentment with her own accomplishment in capturing the scene on film. And then, she calls this a "documentary moment," as if suggesting that what has been recorded is unvarnished reality, and yet Lara and Dyann have been coddled and encouraged to brighten their moods, and the TV crew's presence (with bright lights and all) has surely amped up the girls' emotional states, all leading up to Jane's perfectly timed release of the girls, such that there is very little that is genuine about this "documentary moment"; it is exquisitely formulated for the sake of the show. Jane proceeds to the editing, and again her duplicity comes to the surface: "And so I continued, taking out the stutters and catches from the women's voices, creating a seamless flow in a reality that was no longer theirs and not quite so real anymore." It is curious that she can, in the confines of a single sentence, refer to what is "not quite so real" as "a reality"—either something is *real* or it is not.

It is bad enough that Jane does not seem entirely aware of these minor duplicities or moral inconsistencies. It becomes worse when her shortcomings have direct effects on the women she interacts with. There is the fiasco that the Flowers show becomes, but Jane does not direct that show and hardly deserves the blame. Curiously, though, while Jane claims that her job title was "coordinator" at the time—not director or producer or even camera-woman—she later inflates her role, stating of Suzie Flowers: "The worn fabric of her life tore like tissue under the harsh exposure of my camera; I watched it happen, took aim, exposed her, then shot her in the heart." The only claim regarding Jane's role that seems to be truthful there is that she "watched it happen." If Jane deserves any blame as far as that fiasco is concerned, it is for decidedly ignoring Suzie when she later hounds the studio for a copy of the episode, as if Suzie is nothing more than an obnoxious telemarketer. In July, Jane returns from Quam to find, among other work-related items on her desk, "a couple of messages from Suzie Flowers, which I tossed in the trash." Her excuse?: "I felt bad, but it was Kenji's job to deal with her." But she knows that Kenji has stonewalled her, and Suzie has been trying to contact Jane in particular, person to person. Yet Jane denies her that connection. Then in September, when Kenji tells Jane that "that Flowers woman has been calling almost every day," Jane says, "Sure, Kenji, I'll handle it. Good-bye." She now does assume responsibility for communicating with Suzie; nonetheless, as narrator she then promptly declares, "I had no time for Suzie Flowers today." That is, when she told Kenji she would handle it, she was lying. Kenji finally persuades Jane to call Suzie in January of the new year, after he has already sent her the tape of the show, which improbably resulted in a happy ending. In her presentation of Suzie's happy ending in the context of her own, Jane implicitly takes credit for it.

There is some similarly incriminating miscommunication that takes place between Jane and Helen Dawes. Jane, as the reader knows, is desperately hoping that the Dawes family will be selected by Ueno for presentation on the show. Yet as much as she is hoping for this result, logically she must realize that this will not be the case; Ueno has already professed his preference for the Thayer family, and Jane knows Ueno well enough to realize that nothing about the Dawes family will have made him change his mind. Nevertheless, as Jane tells Helen good-bye at the end of her scouting trip with Ueno, she is unnecessarily theatrical: "'We'll be back,' I said loudly, for Ueno's benefit, as we got ready to leave. 'We'll see you again, soon.'" In her mind she is only trying to manage the circumstance to get Ueno to agree to film the Dawes; but she is doing so by telling what, again, proves to be a lie.

They will not be back, and they will not see Helen again soon, and if Jane had been more sensitive, she would have realized that those were inappropriate things to say to Helen. In a word, she gambled with Helen's emotions in order to get the show she wanted, and she lost—or rather, Helen lost. That Jane yet does not believe she has done anything wrong becomes evident later, when she says with regard to the show's disappointment of the Dawes family, "I can defend myself; that's not the problem. Miss Helen was not my fault. As things go, she barely counts as a casualty at all." Not only does Jane deny fault when, in fact, the fault in communication was hers and hers alone, but she refers to Miss Helen in a dehumanizing way, rendering her no more than an object or an event; the sentence "Miss Helen was not my fault" makes sense only if Miss Helen is being considered not as a human being but as the embodiment of a mistake.

Jane seems to get to the heart of this moral matter when she directly comments on the duplicitous nature of her job. She acknowledges that she occasionally has a "cavalier" attitude—that is, offhand and dismissive—toward the wives, but then suggests that that attitude is actually a "pretense," or insincere display. Already her mental state is more than murky. She continues: "The fact is, I did care, and at the same time I couldn't afford to care, and these two contrary states lived side by side." What is interesting is that Jane seems content to, in a manner of speaking, both care and not care, at any given time favoring whichever of those moral angles is more convenient. She even reduces it to a labeled mental state—"Psychiatrists call this 'doubling'"—suggesting that she might blame the chemistry of her brain (a common practice in the twenty-first century) and take no responsibility for it. Her intent to shed the blame is made startlingly explicit in the closing pages:

> I would like to think of my "ignorance" less as a personal failing and more as a massive cultural trend, an example of doubling, of psychic numbing, that characterizes the end of the millennium....Maybe this exempts me as an individual.

Regardless of whether Jane or her job or the world at large is to blame for her psychology, her habit of "doubling," of being duplicitous, pops up in numerous additional instances that do her discredit. About speaking to the congregation in Harmony, Mississippi, she writes, "I persevered,

speaking slowly and, I hoped, sincerely." Is she really so alienated from her own state of mind that she can only "hope" she is speaking sincerely? Before going to Chicago, she remarks in consecutive paragraphs: "I don't want to see Sloan. That is such a lie. Of course I do. He is picking me up at the airport." Speaking to her own mother, she reveals how practiced she is at emotional concealment: "'I didn't mean to...,' I said in that normal voice I can use even when I'm weeping and my heart is breaking." Despite Jane's default mode of deceit, her mother more than anyone seems attuned to the nuances of her personality:

> This is trouble with you. You *think* you want, you *don't think* you want—always back and forth. Me, when I want, it is with whole heart. I look at wanted thing with eyes straight on. But you! Neither here or there. Your looking always crooked, from side of eye. It has no power to hold. So wanted thing, it slip away from you.

Although she does not appear to intend to, Jane's mother here gives a description that zeroes in on the surprising link between Jane's honorable vocation as a documentarian and her moral wishy-washiness: The documentarian at work can never simply appreciate reality as it is; she must always be looking at the cameraman, or the soundman, or the lighting, or the image in her mind of what the finished product will look like. The documentarian is necessarily at least one step removed from the full experience of immediate reality.

Thus does Jane, being semipermanently removed from reality, arrive at a very unstable conception of the truth itself: "At first I believed in a truth that existed—singular, empirical, absolute. But slowly,...I realized that truth was like race and could be measured only in ever-diminishing approximations." Of course, here she is not referring to actual truth, the truths to be found in actual reality—many really are black-and-white—but to the "truths" that she presents in her documentaries, where one only sees what has been "exquisitely recorded," scenes that are "not quite so real." Based on all her subtle lies and half-truths, it is not clear whether Jane can distinguish the televised sort of truth from actual truth. By the end of the novel, she hardly seems to know what truth is:

> There's no denying, I thought. In the Year of Meats, truth wasn't stranger than fiction; it *was* fiction. Ma says I'm neither here nor there, and if that's the case, so be it. Half documentarian, half fabulist...Maybe sometimes you have to make things up, to tell truths that alter outcomes.

Joichi Ueno, nicknamed "John Wayno," works for BEEF-EX and is a critical husband. (© imtmphoto /
Shutterstock.com)

That last assertion is highly debatable—it could be argued that one never has to make things up in order to tell *truths* of any kind—as is the contention that truth can *be* fiction, that the two can be equivalent; but, like a number of other uncertain statements in Jane's narrative, these two go uncontested. Still, in the end, it is Jane's narrative, and it need not be perfectly truthful to be effective. Readers can ask themselves whether the truths that this novel undeniably conveys would ever have been encountered if they were not encapsulated in this absorbing fictional narrative. If not, Jane's goal, which is truth, indeed justifies Ozeki's means, which is fiction.

Source: Michael Allen Holmes, Critical Essay on *My Year of Meats*, in *Novels for Students*, Gale, Cengage Learning, 2015.

Monica Chiu

In the following excerpt, Chiu points out how Ozeki juxtaposes opposite concepts.

...The novel's plot revolves around Jane Takagi-Little and Akiko Ueno, whose introduction arises through beef. Born in Quam, Minnesota, Jane is the product of a Japanese mother and an Anglo American father. While residing in New York City, she is appointed coordinator for *My American Wife!*, a televised documentary series promoting American beef to Japan-based consumers through the televised depiction of a 1950s fantasy family world reminiscent of *Father Knows Best* or *Leave It to Beaver*. The series' Tokyo-based producer is Akiko's husband, Joichi Ueno, who demands that his wife rate the shows for "Deliciousness of Meat" and "Educational Value, Authenticity, [and] Wholesomeness" of the programs' families (Ozeki 1998:21); spousal disagreements over the series' reality factor—especially considering that "the commercials were to bleed into the documentaries, and documentaries were to function as commercials"—provoke him to verbally, physically, and sexually abuse his wife, more so when he is frequently drunk. Akiko is expected to dutifully prepare the featured meals to "put some meat on her bones" and provide a family heir, preferably a male one.

Meanwhile, Jane is diagnosed with a damaged fallopian tube—she will never provide biological progeny. And beef, she discovers, is the culprit: while pregnant with Jane, her mother was prescribed vitamins containing growth hormones that were initially developed to fatten cattle quickly at the trough. Thought to prevent women from miscarrying, they were later linked to in utero birth defects. Through Jane's and Akiko's struggles with beef, meat production foreshadows a figurative consumption of women who battle both men and infertility.

The chapter's organizing principle is the dichotomy inside/outside given its salience to the permeability of bodily borders (*in*gesting what is *ex*ternal) and given its indispensability for discussing the novel's many related binaries, including but not limited to white/Other, purity/ pollution, production/consumption, true/false, natural/artificial, and fertile /infertile. In a host of critical work, from anthropology to psychoanalysis, from food culture to poststructuralism, "inside" is privileged above "outside" because it allows us the illusion of bodily and intellectual control; if we cannot manage what occurs outside of our bodily borders, at least we can negotiate what flows in and out of them. In religious food taboos, for example, the sullying of one's "clean" corporeal interiority (as a pure spiritual place) occurs through the ingestion of tabooed or unclean alimentary matter. But what is dirty is both complicated and politicized when considering that the Hindu taboo against fowl can be explained as "a negative reaction to their [chicken and egg] use by Moslems, or ... in a desire to distinguish between their [Hindus' clean] way of life and that of tribal peoples who use fowl in ceremonial propitiation" (Frederick J. Simoons 1994:150). Feminist and psychoanalytic critics refer to "dangerous" and "polluted" corporeal social transgressions that disturb any strict division between the two halves of the socially constructed binaries. Homosexuality, for example, vexes the so-called separation of male and female. According to Judith Butler, the porosity and *not* the solidity of sex and gender constructions threaten the seemingly impermeable, unchangeable, and comfortably homogeneous social

> THROUGH JANE'S AND AKIKO'S STRUGGLES WITH BEEF, MEAT PRODUCTION FORESHADOWS A FIGURATIVE CONSUMPTION OF WOMEN WHO BATTLE BOTH MEN AND INFERTILITY."

orders under which all bodies are forced to "harmoniously" operate (1990:132).

In anthropology, "[A]nything which either symbolically or in reality emerges from the body [such as spit, semen, menstrual blood, breast milk, to name a few], or which has been sullied by contact with a body aperture" is dirty, says Lawrence S. Kubie, even if its former existence within the body is deemed proper, clean (1937:391). Take the moisture in one's mouth— the normal, cleansing, digestive bodily product called saliva—which is benign (and alternately clean, useful, pure, sanitary) as long as it remains inside its proper oral cavity. Once ejected, it becomes filthy and impure, as in the invective, "I spit upon you," or the grimaces evoked when a parent "cleans" a child's face with a mouth-moistened handkerchief.

Similar pure/impure designations surround hair and fingernails, considered neutral as they grow within their proper places (on the head, at the ends of fingers). But hair is immediately rendered disgusting as unattached strands on the bathroom floor, and fingernails are dirty as stray, half-moon nail clippings embedded in the carpet or discovered under sofa cushions. More important and more interesting, then, is the tenuous space located within the slash (/), an in-between-ness that "does not respect borders, positions, rules." Mediated by a slash that both unites and separates, the two halves are not mutually exclusive but rather their interdependence invites ambiguity and vulnerability of the two terms' accepted denotations. In a direct reference to Mary Douglas's theory of dirt as "matter out of place," Judith Butler states, "Douglas suggests that all social systems are vulnerable at their margins, and that all margins are accordingly considered dangerous. If the body is synecdochal for the social system *per se* or a site in which open systems converge, then any kind of unregulated permeability constitutes a site of pollution and endangerment" (Butler 1990:132). Butler concludes accordingly:

> What constitutes through division the "inner" and "outer" worlds of the subject is a border and boundary tenuously maintained for the purposes of social regulation and control. The boundary between the inner and the outer is confounded by those excremental passages in which the inner effectively becomes outer, and this excreting function becomes, as it were, the model by which other forms of identity-differentiation are accomplished. In effect, this is the mode by which Others become s—. (pp. 133–134).

The inside/outside dichotomy is therefore nothing but a "crude system of values" according to Kilgour, a rather simplistic hierarchy wherein a good *inside* is too easily privileged above a bad *outside* (p. 4).

That which must be symbolically evicted beyond (bodily, identificatory) borders retains negative metaphoric associations (Other, abject, the maternal, s—), implying that if one intends to retain accepted social systems, the inside must be maintained as a space of the good, the clean, and the pure, while the outside must represent a repository of the bad, the dirty, and the impure. Yet this other's (this rejected's) former existence as part and parcel of an inside interrogates and prohibits any restrictive division between what is self and what is not, between in and out, and between pure and polluted. In rejecting what we loathe, revile, and ultimately fear, we castigate those aspects of ourselves—from which we erroneously think we can so easily separate—that we find mirrored in others. The fact of mutual inexclusivity becomes both problem and cause for the characters in Ozeki's novel on many fronts: for those who fight to keep what is contaminated outside the clean interior of the body; for those who claim to know truth over fiction; and for those who delude themselves into possessing control over what crosses and what remains confined within bodily and national borders. Definitions of clean and dirty, of truth, national good, and healthy food are not definitive, confounding any character's attempts to ingest, literally and figuratively, what is good for him or her.

Food's status as either disgusting or delectable has always pivoted in the space of the slash (/), based on human classification by one (dominant) subset of people for their own finicky and fluctuating tastes in a manner that shapes its

meanings for other groups of people. I return to the wild boar.... It was once considered a food of marginal edibility, deemed palatable for only poor individuals who can hunt and prepare the meat at little cost. But recently the wild boar has been elevated to a sought-after, exotic delicacy, gracing the tables of expensive restaurants for wealthy individuals who prefer that others kill and prepare their meated meals—for a very high price.

Along similar lines, what is coded as "wild," "gamey," and hence "distasteful" or "unrefined" is rarely found at the local meat counter, neatly wrapped in cellophane; rather, such game is shot in the wild and consumed by a population deemed to possess a less sophisticated palate until the food in question becomes the delicacy of the day. Consider, for example, the repugnance by which many Americans in the late 1970s viewed the skunk-, porcupine-, woodpecker-, egret-, and eagle-eating habits of Hmong refugees—an eating pattern structured by wartime necessity. Many Americans continue to be disgusted by the "frog-eating Frenchman and the dog-eating Chinese"; and the inedibility of Japanese sushi was loudly proclaimed until its introduction as an expensive delicacy.

In a broader context, food has (ill-)served as a cultural signifier. When speaking of race relations, food often embodies the palatable side of an "other," a side that many Americans find easier to digest than these so-called others' religious, familial, and social practices. Imbibing what others eat is to embody a cultural difference—to ingest that other—in its most simplistic sense, sating the necessity to exert a more concerted effort toward knowing a particular group of people outside of frequenting a Chinese, Mexican, or Indian restaurant for one's weekly fill of culture.

Furthermore, beef to vegetarians and animal activists represents unnecessary cruelty to animals and has sparked debates over animal rights in research laboratories. Meat's gruesome production, vividly discussed in Upton Sinclair's *The Jungle* (1946) and illustrated in Ozeki's slaughterhouse scenes, reveals larger issues surrounding the rise of unions and prohibitions against child labor as well as more recent laws concerning safe and sanitary working conditions and the standardization of hygienic food processing. The place of food preparation, likewise, has traditionally been a female gendered one, on which Joichi happily capitalizes in his televised images of domesticated women. Yet tradition also notes that the rise of the predominantly male realm of haute cuisine conveniently "borrowed" recipes from its female originators. The "low" of cooking becomes the "high" of cuisine—paralleling how the "low" of pig metamorphoses into the "high" of exotic pork—once it is divorced from women, yet the trace of domestic, female contribution defies any such stark distinction.

If "gamey" sells, "exotic" becomes a convenient advertising euphemism for foods previously considered inedible, elaborating on alimentary categorizations and hierarchizations. Character Joichi's proclamation that "Beef is best" over all other meat poses an interesting foray into food taboos and the changing Japanese diet (Ozeki 1998:12). Joichi, who advocates meat's superiority over the so-called lesser grains of bread and rice, ignores the history of Japan's hesitant acceptance of beef in his television marketing campaigns. That is, consumption of beef was initially forbidden by sixth-century Japanese Buddhism to exhibit mercy toward all living creatures. Much later, the Japanese regarded the product, quite derogatorily, as Western and therefore barbaric. Yet with the rise of modernization and Westernization, and the American occupation of (and influence within) Japan after World War II, the Japanese accepted, even revered, beef. In fact, a dish dubbed "a civilized bowl of rice" contained beef or pork slices, states Emiko Ohnuki-Tierney (1997:166–167). However, the Japanese Eta, the "slaughterhouse caste" who handle cattle butchering and hide tanning, are still castigated as untouchables, the reviled, and the socially abjected, relegating beef production—as socially stigmatizing—considerably less civilized than the act of beef eating itself (Simoons 1994:210). Despite beef's current growing popularity among Japanese youth, meat still takes a backseat to the Japanese staple, rice (Ohnuki-Tierney 1997:168). The stubborn and ignorant Joichi intends, through the aggressive television series *My American Wife!*, to forcefully incorporate beef into the lives and bodies of Japanese citizens.

In the heavily meat-eating West, however, rice is tantamount to bread: the latter may be privileged as a national staple, but it lacks the prestige afforded to beef. Carol J. Adams (1990) reports how, historically, "intellectually superior"

> WHEN I START WRITING THESE NOVELS, I GO INTO THEM WITH A SPIRIT OF INQUIRY, RATHER THAN TO SUBSTANTIATE PREJUDICES I HAD IN THE BEGINNING. IF YOU DON'T DO THAT, YOU CAN'T WRITE GOOD CHARACTERS."

people (men in general and white men in particular) have been urged to eat meat. Adams considers expressions coupling strength and virility with that of beef, such as "beefing something up" or "getting to the meat of the matter." It is no wonder that in many stateside locations, the luxury of consuming a piece of bloody meat is prized far above consuming a loaf of bread (albeit many vegetarians would disagree). . . .

Source: Monica Chiu, "Inside the Meat Machine: Food, Filth, and (In)Fertility in Ruth Ozeki's *My Year of Meats*," in *Filthy Fictions: Asian American Literature by Women,* AltaMira Press, 2004, pp. 135–40.

Andi Zeisler and Ruth Ozeki

In the following interview, Ozeki explains how she made the jump from making documentary films to writing novels.

Ruth Ozeki's acclaimed debut novel, *My Year of Meats*, has probably converted more than a few readers to vegetarianism. Channeling an engaging mix of Upton Sinclair and Haruki Murakami, Ozeki tells the story of Jane Takagi-Little, a Japanese American filmmaker who lands a gig producing a Japanese TV show called *My American Wife!* This romanticization of Middle America—sponsored by U.S. beef exporters—leads Jane on a search for wholesome housewives and the perfect prime rib. Along the way she finds a recipe for beef fudge (!) and begins to discover the queasy reality of bovine growth hormones and force-fed antibiotics—not to mention the horrors of American slaughterhouses. The result is a unique tale of love, cultural identity, and beef.

Ozeki herself was a filmmaker before she became a novelist; after a stint art-directing low-budget horror flicks like *Robot Holocaust*, she began making documentaries about American life for Japanese television, sponsored by the likes of Philip Morris. Her own award-winning documentaries, 1994's *Body of Correspondence* and 1995's *Halving the Bones*, have been shown at Sundance and on PBS.

The 46-year-old Ozeki's ambitious new novel, *All Over Creation*, moves from meat to potatoes with the story of Yumi Fuller, a rebellious daughter who returns to her family's Idaho potato farm—only to find herself at the center of a firestorm involving genetically engineered spuds, guerrilla environmentalism, and shady corporate PR.

Mother Jones spoke to Ozeki from her home in British Columbia about documentary film, genetic modification, and the tricks of mixing politics and fiction.

MOTHER JONES: How did the switch from filmmaking to novels come about?

RUTH OZEKI: It was a financial thing, largely. I had finished a documentary—*Halving the Bones*—about my mother and grandmother, who came from Japan, and I was about $30,000 in credit-card debt. I got a grant to do another screenplay but I didn't have any money to produce it. So I ended up writing *My Year of Meats* instead. It was really a means-of-production problem. It costs so much to make films. With a novel, you can write the whole thing on a ream of paper from Staples for $4.

MJ: My Year of Meats *exposes the way documentaries, like novels, are not always as real as they purport to be. Have you found the two forms to be similar in other ways?*

RO: Even though I was making documentaries, my films had fictional elements to them. I think I like blurring those distinctions because so much of what we see on television purports to be the truth, but it's often largely imaginary—or wishful thinking, or any number of less honorable things. [Laughs.]

MJ: When did you get interested in food production and genetic engineering?

RO: While I was writing *My Year of Meats*. When I started out, I was really writing about documentary filmmaking—about media and television. It was only by researching the novel that I started to become aware of the problems involved in our industrialized system of food production. That's what opened my eyes to it. And of course, once your eyes are opened, you really can't close them again.

MJ: One of your characters says something that I think cuts to the heart of what's troubling about genetic engineering. He says, "We're trying to force alien words into the plant's poem, but we got a problem. Genetic grammar's a mystery, and our engineers are just one click up the evolutionary ladder from a roomful of monkeys, typing random sonnets on a bank of typewriters."

RO: I approached this from a literary perspective. Not to say that there aren't political elements in it; of course there are. But the first time I became interested in this idea of what is natural versus what is artificial was reading Shakespeare—his metaphors of nature in opposition to man's will. When I started writing *All Over Creation*, that really was the driving metaphor. How much do we feel the need to tamper with nature? The book starts out with Yumi's abortion. She's intervening in the natural processes at the age of 14. Later she's given the choice to extend her father's life—to put him on a feeding tube. So those are the two events that sandwich the novel, and in between is this question of genetic modification.

MJ: What kind of research did writing All Over Creation *involve?*

RO: I spent the last four years reading everything I could get my hands on. I visited farms, I visited labs, met people who were breeding potatoes, I collected potatoes in the wild. It was fascinating.

One of the things I realized is that by the time we consumers are aware of these issues, aware of processes like genetic engineering, they're already being done. It's sort of like the war in Iraq: By the time we know about it, it's almost a fait accompli. And that's certainly true with science. From an activist standpoint, it's hard to say, "Stop genetic engineering." It's happening. It has gathered so much momentum at this point that it's not ever going to stop.

MJ: Did your research change your perceptions of genetic engineering?

RO: After talking to the scientists I understand how you can set yourself a problem—like how to breed a potato that's resistant to the Colorado potato beetle. It's so easy to focus only on that problem and get excited by the idea of solving it, and to lose sight of the larger picture. It made me realize that if I had been a scientist instead of a novelist, I probably would be in a lab like that, on the cutting edge of genetic engineering. And it made me glad that I'm a novelist, because I get myopic too. We all do. It's just that as a novelist, there's a limit to how much damage I can do. [Laughs.]

MJ: All Over Creation is told from multiple points of view—much more so than My Year of Meats.

RO: I think I got a little overambitious, the way one does with a second novel. Part of it was raising the bar, and trying to give myself a challenge. But also, I think that if we don't learn to inhabit other people's perspectives, then we're never going to understand why people do what they do.

It was fascinating, and also really heartbreaking, to talk to a farmer who was having to plow half of his crop into the ground because there was no market for the potatoes, or was going bankrupt because the scale of production was just outstripping his ability to keep up. Or to talk to a scientist who was really excited about the work that she was doing. What's fascinating to me is the way that multiple stories go into creating any world—a fictional world, but certainly the world that we live in as well. Of course, I cannot control that world. [Laughs.] I can just control the fictional world.

MJ: As a politically interested writer, how do you write a novel about meatpacking or genetic modification that avoids being didactic?

RO: When I start writing these novels, I go into them with a spirit of inquiry, rather than to substantiate prejudices I had in the beginning. If you don't do that, you can't write good characters.

In this case—genetic engineering—there's no way that I could completely wipe the slate clean and go in prejudice-free. But I wanted to see if I could understand, in a deeper way, how this happens, why it happens, who it's affecting.

MJ: Has the fact that both of your novels are so political caused any problems for them from a marketing standpoint?

RO: I have a wonderful publisher, and I think the reason they support what I write is because it is political. It is kind of amazing, isn't it? I also think that American readers are looking for this kind of content.

A lot of *All Over Creation* is about PR, and so is *My Year of Meats*. It's about media hype and media misrepresentation. They're both novels about what we're fed—both through television

or, literally, on our plate. We're sick of the diet we've had for the last 30 years.

MJ: What's your next project?

RO: I've got another book, a book that I had been working on before *All Over Creation*. It's about the film world. But it's also about the Japanese internment. I had put it aside because I wanted to keep going on the food issues—I was on a roll. This book is more about war. When I put it aside, we weren't in the situation that we're in now. Suddenly, it's become a lot more timely.

MJ: So no more food for a while, then?

RO: I don't know. [Laughs.] Maybe I'll write something sweet and fluffy-for dessert.

Source: Andi Zeisler and Ruth Ozeki, "Ruth Ozeki: When Novel Meets Expose," in *Mother Jones*, Vol. 28, No. 2, March–April 2003, p. 86.

SOURCES

Charles, Dan, "Organic Farmers Bash FDA Restrictions on Manure Use," NPR blog, November 21, 2013, http://www.npr.org/blogs/thesalt/2013/11/21/246386290/organic-farmers-bash-fda-restrictions-on-manure-use (accessed August 10, 2014).

Cheng, Emily, "Meat and the Millennium: Transnational Politics of Race and Gender in Ruth Ozeki's *My Year of Meats*," in *Journal of Asian American Studies*, Vol. 12, No. 2, June 2009, p. 191.

"DES Action USA Key Events," DES Action website, http://www.desaction.org/timeline.htm (accessed August 10, 2014).

Fish, Cheryl J., "The Toxic Body Politic: Ethnicity, Gender, and Corrective Eco-justice in Ruth Ozeki's *My Year of Meats* and Judith Helfand and Daniel Gold's *Blue Vinyl*," in *MELUS*, Vol. 34, No. 2, Summer 2009, p. 43.

"History of the Organic Movement," Organics Institute website, http://theorganicsinstitute.com/organic/history-of-the-organic-movement/ (accessed August 9, 2014).

Kim, Yoo, "Traveling through a 'Hybrid' World: The Politics of Cultural Hybridity in Ruth Ozeki's *My Year of Meats*," in *Foreign Literature Studies*, Vol. 32, No. 1, February 2010, pp. 44–55.

Kuepper, George, *A Brief Overview of the History and Philosophy of Organic Agriculture*, Kerr Center for Sustainable Agriculture, 2010, http://www.kerrcenter.com/publications/organic-philosophy-report.pdf (accessed August 9, 2014).

Ladino, Jennifer, "New Frontiers for Ecofeminism: Women, Nature, and Globalization in Ruth L. Ozeki's *My Year of Meats*," in *New Directions in Ecofeminist*

Literary Criticism, edited by Andrea Campbell, Cambridge Scholars Publishing, 2008, p. 124.

"Mad Cow Disease," Center for Food Safety website, http://www.centerforfoodsafety.org/issues/1040/mad-cow-disease/timeline-mad-cow-disease-outbreaks (accessed August 11, 2014).

"Organic Industry Timeline," Whole Foods Market website, http://www.wholefoodsmarket.com/mission-values/organic-farming/organic-industry-timeline (accessed August 9, 2014).

Ozeki, Ruth L., *My Year of Meats*, Penguin Books, 1999.

Palumbo-Liu, David, "Rational and Irrational Choices: Form, Affect, and Ethics," in *Minor Transnationalism*, edited by Françoise Lionnet and Shu-mei Shih, Duke University Press, 2005, pp. 41–72.

Quan, Shirley N., Review of *My Year of Meats*, in *Library Journal*, Vol. 123, No. 8, May 1, 1998, p. 139.

Review of *My Year of Meats*, in *Library Journal*, Vol. 123, No. 20, December 1998, p. 188.

Review of *My Year of Meats*, in *Publishers Weekly*, Vol. 245, No. 13, March 30, 1998, p. 65.

Tivnan, Tom, "Japanese Tale: The Author, Filmmaker, and Zen Buddhist Priest Impresses with a Beguiling Japanese-Based Coming of Age Story," in *Bookseller*, No. 5557, December 21, 2012, p. 21.

Wilkinson, Joanne, Review of *My Year of Meats*, in *Booklist*, Vol. 94, No. 15, April 1998, p. 1278.

FURTHER READING

Bell, Susan E., *DES Daughters: Embodied Knowledge and the Transformation of Women's Health Politics*, Temple University Press, 2009.

> This volume merits consideration as the definitive history of DES and pregnant women in the United States, covering the period when DES was medically prescribed, the effects it had, the stories of DES daughters, the movement that arose, and what the future holds.

Eisnitz, Gail A., *Slaughterhouse: The Shocking Story of Greed, Neglect, and Inhumane Treatment inside the U.S.*

Meat Industry, Prometheus Books, 2009.

> Eisnitz's journalistic exposé is not a far cry from Jane's fictional one, showing the most despicable aspects of industrial farms' streamlined raising and killing of cows to put the cheapest possible beef on Americans' tables.

Leonard, Christopher, *The Meat Racket: The Secret Takeover of America's Food Business*, Simon and Schuster, 2014.

> In this book, Leonard focuses less on the factory floor of the slaughterhouse and more on the factory offices, discussing how a few companies such as Tyson Foods have come to dominate the mainstream meat industry and prevent legislators from rearranging the market rules in the interest of smaller businesses.

Schoeffel, Melissa, *Maternal Conditions: Reading Kingsolver, Castillo, Erdrich, and Ozeki*, Peter Lang, 2008.

> This critical volume is most valuable if one has read the works of literature covered—including *My Year of Meats*—but the introduction holds value regardless, and one can see here the sorts of works that are considered alongside Ozeki's, by highly esteemed authors like Barbara Kingsolver, Ana Castillo, and Louise Erdrich.

SUGGESTED SEARCH TERMS

Ruth L. Ozeki AND My Year of Meats

Ozeki AND documentary film

Ozeki AND TV industry

meat industry AND hormones OR antibiotics

Japanese culture AND masculinity

Japanese diet AND meat OR fish

pregnancy AND DES

history AND DES

television AND meat industry

capitalism AND consumerism

meat AND scandal

Nineteen Minutes

JODI PICOULT

2007

Jodi Picoult's *Nineteen Minutes* centers on a school shooting in the town of Sterling, New Hampshire. The novel features a large cast of characters and is told from multiple points of view and in a nonchronological narrative format. Picoult presents the shooting and its aftermath from the perspectives of the shooter, the victims, law enforcement personnel, parents, and students. In this way, Picoult attempts to provide a balanced portrait of a fictional event that closely mirrors reality. The book explores questions of blame and judgment, friendship, alienation, and personal identity. Teens and adults in the novel are forced to question who they are and what values matter to them most in the wake of the tragedy. At the heart of the novel, despite its many characters, is the story of Josie and Peter, childhood friends whose relationship is fractured on the fault lines of popularity—Josie does everything in her power to fall on one side, whereas Peter is forever on the opposite side of that divide, always an outcast. The nature of their friendship, and the way the pressure to fit in destroys it, is another focal point of the novel. *Nineteen Minutes* was published in 2007 by Washington Square Press.

AUTHOR BIOGRAPHY

Picoult was born on May 19, 1966, to Myron Michel Picoult and Jane Ellen Friend Picoult. She was born and grew up in Nesconset, New

Jodi Picoult (© *David Levenson* / *Getty Images Entertainment* / *Getty Images*)

York, on Long Island. After earning a bachelor's degree in English from Princeton University in 1987, Picoult went on to study creative writing with the authors Robert Stone and Mary Morris. With the mentorship they provided, she published her first short story, "Keeping Count," in *Seventeen* in 1987. After working on Wall Street, Picoult went on to work in both publishing and advertising. She then returned to school to pursue a master's degree in education at Harvard University. She earned her degree in 1990. While at Harvard, she taught creative writing in Natick, Massachusetts, from 1989 to 1991. She married Timothy Warren van Lear in 1989. Picoult published her first novel, *Songs of the Humpback Whale*, in 1992. She continued to write prolifically for years and published her fourteenth novel, *Nineteen Minutes*, in 2007. More recent works include the novel *Lone Wolf* and the young-adult novel *Between the Lines*, both published in 2012.

PLOT SUMMARY

Part One

MARCH 6, 2007

Nineteen Minutes is structured in a nonlinear format. The first chapter opens on the day of a school shooting, and all subsequent chapters are titled in terms of their chronological relation to that event, such as one year before and five months after. Interspersed between chapters are excerpts from a note written by an unidentified person who is possibly, but not necessarily, the shooter.

In the first chapter, Picoult introduces the primary characters. Alex Cormier, a superior court judge, has a hurried breakfast with her daughter, Josie, before leaving for work and Josie for school. Josie contemplates suicide and feels as though she is an impostor in the world of the popular kids at her high school. Her boyfriend, Matt, makes her feel lucky to have his attention but perhaps undeserving of it. Meanwhile, a police detective, Patrick Ducharme, begins his day. Lacy Houghton is a midwife who is helping to deliver a baby that morning. Her son, Peter, and her husband, Lewis, are at home getting ready for school and work. The scene shifts back to school, where Josie observes and participates in the social dynamics that divide the school between popular and unpopular students. The perspective shifts to a student, Zoe Patterson, in a math class, before switching back to Patrick, who sits in an unmarked police car. He hears reports on his radio of shots fired at Sterling High School. The chaos of the shooting is relayed from Patrick's perspective. Following the trail of blood and bodies and the sound of gunfire, Patrick makes his way to the locker room at the school after he arrives on the scene. Once there, he sees two people on the floor and a boy in wire-rimmed glasses, who puts a pistol to his own head. Patrick deduces the boy is the shooter and instructs him not to move. The boy drops the gun, and another officer, Patrick is dimly aware, removes him from the scene. Patrick discovers that one of the people on the floor is a boy in a hockey jersey and that he is dead. The other is female, and she is moving. She is bleeding but from a cut not a gunshot wound, and she tells him her name is Josie.

SEVENTEEN YEARS BEFORE

In this chapter, Picoult takes the reader back to the time when Lacy had recently given birth to

MEDIA ADAPTATIONS

- *Nineteen Minutes*, narrated by Carol Monda, was published as an unabridged audio CD by Recorded Books in 2007.
- *Nineteen Minutes*, narrated by Carol Monda, was published as an MP3 edition by Recorded Books Audible Audio in 2007.

Peter, her second son. Lacy's other son is Joey, whom she has found to be an easy baby. Alex is pregnant with Josie. Through the course of Josie's pregnancy, Lacy, who meets Alex when she comes to a birthing class, convinces Alex to not give up the baby for adoption. Josie's father is Logan Rourke, Alex's trial advocacy professor. He wants Alex to have an abortion.

HOURS AFTER

In this chapter, the narration returns to the day of the shooting and to Patrick's point of view. At the school, Patrick is managing the crime scene. He and the other first responders are numbering the victims as they are found. The scene switches to Alex, who is in court presiding over a case when word comes about the shooting at the school. Diana Leven, who works for the attorney general's office, is questioning Patrick. She is soon accosted by reporters who want details about what has happened. Meanwhile, Lacy arrives at the school. She thinks about how she has already lost one of her sons and fears now for Peter's life. She recalls the argument she had with Peter the night before. Soon she overhears people talking and realizes that Peter is the shooter. Alex, too, has arrived at the scene and learns that Josie is listed as among the wounded. At the police station, Lacy approaches Patrick and begs to see Peter. As Patrick questions Peter, he thinks about the ten students Peter killed. He tries to talk to Peter about what happened, but Peter will not speak about the shootings. He only cries, until he whispers, "They started it."

Back at the crime scene, Patrick works with the state medical examiner and attempts to retrace Peter's steps. They learn that Matt has been shot twice and that Peter had the makings of a pipe bomb in his car.

Alex visits Josie in the hospital. She has a cut and a concussion. Alex learns that Josie's boyfriend, Matt, has been shot and killed. Alex anticipates that she will be the judge in the case when the shooting goes to trial.

At her home, Lacy attempts to understand what could have led Peter to act as he did. She finds bomb-making materials in his closet and is attempting to put them in a garbage bag when a police officer arrives with a search warrant.

Jordan McAfee, an attorney, receives a call from Lewis Houghton, who asks Jordan to represent his son. Jordan agrees.

Patrick goes to the hospital to talk to Josie, who thinks she has been in a car accident. Alex agrees to let Patrick tell Josie about the shooting.

TWELVE YEARS BEFORE

This chapter opens with Peter Houghton's first day of kindergarten. He is bullied on his very first day of school, but Josie is with him and offers to share her lunch when an older boy hurls Peter's Superman lunch box from the bus.

Alex, who is working as a public defender, considers running for a judicial position.

Peter's father scolds him for losing his lunch box again, and Peter buckles under the weight of being compared to his older brother, Joey, a first-grader. A portion of this chapter is devoted to highlighting Peter's sensitive nature, his being teased and bullied, and Josie's desire to protect him.

Alex becomes a judge and realizes how this will shift the way she parents. She and Lacy argue about the hunting rifles in Lacy's home, rifles that the young Peter and Josie find. Later, Lewis shows Peter how to clean and handle the gun properly and promises to take him hunting with him.

THE DAY AFTER

In this chapter, Picoult describes the way the town of Sterling copes with the tragedy at the high school. Lewis recalls the police search of his home the day of the shooting and how they discovered two of his hunting rifles were missing. Jordan McAfee, Peter's lawyer, meets with him.

Peter is unresponsive but asks his lawyer, "How many did I get?"

Josie leaves the hospital heavily sedated. She resents her mother's concern and ruminates on how it took a shooting for her mother to realize that she and Josie had virtually no relationship.

Patrick reviews evidence in the case. An inconclusive fingerprint on one of the guns leads to further questions about the way the shooting unfolded.

Alex tells Josie she will be the judge in the case and realizes with horror that she never considered the effect of this decision on Josie, who just needs her mother.

Jordan gathers Peter from his cell for his arraignment and tells him that he is charged with ten counts of first-degree murder, along with nineteen counts of attempted first-degree murder. Jordan tells Peter they will enter not-guilty pleas and that Peter is not to say a word.

Josie and her mother attend Matthew Royston's funeral service. Josie makes her way to a podium and addresses the mourners, saying that she is sorry. Her mother consoles her, telling her that she understands that Josie thinks Matt's death was her fault because she could not save him.

Patrick questions Josie. She tells the detective that people noticed Peter because he did not make an attempt to fit in and that people made fun of him. She mentions that they used to work together and that they did not always get along. Josie tells Patrick that after Peter lit a fire at the copy center where they worked, she told on Peter, and he was fired.

Lacy visits Peter in jail and attempts to connect with him. Lacy wonders what she has done as a mother that has led to Peter's becoming a killer. Later, Peter is also visited by Jordan, his lawyer. Peter expresses no remorse for his actions but recounts some of the bullying that made him feel like a victim for so much of his life.

SIX YEARS BEFORE

As of sixth grade, Peter and Josie are still friends, and Josie still comes to Peter's rescue, even though they do not see each other outside of school anymore. At school, the students hear news of the September 11 terrorist attacks that have brought down the two towers of the World Trade Center. The scene shifts to Peter's humiliation on the soccer field. His mother makes him play so that he can try to fit in. He is bullied in the locker room.

Lewis tries to go to work, to do something normal. He is an economics professor at Sterling College. But the dean asks Lewis to take some time off.

Other details of Peter and Josie's middle school experience are captured in this chapter. The turning point in Peter and Josie's friendship comes when both of them have been in on making fun of a girl, Dolores Keating, who has gotten her period in class. Peter has started the teasing and feels for a moment what it is like to belong. When the joke goes too far, Peter tries to stop it. Josie continues to participate and begins to hang out with one of the popular girls, Courtney Ignatio. From Peter's perspective, Josie has made a choice that will forever define them both.

TEN DAYS AFTER

Josie struggles to cope with what has happened. She watches a DVD of her friends and Matt. Lacy and Lewis face swarms of reporters every time they attempt to leave their home.

Ervin Peabody, a professor of psychiatry at the college, decides to run a grief session for the community. Peter is referred to as a monster. The principal discusses resuming classes at a different location. Jordan, Peter's lawyer, is verbally confronted by Courtney Ignatio's father, Mark.

Alex encourages Josie to get out of the house. They try to go out to eat, but Josie panics when she hears a car backfiring.

As Patrick researches the case, he learns that two of the victims were gay, and he wonders whether this influenced Peter's actions.

When Jordan's wife, Selena, meets with Lacy to talk about Peter, Lacy reveals that Peter's older brother, Joey, died after being hit by a car driven by a drunk driver a year before the shooting. She also reveals she found heroin in Joey's room after his death.

Jordan's tires are slashed in his driveway. The police are not in a hurry to take a report from him.

Josie decides to attend school at the new location, a former elementary school. Josie snubs her mother, who has offered to drive her before going to work, and gets a ride with Matt's friend Drew.

Alex struggles through work. She is approached by Patrick, who asks her about Josie. Alex feels comfortable with him. He is the only person who sees her as a person instead of a judge.

Jordan talks to Peter about his dead brother, trying to find a way to use the death to gain sympathy for Peter in court. Peter says that Joey was the person who started the bullying and that he is glad his brother is dead. Jordan also plays a violent video game Peter has created. Jordan explains to Peter that they are waiving the probable cause hearing.

Patrick is called to the scene when Yvette Harvey, the mother of Kaitlyn, a student with Down syndrome who was killed in the attack, commits suicide.

Jordan questions Peter about Josie. Peter reveals that the person he wanted to kill most of all was himself.

ONE YEAR BEFORE

The Houghtons have to put down their dog, whose kidneys are failing. Joey is still alive, and he and Peter are not happy about having to be present at the veterinarian's office, but Peter finds a way to comfort his grieving mother.

The scene switches to Josie, who is lamenting the fact that she never knew her father.

When the narrative moves back to Peter, another bullying scene is presented. In this scene, Joey is in on the verbal attack.

Peter and Josie are working together at the copy center, laughing. Matt comes into the shop and asks Josie to a party. When Matt leaves, Peter asks Josie what it is like to be popular, and she confesses that she feels that if she misses a step, she will fall. Peter sees in this popular Josie the friend he once had and wishes he could still reach her. He wonders why he is not attracted to Josie and wonders whether the boys who bully him are right—that maybe he is gay.

Matt and Josie kiss, even after Peter's school project about popularity ostracizes Josie. Alex prepares for a date. Peter sets a fire in the dumpster at work, trying to set up a situation in which Josie must save him. She does, but she also tells their boss that Peter set the fire. Peter is fired. Matt and Peter have a fistfight. Josie attempts to talk to Matt about not picking on Peter, but she chooses sides and walks away with Matt.

Josie finds her father and shows up at his door. He does not want to have any sort of relationship with her. Matt and Josie have sex for the first time. Later, he is physically abusive with her, grabbing her arm and leaving bruises.

Peter begins to develop a violent computer game. He works with Derek, another ostracized boy who was also reluctantly on the soccer team. Later, Peter goes to a gay bar and is subject to unwanted advances from a stranger. He is rescued by his teacher Mr. McCabe, who is the only teacher killed in the shootings.

Josie and Peter become stuck in an elevator. Josie has recently hurt her ankle. At first she lies about how it was hurt but then later confesses that Matt hit her, causing her to lose her balance and hurt the ankle. Peter asks Josie to kiss him, and she does. He realizes he is not gay but that Josie is the only girl that is right for him. Matt and the janitor pry the elevator door open, and Matt whisks Josie away. When Peter returns home, he learns that his brother is dead.

ONE MONTH AFTER

Lacy finds that women no longer want her to be their midwife. She is being blamed for what Peter has done. Patrick learns that Peter is not gay. Jordan meets with Peter.

Despite some pressure from the prosecutor, Diana Leven, Alex does not recuse herself from the case.

Patrick interviews Josie again, but Josie still cannot remember what happened.

A reporter, Elena Battista, tricks Peter into giving an interview. Patrick connects with Peter about video games.

Lewis is racked with guilt about having taken Peter hunting. Jordan meets with the psychiatrist who interviewed Peter. The psychiatrist, King Wah, likens what Peter went through to the suffering battered women go through.

Alex decides to recuse herself from the case. She begins to date Patrick. Alex tells Josie that she has taken herself off the case, and she attempts to rebuild her relationship with Josie.

Jordan interviews Josie. Patrick and Alex kiss.

THE MONTH BEFORE

Matt forces Josie to have sex without a condom. Peter works up the courage to tell Josie how he feels about her, in an e-mail. Courtney intercepts it and forwards it to Drew, instructing him to send it to everyone. Josie's period is late. Josie finds out about the e-mail that was sent out.

Courtney encourages Peter to talk to Josie, telling him Josie likes him. He approaches her at her lunch table, where he is taunted. Matt pulls down Peter's pants in front of everyone. Josie laughs along with everyone else.

Josie discovers she is pregnant. She researches ways to terminate a pregnancy. She tells Matt, but he does not seem particularly concerned.

Peter steals a gun from his neighbor, who is a retired police officer.

Josie miscarries.

Part Two

FIVE MONTHS AFTER

Jordan is in the process of jury selection for Peter's trial. Alex and Patrick have been in a relationship for four months. Before Patrick sneaks off one morning, Josie makes them both pancakes to let them know of her approval.

Lacy buys Peter a suit for the trial. Lewis finally visits Peter in jail.

Diana Leven, the prosecutor, prepares Drew Girard for the trial. Patrick is also in the room.

The trial begins. Lacy is sequestered with other defense witnesses, including Josie. When Haley Weaver, who was once homecoming queen and is now disfigured from the shooting, testifies, Peter begins to comprehend what he has done.

Josie approaches Peter's mother and apologizes. Lacy is surprised that Josie is in the room with others testifying on Peter's behalf. Josie explains that Peter is her friend.

Drew testifies and points out Peter's unpopularity. He admits to bullying Peter for years and to spamming the e-mail Peter wrote for Josie. Peter's friend Derek testifies on his behalf.

6:30 A.M. THE DAY OF

Peter wakes up thinking of his day and the classes he will attend. But when he accidentally restores the deleted file containing his e-mail to Josie, he takes it as a sign and packs guns instead of books into his backpack.

FIVE MONTHS AFTER

At the trial, Patrick is on the witness stand for four hours. Psychiatrists testify, one for the state and King Wah for the defense. Wah explains that Peter has posttraumatic stress disorder. Peter's history of being bullied and not being protected by adults is detailed. Lacy testifies about the bullying Peter endured. Her testimony is interrupted by a victim's father, who questions Lacy's parenting. Peter takes the stand and does not adhere to the agreed-upon testimony he and Jordan have worked out. He comes across as unsympathetic.

Attempting to redirect the testimony, Jordan intends to call Josie to the stand. In interviews to prepare her for her testimony, Josie says she now remembers that before Peter shot Matt, Matt threatened to shoot Peter with a gun that had fallen out of Peter's backpack. Patrick returns to the school to see whether Josie's new information makes sense.

10:16 A.M. THE DAY OF

In the locker room, when the backpack falls and the gun drops out and slides toward Matt and Josie, Josie, not Matt, picks up the gun and points it at Peter. Peter is pointing the other gun at Matt. Peter asks Josie to let him finish what he has started, and Matt tells Josie to shoot Peter. Matt asks Josie if she is stupid and again tells her to kill Peter. But instead, Josie shoots at Matt, hitting him in the abdomen. She drops the gun and runs to him. Peter approaches and shoots Matt in the head. Peter tells Josie not to tell. She nods and faints.

FIVE MONTHS AFTER

At the trial, the courtroom is shocked at Josie's confession. Patrick's additional investigation at the school has yielded a bullet that lodged in a tree outside the locker room. Peter is soon convicted of eight first-degree murders. He is convicted of second-degree manslaughter in the cases of Matt and Courtney because he had been provoked. Peter commits suicide a month after his conviction.

MARCH 6, 2008

Alex resigns her judicial appointment. Josie has been charged as an accessory to the second-degree murder of Matt and has pleaded guilty to manslaughter with a sentence of five years served. Alex goes back to work as a public defender. She is pregnant with Patrick's child.

CHARACTERS

Elena Battista

Elena Battista is a reporter who pretends to be a college student writing a paper on the effects of bullying. She tricks Peter into talking to her and then prints a story in *Time* magazine.

Alex Cormier

Alex Cormier, a judge, is Josie's mother. During her pregnancy with Josie, Alex considered giving up the baby for adoption because she missed the scheduled date for an abortion. Josie's father is Logan Rourke, a law professor with whom Alex had an affair and who wants nothing to do with Alex's baby. Alex is focused on her career and as the novel opens is aware of the distance that separates her from her daughter. After the shooting, Alex attempts to reestablish a connection with Josie, finally coming to the decision that she must recuse herself from the case in order to better support Josie. She eventually starts seeing Patrick, returns to the public defender's office, and is pregnant with Patrick's baby at the end of the novel.

Josie Cormier

Josie Cormier is Alex's daughter. She was once Peter Houghton's friend. The novel traces the evolution and then devolution of their relationship. It is Josie's quest for popularity that ultimately divides the two friends. In her relationship with Matt, Josie is grateful to him, as a popular boy, for loving her, for allowing her entry into the popular crowd. She allows herself to be physically assaulted by Matt, and he forces her into having sex without a condom. The pregnancy that results ends in miscarriage. Throughout the novel, Josie turns a blind eye to what her new friends do to Peter, just as she often tried to protect him when they were younger. Josie's guilt over her complicity in her friends' treatment of Peter, combined with her resentment of Matt and what he did to her, result in her shooting Matt in the locker room. This twist is not revealed until the end of the novel, when Josie allows herself to remember and confess. Whether she is aware of her role in the shootings before she confesses in court is left ambiguous. Josie is sentenced to five years in a women's penitentiary.

Patrick Ducharme

Patrick Ducharme is a detective who has appeared in previous novels by Picoult. He is characterized by a deep sense of guilt and powerlessness when he is unable to help those in need. He is diligent in his efforts to thoroughly assess the school shooting. Through the course of the novel, he falls in love with Alex Cormier. At the novel's end they are expecting a baby.

Drew Girard

Drew Girard is one of the popular kids at school and is one of Matt Royston's close friends. He is shot but not killed by Peter. He is the person who sends Peter's private e-mail to Josie to the whole student body after Courtney forwards it to him.

Kaitlyn Harvey

Kaitlyn Harvey is a student with Down syndrome whom Peter shoots and kills.

Yvette Harvey

Yvette Harvey is Kaitlyn's mother. She commits suicide not long after Kaitlyn's death.

Joey Houghton

Joey is the older son of Lewis and Lacy Houghton. Peter identifies him as one of his first bullies. Joey is killed by a drunk driver a year before Peter's shooting spree. Later, Lacy finds heroin paraphernalia in Joey's room.

Lacy Houghton

Lacy Houghton is Peter's mother. Picoult gives her a strong and persistent voice within the novel, returning to her perspective repeatedly. As Lacy attempts to cope with what has happened, she unsurprisingly blames herself but at the same time is understandably hurt by the public's criticism of her. She scrutinizes her actions, attempting to see how what she did or did not do over the years contributed to making Peter into the violent young man he has become. Lacy decides that the best she can do now is to find a way to continue to love and support her son.

Lewis Houghton

Lewis Houghton is Peter's father and Lacy's husband. Picoult depicts Lewis as favoring his son Joey over Peter. Yet Lewis makes an attempt to bond with Peter through hunting. Lewis, like his wife, dissects his actions and attempts to understand his role in shaping Peter into a killer. It takes months for Lewis to work up the courage to visit his son in jail, and he reflects on how he let his son down over the years.

Peter Houghton

Peter Houghton is the seventeen-year-old student who guns down fellow students and a teacher, killing ten. Throughout the novel, Picoult traces the bullying Peter endured from kindergarten. She depicts his parents as loving but not connected with Peter in a way that he grasps. He feels isolated from everyone except Josie. After Josie turns her back on him, Peter struggles even more. The bullying is often physical and aggressive and always designed to humiliate Peter with as many people watching as possible. When Peter attempts to win Josie back by sending her an e-mail, it is intercepted by Josie's friend Courtney, who forwards it to her friend Drew, who spams it out to the whole school. Peter learns of this publicly when he approaches Josie at her lunch table and is mocked by her friends. Matt pulls down Peter's pants and underwear in front of everyone, and Josie joins her friends in laughing at him. This is almost the last straw for Peter, who has already been drawing up plans and gathering weapons for an attack on the school. When he accidentally brings up the deleted e-mail file on his computer one morning, he decides that this will be the day he acts. Peter shows little remorse when he is interrogated about what he has done. He does react with some emotion during the testimony of the shooting victims at his trial, and he more than once expresses that he intended to kill himself the day of the shooting. Instead, Peter waits until after his conviction to suffocate himself with his sock.

Courtney Ignatio

Courtney is one of the popular girls at school. She befriends Josie, which begins to bring her under the scrutiny of her other friends. Yet Courtney does not have a problem with humiliating Josie, along with Peter, for the sake of a joke at Peter's expense. Whether she is motivated by jealousy of Josie for being Matt's girlfriend or merely by her own sense of humor, Courtney sends Drew the e-mail Peter sent to Josie, instructing Drew to send it to everyone. Courtney is shot and killed by Peter.

Mark Ignatio

Mark is Courtney's father. He verbally accosts Jordan McAfee during the community grief session.

Dolores Keating

Dolores is the object of teasing when she gets her period in class. Peter instigates the teasing but later regrets it after it goes too far. He tries to protect Dolores but is ineffectual. When Josie participates in the teasing in order to fit in, Peter sees what she is willing to do to be popular.

Diana Leven

Diana Leven is the prosecuting attorney in Peter's case.

Derek Markowitz

Derek is Peter's friend. They both find themselves on the school's soccer team because of pressure exerted by their parents and are equally bad at the game. Derek shares an interest in Peter's violent computer games.

Jordan McAfee

Jordan McAfee is the lawyer who defends Peter Houghton. He has appeared in two of Picoult's previous novels. Jordan struggles to find a way to connect with Peter in an effort to understand him. He searches for signs of remorse in Peter but settles on a defense rooted in the fact that because Peter has been bullied so ruthlessly all of his life, he suffers the same type of trauma that victims of abuse deal with.

Selena McAfee

Selena is Jordan's wife. She aids him by talking to Lacy and Josie, attempting to gather information that might help her husband. Unlike Peter's parents, Selena makes the observation that connects Joey Houghton's death to what happened to Peter. She notes that after Joey's death, Lewis and Lacy were too busy grieving to see or understand what Peter was going through.

Edward McCabe

Mr. McCabe is the only teacher who is shot. He is gay but is discreet about it at school. Peter learns that Mr. McCabe is gay when he goes to a gay bar.

Zoe Patterson

Zoe is the first student to be shot. She is excused from class for an orthodontist appointment. Peter shoots her on the steps of the school as she is leaving; she does not die.

Ervin Peabody

Peabody is a professor of psychiatry at Sterling College. He decides to run a grief session for the community.

Logan Rourke

Logan Rourke is Josie's father. He was once Alex's professor; he wanted Alex to have an abortion.

Matt Royston

Matt is Josie's boyfriend. He is the primary reason Josie, a former friend of Peter's, is accepted into the popular crowd at school, because he is among the most popular of the boys at Sterling High. Matt is possessive of Josie. He insists that he loves her, but he also abuses her. He hits her so that she loses her balance and breaks her ankle and also forces her to have sex without a condom. Josie shoots Matt in the locker room when one of Peter's guns skitters across the floor toward her.

King Wah

King Wah is a psychiatrist who interviews Peter for Jordan. He helps Jordan formulate a defense based on the trauma and humiliation Peter experienced as a result of being bullied.

Haley Weaver

Haley Weaver is one of the popular girls at school. Once the homecoming queen, she is shot by Peter and consequently disfigured. She testifies against him at his trial.

THEMES

Alienation

In *Nineteen Minutes*, Peter Houghton endures severe alienation from everyone around him. He is bullied as early as kindergarten, when older children throw his lunch box from the window of the school bus. Peter is also acutely aware from a young age that his parents seem to favor his older brother, Joey, for whom everything seems to come so easily. As Peter and Joey become older, Joey's bullying becomes more persistent and is just as cruel and demeaning as anything Peter endures at the hands of his classmates. Peter is beaten, stuffed into lockers, and repeatedly publicly humiliated, usually in a crowded place, such as the cafeteria.

Peter's isolation from Josie cuts him deeper than anything else. When they are children, Peter is eager to show Josie his father's guns. Their mothers find out, and Alex, in an attempt to protect Josie, does not allow Josie to spend time with Peter outside of school. In sixth grade, Peter takes an opportunity to be the instigator of bullying instead of the victim. Yet when other kids take the teasing of Delores Keating too far, Peter attempts to halt it. When even Josie participates, taking a stand against Peter for the first time, Peter's descent into complete loneliness and alienation begins. It reaches its climax when Peter realizes how much he still cares for Josie when they are seventeen. In an attempt to tell her how he feels, he sends her an e-mail, which is intercepted by Courtney and distributed by Drew. Josie learns of this when she is taunted by her friends. Afraid of feeling the isolation Peter endures herself, Josie opts to act as if what they have done does not bother her at all. When Peter approaches Josie at her lunch table and her friends reveal the truth about the e-mail, Peter is taken off guard. Matt pulls down Peter's pants and underwear, and Josie and her friends all laugh. It is the height of Peter's humiliation, and Josie participates. The e-mail is Peter's final effort, his grand gesture, his attempt—after not bothering to even try to connect with anyone anymore—to show Josie how he feels about her. The resulting alienation is heightened beyond anything he has experienced thus far.

Josie also feels intense isolation despite her apparent acceptance into the in crowd. Josie has been stealing sleeping pills from her mother and hiding them away so that she will have enough to kill herself one day. She feels as if she is always on the threshold between the isolation Peter feels—which she is acutely aware that he feels—and the precarious place she holds in her group of popular friends. She senses that because of her earlier association with Peter, she is permanently on trial. Josie makes a few weak efforts to ask Matt to not tease Peter or others like him, but Matt ignores them. Josie seems either to fail to grasp that if she were rejected by the popular kids, she would still have Peter and his loyalty and friendship or to simply fail to regard Peter's friendship as enough. Regardless, Josie's rejection of Peter intensifies the alienation they both feel.

Friendship

The friendship between Peter and Josie, and its disintegration, is at the heart of the novel. The

TOPICS FOR FURTHER STUDY

- Watch Michael Moore's *Bowling for Columbine*, the 2002 documentary about gun violence. Moore is known for tackling difficult subjects in a direct and provocative way. Consider the ways in which Moore incorporates his message with statistics about gun violence. Write a report in which you summarize Moore's argument regarding gun violence and gun control. Do you believe, on the basis of the information provided, that Moore's argument is convincing? Why or why not? In what ways does Moore incorporate the motif of bowling? Is this effective?

- Nancy Garden's *Endgame*, published in 2012 by HMH Books for Young Readers, is a young-adult novel focused on a fourteen-year-old boy who is ruthlessly bullied until he takes matters, and his father's semi-automatic weapon, into his own hands. With a book group, read *Endgame* and compare the protagonist, Gray Wilton, to Picoult's Peter Houghton. What similarities do these boys share? In what have their experiences mirrored each other's? In what ways might these bullied youths be different? How do the outcomes of the novels compare? How does each author deliver a message about bullying? How effectively is this message conveyed? Create an online blog that you use as a forum to discuss

these and any other issues that seem pertinent to your group.

- The young-adult novel *The Mariposa Club*, by Rigoberto Gonzalez, who was born in California and raised in Mexico, deals with openly gay teens who have all dealt with some form of bullying. The book was published in 2009 by Alyson Books. Read Gonzalez's novel and consider the ways in which both Hispanic ethnicity and sexual orientation figure into the bullying explored in the work. Examine the plot, characters, and themes and create a presentation—a written report, a poster, or a Prezi or Power-Point presentation—in which you detail these elements.

- Using print and online sources, research the connection between news coverage of school shootings, violent video games, and school shootings. To what extent do experts believe the news media and the gaming world influence school shootings? How do different groups—such as parent groups advocating gun control, the National Rifle Association, and conservative religious groups—discuss this topic? Write a research paper in which you explore and discuss these issues. Be sure to cite all of your sources.

---

relationship is marked out in stages. First, in the chapter "Seventeen Years Before," Picoult outlines the dimensions of the budding friendship between Peter's mother, Lacy, and Josie's mother, Alex. With every instance of bullying that is depicted in the subsequent flashback chapters, through Josie and Peter's sixth grade year, Josie is there with and for Peter, his staunchest ally and fiercest protector. Every time his lunch box is tossed out the window, Josie offers Peter encouraging words and some of her own lunch. Josie even fights off Peter's

attackers on the playground. After a talk with Peter's teacher, Lacy decides to take a new, firmer approach with Peter. In an effort to get him to stand up for himself, Lacy tells Peter that he will not be allowed to play with Josie for a period of time each time he loses his lunch box.

The friendship between Josie and Peer is further tested with the gun incident at Peter's house, after which Josie is no longer allowed to play with Peter after school. The friendship of their mothers, which initially brings Josie and Peter together, begins to disintegrate in a way

Peter endured cruel bullying from his classmates before he broke into violence. (© Sabphoto / Shutterstock.com)

that is destructive to their children. As she grows older, Josie craves other friendships and acceptance. Increasingly she does not want to be associated with Peter, because she does not want to be treated the way he is treated. When she is invited to Courtney's house, Josie feels what it is like to belong, and it becomes increasingly easier for her to sever ties with Peter. She, along with her classmates, teases Delores about her period and drops a tampon on her desk the way the other students do, despite Peter's request that they stop.

Peter's only subsequent friendship is with another outsider, Derek, who is also forced to join the soccer team. They both enjoy violent computer games. Because of their shared experiences with being bullied, Peter instructs Derek to go home the morning of the shooting, thereby sparing him from witnessing or participating in the attack. Josie's other friendships give her the peace of belonging in that she is free from the torture Peter endures. Yet she still seems to have no one to confide in, no one to truly trust. She

feels permanently on edge, as if she is a fraud always on the verge of being discovered. Somehow Josie convinces herself that such treatment and such relationships are better friendships than the one she shared with Peter, in which she was able to be herself. She spends much of the novel denying their friendship, but Peter considers Josie's act of shooting Matt to be an act of solidarity with him. He explains to Jordan after the trial that his reason for not telling Jordan about Josie's involvement was that Josie was his friend once more and he could not break his promise to her that he would not tell.

STYLE

Third-Person Omniscient Narration

In *Nineteen Minutes*, Picoult uses third-person narration that is not limited to any one or two characters. The story is told from the perspective of numerous characters. The reader is given access to the thoughts and feelings—to the interior world—of many of the characters who populate the novel. In this way, the narration is considered omniscient, all-knowing. Third-person narration is storytelling in which the point-of-view characters are referred to by their names or by personal pronouns such as *he* and *she*. This is in contrast to first-person narration, in which the character from whose point of view the story is being told refers to himself or herself as *I*. From the reader's perspective, the benefit of omniscient third-person narration is that a wide range of viewpoints is accessible. In *Nineteen Minutes*, the crime at the center of the plot is considered from the perspective of students—as both witnesses and perpetrators—and from the perspective of law enforcement and the judicial system.

Third-person omniscient narration broadens the reader's understanding of key plot elements. At the same time, it limits to some extent the reader's ability to connect in a deep way with any single character. Additionally, because Picoult uses so many point-of-view characters, the effect can be jarring. Throughout the novel, Picoult uses several main characters as her point-of-view characters: Josie, Peter, Patrick, Alex, Lewis, Lacy, and Jordan. Occasionally she incorporates a minor character as the point-of-view character. For example, on the morning of the shooting, Zoe Patterson, a student, is the point-of-view character for one scene. She sits in class and wonders what it would be like to kiss a guy with braces. Zoe is later one of the students Peter shoots. By selecting a minor character and narrating a scene from his or her perspective, Picoult attempts to provide the reader with an understanding of the shooting and its effects that is both deep as readers are allowed close access to major characters like Peter, the shooter, and broad as readers get a glimpse into the everyday thoughts of the victims of the shooting.

Nonlinear Narrative Format

Picoult relates the events of the novel in a format that is not chronologically sequential. She begins the novel on the day of the shooting. Every other chapter in the novel is framed in relation to that point of reference. Events take place either before or after that turning point and are identified as such in lieu of conventional chapter numbering and chapter titles. For example the chapter that follows the opening is titled "Seventeen Years Before" and the next chapter "Hours After." The reader has the experience of watching a film in which flashback features prominently. Three chapters occur on the day of the shooting. Eight chapters take place after the shooting in a progression from hours after to the day after then ten days after and a month after. Three chapters take place five months after the shooting, during the trial. The last chapter takes place a year after the shooting. Five chapters take place before the shooting: seventeen years before, twelve years before, six years before, one year before, and one month before. The before, after, and day-of chapters are commingled.

Picoult seeks to incorporate the backstory of the way Peter has been bullied all his life and to provide insights into the way primary characters such as Peter and Josie have been parented by blending these past events with the current time as it unfolds after the shooting. Near the novel's end, Picoult flips between the day of the shooting and the trial, emphasizing the relationships between the characters' memories of the event and the ongoing testimony at the trial. As the reader progresses through the novel, moving backward and forward through time, the effect is disorienting. There is a constant effort to contextualize and rethink what has happened and when it is happening. In this way, the structure of the novel mirrors the efforts undertaken by characters in the novel to examine the effects of their past choices on the present situation.

HISTORICAL CONTEXT

School Shootings

In *Nineteen Minutes*, Picoult directly references the school shooting at Columbine High School in Littleton, Colorado, on April 20, 1999. The film *Bowling for Columbine*, a documentary on gun violence directed by Michael Moore, is among the evidence removed from Peter Houghton's room in the novel. Other characters also reference the 1999 shooting. In the Columbine shooting, two teens, Eric Harris and Dylan Klebold, began shooting outside the school then moved inside. In just moments, they killed twelve students and a teacher and wounded more than twenty others. They then killed themselves. On April 16, 2007, a gunman killed thirty-two people and himself at Virginia Tech, a university in Blacksburg, Virginia. Seven years

Josie is traumatized by what happened and cannot remember the details. (© *AntonioDiaz | Shutterstock.com*)

later, it remained the deadliest school shooting in US history. On December 14, 2012, another horrific school shooting occurred at Sandy Hook Elementary School, in Newtown, Connecticut. A heavily armed twenty-year-old man, Adam Lanza, entered the school and killed six adults and twenty children in eleven minutes. He had killed his mother before leaving for the school. All of the children were six and seven years old.

After a shooting at an Oregon high school in June 2014, CNN and other news outlets began reporting the same statistic: In the eighteen months between Sandy Hook and the Oregon shooting, there had been seventy-four school shootings. Writing for *Scientific American,* Frank J. Robertz explored the factors that may influence adolescent school shooters and discussed the way the media to some extent fuel copycat crimes. In discussing signs and symptoms prevalent among shooters, Robertz explored the way elaborate fantasies about violent crimes are sometimes supported by ideas garnered from violent movies, games, and Internet sources. Robertz states, "As fantasies become increasingly important to a disturbed youth, he begins to neglect his real relationships to focus on the mechanics of the deed he has dreamed about." Additionally, signs of depression, an interest in obtaining weapons, an interest in websites pertaining to school shootings and shooters, and access to actual weapons can indicate a potential for violence.

Gun Control Debate

The easy access to weapons that persists in the United States is a topic that receives fresh attention in the wake of each tragic shooting that makes the national headlines. In *Nineteen Minutes,* the shooter, Peter, uses two hunting rifles that belong to his father and two pistols stolen from a retired police officer neighbor to execute his plan. Although Picoult depicts parental conflict—between Lacy and Alex—regarding gun accessibility when young Peter shows Josie his father's guns, the novel fails to take on the gun control debate. Alex has a throwaway line about being pro-firearms, but the novel does not reflect the vehement way this debate resurfaced in the national news media after each school shooting.

In an article for *CBS News*, Lindsey Boerma reported on the stalled efforts of gun control activists in the wake of the Newtown massacre. Boerma notes that in the year after the massacre, "not a single federal law curbing gun violence" was passed. A federal amendment that would have strengthened background checks for gun purchases was voted down, though some states were able to strengthen bans on assault weapons. Boerma cites results of a 2013 CBS poll showing that "85 percent of Americans back a federal law requiring background checks on all potential gun buyers." Legislation and public opinion are perpetually at loggerheads, and this phenomenon continues to resurface. Gun control activists and the 85 percent of Americans who support universal background checks are thwarted by pro-gun lobbyists. As Amber Phillips, writing for the *Las Vegas Sun*, points out, "the pro-gun lobby led by the National Rifle Association is as strong as ever. Gun control legislation has already failed in the Senate." Phillips goes on to explain that in April 2013, Senator Harry Reid "brought legislation for background checks on all commercial gun sales to the Senate floor. But that legislation failed 54–46." Less than a year later, Americans' interest in stricter legislation was declining. Phillips cites January 2014 Gallup poll results indicating that "Americans' support for stricter gun laws fell from 38 percent shortly after Newtown to 31 percent this January."

CRITICAL OVERVIEW

Picoult is widely regarded as a writer who merges the commercial with the literary in her works, and her books regularly reach the top of best-seller lists. *Nineteen Minutes* is no exception. It debuted at the top of best-seller lists. Reviews of the book have been largely favorable, though some journals and papers offer mixed assessments. An anonymous reviewer for *Kirkus Reviews* states that although Picoult is "usually so adept at shaping the big stories with nuance," in *Nineteen Minutes* she "takes a tragically familiar event, pads it with plot, but leaves out the subtleties of character." The reviewer goes on to claim, "Though all the surface elements are in place, Picoult falters in her exploration of what turns a

quiet kid into a murderer." Janet Maslin, writing for the *New York Times*, hinted at the bulkiness of the novel. She comments on the way the Picoult reveals details "in what seems like real time." Maslin further discusses the way Picoult "enlarges the book by adding some history." Summarizing Picoult's style, Maslin states, "However doggedly she belabors the obvious, she writes articulately and clearly, making her all too much of a rarity among popular authors." A less generous review by Jocelyn McClurg in *USA Today* describes Picoult's plot twists as manipulative and notes that "her prose rarely rises above the serviceable." Yet, McClurg concedes, "Picoult knows how to hook you." She further allows that the "very ordinariness" of Picoult's treatment of the tragedy "gives it surprising power."

CRITICISM

Catherine Dominic

Dominic is a novelist and freelance writer and editor. In the following essay, she examines the character of Alex Cormier in Nineteen Minutes, *maintaining that Picoult uses Alex as a means of exploring the theme of judgment.*

The trade paperback version of *Nineteen Minutes* opens with nine quotations from positive reviews from publications such as *Rocky Mountain News*, *Entertainment Weekly*, and *Washington Post*. The reader is reminded that the novelist is a number one *New York Times* best-selling author. These clips praise Picoult's character development, plotting, ability to fuse the literary and the commercial, and ability to tackle moral questions. The scope of the novel is grand, and to her credit, Picoult is able to get into the heads of many characters, all of whom view the shootings at Sterling High School from their own particular vantage point. The cumulative effect of this approach is that Picoult appears to make an effort to be objective. She details Peter's bullying in order to flesh out his psychological trauma. The reader is meant not necessarily to understand how someone could do this but at least to see Peter as a human boy rather than as a monster.

The sheer number of point-of-view characters in *Nineteen Minutes* appears to be an effort on Picoult's part to see the shooting from every angle, to understand all of the perspectives. There is no strength in numbers, however.

❝

PICOULT USES ALEX CORMIER TO EMBODY THE CONFLICT BETWEEN THE WHO-ARE-WE-TO-JUDGE MENTALITY AND THE VERY REAL HUMAN TENDENCY (ALONG WITH THE LEGAL RESPONSIBILITY) TO ACTUALLY JUDGE."

Picoult seems to be implying, as she did in an interview with *Book Browse*, that the shooter could have been anyone, that many teens feel or have felt the way Peter does. In the interview, Picoult states:

> Although the media is quick to list the "aberrant" characteristics of a school shooter, the truth is that [these characteristics] fit all teens at some point in their adolescence! Or in other words—these kids who resort to violence are not all that different from the one living upstairs in your own house, most likely—as scary as that is to imagine.

Parents, lawyers, students, and detectives all contribute their voices to the discussion of the tragic shooting. This seems thorough, like a balanced sampling of the community, like an effort to emphasize a who-are-we-to-judge mentality. Yet under the cloak of objectivity, Picoult does judge and invites the reader to do the same.

Picoult uses Alex Cormier to embody the conflict between the who-are-we-to-judge mentality and the very real human tendency (along with the legal responsibility) to actually judge. This perspective could just as easily have been explored without the clutter Picoult presents in the form of multiple viewpoints. The novel becomes cumbersome with the weight of these additional perspectives and the often extraneous details they provide. When this element of narrative structure is combined with the nonlinear time structure of the book, the effect is chaotic. It could be argued that this is Picoult's intent, to put the reader in a position in which the chaos and confusion of the event and its aftermath are felt in a visceral way. However, for the reader to achieve some sense of clarity or understanding or empathy for any of the characters, the structuring of a chaotic narrative environment becomes detrimental to the novel's success.

Another problem with having so many characters alternate the point-of-view narration is that it creates an illusion of objectivity. The reader feels a false sense of security from the breadth of Picoult's scope. The facts are presented—all of them, apparently, judging from the book's length and the many voices heard throughout the novel—and the reader, like members of the fictional community of Sterling, inevitably forms opinions about what has happened. The reader hears directly from Josie, as both a complicit bullier and a target of bullying through her earlier association with Peter. The reader also sees the world from Peter's perspective, as the object of cruel humiliation and as the killer with apparently no remorse who asks how many kids he got on his spree. The reader is additionally treated to the individual perspectives of Josie's mother and Peter's mother and father. Diana Leven, the prosecutor, is also a point-of-view character from time to time, and Patrick Ducharme, the detective, is repeatedly given point-of-view status. Jordan McAfee, Peter's lawyer, also features relatively prominently as a point-of-view character. These characters all see Peter differently. He is at the center of the story and their thoughts.

With so many characters forming opinions about the matter and with all of these characters flawed in their own particular ways, Picoult seems to be asking, as the introduction to the reader's guide at the novel indicates, Who are we to judge? The reader is compelled to make judgments by the novel's end, just as the characters in the novel are and just as people do in life. Perhaps more than any other character, Alex Cormier, who constantly struggles with her dual roles as mother and judge, reflects on the right and responsibility of members of a community to judge. Is it their rights as parents to judge the way another mother or father parents? Is it their responsibility as members of a society with laws and punishments to judge those who transgress? In Alex, Picoult highlights the struggle between the desire to understand, or to not judge, and the understanding that in this world, in this country, judgment and consequences are required. Although she recuses herself from Peter's case, Alex knows that Peter will still be legally judged for his actions. And whether it is right or fair for him to be judged by the community, he is judged, as he always has been, first as an outsider and then as a monster. Ultimately, Josie is also

WHAT DO I READ NEXT?

- Picoult's young-adult novel *The Storyteller* is a first-person Holocaust narrative. It was published in 2013 by Atria/Emily Bestler Books.

- Ben Mikaelsen is a Bolivian author of Danish descent. He was bullied in school for his Danish ethnicity. In the young-adult novel *Ghost of Spirit Bear*, Mikaelsen writes about a student who volunteers for Native American Circle Justice on a remote Alaskan island instead of going to prison. The book was published in 2008 by HarperCollins.

- Paul Yee's *Money Boy* is a young-adult novel about Ray Liu, a teenage Chinese immigrant, and his attempts to deal with his sexuality and his conservative family. He does not fit in at school or within his family, particularly his stepbrother, who is a good student and dutiful son. Ray prefers playing video games. The book was published in 2011 by Groundwood Books.

- The psychologist Peter Langman's *Why Kids Kill: Inside the Minds of School Shooters*, published by Palgrave Macmillan in 2009, explores the psychological causes of school shootings in an effort to draw attention to signs that can be identified before further tragedies occur.

- R. J. Parker's *Beyond Sticks and Stones: Bullying, Social Media Cyberbullying, Abuse*, published in 2014 by R. J. Parker Publishing, studies the ways in which social media fuel a new array of bullying tactics.

- In *Rampage: The Social Roots of School Shootings*, published in 2004 by Basic Books, Katherine S. Newman, Cybelle Fox, David J. Harding, Jal Mehta, and Wendy Roth study the social causes of shootings and dissect the loner theory.

judged, although the reader is given little information about Josie's or Alex's reaction to that legal judgment.

Alex first feels the pinch of her judge-and-mother quandary when Peter and Josie are young children and looking at Peter's father's guns. Alex reacts as any mother would who sees her daughter in a dangerous situation. At the same time, she recalls her responses to the council that reviewed her application for judgeship. She told the members of the council that she was pro-firearms, that no one has the right to judge someone else. Yet Alex makes the judgment that Peter is not an asset to Josie: "Josie's steadfast loyalty to Peter suddenly seemed to only be a weight dragging her down." Alex determines that Josie needs to make different friends, better friends. After the shooting, Alex is determined to preside over Peter's trial, certain this is the big case of her career, and never questions whether she can be objective, even though Josie was once friends with the shooter and was present at the close of the shooting spree. Alex does decide to recuse herself, though, when she realizes that being there for Josie is more important than presiding over a big case. She admits to Patrick, however, "I'm *good* at being a judge. And lousy at being a mother." Yet after Josie is convicted of manslaughter, Alex resigns her judicial appointment and returns to her job as a public defender because she finds that she can no longer be impartial.

Having witnessed her daughter judged and sentenced, Alex realizes that her feelings as a mother have been interfering with her ability to weigh the evidence in any case in which a child is involved. A judge must uphold a society's responsibility to judge those convicted of a crime, but a mother, Picoult seems to be saying, a mother like Alex operates differently. For Alex, as a mother, "it was not the facts that mattered—only the feelings." This does not say much for Alex in a professional or parental capacity, but it clearly defines the struggle Picoult seeks to highlight: How does one judge when one should not but when one must?

Picoult portrays some characters in a rather damning manner, making her very characterization of them a judgment. Although the multiple perspectives give the illusion of objectivity, Picoult depicts characters such as Courtney and Matt with few, if any, redeeming qualities. As a boyfriend, Matt seems to the casual observer sweet and doting and very much in love with Josie. Yet he is possessive, hits her, rapes her, degrades her in front of his friends, and calls her

Alex faces a difficult dilemma: should she take the case to further her career when it risks further alienating her daughter? (© *Africa Studio | Shutterstock.com*)

stupid. Josie fears him as much as she loves him. She fears the loss of his love more than anything. Rejection by Matt, she is certain, would mean rejection from the fold of popular kids. Matt also is one of the worst abusers of Peter. He physically beats him, and the torment his public humiliation causes Peter is immeasurable. It is easy to judge Matt—he is a bully of the worst kind—and Picoult offers the reader no insights into what has made him this way.

The reader is offered the opportunity to see what Peter has been through, some of the elements that lead him to feel the way he does when he starts shooting. Yet Picoult is silent about what would turn Matt into such a horrible person. The same is true of Courtney, who befriends Josie only to turn on her by reading Josie's private e-mail then sending it to Drew to spam to the student body. Courtney does this as much to hurt Josie as to hurt Peter. But why? Is she jealous of Josie? Perhaps. But this jealousy is not enough to inspire in the reader anything but loathing for Courtney. Why is Picoult silent

about Courtney's background? There is nothing redeemable about her stereotypical mean-girl behavior.

Picoult gives so many characters a point-of-view voice in the novel—an opportunity for characters even as minor as Zoe Patterson to share a thought with the reader—that it is difficult for the reader to learn the lesson who are we to judge? If the reader is given further insights into the thoughts of a killer and of the best friend who betrays him and of the parents who raised these children, all in an effort to make the reader reflect on the idea that no one has the right to judge another, why does Picoult not offer a thought or two in an effort to redeem such vilified characters as Courtney and Matt? In the end, Picoult judges her characters, just as the members of the Sterling community judge one another, and just as the reader judges the characters. They follow Picoult's lead.

Source: Catherine Dominic, Critical Essay on *Nineteen Minutes*, in *Novels for Students*, Gale, Cengage Learning, 2015.

Publishers Weekly

In the following review, the anonymous reviewer praises Picoult's insight into her characters.

Bestseller Picoult (*My Sister's Keeper*) takes on another contemporary hot-button issue in her brilliantly told new thriller, about a high school shooting. Peter Houghton, an alienated teen who has been bullied for years by the popular crowd, brings weapons to his high school in Sterling, N.H., one day and opens fire, killing 10 people. Flashbacks reveal how bullying caused Peter to retreat into a world of violent computer games. Alex Cormier, the judge assigned to Peter's case, tries to maintain her objectivity as she struggles to understand her daughter, Josie, one of the surviving witnesses of the shooting. The author's insights into her characters' deep-seated emotions brings this ripped-from-the-headlines read chillingly alive.

Source: Review of *Nineteen Minutes*, in *Publishers Weekly*, Vol. 254, No. 1, January 1, 2007, p. 31.

Marika Zemke

In the following review, Zemke points out Picoult's interesting use of multiple points of view throughout the novel.

Many things can happen in the span of 19 minutes—fun things, mundane things, and downright horrific things. Best-selling author Picoult (*My Sister's Keeper*) shows just how quickly lives can be changed in this story of a school massacre much like Columbine that is told through the voice not only of the victims but also of the troubled teen who did the shooting. Readers will be pleased to see the return of two favorite characters. Patrick Ducharme, the detective from *Perfect Match*, is assigned to the case, while Jordan McAfee, the lawyer from *The Pact*, finds himself representing the shooter. Picoult has that rare ability to write about an unnerving subject in a way readers will find absorbing. What appears on the surface of a Picoult novel is never as it seems, which is why her books are so popular with book groups. Her 14th novel, perhaps her best, is highly recommended for all public libraries.

Source: Marika Zemke, Review of *Nineteen Minutes*, in *Library Journal*, Vol. 132, No. 1, January 1, 2007, p. 97.

Kristine Huntley

In the following review, Huntley calls the novel "gripping and moving."

Popular and prolific Picoult (*My Sister's Keeper*, 2004, and *The Tenth Circle*, 2006) now tackles the troubling topic of a school shooting. Picoult considers the tragedy—in 19 quick minutes, 10 are dead and 19 are wounded—from several different perspectives, including that of the shooter, a troubled boy named Peter, who was mercilessly picked on at school. The small town of Sterling is rocked by the carnage. Alex Cormier is the superior court judge planning to hear the case, but her daughter, Josie, Peter's only friend during childhood but now a member of the in crowd, was in the midst of the melee. Peter spared Josie, but killed her boyfriend. Two characters from previous Picoult novels are also involved. Charismatic detective Patrick Ducharme rushes into the school and apprehends Peter, and Jordan McAfee agrees to defend the young killer. Every bit as gripping and moving as Picoult's previous novels, *Nineteen Minutes* will no doubt garner considerable attention for its controversial subject and twist ending.

Source: Kristine Huntley, Review of *Nineteen Minutes*, in *Booklist*, Vol. 103, Nos. 9–10, January 1, 2007, p. 57.

SOURCES

Boerma, Lindsey, "One Year after Newtown, Congress Still Stalled on Gun Control," CBS News website, December 14, 2013, http://www.cbsnews.com/news/one-year-after-newtown-congress-still-stalled-on-gun-control/ (accessed August 13, 2014).

Clark, Elizabeth J., "Jodi Picoult," in *Dictionary of Literary Biography*, Vol. 292, *Twenty-First Century American Novelists*, edited by Lisa Abney and Suzanne Disheroon-Green, Thomson Gale, 2004, pp. 278–84.

Fantz, Ashley, Lindsey Night, and Kevin Wang, "A Closer Look: How Many Newtown-like School Shootings since Sandy Hook," CNN website, June 19, 2014, http://www.cnn.com/2014/06/11/us/school-shootings-cnn-number/ (accessed August 13, 2014).

"An Interview with Jodi Picoult," in *BookBrowse*, https://www.bookbrowse.com/author_interviews/full/index.cfm/author_number/601/jodi-picoult? (accessed August 13, 2014).

Maslin, Janet, "After the Shooting Is Over," in *New York Times*, March 16, 2007, http://www.nytimes.com/2007/03/16/books/16book.html?_r=0 (accessed August 13, 2014).

McClurg, Jocelyn, "'Nineteen Minutes': A Tragedy Frightening in Its Banality," in *USA Today*, March 5, 2007, http://usatoday30.usatoday.com/life/books/reviews/2007-03-05-picoult-nineteen-minutes_N.htm (accessed August 13, 2014).

Phillips, Amber, "Despite Harry Reid's Growing Support, Gun Control Legislation Probably Isn't Going Anywhere in Congress," in *Las Vegas Sun*, June 11, 2014, http://www.lasvegassun.com/news/2014/jun/11/despite-harry-reids-growing-support-gun-control-le/ (accessed August 13, 2014).

Picoult, Jodi, *Nineteen Minutes*, Washington Square Press, 2007.

"Remembering the Sandy Hook Elementary Victims," CNN website, http://www.cnn.com/interactive/2012/12/us/sandy-hook-victims/ (accessed August 13, 2014).

Review of *Nineteen Minutes*, in *Kirkus Reviews*, January 1, 2007, https://www.kirkusreviews.com/book-reviews/jodi-picoult/nineteen-minutes/ (accessed August 13, 2014).

Robertz, Frank J. "Deadly Dreams: What Motivates School Shootings," in *Scientific American*, July 30, 2007, http://www.scientificamerican.com/article/deadly-dreams/ (accessed August 13, 2014).

FURTHER READING

Bazelon, Emily, *Sticks and Stones: Defeating the Culture of Bullying and Rediscovering the Power of Character and Empathy*, Random House, 2013.

    Bazelon's work provides an investigation into the causes, effects, and complexities of twenty-first-century bullying. Her study includes an examination of the impact of social media on bullying.

Cook, Philip J., and Kristin A. Goss, *The Gun Debate: What Everyone Needs to Know*, Oxford University Press, 2014.

    The economist Philip Cook and the political scientist Kristin A. Goss examine the research, data, and developments related to gun violence in America. They explore the relationship between mental illness and violent crime and review gun culture in America and the structure of both gun control and pro-gun movements.

Cullen, Dave, *Columbine*, Twelve, 2010.

    Cullen's work is one that is commonly referenced in discussions of school shootings in general and Columbine in particular. His work draws on interviews, police files, the work of FBI psychologists, and the recordings left by the two shooters.

Lysiak, Matthew, *Newtown: An American Tragedy*, Gallery Books, 2013.

    Lysiak is a journalist who in this volume examines the details related to the shooting at Sandy Hook Elementary School. Lysiak draws on interviews, police reports, and previously undisclosed e-mails in an effort to accurately portray the events of that day.

SUGGESTED SEARCH TERMS

Picoult AND Nineteen Minutes

Sandy Hook Elementary shootings

Columbine shootings

Picoult AND gun violence

Picoult AND school shootings

gun control legislation AND school shootings

Bowling for Columbine

school shooting statistics

Picoult AND literary AND commercial fiction

bullying AND school shootings

bullying AND posttraumatic stress

Song Yet Sung

JAMES MCBRIDE
2008

In October 2004, James McBride was fighting writer's block. He was working on a novel about slavery and the Civil War, but it was a struggle. He tried checking in to a hotel for a few days, hoping a change of scene would help, but it was not until McBride was driving home that his problem was solved: On Route 50 near Cambridge, Maryland, he a saw a small roadside sign commemorating Harriet Tubman and was surprised to learn that she had been born nearby. Thinking about Tubman's life—her accomplishments and her bravery—proved to be the inspiration McBride needed. The resulting novel, *Song Yet Sung* (2008), although not directly about Tubman, captures the controversies of her time: the horror and cruelty of slavery and the complicated relationship between slave owner and enslaved.

AUTHOR BIOGRAPHY

McBride was born on September 11, 1957, in Brooklyn, New York, and grew up in the Red Hook housing projects. His father was Andrew D. McBride, an African American minister. His mother was Ruchel Dwajra Zylska (later changed to Rachel Deborah Shilsky), a Jewish immigrant from Poland. McBride never knew his father, who died of lung cancer while his mother was pregnant with him. His mother

James McBride (© *Matt McClain / The Washington Post / Getty Images*)

remarried and had four more children, making McBride the eighth of twelve brothers and sisters.

McBride studied composition at the Oberlin Conservatory of Music in Ohio. After graduating in 1979, he returned to New York and earned a master's degree from the Columbia Journalism School at age twenty-two. While he continued to work on his music, composing and performing, McBride made a living by writing. His work appeared in many publications, including the *Boston Globe*, *People*, the *Washington Post*, *Rolling Stone*, *Essence*, and the *New York Times*.

McBride's first book was *The Color of Water: A Black Man's Tribute to His White Mother* (1996). The memoir tells McBride's own story as well as that of his mother, a remarkable woman. In spite of the prejudice she faced from her own family, her in-laws, and society in general because she was a white woman who married a black man, and in spite of being a young widow with a large family, she felt she succeeded in life, putting all twelve of her children through college. *The Color of Water* was

hugely popular, staying on the *New York Times* best-seller list for two years. McBride's first novel, *Miracle at St. Anna* (2002), was made into movie by Spike Lee in 2008, the same year *Song Yet Sung* was published. McBride's most recent book, *The Good Lord Bird* (2013), won the 2013 National Book Award for Fiction.

As of 2014, McBride splits his time between homes in Pennsylvania and New York. He is an award-winning composer and saxophonist and continues to write and pursue his musical career.

PLOT SUMMARY

The Code

At the beginning of *Song Yet Sung*, Liz Spocott wakes up at Patty Cannon's after a dream of the future. She remembers her escape attempt and her capture, in which she is shot in the head by Little George. She thinks she is dying, but she slowly recovers. The old Woman with No Name explains some of the Code—a secret system of

MEDIA ADAPTATIONS

- In 2009, Audible Audio released an audiobook of *Song Yet Sung* published by Penguin Audio and read by Leslie Uggams. The running time is ten hours and 44 minutes.

communication among the slaves, but Liz is confused by it. George attempts to rape Liz, but she stabs him with piece of metal she finds in the floor beneath her. After Little George is dead, all the slaves in the attic escape, Big Linus carrying the Woman with No Name.

Patty Cannon

Patty Cannon hears about the escaped slaves and is angry and worried about the money she has lost. The members of Patty's gang are introduced: Joe Johnson, the slave boy Eb, Odgin Harris, Hodge Wenner, and Stanton Davis. They specifically discuss Liz, who is called the Dreamer because of her visions.

The Gimp

Tolley comes to speak to Denwood Long, sometimes called the Gimp, asking him to come see Captain Spocott, who wants to hire Denwood to retrieve Liz. Denwood's wife and many of their neighbors superstitiously believe Denwood is to blame for his own son's death because he has put the boy in a basket with a six-legged dog. The boy later catches a fever and dies. Tolley tells Denwood he does not believe Liz can be caught because she is some kind of witch.

The Woolman

While running, Liz finds a young boy caught in a muskrat trap. She frees his leg from the trap and soothes him by giving him sassafras root to chew on. The boy's father, called the Woolman in local legend, sees Liz helping and leaves her some food and clothes.

Big Linus

Sarah and Louie Hughes see someone hiding in the foliage across the cove from their master's pier. Sarah tries to teach their son Gilbert some of the Code, and they leave some oysters out for whoever is hiding, believing it to be a runaway slave. Big Linus comes out of hiding once they are gone, eats the oysters, and takes the boat. The little boat sinks, and Linus is taken by Patty Cannon's gang. He fights them, and Patty shoots him.

Lums

Denwood goes to Captain Spocott's farm and agrees to take the job of finding Liz. After speaking to the captain, Denwood speaks to Lums, one of the plantation's slaves, and learns more about Liz. She has gained her visionary powers after being struck by a cruel overseer who was trying to harm Hewitt, who raised her after her mother died and her father was sold. Liz tried to protect Hewitt and was hit in the head.

Everything in Fives

Liz is still on the run. She remembers a conversation with Uncle Hewitt in which he told her to "lean on the everlasting cross." She meets Wiley on the road. He directs her to a hiding place in an old Indian burial ground and tells her he will send his uncle, Amber, who takes food to Liz and promises to help.

The Sign

Patty Cannon's gang is in Cambridge. They buy supplies at the general store and ask for information about Liz. They learn that Denwood is also looking for Liz.

Eighty Miles

Kathleen Sullivan thinks with fondness and concern about her slaves and questions whether slavery is civilized. She speaks to Amber about getting married, worried that he may be planning to run. She agrees to let him buy his freedom by doing extra work.

The Woolman Declares War

The Woolman is watching the Sullivan farm. He remembers his mother, an escaped slave who taught him how to survive and hide in the wilderness. The Woolman takes his son to town to get treatment for his ankle, which has been mangled in the muskrat trap. The town doctor wants to help, but the Woolman does not understand and thinks his son is being taken from him. He plans to kidnap Jeff Boy Sullivan so that he can bargain to get his own son back.

While helping Jeff Boy plant corn, Amber thinks about his plans for possible escape. There always seems to be a reason for delay. Patty Cannon comes to the farm, and Kathleen firmly sends her away. Amber catches a glimpse of the Woolman but does not believe his eyes.

The Blacksmith
Denwood questions the blacksmith about Liz but learns nothing. Denwood runs into some of the men from Patty's gang.

Discovered
Amber goes to see Liz in her hiding place. They discuss running away and the idea of freedom. Amber kisses her, but Patty's gang interrupts them. Liz and Amber flee, and Patty pursues them.

Snatched by the Devil
The Woolman kidnaps Jeff Boy. Wiley chases them into the forest. Kathleen follows, but the Woolman eludes them. Wiley fears that he and Amber will be blamed for the boy's disappearance. Patty catches up with Wiley and puts a chain on his ankle.

Sounding the Alarm
Ella takes the news of Jeff Boy's kidnapping into town. The constable, Travis House, is out of town, so the deputy, Herbie Tucker, tells Ella to carry the message to Franz Mucheimmer, who runs the general store.

Speak to the Pot
Amber tries to explain his relationship with the Sullivans to Liz. He takes her to Cambridge to see the blacksmith, who tells Amber about Jeff Boy being taken. Liz says she will not go on the "gospel train," but the blacksmith makes it clear she must go because he will not allow her to put others and the Code itself at risk.

Catching Money
Patty's gang goes to see the blacksmith and confront Amber. Amber leads the gang away from town, where Liz is still hiding at the blacksmith's, by telling them that Liz is still at the Indian burial ground.

Spreading the Word
Denwood comes to the Sullivan farm and finds local lawmen directing some watermen, who are out looking for Jeff Boy in their boats. Kathleen slams the door in Denwood's face when she hears that he is a slave catcher. Mary speaks to him, telling about the Woolman and saying that Amber has been acting strangely lately. Mary refuses to tell Denwood anything that may get Wiley in trouble, but she makes a deal with Denwood to help find Liz if he promises not to put Amber at risk.

The Double Wedding Rings
Ducky whispers a message to Clarence. Liz, still at the blacksmith's, has another dream. Stanton and Eb go to the blacksmith's, but the blacksmith distracts Stanton and Ducky distracts Eb just long enough for Clarence to sneak Liz out.

The Woolman Meets Patty
The Woolman has Jeff Boy in his hidden hut. The Woolman sees Patty, Odgin, Hodge, and Wiley moving through the forest. He kills Odgin, causing Hodge to flee, and then tackles Patty. Wiley takes Patty's knife and stabs the Woolman, who disappears into the trees. Wiley takes Odgin's horse and heads for home, leaving Patty on her own.

The Song Yet Sung
Denwood promises Kathleen he will keep an eye out for Jeff Boy. Kathleen and Mary talk, and Mary explains that Denwood has also promised to look for Amber.

Clarence takes Liz out onto the water in a little boat. She has another vision, this time clearly referencing Martin Luther King Jr.'s famous "I Have a Dream" speech. Liz seems to be falling asleep and having dreams more and more often.

Meeting Joe
Wiley, on his way home, meets Joe and Amber. Joe tries to shoot Wiley, but Amber screams at him to run. Amber overcomes Joe and flees on foot. Joe pursues him on horseback. Denwood hears the gunshots and sees Wiley ride by. Denwood stops Amber by hitting him with a branch and then argues with Joe. Joe draws a rifle on Denwood, but the Woolman appears and throws a hatchet at Joe, making his shot go wide. Joe tries to shoot Denwood again with his revolver, but Denwood gets a shot off first, killing Joe.

Finding the Woolman

Wiley tells Kathleen about chasing the Woolman and being caught by Patty. Clarence leaves Liz near the old Indian burial ground. As she makes her way back to her former hiding place, Liz meets the Woolman. She looks at his injuries, and then he leads her to a beach.

Hell in Spite of Redemption

Denwood and Amber discuss Liz. Amber explains his ties to the Sullivans and describes one of Liz's dreams.

Liz's Discovery

Patty and Stanton head for the Indian burial ground. They find Joe's body, and Patty takes his boots, having lost one of her own while chasing Liz and Amber.

The Woolman and Liz have spent the night on the beach, and now he leads her to his hut. She finds Jeff Boy tied to a chair.

Denwood Meets the Woolman

Amber and Denwood find the Woolman's house. Amber sees Liz and calls out to her, but she seems not to notice him until he touches her. She tells him that Jeff Boy is there, safe. The Woolman attacks Denwood, who fires his gun. The shot misses. The Woolman tackles Denwood, and they grapple in the sand. Denwood takes the Woolman's knife and stabs him with it. The Woolman then pulls the knife out of his body and stabs Denwood several times. Denwood is sure the Woolman will kill him, but Liz takes Denwood's gun and shoots the Woolman. She cries at his death.

Showdown

Patty has been watching the action from a distance. Once the Woolman is dead, she approaches with Stanton. She threatens Denwood, Amber, and Liz. When Stanton refuses to look in the Woolman's house for Jeff Boy, Patty shoots and kills him. She coaxes Jeff Boy out of the hut. Amber shouts to Jeff Boy to run. Patty aims her gun at the boy. Denwood, though injured, summons enough strength to knock her gun aside. Kathleen appears and shoots Patty. Denwood dies.

Epilogue

Amber and Kathleen bring Liz back to the creek behind Patty and Joe's tavern. She is weak, presumably because of her repeated head injuries,

and wants to die in the same place where the Woman with No Name has met her end. The Woolman's son is with them. Kathleen has given Amber his freedom and paid the county for the Woolman's son, who is considered unclaimed property. Amber will go to Philadelphia to raise the boy and earn money to repay Kathleen. Liz believes that that boy's descendant will be the man in her dream (Martin Luther King Jr.).

CHARACTERS

Amber

Amber is a slave on the Sullivan farm. He is Mary's brother-in-law and Wiley's uncle. He plans to escape one day, taking Wiley with him, but he feels guilty about leaving Kathleen Sullivan to run the farm on her own, because she has been kind to him. He also cares deeply for Jeff Boy. Amber falls in love with Liz and tries to help her.

Jasper Baxter

Jasper Baxter is the doctor in town who tries to help the Woolman's son while he is in jail.

The Blacksmith

Virgil works as a blacksmith in Cambridge. He uses the rhythm of his hammer strikes to send messages by the Code. Amber asks the blacksmith to help Liz.

Patty Cannon

Patty Cannon is based on a historical figure, Martha "Patty" Cannon, who led a gang that made money by kidnapping slaves and free blacks and selling them for profit. McBride's character is a mixture of terrible and admirable qualities. For a woman of her time, she has accomplished an impressive amount: running a business and leading men. However, she chooses to make her living from the enslavement and misery of others, and she does so without mercy or any apparent remorse.

Clarence

Clarence works as a delivery man at the general store in Cambridge. He plays the role of a harmless older man, but he does his part in spreading messages according to the Code. Clarence takes Liz in a rowboat in an effort to help her escape.

Clementine

Clementine is a slave at the Gables farm who sends coded messages through the quilts she hangs outside to air.

Stanton Davis

Stanton Davis is one of Patty Cannon's gang, although she does not trust him the way she does her other men.

Ducky

Ducky plays the fool, quacking and flapping his arms to earn a few coins from onlookers in Cambridge. He hides behind this foolishness so that he can spread secret messages.

Ella

Ella is one of the slaves on the Gables farm. She carries the message of Jeff Boy's disappearance into Cambridge.

John Gables

John Gables owns the farm next to Kathleen Sullivan's land.

Missus Gables

Missus Gables is John Gables's wife. In contrast to Kathleen Sullivan, who treats her slaves like family, Missus Gables "would reach over the Devil's back before she showed kindness to a colored."

Will Gables

Will Gables is John Gables's son. Will used to make extra money by forcing Big Linus, who was just a boy then, to fight other slaves. When Linus grows into manhood and becomes hard to handle, Will sells him.

Little George

Little George is a slave who belongs to Patty Cannon and helps with her slave-catching business. It is Little George who captures Liz, but when he tries to rape her, she kills him, and all the slaves escape.

The Gimp

See Denwood Long

Odgin Harris

Odgin Harris is one of the men in Patty Cannon's gang. She believes he will be loyal to her because he enjoys the work of slave catching.

Hewitt

Hewitt is the elderly man who raises Liz after her mother dies and her father is sold off the plantation for causing trouble. She remembers him fondly. Hewitt raises several children for Captain Spocott but never marries.

Travis House

Travis House is the constable (or policeman) in the area, but he spends much of the action of the novel out of town.

Drew Hughes

Drew is Louie and Sarah Hughes's older son, who has run away.

Gilbert Hughes

Gilbert is Louie and Sarah Hughes's younger son. Sarah is determined to teach him the Code, although he seems to resent her instruction.

Louie Hughes

Louie is Gilbert and Drew's father and Sarah's husband. His fear makes him hesitant to help escaped slaves.

Sarah Hughes

Sarah is Gilbert and Drew's mother and Louie's wife. She teaches Gilbert the Code and tries to help Big Linus by setting out food for him because she hopes that someone helped Drew when he ran away.

Jenny

Jenny is one of Captain Spocott's slaves. Lums is her husband.

Joe Johnson

Joe is Patty Cannon's son-in-law and a member of her gang. He is not a strong man, letting his mother-in-law control virtually every aspect of his life, including taking over much of the business of his tavern.

Maddy Cannon Johnson

Maddy is Patty Cannon's daughter and Joe Johnson's wife. She dies before the action of the novel, though Joe still misses her. Maddy was nothing like her mother. She was a helpful and kind partner to Joe while he was building his tavern business.

Homer Jones

Homer Jones runs the shop across the street from Franz Mucheimmer's general store in Cambridge.

Big Linus

Big Linus gets his name from his unusual size. He is one of the slaves who escape from Patty Cannon's house with Liz early in the story. He carries the old Woman with No Name because she is too weak to walk on her own. Big Linus is killed when Patty Cannon and her gang try to recapture him.

Denwood Long

Denwood is called the Gimp because of an old injury to his leg. He has been a slave catcher but retires from the work after his son's death, for which he blames himself. When Tolley is sent by Captain Spocott to convince Denwood to catch Liz, he looks at Denwood and thinks "the man [is] dead inside."

Lums

Lums is Jenny's husband and one of Captain Spocott's slaves. Denwood Long questions Lums about Liz's escape.

Mary

Mary is a slave on the Sullivan farm. She is Amber's sister-in-law and Wiley's mother. Her husband, Nate, drowns in the boating accident with Boyd Sullivan, which gives her a kind of bond with Kathleen. Mary is a caring woman, and she fears that Wiley will try to run away someday.

Mingo

Mingo is an almost legendary slave who has a reputation of being very clever. Denwood Long is able to capture him when no one else can.

Moses

Although Harriet Tubman is never mentioned by name, the text refers to "a great woman named Moses." Tubman is sometimes called a Moses to her people, a reference to the biblical story in which Moses leads the Israelites out of slavery in Egypt.

Franz Mucheimmer

Franz runs the general store and the post office in Cambridge. He believes that "he and his wife [are] the only Jews on the eastern shore between Baltimore and Ocean City."

Nate

Nate is Mary's husband, Amber's brother, and Wiley's father. He dies in a boating accident before the story begins.

Dill Reitzer

Dill Reitzer is the captain of the boat that brings the mail into Cambridge City from across the bay.

Liz Spocott

Liz is a runaway slave. As a child, she is hit in the head while trying to protect her surrogate father. From that point on, she has dreams that are visions of the future. Her ability to see the future becomes a kind of legend in the African American community after she escapes from Patty Cannon's attic. Much of the plot of the novel turns on the other characters helping Liz escape. Amber falls in love with her, but she resists his attentions.

Captain Willard Spocott

Captain Spocott is Liz's master. He hires Denwood Long to find her after she escapes. Denwood believes that Captain Spocott has a sexual relationship with Liz and that is why he wants her back so urgently.

Boyd Sullivan

Boyd is Kathleen Sullivan's husband and father to Jeff Boy, Donnie, and Jack Sullivan. Before the story begins, Boyd is lost while out on his boat. Kathleen has not stopped watching for him to return.

Donnie Sullivan

Donnie is one of Kathleen Sullivan's sons.

Jack Sullivan

Jack is one of Kathleen Sullivan's sons.

Jeff Boy Sullivan

Jeff Boy is Kathleen Sullivan's oldest son. He is close to Amber, who stands as a kind of father figure now that Boyd Sullivan is dead. The Woolman kidnaps Jeff Boy in the hope of trading him to get his own son back.

Kathleen Sullivan

Kathleen is a young widow, still mourning her husband's death. She is the mother of three sons. Kathleen is kind to her slaves and trusts them for the most part, though she fears that Amber will run away soon. Kathleen stands up for herself, even against Patty Cannon, but she is vulnerable as a woman alone on an isolated farm.

States Tipton

Tipton is a "deadly slave trader from Alabama." Patty Cannon has borrowed money from him and will not be able to pay him back if she cannot recapture and sell some of the slaves who escape from her attic.

Tolley

Tolley is sent by Captain Spocott to fetch Denwood Long. Spocott wants to hire Denwood to catch Liz.

Herbie Tucker

Herbie Tucker is the deputy constable in Cambridge, working under Travis House.

Virgil

See the Blacksmith

Hodge Wenner

Hodge is one of the members of Patty Cannon's gang. He is very loyal to her, so much so that she believes he will continue working without pay when she loses money because of the slaves' escape.

Wiley

Wiley is Mary and Nate's son and Amber's nephew. He is one of the slaves on the Sullivan farm. He meets Liz on the road and tells Amber about her, wanting to help.

Eb Willard

Eb is a young boy whom Patty Cannon intends to use as a replacement for Little George. He is her only legal slave. He runs errands and delivers messages for Patty's gang.

Woman with No Name

The old Woman with No Name is one of the slaves captured with Liz in Patty Cannon's attic. She tells Liz about the Code, although Liz is confused by her words. Big Linus tries to carry the old woman when they escape from the attic,

but she tells him to put her down. Her death foreshadows Liz's death at the end of the novel.

The Woolman

The Woolman is a shadowy, mysterious figure. Some even doubt he exists until he kidnaps Jeff Boy after his own son is taken into town and put in jail. The Woolman is the son of an escaped slave. Having lived in the wilderness his entire life, he can blend into the trees and the swamps until he is invisible.

The Woolman's Son

Liz helps the Woolman's son when she finds him with his foot caught in an animal trap. After his son ends up in the town jail, the Woolman kidnaps Jeff Boy, hoping to trade for his own captive son.

THEMES

Family

The theme of family runs constantly through *Song Yet Sung*. The characters act in ways that show that they feel family ties strongly. Mary and Kathleen mourn for their husbands, watching the water for the boat months after all hope of return is gone. Mary is fiercely protective of Wiley; she refuses to give Denwood any hint of where Wiley might be, saying, "Long as there's a chance he's living, I won't do it. They'd have to kill me 'fore I tell on my own account." Kathleen is also protective of her children, and after Jeff Boy is kidnapped, she is determined, in spite of her fear and worry, to get him back. In the tumultuous climax of the book, Kathleen even shoots Patty Cannon, who has been threatening Jeff Boy and Amber with a pistol. Jeff Boy's kidnapping is also caused by the pull of family ties: The Woolman's reason for taking the boy in the first place is that he is separated from his own son. Even Patty Cannon seems to feel some loyalty to her son-in-law, though her daughter is no longer around to link the two of them together.

Not all families are made up of blood relatives. Sometimes families are created out of circumstance. The institution of slavery forces unrelated people into living closely, creating some unusual family units. When Denwood questions Lums about Liz, Lums explains that after Liz's mother died and Captain Spocott deemed her father trouble, Hewitt adopted her

TOPICS FOR FURTHER STUDY

- Using traditional and online sources, research the life of Harriet Tubman, who was McBride's initial inspiration for *Song Yet Sung*. While doing your research, look for similarities between Tubman and Liz. If Liz had met Tubman, what do you think they would say to each other? What advice would Tubman offer? How would Liz react? Answer these questions by writing a short story in which you depict a scene in which the two women meet.

- In *Song Yet Sung*, McBride explains how slaves communicated through a code, using the patterns of quilts and rearranging their clothing to send secret messages. People also communicated through spirituals— songs sung while working that usually had religious themes. For example, "Swing Low, Sweet Chariot" is believed to refer to the Underground Railroad. Research African American spirituals to create a presentation for your class. Play recordings of some of the songs for your class, or if you are musically inclined, perform the songs

yourself or with a classmate. Explain the meaning of the songs' symbols and secret messages to the class.

- Read Noni Carter's young-adult novel *Good Fortune* (2010), which centers on a young woman's journey from her life in an African village to a slave ship, then from the cotton fields to working in her master's house, and finally north to freedom. Write an essay comparing Carter's protagonist, Anna, with Liz. Do their outlooks differ because one was born free and the other was born a slave? Are they running toward something or simply running away from captivity?

- Use traditional and online sources to learn about Maryland's eastern shore. Put together a PowerPoint presentation with maps and pictures of the area, including images of the countryside and the waterways. Share your presentation with your classmates to give them a strong impression of the novel's setting.

---

and took care of her. This is not the only time Hewitt raises children. Lums tells Denwood that Hewitt "wouldn't take a wife, no matter how much the captain tried to make him." Perhaps Hewitt does not want to bring more children into a world where they can be sold away. Indeed, the captain cruelly separated Hewitt from the children he raised: "When they was big enough, captain sold off every one of them, except Liz."

On the Sullivan farm, another unconventional family forms. Kathleen is a slave owner, but she treats everyone on her land with kindness. She feels that Amber, Mary, and Wiley are

part of her family, and hers, she felt, was part of theirs. She could not imagine life without them. She believed that they, like her, understood that their collective survival made them dependent on each other, and that made her feel safe.

One might assume that it is much easier for the master to feel this way than for the slave, who has no choice about the relationship or about whether to stay or go, but McBride makes it quite clear that Amber feels the same way. He tells Denwood that Kathleen Sullivan and her sons are "my family in this world. All of 'em." Amber stands in as a father figure for Jeff Boy, now that Boyd is dead. He tells Liz, "I love him like my own."

There was a practice of slaves being given their owners' surnames, as with Liz having Captain Spocott's name. However, the slaves on the Sullivan farm are not identified by any surname. It seems like a contradiction that they do not share Kathleen's name when they all feel like a family, but in truth it reflects the fact that she

The story takes place on Maryland's eastern shore and the Chesapeake Bay. *(© Lone Wolf Photos /*
Shutterstock.com)

does not have the need to dominate her slaves
and reinforce her power of ownership over them
the way masters like Captain Spocott do.

Freedom

In a novel about slavery, it is inevitable that
freedom will be in the characters' minds.
McBride goes to great lengths to explain the
Code, the elaborate system used by the African
American community to pass messages, to help
people to freedom, and to escape the detection of
the white masters and slave catchers. The characters who are slaves act according to the Code,
and even the minor characters are shown doing
their part. Whether they run themselves, pass on
a coded message, send a warning, set out food
for a runaway, or simply look the other way,
people work toward freedom. Those who are
not free can never be content. When Denwood
talks to Lums, who lives on Captain Spocott's
farm, they mention that Patty Cannon might
come "around raising hell," looking for information about Liz. Lums does not seem bothered
by the prospect, saying, "What do it matter to

me? . . . I'm in hell now." His life will always be
hellish because he is not free.

It is not only the slaves who are preoccupied
with the idea of freedom: The masters must consider the idea as well. Kathleen Sullivan's father
tries to get her to move to Ocean City with him
by hinting that her slaves might run away, leaving her helpless. "How can a colored be happy,"
he asks, "if freedom is only eighty miles away?"
Perhaps being so close makes the idea of freedom more tantalizing because it seems more
possible, though plenty of people made a break
for freedom much farther south. From that
point forward, however, Kathleen watches
Amber carefully, wondering how likely he is to
bolt.

In comparing the first scene of the book with
that at the end, one can see the difference that
freedom makes. In the beginning of the novel,
Liz believes she is dying. McBride makes it clear
in the first sentence that Liz is a slave, but her
lack of freedom is compounded by the fact that
she is a runaway caught and now in captivity,

imprisoned in Patty Cannon's attic. Her fevered dreams and memories of her capture give the entire scene a feeling of desperation—Liz is not ready to die. In contrast, at the end of the book, Liz knows that she is dying, but rather than grief or desperation, she seems to go to her death willingly because she is "dying unencumbered, beholden to no one, without even a name." Her freedom brings her peace, even when facing death. As she tells Amber, "Being a slave is a lie. . . . you got to live in a place where you can at least make a choice."

STYLE

Historical Novel

A historical novel comprises a story that takes place in the past. The author makes an effort to realistically recreate the details of that era. The best authors of historical fiction do exhaustive research while working on a novel to ensure that the details are as accurate and plausible as possible. In the author's note at the end of *Song Yet Sung*, McBride thanks scholars who gave him advice and people who worked at the many libraries and museums where he did research. He mentions reading "about twenty-five books and various slave manuscripts and testimonies before putting this novel together." He also explored Maryland's eastern shore and found that with its farms and small towns, "it is a land that even today looks as it did a hundred years ago." Seeing the setting in person and reading the first-hand accounts of slave experiences gave him a framework to build on to make his story come to life.

This is not to say that research is all that is needed. If authors did not also use their imaginations, they would be writing a history book rather than a novel. Historical novels are set in an actual period in history and might even have versions of historical figures as characters, as McBride includes Patty Cannon and Harriet Tubman, but they are still fiction. Authors of historical novels take liberties with historical events to suit their plots or the needs of their characters. However, readers can still learn much from historical fiction, as long as they are sure to do their own research before accepting the elements of any novel as historical fact.

Point of View

Throughout *Song Yet Sung*, McBride switches the point of view of the narrative among numerous characters. McBride uses various perspectives to give insight into the characters and give as much information as possible to the reader. Often the narrative is from a major character like Liz or Amber or Denwood, but sometimes a scene is told from the perspective of a minor character. For example, Ducky has little presence in the novel, but the narrative shifts to his point of view for a brief scene in which he acts up for the townspeople and gets in Clarence's way as he is pushing a wheelbarrow full of oysters. Ducky's antics cause Clarence to lose his balance and spill his load, giving Ducky an opportunity to pass on a message about the blacksmith. By using the point of view of a minor character, McBride shows how widespread the network of helpers is throughout the town, and how they are able to communicate secretly but effectively while distracting onlookers by "eliciting a cascade of laughter from the white pedestrians who watched."

McBride slides the point of view between his characters seamlessly, sometimes right in the middle of a scene. The scene of Big Linus's death is a good illustration of McBride's skill with these transitions. The scene opens with Linus watching Sarah teach Gilbert elements of the code and leave food out. Linus then thinks about the escape from Patty Cannon's basement. That the reader is privy to Big Linus's memory shows how deeply the story is embedded in his point of view. Linus takes the oysters Sarah leaves out for him, shoves off in the little boat, and begins to row. The reader can almost feel Linus's panic when his boat sinks. He feels "as if a water devil had grabbed his chest, then his legs and clung on." Then suddenly Patty Cannon's gang catches Linus. The narrative is still firmly with Linus as he hears their boat creak and feels the net, but then, over the next page or so, McBride gradually alters the perspective until the action is seen from a more neutral stance and then to Patty's point of view, so that by the time Patty fires the gun that kills Big Linus, the narrative has completely shifted to her. It is a difficult change to make in such a short span of text, and many authors do not manage it with the grace that McBride shows in his work.

The waterways and swamps become both obstacles and places of refuge for the runaways. (© Arman Zender /
Shutterstock.com)

HISTORICAL CONTEXT

Harriet Tubman

McBride was inspired to write *Song Yet Sung* by
the historical figure Harriet Tubman. Tubman
was born a slave near Cambridge, Maryland,
around 1820. Unlike many slaves, Tubman had
some stability in her childhood. She had a large
family—she was one of eleven children—that
was lucky to stay together rather than being
separated and sold off to other slave owners.
When she was thirteen years old, Tubman experienced a blow to the head while trying to protect
another slave from an angry overseer. Some say
the injury made her have visions as Liz does in
McBride's novel, though this is likely a folk tale.
Tubman did, however, have seizures through the
rest of her life. Later, Tubman cited her recovery
from this injury as a contemplative time when
she began to question her condition as a slave.

In 1844, Harriet married John Tubman, a
local free black man. Although her husband lacked
ambition and did not seem bothered by her status
as a slave, Tubman researched the possibility that
her mother might have been made free when a
former owner died without a will. This issue was
still unresolved in 1849, when Tubman fled to
Pennsylvania to gain her freedom. Her experience
of escaping without help made her determined to
help others.

As a conductor for the Underground Railroad, Tubman led more than two hundred people to freedom, making more than a dozen trips
into southern slave states, risking her own hard-
won freedom, and then back up north. It is said
that she sang coded songs to communicate to
slaves and runaways. She eventually freed her
parents and all of her siblings. Later in life, Tubman worked as both a spy and a nurse for the
Union during the Civil War.

Underground Railroad

Although McBride does not directly reference
the Underground Railroad, many of the ways
in which the African American community tried
to help runaways are drawn from what is known
about the actual experiences of escaped slaves.

The role of white Americans in the Underground Railroad is often misunderstood. Although white abolitionists helped, especially the Quakers, the Underground Railroad was started, run, and supported by African Americans. Wealthy, educated African Americans in the north contributed money to the cause and arranged legal help. Those from the working class raised money, gathered food and supplies, and provided shelter to runaways.

The Underground Railroad was not a single, unified organization but a network of various groups and routes throughout the northern and upper southern states. Many groups were founded through black churches. One of the most effective stations in the Underground Railroad was fun by free blacks and operated near Baltimore and Washington, DC, helping slaves from farms and plantations throughout Virginia and Maryland.

The number of people actually helped to freedom by the Underground Railroad was small in proportion to the number still enslaved—the Underground Railroad would never have threatened slavery as an institution. Most slaves who escaped set out on their own, although they may have received help down the line. However, the very existence of the organization proved wrong one of the common rationalizations used to justify slavery: that African Americans were somehow inferior or incapable of taking care of themselves or were content with their lots as slaves. It also provided hope to many people living under the horrors of slavery.

CRITICAL OVERVIEW

The critical reception of *Song Yet Sung* has been generally favorable. Many reviewers comment on the quick-moving plot, which Barbara Lloyd McMichael of the *Seattle Times* calls "gripping" and "engrossing." Madison Smartt Bell of the *New York Times* notes that a reader might become so wrapped up in the "well-designed, gripping plot" that he or she "risks turning the pages so fast as to miss some of the richness and subtlety of the writing." Bell does, however, draw attention to the fact that McBride struggles to tie up all the loose ends in his complicated, ambitious story, pointing out that "some elements in the generally masterly plot have to be battered into place at the end."

Writing for the *Washington Post Book World*, David Anthony Durham agrees:

> The novel does have its weaker moments. At times McBride's exposition seems rushed, as if he's got more information to give than time to give it. His action scenes can feel like stage directions for a film.

Several reviewers have commented on McBride's deft touch with dialogue and characterization. Durham praises how

> McBride shows the complexity of his characters' inner lives and dilemmas—particularly his black characters. The cadence of their speech, the way they interact, the small details of their thoughts, desires, fears and hopes: These the author renders with exquisite ease.

Bell also notes that "McBride has a good ear for period black dialect, and a deft touch with all sorts of dialogue."

Critical opinions differ about McBride's incorporation of Liz's dreams of the future. Whereas some believe that it adds an interesting, introspective dimension to the story, others consider it an unnecessary or even confusing addition to an otherwise strong novel. Troy Patterson, in a review in *Entertainment Weekly*, asserts about Liz's dreams that "the reader's never sure what that has to do with anything else." Patterson believes the visions of the future cause the narrative to "spiral into irrelevance . . . undermining its textured take on history." Durham admits, "Some may groan that Liz's prescience is forced, especially as she sees further and further into the future." However, Durham notes McBride's intent: "He is not just interested in staring into an antique, distant past. This past is living. It is linked to the present." McMichael agrees; she sees Liz's visions as McBride's attempt "to indict some aspects of contemporary black culture even as it weaves a story of the slave experience in the antebellum South, and of the varied attitudes and complicities of white folk."

Song Yet Sung has enjoyed quite a bit of popular success. It is a common choice for book clubs and was a *New York Times* best seller. Because of the novel's popularity, the Grammnet Nh production company announced plans in November 2013 to adapt *Song Yet Sung* as a television miniseries. As Bell writes, "*Song Yet Sung* isn't flawless," but the "defects are too small and peripheral to seriously detract from the pleasure or value of this book."

CRITICISM

Kristen Sarlin Greenberg

Greenberg is a freelance writer and editor with a background in literature and philosophy. In the following essay, she examines McBride's skilled portrayal of the depth and complexity of the issue of slavery in Song Yet Sung.

Many books, both fiction and nonfiction, have been written on the subject of slavery. *Song Yet Sung* is a skillful exploration of the theme in that it reflects its complexity. It would be easy to write a novel that simply portrays the torture of living as a slave, for there certainly were many physical, emotional, and psychological abuses forced on people. McBride has done something much more effective than just exposing the evils of the institution because he portrays true-to-life characters who do not see the world in black-and-white terms.

McBride does present the extremes in the spectrum of behavior and opinion. Amber tells Liz about Missus Gables, who lives next to the Sullivan farm and would "reach over the Devil's back before she showed kindness to a colored." Her son, Will, is no better: Just so that he can earn a few extras dollars now and then by gambling, he forces the young Big Linus to fight other slaves. Lums thinks about a man named Mingo, "a troublesome, clever slave" that Denwood Long "tracked . . . for weeks, all the way to Canada." Perhaps Mingo is the sort of person who would fight for his freedom no matter the cost. However, these are minor characters and are barely mentioned. The main players in McBride's story are three-dimensional and complicated, not simplistic.

A comparison of the slave catchers, Patty Cannon and Denwood Long, illustrates the breadth and depth of McBride's characterizations. To modern sensibilities, a slave catcher seems to be the lowest of the low: someone who makes a living by capturing people who have made a break for freedom from unjust and cruel enslavement. Patty Cannon fits this idea of a slave catcher. She is sly, vicious, mercenary, and vengeful. McBride does add touches to her personality to make her human. For example, Patty seems fond of Little George, though she seems to think of him more as a pet than a person, and after he is killed she easily replaces him in her gang with Eb. McBride also presents Patty's fretting about the money she owes to

> **BECAUSE MCBRIDE APPROACHES THE STILL CONTROVERSIAL AND DELICATE SUBJECT OF SLAVERY WITH A SPIRIT OF INVESTIGATION RATHER THAN WITH ANGER AND BITTERNESS—HOWEVER JUSTIFIED SUCH RESENTMENT MIGHT BE—HE FOSTERS THAT SPIRIT IN HIS READERS."**

States Tipton, the "deadly slave trader from Alabama." She fears what Tipton will do if she cannot repay her debt on time. Perhaps the reader finds it hard to actually sympathize with Patty's worries, but these details show McBride's efforts to keep her from becoming a shallow, unrealistic villain. It is true, however, that Patty is even worse than a slave catcher: She is a slave stealer, kidnapping slaves away from their lawful masters and taking free blacks to sell them into slavery. For her, slaves are things, not people.

In contrast to Patty Cannon is Denwood Long. He is a slave catcher not because he enjoys the work or because he wants to profit from the misery of others but because he is good at it and because it is a legitimate profession in that particular time and place. Denwood is far from perfect. He has what in the early twenty-first century would be called anger management issues. At times he is overtaken with a wave of

> rage—the white noise that had drowned his hearing as a young man and carried him from one end of the nation to the other to destroy all that was within in that did not work.

He works, however, to control his anger rather than profiting by his baser nature, the way Patty Cannon does. Denwood's humanity is also illustrated by the grief he feels for his late son. He also clearly regrets chasing his wife away with his grief and anger after their son's death. Although Denwood is a slave catcher, when he interacts with slaves, he speaks to them respectfully rather than treating them like children. Denwood is troubled when he realizes that for slaves like Mary, who would do anything to protect her son,

WHAT DO I READ NEXT?

- McBride's first book was *The Color of Water: A Black Man's Tribute to His White Mother* (1996). The book is a personal memoir, but it also tells the story of McBride's mother, a Jewish immigrant from Poland who married an African American man. She struggled against the racial prejudice of her time and worked hard as the mother of twelve children.

- In *Song Yet Sung*, McBride portrays the complicated relationships between white families and their enslaved black workers. Julius Lester tackles the same delicate issue in *Day of Tears: A Novel in Dialogue* (2005), which tells the story of Emma, who cares for the two young daughters of her master as if they were her own.

- McBride's work is often compared with that of Edward P. Jones, who also writes about the controversial issue of slavery without the rancor that inevitably and understandably bleeds into much of the discussion on the matter. Jones's *The Known World* (2003) is set in antebellum Virginia and features an African American slave owner, adding a twist to an already complex, provocative subject.

- Deborah Ellis has written a series of young-adult novels about Bolivian *cocaleros*, farmers who raise coca, which is used to make cocaine. Many *cocaleros* barely earn enough to survive with their small farms, and their crops are intended for local medicinal use rather than the illegal drug trade. Both *I Am a Taxi* (2006) and *Sacred Leaf* (2008) center on twelve-year-old Diego, whose parents are imprisoned. Diego works as a virtual slave for an illegal cocaine operation and is swept up in politics as he worries about his family.

- William Still, himself the son of slaves and an active member of the Underground Railroad, compiled the stories of escaped slaves in a journal that he published once the Civil War was over. It is often still considered the most complete record of first-hand accounts of the experience. A new edition of the volume, *The Underground Railroad: Authentic Narratives and First-Hand Accounts*, was released in 2007 by Dover Publications.

- Slavery still exists in the modern world. *The Queen of Water* (2011) by Laura Resau and Maria Virginia Farinango, although fiction, is based on Farinango's own experiences after she was sold as a servant, taken out of her village in Ecuador, and forced to work. Only seven years old when her enslavement begins, Virginia fights against the restrictive life, teaching herself to read and eventually finding her way back home.

---

their lives were exact mirrors of his, filled with silent, roaring, desperate human fury and humiliation. He realized at that moment that he despised them even as he admired them. How could you hate someone and like them at the same time?

Although perhaps less dramatic characters than Patty and Denwood, Kathleen Sullivan and Amber are even better illustrations of McBride's commitment to fairly and comprehensively presenting the deep, contradictory feelings people had about slavery. Amber knows that slavery is wrong, and Kathleen is coming to realize that as well, but both must rely on their current situations to feel safe and to keep their family together.

Through Kathleen Sullivan, McBride shows slavery from the perspective of the master. Although Kathleen owns slaves, she is portrayed as a kind, caring, and responsible person. She "grew up with slavery" and sees "it as a necessary evil." However, she is beginning to understand that slavery is wrong:

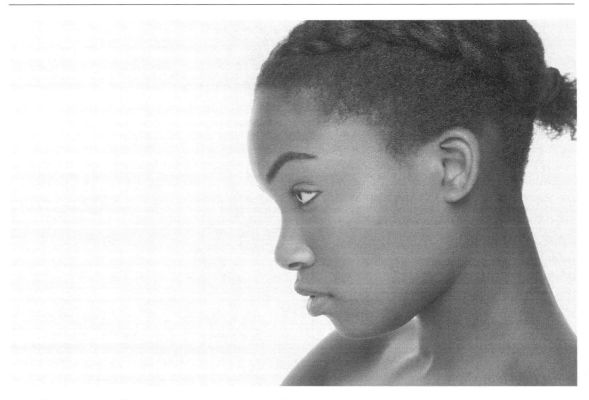

Liz's beauty enthralls Amber, so he tries to help her. (© T Anderson | Shutterstock.com)

the older she got, the more troubling it seemed. She believed the Negro was inferior—was sure of it—but lately she had taken to reading the Bible. . . . The more she read the Bible, the less civilized slavery seemed.

Even more than her reading, the people that Kathleen sees every day seem to convince her that they do not belong in their present lot in life. She sees them as people and respects their abilities and their intelligence. She had even "wanted to teach Amber his letters, but her late husband stopped her." Kathleen has always believed what she has been taught about African Americans needing to be taken care of, but the evidence of her own eyes refutes that:

> No matter what the constables said, no matter what the newspaper and politicians declared about the contented, happy slave, no matter how many songs were sung, poems written, smiling mammies produced, weddings held, promises made, kindnesses offered, children celebrated, and jump-de-broom galas her rich fellow slaveholders held in the Big House on behalf of their beloved Sambos, Aunt Pollys, and Uncle Toms, the eighty-miles-to-the-freedom-line business hung grimly over the eastern shore like a cloud, and Kathleen felt it, every drop of it.

Because she respects and cares for Amber, Mary, and Wiley, Kathleen can no longer see them as inferior or contented while still slaves, which reinforces the idea that keeping them as property cannot be right. She knows that they cannot be oblivious to the possibilities of freedom only eighty miles away from their farm, and she struggles with the realization that they deserve that freedom.

On the other side of coin from Kathleen is Amber, and it is through him that McBride shows the ambiguities from a slave's perspective. Amber is a slave who longs for freedom so much he will not allow himself to marry because he wants nothing to tie him to the Sullivan farm when he finally makes his escape. Kathleen fears that Amber will run: "Everything he did . . . screamed runaway." Indeed, he does plan to leave one day, possibly taking Wiley with him. However, he does not have it in him to be selfish. When Kathleen asks him point blank if he plans to run, he demurs: "All I got is right here. . . . My sister needs me. Wiley needs a man now." He stays for his blood relatives, but another part of the reason he does not leave is his concern that Kathleen will not be able to run the farm without his help. He tells Denwood, "She can't run the place alone." Amber describes the Sullivans, in addition to Mary and Wiley, as "my family in this world. All of 'em." Amber asks Kathleen about the possibility of buying his freedom. She agrees to it and asks what he might do. He answers, "Build me a boat. Take a wife. Get work oystering. Maybe take Jeff Boy fishing. He's my fishing buddy, y'know." Amber imagines an ideal situation, in which he can become free and still maintain his ties with the Sullivan family.

This complex characterization was purposeful on McBride's part. In an interview with NPR, he explains that he "felt that it was important to show people as I believe they really were, as opposed to the stereotypical view of slavery." In the real world, people are not completely evil or angels who never do any wrong. "Good people do bad things," McBride explains, and "bad people do good things." He continues,

> You have to forgive the past. . . . I think only now am I at the age where I've forgiven the past enough to say, "You know what? Slavery was there. Let's talk about it in ways that will help us face tomorrow." . . . Slavery really was a web of relationships. Seeing [it] from that perspective is what kind of propelled this book along.

Because McBride approaches the still controversial and delicate subject of slavery with a spirit of investigation rather than with anger and bitterness—however justified such resentment might be—he fosters that spirit in his readers. This kind of attitude opens people's minds and furthers the discussion rather than dividing people. The subject of slavery in the United States will always be one tied to strong emotions and controversy, and indeed, it should be. There is much to be angry about, to be ashamed of, and to apologize for in that period US history. A novel like *Song Yet Sung*, however, may help society move forward by fairly showing multiple points of view and clearly illustrating the complexity of the issue.

Source: Kristen Sarlin Greenberg, Critical Essay on *Song Yet Sung*, in *Novels for Students*, Gale, Cengage Learning, 2015.

Pam Houston
In the following review, Houston describes McBride's novel as "beautifully paced" and "deeply troubling."

"Chance is an instrument of God," the No Name woman tells Liz Spocott, the beautiful,

twice-escaped slave at the center of James McBride's second novel, *Song Yet Sung* (Riverhead). "And the coach wrench turns the wagon wheel. . . . Scratch a line in the dirt to make a friend. . . . Use double wedding rings when you marry. Tie the wedding knot five times. And remember, it's not the song, but the singer of it. You got to sing the second part twice." Liz doesn't at first understand the meaning of the Code given to her by the No Name woman just before she dies, but she feels the import of the words.

The year is 1850, and on Maryland's Eastern Shore the woods, swamps, and waterways are alive with the movements of runaway slaves—who can sense the freedom that awaits them only 80 miles north across the Pennsylvania state line—and the slave catchers hired to return them to their owners. These Chesapeake backwaters are also home to the watermen: poor, tough, fiercely independent blacks and whites, generations of oystermen who sometimes ferry runaways to safety; and to Woolman, an escaped slave who has avoided capture for years by learning to run like an animal and stand still as a tree; and to the volatile Patty Cannon, who together with her gang of men kidnap runaway slaves, beat them senseless (if not to death), and sell them back into the slave trade heading south.

The Code, intricate and ingenious, allows all those working for the underground railroad (which, on the Eastern Shore, moves in dugout canoes and atop swamp-savvy horses) to communicate through the pattern of a quilt hung on a clothesline, the rhythm of a blacksmith's hammer, or the number of knots tied in a bit of string. But the Code is also an instrument of deep faith, affirming the existence of God and the possibility of freedom—reasons to live in unlivable times—and McBride makes us see why men died rather than reveal it. Gripping, affecting, and beautifully paced, *Song Yet Sung* illuminates, in the most dramatic fashion, a deeply troubling, vastly complicated moment in American history, and asks us to bear witness to both the oppressed and the oppressor in ourselves.

Source: Pam Houston, Review of *Song Yet Sung*, in *O Magazine*, February 2008.

Regis Behe
In the following review, Behe points out the importance of issues of race in Song Yet Sung.

James McBride was stuck. The best-selling author of the memoir *The Color of Water* was trying to write a novel about the Civil War and slavery, but could not make it work.

In October 2004, he was driving the backroads of Dorchester County in eastern Maryland, trying to jumpstart his creativity, when he saw one of those ubiquitous historical markers that no one stops to read. McBride pulled over when he saw the marker commemorated the birthplace of Harriet Tubman, the Civil War-era slave who served the Union Army as a nurse, scout and spy in addition to helping fellow slaves escape to freedom.

McBride—who is also a noted jazz saxophonist—walked around a dead cornfield near the sign. He felt inspired, he felt vibrations, he felt a connection to a mystical world beyond his ken.

"You have to (believe in the mystical) to write that kind of fiction," McBride says of his new book, *Song Yet Sung*. "Every place, every land, every city, every town has its own spirit. Pittsburgh has its own spirit. It's a place where people work hard, people have dreams, they don't complain, they hit it as hard as they can. And when you come into a place like the Eastern Shore, it seems clear once you see the landscape, if you open yourself up to the idea, there was a lot of struggle and a lot of strife and a lot of difficulty that the land represented to people who both loved it and people who were trying to get away from it."

McBride spun *Song Yet Sung* from a combination of history and imagination; "facts are just the blueprint," he says. Liz Spocott is a runaway slave who takes on a legendary status among her fellow slaves on the Eastern Shore. She abets the escape of other runaways from a notorious slave trader, Patty Cannon, who is modeled after a historical figure of the same name.

It's her dreams that set Liz apart—vivid evocations of the present day:

"She dreamed of Negroes driving horseless carriages on shiny rubber wheels with music booming throughout, and fat black children who smoked odd-smelling cigars and walked around with pistols in their pockets and murder in their eyes. She dreamed of Negro women appearing as flickering images in powerfully lighted boxes that could be seen in sitting rooms far distant, and colored men dressed in garish costumes like children, playing odd sporting games and bragging like drunkards—every

bit of pride, decency, and morality squeezed out of them."

It's a harsh passage, but McBride does not back down from what he wrote. To make his point, McBride references Pittsburgh Steelers Lynn Swann and Franco Harris and their classy demeanor when they scored touchdowns.

"Nowadays, a guy scores a touchdown, and all too often he does a jigaboo dance, he stands on his head and looks like an idiot," McBride says. "I had that in mind when I wrote (about) the business of dignity and what dignity represents to black people, and what slaves wanted for themselves and their children and their grandchildren. They wanted them to live a decent life with education and faith as the cornerstone of their existence, and not something as shallow as a football game.

"That's not to say football's not important; I'm delighted as the next guy that the (N.Y.) Giants won the Super Bowl. But ultimately, when you die you don't want to be known as the guy who won the Super Bowl. You want to be known as the guy who tried to help somebody, who tried to spread some joy, some love and peace. I think if slaves came to life now and saw how some of us are living—some of us, not all of us—they'd be disappointed. In fact, if anyone from that era, white or black, was suddenly transported into our times, they would probably be impressed with a lot of what we've done, but they'd be disappointed as well."

If *Song Yet Sung* seems different from other books that have slavery as a theme, it's because of the setting. Maryland's Eastern Shore had a different feel, a different way of life, than most of the American South, and McBride lets the landscape have a role in shaping the story.

That part of the story, at least, came easily for McBride, who is also the author of the novel *Miracle at St. Anna*, which is being made into a movie by Spike Lee.

"Even though the land might have been built up in certain places, the creeks and the rivers and the weather and the land, the air, is still pretty much the same as it was," McBride says. "If you can wipe the current developments from your head, you can see the place as it was."

Song Yet Sung takes on various forms as it progresses—it's by turn an adventure yarn, a history set-piece, a sociological tract. McBride hopes that readers will take all of these elements and use the novel as a way to discuss the issue of race.

"Slavery was really about a web of human relationships, more than slavery," he says. "Obviously, slavery was a dehumanizing, torturous element of American society, but most white people did not own slaves. And those who did not own slaves were as trapped in slavery as those who did own slaves. So I would hope that people would use this book to discuss how we cannot discuss issues of race and class. Because we're all victims, ultimately, of racism, and it's really hard for white people to wrap themselves around that notion."

Source: Regis Behe, "Beliefs Inspire *Song Yet Sung*," in *Pittsburgh Tribune-Review*, February 17, 2008.

Sarah Seltzer and James McBride

In the following interview, McBride explains why he made Denwood Long a sympathetic character.

James McBride's memoir, *The Color of Water*, has become a modern classic, and an adaptation of his WWII novel, *The Miracle at St. Anna*, is being filmed by Spike Lee. McBride's latest novel, *Song Yet Sung* (Reviews, Sept. 24, 2007), takes readers back to America's dark history.

What inspired you to go back to the pre-Civil War era and runaway slaves?

JM: I like the mythology of the Wild, Wild West—the glow, the characters that seem to move from place to place with ease and dignity in heroic ways. And I'm a big history buff. I was casting around for what to do; slavery was the great moral question with lots of adventurous business ripe for exploration. At the age of 50, I was able to divorce myself from some of the hardship of it.

How much of the "code" that the slaves use to communicate is historical, and how much did you take liberties with?

JM: I'd heard and read about the black codes of the underground for years. Whether they really existed, that is a matter of historical debate. That's what compelled me to write the novel. As a musician, having grown up playing many of these songs that pointed the way to freedom, it was something that was very intrinsic in my own soul.

You gave your character Denwood Long a very humane treatment considering the fact that he's a slave catcher. Did you plan that from the outset?

JM: It's something I intended. People are victims of the times they live in. We know that slavery still exists, but does that make us bad people if we don't stop it? You do an injustice to history and to the art when you paint characters as one-dimensional. Denwood Long is in many ways admirable, but he does something terrible.

Liz, the book's character with second sight, has a bleak vision of America's future, which is our present.

JM: I was watching a movie where a prince from the Shakespearean era showed up now, and I thought, what would a slave who was transported to New York tomorrow think? That inspired her "dreams of tomorrow." We've become the people we've dreaded, a consumer society. There used to be lines of people at church and now that happens in Kmart, Costco, Wal-Mart—and I'm as much a consumer as the next person. That's why Denwood Long is important, because he realizes we're all slaves to something. He is all of us, then and now.

Source: Sarah Seltzer and James McBride, "PW Talks with James McBride: Running to Freedom," in *Publishers Weekly*, Vol. 255, No. 1, January 7, 2008, p. 34.

SOURCES

Bell, Madison Smartt, "Prophetic Dreams," in *New York Times*, March 2, 2008, http://www.nytimes.com/2008/03/02/books/review/Bell-t.html?pagewanted = all&_r = 0 (accessed August 2, 2014).

"Biography," James McBride website, http://www.jamesmcbride.com/ (accessed August 2, 2014).

Durham, David Anthony, "So Close to Freedom," in *Washington Post Book World*, February 22, 2008, http://www.washingtonpost.com/wp-dyn/content/article/2008/02/14/AR2008021402344.html (accessed August 2, 2014).

"Harriet Tubman, Biography, Civil Rights Activist (c. 1820–1913)," in *Biography.com*, http://www.biography.com/#!/people/harriet-tubman-9511430#synopsis (accessed August 5, 2014).

"James McBride," American Program Bureau website, http://www.apbspeakers.com/speaker/james-mcbride (accessed August 2, 2014).

"James McBride," New York State Writers Institute website, http://www.albany.edu/writers-inst/webpages4/archives/mcbride.html (accessed August 2, 2014).

Kulman, Linda, "James McBride Blends Fact with Fiction in *Song*," NPR website, http://www.npr.org/2008/02/26/19182838/james-mcbride-blends-fact-with-fiction-in-song (accessed August 2, 2014).

McBride, James, *Song Yet Sung*, Riverhead Books, 2008.

McMichael, Barbara Lloyd, "*Song Yet Sung* a Story of the Slave Experience," in *Seattle Times*, February 15, 2008, http://seattletimes.com/html/books/2004182458 _mcbride15.html (accessed August 2, 2014).

Obenson, Tambay A., "FX Network Will Adapt James McBride's Harriet Tubman–inspired Novel 'Song Yet Sung' as a Mini-Series," in *IndieWire*, November 26, 2013, http://blogs.indiewire.com/shadowandact/fx-net work-will-adapt-james-mcbrides-harriet-tubman-inspired-novel-song-yet-sung-as-a-mini-series (accessed August 1, 2014).

Patterson, Troy, Review of *Song Yet Sung*, in *Entertainment Weekly*, February 1, 2008, http://www.ew.com/ew/article/0,,20175254,00.html (accessed August 2, 2014).

Smith, Jessie Carney, *Epic Lives: One Hundred Black Women Who Made a Difference*, Visible Ink Press, 1993, pp. 529–37.

Yacovone, Donald, "Underground Railroad," in *Encyclopedia of African-American Culture and History*, Vol. 5, 2nd ed., edited by Colin A. Palmer, Macmillan Reference USA, 2006, pp. 2223–26.

FURTHER READING

Burns, Eleanor, and Sue Bouchard, *Underground Railroad Sampler*, Quilt in a Day, 2003.

> Burns and Bouchard explain how quilts were used to communicate secret messages by conductors on the Underground Railroad. Even readers with no intention of sewing will find much to learn about the significance of the symbols and colors used in the historical folk art of quilting.

Clinton, Catherine, *Harriet Tubman: The Road to Freedom*, Little, Brown, 2004.

> This volume is perhaps the first complete, serious biography of Tubman after the brief narratives published before, which were mostly aimed at young children. Clinton's exhaustive research sheds new light on this beloved historical figure.

Draper, Sharon, *Copper Sun*, Simon & Schuster, 2006.

> Draper's young-adult novel centers on Amari, a young woman taken from her African village and sold into slavery, and Polly, an outspoken indentured white girl, who form an unlikely partnership to find their way to freedom.

McBride, James, *The Good Lord Bird*, Riverhead Books, 2013.

> *The Good Lord Bird* won the 2013 National Book Award for Fiction. The novel tells the story of Henry Shackleford, a young escaped slave who hides by pretending to be a girl. Henry becomes involved in John Brown's 1859 raid on Harper's Ferry, one of the events in the controversy surrounding slavery that led to the Civil War.

SUGGESTED SEARCH TERMS

James McBride AND Song Yet Sung

James McBride AND research

Maryland AND runaway slaves

Maryland AND eastern shore

Maryland AND slave catchers

Maryland AND watermen

Maryland AND slavery

Underground Railroad

Harriet Tubman

Patty Cannon

The Storyteller

MARIO VARGAS LLOSA

1987

El hablador, or *The Storyteller*, by Peruvian author Mario Vargas Llosa, puts two different cultures in conflict with each other, asking the reader to think about whether native tribes of the Amazon rain forest should give up their traditional ways and integrate with modern society or be left alone in the jungle. This is not an abstract question: Peru, like most countries today, is multicultural, with a postcolonial legacy. The dominant Western civilization in Lima, represented by institutions structured by the Spanish conquest, is contrasted to the primitive tribal life of the Machiguengas in the rain forest. The Machiguengas, like other tribes, have been exploited, persecuted, and decimated from the sixteenth century to the present. Their identity and way of life are threatened. Is their survival dependent upon modernizing? Or being left alone?

Nobel laureate Vargas Llosa is one of the most influential Latin American writers today, respected for his experimental contributions to the novel form and depictions of the political violence in South American countries. One of the founding authors of the Latin American Boom of the 1960s, in which authors like Carlos Fuentes and Gabriel García Márquez became world famous, Vargas Llosa celebrates storytelling as the most powerful contribution to solving the complex issues of the age. He ran an unsuccessful bid for Peru's presidency in 1990, but his novels, on the other hand, will outlive any political career. Distrusting doctrinaire positions, the

Mario Vargas Llosa (© *Fotonoticias / Getty Images*)

author has evolved his idea of the "total novel," capable of depicting multiple realities without moralizing. In *The Storyteller*, Vargas Llosa alternates chapters depicting Western and Machiguenga points of view, leaving readers to enter these worlds and decide for themselves. This novel, with its vivid portrayal of acculturation issues, is often recommended reading for anthropology students.

AUTHOR BIOGRAPHY

Mario Vargas Llosa was born on March 28, 1936, to Ernesto Vargas Maldonado and Dora Llosa Ureta in Arequipa, Peru. His father was a radio operator in an aviation company but left Vargas Llosa's mother for another woman before the baby was born. Vargas Llosa was brought up by his mother's family in Bolivia, believing his father was dead. His grandfather Llosa was appointed honorary consul for Peru in Bolivia. The Llosas managed a cotton farm in

Cochabamba, Bolivia, where Vargas Llosa spent his happy childhood, unaware he had a father and two half-brothers, Enrique and Ernesto Vargas. Vargas Llosa and his maternal family moved back to Peru, to the coastal city of Piura, when his grandfather got a diplomatic post there. He attended a Catholic elementary school.

At the age of ten, Vargas Llosa moved to Lima and met his father for the first time. His parents got back together and lived in a middle-class suburb of Lima. He attended a Christian middle school from 1946 to 1949. At the age of fourteen, his father sent him to a military school, the Leoncio Prado Military Academy, where he was miserable. He withdrew, finished his studies at Piura, and then worked as a journalist. In 1953, he enrolled in Lima's National University of San Marcos to study law and literature. At the age of nineteen, he married a distant family member, his uncle's sister-in-law, Julia Urquidi, ten years older than he was. This marriage became the material for *Aunt Julia and the Scriptwriter* (1977). In the 1950s, he published short stories. After graduating in 1958, he won a scholarship to continue his studies in Madrid for two years, after which Vargas Llosa and his wife moved to Paris.

After the couple divorced in 1964, he married his first cousin, Patricia Llosa, in 1965. They had three children together. Vargas Llosa's first novel, *The Time of the Hero* (1963), a satire on his time in military school, was a big success. It is considered one of the early masterpieces of the literary period called the Boom, when South American authors were read all over the world for the first time. Vargas Llosa became known for sophisticated techniques and experimentation. A second novel, *The Green House* (1965), about a brothel, won many awards. His third novel, equally important, was *Conversation in the Cathedral* (1969), which attacks the dictatorship of Manuel Odría. In 1971, Vargas Llosa published his doctoral dissertation, *García Márquez: Story of a Deicide*, about the novels of the Colombian writer, Gabriel García Márquez, who, along with Vargas Llosa, was one of the important writers to come out of the Boom.

The War of the End of the World (1981) is an historical account of the massacre of the utopian community in Canudos, Brazil, in 1897. It highlights Vargas Llosa's dislike of fanaticism of any kind. *The Real Life of Alejandro Mayta* (1984) concerns a leftist rebellion. *Who Killed Palomino*

Molero (1986) is a mystery novel. *El hablador* (1987), translated as *The Storyteller* in 1989, is important for its dealing with Peru's multicultural identity. *Death in the Andes* (1993) and *The Notebooks of Don Rigoberto* (1998) were preludes to the author's next major novel, *The Feast of the Goat* (2000), about the Dominican Republic's dictator, Rafael Trujillo. Other novels include *The Way to Paradise* (2003), *The Bad Girl* (2006), and *The Dream of the Celt* (2010). In 2010, Vargas Llosa was awarded the Nobel Prize in Literature, and in 2011, Vargas Llosa was awarded the title of Marqués de Vargas Llosa by the king of Spain. He continues to write and to lecture at various universities.

PLOT SUMMARY

Chapter One

The first-person narrator Mario (a fictional version of the author) says he traveled to Firenze (Florence), Italy, to escape his native country of Peru, but in a window display in the city, he saw photographs of the Peruvian jungle, with native men and women. He went in to find the photos of Gabriele Malfatti documenting the life of the Machiguenga tribe in the Amazon rain forest. The author recognizes the place because he had been there three years earlier. In another photo, he sees the tribal people sitting in a circle listening to an *hablador*, or storyteller, in the center. He feels he recognizes the storyteller.

This chapter is part of the framing story of the narrator's pursuit of the Machiguenga storyteller he saw in the photograph. The chapters of the novel alternate in point of view. The framing story is told from the point of view of Mario the narrator in chapters one and eight, set in Florence, Italy, in the present time (1980s). Mario goes on to tell the story of Saúl Zuratas, a friend he met at college, in flashbacks in chapters two, four, and six, which span the 1950s to the present in the 1980s. The Machiguenga point of view is told by the Machiguenga storyteller himself in chapters three, five, and seven. Sometimes the native storyteller uses a third-person impersonal voice; sometimes he speaks as an "I," telling his experience in the forest; and sometimes he speaks to an audience in second person, "you." Vargas Llosa is known for his experimental narrative techniques, especially his subtle jumps in time, space, and point of view.

Chapter Two

The narrator Mario describes his friend, Saúl Zuratas, as having a dark red birthmark that covers the right side of his face. He has bright red hair, but though ugly, he is a good and likeable person. His nickname is Mascarita, Mask Face. Mario and Saúl attend the same university. Mascarita is a Jew. His father, Don Salomón, is a grocer who has a talking parrot that repeats his son's nickname, "Mascarita." His father insists he enter the University of San Marcos in Lima to study law. While Mario and Saúl are young men at the university in the 1950s, the country is moving from the dictatorship of General Odría to democratic rule. In 1956, Saúl is studying ethnology as well as law and has made several trips to the jungle, fascinated by the primitive culture of the Machiguenga Indians there.

When Mario and Saúl go out to play billiards, Mario witnesses how people treat Saúl rudely because of his birthmark. Mario fights with someone who insults his friend. Saúl sends Mario a letter and a native magic bone of a tapir (a large jungle animal) to calm his anger, explaining anger is not allowed in the Machiguenga tribe because it will distort the sacred lines so humans cannot help to hold up the earth.

Mario asks Saúl to tell him more Machiguenga stories. Saúl sits with his parrot, named Gregor Samsa, on his shoulder. The parrot is named for the main character in Franz Kafka's story *Metamorphosis*, Saúl's favorite book. It is a story about how a man turns into an insect and becomes a loathsome outcast. Saúl feels like an outcast himself because he is Jewish and because of his birthmark. He keeps Mario enchanted, however, telling him Machiguenga myths. Saúl is obsessed with the plight of the people and the rain forest whose destruction is a crime no one cares about. He argues against Mario, who believes the Indians will have to be assimilated into modern life. Saúl thinks the Indians should be left alone to practice their ways, though he admits they are primitive. He himself, with such an ugly birthmark, would have been killed at birth if he had been born into the Machiguenga tribe, which kills babies born with defects. This talk sets up the main argument of the plot: Should the natives be left to their ways or modernized?

Saúl graduates. His professor obtains a scholarship for him to pursue his doctorate in anthropology at the University of Bordeaux, but Saúl turns it down. Mario overhears the professors discussing Saúl's refusal. They believe he turned down the scholarship because he thinks it immoral to study the natives as though they are bugs. Mario and Saúl had discussed whether Saúl identifies with the Machiguengas because he is marginal in society, as they are. Mario loses track of Saúl after graduation and narrates an account of his life by conjecture.

Chapter Three

It is difficult at first to understand who is speaking because of the abrupt change. This chapter is narrated by the Machiguenga storyteller, later identified as Saúl, who supposedly disappeared mysteriously into the jungle to join the tribe. The storyteller speaks as the natives do, in a mythical voice outside time. For the Machiguengas, there are no individuals, only a universe divided by good and evil forces. Interestingly, the storyteller organizes the myths or stories roughly equivalent to the biblical categories: creation, Eden, the fall, exodus, the flood, heaven, hell, gods, and devils. After the primal creation myths, the storyteller tells the history of the Machiguengas. He tries to teach the Machiguengas that their only way to survive is to keep their traditions and avoid the white man's ways.

In the days equivalent to Eden, there was no evil, only the bright light of the sun (the creator, Tasurinchi). The women had pure children. Food was plentiful. There was peace and no war. The people stayed in one place, united. Those who went away came back; this is a way of describing that there was dying and rebirth, but no permanent death. How did it change? The sun started falling, and then the men began to walk to keep it from falling farther, so it would rise again. Perhaps the After started with the battle between sun and moon. Kashiri the moon brought cold and dimmed light, confusion and fear. There were floods and bad weather. Serenity was lost, and men died and did not come back. Tasurinchi told them to keep walking or they would disappear. That was how they became nomads, always moving to outrun evil and death. The people survived and bore sacrifices to keep the world alive, such as the time of the great flood. Even though the people made rafts to float on, they began to drown and did not come back. What happens when the body decays? The soul becomes a *kamagarini* devil or *saankarite* god in worlds above. The people then

began to practice agriculture, clearing the forest and planting. At this time, the moon Kashiri taught people to grow cassava.

Then a vampire bit Tasurinchi while he was sleeping. The Mashcos came (an enemy tribe) and killed the people and burned their houses. Tasurinchi said to keep pure they must keep walking. They left their fields and began walking again, going higher into the mountains around Cerro and the five rivers. The Viracochas (white companies) came to bleed the rubber trees and stole the people to work in their camps.

The narrative suddenly shifts to the present time, but the story still sounds mythical. All the men are called Tasurinchi, after the creator. They do not have personal names. The storyteller ("I") with his parrot went to see Tasurinchi, who lives at the bend in the river. The husband threatens his pregnant wife that if she miscarries again, he will kill her. The storyteller reminds the man the *seripigari* (shaman) saw in the trance that this child would be born walking, and so it was. The man gives the storyteller a net to catch fish and wonders that he travels through the forest alone.

The storyteller tells this tale to Tasurinchi in the forest, who explains to the storyteller about evil sorcerers serving Kientibakori, the evil one, and his devils. The seripigari, the good sorcerer, serves the creator by finding medicine and curing spells. This man tells about the strangers coming up the river who hunt with guns. Tasurinchi, the forest man, sees that the Viracocha (white man) is a devil when he sneezes. Tasurinchi runs away and gathers his family, and they keep walking.

The evil spirit, Kientibakori, sends evil spirits to destroy the tribe, telling them to change their ways, and then they turn into devils, as when Tasurinchi wakes up one day covered with fish scales and a fish tail (a reference to Kafka's story *Metamorphosis*, when Gregor Samsa becomes an insect). There is now a shortage of men; some have become animals and devils. Just as the people being disappearing, they visit Tasurinchi the seripigari (shaman), who meditates and fasts until he becomes a spirit, a saankarite (god). He tells them to go back to their ways and start walking. The ones who try to live with the strangers are no longer men. The storyteller says these are all things he has learned in his travels.

Chapter Four

Mario, the narrator, tells how he became acquainted with the Amazon region in 1958 while at the University of San Marcos. He went on an expedition to the Marañón organized by the Summer Institute of Linguistics. This is a controversial organization of Protestant evangelists who are linguists studying native languages to translate the Bible and convert the natives to Christianity. The narrator remembers this expedition twenty-seven years later while he is in Italy. They visited the linguists and several tribes. The jungles were dark and seemed a primeval world out of the Stone Age. The people still engaged in polygamy and head shrinking.

Mario becomes friends with Dr. Matos Mar, Saúl's advisor in the Department of Ethnology. Mario concludes the Machiguenga way of life cannot be preserved, no matter what one thinks about it. Western and mestizo (mixed race of white and Indian) influences have already corrupted their traditions. By remaining primitive, Mario thinks, they are open to more exploitation. He tells of a village where the headman, Jum, had been tortured for being bilingual and trying to set up independent trading to avoid the white bosses. Mario wonders what the moral of this story is. Does it justify Saúl's idea that the natives cannot assimilate, or that they need to go forward and become educated enough to fight against exploitation?

Dr. Matos Mar thinks Indian sovereignty should be recognized and the whites expelled. Mario thinks, on the other hand, that going forward into civilization is the lesser evil. Matos Mar and Mario discuss the current idea that socialism is the solution, allowing for coexistence of modern and primitive together. Mario thinks back on this optimism of the 1950s about socialism, thirty years later in Italy, and knows it was as naïve as Mascarita's idealism about native life.

The most important event of that trip, however, was meeting Mr. and Mrs. Schneil, evangelists and linguists of the Summer Institute at Yarinacocha. They tell him about the Machiguengas, a tribe dispersed into two factions, one living in higher terrains, beginning to be assimilated with white and mestizo culture, and the group living in the forests, living in isolation. Saúl's group was among the most westernized, for the forest groups had resisted contact. According to the Schneils, the Machiguengas

are depressed and falling apart, poor, living in small groups, constantly on the move. There is a high rate of suicide and decimation from sickness. They try to move them to village settlements where they can be cared for.

Mario seems to like the Schneils but distrusts their evangelical purpose. In a last talk with Edwin Schneil, he learns of the existence among Machiguengas of the storyteller: the *hablador*, or speaker. The storyteller is the communal memory of the tribe.

The narrative shifts suddenly to a conversation that Mario had with Mascarita (Saúl) after coming back from this 1958 trip. It is August 1958, the last time they ever met. Mario tries to tell Mascarita about his fascination with the *hablador* of the Machiguengas. Saúl, though he does not believe in anger, becomes angry as he speaks of the intrusion of the Summer Institute of Linguistics that he believes is backed by powerful, rich Americans. They part as friends, but though Mario writes letters, Saúl never responds. Over the years, Mario remains excited about the idea of the Machiguenga storytellers. He decides to write a novel about them and writes to Saúl to ask his help. There is no reply, but Mario meets a Catholic missionary in Madrid who tells him the myths of the Machiguengas. In 1963 in Paris, Mario meets Matos Mar and learns that Saúl Zuratas went to live in Israel with his father.

Chapter Five

The storyteller visits a Machiguenga who has stolen a woman from the Yaminahua tribe. The other women treat her badly. The man says he did not steal her but traded some food for her, more than she was worth. This reminds him of the story of how the moon Kashiri came down to father the sun by a Machiguenga woman. The moon's wife gave birth to a healthy child who would give heat and light to the world. A jealous woman waited for Kashiri and smeared him with her feces so that he was forever stained. He had to go back to the sky where the stains can still be seen. However, his son is the sun that warms us, and we keep walking to help him rise.

The storyteller tells an animal fable in the first person with himself as the hero. He almost dies in the river and falls from the sky, yet comes back unharmed because he never gives way to anger. Anger is the cause of comets. That gives rise to the story of the angry Machiguenga who turned into the first comet.

The storyteller meets a shaman who can talk to fireflies because he learned to listen. The storyteller also learns to listen respectfully, and the earth and its creatures tell their stories to him. Listening is the source of stories. Knowing stories leads to wisdom. Animals tell the storyteller they were born from men speaking, because the words came true when the first man spoke. The first man was Pachakamue. He kept making things happen with words, so he was killed and his head was buried, but the tongue went on talking and changing the world.

The storyteller visits the herb doctor in the country where the whites are encroaching. The herb doctor is an *hablador* also and tells stories about the whites who came for the rubber and how they took the Machiguengas to their camps. The storyteller is tempted to put down roots and make a hut and garden and take a wife. When he tries to do this, the woman dies. The herb doctor tells him it is a sign. His destiny is to keep moving and tell stories.

Chapter Six

In 1981, the narrator, Mario, was responsible for a Peruvian television show called *The Tower of Babel*, providing quality cultural programming. He is asked to do a piece on the Summer Institute of Linguistics, now a controversial topic. He says he will cover the Machiguengas, remembering his attempt to write a novel about them in the 1960s. He was always puzzled that in all his research he could never discover anything about the storytellers. He had tried to invent a story about them but could never figure out how to represent them convincingly in Spanish. (This story about writing a story is called metafiction, one of Vargas Llosa's main interests in this book.)

Now as he goes to the jungle to film the segment, he meets the Schneils again at the end of their career. They tell him that the Machiguengas have moved into villages. The Bible has been translated into the Machiguengan language, so Mario sees that Saúl's fears are coming true. He feels sad that their culture is disappearing because they are symbolic of all the passing ethnic oral cultures with storytellers, such as the Irish bards.

His crew films the Machiguenga villagers, but he can find out nothing about the storytellers, even speaking to Martín, the bilingual schoolteacher.

Martín evades his questions about storytellers, saying he has never heard of them.

Later, as Mario talks to the Schneils, he tells them his impression that the westernization of the Machiguengas is skin deep. He thinks they are still rooted in their tradition. Their *habladores* have been an inspiration for his own work, and he wishes he could find out more. They explain to him that *habladores* are a taboo subject. Edwin Schneil had, however, met two of them. He describes how one old storyteller talked for hours about gossip, myths, the gods, and animals, with the people sitting in a rapt semicircle around him, as in the photo Mario had seen. Then Mrs. Schneil asks her husband to tell about the other one, the albino storyteller.

Mario is riveted to Schneil's description of a storyteller who had a birthmark on the right side of his face and red hair; he figures it must be Mascarita, Saúl Zuratas. The event had taken place three and a half years ago. The narrator understands the taboo. The natives are protecting Mascarita. Back in Lima, the narrator asks a Jewish friend to trace the Zuratas. Had they gone to Israel? Mario learns that the father died in Lima, and the son disappeared.

Chapter Seven

The storyteller tells the people that before, there were many seripigaris (shamans), but now they are scarce. Perhaps it is because the people are not walking. The wisest seripigari told him the most important thing is not to be impatient; that way destiny will arrive. If you rush, you get confused and make mistakes. One must respect the taboos.

The storyteller tells this wise man about a bad trance he had when he had changed into an insect named Gregor-Tasurinchi. He saw the world differently. He was covered with shame. His family pretended he was all right, but they locked him up. He lived the life of a bug until eaten by a snake. His family was glad he disappeared. (This is a retelling of Kafka's story *Metamorphosis*.)

The storyteller asks the seripigari (shaman) the meaning of his bad trance, and the wise man tells him to forget it; if you remember, you have to keep repeating it. His scarred face has been a suffering that used to eat him up, he admits, but since he has been with the Machiguengas, he has been accepted. He became a storyteller because they listened.

Mascarita tells his own story of becoming a member of the tribe. After he listened to the people to see who they were, they let him walk with them. They started calling him storyteller. He was born a second time. He never understands why they kill their babies who are not perfect, but they do not see him as deformed. They see him as a storyteller. A seripigari told him being born with a scar was not the worst misfortune, which is not knowing one's duty and destiny. Mascarita is now a man who walks, a Machiguenga.

The storyteller tells the story of Jehovah-Tasurinchi and the Jews, making the Jews into persecuted nomads like the Machiguengas. Like the Machiguengas, the Jews did not disappear, no matter what was done to them. They fulfilled their obligations. The storyteller used to think a people must change and become like those who are strong. Now, he knows it is best to be what one is, otherwise, you lose your soul.

Chapter Eight
The narrator is in Firenze in the present time, looking at the famous paintings. He had looked at the exhibition of Amazonian photographs as hard as he had studied Renaissance art. He discusses how the Amazon rain forest has changed over the years. The oil wells came, the drug traffickers, terrorism, and counterterrorism. He wonders whether Saúl Zuratas is with the Machiguengas, for he is sure he is the shadowed storyteller he saw in the photograph. The undying tradition of the native *hablador* is a notion that opens the narrator's heart.

CHARACTERS

Gregor-Tasurinchi
Gregor-Tasurinchi is a character made up by Saúl Zuratas as he tells stories to the Machiguengas. Tasurinchi is the name of their creator, and the word serves as a sort of pronoun used to identify a man. Saúl tells the story of a bad trance when he woke up as Gregor-Tasurinchi, a version of Gregor Samsa, the human turned vermin in Kafka's story *Metamorphosis*. This is Saúl's way of saying that he feels alienated and alone.

Jehovah-Tasurinchi
Jehovah-Tasurinchi is Saúl's invented name for the Jewish God, joining the Jewish name for God and the Machiguenga name for the creator. He tries to tell the Machiguengas the story of the Jews using bits of their mythology.

Jum
Jum is the Aguaruna native headman Mario met in 1958 on his first trip into the Amazon rain forest region to see the Indian tribes. Jum had been tortured by whites and mestizos when he tried to set up a cooperative among the Aguarunas that would bypass the white traders, who exploited the natives. Jum was bilingual, learning to read and write at the Yarinacocha settlement of the Schneils.

Kamagirini
A kamagirini is the Machiguenga name for a little devil, the ones who serve Kientibakori. Bad people can turn into a kamagirini.

Kashiri
Kashiri is the Machiguenga name for the moon god who has both good and bad traits. He teaches the people to grow cassava, but he also brings floods and cold. He fathers the sun by a Machiguenga woman.

Kientibakori
Kientibakori is the Machiguenga name for the evil one, the devil, who tries to trick them into evil ways.

Gabriele Malfatti
Gabriele Malfatti is the Italian photographer in Firenze who displays his photos of his trip to the Amazon rain forest, where he spent two weeks taking photos of the natives in their daily life. His fifty photographs are displayed in a gallery in Firenze where Mario sees the mysterious photo of a Machiguenga storyteller with a half-circle of listeners around him that inspires his tale.

Mario
Mario is the main first-person narrator, a fictionalized version of the author. He is an intellectual writer who attended the National University of San Marcos with his friend Saúl Zuratas in the 1950s. It is Saúl's passion for saving the Machiguengas and his telling their myths to Mario that inspires the subject of the

book. Mario lets us in on how he gathered the materials for the incidents—the meetings with Saúl, the tribes, the Schneils, the photos he saw in Firenze, the TV show he wrote for—all which become the bits for the episodes he puts together to tell the story. Mario is in love with great Western art, evidenced by his visit to Florence to study Renaissance paintings. He is also infatuated with language and writing and the power of storytelling, as a journalist and novelist. The photo of the Machiguenga storyteller becomes a symbol for him of the origin of his art in the ancient oral tradition. Mario fabricates Saúl as the tribal storyteller and shows him in the act of his spontaneous improvisations on traditional themes, adding in his own tales to the tribes. Storytelling is a creative act in every culture. Mario argues by suggestion that as stories evolve and change, so too must the tribe. They cannot remain untouched by the rest of the world, no matter what Saúl may think. He presents both sides of the issue, but it is clear he is on the side of educating and westernizing the natives, and that is what happens over the years.

Martín

Martín is the bilingual Machiguenga schoolteacher and chief of New Light Village in the rain forest. He dresses as a Westerner and knows the Bible. He refuses to talk about the storytellers to Mario because it is a taboo subject.

Mascarita

See Saúl Zuratas.

Mashcos

The Maschcos are an enemy tribe to the Machiguengas.

Dr. José Matos Mar

Dr. Matos Mar is a renowned Peruvian anthropologist from the National University of San Marcos, a real person but the fictional advisor of Saúl Zuritas. Mario the narrator befriends Dr. Matos Mar on a trip to the rain forest, discussing the fate of the Machiguengas as they travel to their villages. Matos Mar believes the Indians should have their sovereignty and that the whites should be expelled from their territory.

General Manuel Odría

General Manuel Odría (1896–1974) was a military dictator and the president of Peru from 1948 to 1956. In the novel, Mario is in college as the country recovers from this dictatorship. Odría stands for all the Latin American military dictators that Vargas Llosa despises.

Pachakamue

Pachakamue is the first man in Machiguenga mythology. He has the power to name things, but as he names, he creates. If he says the name of an animal, it appears. Feared for this power to change things, he is killed by the tribe, and his head is cut off and buried. His tongue keeps speaking underground, however, and continues to change the world.

Saankarite

Saankarite in Machiguenga mythology is a god who resides in heaven. Good souls can become gods after death.

Gregor Samsa

Gregor Samsa is the name of the main character in Franz Kafka's story *Metamorphosis* who wakes up one day to find he has transformed into a vermin or insect. This tale of feeling repulsive and alienated is Saúl Zuratas's favorite story. He tells it to the Machiguengas, and he names his parrot after this character.

The Schneils

In the novel, Edwin Schneil and his wife are Protestant missionaries with the Summer Institute of Linguistics. They come to the Peruvian rain forest to learn the native languages, make dictionaries, and translate the Bible into the native tongues. Their goal is to convert the natives to Christianity and to gather them in settlements to help them survive. The Schneils are based on the real figures of Wayne and Betty Snell from the institute, who studied the Machiguengas and later published their findings.

Seripigari

Seripigari is a Machiguenga shaman, a good sorcerer who can heal and go into trances to help the tribe.

Tasurinchi

Tasurinchi is the name of the Machiguenga creator god, the god of good, associated with the sun. Tasurinchi is also the name of all the male characters, used as a sort of pronoun, because the Machiguengas do not have personal names. The Machiguengas believe they have to keep walking to help the Tasurinchi the sun rise each day.

Viracocha

Viracocha is the Machiguenga name for the white traders, hunters, and rubber bosses who exploit the natives.

Don Salomón Zuratas

Don Salomón Zuratas is Saúl's father, a store owner who moves to Lima and takes up Judaism. He has a Russian or Polish accent and is desolate when Saúl's mother dies. He wants his son to study law at the university. It is reported that he moves with his son to Israel, but he actually dies in Lima.

Saúl Zuratas

Saúl Zuratas is the friend of the narrator, Mario, whom he met at San Marcos University. Saúl is so ugly, with a bright red scar over half his face, that he is shunned or persecuted wherever he goes. Mascarita (Mask Face) is the nickname of Saúl, so named because of the bright red scar or birthmark. He has a shock of bright red hair and speaks slang. Mario, however, frequently refers to him as an archangel because of his goodness. He is also called a monster because of his looks. Saúl becomes passionately interested in studying anthropology instead of law, finally giving up Western life to join the Machiguenga tribe in the jungle as their storyteller. He is acutely aware of his marginal status as a Jew and a disfigured man. His favorite book is *Metamorphosis*, by Franz Kafka. He names his parrot Gregor Samsa after the main character in Kafka's book, which is about alienation. Saúl stays in the jungle because the Machiguengas accept him for himself and listen to his stories. He is depicted as opposite to Mario in character, for Saúl is a utopian or romantic, while Mario is a realist.

THEMES

Latin American Culture

The Storyteller focuses on cultural issues of Peru, especially the question of how to deal with indigenous tribes in the rain forest. The novel brings up problems common to South American countries, such as the contrast of large cities, like Lima, and isolated native populations in the countryside, open to abuse from terrorist groups, drug traffickers, and rubber and oil companies. This novel also mentions dictators, a topic Vargas Llosa highlights in other novels, such as Trujillo, the Dominican dictator in *The Feast of the Goat*. Latin American countries have traditionally been somewhat politically unstable, shifting from democracies to military dictatorships.

The author despises this South American backwardness and tendency to be violent and corrupt. The narrator places his college days during the country's emergence from the dictator, Manuel Odría. He presents the hot debates among intellectuals at the University of San Marcos in Lima about what to do with the indigenous people. Vargas Llosa also brings up the Latin American fascination with socialism and communism. Many South American intellectuals, including Vargas Llosa, were impressed with Fidel Castro and the Cuban Revolution in 1959 that promised to solve problems in that country. The novel gives a sense of Latin American culture with its beautiful and wild countryside, its intense city life, its multicultural conflicts, political upheavals, violence, and its brilliant intellectual life. These extreme paradoxes about Peru and South America are constantly criticized by the author. He, as many intellectuals did, turned to the civility of Europe, going to Madrid or Paris or Italy to escape.

Ethnic Identity

Mario the narrator, like the author, is a sophisticated and cultured man who draws on his vast journalistic experience to write for the TV series *The Tower of Babel*. On his show, he interviews important writers and politicians from South American countries. Mario is interested in cultural justice for the Indian tribes as well, writing a TV segment on the Machiguengas. Nevertheless, his interest and point of view are that of the Western intellectual who tries to solve problems through argument, talk, and the media.

The Machiguenga chapters with the storyteller recounting myths provide a more direct perspective on a primitive oral culture that has not changed for thousands of years. The Machiguengas represent the plight of many ethnic identities, as Mario points out, that have fought for their survival after European colonization. Their ways are so alien to civilization that there is no compromise. If they once start down the path of adapting, their way of life becomes extinct. Mario the narrator represents the author's attempt

TOPICS FOR FURTHER STUDY

- Write a short critical paper showing how Leslie Marmon Silko contrasts white and Indian cultures in *Ceremony* and how Mario Vargas Llosa contrasts white and Indian cultures in *The Storyteller*. Do the contrasts point to the same impressions and conclusions in both novels? What are similarities and differences? Give examples from the novels for your assertions.

- Vargas Llosa has been criticized for trying to write about the Machiguengas when he is a foreigner to that culture. Can he do justice to their way of life? Read and contrast Chinua Achebe's *Things Fall Apart* (1959), an important Nigerian novel describing the precolonial tribal civilization of the Igbo tribe, written by an Igbo member himself. Both authors describe the "primitive" culture practicing infanticide. Is Achebe's view of tribal life more understanding than Vargas Llosa's, or do they come to similar conclusions? Divide the class into two groups: one group will present Vargas Llosa's view of tribal life, and the other will present Achebe's, using passages and incidents from the novels as evidence. Each student should write up the results in a short paper.

- In *The Storyteller*, the characters Jum and Martín are Machiguenga Indians who are trying to assimilate Western culture with varying degrees of success. Read Sherman Alexie's *The Absolutely True Diary of a Part-Time Indian* (2007), a young-adult novel about an Native American teenager going to a white high school. Using a social bookmarking service like Delicious.com, each class member should find and share Internet materials on issues of dealing with being a person of two races and/or two cultures. Discuss the findings with the class, and apply them to Alexie's novel.

- Create a website on endangered cultures and languages around the world with links to information on what is being done to preserve them. Explain the importance of saving cultures and languages, like saving wildlife and habitat. Some readers may wonder why we should try to save languages and ways of life that are in danger of dying out. Do research and compose a group essay answering the question of what it is that ethnic languages and cultures can give to human heritage that is worth preserving, posting it at the front of your website.

- Do a PowerPoint presentation on Rigoberta Menchú, an indigenous Kiche woman from Guatemala who won the Nobel Peace Prize in 1992 for promoting indigenous rights in Guatemala.

- Write a short story that includes something about how you wrote the story or the process of writing the story, so that it becomes metafiction, fiction that refers to the act of writing.

through the character of Mascarita to give the Machiguengas a voice.

Marginalization

Mario confronts Mascarita that perhaps he is so taken with the Machiguengas because they are marginal people in modern society as he is, as a Jew and a man with a physical deformity. The waitress crosses herself when she sees him; he is

bullied until he leaves the pool hall. Saúl does not like being a Jew, but he identifies with their centuries of persecution and even tries to tell the Machiguengas about this other people who have also suffered abuse. That Mascarita is obsessed with being marginal and outcast is obvious from the constant references to Gregor Samsa, the main character in Franz Kafka's fable of alienation, *Metamorphosis*. Like Gregor Samsa, the

The novel examines the debate over whether native peoples should be left alone or "protected" by outsiders. (© Anton_Ivanov / Shutterstock.com)

Jews are treated as vermin to be exterminated. So too are the Machiguengas. Mascarita travels around telling the Indians to resist the white man's ways or they will lose their souls. That is worse than marginalization.

Storytelling

Storytelling ties all the other themes together. The novel's title, *El hablador*, is translated as "storyteller," but literally means "speaker," with the emphasis on oral tradition. Saúl speaks the fables of the Machiguengas to them as their storyteller. Mario the narrator is also a fabulist, or teller of fables. His fable is the fantastic story of Saúl Zuratas, or Mascarita, who disappears into the jungle. Saúl's Machiguenga fables remind the people of their obligation to keep walking as humans to uphold the order of nature. Vargas Llosa uses the theme of fables and storytelling as the true characteristic of human nature, transcending any particular culture.

STYLE

Latin American Novel

Mario Vargas Llosa was a founding writer of the Latin American Boom (*Boom Latinoamericano*) of the 1960s and 1970s, a literary phenomenon that suddenly propelled Latin American novelists into the world limelight. The most famous of these writers were Vargas Llosa from Peru (*The Time of the Hero*), Gabriel García Márquez of Colombia (*One Hundred Years of Solitude*), Julio Cortázar of Argentina (*Hopscotch*), and Carlos Fuentes of Mexico (*The Death of Artemio Cruz*). These writers rejected romantic and realistic styles, influenced instead by modern European and American experimental fiction. Vargas Llosa, for instance, studied the techniques of William Faulkner, Ernest Hemingway, Gustave Flaubert, James Joyce, and Marcel Proust, learning ways to fragment or amplify narrative space and time. His novels use indirect discourse through which the narrator is able to suggest character voice, as well as multiple points of view with subtle shifts between past and present. His style fosters ambiguity and reader involvement, resulting in what he calls a "total novel" that can create a complex and self-sufficient fictional world.

The Boom writers made popular the style known as magic realism that takes into account the rich and mysterious ethnic cultures of South America. A novel may be describing city life and then with no explanation bring in the supernatural beliefs of peasants and Indians. *The Storyteller* has certain traits of magical realism when it includes the narrative of the Machiguenga Indians as a world of magic parallel to the world of civilization. Latin American novels from the Boom to the present are interested in creating defining myths of the Americas and in documenting the violent politics of the region. They tend to combine fantasy and history to do this. Vargas Llosa mentions historical names and incidents side by side with his fantastical account of Saúl Zuratas and his disappearance into tribal life.

Postcolonial Fiction

A criticism of the Boom fiction was that it was too elitist and experimental. It did not address the concerns of common people. Since that time, many writers, including Vargas Llosa, have become more engaged with human rights issues, poverty, violence, and the Spanish colonial legacy that continues to affect indigenous populations. Postcolonial fiction favors magic realism rather than a straight realism. This style ensures that the indigenous cultures with their magical view of nature can be represented.

Postcolonial fiction draws on characters from all classes and races to confront how European domination in the past set up a current society of unjust race and class relationships. *The Storyteller* brings up the problem of what to do with the rain forest natives who resist assimilation. Mario argues they cannot be left alone, while Saúl argues for their privacy. Most postcolonial fiction highlights the confusion of people trying to be traditional and modern at the same time. The case of the Indian Jum who tries to be a businessman and the bilingual village schoolteacher, Martín, are both prime examples in this novel. They are neither in one culture or the other but try to survive by making a hybrid life. Even Saúl, who tries to help the Machiguengas keep their culture, cannot help mixing his own stories in with theirs, making a hybrid mythology.

Metafiction

Metafiction refers to fiction that calls attention to itself as fiction. Readers are not allowed to forget they are reading the construction of an author. *The Storyteller* is metafiction because it discusses how cultures tell their stories. Mario the narrator is fascinated with the image of the Machiguenga storyteller, with all the people gathered in a circle to hear him. His storytelling has an immediacy that the modern novelist lacks, with the printed book being scattered to anonymous readers.

Vargos Llosa puts himself in the book as a character, Mario the narrator, and shows himself creating the fictitious life of Saúl Zuratas. Vargos Llosa contrasts the spontaneous act of storytelling in the jungle to the more conscious construction of art in civilization. For instance, he is in Italy looking at famous Renaissance art. These pieces are expensive and signed by an individual, situated in a particular place and time, like the author's books. Saúl, however, divests himself of his individuality and merges into the timeless forest culture of the Machiguengas. The reader is aware, however, of how Saúl too is constructing his stories, blending their tales with his own.

HISTORICAL CONTEXT

Pre-Columbian Peru and the Spanish Conquest

Peru is a country in northwest South America with a mountainous region (the Andes mountains) and coastal desert on the Pacific Ocean. The interior is rain forest where indigenous tribes like the Machiguenga still live. Peru is notable as the location of ancient Pre-Columbian civilizations, such as Norte Chico, the oldest civilization in the Americas, dating back to the thirtieth century BCE, and the much later Inca Empire. Ruins indicate sophisticated and organized societies in ancient Peru. Coastal cultures excelled at metalwork, pottery, and the Nazca textiles.

The greatest culture was the Inca Empire (1438–1532), the largest dynasty and empire in pre-Columbian America, which included parts of Ecuador, Peru, Bolivia, Chile, and Argentina.

COMPARE
&
CONTRAST

- **1950s:** General Manuel Odría is a military dictator who leads Peru until 1956, while Vargas Llosa is a young man. The dictator novel later becomes a common genre among South American writers who deplore the interference of the military into politics.

1980s: In South America, literary figures are frequently political figures as well. As Vargas Llosa publishes *The Storyteller*, he becomes the leader of the center-right coalition Frente Democrático, on whose platform he runs for president in 1990, hoping to lead Peru to a free-market democracy.

Today: Indigenous people are part of Peruvian politics. Alejandro Toledo, a full Quechuan, was an economist who served as president of Peru from 2001 to 2006. The current president, Ollanta Humala, is Quechuan on his father's side.

- **1950s:** The disappearing Machiguenga tribe in the Amazon rain forest is studied by the Summer Institute of Linguistics, whose members make a dictionary of their language and translate the Bible. Vargas Llosa meets the village chief tortured by the rubber bosses.

1980s: The Summer Institute of Linguistics is seen as an agent of American imperialism, corrupting the native way of life, and it is expelled from many countries and restricted

in Peru. The Snells (the Schneils in the novel), however, leave flourishing settlements, where half the Machiguengas live in safety, bilingual teachers are trained, the natives get medical care, and local trading begins.

Today: Machiguenga villages continue to get westernized advantages that help them survive. Their traditional ways are still practiced, as can be seen in films and on YouTube. In addition, anthropologists study Machiguenga knowledge of medicinal herbs, useful to modern medicine.

- **1950s:** South American writers in the avant-garde Vanguard movement are beginning to be known in other countries but in general, South American writers are still provincial.

1980s: The Latin American Boom of the 1960s has led to an array of brilliant writers known and respected in the world. Some have won the Nobel Prize in Literature, including Gabriel García Márquez and Pablo Neruda.

Today: South American novelists are world leaders in writing politically engaged fiction that is also profound in humane values and experimental form. Vargas Llosa is one of the most prominent among these with a career spanning half a century, culminating in a Nobel Prize in Literature.

Its capital was Cuzco in Peru, and the official language was Quechua. The Inca worshiped the sun god, with the emperor, or Inca, as the symbolic embodiment of the deity. Property was collective, and the religion demonstrated the harmony between humans and nature. A system of roads kept all parts of the empire connected. The spectacular ruins at Macchu Picchu on top of a mountain are thought to be a former royal palace. Macchu Picchu became a mystical symbol for modern artists, such as poet Pablo Neruda of Chile, of the indigenous greatness and unity of South America.

The Spanish conquest of Peru (1532–1572) destroyed the Inca Empire and decimated the indigenous populations through violence and epidemics like smallpox. The Viceroyalty of Peru (1542–1824) was established as a colony of the Spanish Crown at Cuzco in 1534 by Francisco Pizarro. After a period of civil war, the new capital of Lima was founded in 1535. Economic exploitation forced all native Peruvians to produce goods for the Spanish overlords and the Spanish government. Lima had an aristocratic Spanish population with a university and strong military. The colonials fought in wars from 1810 to 1824, with General Antonio José de Sucre beating the Spanish at the Battle of Ayacucho to secure Peru as an independent nation.

The Republic of Peru (1884–1930) created a certain stability until the worldwide economic depression of the 1930s. From 1930 to 1979, Peru alternated between democratic forms of government and military repression. Vargas Llosa grew up during the dictatorship of General Odría (1948–1956). The Cuban Revolution of 1959 encouraged the growth of the Communist Party in South America as a relief from dictatorships, and Vargas Llosa joined the left for a time. Another military coup (1968–1980) by General Juan Velasco Alvarado became part of Peru's ongoing militarism that is criticized in the novel. During the 1980s, drug wars added to the chaos in Peru, along with the terrorism of insurgent groups such as the Shining Path and Túpac Ameru.

Vargas Llosa's Presidential Bid in 1990

Alienated by Peruvian politics as a university student, Vargas Llosa joined many South American intellectuals in supporting the communist revolution of Fidel Castro in Cuba. He rejected the revolution and communism when Castro imprisoned the poet Heberto Padilla in 1971. Slowly, Vargas Llosa abandoned his left-wing ideas for a liberal philosophy embracing human rights and individual liberty, opposing authoritarianism of any kind. In the 1980s, conditions worsened in Peru with the terrorist actions of the rebel groups Shining Path (Sendero Luminoso) and Túpac Ameru. In 1983, a group of white journalists was massacred in the Amazon rain forest. Vargas Llosa was appointed to the investigatory commission, which found that indigenous villagers were responsible. The Peruvian press criticized him for racial prejudice. Scholars began to accuse him of seeing indigenous cultures as primitive and championing Western modernity. These issues are at the heart of his 1987 novel, *The Storyteller*.

Peru was afflicted in the 1980s with problems involving the assimilation of rain forest tribes, political terrorism and instability, militarism, and economic issues. In 1987, the year *The Storyteller* was published, Vargas Llosa became the liberal leader of the Movimento Libertad, creating a coalition with conservative leaders. The result was the center-right coalition, Frente Democrático, on whose platform he ran for

president in 1990. He proposed an economic austerity program that included privatization, a market economy, free trade, and dissemination of private property. Although he won the first round of the election, he was defeated in the final round by Alberto Fujimori, a more moderate Japanese agricultural engineer. Vargas Llosa's memoir, *A Fish in the Water* (1993), gives his account of this election. After this defeat, Vargas Llosa became a dual citizen of Spain and Peru and focused on writing, dividing his time between Madrid, London, and Lima. He tends to see Peru as still plagued by primitive violence and authoritarianism unworthy of a civilized nation.

The Machiguenga

The Machiguengas, the featured people of *The Storyteller*, are an indigenous people living in the Amazon basin jungle of southeastern Peru, the area around the Urubamba, Madre de Dios, and Manu Rivers near the borders of Bolivia and Brazil. They are basically hunter-gatherers in lifestyle, hence the constant emphasis that they must keep walking. They practice swidden, or slash and burn agriculture, growing cassava, manioc, bananas, maize, cotton, peanuts, chili peppers, and other crops in cleared forest gardens. Their meat comes from the rodent called paca, from fish, and some game. The people live in huts thatched with palm leaves and wear homemade tunics called cushmas. Although the Machiguengas, like other Amazon tribes, have extensive herbal medicines, now being studied by ethnobiologists, they have succumbed in large numbers to Western diseases and infections to which they have no immunity. Depicted in the novel as a primitive people who kill infertile wives and infants with defects, they have an elaborate animistic religion that includes good and evil spirits, with shaman figures mediating the spiritual world. Every human, animal, and plant has a proper place, with taboos and courtesies required in daily behavior. The Machiguenga language is in the Arawakan family, spoken in Peru.

Traditionally, the Machiguena are nomads, but many have now settled in villages. The Catholic Church and, later, Evangelical missionaries such as the Schneils in the novel created outposts or settlements where the natives could be converted, trade, and get medicine. The Summer Institute of Linguistics sponsored by the National University of San Marcos in Lima

Saul Zuratas tries to leave his modern life behind and settle with an indigenous tribe in the Peruvian jungle. (© Lukasz Janyst | Shutterstock.com)

where Vargas Llosa was a student allowed bilingual missionaries from the United States to document Machiguenga language and life from the 1950s. In the novel, Saúl Zuratas objects to the Summer Institute as intrusive; it was finally restricted in its activity in Peru in the 1980s. The creation of Manu National Park in 1974 has become a sort of reservation for several tribes of indigenous people of the area, including Machiguengas. In this park, Machiguengas have access to clean water, health care, and Western communication but are free to follow traditional ways, safe from the slavery and kidnapping practiced by rubber and lumber companies that used the natives for free labor.

CRITICAL OVERVIEW

Vargas Llosa gained international recognition with his very first novel in 1962, *The Time of the Hero*. He was in his twenties and already winning prizes for his technical mastery of the novel, his

contemporary themes, and his experimental style. In Peru, however, his novel was publicly burned because he had criticized Peru's military. Since then, Vargas Llosa has been a controversial figure, both politically and among fellow artists, though his literary reputation never falters. Instead of embracing his native country, his novels investigate the dark side of Peruvian and South American life, with its corruption and violence. *The Storyteller*, written twenty-five years after his first success, continues to present a clear and multifaceted look at his country's problems, without whitewashing or optimism.

In a 1984 review of the author's fourth acclaimed novel, *The War of the End of the World*, for the *New Republic*, Salmon Rushdie calls Vargas Llosa the "Peruvian Master" of the novel and speaks of his "appalling and ferocious" political vision, moving from his early interest in complex form to complex ideas. In a 1991 review of *El hablador* (*The Storyteller*) for *Hispanic Review*, Peter Standish comments on the metafictional structure, as well as the depth of the meaning the author creates about the role of the storyteller: "*El hablador* is a story (fable) told by one self-aware storyteller (fabulator) about another, who is also telling stories including other stories." Standish notes the ambiguity of the title, for *hablador* in Spanish can be a negative term used to describe someone who is a gossip or someone who makes up stories. Therefore, this is not merely a celebration of the storyteller but an investigation into his responsibility.

An article for *Kirkus Reviews* in 2003 examines Vargas Llosa's published collection of journalism called *The Language of Passion: Selected Commentary*, noting that the author began as a journalist and continues to shape public opinion with "contrarian musings on such matters as Third World development, free markets, and modern literature." This spirit of controversial public debate carries over into his novels, such as *The Storyteller*, which includes a scene of the journalist at work, producing the TV show *The Tower of Babel*.

Guadalupe Martí-Peña admires the novelist's use of language, not as escape, but to engage in real-life issues. In "The Power of Imagination: Mario Vargas Llosa" in *Romance Notes* for 2009, she comments on his use of fiction as an investigative tool: "Making sense of other people's lives means to read or misread their stories. As our common human destiny, we cannot escape words and interpretation." Her comment elucidates how the author uses fiction to highlight the difficulties of understanding others in a multicultural country, as he does in *The Storyteller*.

Finally, in "More Equal than Others," an article for the *New Statesman* in 2010, Isabel Hilton presents an overview of Vargas Llosa's tumultuous career, after he won the Nobel Prize in Literature that year. She concludes that in spite of his public quarrels, his work explores "the individual's struggle for self-realisation against oppression from both right and left." He is acknowledged as a major influence in South American and postmodern fiction.

CRITICISM

Susan K. Andersen

Andersen holds a PhD in English and is a former university professor of literature. In the following essay, she considers Vargas Llosa's use of the storyteller as both theme and technique in The Storyteller.

> IN A POSTMODERN, POSTCOLONIAL WORLD, THERE ARE NO PURE STORIES OR PRISTINE CULTURES TO SAVE, ONLY A VAST WEB OF INTERTEXTUALITY, MIXED OR HYBRID STORIES THAT KEEP UNFOLDING BECAUSE OF THE IRREPRESSIBLE NATURE OF STORYTELLERS."

Mario Vargas Llosa alternates Western and Machiguenga points of view in *The Storyteller*. The narrative is also split between two characters, Mario the narrator and Saúl Zuratas, who goes native and becomes a Machiguenga storyteller. Vargas Llosa does this to contrast the cultures, without choosing one over the other. From examining these diverse points of view and levels of reality, however, Vargas Llosa means to show there is no going back. The native populations of Peru will have to modernize in order to survive. Vargas Llosa shows this subtly through the theme and narrative device of the storyteller. In a postmodern, postcolonial world, there are no pure stories or pristine cultures to save, only a vast web of intertextuality, mixed or hybrid stories that keep unfolding because of the irrepressible nature of storytellers.

Vargas Llosa, like other South American writers, seeks social justice and uses writing as a form of protest, as Braulio Muñoz has pointed out in *Storyteller: Mario Vargas Llosa Between Civilization and Barbarism*. The author depicts Peru as a place of brutality and corruption, poised between civilization and barbarism. As is shown in *The Storyteller*, both white and native cultures have their dark and violent sides. Vargas Llosa does not romanticize either one.

The story opens with the narrator remembering meeting the Machiguengas on a trip to the Amazon, seeing a boy with his face eaten away by ulcers. It is a hard life, the people becoming nomads when violence or poverty forces them to keep walking. The book closes with the narrator commenting on whether life has improved for the tribe since moving into villages. He thinks of the oil wells and the Indians forced to work for them, the drug traffic, the killings of rival gangs, the

WHAT DO I READ NEXT?

- Isabel Allende's *The House of the Spirits* (1982) is an example of magic realism with myth and fact interwoven in this tale of three generations of Trueba women in Chile leading to the dictator Pinochet's takeover in 1973 and murder of the author's uncle, President Allende.

- The 1991 novel by Dominican American writer Julia Alvarez, *How the García Girls Lost Their Accent*, tells the story of four sisters forced to flee to New York with their family from the Dominican Republic because of the dictator, Trujillo, the same dictator Vargas Llosa writes of in *The Feast of the Goat*. The novel begins in their adult lives and goes back to their childhood in the Dominican Republic, showing their hardships in adapting to a new culture and in their confusion of identity.

- Hiram Bingham's *Lost City of the Incas*, originally published in 1948, recounting his 1911 discovery of Macchu Picchu, was republished in 2003 by Phoenix Press with illustrations. A possible Indiana Jones prototype, Bingham was a Harvard professor, amateur archaeologist, and later, American senator.

- Allen Johnson's *Families of the Forest: The Matsigenka Indians of the Peruvian Amazon* (2003), published by the University of California Press, is an ethnolographical study of the Machiguengas as a society originally organized in small self-sufficient units.

- Gabriel García Márquez's *Love in the Time of Cholera* (1988) is a love story set between the late 1870s and the early 1930s in Colombia, illuminating Latin American culture as it transitions to a modern age. Márquez was a model for Vargas Llosa's own fictional theories and is considered another important Latin American author today.

- Sally Morgan's *The Flying Emu and Other Australian Stories* (1993) are original animal fables told by an aboriginal young-adult author from tales she heard in her childhood.

- *The No. 1 Ladies Detective Agency* (2003) by Alexander McCall Smith is another tale, like *The Storyteller*, about a racial group different from the author's own. His heroine, Precious Ramotswe, is an African detective folk hero of Botswana, highlighting the history and culture of that country. The author is a Scotsman.

- Vargas Llosa's *The Time of the Hero* (1962) was instantly successful and among the first novels of the Latin American Boom of the 1960s. It is a satire on the military school his father forced him to attend.

---

military, and the terrorism and counterterrorism in ongoing political instability. The Machiguengas have no idea what it is about, just that history repeats itself. Vargas Llosa does not try to give a solution, just a discussion of options.

In his 1991 book, *A Writer's Reality*, Vargas Llosa talks about how novels were forbidden in the Spanish colonies of Peru by the Spanish Inquisition. He notes that the Inquisitors were aware of the power of the novel before writers were. Since then, the novel has had its revenge with the "novelization of our whole life." In the novels of the Boom writers, for instance, "History and literature, truth and falsehood, reality and fiction mingle," as in Gabriel García Márquez's *One Hundred Years of Solitude*, a mixture of facts from the author's family history and magic storytelling about the Colombian countryside. The novel symbolizes the irrational development of South America, a continent of superstition and acting out of violent fantasies in its political isolation.

M. Keith Booker, in *Vargas Llosa among the Postmodernists*, asserts that though the author does not endorse utopian solutions, he is a utopian at heart. Vargas Llosa suggests the *hablador* as a kind of ideal figure able to make a difference for his people in the act of communal storytelling. Similarly, Vargas Llosa passionately argues that the "total novel," the kind written by Western authors like García Márquez and himself, creates a new open-ended universe that offers, if not solutions, at least a range of possible positions for the reader to consider. For this reason, Vargas Llosa calls the novelist a deicide, or god killer, who takes God's place and creates an alternative reality. Vargas Llosa gives both the native and Western storytellers in *The Storyteller* the power to engage with reality as they find it and to modify it. He celebrates this as one of the nobler human traits, as illustrated by the *hablador* in his tale of the first Machiguenga man, Pachakamue, whose speech came true: Every time he spoke he created animals and events. The people disliked this and killed him and buried his head, thinking they were saving the world from disorder, but Pachakamue's tongue still moved, and he "went on transforming things so they would be like his words." The moral is that you can kill a storyteller but you cannot kill stories. They spread, change, and transform themselves and the world.

In the novel, Mario accuses Saúl of being involved in *indigenismo*, the movement in the 1920s when some Peruvian writers began to champion the cause of indigenous people. They brought to light the Black Legend, the stories of the cruelty of the Spanish conquest, extracted from the chronicles of the conquerors themselves. In *Literature of Latin America*, Rafael Ocasio claims that though Vargas Llosa does not romanticize the natives as the *indigenismos* did, he treats them in a positive light. The author does not endorse one character or point of view, however, so that readers may enter the narrative space on their own. A common criticism of Vargos Llosa, however, is summarized by Muñoz in the charge that he is like a tourist in his own country, not really knowing the natives or their language. This brings up the question of whether someone of one race has the right to be a representative of another race. Until there are Machiguenga novelists to answer his narrative, Vargas Llosa has the field to himself, showing the natives through the eyes of characters who are non-native, like Mascarita. Although Mascarita tries to do the Machiguengas justice, claiming to have become one of them, he is always the outsider, with his scar and Jewish background.

In fact, scholars question where Vargas Llosa got the figure of the *hablador*, as Fiona J. Macintosh points out in "Innocence and Corruption: *Who Killed Palomino Molero?* and *The Storyteller*." Mario the narrator admits that he believes Saúl Zuratas is the *hablador* in the photograph, though he cannot prove it. What is even more interesting is that there is no objective or historical evidence of Machiguenga storytellers as described by the author. Vargas Llosa met Wayne and Betty Snell from the Summer Institute of Linguistics (the Schneils in the novel), but they never published anything on the existence of such a figure in their studies. The author does acknowledge Father Joaquin Barriales, O. P., as the collector and translator of many of the Machiguenga myths that appear in the book. Unlike his character Saúl Zuratas, the author got the stories in a second-hand written form. The *hablador* is thus a charming and magical myth created by Vargas Llosa.

Vargas Llosa created both the Western and Machiguenga storytellers, Mario and Saúl, two characters who are in dialogue with each other, discussing the issues of the Machiguenga future. Saúl asks, "Do our cars, guns, planes, and Coca-Colas give us the right to exterminate them because they don't have such things?" Mario counters with the charge that Saúl wants to protect the "way of life and the beliefs of a handful of tribes still living, many of them in the Stone Age" while the rest of the country abstains from developing itself. Mario invokes the stereotype of the natives as interested in animism and head shrinking, while Saúl answers, "They have a deep and subtle knowledge of things that we've forgotten. The relationship between man and Nature, for instance." The author dramatizes the debate, not only with the two storytellers on opposing sides, but also with contrasting vignettes of the cultures themselves—the jungles versus Lima and Florence, Italy.

With the alternating chapters and storyteller/narrators, the narrative seems set up as a straight contrast of cultures and values. The very stark difference makes the point that bridging the gap is almost impossible. Even though Mario at the end laments that the Machiguengas are going downhill, and nothing ever seems to change in the political atmosphere of Peru, the narrative provides a subtle shift in this deadlock.

Some chapters feature Mario Vargas Llosa as a character in his own novel, working at a radio station and visiting local pubs in Lima. *(© Klaus Ulrich Mueller / Shutterstock.com)*

Vargas Llosa creates the shift with the narrative technique he calls "communicating vessels" in *Letters to a Young Novelist*. This book is actually a detailed study of his own practices on using plot, narrative, time, space, and levels of reality to make what he calls the total novel, a narrative able to properly represent and recreate the world. In *The Storyteller*, for instance, there are two story lines going at once: what happens to Mario as he searches for the *habladores* and what happens to Saúl Zuratas after his disappearance. These two plot lines he calls vessels. They appear to be separate or parallel vessels, depicting white and native cultures, but there is a subtle interaction. The two vessels are communicating or merging at various points. He defines communicating vessels as "two or more episodes that occur at different times, in different places, or on different levels of reality but are linked by the narrator so that their proximity or mingling causes them to modify each other."

The two plots leak into one another through the narrators or storytellers. Eventually, we find out that the Machiguenga storyteller is Saúl

Zuratas, a Westerner and Mario's university friend. Saúl recounts not only native cosmology to the natives, but soon he is also mixing in his own stories with theirs, the same ones we were introduced to while he argued with Mario in Mario's narrative, such as the struggle of the Jews and Kafka's story *Metamorphosis*. It appears Saúl's motive in telling stories is to urge the natives to stay away from the white world and to keep their own ways. Yet he introduces Western stories about Jews, Christ, the Bible, and Kafka, retold as their own myths, but with values attached to these stories that do not reflect their own. The rain forest tribes kill deformed babies and suspicious strangers, but in Mascarita's tales, he inserts examples of tolerance over taboo. In one episode, he tells how he was dying of sickness in the forest, unable to move. The tribe that finds him debates whether to kill him, their usual practice, but instead, they give him food. Saúl is modifying their culture from within. He actually confirms Mario's thesis that the Machiguengas cannot remain unchanged in the modern world. It is a world of mixing values, races, and stories. It does not require a policy decision; they will modernize by default.

Mario does not try to pretend that the Machiguenga chapters are the authentic production of a native storyteller. He lets the reader in on how hard it was to make those chapters sound convincing, since he is a Spanish-speaking intellectual trying to write from a native point of view. He admits he is conjecturing the story of Saúl's disappearance but engages the reader's help by creating a mystery, and the scenes he constructs afford glimpses of what Saúl's story could have been. The novel is a metanarrative with an invented storyteller inventing another storyteller. Mario merges all storytellers into one grand archetype: "All the people or institutions everywhere in the world that might resemble or in any way be associated with the Machiguenga storytellers had held an immediate fascination for me."

In this way, Vargas Llosa seems not to favor one culture over the other, but rather, to favor the storyteller who is the carrier of culture in every society. Vargas Llosa may stir controversy over whether he has a right to tamper with another culture's stories, but, like the buried head of Pachakamue with its tongue still wagging, there is no stopping the propagation of stories or the storyteller's imagination. In the end, most agree that Vargas Llosa's novel does bring the dark plight of the Machiguengas into public light in the interest of social justice.

Source: Susan K. Andersen, Critical Essay on *The Storyteller*, in *Novels for Students*, Gale, Cengage Learning, 2015.

Jean O'Bryan-Knight

In the following excerpt, O'Bryan-Knight examines the significance of Peru's politics in The Storyteller.

. . . In his novel *The Storyteller* (1987), released shortly after he wrote the "Foreword" to *The Other Path*, Vargas Llosa offers us another minor character whose desire is to participate directly in the free market, and in this case the results are tragic. As in *The Real Life of Alejandro Mayta*, *The Storyteller* features a narrator who is a novelist in the process of writing a novel. The novel in question is the story of an anthropology student, Saúl, who 'goes native,' abandoning intellectual life in Lima in order to join a prehistoric tribe in the jungle, the Machiguenga. Alternating between chapters set in

> LIKE HIS LITERARY PREDECESSORS, IN HIS DEPICTION OF JUM, VARGAS LLOSA, A NON-INDIAN INTELLECTUAL WRITING FOR A NON-INDIAN URBAN READERSHIP ABOUT THE INDIAN IN THE STATE OF NATURE, DESCRIBES THE INDIAN IN A WAY CONSISTENT WITH HIS OWN WORLDVIEW."

urban landscapes and those set in the forest, the novel establishes a fascinating counterpoint between the two cultures that make up Peru: one industrialized and literate, the other premodern and oral. As the novel alternates between these two worlds, it invites the reader to ponder difficult questions about the benefits of assimilation versus isolation of fragile minority cultures.

In chapter four of *The Storyteller* the unnamed narrator recalls that, during his first trip to the jungle in 1958, he visited the Aguaruna settlement of Urakusa, where he had his first encounter with a victim of torture, Jum. Working through an interpreter, the narrator learns that a posse of whites and mestizos, comprising all the civilian authorities of the town Santa María de Nieva and a soldier from one of the bases on the frontier, descended on the indigenous settlement one day. They burned huts, raped women, beat the men who tried to defend themselves, and carried off Jum, the tribal leader. Back in Santa María de Nieva, Jum was publicly tortured, an act the interpreter describes in horrifying detail, "They flogged him, burned his armpits with hot eggs, and finally hoisted him up a tree the way they do paiche, large river fish, to drain them off." After a few hours he was released and allowed to return to his village. The purpose of this brutality was retaliation. Jum had angered his attackers by exercising his economic freedom by organizing a cooperative among the Aguaruna settlements of the Alto Marañón.

Chief Jum was a clever and determined man who was identified as a strong leader by the Summer Institute of Linguistics missionaries working in his settlement. They arranged to have him study in the town of Yarinacocha in order to train to become a bilingual teacher who would be capable of teaching his people to read and write in their own language. Although the program did not realize the lofty goal of bringing literacy to the Amazonian tribes, in Jum's case it did have the effect of putting the chief in contact with "civilization" in Yarinacocha—with unintended consequences. There he discovered that he and his people were being exploited by the white and mestizo middlemen with whom they traded rubber and hides. The middlemen set the prices for the raw materials and then paid the Indian suppliers in goods for which they also determined the value. When the clever *cacique* realized that his people could sell their raw materials in the cities for greater profit and buy their goods at better prices there as well, he informed the middlemen of Santa María de Nieva that he would no longer trade with them. Right after Jum communicated this decision, he was punished. As the posse tortured Jum, they told him repeatedly to forget about the cooperative.

The narrator, while reflecting on Jum's sad story, mulls over a particular articulation of the so-called indigenous question, which has been debated among Peruvian intellectuals for over a century. Given that the Urakusa dwellers live in a state of abject exploitation, what should be done to better their lot? Should they move backward toward the isolation they knew before coming into contact with Western civilization? This might be achieved by herding them into protected reservations where they could continue living according to their ancient traditions. Or should they move forward toward economic integration by establishing their cooperative and gaining the economic security that would allow them to enforce their physical security? It is clear that the narrator, as a young man in his twenties, believes the answer is assimilation, and he suspects that his old friend Saúl would disagree:

> Would he admit that in a case like this it was quite obvious that what was to Urakusa's advantage, to Jum's, was not going backward but forward? That is to say, setting up their own cooperative, trading with the towns, prospering economically and socially so that it would no longer be possible to treat them the way the "civilized" people of Santa María de Nieva had done. Or would Saúl, unrealistically, deny that this was so, insist that the true solution was for the Viracochas to go away and let the inhabitants of Urakusa return to their traditionally way of life?

At the time he is reflecting on Jum's story in the 1950s the narrator obviously equates progress with the advent of socialism. (In this respect, he looks a lot like the young Vargas Llosa on whom he is clearly modeled.) He sees the Urakusas' problem in terms of class conflict that could be resolved through the successful transition to socialism:

> By substituting for the obsession with profit—individual gain—the idea of service to the community as the incentive to work, and reintroducing an attitude of solidarity and humanity into social relations, socialism would make possible that coexistence between modern and primitive Peru that Mascarita thought impossible and undesirable. In the new Peru, infused with the science of Marx and Mariátegui, the Amazonian tribes would, at one and the same time, be able to adopt modern ways and to preserve their essential traditions and customs within the mosaic of cultures that would go to make up the future civilization of Peru.

This socialist solution never pans out for the Urakusa, and we can infer from his comments elsewhere in the novel that the narrator eventually distances himself from that political position. *The Storyteller*, however, does not focus on the efficacy of any particular economic plan but on the inevitability of assimilation. Looking back on the ideas of his youth some three decades later, the narrator understands that it was highly romantic of him to believe that industrial development, whether socialist or capitalist, would preserve rather than annihilate the fragile forest cultures. As he writes in the 1980s, Machiguenga culture is well on the way to extinction, and its only possibility for preservation is in texts such as the one the novelist-narrator is writing.

The appearance of Jum in this novel, therefore, is all the more interesting. The Urakusa chief, as we have seen, is no socialist. (As soon as he saw the market's potential, he was eager to exploit it.) I would argue that his presence in *The Storyteller*, however brief, constitutes a persuasive little plug for a market-oriented economy. This implication was lost on the narrator when he was a young socialist blinded by his utopian ideals but should not be lost on the attentive reader. We do not have to look too hard to see that as a free marketeer Jum embodies the neoliberal notions of his creator, author Vargas Llosa. In addition to being a creative and resourceful human being, the chief is motivated by profit, naturally acquisitive, and capable of understanding money and the market. By representing the Indian in a way that is consistent with his own market-oriented ideology of the mid-1980s, the novelist is actually following a pattern established by earlier works of Andean indigenism. Earlier in the twentieth century non-Indian authors such as the Ecuadorian Jorge Icaza and the Peruvian José María Arguedas wrote novels for their white and mestizo urban readership in which they represent the Indian in his rural environment as a natural communist, a portrait consistent with their own leftist worldviews. Like his literary predecessors, in his depiction of Jum, Vargas Llosa, a non-Indian intellectual writing for a non-Indian urban readership about the Indian in the state of nature, describes the Indian in a way consistent with his own worldview. By making the utterly sympathetic *cacique* of the Urakusa a natural capitalist, Vargas Llosa continues the indigenist tradition, albeit with very different political implications....

Source: Jean O'Bryan-Knight, "'Let's Make Owners and Entrepreneurs': Glimpses of Free Marketeers in Vargas Llosa's Novels," in *Vargas Llosa and Latin American Politics*, edited by Juan E. De Castro and Nicholas Birns, Palgrave Macmillan, 2010, pp. 56–59.

Braulio Muñoz

In the following excerpt, Muñoz discusses the cultural importance of the storyteller figure.

...THE QUIXOTIC QUEST

In the late eighties, armed with the conviction of the strength of his vision—and perhaps urged by blind, ancient forces deposited by childhood traumas—Vargas Llosa set out into the Peruvian political world in the quixotic quest to straighten what needed straightening. Since, willing himself to succeed, he had become a supplanter of God in fiction—despite the high hurdles that a country like Peru, barbaric and sad, had put in his path; since he had willed himself into an international citizen by jumping the fences of barbarism, he believed he could help others, less fortunate or less gifted, to achieve their potential and do something similar for themselves.

To this end, as he had learned to do in literature, Vargas Llosa was willing to borrow the necessary weapons from the local and international culture—freely. If first he had armed himself with the rhetoric of Marxism, he now found in neoliberalism the ideology best suited for the daily deicidal act to be carried out by all Peruvians. Marx was exchanged for Popper as Sartre was for Camus. But the exchange did not

> HIS DEFEAT BY THE WORLD HAD NOT PRODUCED A RETREAT BUT A RETURN."

erase all earlier valuations and hopes. For, much as Marx had done in the nineteenth century, Vargas Llosa rose ready to bid all Peruvians, as authors of their own fate, to reinvent their world and themselves in the process.

Unlike Freud, who coyly claimed not to have the courage to rise before humanity as a prophet, Vargas Llosa did not find daunting the prospect of presenting himself as a messianic figure. On the contrary, his Will to Truth and Will to Power found there a worthy field of resistance. As he had done in the quixotic quest to produce the Good Lie while standing in a cursed land, he now saw himself as a world-historical politico, ready to tackle a new goal against impossible odds. Indeed, "if the decadence, impoverishment, terrorism and constant crises had not made governing the country an almost impossible challenge, it would never have entered my head to take on the task."

The Quixote quest has its proper animus and limitations. The quixotic hero never understands failure as the result of his own shortcomings. To him, failure always issues from the intractability of the world. Failure may even come from exhaustion; but never from the misplacement of emotions or the erroneous understanding of things. In his messianic moments, the quixotic hero may even understand failure as a fateful event. In that case, his self-proclaimed tragic effort confers on him nobility. In Peru, Vargas Llosa anticipated, all heroes so far have been defeated.

THE STORYTELLER

From the troubadours of the *sertón* in Brazil to the Seanchaí of Ireland, Vargas Llosa has noted, the Storyteller is someone who rekindles the fire of collective memory. Like Walter Benjamin, he envisions the Storyteller as a transmitter of collective wisdom, hopes, and desires.

Benjamin believed the Storyteller was a character of the past, a character whose voice was finally drowned by the metallic, impersonal noises of modernity. A man born in Peru, at the fringes of the modern world, in a land where *habladores* still make a living performing on the streets, cutting through the veil of ideology and custom, exposing collective wounds, raising a mirror to collective feelings and failings, Vargas Llosa believes the Storyteller has metamorphosed but endures. Unlike Lukacs and Benjamin, who conceived of the novel as a bourgeois form par excellence and hence utterly allied with the powers of modernity against the dream-bird that hatched the egg of desire in more placid times, Vargas Llosa not only makes room for the Storyteller as a character in his literary creations, he aspires to be one himself.

COMMUNION

The strength of the vision of the Storyteller is grounded in the strength of his culture. The world beyond, threatening or becoming, must be appropriated through the webs of meaning particular to that culture. To be equal to his task, therefore, the Storyteller must find a home within his culture. His place need not be a coveted nor even a respected one; but it is indispensable that the Storyteller's audience stir under the impact of his words ricocheting in the deep recesses of a psychological communion. In this sense, the image of the Storyteller and that of the prophets of old—foretellers of disasters and admonishers of those unable or unwilling to follow the path of covenant and salvation—fuse into one.

A PERUVIAN STORYTELLER

Despite his repeated renunciations, Vargas Llosa is a Peruvian—not European—Storyteller. He draws strength from his own complex, if not damned, culture. Like prophets of old, he feels shame, anger, and pity for the barbarous land. But, by his own admission, he cannot remove the call of the land and its people from under his skin. He knows he must see the world through the prism of the culture that nurtured him to adulthood and bestowed upon him heaps of pain and shame. This is why, in one way or another, most of his major literary efforts are about Peru. He feels that cursed land in his bones, and the more he looks to distance himself, the closer he draws to it emotionally, metaphysically. The telluric—a *huachafo* term—envelops him.

IDEALIZATIONS

Vargas Llosa has never offered a Good Lie about Europe or America. This is not because he

really does not know Europe or America the way he knows his own land. Not only does he appear to have spent more time in Madrid, London, or Paris than in Loreto or Cusco, but inadequate knowledge has never been a serious deterrent to writing fiction. It is certainly not a deterrent to a quixotic hero. What to make, then, of the fact that Vargas Llosa feels free to write about Iquitos and the Andes critically without much apprehension of misrepresenting things, whereas his remarks on the shortcomings of Western culture, on the other hand, are proffered, here and there, muffled by care and deference? Why has he not—so far, at least—engaged, critically, the culture he so admires and to which he wishes to belong? Because like other Peruvians of his class, he idealizes those lands. Furthermore, as ideal-typical and utopic, they play a pivotal role in his posture as writer/Storyteller: the idealized West becomes his measuring rod for all that is human. An inability to imitate those Others is punishable by economic backwardness and political barbarism. Europe and America, it seems, play a role similar, though in reverse, to that of the Philistines in the ancient drama of the Jewish people.

REINVENTIONS

The role of the Storyteller/prophet could not be more difficult than in Peru—a cursed and chaotic land, inhabited by individuals embodying antagonistic cultures, languages, and values, and hence necessitating either the rule of a ruthless strongman or, perhaps, the gifts of a Storyteller, to bring order into chaos and unite individuals into a people, according to Vargas Llosa. In other words, as for some prophets of old, the task of the Storyteller in Peru is to invent a new identity, a new Truth, a new Nation. This means the Storyteller must reinterpret the past, understand the present ruthlessly, and, grounded on such insights, carry the project of reinvention forward into the future. Perhaps that was why Vargas Llosa entered politics, against his better judgment and seemingly against his own interests: in Peru, the Storyteller had to become a politico.

CHARISMA

In his discussions on charisma, Max Weber noted that the role of prophet cannot be enacted without the willingness to assent on the part of those for and to whom the charismatic leader speaks. When it comes to changing the world, prophets can only do so much. Similarly, the task of the writer/Storyteller is nearly impossible unless his culture has already woven into existence the expectation that culture bearers have not only the right but the duty to demand sacrifices and constancy in action even against overwhelming odds. Vargas Llosa believes such is the case in Latin America in general and Peru in particular. As a culture bearer, he has always felt he was being asked to be oracle, wisdom personified, priest, mentor, teacher, father, and caudillo. Reluctantly, he prepared himself to obey the demand.

Charisma, particularly in modern times, is very seldom transferable. Few great military leaders, for example, become elder statesmen or high priests. Few great writer/critics become presidents of their countries. This makes it remarkable that, on hearing the demands of his people, Vargas Llosa took a chance and advanced the claim. He did his best not to falter. He began by accepting that he was different from the Many. He accepted his condition as marginal man; perhaps an extraordinary man for extraordinary times. He declared himself prepared to show his mettle and, by his own account, endangered his life for the sake of the cause. At the same time, he declared himself utterly attached to principles, a rebel against the up-to-then immoral ways of conducting public affairs. And, for a while, he had the ears and hearts of the Many, who seemed to appreciate his courage and sacrifices.

Then, perhaps because the Many saw the price of reinventing themselves as too high, or perhaps because it eventually became clear that the voice of the fabulist mingled freely with that of the statesman, that the evils he denounced were not as altogether intractable as he believed, that the hopes he offered were squalid in comparison to other long-standing hopes, that his dream of a prosperous land was based on a neo-liberal ideology with all the limitations that reality visits upon all such constructions, the people walked away. In the end, his proclaimed self-immolation—neglect of his creative powers, distaste for pressing the flesh of the Many—was not sufficient to retain them.

THE INTRACTABLE WORLD

After the defeat, Vargas Llosa and his closest allies looked around for reasons. They were led to the recapitulation of old truths: the people are still like children. They are credulous, steeped in myth and magic, hoping for a false messiah to save them, and easily led astray by

> **THE STORYTELLER SPEAKS WITH THE VOICE OF THE LATE 20TH CENTURY, NOT MERELY IN ITS ECOLOGICAL CONCERN FOR THE DESTRUCTION OF THE RAIN FOREST, BUT MORE CENTRALLY IN ITS VISION OF THE PRECIOUS PARTICULARISM OF HUMAN CULTURES."**

would-be Storytellers who sacrifice the sacrosanct role for the sake of material rewards. The writer/Storyteller had offered a truer language and self-immolation as an antidote to the weight of a twisted tradition. It was not enough. And so, his quixotic will spent, he claimed a role as eternal outsider. He would dispense counsel through his art; he might approximate the exemplary prophets of old. His defeat by the world had not produced a retreat but a return.

Source: Braulio Muñoz, "The Storyteller," in *A Storyteller: Mario Vargas Llosa between Civilization and Barbarism*, Rowman & Littlefield Publishers, 2000, pp. 90–94.

Robert Alter

In the following review, Alter explains why he thinks the first-person narrator weakens the book.

This intriguing work of fiction is less a novel than an illustrated meditation, on the nature of culture and the relation of narrative to culture. The unnamed first-person narrator is a thinly fictionalized stand-in for Mario Vargas Llosa. He is the same age; has the same educational background; produces a television program, as in fact Vargas Llosa did, called "The Tower of Babel" (a kind of Peruvian "60 Minutes"); and writes his story in a sultry season in Florence, where Vargas Llosa actually began *The Storyteller* in the summer of 1985. The only character besides the narrator with more than a walkon role is Saul Zuratas, the narrator's Jewish friend from his university years in Lima, but Zuratas is more an idea or an obsession than a realized novelistic character.

The two men have not seen each other for almost 30 years. Teasing hints and clues-an ambiguously shaded face in a photograph of Amazonian natives, ripples of rumor emanating from the Amazon-lead the narrator to conclude that his old friend has sloughed off both his Peruvian and his Jewish identity, plunged into the primal world of the great rain forest, and surfaced in the Machiguenga tribe as a traditional hablador, a spellbinding speaker and storyteller. This central fact of the plot, as the narrator himself recognizes, is a little improbable, and Vargas Llosa tries, somewhat surprisingly, to build a bridge from Lima to the jungle, from the 20th century to the stone age, through Saul Zuratas's jewishness.

The correspondences between jew and Machiguengan are intimated early on, and then spelled-out (perhaps too explicitly) late in the book when Zuratas as storyteller recounts in Machiguengan terms the history of the Jews. Both peoples are uprooted, banished by invading foreigners with superior technology; both become wanderers (the Machiguengas call themselves "the men who walk"); both stubbornly cling to their language, their traditions, their intricate tapestry of taboos, through all of which they constantly affirm, against the threat of seeming chaos, "the order that reigns in the world."

The addiction to storytelling as the vehicle of vital wisdom that is sometimes transparent, sometimes baffling, is represented as another essential link between Machiguengan and Jew. In his pre-Amazonian years, Zuratas, an assimilated jew, makes visible contact with just one serious expression of Jewish culture: the fiction of Kafka. The story that particularly fascinates him is "The Metamorphosis," no doubt because he himself, like the protagonist Gregor Samsa, is a pariah figure, half his face frighteningly disfigured by a strawberry-blotch birthmark.

The stories Zuratas tells his Machiguengan audiences-conveyed in long chapters intercalated in the narrator's reflective account of his own pursuit of the traces of his vanished friend-evoke a magical world in which weird transformations from man to animal are everyday occurrences. When, near the end of the book, Zuratas retells to his Amazonian listeners the story of Samsa's metamorphosis into a "buzz buzz bug," this tale invented by a Prague Jew seems absolutely at one with their experience of a radically unstable reality, inhabited by quirky and dangerous spirits, exposed to mercurial changes in forms of being, yet somehow held in check by the shaping power of narrative.

By a technical tour de force, Vargas Llosa makes us see an affinity between Kafka and native storyteller, between jew and Machiguengan, but it must also be said that the set of correspondences he proposes sometimes seems more like Dr. Johnson's definition of the metaphysical conceit: "a violent yoking of heterogenous elements." The Jews and the Machiguengas may both be tradition-haunted people, but the jews have also been, after all, a people cut off from nature; cerebral; caught up in the exegetical intricacies of a culture conspicuously tied to the written word; and in the view of some of their vigorous internal critics in the modern era, not primitive enough by half. Or, on the contrary, if one chooses to adopt the more celebratory self-evaluation of Freud in Moses and Monotheism, the jews are, above all, the people who renounced instinctual gratification for the sake of intellectual labor-which is rather unlike the route of Amazonian tribal culture.

The Storyteller speaks with the voice of the late 20th century, not merely in its ecological concern for the destruction of the rain forest, but more centrally in its vision of the precious particularism of human cultures. In this respect, the novel can be read as a pointed reversal of *Heart Of Darkness*. It is conceivable that Vargas Llosa is deliberately alluding to Conrad. Both books are written out of a guilty consciousness of the effects of colonialism, but to opposite effects. In *Heart of Darkness*, Kurtz, the Westerner who goes native, discovers behind his own thin facade of civilization-bearer a deep affinity with the demonic that is manifested in the savage rites of the Congolese. Beneath surface distinctions between black and white, African and European, lies a universal human potential for depravity ("The horror! The horror!") that at best can be camouflaged by a veil of lies, as Marlow the narrator does for the sake of Kurtz's fiancee.

By contrast, what Vargas Llosa's lapsed Westerner discovers on the banks of the Amazon is not the universal darkness of human nature, man's vocation for chaos, but instead one of the many primal languages of human culture, untainted by high technology, mass society, and secularization. The Machiguengas reveal to Zuratas the possibility of a primeval integrity, rooted in a nurturing sense of tradition, of community, of transmissible wisdom, and, above all, of a pervasive correspondence between the spirit of man and the spirits of Nature."

The obvious danger of this whole conception of the Amazonians is that it could easily decline into a latter-day version of the Noble Savage, a trap of sentimentalization that at one point the narrator explicitly says he wants to avoid. Vargas Llosa cannot entirely escape this trap because the basic premise of his plot is, after all, the pristine wholeness of primitive culture, but he can at least mitigate the sentimentality in the way he realizes the Amazonian world. The persuasiveness, then, of the book as a whole hangs on Vargas Llosa's ability to meet the daunting technical challenge of the Zuratas chapters, which as he himself put it, "was the difficulty of inventing, in Spanish and within logically consistent intellectual framework, a literary form that would suggest, with any reasonable degree of credibility, how a primitive man with a magico-religious mentality would go about telling a story."

Style has its own moral imperatives, and I think Vargas Llosa avoids blatantly sentimentalizing his savages by creating a style for his storyteller that is at once rough-hewn and crafted, without adjectival insistence or syntactic complications, focused on the gritty concreteness of the physical world and attuned to its animistic presences. (His stylistic success is beautifully conveyed in Helen Lane's English version.) At one point the storyteller explains how he taps an ultimate source for his tales by "listening, carefully, respectfully," to the rain forest through which he walks:

> The things you'd least expect speak. There
> they are: speaking. Bones, thorns. Pebbles,
> lianas. Little bushes and budding
> leaves. The scorpion. The line of ants
> dragging a bottly back to the anthill. The
> butterfly with rainbow wings. The hummingbird.
> The mouse up a branch speaks,
> and circles in the water.... The little stone
> you can hardly see, it's so small, sticking
> out of the mud. Even the louse you crack in
> two with your fingernail has a story to tell.
> If I could only remember everything I've
> been hearing. You'd never tire of me,
> perhaps.

As conventional syntactic ordering is displayed by this chain of noun clauses and brief simple sentences, the sheer presence of natural things obtrudes, as it might in a consciousness different from a modern man's. Both the language-shorn as it is of evaluative and descriptive elaboration-and the things described break the frame of the aesthetic and attitudinal hierarchies in which we are accustomed to imagine the world: bones, thorns, bottly, butterfly, hummingbird, mouse, louse, and stone are set at one level as things that speak to the storyteller. Nature is a realm of odd and often raucous presences, quite unlike, say, the gently semantic universe, suffused with hidden light, of Wordsworth's poetry. And if the lyric catalog is vaguely reminiscent of Modernist poetry, that is a happy congruence, which in part may reflect the fascination with the primitive in early 20th-century literature.

The Machiguengan world revealed in Zuratas's stories is not "noble" but earthy, naive in some ways and shrewd in others, crude, sometimes cruel, scary and funny, and always buoyed up by an unmodern sense of the culture sustaining efficacy of telling the tale. Here, for example, is the hablador in a mood of fantastic humor, recounting how Tasurinchl, the creator-god and culture-hero (who is sometimes blurred with the storyteller), suffers a wasp sting on his penis, which then swells to epic proportions: The birds perched on it to sing, thinking it was a tree. When Tasurinchi urinated, a cataract of warm water, foamy as the rapids of the Gran Pongo, came out of its big mouth. Tasurinchi could have bathed in it, and his family too, maybe. He used it as a seat when he stopped to rest. And at night it was his pallet.

The Zuratas chapters of *The Storyteller* are arresting because Vargas Llosa has found in them a style that vividly manifests the otherness of primitive culture at the same time that it intimates certain abiding connections with our own culture; this accounts for the force of the retelling of Kafka's "Metamorphosis," with no real violation of the German story, in Amazonian idiom. It may be something of an anthropological cliche to say that without stories there is no human culture, but Vargas Llosa makes the meaning of the notion vividly concrete by showing through Zuratas's tales how the act of narrative invention gives us a human handle on birth, sex, and death; sky, earth, and water; pain and healing; animal, vegetable, and human-everything that inspires perplexity and wonder and threatens to defy human control.

Vargas Llosa's book is poorer, however, for its patently exemplary character. The outsider who joins the outsider people in order to take up one of the primary tasks of civilization from time immemorial is meant to be an example to all of us moderns, marooned in a wasteland created by technology, mindless individualism, and rampant secularization. The narrator, constantly ruminating on the bizarre destiny of his friend Saúl, has a propensity to spell out meanings that might better have been left implicit. I would have preferred the book to end not with the narrator, who provides a series of reflections on the Machiguengan sense of history (it is not a forward march but goes round and round), the importance of their myths, and the reasons for Zuratas's going native, but rather with the last note of the immediately preceding Zuratas chapter: the storyteller in the jungle, a pet parrot perched on his head, cawing out the name that people called its master in his now forgotten life in Lima-Mascarita, the Masked One.

Source: Robert Alter, Review of *The Storyteller*, in *New Republic*, Vol. 202, Nos. 2–3, January 8, 1990, p. 41.

SOURCES

Booker, M. Keith, *Vargas Llosa Among the Postmodernists*, University of Florida Press, 1994, pp. 122–23.

Gerdes, Dick, *Mario Vargas Llosa*, Twayne's World Author Series: Latin American Literature, No. 762, Twayne Publishers, 1985, pp. 1–17, 63, 83, 90, 92.

Hilton, Isabel, "More Equal than Others," in *New Statesman*, Vol. 139, No. 5023, October 18, 2010, pp. 40–41.

Macintosh, Fiona J., "Innocence and Corruption: *Who Killed Palomino Molero?* and *The Storyteller*," in *The Cambridge Companion to Mario Vargas Llosa*, edited by Efrain Kristal and John King, Cambridge University Press, 2012, pp. 81–82.

Martí-Peña, Guadalupe, "The Power of Imagination: Mario Vargas Llosa," in *Romance Notes*, Vol. 49, No. 1, Fall 2009, pp. 101–109.

Muñoz, Braulio, *A Storyteller: Mario Vargas Llosa between Civilization and Barbarism*, Rowman & Littlefield Publishers, 2000, pp. 2, 4, 44–45.

Ocasio, Rafael, *Literature of Latin America*, Greenwood Press, 2004, p. 114.

Review of *The Language of Passion: Selected Commentary*, in *Kirkus Reviews*, Vol. 71, No. 5, March 1, 2003, p. 371.

Rushdie, Salman, "Peruvian Master," in *New Republic*, Vol. 191, No. 15, October 8, 1984, pp. 25–27.

Standish, Peter, "Vargas Llosa's Parrot," in *Hispanic Review*, Vol. 59, No. 2, Spring 1991, pp. 143–51.

Vargas Llosa, Mario, *Letters to a Young Novelist*, translated by Natasha Wimmer, Farrar, Straus and Giroux, 2002, p. 124.

———, *The Storyteller*, translated by Helen Lane, Farrar, Straus and Giroux, 1989, pp. 21, 26, 100, 135, 164.

———, *A Writer's Reality*, edited by Myron I. Lichtblau, Syracuse University Press, 1991, p. 25.

FURTHER READING

Camus, Albert, *The Plague*, translated by Stuart Gilbert, Vintage, 1991.

> Camus was one of the important influences shaping Vargas Llosa's theme of turning away from extremist and doctrinaire values (as he found in religion or in communism) for humane, tolerant, and engaged relationships with others. *The Plague* demonstrates human solidarity during a time of crisis.

Davis, Patricia M., *Reading Is for Knowing: Literacy Acquisition, Retention, and Usage Among the Machiguenga*, Publications in Language Use and Education, Vol. 1, SIL Publication, 2004.

> One of the studies published by the Summer Institute of Linguistics, this volume builds on research originally done by Wayne and Betty Snell (the Schneils in the novel). The Summer Institute of Linguistics, though controversial, has been responsible for much of the knowledge and preservation of Machiguenga language and culture.

Rossman, Charles and Allen Warren Friedman, eds., *Mario Vargas Llosa: A Collection of Critical Essays*, University of Texas Press, 2011.

> This is an important collection of essays on the author in English (most published criticism on Vargas Llosa is in Spanish). Essays on individual novels as well as more general articles are included.

Stam, Orin, Ivan Degregori, and Robin Kirk, eds., *The Peru Reader: History, Culture, Politics*, The Latin American Readers, 2nd rev. ed., Duke University Press, 2005.

> Chapters are included on ancient civilizations, colonial rule, the republic, the Amazonian Indians, and the rubber and lumber booms, as well as contemporary politics.

Vargas Llosa, *A Fish in the Water: A Memoir*, translated by Helen Lane, Farrar, Straus & Giroux, 1994.

> The memoir is organized like many of his novels, with alternating chapters where Vargas Llosa tells about his early days as an author of the Boom, juxtaposed against his political career running for president.

SUGGESTED SEARCH TERMS

Mario Vargas Llosa

El hablador

The Storyteller AND Mario Vargas Llosa

Latin American AND literature

Latin American AND novel

Peruvian literature

Summer Institute of Linguistics

Manu National Park

Amazon rain forest tribes

history AND Peru

Tobacco Road

ERSKINE CALDWELL
1932

Erskine Caldwell's 1932 novel *Tobacco Road* is a familiar foundation of popular American culture, though few people have heard of it directly. Particularly through its popularization in debased versions in theater and film, it helped to establish the stereotype of the southern "redneck" or "poor white trash." Popular culture phenomena like the television series and film *The Beverly Hillbillies* or the character Cletus the Slack-Jawed Yokel on *The Simpsons* are deeply indebted to *Tobacco Road*. The true nature of *Tobacco Road* is quite different, however. Written at the height of the Great Depression, it is a careful laying out of the evidence in favor of socialist economic reforms even more extensive than those carried out through the New Deal in order to relieve the desperate conditions of all poor Americans, exemplified by the poor southern white farmers whom Caldwell's father had ministered to as a clergyman and whose aid Caldwell made his life's work. *Tobacco Road* is at the same time an intensely traditional work, glorifying the dignity of working on the land.

AUTHOR BIOGRAPHY

Erskine Preston Caldwell was born on December 17, 1903, in Morleand, Georgia. Caldwell's father, Ira, was a Presbyterian minister whose work caused the family to move from one small

Erskine Caldwell (© *Ulf Andersen / Getty Images*)

town to the next throughout the South during Caldwell's youth, allowing him to witness the desperation of the poorest levels of society firsthand. The elder Caldwell worked as a social reformer, trying to better the lives of his parishioners by working for social and economic reform, including involvement in the pseudoscience of eugenics. From an early age Caldwell was determined to be a writer. He attended Erskine College but did not finish his degree, concluding that life experience was more important. He initially worked as a milkman in order to more closely observe the lives of the poor. F. Scott Fitzgerald noticed Caldwell's short stories and essays published in small regional journals and aided the publication of his first collection of short stories, *American Earth*, in 1930. Caldwell soon began work on novels, publishing *Tobacco Road* in 1932 and *God's Little Acre* in 1933. His novels exclusively deal with the criticism of the institutional poverty and racism endemic in the South. Collectively, Caldwell's novels are sometimes called the "Cyclorama of the South." Caldwell gained national fame and a huge reading audience after the adaptation of

Tobacco Road for the stage in 1933. Caldwell also wrote essays and gave public lectures calling for social and economic reform to help the poor. Caldwell was denounced by the southern establishment as a critic of southern culture, particularly on racial issues. He was also prosecuted for obscenity due to the sexual themes in his writing, though he was exonerated at trial. With his second wife, photographer Margaret Bourke-White, Caldwell published in 1937 *You Have Seen Their Faces*, a photo-documentary of poor southern white life. Caldwell's political views were socialist, but he did not embrace any socialist or communist party, since he believed the influence of the Soviet Union was corrupting American socialism. Nevertheless, during World War II he worked as a photo journalist in the Soviet Union, conveying the war in Russia to an American audience. He also began editing in 1941 the American Folkways series, which documented different American rural cultures.

After the war, Caldwell's work found an even wider reading public when his books were published as cheap paperbacks with exploitative cover art, falsely suggesting they were pornographic and hiding their real social significance. This factor, as well perhaps as the general backlash against socialism in the 1950s, caused his literary reputation to decline. For the next twenty years he settled into a regular pattern, traveling the world for half of the year and writing for the other half. Besides writing a total of twenty-five novels, he produced several works of autobiography, including *Call It Experience* (1951), and travel writing, including *Deep South* (1968). After the early 1970s, Caldwell was effectively in retirement. A lifelong smoker, he suffered from emphysema and died of lung cancer on April 11, 1983, in Paradise Valley, Arizona.

PLOT SUMMARY

Chapter I

On a country road outside Augusta Georgia, Lov Bensey is walking back to his house from town, where he has bought a sack of turnips. Ordinarily, he is careful on such occasions to avoid the nearby Lester farm because he is fearful that the poverty of the Lesters, who are on the verge of starvation, might drive them to steal his turnips. But he takes the risk because he has an urgent request for Jeeter, the patriarch of the Lester family. Lov is married to Pearl, the twelve-year-old daughter of Jeeter. But Pearl has not slept with her husband, and indeed refuses to talk to him and spends most of her time avoiding him, and Lov wants her father to persuade her to do what he considers her wifely duty. Jeeter says he will, in exchange for the turnips, complaining that his own crop of turnips was destroyed by worms. Lov considers what he is asking is Jeeter's duty, and so refuses to pay him. Jeeter's mother's hunger reaches a fever pitch from seeing the turnips, so she goes into the kitchen and lights a fire in the wood stove, hoping that if she takes this step in faith, God will somehow provide lunch for her and the family.

Chapter II

Lov infuriates the Lesters by eating turnips in front of them. They have been living on a thin stew made by boiling bacon, but even that has given out, and it is unclear what they will eat in the immediate future. Jeeter and Lov discuss their poverty in religious, apocalyptic, terms, suggesting that it is God's judgment. Jeeter had

MEDIA ADAPTATIONS

- *Tobacco Road* was adapted as a stage play with major plot changes in 1933 by Jack Kirkland. Playing both on Broadway and in touring companies, the play was phenomenally successful and laid the foundation for the popularity of Caldwell's novelistic career.

- *Tobacco Road* was filmed in 1941 by John Ford. The screenplay was based on the novel rather than the play but again had major plot changes.

- Coincident with the release of the film, *Tobacco Road* was satirized by Jack Benny on the March 23, 1941, episode of his radio show.

- *Tobacco Road* was also satirized (as *Nicotine Alley*) by Fred Allen on the March 19, 1941, episode of *Texaco Star Theater*.

- Thanks largely to the popularity of the play, the stereotypes of *Tobacco Road* have entered popular culture and form the foundation of many television shows and films, such as *The Beverly Hillbillies*.

- *Tobacco Road* has been adapted by Recorded Books as an audiobook read by Mark Hammer (2011). The running time is six hours 34 minutes.

worked as a sharecropper, but his patron had retired and left the county and now he cannot hope to get the credit he needs to buy cotton seed and fertilizer. The only source of income he has left is selling as fuel the brushwood that grows on his land, and he is busy trying to repair the tire of his car so he can take a load of brushwood into Augusta.

Chapter III

Jeeter's daughter Ellie May (whose face is deformed by a cleft upper lip) now begins to flirt with Lov. She succeeds in getting a turnip for herself, but more importantly, enticing him away from the sack. Jeeter's son Dude watches them intently since he believes they are actually going to have sex, there in the open, in front of the whole family. Dude is not able to understand the real reason behind her seduction however, but the point is explored to show that poverty has reduced the Lesters to the level of animals. A group of young black men, who happen to be walking along the road, also stop to watch.

Chapter IV

At the crucial moment, the Lesters go into action to steal Lov's turnips. Jeeter dashes to grab the sack and carry it off into the woods. At the same time Ellie May gets Lov in a wrestling hold while Ada (Jeeter's wife) and the grandmother come and poke and hit him with sticks, stunning him with a blow to the head. Unable to fully realize what is happening, Dude goes on talking to Lov in a normal manner. He describes how black railroad employees throw coal from freight cars into black villages they pass since the fuel is too expensive for the people to buy. He suggests that since Lov works loading coal onto trains he could similarly steal all the coal he needs. When Lov finally recovers, he leaves in disgust.

Chapter V

Dude finds Jeeter hiding in the woods, where he has eaten most of the turnips. He does not offer any to his son, but Dude simply takes them from Jeeter's pockets by virtue of the fact that he is larger and stronger than his father. They go back to the house, where Jeeter intends to give the few remaining turnips to Ada and Ellie May, and perhaps one even to his mother. But they find that Bessie Rice is there. She is a preacher who makes rounds ministering to the local poor and is well known to the Lesters. Like Ellie May, she has a facial deformity: there is no cartilage in her nose, leaving it a formless lump. She says that Jesus came to her in her kitchen and told her to come and pray for Jeeter. They all agree that this is no coincidence, since she has arrived just after Jeeter committed the deadly sin of stealing food to feed his starving family. She nevertheless accepts and eats the remaining turnips that Jeeter gives her. After she prays for God to forgive Jeeter, she mentions that she is looking for a husband. (Her first husband, from whom she inherited her position as a preacher, had died the previous year.) Jeeter suggests that under different circumstances he might be interested (and she admits she would favor Jeeter too, except for his poverty) but he does not press

the point, since, as he says, Ada (who is standing right next to them) does not like to hear him talk about his marrying other women.

Chapter VI

Jeeter asks Bessie to say a special prayer for Dude. Dude is reluctant, since he does not like to kneel, but he is all for it when he finds it will involve her laying hands on him and allowing him to embrace her. He has no interest in the prayer, but rather in the erotic contact. Jeeter then complains to Bessie of God's injustice in cursing Ellie May with her cleft lip. Bessie responds that God does nothing unjustly, and says the good in Ellie's May's lip is perfectly obvious. Jeeter then demands to know what that good could be, and Bessie tells him that his daughter having what he considers a repulsive deformity prevented him raping her. Jeeter does not deny that he would ever have done such a thing, but mentions innumerable acts of adultery he committed when he was a sinner; he suggests that many of the children in local families are his rather than their putative fathers.

Long after her prayer has ended, Dude and Bessie's mutual caressing does not end, exciting comment form the Lesters. Bessie offers in excuse that she is thinking of marrying Dude but will have to pray about it before making a decision. She thinks too that he might become suitable to act as her partner in preaching.

Chapter VII

The narrator recounts the history of the Lester family. Jeeter's grandfather had owned a large plantation centered around the land where the Lesters still live as tenant farmers. Jeeter's father had inherited half of the plantation, but each year the tax bill was more than he could pay, and a parcel of land had to be auctioned off to meet the bill. Once the land was depleted for growing tobacco, the farming switched to cotton, for which the soil was unsuitable and which required increasing application of fertilizer (guano). When Jeeter's father died, the remaining land was auctioned off to pay taxes. Jeeter worked for many years as a sharecropping tenant for one of the new owners, until the owner finally abandoned the enterprise as unprofitable, leaving Jeeter as a squatter, unable to farm for lack of capital.

Chapter VIII

The narrator explores Ada's and Jeeter's obsession with death. Both share the greatest anxiety that they be buried in formal clothing that they are too poor to buy. Ada in particular misses seeing their twelve surviving children, who, once they left to find jobs in cotton mills or other economic opportunities, have had no contact with the family. For all the Lesters know, there are letters from their children waiting for them in the local post office, but Jeeter, who rarely accomplishes anything he plans to do except for farming, has not actually bothered to check for many years.

Chapter IX

On what is only the second day of the narrative, Bessie returns to the Lester farm early in the morning and announces that God has authorized her to marry Dude. Dude is persuaded by the prospect of being able to drive the car that Bessie also announces she intends to buy that day. They walk several miles into the town of Fuller, Dude running ahead in anxious anticipation of being able to honk a car horn as much as he wants.

Chapter X

Once in Fuller, Dude and Bessie go first to a Ford dealership to buy a new car. The dealer takes full advantage of her gullibility, charging her twice what she need have paid, as well as defrauding her over the licensing fee. Their next stop is the city hall to get a marriage license. The clerk is reluctant to give it to them since Dude is underage, but Bessie threatens to stand in the office and pray for him until he capitulates. Once he learns that Dude is Jeeter's son he concedes that Jeeter would not object to the marriage, recalling the case of Pearl, who was exceptionally young to marry, even in that time and culture.

Chapter XI

Dude drives Bessie back to the Lester farm, incessantly honking the horn and driving so recklessly that he damages some of the springs in the car. Dude and Bessie go into the house, where Bessie, as a preacher, performs their religious marriage ceremony herself. This consists of praying while the two of them hold onto the marriage certificate, as though it were a talisman charged with sympathetic magic. They then retire to Dude's bed to consummate the marriage.

Chapter XII

The Lesters peer in through the windows to watch Dude and Bessie have sex; Jeeter even props a ladder against the window to get a better view. Afterwards, Jeeter confesses to Bessie that he became excited watching them, and that really he ought, on the Biblical principle of plucking out the offending eye, to castrate himself. Bessie agrees. However, Jeeter realizes that this is one of the many things he plans but will put off indefinitely. Later, Jeeter advises Ellie May that she ought to hang around the local saw mill and try to seduce one of the workers there into marrying her. This causes her to run off in tears, but Jeeter cannot imagine why.

Chapter XIII

Desperately planning to plant a crop this season, Jeeter recalls the last crop he was able to plant. Planting a crop would cost Jeeter about two hundred dollars to buy seed and fertilizer. No merchant in Fuller would give him the goods on credit, and the bankers in Augusta would not loan him the money without collateral. About seven years earlier, one of the bankers had suggested he try a loan company (similar to the payday loan companies that still operate today). They had given him the money, but, though it was apparent he would not have any money to make payments until the cotton was harvested, they demanded monthly interest payments. When Jeeter failed to pay the interest, it was simply added to the principle, increasing each monthly interest charge in turn. When he finally sold his crop for three hundred dollars, they explained to Jeeter that he also owed large fees of at least fifty dollars, or 25 percent of the original loan. He made seven dollars for a year's labor. However, he had borrowed a mule for plowing from a neighbor and had been given credit on the ten-dollar fee, so he actually lost three dollars, for which his neighbor was still dunning him.

Chapter XIV

Bessie and Dude go for a celebratory drive around the county. When they return, the left headlight and fender of the car have been destroyed. But, since this does not interfere with the operation of the car, no one minds it. They explain that during the one brief interval when Dude had stopped honking the horn to stare at a turpentine still on the roadside, he had hit a wagon. In fact, the accident had overturned the wagon, crushing the driver underneath, probably killing him. They did not stop to find out, since the driver was black and what happened to him hardly mattered, in their view. During the ride, they had paid calls on many of the families that counted Bessie as their preacher. Most of them disapproved of the marriage owing to Dude's age, but they objected more to the extravagance of buying a new car. Since her house is even more dilapidated than Jeeter's, Bessie and Dude will live in the Lester household. As they go to bed Jeeter and Bessie flirt.

Chapter XV

In the morning Ada denounces Bessie, preacher or not, as a hussy. Dude and Jeeter load Bessie's car with scrub oak and the three of them drive toward Augusta in the hope of selling it for firewood. Dude's reckless driving does more damage to the car, and it eventually stops, fortunately next to a gas station. The mechanic advises them that they were driving with too little oil (another cheat on the part of the Ford dealer) and the engine has suffered irreparable damage. Nevertheless, Bessie uses her last two dollars to buy more oil and they press on, Dude incessantly honking. They seem unable to appreciate how soon it will be until the car stops running altogether.

Chapter XVI

Jeeter is unable to sell the green scrub oak on the streets of Augusta. Eventually they sell the car's spare tire in order to buy food and also pay for a hotel. They are excited because none of them has ever stayed in a hotel before. The clerk puts them in a single room with only one bed, but he shortly returns and takes Bessie off to another room he claims has opened up. Jeeter thinks it strange he is not the one moved, since Dude and Bessie are a married couple, but he attributes it to the strange ways of city folks. Unknowingly, they have checked into a hotel that caters to prostitutes, and the clerk, thinking Bessie must be a prostitute, takes her on rounds from room to room, selling her to the male guests. When they are reunited in the morning, Bessie comments how much she enjoyed herself and wants to go back to that hotel soon. The clerk seems to have kept any fees that were collected.

They are still unable to sell their wood, and Jeeter eventually abandons it and burns it to prevent anyone taking it for free, and they return to the farm.

Chapter XVII

The next morning Jeeter determines that he wants to go and see his son Tom. He has heard that Tom has a well-paying job in the next county as the supervisor of a facility manufacturing railroad ties. Jeeter wants to ask him for money. Bessie and Dude drive off without him, however. When they return in the evening, they reveal that they in fact went to see Tom. They report that he has no intention of visiting the farm or giving Jeeter money, and that he in fact cursed his father. Jeeter is at a loss to understand this since Tom was the only one of his children who did not hit him or throw rocks at him.

Bessie runs a regular church service at an old school house every Sunday. The coming Sunday Dude is going to start preaching, denouncing men wearing black shirts. Even Jeeter doesn't see much potential in the subject. Bessie says that to her way of thinking, preaching must always be against something; in other words, her religion is always prescriptive, limiting, and controlling.

Bessie blames Jeeter for the damage to her car incurred on the trip to Augusta and tells him he can no longer ride in it. He responds by telling her to get off his land. When she points out that Jeeter owns no land, he and Ada begin attacking her with their fists and sticks. She and Dude scramble into the car and drive off, running down Mother Lester in the process.

Chapter XVIII

Lov comes running up to the Lester farm. He reports that Pearl has run away to Augusta. He cannot imagine that she could have been provoked by what he had done that morning when he attempted to tie her down to his bed and rape her, before she was finally able to squirm out of his grasp. At first Lov thought she must just have hidden in the forest as she regularly did, but the truck driver who delivers the coal to Lov's work station mentioned he saw her walking on the road near Augusta. Jeeter advises Lov that Pearl is no more likely to come back to him than any of his other daughters who ran off to work in the cotton mills. He suggests Lov take Ellie May as a replacement for Pearl. He provisionally accepts but has to get back to work. Before he leaves, they notice that Mother Lester has finally died after crawling a few feet toward the house from the spot where she had been run down. Jeeter proceeds to bury her. Ellie May is anxious to go and live with Lov; probably because it will mean she will eat regularly. Jeeter expects that she will now steal food from Lov and bring it back to him and Ada.

Chapter XIX

A few days later, Jeeter burns off the brush from his fields. He hopes that after taking this first step in planting a crop, God will somehow provide him with the seed and fertilizer he needs to complete the work. He is using the same type of thinking that Mother Lester did when she lit a fire at lunchtime every day, hoping that if she did that, God would somehow procure lunch for the family. During the night, a wind storm whips up the fire and spreads it to the Lester house. It quickly burns down, killing Ada and Jeeter before they knew what was happening. At dawn, other local farmers see the fire and come to try to help, but they are too late. Bessie too is there and says that the Lesters were killed by God according to the curse she placed upon them, but no one pays any attention to her. Lov and the other farmers bury the remains. They agree that since Jeeter's way of life as a farmer was no longer possible, he is better off dead. The closest thing to a funeral service comes when Dude and Bessie drive Ellie May and Lov back to his house for breakfast. Dude honks all the way, stopping only to say that he has been seized by a powerful desire to plant a cotton crop.

CHARACTERS

Lov Bensey

Lov works shoveling coal onto locomotives at a railroad siding. He makes only one dollar a day but is the only character in the book to be employed at all. The ironically named Lov is a study of human depravity. Within the first pages of *Tobacco Road*, the reader learns that a few months ago, during the previous summer, he had married Pearl Lester, who was twelve years old at the time. While marriage at such a young age was not uncommon in the rural South of that era, Lov is a true pedophile. Pearl is still prepubescent and it is precisely her childish features that attract him to her, as he admits, to an extraordinary degree. He says, "She's such a pretty little girl—all them long yellow curls hanging down her back sort of gets me all crazy sometimes." Wearing long hair not put up was a mark

of childhood (even Ada is careful to put up her hair every morning). Pearl's father Jeeter, says of her: "Pearl ain't nothing but a little gal yet. She don't even look like a woman so far." When Pearl refuses to cohabit with her husband or even to speak to him—indeed Pearl spends most of her time hiding from him—Lov tries to subjugate her with violence:

> He kicked her, he poured water over her, he threw rocks and sticks at her, and he did everything else he could think of that he thought might make her talk to him. She cried a lot, especially when she was seriously hurt, but Lov did not consider that as conversation.

Lov is incapable of blaming his own cruelty for his wife's silence: "Sometimes I think it's just the old devil in her," he says. "To my way of thinking, she ain't got a scratch of religion in her. She's going to hell-fire when she dies, sure as day comes." Lov blames his victim and imagines a vast cosmic apparatus that will help him torment her for all of eternity. Yet in his community Lov is counted as a virtuous man. Caldwell's method is simply to narrate circumstances without comment and let readers draw their own conclusions. Caldwell believes that Lov has sunk to this inhuman condition because of the oppression of poverty, and by showing its utter depths he hopes to inspire the reader to work against it.

Pearl Bensey

Pearl is the youngest Lester child (however, Jeeter is not her father), and is married to Lov Bensey, the only man in the area with a steady job. The novel begins with Lov's complaints to Jeeter about her behavior. She has never slept with him, avoids him insofar as possible, and does not even speak to him. But Caldwell reveals this is part of a larger problem with her: "Pearl had never talked, for that matter. Not because she could not, but simply because she did not want to." The matter is not so simple, however. As always, Caldwell wants readers to draw their own conclusions. The Lester family is riddled with birth defects, and Pearl's lack of speech, shared with her mother, and no doubt inherited from her, is probably to be understood as a form of mental retardation brought about by inbreeding, another result of the poverty that oppresses the world of *Tobacco Road*.

Ada Lester

Ada is Jeeter's wife and the mother of the seventeen Lester children. Of these only Dude and

Ellie still live at home. Some, like Pearl, left to marry, and others escaped the poverty of the Lester household by working in the mills. Five had died in infancy. At the beginning of their marriage, Ada was standoffish to Jeeter, as Pearl is to Lov, but the crushing weight of their poverty eventually made her more compliant. She remains perhaps the most human of the Lesters. She is, for example, desperate to see her daughter Pearl, who had not visited her since her marriage to Lov, as well as her other children. She is conscious that she is slowly dying of pellagra, a dietary disease caused by a lack of niacin. Like all the Lesters, Ada is addicted to snuff, a form of tobacco. While tobacco use is considered relatively acceptable in society, especially in the 1930s, Ada's desire for snuff exceeds her hunger. She is conscious that it caused all of her teeth to fall out by her early twenties, but she is powerless to stop desiring it, preferring it to food.

Dude Lester

Dude is the last Lester boy still living at home at the time of *Tobacco Road*. He is sixteen years old at the time of the novel. He is insolent, disrespectful, and lazy. To the Lesters' way of thinking, "Dude did not have very much sense," probably meaning that he has a mild intellectual disability. Even as he is starving he dwells on the most childish subjects. When Lov has been knocked unconscious in his fight with the Lester women, Dude is unable to comprehend what is going on and tries to make small talk with him:

> Why don't the [railroad] firemen blow the whistle more than they do, Lov?...If I was a fireman, I'd pull the whistle cord near about all the time. They make a noise about as pretty as an automobile horn does.

Despite Dude's mental impairment, Bessie thinks that he has all the qualities necessary to become a successful preacher. He is a large and presumably handsome young man, and Bessie must consider these attributes more essential to preaching than theological learning or wisdom. His only interest in his marriage is the opportunity to drive Bessie's car and honk the horn.

Ellie May Lester

Ellie May is one of the Lester children and suffers from a birth defect:

> Ellie May's upper lip had an opening a quarter of an inch wide that divided one side of her mouth into unequal parts; the slit came to an abrupt end almost under her left nostril. The upper gum was

> low, and because her gums were always fiery red, the opening in her lip made her look as if her mouth were bleeding profusely.

Because of this deformity she has never had a prospect of marriage and lives with her parents, though she is essentially estranged from them, a spectator rather than a participant in their lives.

Jeeter Lester

Jeeter is the patriarch of the Lester family. The productivity of his farm has dwindled over the years, largely because it at best produced a bare living for his family, leaving no way to secure the capital necessary to replace livestock or buy seed. The decadent heir of a once prosperous landowning family, he and his family live in the direst poverty on the verge of starvation. He is, in his own estimation, an incorrigible sinner, particularly given to adultery, and even a threat to his own daughter. He is irresolute and lazy: "There were always well-developed plans in Jeeter's mind for the things he intended doing; but somehow he never got around to doing them." His one worthwhile passion is for the land, but economic circumstances prevent him from farming.

Old Mother Lester

Mother Lester is Jeeter's mother. While one might expect the elderly to be respected in a traditional culture, she is despised and spurned by her family because she had no economic value and, in their desperate straits, no other considerations can be taken into account. Her descendants hold her in such low regard that, "If she had gone to the thicket and had not returned, no one would have known for several days that she was dead." In fact, her own son Jeeter beats her for stealing food. Like Ada, she suffers from pellagra. Her dehumanization is marked by the fact that her name is never mentioned in the novel.

Bessie Rice

Bessie Rice is a preacher who visits the Lester family. In the South of the era of *Tobacco Road*, Christian denominations existed on a scale from High Church to Low Church, depending on matters such as church hierarchy, centralization of education for pastors, adherence to traditional rituals, and so forth. (High Church and Low Church were originally names for different strains of Anglicanism, but afterwards gained a wider usage.) Black denominations had a similar but parallel hierarchy. The scale from High Church to Low Church corresponded in some degree to economic status. Church members at any point on the scale might dismiss those higher on the scale as theologically unsound, and despise those beneath them as socially inferior. Bessie is not identified with any particular denomination but despises hard-shell or primitive Baptists, a decidedly Low Church denomination, as corrupt ritualists. She became a preacher when her husband, who was a preacher, died and she took on the family business, so to speak. She never attended a seminary and has no specialized training, such as in reading Hebrew or Greek or in systematic theology. Indeed, she seems to have scarcely any familiarity with the Bible at all; when she attempts to offer theological teaching, she generally gives truisms from poor southern culture that directly contradict Biblical teaching. In fact, she cannot read at all (nor can any character in the novel). Her husband also left her eight hundred dollars (about as much Lov would make in three years of labor, for comparison) from an insurance policy, but she is carefully hoarding this for some purpose she believes God will reveal to her. She is otherwise nearly as poor as the Lesters. Like Ellie May, she suffers from a congenital deformity, in her case the lack of cartilage in her nose. Despite her profession, she is markedly lascivious.

THEMES

Realism

Literary realism, as the name implies, is the desire to use the art of literature to convey a valid impression of real life, as if literature could become a type of sophisticated journalism. For Caldwell, realism meant a commitment to his social conscience. In his memoir about his education as a writer, *Call It Experience*, Caldwell says, "I wanted to write about the people I knew as they really lived, moved, and talked." Caldwell considered it more useful to his writing to drop out of school without a degree to work and live among ordinary people, that is, ordinary poor people. He intended to use realism as a way of showing his readers the plight of the poor, rubbing their faces in it, and in this way call for social reform. This is why *Tobacco Road* takes as its subject a family that is starving in the richest culture that has ever existed, because of

economic injustices that are quite beyond their understanding. He wants to show the reality of poverty in a way that cannot be denied and will lead to a call for action and reform. The drive for realism is also behind Caldwell's forthright depiction of sexuality, since it is one of the most important parts of human life, a concern that would often find his works derided as pornographic.

Surrealism

Surrealism was an artistic movement that flourished in Europe in the 1920s and 1930s, exemplified by the works of painter Salvador Dalí, photographer Man Ray (an American who lived and worked in France), filmmaker Luis Buñuel, and its ideologue, Andre Breton. The goal of surrealism was to explore the dreamlike world of the human unconscious as a source of artistic inspiration. Surrealism borrowed much of its formal content from Freudian psychoanalysis and aligned itself politically with communism, in recognition of the pervasive power of greed and the will to dominate others in human society. Caldwell had no formal contact with surrealism and probably would have reacted unfavorably to an association of his work with it, but *Tobacco Road* contains many elements that are hard to characterize as other than surrealist. His characters uniformly engage in long, brooding silences that are either left mysterious or serve as the occasion for the exploration of a chain of unconscious thoughts and memories that are constantly roiling below the surface and which drive outward action in a wholly irrational way. The extreme poverty of the Lesters forces them to act on the most primitive drives of hunger and desire, stripping away the veneer of civilization that separates humans from animals. Their private feelings are free to erupt in violence and perversion. In effect, their poverty forces the Lesters to live in complete isolation from the standards of bourgeois society.

If this was not precisely the ideal of the surrealist movement, it was the state which they wanted to explore, since they rejected bourgeois culture as hypocritical and stifling of human freedom. For the surrealists, the Lesters might have become something like noble savages, liberated from social convention, but for Caldwell their poverty is oppressive precisely because it isolates them from the niceties of bourgeois culture. Luis Buñuel explored similar themes in his film *Land Without Bread*

TOPICS FOR FURTHER STUDY

- *Far and Beyon'* (2002) is a young-adult novel about a poor farming family in Botswana. The family must not only overcome poverty but also struggle against HIV. They are too poor to obtain any modern medical treatment but must rely on traditional healing and magic. Write a blog post comparing *Far and Beyon'* and *Tobacco Road*. Points of interest might include the role of religion and ritual in the novels and the economic situation of the two families. Invite your classmates to comment on your blog

- The collective farming practices that Caldwell advocates in *Tobacco Road* are an example of anarcho-syndicalism (a political theory that was partially put into practice in Spain during the Republican era in the 1930s). Research anarcho-syndicalism and write a paper demonstrating how it would have benefited the Lesters and their neighbors. Some places to start your research are Rudolf Rocker's *Anarcho-Syndicalism: Theory and Practice* (1938) and Noam Chomsky, *On Anarchism* (2005).

- The first refutation of the pseudoscience of eugenics was made in a series of essays by Thomas Huxley in the 1890s (collected in *Evolution and Ethics*). Although eugenics has been discredited in the mainstream, it thrives on fringe websites on the Internet, where it is often called by the euphemism *race realism*. Research the major ideas of the contemporary eugenics movement and criticize them in a class presentation using Huxley's arguments.

- Using the Internet, research the New Deal antipoverty programs that were implemented during the Roosevelt administration, a few years after the time of *Tobacco Road*. Write a paper demonstrating how they could have helped the Lesters.

- Caldwell's attention to vivid detail and surrealist style in *Tobacco Road* call out for treatments of its subject matter in other forms; it is no mistake that the story rose to prominence first as a drama and has also been used for film adaptation and satire. Use a passage from the novel as inspiration either for a poem, drawing, or painting.

(1933), a documentary in which he uses hyperrealism to show the effects of the most extreme poverty on the mountain villagers of the Las Hurdes region of Spain. Just as *Tobacco Road* is a call for social justice, *Land without Bread* was a propaganda film meant to elicit support for the Republican side in the Spanish Civil War. Both Caldwell and Buñuel were also fascinated by the role of poverty and malnutrition in causing intellectual disability. Caldwell also arranges in *Tobacco Road* scenes that are only comparable to a surrealist tableau, for example, in Dude's minute observation of the ants crawling over the naked, unconscious body of his sister Ellie May. One of the most widely known surrealist images is a body swarming with ants, found in many of Dalí's paintings as well as in Bunuel's *Un Chou Andalou* (1929), whose script was cowritten with Dalí. Other scenes in the novel seem typically surreal in their undermining of bourgeois propriety, such as the uncontrollable laughter among the mourners at Jeeter's father's funeral when they see that his face has been eaten away by rats in his coffin, or the Lesters crowding in to see the consummation of Dude and Bessie's marriage. Bessie's enjoyment of her night of prostitution also shows the release of animal passions from bourgeois restraint. The blitheness with which Jeeter discusses castrating himself is surely informed by the popularity of Freud among American intellectuals during the 1920s and 1930s, rather than Caldwell's observation of rural life.

The novel portrays the difficult situation of Southern tenant farmers. *(© Ehrman Photographic / Shutterstock.com)*

STYLE

Satire

There is a fine line between tragedy and comedy. Satire straddles this line, dealing with themes that might seem grave and serious, but in an exaggerated and distorted way so that they become comic. It is indeed possible to miss the most subtle satire, since it depends on imitating the serious. Caldwell's subject matter in *Tobacco Road* is certainly serious, even tragic, but is often presented in a way that is so extreme that it is difficult to believe that he is not aiming for a satirical effect. The main theme of the novel is the poverty of its characters, and the masses of real people they represent, and the iniquitous social system that keeps them in poverty. Caldwell explores this theme at the very beginning of the novel in the matter of some turnips, and he treats it satirically. The main character Lov wants to discuss something quite different with his father-in-law Jeeter, but considers it unfortunate that he must stop by Jeeter's house while he is on the way home from the store, carrying a sack of turnips. The point of the scene is to show

that Jeeter's family is so poor that they are on the verge of starvation and hunger so powerfully for the turnips that they are prepared to steal them. The narrator explains:

> Usually when [Lov] came by the Lester place with turnips . . . he left the road half a mile from the house and made a wide circle through the fields, returning to the road a safe distance beyond.

Jeeter and his children incessantly question Lov about the bag he is carrying. Once he admits it contains turnips, the narrator reports of Jeeter:

> It did not occur to him that Lov had bought them with money; Jeeter had long before come to the conclusion that the only possible way a quantity of good could be obtained was by theft.

And, indeed, he had often raided his neighbor's turnip fields, but lately even these had given out.

Although it is tragic that people are driven to contemplate theft because of hunger, the characters' drooling over the prospect of eating raw turnips (which most people in the United States, even in the 1930s, would hardly have considered food) and their willingness to commit theft, assault, and possibly murder to do so, is ridiculous. The scene is tipped over to the side of comedy when the reader considers the role of the turnip in literature. The turnip was an important symbol in ancient Roman literature and Roman ideology. Roman aristocrats at the end of the republic and the beginning of the empire lived in a world of unprecedented wealth as well as unprecedented political and social corruption. They wanted to believe that they could aspire to better things and told stories about the ancient virtues of their ancestors as a model for their hopes. Romans at the founding of the city were reported as being so poor that they had to live on a diet of turnips. But this became a source of virtue: A man who was satisfied with turnips could not be tempted, for example to betray his country, with gold (Plutarch, *Life of Cato the Elder*, 2.2). The virtuous poverty of the first Romans made everyone equal: even the first king, Romulus, lived on turnips, and continued to do so in heaven, since he wanted nothing grander. But even Romans could see how ridiculous this trope is and singled it out for their own satire (Seneca, *Apocolocyntosis* 9.5; Martial, *Epigrams* 13.16). Caldwell inverts tradition, always a sign of satire. For him, poverty does not lead to good old-fashioned virtue (a trope in stories about Abraham Lincoln the rail splitter, as well as Romulus) but rather to vice, because in the real world poverty leads to degradation.

The matter of the turnips is representative of a great many conceits in the novel, where matters of the utmost seriousness to the characters cannot help but appear ridiculous to the reader. Caldwell keeps an unresolved tension between the pathetic and the ridiculous, but adaptations, including the John Ford film version, often treat the story as straight comedy.

Dialect

Part of Caldwell's realist technique in *Tobacco Road* is the use of the English dialect of rural northern Georgia in the speech of his characters, in distinction to his own narrative voice, which speaks in standard English. This can be seen, for example, in Jeeter's initial greeting to Lov: "Ain't no sense standing out there. Come in and rest yourself." A greeting is very apt to demonstrate the character of the novel's language, since greetings tend to be highly formulaic. In this case, the attempt to mirror heard speech begins with simple conversational elements that are not truly dialectical, for example, the omission of *there* from the beginning of the statement. This word is often omitted without loss of comprehension by the hearer and is said to be understood. A more truly dialectical element is the use of *ain't* rather than the more standard *is not*. Students are often told that *ain't* is incorrect, or even that it is not a word, but it is a local variation or dialectical word. It is part of a coherent pattern of speech that does not rise to the level of another language but is nevertheless particular to a social and geographically connected group of speakers, whose natural speech is different from the formal usage sanctioned by education and government. There is no objective basis for saying that either the dialect or the standard is correct. Another dialectical element is the use of *rest* as a reflexive verb rather than an intransitive. Jeeter invites Lov not to rest, but to rest himself.

The dialect of the rural South is descended from the regional dialect of the English West Country, whereas standard British English is based on the dialect of Oxfordshire. Standard American English is strongly marked by Standard British English but is more generally a negotiation between various regional American dialects. The dialectical words and structures that Caldwell uses are actually quite mild compared to what he must have heard while living in the rural South. His purpose is to suggest the dialect, without fully reporting it in a manner that in some instance might lead to incomprehension by standard speakers. The dialect of Caldwell's characters also includes racial slurs that were used completely unselfconsciously in the 1930s (although Caldwell clearly disapproved of them and uses more neutral phrases in his narration) as well as terms like *harelip* that have since been deemed politically incorrect.

HISTORICAL CONTEXT

Tobacco Road

The term *tobacco road* is used by historians and within the tobacco industry to refer to the area stretching from Virginia through North Carolina and into Georgia, where tobacco has traditionally been cultivated. For Caldwell, the phrase described the dirt road that runs by the Lester farm, which was originally formed by the transport of barrels of tobacco. Caldwell uses it as a symbol of economic failure since

COMPARE & CONTRAST

- **1930s:** The United States is in the throes of the Great Depression, a severe economic downturn partly caused by rampant speculation on Wall Street in the preceding decades.

  Today: The United States is still recovering from the Great Recession of 2008–2009, which was the most severe economic crisis since the Great Depression. Recovery has been slow and uneven, but unemployment is falling and more jobs are being created. In the second quarter of 2014, for example, the Gross Domestic Product grew by 4.0 percent, after contracting in the first quarter. In June and July 2014, private employers added a total of almost five hundred thousand jobs.

- **1930s:** There is little consciousness of the dangers of tobacco addiction.

  Today: The dangers to health of tobacco are widely known, and the government takes at least some steps, in the form of taxes and propaganda, to discourage its use.

- **1930s:** Millions of people have been thrown out of work by the Depression, and the government has little means of helping the indigent, although programs like food distribution begin later in the 1930s. The only help the Lesters have available is to move to the poor farm, a county-run establishment for the worst off.

  Today: The government has many programs, such as welfare, food stamps, and Medicare, that would be available to help people in the Lesters' position.

tobacco, and the cotton that replaced it after the Civil War, depleted the soil and created an economic prosperity that was doomed to failure. Poor farmers, however, are remarkably resistant to change, and their culture made it difficult for them to help themselves by using modern agricultural practices that might have produced a better result.

Eugenics

Eugenics is a pseudoscience that called for the improvement of humanity through selective breeding. It was extraordinarily popular among intellectuals in the nineteenth and early twentieth century, though it was completely discredited during the Holocaust carried out by Nazi Germany before and during World War II. Based on a false understanding of evolution, eugenics held that the human race was declining because "inferior" people were producing more children than "superior" people. Aside from the immorality in determining the inferior and the superior, the premise is false, because selective breeding, when it is applied to domestic plants and animals, produces organisms that are fitted only to an artificial environment and less able to compete against wild varieties; for example, garden varieties of flowers have to be protected from competition with weeds, which would soon overwhelm any garden without the intervention of the gardener. Selective breeding produces organisms that are less fit, not more fit as eugenics argued.

Caldwell's father, Ira, was a proponent of eugenics. He carried out his own eugenic studies and tried to intervene in the lives of the poor families he served as a clergyman. When he discovered that people would not willingly marry a spouse picked for them by a third person, he supported forced sterilization of the "inferior" (which was legally sanctioned in thirty American states at the time). An unexamined axiom of eugenics was that it was always the poor who were deemed degenerate as opposed to the rich, as though genetic fitness corresponded to economic prosperity. In this way, eugenics was closely aligned with racism. Caldwell's characters in *Tobacco Road* are based on the subjects of his father's studies, particularly in the case of Ellie

The opening scene of the novel, in which the entire Lester family tries to steal a bag of turnips, is a prime example of Caldwell's strange mixture of sad desperation and black humor. (© duckeesue | Shutterstock.com)

May's cleft lip (which can be an inherited condition, but which can also arise from environmental factors during gestation) and Bessie's Rice's nose (the cause of which, genetic or otherwise, could not have been determined in the 1930s). Caldwell shared his father's belief that the rural poor were genetically deteriorating, but thought that the condition should be remedied by general improvement of their circumstances. He was, however, willing to countenance forced sterilization, the option generally supported by government officials and community leaders of the era, if other improvements could not be achieved.

In *Tobacco Road*, Caldwell, does not make an explicit call for some kind of eugenic intervention, but presents his idea through the evidence he shows in the expectation that readers will draw the same conclusion as he does. If Caldwell thought the situation of the poor could be improved so that they could adopt bourgeois social conventions, their problem would be solved. Besides the physical deformities, Dude's intellectual impairment is probably meant to be understood as being due to genetic factors. Clearly Caldwell believed the culprit was inbreeding. The well-developed themes of adultery and incest in the novel lead to the conclusion that the poverty of his characters is responsible for their genetic decline. Those already genetically inferior are not, as they ought to be, excluded from marriage and breeding by the norms of bourgeois society, while their disregard of marriage will lead to many half-siblings marrying without knowing their relationship. His argument, however, apart from the general unsoundness of eugenics, collapses under the weight of its unexamined assumptions, for example that adultery is linked to class, or the idea of determining genetic causation of a given condition, which was impossible in the 1930s.

CRITICAL OVERVIEW

Caldwell's work went largely unnoticed until the success of the 1933 dramatization of *Tobacco Road*. Critics quickly elevated him to the status of a great American novelist, the peer of Faulkner or Hemingway. His reputation declined after the 1930s, however, because he allowed his novels (which had excellent sales) to be marketed to a lowest-common-dominator audience, sold on the strength of their sexual content, with lascivious cover illustrations, in drugstore checkout lines. Because of this, Caldwell became an object of public ridicule in the 1950s.

With the distance of time, Caldwell's work has again become the focus of critical attention, and he is increasingly being restored to his position as one of the prominent American novelists of the twentieth century. His extensive papers, still largely unpublished, are housed at Dartmouth College and at the Caldwell Museum in his birthplace, Moreland, Georgia. The renaissance of Caldwell studies began in the 1990s with two biographies: *Erskine Caldwell: The Journey from Tobacco Road* (1995), by Dan B. Miller, and Wayne's Maxon's *The People's Writer: Erskine Caldwell and the South* (1995). An obvious topic regarding Caldwell for postmodern criticism is eugenics. Karen A. Keely, among others, in "Poverty, Sterilization, and Eugenics in Erskine Caldwell's *Tobacco Road*," notes that as much as Caldwell is drawn to help the rural poor, he is more viscerally repulsed by them, in line with the class divisions in southern culture, and wants to control, and if necessary, eradicate them. She finds *Tobacco Road* "a deeply cynical novel that condemns America's economic *modus operandi* for the living conditions of the poor but also condemns those poor as being permanently beyond help." Also, in the seminal *Reading Erskine Caldwell* collection, Natalie Wilson focuses on Caldwell's portrayal of the body in *Tobacco Road*:

> In particular, the novel focuses on the differing body as an economic burden. Whether this "difference" is linked to poverty, disease, or physical deformity, the text repeatedly suggests the physical cost of living in the Depression-era South.

She finds, however, in distinction to those who focus on eugenics in *Tobacco Road*, that the fault lies not in the bodies of the Lesters but in their society: "Caldwell points an accusing finger not at the Lesters themselves, but at a blood

> IN *TOBACCO ROAD*, CALDWELL LAYS OUT THE EVIDENCE OF THE PLIGHT OF THE POOR AND EXPECTS THE READER TO BE SHOCKED BY THE DEGRADATION OF THEIR CONDITION INTO ADOPTING A REFORMIST ATTITUDE."

hungry economic system that exploits the body for its labor, and then, when it is used up, disposes of it." In another essay in *Reading Erskine Caldwell*, Bert Hitchcock explores Caldwell's debt to the tradition of southern humor. Caldwell's humor is never simply funny, Hitchcock notes, but arises from a situation that would be too horrible to bear if the reader did not laugh at it. Hitchcock cites the struggle over the sack of turnips in the first chapters of *Tobacco Road* as an example.

CRITICISM

Bradley A. Skeen

Skeen is a classicist. In the following essay, he examines Tobacco Road *as a work of socialist propaganda.*

Precisely because the 1930s was the era of the Great Depression, it was also a high point of socialism in the United States. Because of their desperate economic situation, workers were ready to band together in trade unions to protect themselves from exploitation by their employers and to demand intervention by the government in the economy. The socialist and communist parties also attracted a high number of members, especially among intellectuals who saw the Depression as a sign that capitalism had failed (many were later persecuted for this during the Cold War, in the Red Scare of the 1950s). There was also a strong reaction against socialism by conservative elements in society who not only wanted to protect their own economic interests against workers but also saw any form of social change as a moral decline.

Caldwell's life and work among the poor in the rural South persuaded him that socialist

WHAT DO I READ NEXT?

- *God's Little Acre* (1933), Caldwell's next novel after *Tobacco Road*, is almost equally well known. Set on the rural outskirts of Augusta (this time over the South Carolina border), the novel develops the theme of the economic exploitation of the poor, centering around a strike by mill workers.

- *The Good Earth* (1931) is a Pulitzer Prize–winning novel by Pearl S. Buck that is set in a community of poor farmers in China during the early part of the twentieth century.

- *Old Yeller* (1956), by Fred Gipson, is a young-adult novel that won a retroactive Newbery Honor in 1968. It tells the story of a family of poor farmers in rural Texas.

- Harvey L. Klevar's 1993 biography, *Erskine Caldwell*, is more popularizing than the later work on Caldwell that began in the late 1990s.

- *You Have Seen Their Faces* (1939), by Caldwell and his wife, Margaret Bourke-White, is a photo essay documenting poverty in the rural South.

- *Deep South: Memory and Observation* (1968) is the most important of Caldwell's memoirs.

- *Flags in the Dust* (1973) is a novel by William Faulkner chronicling the decay of an aristocratic southern family, with a very different focus and depiction of southern culture from Caldwell's. An abridged version was published in 1929 under the title *Sartoris*.

reforms were necessary, but he never used the name socialism because of the reaction it would provoke among the rich and influential who actually had the power to help, or not help, the poor, and also because he was in other respects quite conservative himself. In *Tobacco Road*, Caldwell lays out the evidence of the plight of the poor and expects the reader to be shocked by the degradation of their condition into adopting a

reformist attitude. He gives only the slightest hints of the reforms he considers necessary, although he stated them much more directly in public lectures he gave throughout the 1930s. In the novel, he does give a thumbnail sketch of his program:

> An intelligent employment of his land, stocks, and implements would have enabled Jeeter [and his neighbors]...to raise crops for food, and crops to be sold at a profit. Co-operative and corporate farming would have saved them all.

He is proposing a land reform in which farmers' fields would be transferred from the ownership of their often absentee landlords to collectives of farmers who would be able to manage their own affairs and who could keep all the profit from their labor. He also thought that agricultural workers should bargain collectively with their employers. The education to enable the farmers to work their land effectively, as well as the initial credit that they would need to start, would have to be provided by the government. Even Jeeter realizes that the tightening of credit following the 1929 stock market crash was strangling small-scale agriculture:

> I don't know what's going to happen to me and my folks if the rich don't stop bleeding us. They've got all the money, holding it in the banks, and they won't lent it out unless a man will cut off his arms and leave them there for security.

Much of the novel is devoted to illustrating the impossibility of a farmer like Jeeter obtaining credit, and the exploitative terms that would come with it, even if he were able to get it. In essence, Caldwell thought that workers should benefit from their own labor, rather than the benefit going to those whose only contribution was capital.

Caldwell's recognition that socialist reforms were necessary is balanced by an innate social conservatism. Caldwell expresses this in the novel through his romantic, lyrical rhapsodizing of Jeeter's connection to the land:

> I think more of the land than I do about staying in a durn cotton mill. You can't smell no sedge fire up there, and when it comes time to break the land for planting, you feel sick inside but you don't know what's ailing you.... out here on the land a man feels better than he ever did. The spring-time ain't going to let you fool it by hiding away inside a durn cotton mill. It knows you got to stay on the land to feel good. That's because humans made the mills. God made the land.... That's how I know better than to go up there like the rest of them. I stay where God made a place for me.

Caldwell considers this attitude virtuous and a valid source of meaning in the farmers' lives. But at the same time he recognizes that the primitive nature of the connection of the rural poor to the land is an impediment to their successful farming that has to be overcome with education. Caldwell illustrates this in *Tobacco Road* through the farmer's positive resistance to modernization. The owners of the land Jeeter and his neighbors farmed simply abandoned it because agriculture could no longer be operated at a profit on it. A large part of the problem was the reluctance of the poor farmers to adopt modern, scientific methods of farming. The owners saw no point in even attempting to make them do so over their resistance. An example of this resistance is as follows:

> In the spring, the farmers burned over all of their land. They said the fire would kill the boll weevils.... But the real reason was because everybody had always burned the woods and fields each spring, and they saw no cause for abandoning life-long habits.

In fact, the fires did nothing for pest control and destroyed the wild pines that grew on the land that would at least have produced timber to sell and use (for example, in the repair of housing) with no effort on the farmer's part. The fact that the Lesters die in a house fire started by burning the fields is a symbolic representation of the ignorance destroying the rural poor as a class.

Another factor of great interest to Caldwell is the means of social control within traditional society used to keep the poor from realizing that they are oppressed and demanding social betterment. A simple example of this considers the inferior role of women in traditional culture. Ada Lester, for instance, has completely internalized the patriarchal views of her society, believing, "Women ain't good for nothing but to marry and work for men." So long as she thinks like this it will not occur to her to demand change to better her situation or her family's. The racism that was so prominent in American culture in the first half of the twentieth was also, paradoxically, a means of social control against the poor whites who were the most racist. The Lesters are shown to be barbaric racists who think nothing of stealing from and even killing blacks (many of Caldwell's later works are propaganda against the southern institution of lynching blacks). But so long as they are racists they will have a sort of safety valve against considering their own position. They will believe that they have a superior position because

they know that there is a class worse off and more despised than themselves. They are led to believe that, no matter how badly off they are, they can take a special pride merely in the status of being white. Indeed, the only time the Lesters feel shame is when they do or suffer something that will embarrass them in front of their black neighbors. Any idea of gender or racial equality is a threat to the traditional culture that oppresses poor white men, so traditional culture keeps them ignorant of any more enlightened ideas that could undermine these forces of social control. The aristocratic class in the South that controlled state governments preferred to spend money to sterilize poor whites than to educate them.

But the chief form of social control that Caldwell criticizes is religion. Modern criticism of religion had long asserted that it was used as a means of social control to keep the poor in their place. Karl Marx made a famous expression of this idea in *Toward a Critique of Hegel's "Philosophy of Right": Introduction*, in 1844:

> *Religious* suffering is the *expression* of real suffering and at the same time the *protest* against real suffering. Religion is the sigh of the oppressed creature, the heart of a heartless world, as it is the spirit of spiritless conditions. It is the *opium* of the people.

This means that religious hope is used as a distraction from real suffering. So long as the poor believe that God will improve their situation, whether in this life or the next, they will be less intent on effective action for real change that would improve their lives. Indeed, religion is often used to characterize such action as sinful. Part of the socialist program, therefore, was to make the poor see the hope that religion might alleviate their oppression as an illusion meant to keep them from demanding a real end to their oppression: "The abolition of religion as people's *illusory* happiness is the demand for their *real* happiness. The demand to abandon illusions about their condition is *a demand to abandon a condition which requires illusions*."

Sigmund Freud, in *The Future of an Illusion*, extends Marx's analysis. He realizes that "the great mass of the uneducated and the oppressed ... have every reason for being enemies of civilization" because civilization is so organized as to transfer the profit from their labor to the aristocratic classes and that this arrangement is what makes them poor and fills their lives with suffering. Religion is used to persuade them of the illusion that the current system of civilization is just and that by

Dude is more interesting in driving Bessie's new Ford than in marrying her. (© *Richard Thornton | Shutterstock.com*)

adhering to it they will receive social justice at some future time. Religion is used to make the idea of actual revolutionary social change unthinkable by providing a false hope of revolutionary social change in the future. It is therefore in the interest of the rich who benefit from the current social and economic arrangements that "either these dangerous masses must be held down most severely and kept most carefully away from any chance of intellectual awakening, or else the relationship between civilization and religion must undergo a fundamental revision."

Caldwell illustrates the role of religion in preventing the Lesters from thinking of any kind of social change without invoking the inflammatory names of Marx or Freud. Jeeter recognizes that he is oppressed by the rich, but believes that someday God will intervene to stop this oppression. He also believes that if he tries to change his situation, or even complains about it, he will not receive God's reward but will instead receive divine punishment:

> Some of these days He'll bust loose with a heap of bounty and all us poor folks will have all we want to eat and plenty to clothe us with. It can't

always keep getting worse and worse every year... God, He'll put a stop to it some of these days and make the rich give back all they've took from us poor folks. God is going to treat us right. He ain't going to let it keep on like it is now. But we got to stop cussing Him when we ain't got nothing to eat. He'll send a man to hell and the devil for persisting in doing that.

So long as Jeeter thinks like this he will do nothing to change social relationships in order to get as much as he wants to eat and enough to clothe his family in the here and now.

Caldwell goes further and characterizes religious belief as a kind of magic spell. Old Mother Lester "was always hoping that God would provide for them if she made a fire in the kitchen at meal-time." She turns to ritual action as though it was an effective means of realizing her basic desire to have enough to eat. Magic is a last resort to fulfill a desire that cannot be realized in reality. But because she has internalized the illusions of religion offered her by society, she is satisfied by carrying out this ritual rather than working to bring about social change. Jeeter does the same thing on a larger scale when he lights the fire that eventually kills him, believing that if he takes the first step of cultivation, God will somehow provide the means to complete his work. Persisting in religious belief is deadly to the poor, Caldwell thinks.

Source: Bradley A. Skeen, Critical Essay on *Tobacco Road*, in *Novels for Students*, Gale, Cengage Learning, 2015.

Wayne Mixon

In the following excerpt, Mixon describes the reaction of southerners to a play adapted from Tobacco Road.

. . . Although the novel upon publication had elicited little outrage against Caldwell in the South, reaction to the play rained torrents of vilification on him. Few were the voices raised in his defense, such as that of an Augusta woman who confessed her impatience with a false pride "that takes offense at any allusion to the existence of possible imperfections within a certain area." If the novel *Tobacco Road* "be propaganda in the interest of humanity," wrote Marguerite Stefan, "it has nevertheless enough literary merit to stand on its own feet as a piece of naturalistic fiction distinguished by some very good characterization, description, and even a certain kind of pathos." Many commentators discussed novel and play interchangeably, and some attributed authorship of the play to Caldwell.

Laughing at the antics of Tobacco Road's denizens, Yankees ignorant of the South considered the Lesters typical of the region—such was a common complaint from southerners. Georgians led the chorus of denunciation. "Erskine Caldwell's pot boiler and Georgia disgracer, . . . perhaps the filthiest story that was ever written about human beings . . . was typical of nothing—except depraved imaginings," the *Macon Telegraph* editorialized. The *Atlanta Georgian* defended the condemnation of the novel by the state's clubwomen "because they have the best interest of their state at heart." *Tobacco Road*, the writer continued, had caused "the most dreadful abuse of Georgia, whose good name is more important than any literary gem!" On the floor of the United States House of Representatives, a Georgia congressman denounced the novel as an "untruthful, undignified, undiplomatic and unfair sketch of Southern life." After Chicago banned the play, Georgia's governor, Eugene Talmadge, commended the mayor for preventing

> " BY HIS ACCOUNT, HE HOPED TO AWAKEN PEOPLE OF GOODWILL, ESPECIALLY SOUTHERNERS, TO THE REALITY OF SUCH DESTITUTION AS *TOBACCO ROAD* PORTRAYED."

"misrepresentation" of the South. A Tennessean who had seen the play in New York agreed with the Georgians. In a letter to the *New York Times* that was reprinted approvingly in southern newspapers, he expressed resentment of northerners' beliefs that the drama was "an accurate picture . . . of the conditions in the South." He proceeded to describe the horrible sights that he had witnessed on the streets of New York and added that such conditions were "no more a true picture of New York as a whole" than *Tobacco Road* was of the South.

When, more than four years after the play's debut on Broadway, a road company brought the production south for the first time, the furor reached an unprecedented level. Not only was the play a calumny on the South, many southerners contended, it would also corrupt public morals, particularly those of the young and impressionable. Few had the temerity publicly to defend the play as had W. J. Cash earlier. "I defy anybody with a grain of grit," Cash had written in the *Charlotte News*, "to read Caldwell's book or see his play [*sic*], and still believe that it might conceivably move any youth not a raving lunatic to imitation—or that it would do anything but goad him to headlong flight away from anything which reminds him of it. The thing, indeed, is a terrific sermon—and in other senses than the social one Caldwell intends." Heedless of such remonstrances, some southern cities refused to book the play, and in many places where it was performed—even in New Orleans—it was heavily censored.

Georgians were especially uneasy. When word arrived that the play was scheduled to be performed in Augusta, the police chief in Wrens asked the sheriff of Richmond County to ban it because "the Caldwells have created a great deal of excitement with their books and writings in reference to Richmond and Jefferson counties."

Despite the objections of lawmen, clubwomen, churchmen—from Baptist to Catholic—newspaper editors, and other defenders of decency, *Tobacco Road* came to Georgia and played to overflow crowds in Savannah, Augusta, and Atlanta. Everywhere, the audiences laughed—loud, long, and often. In Augusta, tenant farmers from Tobacco Road, brought by Caldwell's father, shared the mirth. Ira also took the play's cast to Tobacco Road; subsequently, the actors sent a portion of their salaries to him to help provide for the needy.

Here and there over the South, some viewers protested that the play distorted the novel. A Georgian lamented that "the love-of-the-land theme is subordinated and the comedy emphasized." A Tennessean deplored "the excess of filth and the total lack of any redeeming purpose" as well as the failure to probe "the deeper human implications of the tenant farmer problem." An Alabaman pointed out that though the novel's "primary aim" was "to portray the miserable plight of the tenant farmer in all its hopelessness," the play had made "lewdness the most striking quality of the work."

Occasionally, critics who held the novel in high regard felt compelled to defend the play as well, or at least its right to be performed. In doing so, they demonstrated that the novel *Tobacco Road* had made the kind of impact, at least on some southerners, that its author had intended. Believing that the play was an extension of the novel, Caldwell's friends Earl L. Bell of the *Augusta Herald* and Frank Daniel of the *Atlanta Journal*, who admired him as a person and who esteemed his work, wrote moving defenses of both the novel and the play. To Bell, it was salutary that Augustans, who had been "busy building polo fields and checking golf scores," should witness "the tragedy of the lowliest white agricultural element struggling against crushing odds because of their love of the land." Granting that *Tobacco Road* was "untypical," Bell nonetheless insisted upon its veracity. "As for this reviewer," he concluded, "who has seen Richmond County sharecropper children so famished that they snatched raw beef liver off the kitchen table before it could be cooked and ran off with it like so many little wolves—well, it is not for him to hurl the ugly word at Jeeter Lester's Boswell."

To Daniel, who believed that Caldwell was the greatest writer in Georgia's history, *Tobacco Road* was "a work of great power and great beauty." The stage version had impressed "on the minds of millions of people" the shocking conditions of the South's rural poor and for that reason alone had served "an admirable purpose." For the first time, Daniel said, a writer had spoken for people—the Lesters of the South—"who cannot speak for themselves." In an impassioned rebuke of his fellow southerners who contended that *Tobacco Road* was not typical of conditions in the South, Daniel responded that those making the charge never seemed "to make any effort to determine just how frequent such conditions are." Furthermore, he asked, "how general must starvation and degradation become before it may permissibly be deplored? If there is even one instance in the world of a condition like that presented in 'Tobacco Road,' isn't that single case too general?...How can anyone who has lived through the past decade deny that need is everywhere, with its consequences to body and mind and soul?" The erudite Daniel also asked his readers to decide whether the situation in *Tobacco Road* was more rare than circumstances portrayed in works by Sophocles, Shakespeare, Goethe, and Chekhov.

The South Carolinian J. H. Marion Jr. also ringingly defended *Tobacco Road*, as novel and as play. In an article published in the *Christian Century* early in 1958, Marion averred that Caldwell had "impressively brought to light" the "scabrous horrors" that lay "beneath the surface of cropper life." To the critics who cried that "Caldwell's pictures of poor-white life are caricatures, his characters grotesque," Marion responded: "One could only wish they were!" Caldwell's grimly realistic portrayal of rural poverty, he concluded, had the effect of "not letting southerners live in a world that is only a painted lie."

Caldwell did not want merely to confirm the converted such as Bell, Daniel, and Marion. By his account, he hoped to awaken people of goodwill, especially southerners, to the reality of such destitution as *Tobacco Road* portrayed. To the incessant charge that such conditions were not typical of the South, he responded, "perhaps the great error of my life was in not appending a preface to 'Tobacco Road' stating that the story did not pretend to typify the entire South, but that it was my purpose merely to sketch a representative family among five million persons who are actual residents on Tobacco Road, who are likely future residents there. As it is, we have the spectacle of a man entering a room full of people, crying 'Thief,' and seeing nearly every person present in the act of running away." If the story *Tobacco Road* told was exceptional, it was nonetheless legitimate, Caldwell insisted. The actions of the characters, he told a newspaper interviewer, "are not mere imagining on my part. They grow out of the environment." Nor did he consider the story obscene, because the characters "do not live consciously in a lurid or dirty way."

Caldwell contended that *Tobacco Road* could have been set in any part of the cotton belt from the Carolinas to Arkansas, where "economic slavery, subtropical climate, and *depleted* soil . . . [had converged] upon a group of people over a long term of years." Throughout that time, little had been attempted to alleviate a worsening situation. Politicians, whose "static ignorance . . . is a thing to marvel at," bore much of the blame. So did the church. With the exception of a few socially conscious ministers, preachers for the past fifty years had been unduly concerned "to save the heathen" elsewhere in the world, although their "own people were being subjected to the economic bloodsucking of the landlord-elders and the politician-deacons." The result of this unholy alliance of church and state was that "the South has not only produced a coolie serfdom but, more than that, has turned around and deliberately kicked it in the face." Precisely because he loved the South, Caldwell wrote, "I insist upon such a story as 'Tobacco Road' as a means of exposing the shame of its civilization." The play, wherein, according to Caldwell, "sex and profanity are incidentals," was bringing much-needed attention to the South's decay, whose "stench is a complacent nation's shame." He hoped that "with the help of science, economics, sociology, and common humanity" the expansion of Tobacco Road could soon be halted and that "eventually it could be wiped completely off the map."

When *Tobacco Road* concluded its record-setting run on Broadway in the spring of 1941, the *Montgomery Advertiser*, in an editorial reprinted in other southern newspapers, assessed the reasons for the "phenomenal appeal of Erskine Caldwell's play [*sic*]." Not its sociological aspects or its libel of the South but its "unique humor" was the source of the play's popularity. "Its lusty, often lewd, lines evoked gales of laughter North, South, East and West."

Yet the *Advertiser* admitted that *Tobacco Road* had dramatized "some very real problems which we Southerners have been slow to face." Nearly three years before, the same newspaper had credited the play with a social achievement that was more concrete-inspiring the Rosenwald Foundation to fund a study of sharecropper conditions that had produced "considerable good." Other southern newspapers agreed that the play, and the novel, had been socially constructive . . . .

Source: Wayne Mixon, "The Godforsaken South: The Fiction of the Thirties," in *The People's Writer: Erskine Caldwell and the South*, University Press of Virginia, 1995, pp. 59–63.

SOURCES

Caldwell, Erskine, *Call It Experience: The Years of Learning How to Write*, Duell, Sloan and Pearce, 1951, p. 35.

———, *Tobacco Road*, Modern Library, 1960.

Cook, Sylvia J., "Erskine Caldwell: Modernism from the Bottom Up," in *Reading Erskine Caldwell: New Essays*, edited by Robert L. McDonald, McFarland, 2006, pp. 58–76.

Devlin, James E., *Erskine Caldwell*, Twayne's United States Authors Series No. 469, Twayne, 1984, pp. 1–48.

Freud, Sigmund, *The Future of an Illusion*, translated by James Strachey, W. W. Norton, 1961, pp. 49–50.

Hitchcock, Bert, "Well, Maybe Just This Once: Erskine Caldwell, Old Southwest Humor, and Funny Ha-Ha," in *Reading Erskine Caldwell: New Essays*, edited by Robert L. McDonald, McFarland, 2006, pp. 27–45.

Keely, Karen A., "Poverty, Sterilization, and Eugenics in Erskine Caldwell's *Tobacco Road*," in *Journal of American Studies*, Vol. 36, No. 1, 2002, pp. 23–42.

Marx, Karl, *Toward a Critique of Hegel's "Philosophy of Right": Introduction*, in *Selected Writings*, edited by Lawrence H. Simon, translated by Lloyd D. Easton and Kurt H. Guddat, Hackett, 1994, pp. 27–39.

Maxon, Wayne, *The People's Writer: Erskine Caldwell and the South*, University of Virginia Press, 1995, pp. 37–90.

Miller Dan B., *Erskine Caldwell: The Journey from Tobacco Road*, Alfred A. Knopf, 1995, pp. 89–127.

Mutikani, Lucia, "U.S. Economy Back on Track with Strong Second-Quarter Rebound," in *Reuters*, July 30, 2014, http://www.reuters.com/article/2014/07/30/us-usa-economy-idUSKBN0FZ09P20140730 (accessed September 10, 2014).

Wilson, Natalie, "Social Justice Embodied: Caldwell and the Grotesque," in *Reading Erskine Caldwell: New Essays*, edited by Robert L. McDonald, McFarland, 2006, pp. 114–30.

FURTHER READING

Caldwell, Erskine, *Georgia Boy*, Duell, Sloan and Pearce, 1943.

> Reissued by the University of Georgia Press in 1995, Caldwell considered this his favorite book. Lighter in tone than *Tobacco Road*, it nevertheless deals with Caldwell's themes of economic exploitation of the poor and their consequent moral degeneracy. It takes the form of a series of interlocked short stories about a rural family. It was adapted as a remarkably unsuccessful Broadway play.

————, *Trouble in July*, Duell, Sloan and Pearce, 1940.

> In this novel, reissued by the University of Georgia Press in 1999, Caldwell shifts his focus to race relations in the rural South. It builds its plot around a lynching.

McDonald, Robert L., *Erskine Caldwell: Selected Letters*, McFarland, 1999.

> This is the only publication of any of Caldwell's papers. It is particularly useful for the extensive annotations tying the letters back to Caldwell's life and work.

MacDonald, Scott, ed., *Critical Essays on Erskine Caldwell*, G. K. Hall, 1981.

> Scott collects a group of older studies of Caldwell.

SUGGESTED SEARCH TERMS

Erskine Caldwell

Tobacco Road

realism

surrealism

socialism

opium of the masses

Great Depression

eugenics

satire

Glossary of Literary Terms

A

Abstract: As an adjective applied to writing or literary works, abstract refers to words or phrases that name things not knowable through the five senses.

Aestheticism: A literary and artistic movement of the nineteenth century. Followers of the movement believed that art should not be mixed with social, political, or moral teaching. The statement "art for art's sake" is a good summary of aestheticism. The movement had its roots in France, but it gained widespread importance in England in the last half of the nineteenth century, where it helped change the Victorian practice of including moral lessons in literature.

Allegory: A narrative technique in which characters representing things or abstract ideas are used to convey a message or teach a lesson. Allegory is typically used to teach moral, ethical, or religious lessons but is sometimes used for satiric or political purposes.

Allusion: A reference to a familiar literary or historical person or event, used to make an idea more easily understood.

Analogy: A comparison of two things made to explain something unfamiliar through its similarities to something familiar, or to prove one point based on the acceptedness of another. Similes and metaphors are types of analogies.

Antagonist: The major character in a narrative or drama who works against the hero or protagonist.

Anthropomorphism: The presentation of animals or objects in human shape or with human characteristics. The term is derived from the Greek word for "human form."

Anti-hero: A central character in a work of literature who lacks traditional heroic qualities such as courage, physical prowess, and fortitude. Anti-heroes typically distrust conventional values and are unable to commit themselves to any ideals. They generally feel helpless in a world over which they have no control. Anti-heroes usually accept, and often celebrate, their positions as social outcasts.

Apprenticeship Novel: See *Bildungsroman*

Archetype: The word archetype is commonly used to describe an original pattern or model from which all other things of the same kind are made. This term was introduced to literary criticism from the psychology of Carl Jung. It expresses Jung's theory that behind every person's "unconscious," or repressed memories of the past, lies the "collective unconscious" of the human race: memories of the countless typical experiences of our ancestors. These memories are said to prompt illogical associations that trigger powerful emotions in the reader.

Often, the emotional process is primitive, even primordial. Archetypes are the literary images that grow out of the "collective unconscious." They appear in literature as incidents and plots that repeat basic patterns of life. They may also appear as stereotyped characters.

Avant-garde: French term meaning "vanguard." It is used in literary criticism to describe new writing that rejects traditional approaches to literature in favor of innovations in style or content.

B

Beat Movement: A period featuring a group of American poets and novelists of the 1950s and 1960s—including Jack Kerouac, Allen Ginsberg, Gregory Corso, William S. Burroughs, and Lawrence Ferlinghetti—who rejected established social and literary values. Using such techniques as stream of consciousness writing and jazz-influenced free verse and focusing on unusual or abnormal states of mind—generated by religious ecstasy or the use of drugs—the Beat writers aimed to create works that were unconventional in both form and subject matter.

Bildungsroman: A German word meaning "novel of development." The *bildungsroman* is a study of the maturation of a youthful character, typically brought about through a series of social or sexual encounters that lead to self-awareness. *Bildungsroman* is used interchangeably with *erziehungsroman*, a novel of initiation and education. When a *bildungsroman* is concerned with the development of an artist (as in James Joyce's *A Portrait of the Artist as a Young Man*), it is often termed a *kunstlerroman*.

Black Aesthetic Movement: A period of artistic and literary development among African Americans in the 1960s and early 1970s. This was the first major African-American artistic movement since the Harlem Renaissance and was closely paralleled by the civil rights and black power movements. The black aesthetic writers attempted to produce works of art that would be meaningful to the black masses. Key figures in black aesthetics included one of its founders, poet and playwright Amiri Baraka, formerly known as LeRoi Jones; poet and essayist Haki R. Madhubuti, formerly Don L. Lee; poet and playwright Sonia Sanchez; and dramatist Ed Bullins.

Black Humor: Writing that places grotesque elements side by side with humorous ones in an attempt to shock the reader, forcing him or her to laugh at the horrifying reality of a disordered world.

Burlesque: Any literary work that uses exaggeration to make its subject appear ridiculous, either by treating a trivial subject with profound seriousness or by treating a dignified subject frivolously. The word "burlesque" may also be used as an adjective, as in "burlesque show," to mean "striptease act."

C

Character: Broadly speaking, a person in a literary work. The actions of characters are what constitute the plot of a story, novel, or poem. There are numerous types of characters, ranging from simple, stereotypical figures to intricate, multifaceted ones. In the techniques of anthropomorphism and personification, animals—and even places or things—can assume aspects of character. "Characterization" is the process by which an author creates vivid, believable characters in a work of art. This may be done in a variety of ways, including (1) direct description of the character by the narrator; (2) the direct presentation of the speech, thoughts, or actions of the character; and (3) the responses of other characters to the character. The term "character" also refers to a form originated by the ancient Greek writer Theophrastus that later became popular in the seventeenth and eighteenth centuries. It is a short essay or sketch of a person who prominently displays a specific attribute or quality, such as miserliness or ambition.

Climax: The turning point in a narrative, the moment when the conflict is at its most intense. Typically, the structure of stories, novels, and plays is one of rising action, in which tension builds to the climax, followed by falling action, in which tension lessens as the story moves to its conclusion.

Colloquialism: A word, phrase, or form of pronunciation that is acceptable in casual conversation but not in formal, written communication. It is considered more acceptable than slang.

Coming of Age Novel: See *Bildungsroman*

Concrete: Concrete is the opposite of abstract, and refers to a thing that actually exists or a description that allows the reader to experience an object or concept with the senses.

Connotation: The impression that a word gives beyond its defined meaning. Connotations may be universally understood or may be significant only to a certain group.

Convention: Any widely accepted literary device, style, or form.

D

Denotation: The definition of a word, apart from the impressions or feelings it creates (connotations) in the reader.

Denouement: A French word meaning "the unknotting." In literary criticism, it denotes the resolution of conflict in fiction or drama. The *denouement* follows the climax and provides an outcome to the primary plot situation as well as an explanation of secondary plot complications. The *denouement* often involves a character's recognition of his or her state of mind or moral condition.

Description: Descriptive writing is intended to allow a reader to picture the scene or setting in which the action of a story takes place. The form this description takes often evokes an intended emotional response—a dark, spooky graveyard will evoke fear, and a peaceful, sunny meadow will evoke calmness.

Dialogue: In its widest sense, dialogue is simply conversation between people in a literary work; in its most restricted sense, it refers specifically to the speech of characters in a drama. As a specific literary genre, a "dialogue" is a composition in which characters debate an issue or idea.

Diction: The selection and arrangement of words in a literary work. Either or both may vary depending on the desired effect. There are four general types of diction: "formal," used in scholarly or lofty writing; "informal," used in relaxed but educated conversation; "colloquial," used in everyday speech; and "slang," containing newly coined words and other terms not accepted in formal usage.

Didactic: A term used to describe works of literature that aim to teach some moral, religious, political, or practical lesson. Although didactic elements are often found in artistically pleasing works, the term "didactic" usually refers to literature in which the message is more important than the form. The term may also be used to criticize a work that the critic finds "overly didactic," that is, heavy-handed in its delivery of a lesson.

Doppelganger: A literary technique by which a character is duplicated (usually in the form of an alter ego, though sometimes as a ghostly counterpart) or divided into two distinct, usually opposite personalities. The use of this character device is widespread in nineteenth- and twentieth-century literature, and indicates a growing awareness among authors that the "self" is really a composite of many "selves."

Double Entendre: A corruption of a French phrase meaning "double meaning." The term is used to indicate a word or phrase that is deliberately ambiguous, especially when one of the meanings is risqué or improper.

Dramatic Irony: Occurs when the audience of a play or the reader of a work of literature knows something that a character in the work itself does not know. The irony is in the contrast between the intended meaning of the statements or actions of a character and the additional information understood by the audience.

Dystopia: An imaginary place in a work of fiction where the characters lead dehumanized, fearful lives.

E

Edwardian: Describes cultural conventions identified with the period of the reign of Edward VII of England (1901-1910). Writers of the Edwardian Age typically displayed a strong reaction against the propriety and conservatism of the Victorian Age. Their work often exhibits distrust of authority in religion, politics, and art and expresses strong doubts about the soundness of conventional values.

Empathy: A sense of shared experience, including emotional and physical feelings, with someone or something other than oneself. Empathy is often used to describe the response of a reader to a literary character.

Enlightenment, The: An eighteenth-century philosophical movement. It began in France but had a wide impact throughout Europe and America. Thinkers of the Enlightenment valued reason and believed that both the individual and society could achieve a state of perfection. Corresponding to this essentially humanist vision was a resistance to religious authority.

Epigram: A saying that makes the speaker's point quickly and concisely. Often used to preface a novel.

Epilogue: A concluding statement or section of a literary work. In dramas, particularly those of the seventeenth and eighteenth centuries, the epilogue is a closing speech, often in verse, delivered by an actor at the end of a play and spoken directly to the audience.

Epiphany: A sudden revelation of truth inspired by a seemingly trivial incident.

Episode: An incident that forms part of a story and is significantly related to it. Episodes may be either self-contained narratives or events that depend on a larger context for their sense and importance.

Epistolary Novel: A novel in the form of letters. The form was particularly popular in the eighteenth century.

Epithet: A word or phrase, often disparaging or abusive, that expresses a character trait of someone or something.

Existentialism: A predominantly twentieth-century philosophy concerned with the nature and perception of human existence. There are two major strains of existentialist thought: atheistic and Christian. Followers of atheistic existentialism believe that the individual is alone in a godless universe and that the basic human condition is one of suffering and loneliness. Nevertheless, because there are no fixed values, individuals can create their own characters—indeed, they can shape themselves—through the exercise of free will. The atheistic strain culminates in and is popularly associated with the works of Jean-Paul Sartre. The Christian existentialists, on the other hand, believe that only in God may people find freedom from life's anguish. The two strains hold certain beliefs in common: that existence cannot be fully understood or described through empirical effort; that anguish is a universal element of life; that individuals must bear responsibility for their actions; and that there is no common

standard of behavior or perception for religious and ethical matters.

Expatriates: See *Expatriatism*

Expatriatism: The practice of leaving one's country to live for an extended period in another country.

Exposition: Writing intended to explain the nature of an idea, thing, or theme. Expository writing is often combined with description, narration, or argument. In dramatic writing, the exposition is the introductory material which presents the characters, setting, and tone of the play.

Expressionism: An indistinct literary term, originally used to describe an early twentieth-century school of German painting. The term applies to almost any mode of unconventional, highly subjective writing that distorts reality in some way.

F

Fable: A prose or verse narrative intended to convey a moral. Animals or inanimate objects with human characteristics often serve as characters in fables.

Falling Action: See *Denouement*

Fantasy: A literary form related to mythology and folklore. Fantasy literature is typically set in non-existent realms and features supernatural beings.

Farce: A type of comedy characterized by broad humor, outlandish incidents, and often vulgar subject matter.

Femme fatale: A French phrase with the literal translation "fatal woman." A *femme fatale* is a sensuous, alluring woman who often leads men into danger or trouble.

Fiction: Any story that is the product of imagination rather than a documentation of fact. Characters and events in such narratives may be based in real life but their ultimate form and configuration is a creation of the author.

Figurative Language: A technique in writing in which the author temporarily interrupts the order, construction, or meaning of the writing for a particular effect. This interruption takes the form of one or more figures of speech such as hyperbole, irony, or simile. Figurative language is the opposite of literal language, in which every word is truthful, accurate, and free of exaggeration or embellishment.

Figures of Speech: Writing that differs from customary conventions for construction, meaning, order, or significance for the purpose of a special meaning or effect. There are two major types of figures of speech: rhetorical figures, which do not make changes in the meaning of the words, and tropes, which do.

Fin de siecle: A French term meaning "end of the century." The term is used to denote the last decade of the nineteenth century, a transition period when writers and other artists abandoned old conventions and looked for new techniques and objectives.

First Person: See *Point of View*

Flashback: A device used in literature to present action that occurred before the beginning of the story. Flashbacks are often introduced as the dreams or recollections of one or more characters.

Foil: A character in a work of literature whose physical or psychological qualities contrast strongly with, and therefore highlight, the corresponding qualities of another character.

Folklore: Traditions and myths preserved in a culture or group of people. Typically, these are passed on by word of mouth in various forms—such as legends, songs, and proverbs—or preserved in customs and ceremonies. This term was first used by W. J. Thoms in 1846.

Folktale: A story originating in oral tradition. Folktales fall into a variety of categories, including legends, ghost stories, fairy tales, fables, and anecdotes based on historical figures and events.

Foreshadowing: A device used in literature to create expectation or to set up an explanation of later developments.

Form: The pattern or construction of a work which identifies its genre and distinguishes it from other genres.

G

Genre: A category of literary work. In critical theory, genre may refer to both the content of a given work—tragedy, comedy, pastoral—and to its form, such as poetry, novel, or drama.

Gilded Age: A period in American history during the 1870s characterized by political corruption and materialism. A number of important novels of social and political criticism were written during this time.

Gothicism: In literary criticism, works characterized by a taste for the medieval or morbidly attractive. A gothic novel prominently features elements of horror, the supernatural, gloom, and violence: clanking chains, terror, charnel houses, ghosts, medieval castles, and mysteriously slamming doors. The term "gothic novel" is also applied to novels that lack elements of the traditional Gothic setting but that create a similar atmosphere of terror or dread.

Grotesque: In literary criticism, the subject matter of a work or a style of expression characterized by exaggeration, deformity, freakishness, and disorder. The grotesque often includes an element of comic absurdity.

H

Harlem Renaissance: The Harlem Renaissance of the 1920s is generally considered the first significant movement of black writers and artists in the United States. During this period, new and established black writers published more fiction and poetry than ever before, the first influential black literary journals were established, and black authors and artists received their first widespread recognition and serious critical appraisal. Among the major writers associated with this period are Claude McKay, Jean Toomer, Countee Cullen, Langston Hughes, Arna Bontemps, Nella Larsen, and Zora Neale Hurston.

Hero/Heroine: The principal sympathetic character (male or female) in a literary work. Heroes and heroines typically exhibit admirable traits: idealism, courage, and integrity, for example.

Holocaust Literature: Literature influenced by or written about the Holocaust of World War II. Such literature includes true stories of survival in concentration camps, escape, and life after the war, as well as fictional works and poetry.

Humanism: A philosophy that places faith in the dignity of humankind and rejects the medieval perception of the individual as a weak, fallen creature. "Humanists" typically believe in the perfectibility of human nature and view reason and education as the means to that end.

Hyperbole: In literary criticism, deliberate exaggeration used to achieve an effect.

I

Idiom: A word construction or verbal expression closely associated with a given language.

Image: A concrete representation of an object or sensory experience. Typically, such a representation helps evoke the feelings associated with the object or experience itself. Images are either "literal" or "figurative." Literal images are especially concrete and involve little or no extension of the obvious meaning of the words used to express them. Figurative images do not follow the literal meaning of the words exactly. Images in literature are usually visual, but the term "image" can also refer to the representation of any sensory experience.

Imagery: The array of images in a literary work. Also, figurative language.

In medias res: A Latin term meaning "in the middle of things." It refers to the technique of beginning a story at its midpoint and then using various flashback devices to reveal previous action.

Interior Monologue: A narrative technique in which characters' thoughts are revealed in a way that appears to be uncontrolled by the author. The interior monologue typically aims to reveal the inner self of a character. It portrays emotional experiences as they occur at both a conscious and unconscious level. images are often used to represent sensations or emotions.

Irony: In literary criticism, the effect of language in which the intended meaning is the opposite of what is stated.

J

Jargon: Language that is used or understood only by a select group of people. Jargon may refer to terminology used in a certain profession, such as computer jargon, or it may refer to any nonsensical language that is not understood by most people.

L

Leitmotiv: See *Motif*

Literal Language: An author uses literal language when he or she writes without exaggerating

or embellishing the subject matter and without any tools of figurative language.

Lost Generation: A term first used by Gertrude Stein to describe the post-World War I generation of American writers: men and women haunted by a sense of betrayal and emptiness brought about by the destructiveness of the war.

M

Mannerism: Exaggerated, artificial adherence to a literary manner or style. Also, a popular style of the visual arts of late sixteenth-century Europe that was marked by elongation of the human form and by intentional spatial distortion. Literary works that are self-consciously high-toned and artistic are often said to be "mannered."

Metaphor: A figure of speech that expresses an idea through the image of another object. Metaphors suggest the essence of the first object by identifying it with certain qualities of the second object.

Modernism: Modern literary practices. Also, the principles of a literary school that lasted from roughly the beginning of the twentieth century until the end of World War II. Modernism is defined by its rejection of the literary conventions of the nineteenth century and by its opposition to conventional morality, taste, traditions, and economic values.

Mood: The prevailing emotions of a work or of the author in his or her creation of the work. The mood of a work is not always what might be expected based on its subject matter.

Motif: A theme, character type, image, metaphor, or other verbal element that recurs throughout a single work of literature or occurs in a number of different works over a period of time.

Myth: An anonymous tale emerging from the traditional beliefs of a culture or social unit. Myths use supernatural explanations for natural phenomena. They may also explain cosmic issues like creation and death. Collections of myths, known as mythologies, are common to all cultures and nations, but the best-known myths belong to the Norse, Roman, and Greek mythologies.

N

Narration: The telling of a series of events, real or invented. A narration may be either a simple narrative, in which the events are recounted chronologically, or a narrative with a plot, in which the account is given in a style reflecting the author's artistic concept of the story. Narration is sometimes used as a synonym for "storyline."

Narrative: A verse or prose accounting of an event or sequence of events, real or invented. The term is also used as an adjective in the sense "method of narration." For example, in literary criticism, the expression "narrative technique" usually refers to the way the author structures and presents his or her story.

Narrator: The teller of a story. The narrator may be the author or a character in the story through whom the author speaks.

Naturalism: A literary movement of the late nineteenth and early twentieth centuries. The movement's major theorist, French novelist Emile Zola, envisioned a type of fiction that would examine human life with the objectivity of scientific inquiry. The Naturalists typically viewed human beings as either the products of "biological determinism," ruled by hereditary instincts and engaged in an endless struggle for survival, or as the products of "socioeconomic determinism," ruled by social and economic forces beyond their control. In their works, the Naturalists generally ignored the highest levels of society and focused on degradation: poverty, alcoholism, prostitution, insanity, and disease.

Noble Savage: The idea that primitive man is noble and good but becomes evil and corrupted as he becomes civilized. The concept of the noble savage originated in the Renaissance period but is more closely identified with such later writers as Jean-Jacques Rousseau and Aphra Behn.

Novel: A long fictional narrative written in prose, which developed from the novella and other early forms of narrative. A novel is usually organized under a plot or theme with a focus on character development and action.

Novel of Ideas: A novel in which the examination of intellectual issues and concepts takes precedence over characterization or a traditional storyline.

Novel of Manners: A novel that examines the customs and mores of a cultural group.

Novella: An Italian term meaning "story." This term has been especially used to describe fourteenth-century Italian tales, but it also refers to modern short novels.

O

Objective Correlative: An outward set of objects, a situation, or a chain of events corresponding to an inward experience and evoking this experience in the reader. The term frequently appears in modern criticism in discussions of authors' intended effects on the emotional responses of readers.

Objectivity: A quality in writing characterized by the absence of the author's opinion or feeling about the subject matter. Objectivity is an important factor in criticism.

Oedipus Complex: A son's amorous obsession with his mother. The phrase is derived from the story of the ancient Theban hero Oedipus, who unknowingly killed his father and married his mother.

Omniscience: See *Point of View*

Onomatopoeia: The use of words whose sounds express or suggest their meaning. In its simplest sense, onomatopoeia may be represented by words that mimic the sounds they denote such as "hiss" or "meow." At a more subtle level, the pattern and rhythm of sounds and rhymes of a line or poem may be onomatopoeic.

Oxymoron: A phrase combining two contradictory terms. Oxymorons may be intentional or unintentional.

P

Parable: A story intended to teach a moral lesson or answer an ethical question.

Paradox: A statement that appears illogical or contradictory at first, but may actually point to an underlying truth.

Parallelism: A method of comparison of two ideas in which each is developed in the same grammatical structure.

Parody: In literary criticism, this term refers to an imitation of a serious literary work or the signature style of a particular author in a ridiculous manner. A typical parody adopts the style of the original and applies it to an inappropriate subject for humorous effect. Parody is a form of satire and could be considered the literary equivalent of a caricature or cartoon.

Pastoral: A term derived from the Latin word "pastor," meaning shepherd. A pastoral is a literary composition on a rural theme. The conventions of the pastoral were originated by the third-century Greek poet Theocritus, who wrote about the experiences, love affairs, and pastimes of Sicilian shepherds. In a pastoral, characters and language of a courtly nature are often placed in a simple setting. The term pastoral is also used to classify dramas, elegies, and lyrics that exhibit the use of country settings and shepherd characters.

Pen Name: See *Pseudonym*

Persona: A Latin term meaning "mask." *Personae* are the characters in a fictional work of literature. The *persona* generally functions as a mask through which the author tells a story in a voice other than his or her own. A *persona* is usually either a character in a story who acts as a narrator or an "implied author," a voice created by the author to act as the narrator for himself or herself.

Personification: A figure of speech that gives human qualities to abstract ideas, animals, and inanimate objects.

Picaresque Novel: Episodic fiction depicting the adventures of a roguish central character ("picaro" is Spanish for "rogue"). The picaresque hero is commonly a low-born but clever individual who wanders into and out of various affairs of love, danger, and farcical intrigue. These involvements may take place at all social levels and typically present a humorous and wide-ranging satire of a given society.

Plagiarism: Claiming another person's written material as one's own. Plagiarism can take the form of direct, word-for-word copying or the theft of the substance or idea of the work.

Plot: In literary criticism, this term refers to the pattern of events in a narrative or drama. In its simplest sense, the plot guides the author in composing the work and helps the reader follow the work. Typically, plots exhibit causality and unity and have a beginning, a middle, and an end. Sometimes, however, a plot may consist of a series of disconnected events, in which case it is known as an "episodic plot."

Poetic Justice: An outcome in a literary work, not necessarily a poem, in which the good are rewarded and the evil are punished, especially in ways that particularly fit their virtues or crimes.

Poetic License: Distortions of fact and literary convention made by a writer—not always a poet—for the sake of the effect gained. Poetic license is closely related to the concept of "artistic freedom."

Poetics: This term has two closely related meanings. It denotes (1) an aesthetic theory in literary criticism about the essence of poetry or (2) rules prescribing the proper methods, content, style, or diction of poetry. The term poetics may also refer to theories about literature in general, not just poetry.

Point of View: The narrative perspective from which a literary work is presented to the reader. There are four traditional points of view. The "third person omniscient" gives the reader a "godlike" perspective, unrestricted by time or place, from which to see actions and look into the minds of characters. This allows the author to comment openly on characters and events in the work. The "third person" point of view presents the events of the story from outside of any single character's perception, much like the omniscient point of view, but the reader must understand the action as it takes place and without any special insight into characters' minds or motivations. The "first person" or "personal" point of view relates events as they are perceived by a single character. The main character "tells" the story and may offer opinions about the action and characters which differ from those of the author. Much less common than omniscient, third person, and first person is the "second person" point of view, wherein the author tells the story as if it is happening to the reader.

Polemic: A work in which the author takes a stand on a controversial subject, such as abortion or religion. Such works are often extremely argumentative or provocative.

Pornography: Writing intended to provoke feelings of lust in the reader. Such works are often condemned by critics and teachers, but those which can be shown to have literary value are viewed less harshly.

Post-Aesthetic Movement: An artistic response made by African Americans to the black aesthetic movement of the 1960s and early '70s. Writers since that time have adopted a somewhat different tone in their work, with less emphasis placed on the disparity between black and white in the United States. In the words of post-aesthetic authors such as Toni Morrison, John Edgar Wideman, and Kristin Hunter, African Americans are portrayed as looking inward for answers to their own questions, rather than always looking to the outside world.

Postmodernism: Writing from the 1960s forward characterized by experimentation and continuing to apply some of the fundamentals of modernism, which included existentialism and alienation. Postmodernists have gone a step further in the rejection of tradition begun with the modernists by also rejecting traditional forms, preferring the anti-novel over the novel and the anti-hero over the hero.

Primitivism: The belief that primitive peoples were nobler and less flawed than civilized peoples because they had not been subjected to the tainting influence of society.

Prologue: An introductory section of a literary work. It often contains information establishing the situation of the characters or presents information about the setting, time period, or action. In drama, the prologue is spoken by a chorus or by one of the principal characters.

Prose: A literary medium that attempts to mirror the language of everyday speech. It is distinguished from poetry by its use of unmetered, unrhymed language consisting of logically related sentences. Prose is usually grouped into paragraphs that form a cohesive whole such as an essay or a novel.

Prosopopoeia: See *Personification*

Protagonist: The central character of a story who serves as a focus for its themes and incidents and as the principal rationale for its development. The protagonist is sometimes referred to in discussions of modern literature as the hero or anti-hero.

Protest Fiction: Protest fiction has as its primary purpose the protesting of some social injustice, such as racism or discrimination.

Proverb: A brief, sage saying that expresses a truth about life in a striking manner.

Pseudonym: A name assumed by a writer, most often intended to prevent his or her identification as the author of a work. Two or more authors may work together under one pseudonym, or an author may use a different name for each genre he or she publishes in. Some publishing companies maintain "house pseudonyms," under which any number of authors may write installations in a series. Some authors also choose a pseudonym over their real names the way an actor may use a stage name.

Pun: A play on words that have similar sounds but different meanings.

R

Realism: A nineteenth-century European literary movement that sought to portray familiar characters, situations, and settings in a realistic manner. This was done primarily by using an objective narrative point of view and through the buildup of accurate detail. The standard for success of any realistic work depends on how faithfully it transfers common experience into fictional forms. The realistic method may be altered or extended, as in stream of consciousness writing, to record highly subjective experience.

Repartee: Conversation featuring snappy retorts and witticisms.

Resolution: The portion of a story following the climax, in which the conflict is resolved.

Rhetoric: In literary criticism, this term denotes the art of ethical persuasion. In its strictest sense, rhetoric adheres to various principles developed since classical times for arranging facts and ideas in a clear, persuasive, appealing manner. The term is also used to refer to effective prose in general and theories of or methods for composing effective prose.

Rhetorical Question: A question intended to provoke thought, but not an expressed answer, in the reader. It is most commonly used in oratory and other persuasive genres.

Rising Action: The part of a drama where the plot becomes increasingly complicated. Rising action leads up to the climax, or turning point, of a drama.

Roman à clef: A French phrase meaning "novel with a key." It refers to a narrative in which real persons are portrayed under fictitious names.

Romance: A broad term, usually denoting a narrative with exotic, exaggerated, often idealized characters, scenes, and themes.

Romanticism: This term has two widely accepted meanings. In historical criticism, it refers to a European intellectual and artistic movement of the late eighteenth and early nineteenth centuries that sought greater freedom of personal expression than that allowed by the strict rules of literary form and logic of the eighteenth-century neoclassicists. The Romantics preferred emotional and imaginative expression to rational analysis. They considered the individual to be at the center of all experience and so placed him or her at the center of their art. The Romantics believed that the creative imagination reveals nobler truths—unique feelings and attitudes—than those that could be discovered by logic or by scientific examination. Both the natural world and the state of childhood were important sources for revelations of "eternal truths." "Romanticism" is also used as a general term to refer to a type of sensibility found in all periods of literary history and usually considered to be in opposition to the principles of classicism. In this sense, Romanticism signifies any work or philosophy in which the exotic or dreamlike figure strongly, or that is devoted to individualistic expression, self-analysis, or a pursuit of a higher realm of knowledge than can be discovered by human reason.

Romantics: See *Romanticism*

S

Satire: A work that uses ridicule, humor, and wit to criticize and provoke change in human nature and institutions. There are two major types of satire: "formal" or "direct" satire speaks directly to the reader or to a character in the work; "indirect" satire relies upon the ridiculous behavior of its characters to make its point. Formal satire is further divided into two manners: the "Horatian," which ridicules gently, and the "Juvenalian," which derides its subjects harshly and bitterly.

Science Fiction: A type of narrative about or based upon real or imagined scientific theories and technology. Science fiction is often peopled with alien creatures and set on other planets or in different dimensions.

Second Person: See *Point of View*

Setting: The time, place, and culture in which the action of a narrative takes place. The elements of setting may include geographic location, characters' physical and mental environments, prevailing cultural attitudes, or the historical time in which the action takes place.

Simile: A comparison, usually using "like" or "as," of two essentially dissimilar things, as in "coffee as cold as ice" or "He sounded like a broken record."

Slang: A type of informal verbal communication that is generally unacceptable for formal writing. Slang words and phrases are often colorful exaggerations used to emphasize the speaker's point; they may also be shortened versions of an often-used word or phrase.

Slave Narrative: Autobiographical accounts of American slave life as told by escaped slaves. These works first appeared during the abolition movement of the 1830s through the 1850s.

Socialist Realism: The Socialist Realism school of literary theory was proposed by Maxim Gorky and established as a dogma by the first Soviet Congress of Writers. It demanded adherence to a communist worldview in works of literature. Its doctrines required an objective viewpoint comprehensible to the working classes and themes of social struggle featuring strong proletarian heroes.

Stereotype: A stereotype was originally the name for a duplication made during the printing process; this led to its modern definition as a person or thing that is (or is assumed to be) the same as all others of its type.

Stream of Consciousness: A narrative technique for rendering the inward experience of a character. This technique is designed to give the impression of an ever-changing series of thoughts, emotions, images, and memories in the spontaneous and seemingly illogical order that they occur in life.

Structure: The form taken by a piece of literature. The structure may be made obvious for ease of understanding, as in nonfiction works, or may obscured for artistic purposes, as in some poetry or seemingly "unstructured" prose.

Sturm und Drang: A German term meaning "storm and stress." It refers to a German literary movement of the 1770s and 1780s that reacted against the order and rationalism of the enlightenment, focusing instead on the intense experience of extraordinary individuals.

Style: A writer's distinctive manner of arranging words to suit his or her ideas and purpose in writing. The unique imprint of the author's personality upon his or her writing, style is the product of an author's way of arranging ideas and his or her use of diction, different sentence structures, rhythm, figures of speech, rhetorical principles, and other elements of composition.

Subjectivity: Writing that expresses the author's personal feelings about his subject, and which may or may not include factual information about the subject.

Subplot: A secondary story in a narrative. A subplot may serve as a motivating or complicating force for the main plot of the work, or it may provide emphasis for, or relief from, the main plot.

Surrealism: A term introduced to criticism by Guillaume Apollinaire and later adopted by Andre Breton. It refers to a French literary and artistic movement founded in the 1920s. The Surrealists sought to express unconscious thoughts and feelings in their works. The best-known technique used for achieving this aim was automatic writing— transcriptions of spontaneous outpourings from the unconscious. The Surrealists proposed to unify the contrary levels of conscious and unconscious, dream and reality, objectivity and subjectivity into a new level of "super-realism."

Suspense: A literary device in which the author maintains the audience's attention through the buildup of events, the outcome of which will soon be revealed.

Symbol: Something that suggests or stands for something else without losing its original identity. In literature, symbols combine their literal meaning with the suggestion of an abstract concept. Literary symbols are of two types: those that carry complex associations of meaning no matter what their contexts, and those that derive their suggestive meaning from their functions in specific literary works.

Symbolism: This term has two widely accepted meanings. In historical criticism, it denotes an early modernist literary movement initiated in France during the nineteenth century that reacted against the prevailing standards of realism. Writers in this movement aimed to evoke, indirectly and symbolically, an order of being beyond the material world of the five senses. Poetic expression of personal emotion figured strongly in the movement, typically by means of a private set of symbols uniquely identifiable with the individual poet. The principal aim of the Symbolists was to express in words the highly complex feelings that grew out of everyday contact with the world. In a broader sense, the term "symbolism" refers to the use of one object to represent another.

T

Tall Tale: A humorous tale told in a straightforward, credible tone but relating absolutely impossible events or feats of the characters. Such tales were commonly told of frontier adventures during the settlement of the west in the United States.

Theme: The main point of a work of literature. The term is used interchangeably with thesis.

Thesis: A thesis is both an essay and the point argued in the essay. Thesis novels and thesis plays share the quality of containing a thesis which is supported through the action of the story.

Third Person: See *Point of View*

Tone: The author's attitude toward his or her audience may be deduced from the tone of the work. A formal tone may create distance or convey politeness, while an informal tone may encourage a friendly, intimate, or intrusive feeling in the reader. The author's attitude toward his or her subject matter may also be deduced from the tone of the words he or she uses in discussing it.

Transcendentalism: An American philosophical and religious movement, based in New England from around 1835 until the Civil War. Transcendentalism was a form of American romanticism that had its roots abroad in the works of Thomas Carlyle, Samuel Coleridge, and Johann Wolfgang von Goethe. The Transcendentalists stressed the importance of intuition and subjective experience in communication with God. They rejected religious dogma and texts in favor of mysticism and scientific naturalism. They pursued truths that lie beyond the "colorless" realms perceived by reason and the senses and were active social reformers in public education, women's rights, and the abolition of slavery.

U

Urban Realism: A branch of realist writing that attempts to accurately reflect the often harsh facts of modern urban existence.

Utopia: A fictional perfect place, such as "paradise" or "heaven."

V

Verisimilitude: Literally, the appearance of truth. In literary criticism, the term refers to aspects of a work of literature that seem true to the reader.

Victorian: Refers broadly to the reign of Queen Victoria of England (1837-1901) and to anything with qualities typical of that era. For example, the qualities of smug narrowmindedness, bourgeois materialism, faith in social progress, and priggish morality are often considered Victorian. This stereotype is contradicted by such dramatic intellectual developments as the theories of Charles Darwin, Karl Marx, and Sigmund Freud (which stirred strong debates in England) and the critical attitudes of serious Victorian writers like Charles Dickens and George Eliot. In literature, the Victorian Period was the great age of the English novel, and the latter part of the era saw the rise of movements such as decadence and symbolism.

W

Weltanschauung: A German term referring to a person's worldview or philosophy.

Weltschmerz: A German term meaning "world pain." It describes a sense of anguish about the nature of existence, usually associated with a melancholy, pessimistic attitude.

Z

Zeitgeist: A German term meaning "spirit of the time." It refers to the moral and intellectual trends of a given era.

Cumulative Author/Title Index

Sinclair, Upton
    The Jungle: V6
Sister Carrie (Dreiser): V8
Slaughterhouse-Five (Vonnegut): V3
The Slave Dancer (Fox): V12
Smiley, Jane
    A Thousand Acres: V32
Smilla's Sense of Snow (Høeg): V17
Smith, Betty
    A Tree Grows in Brooklyn: V31
Smith, Zadie
    White Teeth: V40
Snow Country (Kawabata): V42
Snow Falling on Cedars (Guterson):
    V13
So Far from the Bamboo Grove
    (Watkins): V28
So Long a Letter (Bâ): V46
Solzhenitsyn, Aleksandr
    One Day in the Life of Ivan
      Denisovich: V6
Something Wicked This Way Comes
    (Bradbury): V29
Song of the Lark (Cather): V41
Song of Solomon (Morrison): V8
Song Yet Sung (McBride): V49
Sons and Lovers (Lawrence): V45
Sophie's Choice (Styron): V22
Soul Catcher (Herbert): V17
The Sound and the Fury (Faulkner):
    V4
The Sound of Waves (Mishima): V43
Spark, Muriel
    The Prime of Miss Jean Brodie:
      V22
Speak (Anderson): V31
Spiegelman, Art
    Maus: A Survivor's Tale: V35
Spinelli, Jerry
    Stargirl: V45
St. Dale (McCrumb): V46
Staples, Suzanne Fisher
    Shabanu: Daughter of the Wind:
      V35
Stargirl (Spinelli): V45
Staying Fat for Sarah Byrnes
    (Crutcher): V32
Stead, Christina
    The Man Who Loved Children:
      V27
Stein, Gertrude
    Ida: V27
Steinbeck, John
    Cannery Row: V28
    East of Eden: V19
    East of Eden (Motion picture):
      V34
    The Grapes of Wrath: V7
    The Grapes of Wrath (Motion
      picture): V39
    Of Mice and Men: V1
    The Moon is Down: V37

The Pearl: V5
The Red Pony: V17
Tortilla Flat: V46
Steppenwolf (Hesse): V24
Stevenson, Robert Louis
    Dr. Jekyll and Mr. Hyde: V11
    Kidnapped: V33
    Treasure Island: V20
Stockett, Kathryn
    The Help: V39
Stoker, Bram
    Dracula: V18
    Dracula (Motion picture): V41
The Stone Angel (Laurence): V11
The Stone Diaries (Shields): V23
Stones from the River (Hegi): V25
The Storyteller (Vargas Llosa): V49
Stowe, Harriet Beecher
    Dred: A Tale of the Great Dismal
      Swamp: V47
    Uncle Tom's Cabin: V6
The Strange Case of Dr. Jekyll and
    Mr. Hyde (Stevenson): see *Dr.*
    Jekyll and Mr. Hyde
The Stranger (Camus): V6
Stranger in a Strange Land
    (Heinlein): V40
The Street (Petry): V33
Strout, Elizabeth
    Olive Kitteridge: V39
Styron, William
    Sophie's Choice: V22
Sula (Morrison): V14
Summer (Wharton): V20
Summer of My German Soldier
    (Greene): V10
The Sun Also Rises (Hemingway): V5
Sunrise over Fallujah (Myers): V45
Surfacing (Atwood): V13
Swallowing Stones (McDonald): V45
Swamplandia! (Russell): V48
Swarthout, Glendon
    Bless the Beasts and Children: V29
The Sweet Hereafter (Banks): V13
Sweetgrass (Hudson): V28
Swift, Graham
    Waterland: V18
Swift, Jonathan
    Gulliver's Travels: V6

T

Tagore, Rabindranath
    The Home and the World: V48
A Tale of Two Cities (Dickens): V5
The Talented Mr. Ripley
    (Highsmith): V27
Tambourines to Glory (Hughes): V21
Tan, Amy
    The Bonesetter's Daughter: V31
    The Joy Luck Club: V1

    The Joy Luck Club (Motion
      picture): V35
    The Kitchen God's Wife: V13
    The Hundred Secret Senses: V44
Tan, Shaun
    The Arrival: V42
Tangerine (Bloor): V33
Tar Baby (Morrison): V37
Tarkington, Booth
    The Magnificent Ambersons: V34
Tashjian, Janet
    The Gospel according to Larry:
      V46
Tears of a Tiger (Draper): V42
Ten Little Indians (Christie): V8
The Tenant of Wildfell Hall (Brontë):
    V26
Tender Is the Night (Fitzgerald): V19
Tess of the d'Urbervilles (Hardy): V3
Tex (Hinton): V9
Thackeray, William Makepeace
    Vanity Fair: V13
That Was Then, This Is Now
    (Hinton): V16
Their Eyes Were Watching God
    (Hurston): V3
them (Oates): V8
Thin Wood Walls (Patneaude): V46
Things Fall Apart (Achebe): V2
The Third Life of Grange Copeland
    (Walker): V44
The Third Man (Greene): V36
This Side of Paradise (Fitzgerald):
    V20
A Thousand Acres (Smiley): V32
Three Junes (Glass): V34
The Three Musketeers (Dumas): V14
Through the Looking-Glass: V27
The Time Machine (Wells): V17
Time's Arrow; or, The Nature of the
    Offence (Amis): V47
To Kill a Mockingbird (Lee): V2
To Kill a Mockingbird (Motion
    picture): V32
To the Lighthouse (Woolf): V8
A Town Like Alice (Shute): V38
Tolkien, J. R. R.
    The Hobbit: V8
    The Lord of the Rings: V26
Tolstoy, Leo
    Anna Karenina: V28
    War and Peace: V10
Tom Jones (Fielding): V18
Too Late the Phalarope (Paton): V12
Toomer, Jean
    Cane: V11
To Sir, With Love (Braithwaite): V30
Tobacco Road (Caldwell): V49
The Tortilla Curtain (Boyle): V41
Tortilla Flat (Steinbeck): V46
Toward the End of Time (Updike):
    V24

Cumulative Nationality/Ethnicity Index

Cumulative Nationality/Ethnicity Index

Tolstoy, Leo
  Anna Karenina: V28
  War and Peace: V10
Turgenev, Ivan
  Fathers and Sons: V16
Yezierska, Anzia
  Bread Givers: V29

Scottish

Grahame, Kenneth
  The Wind in the Willows: V20
Laird, Elizabeth
  A Little Piece of Ground: V46
Rankin, Ian
  Watchman: V46
Scott, Walter
  Ivanhoe: V31
Spark, Muriel
  The Prime of Miss Jean Brodie: V22
Stevenson, Robert Louis
  Kidnapped: V33
  Treasure Island: V20

Senegalese

Bâ, Mariama
  So Long a Letter: V46

South African

Coetzee, J. M.
  Dusklands: V21
Courtenay, Bryce
  The Power of One: V32
Gordimer, Nadine
  July's People: V4

Gordon, Sheila
  Waiting for the Rain: V40
Head, Bessie
  When Rain Clouds Gather:
    V31
Magona, Sindiwe
  Mother to Mother: V43
Paton, Alan
  Cry, the Beloved Country: V3
  Too Late the Phalarope: V12

Spanish

de Cervantes Saavedra, Miguel
  Don Quixote: V8
Jiménez, Juan Ramón
  Platero and I: V36

Sri Lankan

Ondaatje, Michael
  The English Patient: V23

Swedish

Spiegelman, Art
  Maus: A Survivor's Tale: V35

Swiss

Hesse, Hermann
  Demian: V15
  Siddhartha: V6
  Steppenwolf: V24

Trinidad and Tobagoan

Naipaul, V. S.

  A Bend in the River: V37
  Half a Life: V39

Turkish

Pamuk, Orhan
  My Name is Red: V27

Ukrainian

Roth, Henry
  Call It Sleep: V47

Uruguayan

Bridal, Tessa
  The Tree of Red Stars: V17

Vietnamese

Duong Thu Huong
  Paradise of the Blind: V23

West Indian

Kincaid, Jamaica
  Annie John: V3

Zimbabwean

Dangarembga, Tsitsi
  Nervous Conditions: V28

Subject/Theme Index

143.00   6/15

LONGWOOD PUBLIC LIBRARY
800 Middle Country Road
Middle Island, NY 11953
(631) 924-6400
longwoodlibrary.org

LIBRARY HOURS

Monday-Friday	9:30 a.m. - 9:00 p.m.
Saturday	9:30 a.m. - 5:00 p.m.
Sunday (Sept-June)	1:00 p.m. - 5:00 p.m.